Praise for *The Design of Sites*

"Stop reinventing the wheel every time you design a Web site! *The Design of Sites* helps you rethink your Web sites in terms of genres and patterns. Once you have identified the patterns and applied the best practices for those patterns as outlined in this book, you will reduce your design effort by 50 percent . . . at least!"

PAWAN R. VORA
Vice President, Information Architecture, Seurat Company

"The content [in *The Design of Sites*] could make a novice into a seasoned professional over a weekend. Many companies pay a fortune for the information contained in the book's primary chapters."

JOHN CILIO
Global marketing manager for the Web site of a leading international supplier of computer hardware, software, and services

"This book has many handy checklists for what you should and should not do in creating a conventional Web site. Just following the authors' suggestions would put your site in the top few percent for readability and usability."

JEF RASKIN
Creator of the Macintosh computer and author of *The Humane Interface*

"Now that *The Design of Sites* has made its appearance, we won't have to put up with those poorly designed Web pages. These authors have captured patterns from successful Web designers, including their own experience in consulting and teaching, and have made this information accessible to all of us. The book is readable yet full of worthwhile information—a valuable addition to any Web designer's bookshelf."

LINDA RISING
Independent consultant and author of *The Patterns Handbook*, *The Pattern Almanac 2000*, and *Design Patterns in Communications Software*

"[*The Design of Sites*] bridges the gap from theory to practice and makes it possible for people in the Web-design space to use user-centered design principles in their work—without having to undertake extensive training."

MAYA VENKATRAMAN
Human interface engineer, Sun Microsystems

"The coverage [in *The Design of Sites*] is excellent—issues go beyond the traditional 'design the best page' focus and do a good job of showing the context. I haven't seen any other book with the kind of breadth this has."

TERRY WINOGRAD
Professor of computer science, Stanford University, and editor of *Bringing Design to Software*

The Design of Sites

The Design of Sites

Patterns, Principles, and Processes for Crafting a Customer-Centered Web Experience

DOUGLAS K. VAN DUYNE

JAMES A. LANDAY

JASON I. HONG

✦ Addison-Wesley

Boston • San Francisco • New York • Toronto • Montreal
London • Munich • Paris • Madrid
Capetown • Sydney • Tokyo • Singapore • Mexico City

The publisher offers discounts on this book when ordered in quantity for special sales. For more information, please contact:

U.S. Corporate and Government Sales
(800) 382-3419
corpsales@pearsontechgroup.com

For sales outside the U.S., please contact
International Sales
(317) 581-3793
international@pearsontechgroup.com

Visit Addison-Wesley on the Web: www.awprofessional.com

Library of Congress Cataloging-in-Publication Data

van Duyne, Douglas K.
    The design of sites : patterns, principles, and processes for crafting a customer-
  centered Web experience / Douglas K. van Duyne, James A. Landay, Jason I. Hong.
        p. cm.
    Includes bibliographical references and index.
    ISBN 0-201-72149-X
    1. Web sites—Design. I. Landay, James A. II. Hong, Jason I. III. Title.

TK5105.888 .V36 2002
005.7'2—dc21   2002018324

ISBN 0-201-72149-X
Text printed on recycled and acid-free paper.
2 3 4 5 6 7 QWT 06 05 04 03
2nd Printing   February 2003

Contents at a Glance

Contents

PATTERN GROUP E Building Trust and Credibility 315

Trust is essential to establishing a relationship with customers. Without trust and credibility, visitors have no reason to believe (or purchase) anything on your Web site. This pattern group discusses the trust and credibility issues critical to good Web site design.

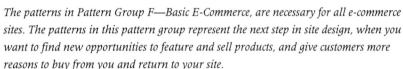

Foreword

Ever since Christopher Alexander wrote his seminal *A Pattern Language,* many have spoken about the need to extend his idea for identifying and illuminating patterns of successful architectural experiences into other design realms. To date, few attempts have borne any fruit, but in this book, Douglas van Duyne, James Landay, and Jason Hong have succeeded in describing patterns in the online world in a way that fulfills both the intent and promise of Christopher Alexander's original book. These authors have done an excellent job of analyzing models and describing them in detail. And in translating Alexander's approach into this new medium, they prove that even after 25 years, it is still valid. They have done a thorough job of discovery, synthesis, and presentation that is a credit to Alexander's approach and standard.

In my experience with interactive media, dating well before the Web's rise, designers, engineers, clients, and marketers have always been looking for ways of communicating new functionality to customers, participants, members, and other system users. Most new functions require new conventions, and these are often confusing at worst, unfamiliar at best, and very often unsettling. It takes time for conventions to appear. For example, the beveled button, now a style that reminds us of interactive or digital design from the late 1980s, was an early convention that helped people differentiate the objects on a screen that performed actions from those that were merely labels, titles, decorations, or other content. The underlying need being addressed here is helping people better identify controls, available actions, and interactive flow. There will always be needs for new functions and the need to make the interaction of those new functions clear to people. Therefore, new conventions (and eventually standards) will always be evolving.

I have seen these design problems and solutions develop for the last 14 years. From early screen designs for kiosks and presentations to CD-ROMs, online services, and the Web, each medium has offered new opportunities and presented designers with new problems. Indeed, the interfaces for computers themselves (such as applications and operating systems), distinct devices (such as PDAs, mobile phones, and stereo equipment), and even the print medium are still evolving ecosystems of communication—some successful, many not. You can see design conventions at work on the displays of modern copiers as well as tax forms and voting ballots. Our visual language, from which patterns emerge, is not relegated to one medium but is built from all media with which we interact.

Although the Web is still a new medium—barely ten years old—through mostly trial and error some standards have arisen that establish conventions of organization and communication. Not all of these have been ideal, of course, but most conventions have, at least, contributed to the development of a common language for people to understand when using a Web site. This book helps illuminate that language, describing how to use it to maximum effect.

For example, the placement of corporate or Web site branding in the upper left corner is a reaction to the fact that this is really the only area of the page that one can consistently expect to be visible in all conditions (screen sizes and resolutions, page sizes and locations, type sizes and styles, and so on). This standard placement has become one of the most common practices on the Web, and it is described in this book as only one of many such conventions. Although this is a simple example, other examples governing more sophisticated interactions, such as those for commerce or communication, offer equally important insights into successful and important conventions that designers and engineers can potentially follow.

Most design processes seek to distill the information or data to be presented and arrange it on the page or screen as a designer sees fit, given the available resources and design preferences. How the pages of a Web site fit together, and how this organization (or lack thereof) is represented, is a different process entirely, but one also governed mostly by personal design preferences. This book introduces a new process to consider that summarizes an amalgam of successful solutions and distills them into some basic models to follow. This approach represents a synthesis of the best current thinking on the Web and an approach that closely aligns with most users' experiences and expectations. To be sure, this is not the only way to design, and it may not be the best approach in every case. However, it represents a new way to design Web sites that should not be ignored.

This isn't to say that design is dead or that every model must be followed exactly. The models here are great guidelines that give designers an option to start with a predefined, successful framework that they can modify at will to solve their particular design constraints. Whereas many designers may view this as a way of limiting design freedom, others will see it as a way of reaching better solutions faster and finding new, higher levels on which to concentrate their drive to innovate.

By no means should this book be seen as a complete document, because the language of online communication is still evolving, but it is the best record to date of the predominant vocabulary and grammar of this language. There are still more interactions to be developed and online experiences to be defined. No doubt, future editions will evolve along with this language.

Nathan Shedroff
Author of *Experience Design* and cofounder of **vivid** studios
January 19, 2002

United Flight 60, somewhere over the Pacific Ocean
between Honolulu and San Francisco

Preface

You are probably wondering how this book is any different from the numerous other Web design books out there. This unique book is not about programming or any specific technology. Nor is it a quick fix for all of the problems you and your team will face in developing a Web site. No single book can do that. What this book does offer are principles, processes, and patterns to help you develop successful customer-centered Web sites. With this customer-centered focus, your Web site can be relevant, self-explanatory, and easy to use.

Creating a Web site is easy. Creating a successful Web site that provides a winning experience for your target audience is another story, and that is what this book is about. And when you're finished reading it, it will be a valuable reference tool to keep on your desk. You can turn to it again and again as you design, redesign, and evaluate sites.

Your target customers[1] will differ. Depending on your business, they might be members in a club, students of a university, concerned citizens, or paying shoppers. The goals of each of these audiences will also vary, but the challenge for you is the same: creating an interactive interface that provides tangible value to the people who go to your site.

The patterns in this book provide you and your team with a common language to articulate an infinite variety of Web designs. We developed the language because we saw people solving the same design problems over and over at great time and expense. The patterns examine solutions to these problems. We present the best practices from our consulting experience, our research experience, and our Web development experience—gathered in one place. In *The Design of Sites* we give you the tools to

---

[1] We use the term *customers* to mean any person who will use the Web site you are designing. We use the term *clients* to mean the people for whom you are doing the work, the people providing the funding.

understand your customers better, help you design sites that your customers will find effective and easy to use, shorten your development schedules, and reduce maintenance costs.

If you do not have "customers," think of *target audiences*. One focus of the book is the design of e-commerce Web sites; however, you can successfully apply the majority of the content to make any Web site better.

Who Should Read This Book?

This book is written for anyone involved in the design and implementation of a Web site. Its focus is tilted more toward Web design professionals, such as interaction designers, usability engineers, information architects, and visual designers. But this book is also written to be a resource for anyone on a Web development team, from business executives to advertising managers to software developers to content editors. The best possible team will understand and buy into the customer-centered design philosophy because every person on the team influences how the Web site is shaped and formed.

Web Design Professionals • Start with Chapters 1 and 2 to understand the motivation for customer-centered design and the patterns approach to Web design. If you already have a strong background in the principles (Chapters 3 and 4) and processes (Chapter 5) of customer-centered design, you can skim these chapters and move quickly to the patterns themselves (Part II of the book). If you have less experience, the three chapters on customer-centered design and development (3 through 5) should prove useful for whatever kind of Web site you're developing.

Business Managers • Read Chapters 1 through 5 to understand the business consequences of ignoring customer-centered design, as well as to learn the principles and processes required to build a customer-centered site. E-commerce sites pose the greatest risk of project failure. These chapters show techniques you can use to reduce this risk, decrease feature creep, and minimize implementation and maintenance costs. Customer-centered design will also help you shorten development schedules and increase overall customer satisfaction—and consequently client satisfaction too.

Business Clients • If you are the client who funds development of a Web site, read the first five chapters. Because you are paying, you will be especially interested in why there is such an urgent need for a strong customer focus, and in what steps design teams can take to ensure that your customers' needs are met. You will see why these steps will actually reduce your costs and give you happier, more loyal customers.

Benefits of Using *The Design of Sites*

We know that improving your customers' Web experience will take more than reading this book. The principles, processes, and patterns in this book are not a magic solution to your problems. However, by putting them into practice in the design and evaluation of your Web sites, you will improve the overall customer experience. Success requires an extreme focus on customer needs, but one that will pay off in the long run. Your work will result in improved customer satisfaction, a balanced approach to Web design, and incremental improvement of design practices, as described in the sections that follow.

Improved Customer Satisfaction • By focusing on your customers throughout the development process, you will discover their needs, design Web sites for those needs, and evaluate your designs to ensure that those needs are met. You will test your site iteratively with representative customers to make certain that you work out the majority of problems *before* they cause serious problems and *before* they become expensive to fix. Customer-centered design concentrates on making sure that you're building the right features on your Web site, and that you're building those features right!

A Balanced Approach to Web Design • Too many books read like ancient scripture, as in, "Thou shalt do this" and "Thou shalt not do that." Such approaches are too dogmatic for Web design, which needs to be flexible and adaptable to a wide range of situations. The Web has led to more customer diversity, as well as a wider range of customer goals and tasks than was commonly seen in the past. We acknowledge, however, that customer needs must also be balanced with your business goals, usability requirements, aesthetics, and technological constraints.

That's why we have aimed for general principles, processes, and patterns that can be applied to many Web site genres. We have integrated the three in one book because each is part of a comprehensive solution: The patterns provide a language for building Web sites; the principles and processes provide instructions for how to use the language.

Incremental Improvement of Design Practices • It is unlikely that anyone has time to read and put into practice an entire book about designing customer-centered Web sites in a short period of time. So we have divided this book into many small, digestible parts. The first five chapters describe the key ideas behind customer-centered design. The rest of the book is devoted to Web design patterns that can be applied to practically any Web site. You can skip around, mix and match, skim, and sample what you need. *This is not a book that you must read from cover to cover.*

The ideas in this book do not require wholesale adoption. You can take small parts at a time and try them out to see what works for you. In fact, we encourage many small steps instead of a few big leaps because it takes time to become practiced in the many ideas presented here. For example, you could improve your design practices by using the design patterns that make up the bulk of this book. Or you could use just some of the techniques described in the first part of the book, such as observing some representative customers using your site. Though often a humbling process, making such observations will help ground your intuitions of the way your customers think, and in the long run improve the overall design of your site.

Conventions Used in This Book

The following typographical conventions are used in this book:

- **Web pages and Web sites** that we reference are set in blue text.
- **Pattern names** are identified as follows:

  PATTERN NAME (A2)

  where the letter in parentheses represents the pattern group and the number is the pattern number. In this case "A2" means the second pattern in pattern group A. Each use of a pattern in the text is also accompanied by a color-coded, circular icon in the margin (as illustrated to the right of the pattern name example above). The color indicates the pattern group. These icons are also shown on each page of the respective pattern.
- **Chapter and pattern group names** are also represented in the book by color-coded icons. The first five chapters use square icons with the chapter number inside the square, and the pattern groups use diamond-shaped icons with the group letter inside the diamond. For example, in the margin here are the icons associated with Chapter 1 and Pattern Group C, respectively. Throughout the book, such icons are shown in the margin of the text wherever a specific chapter or pattern group is mentioned.
- **HTML tags and code examples** are set in constant-width type.

Disclaimer

We use many screen shots of Web sites in this book to illustrate examples of good and not so good design. We offer kudos to the Web teams and companies that made the good designs. However, the examples of not so good design should not be construed as attacks on the Web sites in question or the companies responsible for those sites. Wrestling the technological, economic, and organizational beasts can be quite an endeavor, and change can be slow, even in Internet time. Besides, we are all still learning. We are all in this together.

We Would Like to Hear from You

Please send us your comments, questions, and any errata. Although we cannot update your copy, we will organize your feedback at http://www.designofsites.com/feedback/.

We are especially interested in finding out how well particular patterns worked for you and hearing your suggestions for improving them. We plan to share new patterns that you have discovered with other readers of the book!

You can reach us at doug@netraker.com, landay@cs.berkeley.edu, and jasonh@cs.berkeley.edu, or through our publisher at AWPro@aw.com.

Douglas van Duyne, James Landay, and Jason Hong
Berkeley, California, January 2002

Acknowledgments

We give thanks to all the designers who have come before us, our spouses, the team of dedicated visionaries at NetRaker, and our colleagues and students at the University of California, Berkeley, who gave us early feedback on this work. We would especially like to thank Mark Newman, whose study of Web designers was the basis for the design process that we describe in Chapter 5. We thank the people who participated in the CHI 2000 Workshop on Design Patterns for their comments on our early ideas. We also thank Christopher Alexander, who originally developed the concept of design patterns in *A Pattern Language: Towns, Buildings, Construction* (Oxford University Press, 1977).

Several people helped with the final production of the book. We would like to thank Mary O'Brien, our editor at Addison-Wesley. Thanks especially to Dianne Jacob for helping create the proposal and editing many versions of the book. Thanks to Tyrrell Albaugh for smoothing the production of the book, which was also much improved by Stephanie Hiebert, who copyedited our draft. Special thanks to Colleen Stokes for her initial cover and pattern format designs. Thanks to Sarah Vilaysom for her extensive help with collecting, editing, organizing, and managing the images in the book. And thanks to Matthew Tarpy for his help in collecting several of the screen shots illustrating the patterns and to Mandy Erickson for obtaining permissions to use these images here. We appreciate the many reviewers who gave us great feedback on the drafts of this work, including Mitchel Ahern, Linda Brigman, John Cilio, Sunny Consolvo, Sally Fincher, Åsa Granlund, Jeff Johnson, Jef Raskin, Ross Teague, Ken Trant, Maya Venkatraman, Pawan Vora, John Wegis, and Terry Winograd.

Foundations of Web Site Design

Customer-Centered Web Design   1

One day, while walking down the street, a man encounters a talking dog. Flabbergasted, the man dashes off to tell his friend. As they both rush back to find the talking dog, his friend asks, "A talking dog? What did it say?" The man replies, "Who cares, it's a talking dog!"

A few years ago, the Web was just like the talking dog. It was so new, so fascinating, that its content did not matter. Anybody could create a Web site, and it was fun just to be there. People put Web cameras on coffee makers, on fish tanks, and sometimes even on themselves. People created elaborate Web sites devoted to arcane obsessions, from cult television shows to fetishes too bizarre to put in print.

But then the first commercial Web sites appeared, and for better or worse, the Web took its first few steps growing up.

Since then, designers have explored literally thousands of ideas in an effort to understand and make use of this new medium. The Web is no longer a rambunctious toddler, touching and tasting and trying out every new thing within reach. The Web is maturing, and the problems faced by today's Web developers are the same ones faced by any industry as it matures: More and more people are starting to care about factors like value, convenience, and ease of use over the novelty of the technology itself.

Customer-centered design deals with this change in priorities. In this chapter you will discover the thinking behind customer-centered design, and learn how to apply it to your projects using the principles, processes, and patterns we present.

The Evolution of Web Design   <u>**1.1**</u>

The First Generation • The mantra was "build it, and they will come." Talented individuals and large crews alike built Web sites. These creative and visionary people managed everything from business planning to graphic design and software development in this new medium. But, having built the site, they could say only that they had a Web site. They could not say how their site was performing from the customer's perspective, and what relationship the site had to the business's bottom line.

The Second Generation • The mantra was "advertise that you sell it online, and they will come." Start-ups invested large amounts of capital into expensive ads to drive visitors to their e-commerce sites. Even established companies put ".com" on their letterhead and ran costly campaigns to let people know they hadn't been left behind.

Unfortunately, this strategy did not work because Web design was complex and still misunderstood. *For the first time, organizations were building interactive computer interfaces to their products and services.* This proved to be a difficult task to execute well. In fact, building a Web site too quickly made its probability of being both compelling and easy to use practically zero.

The Third Generation • Today the focus has shifted to constructing powerful Web sites that provide real value and deliver a positive customer experience. When visitors consistently give a Web site high marks for content, ease of use, performance, trustworthiness, and overall satisfaction, we call it a **customer-centered Web site.**

We use the term *customer* rather than *user* for three reasons. First, only two industries refer to their customers as *users:* drug dealers and computer companies. We hope to help break this connection between the two. Second, and more importantly, the term *customer* evokes the fact that successful Web sites account for issues that go beyond ease of use and satisfaction, such as trustworthiness, brand value, and even how well a company's traditional interactions with the customer work, such as telephone-based customer service or the return of merchandise.

Finally, taking a cue from Beyer and Holtzblatt's *Contextual Design,* we use *customer* to refer to anyone who uses or *depends* on the site. Customers can be administrators, partners, managers, and producers, among others. To manage the site, many of these individuals will see a completely different interface. We chose the term *customer* because it is more expansive

Figure 1.1

The key issues driving customer-centered Web design

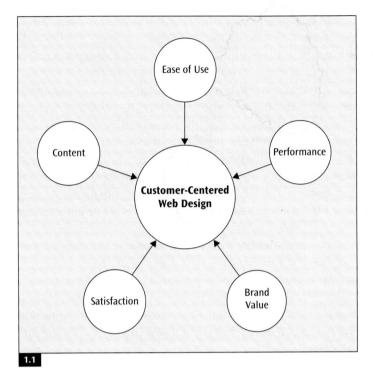

1.1

than *user,* referring to all of these individuals and their myriad needs. Consideration of these additional factors is what differentiates customer-centered design from other design approaches (see Figure 1.1).

The challenge to be customer centered exists for all enterprises: large multinationals, government agencies, internal corporate services, small businesses, and nonprofit organizations, to name just a few. General Motors, for example, must manage its customer experience for more than 300 end-customer, supplier, and distributor Web sites. Government sites, with responsibilities to help the citizenry and other agencies, need to satisfy "customer" requirements as well. Intranet applications that optimize a corporation's workforce must provide positive experiences to employee "customers."

1.2 The Importance of Customer-Centered Design

Over the years we have learned that the criteria for building customer-centered Web sites are based on providing a positive experience for all customers, whether those customers are there to find information, to be part of a community, to purchase items, or to be entertained. This focus is called **customer-centered design.** Customer-centered design increases the value of Web sites through better design and evaluation. It is about how you empathize with customers, understanding their needs, the tools and technologies they use, and their social and organizational context. It is about how you use this understanding to shape your designs, and then test those designs to ensure that the customers' needs are met.

Why go to all this trouble? What will happen if you don't? Suppose your site overruns its budget or schedule. Management could pull the plug before it is completed. Or what if your Web site is finished but turns out to be too hard to learn or use? Customers may visit your site once and never return.

With customer-centered design, you do the work up front to ensure that the Web site has the features that customers need, by determining and planning for the most important features and by making certain that those features are built in a way that customers will understand. This method actually takes less time and money to implement in the long run. In short, customer-centered design helps you build the right Web site and build the Web site right!

Here is an example underscoring the importance of customer-centered design. A few years ago, IBM found that its Web site was not working well. Quick analysis revealed that the search feature was the most used function. The site was so confusing that IBM's customers could not figure out how to find what they wanted. IBM also discovered that the help feature was the second most popular function. Because the search feature was ineffective, many people went to the help pages to find assistance. Paying close attention to customer needs, IBM redesigned the site from the ground up to be more consistent in its navigation. A week after launching the redesigned site, reliance on the search and help features dropped dramatically and online sales rose 400 percent.

This is just one of many stories highlighting the increasing importance of good design. But does good Web design really affect the bottom line? You bet! Web sites founded on solid fundamentals and extensive customer research can make the difference between success and failure. A clear, easy-to-use, and customer-centered Web site can help garner better reviews and ratings, reduce the number of mistakes made by customers, trim the time it takes to find things, and increase overall customer satisfaction. Furthermore, customers who really like a Web site's content and quality of service are more likely to tell their family, friends, and coworkers, thereby increasing the number of potential customers. A great example of this result is Google, which has become the dominant search site with little or no advertising. It simply works better than most other search sites, and customers tell their friends about it.

There is also a strong correlation between increased satisfaction and increased profits for commercial Web sites. Underscoring this point, NetRaker's research shows that increasing customer satisfaction by just 5 percent can lead to a 25 percent or greater increase in revenues. This increase comes from customers who can find products and services more easily—customers who will return in the future—as well as the corresponding reduction in support costs. The decrease in support costs comes from a lower number of phone calls, e-mails, and instant messages to help desks, as well as a lower number of returns on products.

The stakes are higher now than ever before. Commercial Web sites that are not relevant, fast, trustworthy, satisfying, and easy to use will find it difficult to attract new customers and retain existing ones, especially if competitors are only a click away.

Providing Tangible Value

Yahoo! is one of the top Web sites out there today, and it's likely to remain near the top for the foreseeable future. Why? Is it because it has slick graphic design? Hardly. Yahoo!'s homepage only has around ten graphical images, and most of its other pages have less than a dozen. Yahoo! is always pointed out as the poster child of boring interfaces. Is it because Yahoo! uses the latest browser technologies? You would actually be hard-pressed to find Web pages on Yahoo! that use Macromedia Flash plug-ins or other bleeding-edge technologies. (In fact, the games section was the only part of Yahoo! we could find that used technology beyond HTML and basic JavaScript.)

So why is Yahoo! so popular? It's pretty simple actually: Yahoo! provides quality services that are useful, fast to download, and easy to use. One of the reasons it is such a popular Web site is that interaction design and usability research are integral parts of Yahoo!'s development process. Yahoo! discovers its customer needs through field studies, interviews, and usability evaluations, and then it tailors its designs to match customer needs.

People will leave your Web site if they

- Are frustrated
- Think it is too much effort to navigate the site
- Think you don't have the product or service they are looking for
- Get big surprises that they don't like
- Feel it takes too long to load

You cannot afford to abandon a single customer.

Even if your site does not have direct competitors, as is the case with educational institutions and corporate intranets, it can benefit from being customer centered. Simple, clean, and well-designed Web sites can cut down on wasted time for customers, reduce Web site maintenance costs for clients, and improve overall satisfaction.

The First Steps We Took to Unify Design, Usability, and Marketing

1.3

In 1997 we noticed that a few companies had dramatically jumped ahead of the competition and were now leaders on the Web. These companies had publicly stated and acted on making the customer experience their top priority, and they raised the bar for everyone.

While we were actively helping clients develop sites in an ever more competitive environment, we realized we had to move beyond the traditional boundaries of usability, market research, and software design. It was not an easy task, because our clients had committed to these means at varying levels, in different parts of the organization that usually did not talk to one another.

Drawing on our experience in design, consulting, marketing, communications, and human–computer interface research, we evaluated our clients' Web sites on many levels. We discovered that although a customer focus existed, often it was not reflected on the Web sites. We also discovered that some clients were not improving the customer experience on their Web sites at all. This was not surprising, considering that these companies did not have a clear Web strategy. It was not uncommon to see a client's Web design team with an inadequate budget and little authority to integrate operations with the rest of the company.

Sometimes our clients were simply too busy trying to stay afloat to care about getting a full wind in their sails. One Web business we studied thought that it was doing very well with its health-related news, information, and products. It was receiving thousands of Web-based orders per week. It spent heavily on advertising to drive people to its site, and as advertising spending increased, so did sales. Our team evaluated the ease of use of its site, doing some customer research over a short period of time (later we will show you how you can run studies like this yourself). We looked at many factors, from first impression, to ease of use, to overall satisfaction.

We found some surprising results that led us to important conclusions. The developers of the site had done a great job of creating a powerful first impression. All the customers in our research panel liked the site, thought it looked easy to use, and said it appeared to have relevant content.

But then in the next step we asked the same customers to use the site to carry out a realistic task: finding products for the common cold. Only 30 percent of the customers could find products for colds, or for any other medical condition at all. This research suggested that about 70 percent of customers who came to the site to solve particular health problems could not find what they were looking for. This result provided a direct causal link between human–computer interface problems and lost revenue. The cost of dissatisfied customers abandoning this site could have reached into the millions of dollars over the course of a year.

Our experience with the health site is not uncommon. The bottom line is that poorly designed Web sites frustrate people, fritter away customer loyalty, and waste everyone's time.

1.4   Why We Prefer Customer-Centered Design

One way to explain the value of customer-centered design is to compare it to other design styles. In this section we look at four styles centering in turn on the user, the company, technology, and the designer.

User-Centered Design • Customer-centered design is most closely related to what is known as **user-centered design,** an effort pioneered in the 1980s for engineering useful and usable computer systems. Customer-centered design builds on user-centered design, adding concerns that go beyond ease of use and satisfaction. In particular, it also focuses on the fusion of marketing issues with usability issues.

On the Web it is much easier to get an audience than by traditional means, but you also want to convert Web site visitors to customers and then keep them coming back. Unlike someone selling shrink-wrapped software to a customer who buys before using it, you want to convince Web site visitors to become customers and make their first use enjoyable—all at the same time. Pay special attention to business goals, marketing goals, usability goals, and customer experience goals. These goals often conflict with each other, and you will be able to find a balance among them only if you are aware of them all at once. These issues are much more intertwined and harder to design for on the Web than for shrink-wrapped software.

Company-Centered Design • A style that used to be quite popular among Fortune 500 companies is what we call **company-centered design.** Here the needs and interests of the company dominate the structure and content of the Web site. The fatal flaw is that what companies think should be on a Web site is not necessarily what customers need or want. You have probably seen Web sites that are organized by internal corporate structure, with sparse information about the products and services they offer. These kinds of sites are derisively termed **brochureware.** They contain little useful information and completely ignore the unique capabilities of the Web as a medium. Brochureware sites are acceptable only if they are a short-term first step toward more sophisticated and more useful sites.

Another example of company-centered design is the use of jargon known only to those in the business. One of our friends recently wanted to buy a digital camera. As an amateur, he wanted a camera that was easy to use, one that would help him take clear pictures. But instead, most of the sites bombarded him with terms like *CCDs, FireWire, PC card slots,* and *uncompressed TIFF mode*. The fact that he didn't know what these terms meant embarrassed him. He was put off and confused. The companies had made the wrong assumption about their customers' knowledge. None of them answered the simple question of which camera was best for amateurs. This is an example of why company-centered design is almost always a bad style.

Technology-Centered Design • Sites constructed on the basis of **technology-centered design** are often built with little up-front research about business needs and customer needs—just a lot of hacking and caffeine. We have all seen these kinds of Web sites—the ones overloaded with animation, audio, and streaming banners. The problem with this approach is that it often results in amateurish Web sites that are not useful, usable, or desirable. Technology-centered Web sites were pervasive in the early days of the Web, but thankfully they are becoming less common as the Web matures.

Designer-Centered Design • Designer-centered design (also known as **ego-centered** design) is still popular in certain circles. One designer was quoted in a popular industry rag as saying, "What the client sometimes doesn't understand is the less they talk to us, the better it is. We know what's best." This is exactly what we mean.

Don't get us wrong, though. Some design teams have deep-seated creative urges that are matched only by their incredible technical ability. They can create sites that are cool, edgy, and loaded with the latest technologies. In some cases, this is exactly the image a company wants to project. Unfortunately, these kinds of sites can also be slow to download, as well as hard to use, and they may not work in all Web browsers. Designer-centered design is fine for some art Web sites, but not for e-commerce or informational sites whose livelihood depends on a large number of repeat visitors.

In company-centered design, designers give no thought to why people would visit the company's Web site and what they would want to do

---

Top Ten Signs That Things Are Going Badly

1. "Our Web site is intuitive and user-friendly."
2. "We need to start doing some usability tests before our launch next month."
3. "We can use [XML / SOAP / insert other buzzword technology] to fix that."
4. "If you stop and think about how the interface works for a second, it makes complete sense."
5. "How can our customers be so stupid? It's so obvious!"
6. "Well, they should RTFM!"[1]
7. "We don't need to do any user testing. I'm a user, and I find it easy to use."
8. "We'll just put an 'Under Construction' sign there."
9. "Shrink the fonts more so that we can put more content at the top."
10. "We need a splash screen."

---

[1]   Read The *Fantastic* Manual.

there. In technology-centered design, technology is an end rather than a means of accomplishing an end. In designer-centered design, the needs of other people are placed beneath the creative and expressive needs of the design team. Contrast these styles with customer-centered design, which emphasizes customers and their tasks above all, and sees technology as a tool that can empower people.

Company-centered, technology-centered, and designer-centered design styles were understandable in the early days of the Web when designers were still finding their way. In the old worldview, few people really considered what customers wanted. Now, successful and easy-to-use sites like amazon.com, yahoo.com, and ebay.com are designed from the ground up to meet the needs of their customers. In the new worldview, your careful consideration of customers, as reflected in your Web site, will help you achieve long-lasting success.

Nine Myths of Customer-Centered Design   1.5

Why do so many organizations not embrace customer-centered design? We are here to dispel the myths that keep companies from moving forward with customer-centered design.

Myth 1: Good Design Is Just Common Sense • If Web site design is just common sense, why are there so many bad Web sites? Thinking that design is just common sense leads us to think that we know what everyone needs and wants. Time and time again, however, this notion has been shown to be incorrect.

Web design teams always have to keep in mind that they are not the customers. They cannot always predict the way customers will think or act. In addition, they know too much about how the Web site works. They cannot look at it in the same way that customers will. They could avoid this problem by observing and talking to customers and getting feedback from them as often as possible.

Myth 2: Only Experts Create Good Designs • Although experts might apply customer-centered design techniques more quickly or conduct more rigorous analyses, anyone can understand and use these techniques. Anyone can create a good design if they devote themselves to it.

Myth 3: Web Interfaces Can Be Redesigned Right before Launch • Sentiments like "we'll spend a few days working on our site's interface" or "we'll solve the interface problems after all the programming is done" are common. However, these ideas assume that the Web site has the right features and that those features are being built correctly. These are two very risky assumptions that can be costly to fix, especially if the Web site is near completion. Customer-centered design helps minimize these risks by getting constant feedback on designs so that the Web site will be in good condition the day it is launched.

Myth 4: Good Design Takes Too Long and Costs Too Much • Customer-centered design does add some up-front costs because you will be talking to customers, creating prototypes, getting feedback on those prototypes, and so on. However, customer-centered design can considerably reduce **back-end costs**—that is, costs incurred as a result of responding to customer dissatisfaction, through help desk calls, returned purchases, general Web site maintenance, and so on. Evaluate the trade-off between spending more time and money at the start of your project and losing revenue over the long run.

Customer-centered design can even reduce the total development time and cost because it focuses on finding problems in the early stages of design when they are still easy to repair, preventing them from ever causing serious problems that are time-consuming and expensive to fix. We know that your team will not always have the time and budget to do everything possible, so we try to lay out the trade-offs among the different actions you could take to improve your site. This book discusses many effective approaches you can use to test your assumptions and to test your Web site, to make sure that it is a winner in the long run.

Myth 5: Good Design Is Just Cool Graphics • An aesthetically pleasing design is an important part of any Web site because it helps communicate how to use a particular interface and it conveys a certain impression. However, graphics are only one part of the larger picture of what to communicate and how. Customer-centered design takes into account what customers want, what they understand, what tasks they perform, and the context in which they do things. Cool graphics by themselves do not address these issues.

Myth 6: Web Interface Guidelines Will Guide You to Good Designs • Web interface guidelines are a good checklist to ensure that the final design has no obvious minor problems. Guidelines address only how a Web site is implemented, however. They do not address what features a Web site should have, the overall organization of the Web site, or the flow between individual Web pages. In contrast, the design patterns described in this book are generative. Using them will help you create solutions to your design problems. Furthermore, guidelines do not address the trade-offs of Web site development. Customer-centered principles, processes, and patterns, on the other hand, do take these issues into account.

Myth 7: Customers Can Always Rely on Documentation and Help • Documentation and help are important; however, customers are unlikely to be patient enough to sift through a great deal of documentation just to use a Web site. Documentation and help are the last resorts of a frustrated customer.

Think about it this way: When was the last time you read a help page? Did you wish the design team had gone the extra mile in the first place to make using the site straightforward so that you would not need to read the help? Customer-centered design provides tools to see the world from your customers' eyes, to help you understand their worldview, and then to design Web sites to fit their needs.

Myth 8: Market Research Takes Care of Understanding All Customer Needs • Although market research is invaluable for helping to understand customer attitudes and intentions, it does not suffice when it comes to understanding customer behavior. Be careful also about using market research to create lists of customer feature requests. Implementing a laundry list of new features might satisfy customers who have asked for a particular feature, but all these features are more likely to get in the way of offering most of your customers a successful customer experience.

What customers *say* in a market research study can be useful as well, but when it comes to interfaces, what they *do* is critical. That's why market research must be balanced with direct observation. A customer-centered design team uses a variety of techniques—from observations to interviews—to elicit true customer needs and focus on the areas that will be most important for most customers.

Myth 9: Quality Assurance Groups Make Sure That Web Sites Work Well • Software testing is key to ensuring that you are not launching a buggy, poorly performing site. Although quality assurance is important, its purpose and focus are different from those of customer-centered design. Software testing is often technology driven rather than customer driven. Expert testers try to make sure the product does what the specification says it should. This is different from seeing what happens with real customers working on real problems.

More importantly, Web sites often are tested only *after* being built. At that point it is too late to make major changes. Software testing can help you find and fix only coding mistakes, not major design mistakes. Customer-centered design, in contrast, focuses on quality from the very start—before anyone has written a line of code.

1.6 Applying Customer-Centered Design

Over time we have evaluated the best practices to use when designing powerful, compelling, and useful interactive Web sites. We realize that designers need concepts they can quickly integrate into their Web site design practices, as well as a process that can be applied universally, from entertainment sites to e-commerce sites, from sites for informal clubs to sites for large corporations. On the basis of our experiences, research, and discussions with other Web designers, we have refined our ideas on customer-centered design into three parts: principles, processes, and patterns.

Principles • These high-level concepts guide the entire design process and help you stay focused. For example, as we state in one of our key principles, you must acquire a deep understanding of your customers' needs. Another major principle is to design your Web site iteratively, moving from rough cuts to refined prototypes, before creating the production Web site. These principles, described in Chapters 3—Knowing Your Customers: Principles and Techniques and 4—Involving Customers with Iterative Design, can be applied to any design problem and are the foundation for the patterns we describe in the second half of the book.

Processes • This is how you put the principles into practice. In Chapter 5—Processes for Developing Customer-Centered Sites, we describe our Web site development process, a guide that explains the major steps and milestones for developing a Web site. We also provide a collection of how-to tips, such as how to conduct a focus group, how to run a survey, and how to do a usability test (most of these tips are included in the appendixes). If your firm has similar processes, use Chapter 5 to update your process so that the key principles of customer-centered design are supported.

Patterns • Design patterns solve recurring design problems, so you can use pattern solutions to design your sites without reinventing the wheel. Patterns are a **language**, a common vocabulary that allows you and your team to articulate an infinite variety of Web designs.

These patterns let you focus your energies on solving new problems, rather than problems that have been worked out hundreds of times before. But design patterns do not make cookie-cutter sites—far from it. Because no two businesses are the same, we created the design patterns for you to tailor to your particular business needs. This book shows you how to create an overall solution that works for your customers and your business.

Using the Principles, Processes, and Patterns

Design is about making informed trade-offs between competing constraints. Customer-centered design tries to make these trade-offs clearer, but only you can solve the problems. The principles help you decide between different process activities at a particular step of your project. For example, when deciding between iterating on a paper design one more time versus building a high-fidelity version of the design, you might decide to stick with paper because you can easily bring in potential customers to evaluate the design.

You can also use the principles to help you decide among different design solutions you developed using the patterns. Say, for example, that you are not sure whether your branding is prominent enough during checkout on your site. You could use online surveys, a common tool of market researchers, to quickly see what potential customers think.

Take-Away Ideas   1.7

Your opportunities on the Web are vast, but so are the difficulties of delivering a site that customers will give high marks for content, ease of use, performance, trustworthiness, and overall satisfaction. These problems are not insurmountable if you solve them with the set of principles, processes, and patterns we have described.

In the rest of this book you will find more reasons to implement customer-centered design, descriptions of techniques to use in your current projects, and dozens of design patterns proven to enhance your customers' experience. Guidelines for instituting customer-centered design will help you through the process.

This book is meant as the first step in an ongoing conversation to improve the Web. We have not identified all of the useful Web design patterns. New patterns will be found, and the patterns we describe here will evolve as new techniques are invented and customer knowledge and skills change. We encourage you to join in the conversation and keep moving the Web toward the new, raised bar for success.

Making the Most of Web Design Patterns   2

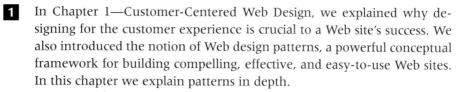

1 In Chapter 1—Customer-Centered Web Design, we explained why designing for the customer experience is crucial to a Web site's success. We also introduced the notion of Web design patterns, a powerful conceptual framework for building compelling, effective, and easy-to-use Web sites. In this chapter we explain patterns in depth.

We do not expect you to read through all of the patterns in this book from start to finish. Instead, we show you ways to explore the patterns so that you can quickly find the right patterns for your needs.

2.1 What Are Patterns?

Patterns communicate insights into design problems, capturing the essence of the problems and their solutions in a compact form. They describe the problem in depth, the rationale for the solution, how to apply the solution, and some of the trade-offs in applying the solution.

Patterns were originally developed by the architect Christopher Alexander and his colleagues, in a 1977 groundbreaking book called *A Pattern Language: Towns, Buildings, Construction* (Oxford University Press). Patterns, he said, can empower people by providing a living and shared language "for building and planning towns, neighborhoods, houses, gardens, and rooms." Alexander intended for patterns to be used by everyday people to guide the process of creation, whether designing a house for themselves or working with others designing offices and public spaces. By creating a common language, would-be designers could discuss and take part in the design of the spaces in which they worked, lived, and played. Alexander's patterns were also a reaction against contemporary architectural design, which he felt did not take enough of human needs, nature, growth, spirituality, and community into consideration.

Alexander's emphasis was on an entire language for design. He felt that individual, isolated patterns were of marginal value. By connecting related patterns, and by showing how they intertwine and affect one another, he believed he could create an entire pattern language that was greater than the sum of the individual parts.

Likewise, Web design patterns make up a *language* that you can use in your daily work. In fact, though you may not know it, you may already be using some form of pattern language to articulate and communicate your designs. The patterns might reflect your own experiences using the Web. You might have picked them up from another site. They could even come from an insight you learned from a successful design you developed in the past.

Our Web design pattern language focuses on your customers and their needs. This book is a reaction to the multitude of design patterns implicitly in use that do not take a customer-centered design approach.

Many of our patterns reflect how your customers understand and interact with Web sites. When people go online, they do not start with a blank slate. They take with them all of their experiences, their know-how, and their understanding of how the world works. By now they recognize common signposts such as blue links and buttons, and well-known processes such as sign-in and shopping cart checkouts, as powerful ways of making any single site easy to use.

Some patterns reflect abstract qualities that make great Web sites—qualities such as value, trust, and reliability. You will integrate traits like these into the design of the entire Web site, and reaffirm and reinforce them at every point of contact with your customers. These patterns describe the essence of these abstract qualities and how they can be incorporated into the whole Web site.

A Sample Pattern

2.2

Let's start with a pattern that may already be familiar to you: ACTION BUTTONS (K4).[1] These buttons solve a common problem that customers encounter on Web sites: knowing what can and cannot be clicked on. By adding shading to an otherwise flat button, you make it easier for people to find your links. This visual illusion works because it takes advantage of what people already know about physical buttons (see Figure 2.1).

---

1 Patterns in this book are referenced in SMALL CAPITAL LETTERS. The part in parentheses, "K4," means to go to Pattern Group K—Making Navigation Easy and then to the fourth pattern in that section.

Figure 2.1

People know how to use three-dimensional buttons.

Figure 2.2

Buttons in modern graphical user interfaces appear three-dimensional, to make them look as if you can press on them. You can take advantage of this knowledge by making the most important buttons on your Web site look three-dimensional too.

Figure 2.3

The gray **Search** button on the right-hand side is an example of an HTML action button. HTML action buttons can be specified in HTML and are created by the Web browser.

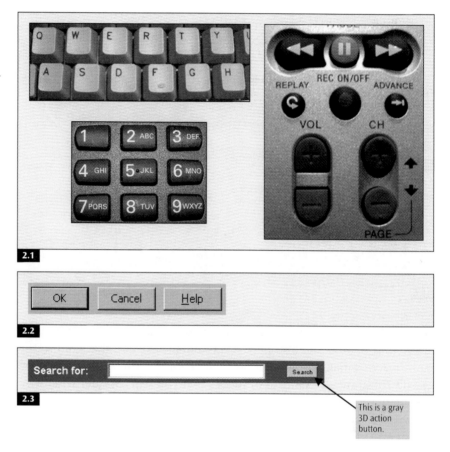

This is a gray 3D action button.

Graphical user interfaces have become another form of transferable knowledge. People who use computers learn that they can press on buttons with their mouse (see Figure 2.2). This becomes a learned behavior that can be transferred to how people perceive and interact with Web sites.

(K4) There are two kinds of ACTION BUTTONS (K4): HTML action buttons and graphical action buttons. HTML buttons are specified in HTML, so you have little control over how they are displayed. Figure 2.3 shows an example of an HTML button.

eBay and Amazon.com provide two examples of Web sites that use graphical action buttons on their homepages (see Figures 2.4 and 2.5). These buttons are often implemented as a single image that may contain multiple buttons.

But making buttons look three-dimensional is not the end of the story. What size should these buttons be? Bigger buttons are easier to see and

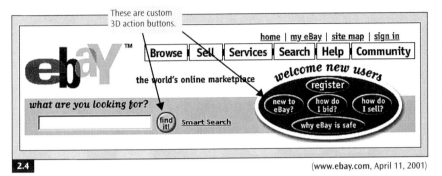

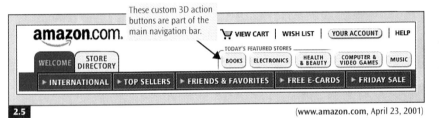

Figure 2.4

eBay uses graphical action buttons for the **find it!** button and for the buttons on the right, such as **register** and new to eBay?

(www.ebay.com, April 11, 2001)

Figure 2.5

Amazon.com uses graphical action buttons for its featured stores.

(www.amazon.com, April 23, 2001)

easier to click on, but they take up more space. In addition, if you have an image link, should you also have a redundant text link that goes to the same place? Finally, how does using images as links affect download speed? These are all examples of **forces** that you will consider when you use the patterns. The forces are the key issues that come into play when you are trying to solve a particular design problem. Within each pattern we include these forces and provide guidance for how to resolve the issues. For example, to improve the download speed of your ACTION BUT-TONS (K4), you might use FAST-DOWNLOADING IMAGES (L2).

The preceding explanation of ACTION BUTTONS (K4) has all the essential ingredients of a pattern. It explains the basic problem and describes the general solution. It also points out the forces exerting themselves on a design, and the many decisions and trade-offs that must be made if you use the pattern. Most importantly, it refers to other related patterns that affect how the pattern in question will be used.

As in Alexander's pattern language, each pattern is connected to certain higher-level patterns and to certain lower-level patterns. The pattern helps complete the higher-level patterns that are "above" it, and it is completed itself by the lower-level patterns that are "below" it. ACTION BUTTONS (K4), for example, help complete a PROCESS FUNNEL (H1), where moving from step to step requires a clear call to action. Similarly, ACTION BUTTONS (K4) may be completed with FAST-DOWNLOADING IMAGES (L2).

The benefit of using patterns is that they embody design experience that all of us as a community have developed and learned. A given pattern may not necessarily be the best solution in every case, but it tends to work in practice.

In the next section we describe the specific format of the patterns presented in this book. If you have ever seen patterns in other domains (such as software design or architecture), you will notice many similarities.

2.3   How to Read a Pattern

The patterns in this book have a more formal format than what you have read up to this point. Each pattern has six parts: name, background, problem, forces, solution, and other patterns to consider. See Figure 2.6 for an example.

The pattern name is the name we gave the solution. It consists of a phrase that you can use in a sentence, such as "What is the name of that PAGE TEMPLATE (D1)?" Each pattern name is written in SMALL CAPITAL LETTERS, so you can quickly identify it on a page. Each pattern also has a pattern number, such as A9. The letter identifies the group to which the pattern belongs. Throughout the book we also flag patterns in the margins with small callouts (such as **A9**). These callouts are also color-coded to match the corresponding pattern group. Each pattern group is also color-coded on the edge of the page so that you can find the group you want by looking at the edge of the book. Following the pattern name is the sensitizing image, a sample implementation of the solution. It shows how the solution might appear on a finished site.

Next comes the background, which provides context for the pattern, describing any other patterns that lead to this pattern and how they are related, as well as the scope of this pattern.

The next part is the problem, a concise statement, in **boldface,** of the specific problem that this pattern addresses.

The forces follow the problem, describing it in more detail, examining how people, their tasks, the technology, and society affect the design problem.

Next is the solution. Also set in **boldface,** the solution is a succinct statement of how to solve the problem. We also provide a sketch so that you can visualize the solution.

Finally, we discuss the other patterns to consider. Here we recommend more detailed patterns that help complete this pattern. You should examine and choose these according to your needs.

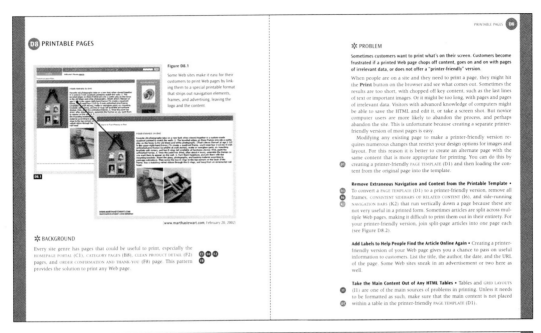

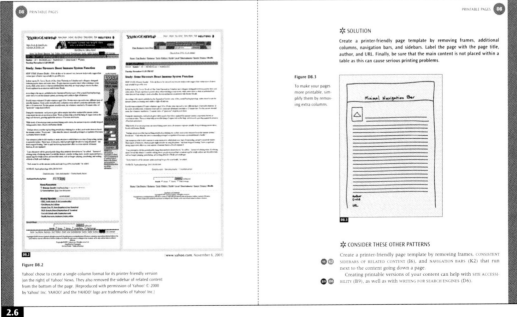

Figure 2.6

Every pattern has the same elements in identical order so that you can quickly find the information you need.

2.4 How to Use the Patterns

Pattern groups are organized by letter and by name, as Table 2.1 shows. Each pattern group contains a collection of thematically related patterns. For example, if you wanted to improve the search feature on your Web site, you would go to Pattern Group J—Making Site Search Fast and Relevant. Or if your testing showed that customers were having problems navigating your Web site, you would consult the patterns in Pattern Group K—Making Navigation Easy.

Generally speaking, the earlier the pattern group in this scheme, the earlier it should be used in the design process. For example, Pattern Groups A and B discuss Web site genres and creating a navigation framework for the entire Web site, respectively. Continuing, Pattern Group F looks at basic e-commerce issues, and Pattern Group H contains patterns that help customers complete tasks. These patterns are useful after you set the high-level goals and design of your Web site. Moving to the end, Pattern Group K deals with things like links and navigation bars, and Pattern Group L looks at speeding up a Web site.

Each pattern identifies related patterns in its sections on background, forces, and other patterns to consider. This network of patterns provides you with a way to quickly collect the patterns you need to complete your design. You can use the rich pattern vocabulary to articulate an almost infinite number of designs.

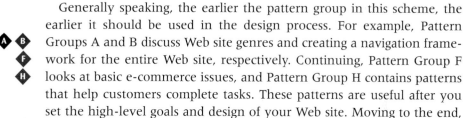

Table 2.1 Pattern Groups

A	Site Genres
B	Creating a Navigation Framework
C	Creating a Powerful Homepage
D	Writing and Managing Content
E	Building Trust and Credibility
F	Basic E-Commerce
G	Advanced E-Commerce
H	Helping Customers Complete Tasks
I	Designing Effective Page Layouts
J	Making Site Search Fast and Relevant
K	Making Navigation Easy
L	Speeding Up Your Site

An Example of Using Patterns

This example tells the story of a designer who discovers a costly Web site problem and uses the patterns presented in this book to deploy a customer-centered solution.

Sarah is part of the design team for an e-commerce Web site. Because the team is small, she has many responsibilities, including designing and evaluating the usability of the site.

While examining the Web site statistics, such as data from server logs, Sarah discovers that most customers are spending a fair amount of time on the site. However, many people appear to be abandoning their shopping carts and leaving the Web site right at checkout, before a sale is successfully closed. This problem is clearly something she needs to fix as quickly as possible.

Sarah brings up the problem at the design team's weekly meeting. It turns out that everyone knows that the Web site checkout has numerous problems, but no one has a solution. In a heated discussion team members voice their opinions, but the meeting ends with no resolution.

After the meeting Sarah checks if there are any design patterns that might help. Because this is an e-commerce problem, she starts with Pattern Group F—Basic E-Commerce, quickly skimming through the patterns there.

The first pattern that catches her eye is QUICK-FLOW CHECKOUT (F1). The problem statement seems to match the problem her Web site faces: "An e-commerce shopping experience will not be enjoyable, or worse, a purchase might not be completed, if the checkout process is cumbersome, confusing, or error prone." This pattern points out several problems with checkouts, including hidden charges, tedious text entries, confusing links, extra buttons, and complicated instructions. Sarah's team took special care to address the issue of hidden charges when they first designed the site because that was something that bothered them on other e-commerce Web sites. She finds, however, that a few links on the site still have confusing names.

Sarah also sees that several other patterns are referenced, including PERSONAL E-COMMERCE (A1). This pattern is in a group that comes before QUICK-FLOW CHECKOUT (F1), indicating that it is a more abstract pattern. Skimming over the PERSONAL E-COMMERCE (A1) pattern, she sees that it describes qualities of e-commerce sites in general, such as privacy, convenience, and returns. Although she finds that the PERSONAL E-COMMERCE (A1) pattern might be useful in the future, she decides that it is too high level for what she needs right now.

(F3) Another referenced pattern, SHOPPING CART (F3), looks more promising because it describes the features needed to make shopping carts useful. One important design question is how long unpurchased items stay in a shopping cart before they are automatically removed. Premature clearing of shopping carts may lead to lost sales because customers who return to a Web site might find that all the time they spent finding the items they wanted to buy was wasted. Sarah makes a mental note to ask the developers on the design team how long items are kept in the Web site's shopping carts. (It turns out to be just one hour.)

(F1)
(H1) QUICK-FLOW CHECKOUT (F1) also mentions a pattern called PROCESS FUNNEL (H1). Looking this pattern over, Sarah sees that process funnels are a sequence of pages designed to help people complete extremely specific tasks. Special care is taken to make instructions concise, to minimize extraneous links that might lead customers out of the process funnel, and to shorten the number of steps required for completing the process funnel. Thinking about the current checkout process, Sarah realizes that some of her site's pages are heavy with text instructions. There are also a few pages with links that could accidentally lead people out of the checkout process.

After studying the patterns, the forces, and the solutions, Sarah understands many of the shortcomings of her team's current checkout design. Using her site's existing design as a starting point, she can now quickly sketch design alternatives for a new checkout process, combining and modifying the solutions that the patterns describe.

After creating three possible solutions, using the patterns as a guide, she asks for informal feedback from the members of her design team. They identify some problems with her proposed designs and point out which changes will be easy to implement and which will not. Sarah uses this feedback to sketch another set of design alternatives, again using the patterns and her team's suggestions.

Sarah knows that a key principle of customer-centered Web design is keeping customers in the loop throughout the design process. She decides to run a quick evaluation with some representative customers. For this round of evaluations, Sarah decides that informally talking to and observing five participants is enough to get a pretty good idea of what the big problems are with the current site. She recruits five people that live nearby, visiting them in their homes. Offering a gift certificate and a free T-shirt makes recruiting pretty easy.

First she asks her recruits to try the old checkout process, so that she can get a better feel for the problems they encounter. Then she shows them her sketches for the new checkout process and gets feedback on the early designs.

While observing the participants, she realizes that she has anticipated many of the problems correctly. A customer named Fred, for example, clicks on the wrong link while in the checkout sequence, thereby accidentally exiting the process funnel. Although he is momentarily confused, Fred figures out what happened and hits the **Back** button. However, all of the information that he had just typed has disappeared, and he has to enter it all over again. Sarah marks this event down as a critical error.

Sarah also discovers a few new things that the design team did not realize were problems. Two of the participants have serious problems finding the button that takes them to the third step of the checkout. The correct button is at the bottom of the page. However, these two have fairly old computers, and their monitors are small enough that this button is not visible on their Web browser unless they scroll down. (This is why Fred clicked on the wrong link and fell out of the checkout process funnel.)

Although all five participants successfully complete the checkout sequence, none of them think it is very easy, and all of them suggest that the process reflects poorly on the Web site. Sarah also realizes that this result is probably an example of testing bias. Given all the problems with the Web site, she doubts that the participants would have finished the task if she had not been sitting beside them.

After the evaluation, Sarah takes out the sketches she created from the patterns and prior discussion with her team. She shows them to the participants, one at a time, asking them where they think each link will take them if they click on it, and whether the content on the page makes sense.

All five participants like the design sketches and think each one has more potential than the existing checkout process. However, one of the three design alternatives stands out as the one they like best. Sarah makes a note to explore this design alternative in greater detail.

At the next team meeting, Sarah presents the results of the evaluation. She describes many of the problems that her group of participants experienced and presents ideas on how to fix them. One team member mentions that the HIGH-VISIBILITY ACTION BUTTONS (K5) pattern addresses the problem of clicking on the wrong links in a process funnel.

Everyone agrees that the existing checkout process is broken and needs to be replaced as quickly as possible. Sarah presents sketches for the design alternative that her recruited participants said was best. The discussion focuses on prioritizing the features. After a brief debate, the team quickly reaches a consensus on the most important features for the next version of the checkout. They start looking to see if any design patterns apply, and they get to work on refining the new design.

2.6 Take-Away Ideas

The bulk of this book contains design patterns that you and your team can start using today. With these design patterns you can design a site from scratch, redesign a section of a site, or fix a particular problem on a page. Every design still requires your creativity, intuition, and testing to make the solutions effective. Our patterns direct your creative energies to solving new problems, as opposed to reinventing the wheel. In the words of literary critic Lionel Trilling, "Immature artists imitate. Mature artists steal."

The key here is to consider your options in context. If the goal of your site is to challenge your visitors, then many of the design patterns may not apply. But for any business or government site, the goal is to maximize your customer experience. This means that you will want to provide valuable, useful, and usable navigation structures and make it easy to find information and complete tasks successfully. For these kinds of sites, our patterns provide design solutions that work.

Knowing Your Customers: Principles and Techniques

A gulf between a design team and the end customers is a fundamental problem inherent in Web site design, whether the Web site is for entertainment, e-commerce, community, or information purposes. To bridge this gulf, you need to focus on customer-centered design. At the heart of customer-centered design are two principles:

1. Know your customers (covered here).
2. Keep your customers involved throughout the design and implementation process (covered in Chapter 4—Involving Customers with Iterative Design).

Knowing Your Customers Helps You Choose Patterns • So far, we have explained why good Web site design is important, and we have presented customer-centered design as the way to create successful Web sites. We have also introduced Web design patterns as one part of customer-centered design, and we have shown how you can use the patterns to create effective Web sites. However, Web design patterns by themselves are not enough. This chapter presents the next part. Knowing your current and prospective customers will help you choose patterns that are relevant to your site design, as well as help you decide between competing trade-offs when you are customizing patterns for your design situation.

To Know Your Customers, You Need Some Special Techniques • In this chapter you will learn the importance of having a deep understanding of your customers, their tasks, the technology available to them, and their social and organizational context before implementing your Web site. Then you will discover the techniques you can use for gaining such understanding, such as task analysis, scenario building, customer interviews, and analysis of existing Web sites.

Take It a Step at a Time • You do not have to adopt these principles all at once. In fact, it is best to take many small steps instead of one big leap. Chapter 5—Processes for Developing Customer-Centered Sites, explains how to go forward, outlining steps and deliverables for a customer-centered design process. If you are already an expert on customer-centered design and the design process, just skim Chapters 3 through 5 or skip right to the patterns in the second part of the book.

5

Principles for Knowing Your Customers

3.1

As you do when you're building any other relationship, you want to become intimate with the lives of your customers. This will not happen overnight. There is no secret formula. Fortunately, though, there are tried-and-true ways to learn about your customers. Before we discuss any of these techniques, let's understand what it means to *know your customers*. This principle really is many principles wrapped into one.

You Are Not Your Customers

One of the most important things that design teams must learn is that *they are not the customers*. Although it might sound obvious, this idea is not always integrated into the way design teams work. Customers do not have the same experiences, do not think the same, do not talk the same, and do not perform things in the same way as the design team does. This means that design teams cannot rely exclusively on their own intuition and experience when creating Web sites.

Understand the Elements, Balance the Forces

To understand your customers, consider the competing elements of every design: your customers, their tasks, their technology, and their social context (see Figure 3.1). Each of these elements has certain capabilities and limitations that exert forces on your design. To create a successful site, you must understand and balance these forces so that none dominates and each is considered in your final design. The principles and patterns in this book will help you balance your design. Let's begin by understanding the elements in more detail.

Understand Your Customers as People

If you understand the needs of your customers, you can use the information about them to shape your design. There are two ways of thinking

Figure 3.1

Customer-centered design is about understanding people, their tasks, the technology available, and how these issues sit within the social and organizational context of the customer and potentially the client who is having the Web site built.

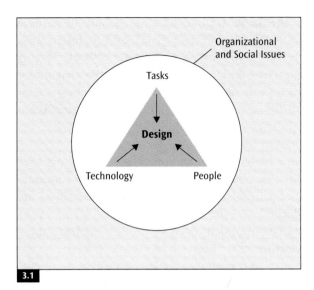

about this. One way is to understand people as individuals. The other way is to understand the basic characteristics of people in general.

Your Customers Are Different • Understanding people as individuals means having detailed profiles of customers, such as their demographics, attitudes, behaviors, knowledge, skills, and any other characteristics that can have a strong influence on the overall structure, design, and content of a Web site. For example, do the target customers care a lot about aesthetics, or do they prefer a simple and functional Web site? Who are the people who will visit the site? Are they children, young adults, seniors, or a combination of these? What level of education do they have? What other Web sites do they currently use? How experienced are they in using computers and the Web?

Understanding people as individuals also means learning the specific skills and language of your customers. If you were building a Web site for medical professionals, for example, you would probably study the terms and idioms in use in the medical profession, and carefully test the wording on the Web site for comprehension and correctness. On the other hand, if you were designing a Web site for premed students, you could not make the same assumptions. Instead, you would have to try to use the vocabulary and concepts that they understand, and test for those terms.

Your Customers Are Also the Same • Understanding people in general means knowing the fundamentals of human physical and cognitive abilities—how the human visual, motor, and memory systems work. Factors like these influence the structure and layout of individual Web pages. For example, how many things can an average person remember? What kinds of color deficiency, also known as color blindness, are most common? How well can people click on really small Web buttons? What sort of response time is required to support hand–eye coordination?

Knowledge of basic human abilities comes from the fields of cognitive psychology, human factors, ergonomics, and human–computer interaction. Although they are critical to superior design, these disciplines are also quite involved and can take years to master. To accelerate your learning process, we have incorporated many of the lessons from these fields into the design patterns in this book.

For example, the time it takes a person to move a mouse to a target is proportional to the distance to the target divided by the target size (this concept is known as Fitts's Law). In other words, buttons that are small or far away are harder to click on than buttons that are large or nearby. Two patterns influenced by Fitts's Law are DESCRIPTIVE, LONGER LINK NAMES (K9) and ACTION BUTTONS (K4). Fitts's Law will guide you in deciding how large links and buttons should be, ensuring that the ones on your Web site will be large enough to click on quickly.

As another example, about 8 percent of men and 0.5 percent of women in North America have some form of color vision deficiency. The most severe form, and the one that is most commonly known, is red–green deficiency. If you are designing a site targeted primarily at men, one in 12 of them might not be able to easily distinguish between red and green. Figure 3.2 shows feedback given to customers on problems with completing their form data that requires them to discern the difference between red and green. Would customers with color-deficient vision notice this subtle difference? One of our colleagues observed a test participant giving up on a purchase at this stage. It turned out that he had red–green color deficiency and he could not recover from an error because he could not see what he had done wrong.

It can be a challenge to balance the information from all the fields we have mentioned with Web design. The design patterns we present mix theory, research, and practical experience to provide solutions that work. For example, DESCRIPTIVE, LONGER LINK NAMES (K9) will help your customers navigate to the right page, but they also fill up more screen space and take longer to read. There is an intrinsic trade-off here between differing principles that have to be balanced to achieve the right effect.

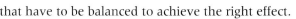

Figure 3.2

It might be tempting to use red to highlight an error. Because many people have red–green color deficiency, however, it is not a good idea to depend on their ability to distinguish differences that are communicated through those colors alone.

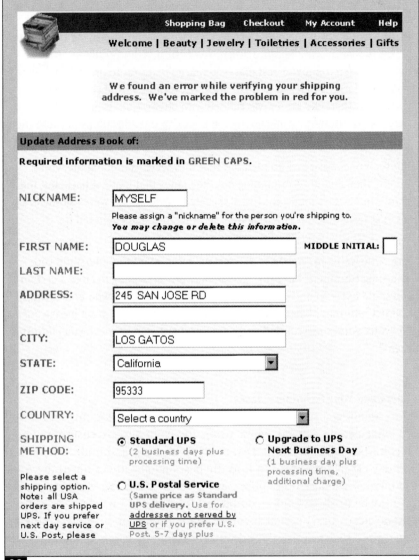

Customers Who Don't Return

During World War II some researchers were working on improving the armor on U.S. fighter planes. Because weight is a critical factor for planes, they needed to determine the best places to place the armor to protect the plane and the pilot. They looked at the planes that returned from combat, noting the places where the armor was riddled with enemy bullets. In their report they stated that more armor should be added to these locations because they seemed the most likely to be hit.

But then one researcher pointed out that they were examining the wrong things: They should be examining not the planes that made it back, but the planes that were shot down! The planes that made it back were not the ones hit in critical locations and thus were not the ones that could tell the researchers where more armor was needed.

The same is true for Web sites. It's certainly important to understand your returning customers, but they have already proven willing to cross a certain threshold to use your Web site. What about the customers who are leaving and not returning? What barriers are keeping these people from using your Web site? What concerns and needs do they have, and how can you address them?

Understand Your Customers' Tasks

Understanding customers' **tasks** means explicitly cataloguing and scripting what people can do when using the Web site. A customer might describe her task like this: "I want to send my grandmother an online birthday card," or "I want to find the best digital camera for under $500 and buy it." The task description says *what* the customer wants to do, but not how he or she would accomplish it.[1]

At a more fundamental level, though, understanding tasks also involves thinking critically about how your Web site can help streamline or even augment what people do today.

As a negative example, consider what happened to one of us while looking for a refund form on a company's Web site. The first task was to find this form online, but the site was so confusing that it was impossible. The company did not understand that this might be a common task that its customers would want to perform. In addition, the company's search

---

1 Some authors refer to abstract tasks like this as *goals*. We use the terms *task* and *goal* interchangeably here.

engine was relatively useless. Even after the right page was located through an *Internet* search engine, the only information the site provided was a fax number to request the right form.

If the design team had performed a **task analysis**, they might have discovered this task and streamlined it by letting people download the right forms and print them for themselves. A task analysis would have articulated the things people do, the things they act on, and the things they need to know. Taking their analysis one step further, the team could augment how the task is done today by having an online form that people can fill out and submit electronically.

You might be thinking, "What does it matter? He spent half an hour to find the right Web page, but he still got what he wanted in the end." That is true, but consider these issues: First, how many people do you think he told about this bad experience? Second, do you think he will ever buy something from this company again? We rest our case.

Reducing Work • Design teams should consider how they might help reduce the amount of work customers have to do. One way to do this is

The Importance of Understanding Tasks

Here's a story about why it is important to understand the customer's tasks *before* starting to implement your design. A small dentist's office decided to automate its billing, switching from paper-based forms to electronic versions. Hoping to reduce costs in the long term, the dentist spent a nontrivial amount of money to hire a programming team to develop a new system.

When the system was finished and deployed, however, all of the dentist's assistants were extremely dissatisfied with the new system, almost to the point of rejecting it entirely and going back to the paper-based forms. If the programmers had taken a closer look at how the paper forms were used, they would have noticed that many of them had handwritten notes in the margin.

It turns out that the assistants often wrote reminders, such as, "This patient's insurance takes longer than most," on the forms. But the system simply did not support this kind of flexibility. A careful analysis of the existing tasks could have revealed this use of notes, and the appropriate flexibility could have been designed into the system. Instead, the dentist's office ended up paying a lot of money for an inflexible system that did not please the assistants.

to use a metaphor that people already know. Spreadsheets did this by using a metaphor to existing paper spreadsheets. E-commerce sites do this by using metaphors to things in real stores, such as a SHOPPING CART (F3). However, replicating an existing interface is not always the best approach. For example, a design team could create a Web-based telephone directory by taking images of real telephone directory pages, sticking a page at a time on the screen, and adding buttons to turn the pages. Now, whether they *should* do this is the real question.

F3

This approach ignores the problems with existing telephone directories and fails to take advantage of the Web medium. It takes time to find a listing in paper-based telephone directories, even if you know the exact spelling. Paper directories are also hard to use if you know only part of a listing. A better approach would be to take advantage of the computer's abilities to do fast searches and to make partial and close matches.

Task Training • One factor to consider with regard to understanding tasks is how much training is involved. For example, engineers spend many years learning very specific terms and procedures. A Web site targeted at professional engineers might assume a certain level of knowledge. However, a Web site targeted at homeowners interested in maintaining their homes on weekends cannot make the same assumption. It is your job to decide how much hand-holding customers need.

One of the myths of the usability field is that everything needs to be intuitive on first use. Certainly this is true for kiosks at tourist sites or handheld tour guide devices—things a person might use only once. But in many cases, with a little training your customers will become highly effective using the tools you provide.

There is a real difference between ease of learning and ease of use. For example, kazoos and triangles are walk-up-and-use musical instruments, but they are not all that interesting. With many years of practice, however, people can master playing a difficult instrument such as a violin, and in some cases become creators of music instead of just consumers. Computer pioneer Douglas Engelbart said it best: "If ease of use was the only valid criterion, people would stick to tricycles and never try bicycles." (This notion of training the customer or relying on the customer's existing training is one of the key ideas behind the Web design patterns in this book. People become accustomed to operating in a certain way on the Web, and in many cases it makes sense to take advantage of this knowledge.)

Design teams have to be careful, though, because it is far too easy to use the bicycle-versus-tricycle argument as an excuse for poor Web design. You should know how much training customers are realistically willing to undergo. Paul Saffo, the noted futurist, writes:

> We do not use tools simply because they are friendly. We use tools to accomplish tasks, and we abandon tools when the effort required to make the tool deliver exceeds our threshold of indignation—the maximal behavioral compromise that we are willing to make to get a task done.

Customers often do not take kindly to having to train to use a product. In this way, Web sites are different from desktop software. With desktop software, customers have already invested a fair amount of time and money purchasing and installing the software, and thus have a motivation to learn how to use it. With Web sites, it is just the opposite. Customers are not likely to buy something on a Web site or avail themselves of its services if they have to spend lots of time learning to use it, unless they can see that it provides significant benefit. For example, it is highly unlikely that customers will spend more than a few minutes learning how to use an entertainment Web site. On the other hand, look at how kids attach themselves to video games. They are willing to learn fairly complex controls because they think the game will be a lot of fun.

Helping People Become Experts • You should also consider how your Web site could help people to *become* experts faster. For example, going back to the example of the Web site for homeowners, it is probably not a good idea to scare off newcomers by having lots of complex terms and diagrams on the homepage. However, the Web site could gently introduce a few basic terms, and maybe even have an online dictionary containing all the commonly used terms.

The Web site could also have a section for beginners, filled with tutorials, basic diagrams, and interesting war stories, all designed to draw them in. Sample home projects could be ranked by difficulty so that homeowners would have some way of knowing what is easy and what is not. The Web site could also support a community, as illustrated by COMMUNITY CONFERENCES (A3), in which people could ask questions and slowly learn the ropes of taking care of, maintaining, and adding onto their homes. By providing many ways to learn and many places to fall back on, and by making it fun, design teams can "hide" the amount of training required and create a more gentle slope to gaining expertise.

Understand the Technology

Do you know which tools your customers have at their disposal, which tools are available to you, and what the capabilities and limitations of these tools are? For example, how many of your customers have fast Internet connections? If most people have slow network connections, using a lot of large images is not a good idea. By understanding how the Internet works, you can design Web pages that are faster to download. See Pattern Group L—Speeding Up Your Site, for more information.

Technology is a broad issue, but unfortunately it is either completely ignored or given too much primacy in designs. When Web design teams overlook the fact that many of their customers do not have the latest Web browser and plug-ins, they wind up with customers who are puzzled because they see nothing at all on the Web site. (This is not as uncommon as you might think. Just try surfing the Web with JavaScript turned off and you will see what we mean.) When technology becomes the central factor in Web design, it becomes technology for technology's sake. The customer's needs are certainly not being met on sites like this.

Design teams need to know what is possible with current technologies, and the relative advantages and disadvantages of each technology. For example, do you know the differences between a GIF image and a JPEG image? When is it better to use one over the other? (See FAST-DOWNLOADING IMAGES (L2) for more information on this topic.) The Web design patterns in this book address some of these issues, but you can get more detail from books that focus on these subjects, such as those included in the Resources section of this book.

Here's an example of what happens when human abilities and the technological constraints that affect them are not considered in Web site design. Fast response times help maintain a sense of continuity in a task flow. Generally speaking, response times on the order of 100 milliseconds are needed for things like dragging icons and typing text. Response times on the order of 1 second (1,000 milliseconds) are required to maintain an uninterrupted flow of thought when completing a routine action like clicking on a button. Now, you could read about these response times in a news article or a book on human factors and decide that all the pages on your site must be viewable by customers in less than a second. Although this notion is well-intentioned, given the current state of networking and Web technology, this is a completely unrealistic goal. Although they should never be the driving factor, technological constraints should still be considered as part of a Web site's design: people and tasks first, technology second.

Be extremely wary of religious wars. If you talk to enough Web designers, you will meet a few that are slavishly devoted to a specific technology, such as Macromedia Flash. Such viewpoints lead to narrow and severely unbalanced views of the world, putting technology ahead of client goals and customer needs. Remember, if all you have is a hammer, everything looks like a nail. Technology is a tool for helping people get things done—nothing more, nothing less.

Understand Your Customers' Social Issues

Framing how people, tasks, and technology fit within a broader social and organizational context means considering how these social issues broaden the scope of design, putting things into the context of the big picture. Suppose you're designing a Web-based group calendaring system. You will need to know who has an online calendar. You will also ask how groups decide to have meetings. Does a manager decide, or is it a consensus process? These are all organizational questions that will help you design the interface to best meet the needs of your customer.

The importance of looking at organizational issues is illustrated quite nicely by Leysia Palen's 1999 study of online group calendars at two large technology companies. Palen found that it is wise to pay attention to the culture of the company when setting the defaults for enterprise-wide software. For example, should a shared calendar show only that a person is busy, or should it show exactly what the person wrote down for that time slot? This question must take into account personal privacy, company security, and control over the group's personal time. The research found that the preferences for these defaults were vastly different in the two organizations.

Palen's research showed that the success or failure of a group calendaring system lies not only in the functionality it provides, but also in default settings. You could argue that all that is needed to fix the problem is a feature that lets individuals customize this kind of information, but the study showed that over 80 percent of the people maintained the defaults. This is an important lesson for any human–computer interface design. Even if you build in a lot of flexibility, your customers will probably use the default settings. The choice for your defaults thus will have a major impact on the success or failure of your site. Again, your customers' successful adoption of new software often depends on how it fits into existing social and organizational contexts.

It is also valuable to understand the flow of work through an organization. Say you were building a new Web-based programming tool. Many enlightened designers might consider just watching programmers and how they work. Although this is a good first step, it actually leaves quite a bit out. We would also want to understand how the programmers interact with quality assurance engineers, designers, technical writers, and marketers. When do these interactions occur? What kinds of things happen during these interactions? Answers to these questions could critically influence your design.

The growing importance of online communities provides another reason to look at social and organizational issues. Before the Web, the concept of online communities was limited to dial-up bulletin board systems, newsgroups, and e-mail lists. The Web has expanded on these early outposts and proliferated the idea that groups tied together by shared interests or by common values can find a place together in cyberspace. Paying close attention to social and organizational factors can help you see how a Web site will explicitly support a specific group and build a community, cementing a longer-term relationship with customers.

Usually the organizational issues will be about the customer's organization, but sometimes it might be useful to look into organizational issues of the client. The client might have high-level goals for the Web site that are different from the high-level goals or tasks that you found to be important to customers. Resolving these differences up front might be the difference between success and failure of the project.

Techniques for Knowing Your Customers   3.2

We have described what it means to understand the elements of every design: people, tasks, technology, and social issues. Here we describe specific techniques that you can use to gain this understanding. Techniques such as task and customer analysis, observations, interviews, surveys, focus groups, and Web site evaluations help you characterize target customers and their needs. Some of these techniques are good for qualitative information, others for quantitative. The key is to use a mixture of techniques to get a more complete picture of who your customers are and what they *need*.

The word *need* here is important. One of the major problems with traditional software engineering methodologies is that they have focused on what clients say they *want*. The difference between what clients ask for and what customers need has led to many project failures in the past.

Customers themselves cannot easily express what they need.[2] The methods we present here focus on finding out what these needs are.

One of the problems you will repeatedly face is finding your target customers, and getting them to help out. Are they too busy? Perhaps you can buy their time by offering T-shirts, coffee mugs, or gift certificates. Are they still too busy? See if there is an alternative but similar audience. For example, medical doctors are often too occupied to take surveys or to participate in Web site evaluations, but first-year medical students might help out instead. Although students may not be the exact target customers, they are a pretty good approximation.

What if you have no idea who your potential customers are? This is where traditional market research techniques come to bear. Running focus groups and surveys, by telephone or online, with different types of potential customers, can help your team focus on the kinds of people who will be attracted to your Web site. This type of research should be conducted before you start designing the site.

Run a pilot test before showing your site to potential customers. Have some friends first try out your survey, focus group, or Web site evaluation to work out any kinks in the wording or procedure. Analyze the pilot test data to make sure that the data you're collecting is the data you want. This will help minimize the problems you will encounter when you collect and analyze information for real.

Start a Task Analysis

One of the first steps, before doing any kind of design work or implementation, is a **task and customer analysis**.[3] A task analysis will help you understand what your customers do now and how they do it, and it will provide ideas for what your customers could do with your Web site. The key to task analysis is to first identify the target customer population, find people representative of that population, and then find out what they do.

When starting a task analysis, use your intuition and experience, as well as informal interviews with task experts, to answer questions that

---

2 Customers *are* good at using a Web site and being able to say that it is something they do not need. This is where the iterative design techniques described in Chapter 4—Involving Customers with Iterative Design come into play.

3 Our use of the term *task analysis* differs slightly from the traditional definition. We have added customer analysis to this phase. This means you use task analysis to find out about your customers' tasks, as well as to find out who your customer is—that is, to know your customer.

characterize the target audience. Later you can use other techniques, such as observations, surveys, and evaluation of competitors' Web sites to answer the questions in more detail. If you are revising an existing Web site, you can also evaluate it. Successful design teams often use a combination of these techniques to develop a meaningful understanding of customers and their needs.

The sections that follow describe some sample task analysis questions. As you might have expected, they are organized into four categories: people, tasks, technology, and social issues.

People • Who are the customers? What are their interests? What are their ages? Are they children, young adults, adults, senior citizens, or a combination? What level of education do they have? What kind of vocabulary do they use? What kind of computer skills do they have? Are they expert computer users? Are they novices? What is their income range? What is their reading ability? Do they have any physical constraints, such as poor vision or poor hearing? What is important in their lives?

Tasks • What are your customers' current offline tasks? What tasks do they do on other Web sites? What do they come to your current Web site to do? What specific tasks do they want to do there? How are the tasks learned? Are the tasks things they will do many times, or just a few times? What tools and information do they need to accomplish their tasks? How often do they do their tasks? Are there time constraints? Do the tasks need to be done within a certain period of time? What happens if they do not complete a task? What do they do for help if they cannot complete a task? In what ways can they recover?

Technology • What kind of equipment and tools do your customers have? What kind of Web browsers do they use? What kind of plug-ins do they have? What other kinds of software do they have and use? What monitor sizes do they have? How fast are their network connections?

Social Issues • What kind of social or organizational factors affect your customers? Where will they do their tasks? In what environment do they do their tasks? Is it noisy or quiet? Is it a stressful environment? Is it an office environment? Do they work at home? Do they use a public kiosk or a shared computer? Is security an issue? Do they work late at night? Do they work during peak Internet traffic hours? What is the relationship between the customer and the data? Is it public data? Is it highly sensitive private data? Is the data shared with coworkers? Is it shared with family members?

Experts might ask how you can answer these questions without first doing an in-depth field study, in which you watch customers in action. We think these techniques work best used in tandem. Your task analysis can inform your field observations and interviews, and your interviews and observations can inform your task analysis. You will always have some assumptions going into a field study, and it is advantageous to make those explicit, as the task analysis lets you do. On the other hand, it is unwise to invest too much time in a task analysis before studying real customers. You might become too committed to your initial analysis and have a hard time letting evidence from the field overturn your assumptions.

Quick-and-dirty task analysis before interviewing helps you focus the field investigation. Usually time and resources do not realistically permit an unstructured "let's go in and see what we see" study, so you have to figure out which customers do the tasks you want to focus on.

Build Scenarios

After your initial task analysis, create scenarios illustrating what people would use your Web site for. **Scenarios** are stories rich in context that focus more on *what* people will do than on *how*. (If your background is software engineering, you may be more familiar with the term *use cases*.) Here's an example of a scenario for a hypothetical Web site called ebirthdayz.com that specializes in helping customers shop for gifts:

Victoria is a bright young college student looking for a gift for her younger sister, who is turning 16 in two weeks. Like most college students, Victoria is on a tight budget, but she wants to get something memorable and useful for her sister on this important birthday for a young girl. She's heard some of her friends talk about ebirthdayz.com, so she decides to check it out. On the ebirthdayz.com homepage, she sees that the Web site has a gift recommendation feature. Victoria finds the recommendations screen and views gifts based on her sister's age and general interests, as well as her own limited finances. The site shows some suggestions, and Victoria chooses a popular favorite and buys it, including gift wrapping. Total time spent: 20 minutes.

A scenario tells us something about customers and their characteristics, the tasks they want to accomplish, and the context of their use of the site (in this case Victoria's sister's sixteenth birthday, which is important to Victoria).

It is useful to create many different scenarios for each of the several types of customers that you expect to come to your Web site. These detailed illustrative customers are often referred to as **personas**. Get lots of detail about your personas: name, background, what they do, where they live, and so on. Make these details as real as possible. You can put some of these details right in the scenarios, or you might put some only in a document where you describe your personas. Having real people in mind is even better because you can get more details later, when you need them.

Refer to the details when deciding between different ways of carrying out a design. You might ask, "Would Victoria use this feature for sending business gifts to colleagues? No, she is a college student and probably does not have a need for business gifts. This feature would be irrelevant to this type of customer." Reuse scenarios throughout the design process as a check, to see whether your design decisions still make sense in relation to the scenarios.

Sometimes scenarios include photographs or sketched storyboards. A **storyboard** is a sequence of Web pages you create to give a rough idea of how a person would accomplish a given task. The storyboard in Figure 3.3 shows some rough cuts of how people would select different musical genres on a PDA-based music Web site. Although you might be tempted to use software tools to make nice-looking storyboards, there are many good reasons to defer doing it at this stage (see Section 4.4, Rapid Prototyping, in Chapter 4—Involving Customers with Iterative Design, for **4** more information).

Again, note that scenarios do not say much about how things are accomplished. The first of the two preceding scenarios does not say where the gift recommendation feature is located, nor does it give specifics of how the gift recommendations are organized. At this early stage it is more important to determine whether the gift recommendation feature is a good idea at all before getting too detailed. Have the design team "walk through" a scenario to see if it makes sense. Is it a compelling story? Does it feel useful? Does it have a good UP-FRONT VALUE PROPOSITION (C2)? Are **C2** there any obvious problems with it?

Rich scenarios help you try out design ideas before even building software. They can also provide an idea of which genre patterns and other high-level patterns might be appropriate. Our scenario with Victoria, for example, would tell us that we should look at the PERSONALIZED

Figure 3.3

This sketched story-
board shows how a
customer would
accomplish one task
using the design of a
music site targeted at
PDA users.

RECOMMENDATION (G3) and GIFT GIVING (G6) patterns in Pattern Group
G—Advanced E-Commerce. These patterns would be necessary, in addition to the patterns in Pattern Group F—Basic E-Commerce, to support
the customer goals in the Victoria birthday scenario. Having several personas and scenarios will help you determine which other patterns might
also apply.

Scenarios are also useful for describing to clients and customers what a
Web site will offer. They tell us about particular customers, describing
their situations and what they're trying to accomplish.

Choose Tasks

We have already mentioned that you can create several scenarios that
illustrate your personas accomplishing a variety of goals or tasks. How
do you choose these tasks, and what should they look like? These tasks
will come from your initial task analysis and will be enriched by later
observations and interviews with real customers. The tasks in your scenarios should be *detailed*, providing specifics about the customers and
the situations. Remember that a task description does not say how it is
accomplished.

The tasks in your scenarios should also be *representative;* that is, they should be real tasks that customers or prospective customers currently or eventually want to accomplish. You might say, "I'm inventing something new; nobody has ever done the tasks my site will allow!" Your site might allow someone to do things in a new way, but it is quite rare to invent something entirely new. For example, before sites like evite.com, you could not use a Web site to invite your friends to a party and check on their RSVPs. But the task itself is not new. People had parties before the Web was created, and they needed to invite people and see who was coming. Instead of a Web site, they used letters, phone calls, and even e-mail to accomplish the same task.

The tasks you choose for your scenarios should also be *common* or *important*. Common tasks are those that will be done frequently. For an invitation site, for example, creating a new invitation and sending it out will be a common task. Important tasks are those that must be done correctly or there will be unfortunate consequences. Again, on our invitation site it is important that customers have the ability to create an account with their name and e-mail address registered correctly, so that people they invite will know who is sending the invitation. Getting this wrong would not make the site very useful.

Finally, make sure that the tasks you use describe a *complete* activity— that they are entire tasks, not subtasks or pieces of a task. Thinking about complete activities forces us to consider how features will work together, which is important because the tasks in your scenarios will become the basis for the site design and for the tasks used in future customer tests of the site.

Imagine that you're creating a Web-based banking site. You might decide that there are three different scenarios, each with a different task: (1) checking a savings account balance, (2) checking a checking account balance, and (3) transferring funds between savings and checking accounts. If you develop these three features independently and then later test them, they might work just fine. Unfortunately, you might also end up with an awkward design and not know it until the site launches.

A more realistic, complete task is a combination of the three subtasks just described to achieve a common customer goal: "Make sure that I have enough money in my checking account to cover the last check I wrote." This task would require first a verification that the checking account had sufficient funds. If not, the customer would next check the balance in savings and then move some money from savings to checking. If your banking site were designed to support only the three subtasks, using them in combination might be tedious. For instance, the design might require going back to a main menu to select a new operation. Only by knowing about complete, realistic tasks in advance would you be able to smoothly support these tasks in your design.

The task analysis and sample scenarios generated so far are based on your knowledge and intuition, as well as on any interviews and observations you might have carried out with prospective customers. In the next section we describe in more detail the techniques you can use to get feedback from customers. In addition to helping you complete your initial analysis, these techniques can help you see if the analysis and scenarios are correct.

Observe and Interview Customers

Techniques for observing and interviewing customers can be quick and informal, consisting of conversations over coffee, or having customers show you what they do now in their homes or at work. We have found that most people are willing to help, especially if you explain that you're using the information to improve your site for them. And paying for coffee or lunch doesn't hurt.

Ethnographic Approaches Can Be Used to Observe • Ethnography is a more formal technique used in sociology and anthropology to observe and interact with people. Ethnographers study people in their normal environments. The advantage that ethnography has over techniques such as interviews and surveys is that you can watch what people *actually* do, as opposed to what they *say* they do. You can also ask them questions while they show you what they do, to verify your inferences. You can see the people with whom they communicate, the tools they use, and the kinds of things they create—things that may be difficult for participants to remember or explain when taken out of context. Although a rigorous ethnographic observation can be difficult and time-consuming, a more informal and "ethnographically inspired" field study can be fast and still yield valuable information that can drive the design.

For example, if you are building a banking site, your ethnographic research might include visiting a bank for a day and studying all the different types of transactions that customers perform with the teller. Because you are also extending banking capabilities into the home, you might also study the financial activities people do at home, such as paying bills, checking balances, and transferring money. Ethnographically inspired observation is easier than you might think. First recruit some participants and ask if you can follow them around for a day or two and watch what they do. If they don't mind, use a digital camera to take pictures of their workplace or home. These pictures will make it easier to describe what you learned to your clients and to the rest of your design team.

In addition, see what kinds of Web sites people visit. Ask them to take you through your Web site or through a competitor's Web site. Ask them what they like and dislike about the sites. Look at the kinds of tools they use and note the kinds of information they use to make decisions. Ask questions to make sure you understand what they're doing. Run your interpretations by the customers to see if you're right. Look for any sign of disagreement, even signs as subtle as "Huh?," "Umm," and "Yes, but . . ." Customers will feel uncomfortable until you phrase the question correctly, but they may be hesitant to come right out and say so.

Follow Up with Informal Interviews • Tell any customers you interview what the Web site is supposed to do, and ask them what kinds of things they would like to do. Ask if they have any ideas about how they would organize and structure parts of the Web site. Show them sketches and scenarios and ask what they think about these conceptualizations (do not show these sketches too early in the observation or interview because doing so might bias the customers). Although they cannot develop the design for you, customers can certainly provide a lot of useful information.

When talking to customers, phrase your questions carefully. Do not lead people toward a certain answer. Questions that do not lead to a simple yes or no answer are preferable. For example, questions like "Would you like this feature?" do not work well because most people will just say, "Yeah, sure, why not?" You want to ask questions that get people talking so that you can hear what they're thinking.

A better way of asking a question is to show two alternatives and ask people what they think. It is difficult to judge something by itself. It is easier to compare the differences between two approaches.

Another way of phrasing the question is to give people a list of features and ask them to state how important each feature is on a scale from 1 to 7, with 1 being "not important" and 7 being "very important."

Recording observations and interviews using an audio recorder can make your job much easier and the data you collect more reliable. It's hard to keep up with taking notes while you're watching someone in action and speaking to them. Use your notes to record only the most important things and remember to write down the time that these events occur. This information will make it easier to find the corresponding place

Asking Interview Questions

Here are some tips for interviewing people about their work practices.

Avoid Interruptions • Turn off all cell phones and find a quiet place that will not have any distractions. If possible, conduct your interviews in customers' normal environments, such as work or home, so that they can show you things while they're talking. In such cases the interviews are more like ethnographic observations.

Start with Easy Questions First • Wait to pose the harder questions until after the interviewee has talked for a while and is more comfortable speaking with you.

Ask Open-Ended Questions • Avoid asking simple yes or no questions. Ask questions that will get your interviewees to talk about their thoughts and experiences. Short questions that result in long answers are good—for example, "What do you like best about the current site, and why?"

Be Nonjudgmental and Accepting • Try not to be confrontational or condescending. It is not your job to judge what your interviewees are doing; it is to learn how to make your Web site fit your customers better.

Listen • These are interviews, not conversations, so let the interviewees do the talking. While they are talking, note anything important and write down follow-up questions. Interrupt only if you need a clarification or if they start digressing. Give feedback, such as nodding your head and saying, "Mm-hmm," to let your interviewees know you're listening. It is also all right to have extended periods of silence to let them collect their thoughts.

in the audiotape later. Transcribing your audiotapes can be tedious and time-consuming, but having a transcript is valuable for noticing subtle issues that you might have missed and helping you confirm inferences you might have made. There are several services that will transcribe audiotapes for a modest price. We recommend that you take advantage of such a service if you can.

Organize the Information You Discover • Your observations and interviews will result in a lot of data. Organize and make sense of that information. In **affinity diagramming,** for example, you arrange all the individual points and concepts you have gathered on a wall-sized, hierarchical

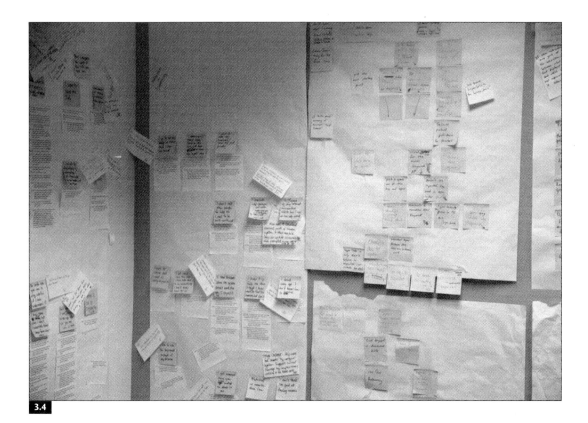

3.4

diagram (see Figure 3.4). Write each concept on a Post-it note. Group related concepts together, and draw lines between related concepts in different groups. Use different colors to denote groups and even groups of groups, creating a hierarchy. The affinity diagram gives your team a visual explanation of the customer's problems and needs, all in one place. Affinity diagrams can eventually become the basis for your initial information architecture, and they are good starting points for scenarios and storyboards.

Card sorting is another technique for determining the best site organization that is easy to carry out. It helps you understand how to group items so that people will be able to find what they're looking for by recognizing the groups. It also helps you find and fix terminology that would be hard for customers to understand.

To understand card sorting, imagine you wanted to organize a deck of cards. You could organize the cards by suit, separating them into clubs,

Figure 3.4

An affinity diagram organizes the information resulting from your interviews. Over time, this diagram can result in a site map representing the site's information architecture.

spades, hearts, and diamonds. However, the cards could also be organized validly by number, that is, grouping all four kings together, all four queens together, and so on. Alternatively, you could organize the cards by color, separating the red cards from the black cards. Because these would be relatively large groups, it might make sense to further subdivide the red cards, by suit or by number.

Likewise, there are many ways of organizing Web pages. The point is that there are many valid ways of organizing content, and it all depends on what you need. You group pages in a way that makes sense, and then later you name the resulting categories. Variations of the card-sorting method include sorting the categories into subcategories, or even asking customers to carry out the card sorting.

Card sorting can be a useful exercise if you need to create or validate the organization of a site. For example, suppose your site starts with the following content:

Depending on your target customer, your sort might come out differently. If these were categories for a grocery site, you might sort them as follows:

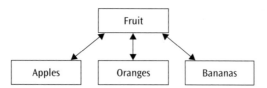

If customers were particularly concerned about freshly picked, locally grown fruit, you might sort the cards in this way:

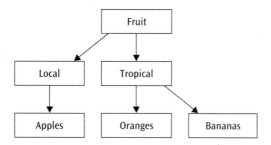

If customers were concerned about pesticide use, you might sort the cards like this:

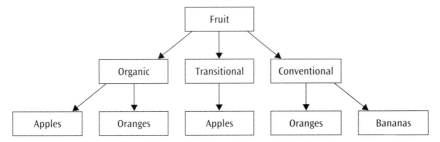

Just for the sake of argument, a botanist would probably sort the cards completely differently, maybe like this:

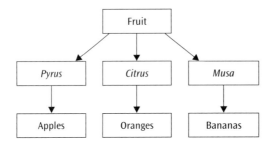

If you carry out a card-sorting activity with several customers or other team members, cluster the resultant groupings to understand where they agree and where they do not. Pay attention to items about which consensus could not be reached. Would renaming the item improve things? Some items might fit into several categories. An easy way to visualize the data is to use IBM's EZSort or NIST's WebCAT (see the Resources section later in the book for details on downloading these tools). Asking these questions about where to put each content item and what to call the categories will help create the most customer-friendly content structure possible.

Know the Limits of These Techniques • Sometimes it is useful to observe how people work for at least a few days. The amount of information you learn about your customers during this time will be tremendous. However, it is difficult to capture some kinds of information in such a short time. For example, how do the environment or priorities change for families during events such as holiday seasons or childbirth? If you observed a family for just one or two days, you would probably miss things like this.

Unfortunately, few of us have the time to carry out interviews and observations at this level of depth. This is one of the trade-offs you will have to consider, depending on your situation and the type of site you're attempting to design. Extended fieldwork might not be as useful for a site that customers occasionally come to for e-commerce transactions, but it may be crucial to spend lots of time on this type of field study for a Web application that someone will use for much of the day, every day.

Survey Your Customers

Traditionally used in market research, surveys are another useful way of finding out about your customers and helping you confirm who should be your target audience. Surveys are used to gather a great deal of information from lots of people. If you are planning to revise your Web site, consider adding a survey on the existing Web site to get feedback from current customers about what they like and do not like. Use a combination of multiple-choice and free-form questions. Multiple-choice questions make your data analysis task easier and allow the respondent to move through your survey faster. Free-form responses let people write at length about what is right (and what is wrong) with the existing Web site.

Surveys can be delivered in several different ways. You can survey people in person. One especially effective technique is to approach people coming into a shopping mall and ask them whether they would like to help improve a Web site. Mailing surveys to your target audience or using a market research firm to ask survey questions over the phone are also common techniques. When mailing surveys, be careful to get responses from a representative sample of customers. This problem largely goes away with telephone sampling. All three of these techniques can be expensive and take a lot of time to get results.

The Web opens up the opportunity to carry out survey-based research online. Several firms offer this service, or you can have your development team build a simple survey tool for you. Web-based surveys can be delivered via e-mail to research participants (from your customer list or from a list you buy from a market research firm), in pop-up windows to a randomly sampled set of visitors to your site, or as a link on a feedback page. This flexibility offers you a powerful way to get survey results about your customers quickly.

Convincing people to participate in a survey usually requires some enticement. Offer potential participants a chance to win a prize in a drawing, a T-shirt, a coffee mug, or cash.[5] The reward you offer will depend on

---

5 It is amazing what well-paid people will do for a free T-shirt or coffee mug that costs maybe five U.S. dollars.

how much time the survey takes to complete. The longer it is, the more you have to "pay." What you pay might range anywhere from $15 to $100 (U.S.). This, along with the fact that people will simply stop participating in a survey that is too long, is one reason to make your survey take less than 15 minutes to complete. This is especially true for Web-based surveys, where people will give up even more quickly. The reward will also depend on the type of participant you are trying to recruit. It is not unusual to offer executive-level participants cash compensation or a donation of $200 or more to their favorite charity in exchange for 45 minutes of their time.

Surveys can be tricky, though. At best, you can get a lot of data and make conclusions that are based on quantitative results. This can be helpful for convincing others in your organization about the usefulness of the results. Unfortunately, when you want to make quantitative conclusions, you need to be sure that those conclusions make sense from a statistical perspective. Surveys have to be designed properly to give you **reliable data**—results that would be found consistently if you ran the survey over and over with the same type of audience under the same conditions. Also make sure you have enough participants, and get a high enough response rate so that you achieve **statistical validity**—results that are highly likely to be right.

A lot of the survey work we have seen on the Web simply falls down on one or both of these issues. We recommend that you work with a firm that has expertise in this area, as well as read a good book on survey design to understand the full impact of drawing conclusions on poorly collected data.

Another issue to watch out for is that surveys report on what people *say*, not on what people *do*. A lot of research has found that what people say does not always correspond to what they do. This is especially true when people have to reconstruct specific details about what they do on the Web. People can remember things at a high level, but they tend to quickly forget the details. Despite these shortcomings, surveys have been proven very effective over and over for determining the target market, product and concept feasibility, price elasticity, attitudinal and brand image, general opinions, and preferences. Ultimately, however, if you want to know what people really do, or are going to do, you should watch them in action.

Run Focus Groups
Focus groups are commonly used by market researchers to find out about customers and their opinions. In a **focus group**, a handful of peo-

ple (6–12) who are representative of target customers are brought into a meeting as a group. They may or may not know each other beforehand. As in the interviewing process already described, people are asked questions about competitors' Web sites and about the proposed Web site. If you are revising your Web site, you might ask the focus group what they like and dislike about the site. If you are creating a new Web site, ask them the same questions about your competitors' Web sites. Get their feedback on the proposed Web site by showing them sketches or pictures of how it will work. It is also common to present scenarios of future use to see how these ideas resonate with the group.

Just like the Boy Scouts, focus groups have the motto "Be prepared!" Do not go in blindly and hope you will find useful information. Identify what you want to find out. Have an idea of what you're looking for, and make sure that all of the questions you ask will help you learn whether you're going in the right direction. Also be ready for criticism. Although it may sting a little in the short run, it will result in higher-quality designs in the end. Other members of the development team or management can sit in on these meetings. Hearing comments directly from customers is much more convincing than reading reports. Be sure to keep the number of these insiders low so that you don't overwhelm the focus group.

Focus groups are difficult to run well. Often the moderator can be too controlling and drive the group to conclusions that he or she would like to see. Another common problem is that an individual in the group dominates and causes groupthink to emerge as the other members defer. You will have to get the dominating person to quiet down so that you can draw other members out. Find moderators who have experience running a focus group because they will be familiar with these problems and know how to handle them gracefully.

Note also that you may get different results, depending on the chemistry of the people in the group. Sometimes your results will be positive, sometimes negative, and very negative—all in response to the same questions and the same examples. For this reason it is usually a good idea to run a focus group several times, with different types of people, in different geographic locations. Also be careful in your recruiting to avoid **professional respondents**, focus group members who make money on the side by going from group to group. You want to get people who are representative of your customers, not people who are just conveniently available.

One caveat about focus groups is that, like surveys, you can learn only what people *say*, but not necessarily what they actually *do*. In other words, you can learn a lot about their attitudes and their perceptions, but not much about what they might do in practice. This is why focus groups are more useful for the early stages of design, when you are more interested in finding out about your customers than in trying to evaluate what they will do with a Web interface that you have not yet built or even prototyped. This kind of information is still valuable, but it should be supplemented with the other techniques described here.

Analyze Existing Web Sites

Another way of getting information about potential customers and their needs is to ask them to evaluate existing Web sites. Use your existing Web site or a competitor's Web site to get a feel for what's right and what's wrong. Recruit some representative customers, and observe what they say they want to do on the Web site, what they actually do, and what steps they take to do it. Make note of the kinds of mistakes they make, and pay special attention to what they say they like and don't like. You might also want to have a questionnaire that they can fill out, to learn more about their demographic information and their interests and subjective ratings. In Chapter 4—Involving Customers with Iterative Design, we discuss in more detail how to do this.

4

Start your analysis by finding all the people who sent you e-mail about your Web site. Whether they suggested a new feature or criticized a feature that did not make sense, these are the customers who cared enough to make a comment about your site in the first place. If they live close enough, consider asking if you can visit them for an interview, or if they can come to your office to help evaluate the Web site.

But do not rely only on this type of customer. Because they have voluntarily sent a complaint or suggestion, such customers have already been self-selected as having a certain type of personality or level of expertise that may differ from that of the rest of your customers. Make an effort to find a wide range of people who are representative of your overall customer base.

Take-Away Ideas

3.3

A customer-centered design process involves first knowing who your customers are and keeping them involved throughout the design process. In knowing your customers, you will learn their skills and knowledge (people), what they want to do on your site (tasks), the equipment and software they use (technology), and the larger social and organizational context in which they work, play, and live (social issues).

The potential customers visiting a Web site, the things they want to accomplish, the technologies available to them, and their social and organizational contexts are all highly variable. This is why you need a good understanding of these variables before starting implementation. The methods we have described in this chapter may seem too time-consuming if you haven't used them before. Start with one at a time. Run a few informal surveys or interviews of your customers early in the design process for a new project. As you become more comfortable with the process and its benefits, add more.

If you don't know your customers, it is easy to build features that customers consider only marginally useful or even useless. It is also easy to overlook features that customers deem important. And even if the selected features are right, it is just as easy to build them incorrectly, by organizing the information in a confusing manner, using unfamiliar terms, or by having an error-prone navigation scheme that makes the features impossible to find. Chapter 4—Involving Customers in Iterative Design and the pattern groups will help you build the features right.

Involving Customers with Iterative Design 4

The primary principle of customer-centered design is know your customers, as discussed in Chapter 3—Knowing Your Customers: Principles and Techniques. Now you will learn three related principles: keep the customers involved, conduct rapid prototyping, and evaluate your designs. Omitting any of these principles from your design processes is a major risk. Studies by the Standish Group International have attributed many of information technology's frequent project failures to a lack of end-customer input.

Iterative design addresses this problem by calling for setting measurable goals and repeatedly refining and testing design prototypes with customers until the final design meets or surpasses those goals. Your goals can be high-level and strategic, such as increased customer satisfaction or increased sales. They can also be short-term and tactical, such as reduced time to find items or fewer mouse clicks to check out and complete a purchase.

4.1 The Iterative Design Process

Iterative design involves taking an existing design and reworking it until it fits the needs of customers. This process is widely considered to be a valuable technique for designing interfaces, but at a more fundamental level iterative design acknowledges that *no design team is perfect.*

Teams are made of people, and people do not always know the right answers. It is difficult to have complete information about the needs of customers and clients. Iterative design compensates for these shortcomings, letting you continually improve a design. The key to iterative design is quickly creating design prototypes that are good enough to provide feedback but flexible enough for significant changes to be made down the

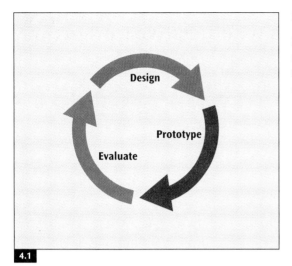

Figure 4.1

Iterative design is an ongoing cycle composed of three steps: design, prototype, and evaluate.

4.1

line. The goal is as much iteration as possible to solve as many problems as possible early, when they are inexpensive to fix.

The iterative design process has three steps: design, prototype, and evaluate (see Figure 4.1). In the design step, teams consider business goals and customer needs, setting measurable goals and developing design concepts. In the prototype step, teams develop artifacts as basic as scenarios and storyboards, and as complex as creating running Web sites, that illustrate how the site will accomplish these goals. In the evaluate step, teams assess the prototypes to see if they meet the desired goals. The results are then used to inform the design in the next iteration, and the entire process repeats until the goals have been met. However, sometimes scheduling and budgeting constraints force work to begin on the final production site before all the goals have been met.

Use design patterns to help you move quickly through each step of iterative design. During the initial design stage, use the information you learned about your customers, the genre patterns, and other high-level patterns to rough out the basic features your site will need. Use the more detailed, low-level patterns to help you storyboard and prototype Web pages for specific scenarios. After evaluating your prototypes with customers, clients, and other team members, use the patterns again to find solutions to the particular problems they encountered. Use these solutions in the next design iteration.

Before working on the final production site, go through this iterative cycle several times in the early stages of design and *make simple prototypes instead of full-fledged sites.* Real Web sites can take several weeks or months to implement, and by the time a site is completed and ready for evaluation, it might already be too expensive and time-consuming to fix.

In contrast, prototypes can be created in just a few hours or days. The prototypes will not have all the features of a finished site, and many features will be faked, but they will be real enough to give customers a flavor of what the final site will be like. In this way you can get a lot of feedback about what works and what does not work. (We talk more about how to create prototypes in Section 4.4, Rapid Prototyping.)

4.2   Reasons to Use Iterative Design

There are three main reasons to use an iterative design process:

1. It will help you find problems while they are still inexpensive and easy to fix.
2. It ensures that you are building a site that has the features your customers need.
3. It ensures that you are building those features in a way that your customers can use.

Fixing Errors While They're Still Inexpensive and Easy to Fix

Why is it important to fix errors as early as possible? It has been well documented in many disciplines that fixing errors in later phases of design can be expensive. The famous architect Frank Lloyd Wright said it best: "You can use an eraser on the drafting table or a sledgehammer on the construction site." In the realm of software development, a general rule of thumb is that errors cost about *ten times* more effort and money to fix late in the process than if they are caught in an earlier phase. Watts Humphrey and others in the field of software engineering have even documented costs on the order of 100 to 1,000 times more effort and money to fix problems after deployment.

Why does it cost so much to make downstream changes? There are three reasons: (1) All the deliverables generated in later phases of design have to be made consistent with the proposed changes. (2) Sometimes one change forces other changes to be made so that everything will work correctly. (3) Most importantly, anything that causes a change in the software source code and HTML is expensive. Think about the time to change a simple sketch versus the time to rewrite the code that implements the ideas in the sketch.

Suppose you already have a Web site but want to add LOCATION BREAD CRUMBS (K6), tiny markers like "Home > About > History," at the top of each page so that your customers always know where they are in the site. Not only does this change have to be made on every page, but you also have to redesign the overall page layout to accommodate that change. Style sheets and other template mechanisms may make the technical part of this change much easier, but you will still have to make significant design and layout changes so that it all makes sense.

Now this is just a trivial change. Imagine the kind of effort it would take to make more involved changes, such as altering the way information is organized on the site or adding a significant feature that requires new code. Add these costs to what was spent in the first place, and you will see why downstream changes are expensive.

Building the Right Site, and Building the Site Right

What kinds of mistakes are made on Web sites? Figure 4.2 divides the problems by feature and implementation. The top right-hand quadrant shows the right feature but the wrong implementation. For example, a SHOPPING CART (F3) is definitely the right feature for an e-commerce site, but it could have implementation problems that make it hard for customers to check out and finalize purchases. Iterative design and testing will help you discover these types of problems.

The bottom left-hand quadrant shows the wrong feature but the right implementation. For example, providing extremely sophisticated search features for power users is not very useful if most of your customers cannot even understand the basic search capabilities.

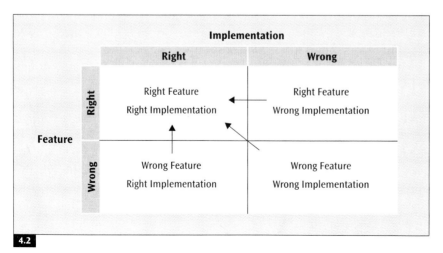

Figure 4.2

Iterative design helps design teams find the features customers need (the "right" features) and make sure those features are implemented correctly (the "right" implementation).

4.2

The bottom right-hand quadrant shows the wrong feature and the wrong implementation—a design that is not useful *and* does not work correctly. A good design process, like the one presented in Chapter 5—Processes for Developing Customer-Centered Sites, should filter out most of these sorts of problems.

Ultimately, you want to be in the top left-hand quadrant, with the right features and the right implementations of those features. Iterative design helps push you toward the top left by getting constant feedback from customers about features and their implementation.

To summarize, design mistakes are costly, and it pays off in the long run to find them as early as possible in the development cycle. This is why rapid iterative design is so important in the early phases: It helps teams find and root out as many problems as possible *before* the site is deployed.

4.3 Designing with Goals and Principles in Mind

Design is a process that is driven by both goals and principles. Goals come directly from analyzing your business and customer needs (see Chapter 3—Knowing Your Customers: Principles and Techniques). Design principles come from research in human–computer interaction, as well as graphic design. Following these design principles as you iterate on your design will help you reach your goals. Most of these goals and principles will apply whether you're working on your site's information architecture, navigation design, or graphic design.

Setting Measurable Design Goals

What does it mean to "get the site right"? This is where business, usability, and customer experience goals come into play. Some possible design goals include the following:

- Faster task completion
- Successful completion of more tasks
- Greater ease of learning
- Commission of fewer errors
- Abandonment of fewer shopping carts
- Greater pleasure or satisfaction
- More fun
- Increased visitor-to-customer conversion rate
- Increased customer repeat visits
- Increased revenue

Studies we have carried out show that achieving many of the usability and customer experience goals, such as giving a more satisfying experience, have a direct impact on achieving business-related goals such as increased customer repeat visits.

The key to achieving all of these goals is testing and measuring. The rest of this section outlines examples of tests and measures you can undertake to assess your progress toward your design goals.

For example, suppose you want to know how long it takes to complete common tasks, such as checking out and finalizing a purchase. In this case, task completion time is an important metric. You could measure the time it takes to complete these tasks by recruiting representative customers to try out the site. Time how long it takes them to finish each task. See if they complete their tasks successfully. Observe where they have problems, and see if you can find commonality among the problems. Are the problems occurring in the same places? Are they navigation errors? Are they problems with the search feature? See if an existing design pattern from this book can help. Implement the necessary changes and retest to see if you solved the problems.

Say you find out from your server logs that customers who start to post messages in the community section of your site have a low rate of completing the postings. A follow-on usability study confirms that customers are distracted in the middle of the posting process and tend to follow some tangential links, never to return. This finding might indicate a good place to apply a PROCESS FUNNEL (H1), which will help your customers go
through the steps of completing their initial task—posting a message.

Another approach to achieving your design goals is to compare two different prototypes to see which one works best. You might find that with one of the designs, customers are 20 percent faster on average than with the other design. A similar approach is to compare the new site design to the existing design or the design of one of your competitors.

Alternatively, you might want to know how quickly customers get up to speed using the sites. Finding this out can be harder than it sounds. You could measure how many hours of use customers need on average to complete a particular set of tasks successfully. Or you could measure how many tasks customers complete in a certain amount of time. Both of these forms of ease-of-learning measures can be used to compare your site designs to one another and to the competition.

Or you could measure and compare the average number of errors made on each site. If your customers make errors and become confused, they will not be able to buy your products. To measure errors, first define them. Is it an error when a person clicks on the browser's **Back** button? For example, say the customer is purchasing five cartridges of printer toner online. As he finishes the checkout process and fills out a form with his credit card number and address, he notices he forgot to change the quantity on the order form on the previous page. The customer has to go back to fill it in, and then when he goes forward the billing information might be lost. Is this an error? Probably. You have to define what you're measuring.

Sometimes you can look at specific pieces of your site that do not necessarily indicate an interface problem but might indicate a general problem with your content or policies. For example, many sites measure the rate of shopping cart abandonment before checkout. Customers might abandon their shopping carts if they cannot find all the products they want to purchase. Or the checkout process might be too long (this problem is addressed in QUICK-FLOW CHECKOUT (F1)). Another explanation is that your prices are higher than a competitor's, and people are just there to comparison shop. A fourth explanation could be that customers are surprised at how high the sales tax or shipping and handling costs are and decide to leave. At any rate, the abandoned–shopping cart metric is certainly tied to your business's revenue numbers.

The key to any of the numerical measurements discussed so far is to make sure you're presenting numbers that make sense. This is where statistics and research design come into play. As we mentioned in Chapter 3—Knowing Your Customers: Principles and Techniques, when designing surveys and usability studies you want to ensure that your numerical results are both reliable and valid. Be certain you have enough research participants to get statistically significant results. Often 20 to 50 participants might be required, depending on the variability in their background and performance.

You might also want to look at more subjective metrics. Do your customers find your site more pleasing or satisfying than the last version of the site, or your competitors' sites? Is your site fun? You can measure responses to questions such as these on an ongoing basis to understand how your site and your customers' opinions change over time. This information will help you know when you need to conduct more in-depth research. Again, these numbers can be tied directly to your bottom-line revenue or profit.

You can measure these subjective issues with surveys. Online surveys are easy to create and can be sent to a representative sample of your customers, or they can be made available on one of your Web pages. Target additional surveys for specific pages, or for times when customers take specific actions. Would you like to ask visitors why they abandoned their shopping carts? You can ask them with a survey, right when it happens!

The design goals we have talked about so far are only an approximation of the higher-level client and business goals. For example, shorter task completion time and fewer abandoned shopping carts are important metrics to work toward, but the business goal for an e-commerce site is to increase revenue. The problem is that you simply cannot gather this kind of metric using prototypes. Still, prototypes are good enough to provide useful feedback that will bring you closer to the overall goals.

Design Principles

Design goals represent the destination you want to reach when you're finished building a Web site. Design principles guide you to that destination. The patterns in this book were guided by design principles, as well as by observation of what has worked well for customers. Here we present some basic design principles that you can use to tailor the patterns to your particular situation. Entire books could be written about these principles. The seven that we present are based on those from some of the most respected sources, specifically Ben Shneiderman's eight golden rules of interface design, Jakob Nielsen's ten heuristics, and Edward Tufte's musings on information presentation:

1. **Be consistent throughout.** Consistency applies across several dimensions. Use a consistent sequence of actions to carry out similar tasks. Pages should have consistent color, layout, and fonts. For example, your NAVIGATION BAR (K2) should be in the same place on every page, and ACTION BUTTONS (K4) that do the same thing should appear in the same general location across different parts of the site. Use identical terms in different places across the site. Make your site consistent with the real world: Follow real-world conventions, and use FAMILIAR LANGUAGE (K11) by using terms that your customers will understand rather than technical jargon.

2. **Offer informative feedback.** Make the status of the system visible, and keep your customers informed about what's going on. For example, this is the principle behind SECURE CONNECTIONS (E6), which lets customers know whether the information they are about to send over the Internet will be safe.

3. **Rely on recognition over recall.** Short-term memory is the key limitation in human cognition. Reducing the short-term memory load is easy if people can *recognize* what they need to know from visible objects, actions, options, and directions. The memory load is much higher if

they need to *recall* this information from memory with no visual aids. This is why a visual human–computer interface like that of the Macintosh or Windows is easier to learn than a command language–based interface like DOS. This is also why ACTION BUTTONS (K4) always have a textual label to go along with the graphical icon.

4. **Help customers prevent and recover from errors.** Errors cause frustration, poor performance, and a lack of trust in your site. PREVENTING ERRORS (K12) will help avoid many of these problems. Unfortunately, no matter how well you design the site, humans will make occasional errors. Help people recover from errors by presenting MEANINGFUL ERROR MESSAGES (K13). Tell them what happened and how to recover, or better yet, offer to automatically carry out the steps that would help them recover from the error.

5. **Support customer control and freedom.** Customers should sense that their actions determine the site's responses, and that they are not being forced down a fixed path. Providing MULTIPLE WAYS TO NAVIGATE (B1) is one example of how to support this attitude on your site. It also means that the customer is given easy exits, such as undo and redo, for mistaken choices. The browser's built-in **Back** and **Forward** buttons and LOCATION BREAD CRUMBS (K6) are both mechanisms that give customers easy exits on the Web.

6. **Help frequent customers use accelerators.** Keyboard shortcuts are important for expert customers. Your site can support frequent actions automatically. For example, your site can store information such as shipping addresses so that your customers do not have to retype this information every time they come to that page. Design an ACCOUNT MANAGEMENT (H4) interface that makes it easy for your customer to see and change this stored information.

7. **Strive for aesthetic and minimalist design.** Clean aesthetics make using your site a pleasing experience. A GRID LAYOUT (I1) is one common technique you can use to ensure that your site has a clean, understandable look. Well-designed type, images, and graphical elements communicate how the site works. Often visual elements are overused. If removal does no harm to the site, take out irrelevant information and graphics from all pages. Every extra element draws attention away from the ones that matter.[1]

---

1 As Edward Tufte says, "Graphical excellence is that which gives the viewer the greatest number of ideas in the shortest time, with the least ink in the smallest space."

These principles sometimes conflict. Use your best judgment to resolve these conflicts. For example, supporting individual control and freedom may conflict with helping customers prevent errors. Sometimes, as in the case of a PROCESS FUNNEL (H1), restricting control and freedom can help customers complete their tasks. Use these restrictions judiciously. We have tried to make these conflicts apparent when discussing the forces for each pattern in Part II of the book.

Information Architecture, Navigation Design, and Graphic Design

No matter what form of design you're carrying out—information architecture, navigation design, or graphic design—use the design goals and principles we have described to guide your work. **Information architecture** means identifying, structuring, and presenting groups of related content in a logical and coherent manner.[2] **Navigation design** means designing methods so that customers can find their way around the information structure. **Graphic design** means developing the visual communication of information, using elements such as color, images, typography, and layout. Information and navigation design are typically done before graphic design.

Figure 4.3 shows how these three types of design relate to one another, as well as how usability evaluation and traditional human–computer interface design fit into the picture. All three approaches to design are necessary. A graphic design that is rich with images cannot compensate for a poor information architecture. Likewise, a clean information architecture cannot make up for a navigation design that hides the location of all the navigation elements.

Rapid Prototyping   4.4

As we said earlier, a key principle of iterative design is rapid prototyping—quickly creating rough-and-ready mock-ups that provide useful feedback. These prototypes can help reduce risk, lead to smaller and less complex systems, and nail down what customers really need. In the sections that follow we describe how to do rapid prototyping, beginning

---

2 There is an ongoing (and sometimes heated) debate in the design community about the delineation between *information architecture* and *information design*. In general, information architecture focuses more on things like structure and language, while information design concentrates on presentation and perception. However, distinctions between these two fields are still very blurry. Information architecture and information design represent a convergence of multiple disciplines with different backgrounds, vocabularies, and cultures. The key here is to go beyond these superficial differences and to focus on what they all have in common: helping customers find, understand, and manage complex information.

Figure 4.3

The spaces of information architecture, navigation design, graphic design, and usability evaluation overlap. Traditional human–computer interface design is primarily navigation design and usability evaluation, with a touch of information architecture and graphic design.

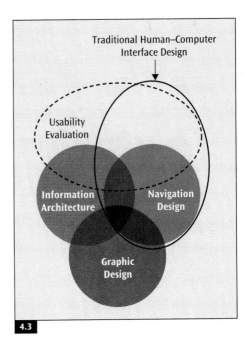

4.3

with a description of the different design artifacts that are created during iterative Web site design.

Site Maps, Storyboards, and Schematics

Typically, early in the design and prototyping phases you develop three kinds of design artifacts: site maps, storyboards, and schematics. A **site map** is a high-level diagram showing the overall structure of a site (see Figures 4.4 and 4.5). It is used primarily to reflect an understanding of the information structure or architecture of the site as it is being built and, to a limited extent, the navigation structure, or **flow** through the site.

A **storyboard** is a sequence of Web pages depicting how a customer would accomplish a given task (see Figures 3.3 and 4.6). Use storyboards to illustrate important interaction sequences, or flows through a site. When showing ideas to a client, you can accompany storyboards with a narrative about the task that the customer is trying to accomplish. That is, you might show the client the complete **scenario** you developed, or at least a small piece of it.

Schematics are representations of the layout and content that will appear on individual pages (see Figure 4.7). They are usually devoid of images, though they may indicate, with a label, where to place an image.

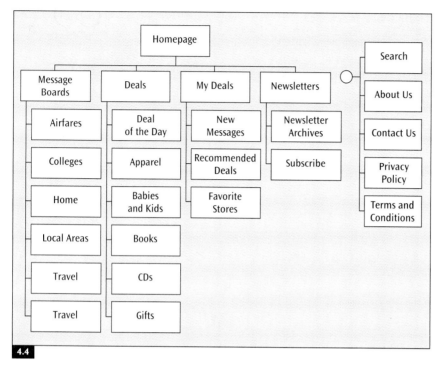

Figure 4.4

A site map is a high-level diagram that depicts the overall organization of a site. This site map shows the structure of a Web site that helps people find online deals and electronic coupons. The set of pages on the right represent a NAVIGATION BAR (K2) that is available on every page.

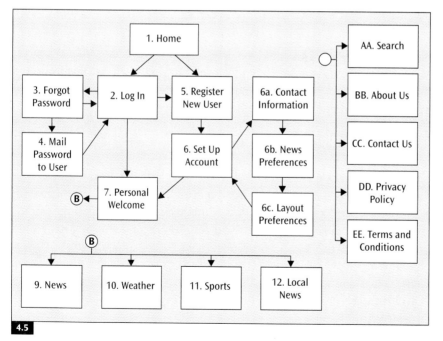

Figure 4.5

This site map shows part of the structure and flow of a personalized news site. (This design has a problem: It forces people to sign in before they see any content. See the SIGN-IN/NEW ACCOUNT (H2) pattern for more details.)

Figure 4.6

Storyboards show the steps a customer would take to accomplish a task. This storyboard shows how a customer interacts with a site that lets groups of friends find, recommend, and share things with each other.

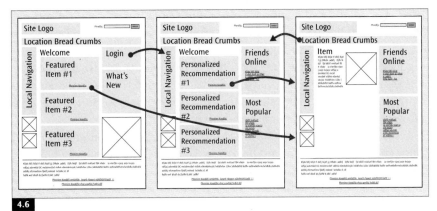

Figure 4.7

These two examples of schematics have the feel of complete individual Web pages.

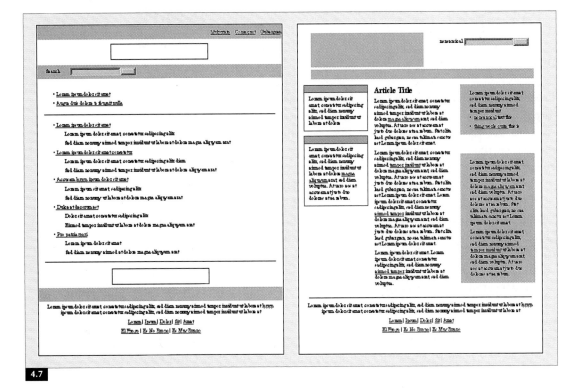

The fonts, colors, and layout are often quite preliminary, not indicating a final decision, but instead giving the graphic designer hints about which information needs to be highlighted or grouped together.

You probably noticed that the illustrations of site maps, storyboards, and schematics here look pretty basic. At this stage they are just abstract representations, not to be taken literally. Their point is to get the big ideas across, without the irrelevant details that distract reviewers.

Research we carried out with Mark Newman, a human–computer interaction researcher, found that often designers first sketch out all three of these representations on paper (see Figures 3.3, 4.8, and 4.9). Before showing these representations to clients or customers, many designers like to clean them up by creating electronic versions. Others are comfortable showing the informal, sketched representations to get earlier validation and keep the discussion focused on the important issues. It really depends on your clients and their expectations. If you manage their expectations well, your clients will understand why you are showing them rough sketches.

Progressive Refinement, from Low Fidelity to High Fidelity

The great thing about prototypes is that they can be created quickly and used to get feedback from customers. Low-fidelity prototyping is one technique that many designers use to accomplish this task. In **low-fidelity prototyping**, you use paper, whiteboards, Post-it notes, and markers to create rough cuts of a Web site. That's it. Sketches are low-fidelity ("low-fi") when they are far from the final design in both their visual and interactive details. For example, Figure 4.9 shows hand-drawn graphics and handwritten text, much of it represented by squiggly lines. In addition to sketching, you can use cut, copy, and paste techniques with scissors, glue, and photocopying machines.

Using a set of low-fidelity pages, you can test a design with representative customers. Sit them down in front of your sketches and ask how they would complete a particular task. On the basis of the customer's verbal responses or pointing, one of your teammates can "play computer" and flip to a new page to show the designed output of the site. Observing what customers do on these low-fi designs will give you valuable information about how to refine your early design ideas. This type of prototyping and testing can let you iterate through an entire cycle of design, prototype, and evaluate in less than a day.[3]

---

3 Read Mark Rettig's article "Prototyping for Tiny Fingers" (see the Resources section later in the book) for a great how-to on creating low-fidelity prototypes and testing them with customers.

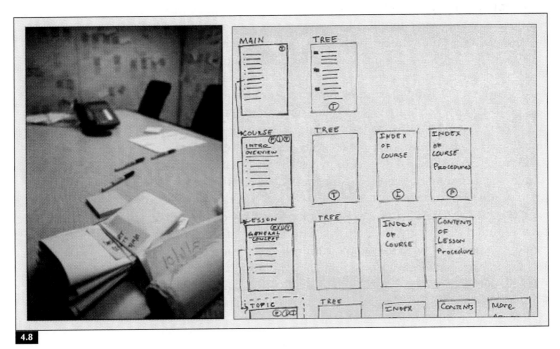

4.8

Figure 4.8

Create site maps on walls, using pens, papers, and Post-it notes (left). This technique, known as *affinity diagramming*, lets multiple team members brainstorm simultaneously and provides a large, immersive display for working on large sites. When you are finished brainstorming, write the site map down on paper (right) or take a digital photo to capture the design.

Figure 4.9

A low-fidelity prototype is a quickly created rough sketch that gives an overall feeling of what is needed on the page, without going into unnecessary detail. This sketch illustrates the main functionality available at a Web-based custom jewelry store.

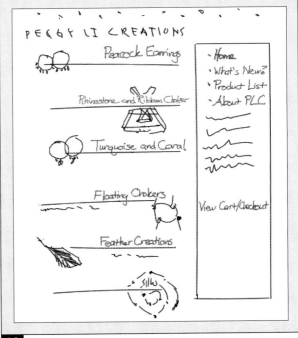

4.9

Our personal experience has shown that it is *at least* 10 to 20 times easier and faster to create a low-fidelity prototype than an equivalent high-fidelity ("hi-fi") prototype. By **high-fidelity prototype**, we mean one that looks polished and complete, created with computer-based tools such as Macromedia Dreamweaver or Adobe Photoshop (see Figure 4.10). We are not saying that you do not need hi-fi prototypes—just that you do not need them in the *early stages of design*. It is not worth the effort of focusing on colors, fonts, and alignment when there are more important issues like organization and overall site structure to worry about.

Another advantage of low-fi prototypes is that because specific programming or graphic design skills are not required, the contributions and insights of each team member can be easily integrated into the design. Even CEOs have been observed creating low-fi prototypes! Creating low-fi prototypes and evaluating them with customers is a good team-building experience, even for people with roles that traditionally do not include interaction with customers. By doing this, you will get everyone on the same page about what customers really need. You will find that it is a lot more effective and fun to create low-fi prototypes than to argue endlessly about what customers *might* want.

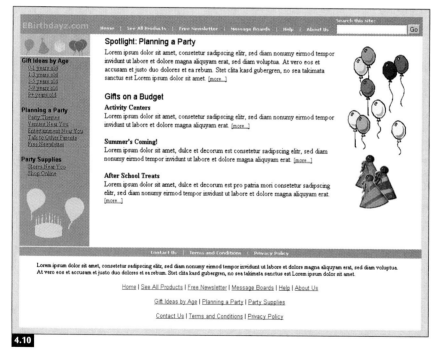

Figure 4.10

A high-fidelity prototype, such as this one, is detailed and rich with typography, color, and graphics.

Avoid Computer-Based Tools in the Early Design Stages • Research shows that designers who work out conceptual ideas on paper tend to iterate more and explore the design space more broadly, whereas designers using computer-based tools tend to take only one idea and work it out in detail.

Nearly every one of the designers we have talked to has observed that *the discussion is qualitatively different when people are presented with a high-fidelity prototype*. Clients often respond with comments like, "I do not like your color scheme," or "These two buttons need to be aligned correctly." When presented with a low-fidelity prototype, however, clients are more likely to say something like, "These labels on the navigation bar do not make sense to me," or "You're missing a link to the shopping cart here on this page." In other words, with low-fidelity prototypes, which lack irrelevant details like color, font, and alignment to distract the eye, people focus on the interaction and on the overall site structure.

All of the tools used in Web design today focus on creating finished products. Tools like Microsoft FrontPage, Adobe GoLive, and Macromedia Dreamweaver help you create production Web sites, not early prototypes. Other tools used by designers, such as Microsoft Visio, Macromedia

---

What's in a Paper Prototyping Kit?

It's a good idea to create a paper prototyping kit, a small box of goodies for making paper prototypes that everyone on your team can access. Here's a shopping list of supplies that no kit would be complete without:

Lots of paper (both white and colored construction paper)
Lots of index cards
Lots of Post-its
Transparencies
Scotch tape
Scissors
An Exacto knife
Paste (try not to eat too much of it)
Markers (with lots of colors)
Pens
Rulers
Duct tape (hey, you never know when it will come in handy)

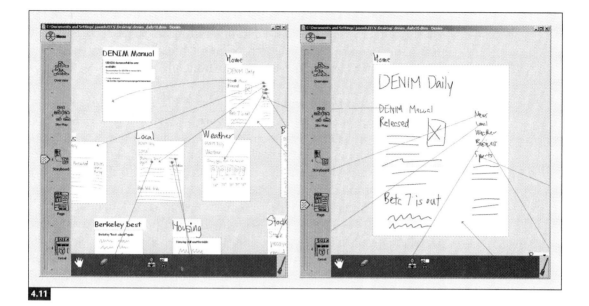

4.11

Director, Adobe Illustrator, and Adobe Photoshop have the same problem. Until tools that support the progression from low-fidelity to high-fidelity prototypes become widely available, we advocate that you delay using computer-based tools. Incidentally, we have developed a research-quality tool called DENIM that allows you to "sketch" low-fidelity prototypes on a computer (see Figure 4.11).[4]

When You're Ready, Switch to Computer-Based Tools • When should you move to computer-based tools? It depends on your work practices. If you find that you absolutely must save designs and e-mail them to others, you might be ready. Design teams often want to switch to using a computer when they are presenting to clients. In our interviews, the general consensus was that you should not show low-fidelity sketches to clients because they are perceived as unprofessional. However, high-fidelity mock-ups take too long to create, and again they have the drawback of directing the discussion toward extremely fine details. One solution is to go ahead with sketches and, as we mentioned before, manage clients' expectations by explaining that you're using sketches instead of computer-based designs to speed up the iteration process and to focus on the right issues at this stage.

Figure 4.11

These are two screen shots of DENIM, a sketch-based Web site design tool for the early stages of design. DENIM allows you to quickly sketch Web pages, create links among them, and interact with them in a run mode. You can use zooming to integrate the different ways of viewing a site, from site map to storyboard to individual pages.

---

4 If you are ambitious, try out DENIM at **guir.berkeley.edu/denim**.

Another solution is to use what we call **medium-fidelity prototypes** (see Figure 4.12). Medium-fidelity prototypes have many more details about content, but they do not distract clients or customers with fonts, colors, and graphics. Medium-fidelity prototypes are a good compromise if you need to present mock-ups.

At some point your team will have most of the major structural and interaction issues hammered out and satisfactorily tested with customers. This is a good time to create high-fidelity prototypes—ones that are richer and closer to what the final site will look and feel like. You will probably create them with HTML and graphic design tools such as Illustrator and Photoshop.

Again, the key here is to fake it! For example, suppose your site lets people view stock prices. You do not have to show the real prices, or even real graphs. Just create one or two sample images and use them for all of the graphs. You will show enough to give people the feel of the final site. As another example, if you are building a site that uses personalization technology to improve the customer experience, when applying PERSON- ALIZED CONTENT (D4) you might mock up the customization at this stage and make it look the same for all of your test participants.

Figure 4.12

A medium-fidelity prototype is a cleaned-up illustration that shows more detail about content, without specifying typography, color, or graphics. This kind of prototype is often shown to clients in lieu of low-fidelity or high-fidelity prototypes.

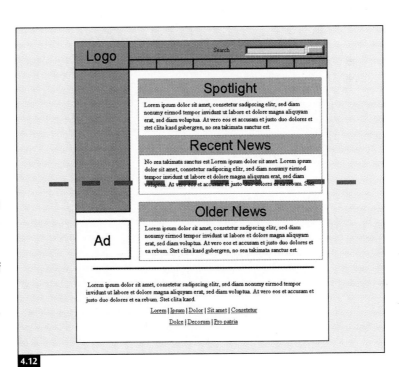

Horizontal and Vertical Prototypes

In the very early stages of design, you often want to create prototypes that show a broad swath of what the eventual Web site will support. These **horizontal prototypes** might show the top-level pages, but without much depth behind them (see Figure 4.13). The homepage might have all the links you expect to have, and each will take you somewhere, but any links from those second-level pages that implement specific features will not exist yet. These prototypes are good for making sure the basic features of the site are present and organized logically.

In contrast, sometimes you will want to flesh out and test the steps that a customer will go through to complete a particular task, such as SIGN-IN/NEW ACCOUNT (H2). A **vertical prototype** implements only the key 〔**H2**〕 pages along the path for completing a particular task. This step is appropriate when a complex feature is poorly understood or needs to be explored further. You will not yet support any links that connect to other tasks or other parts of the site.

Often you will want to combine these two techniques, as in Figure 4.13. Prototype the entire top level of the site with a horizontal prototype to give a flavor of what will be on the site. Then focus on one particular feature, and use the vertical approach to prototype the pages illustrating that feature in detail.

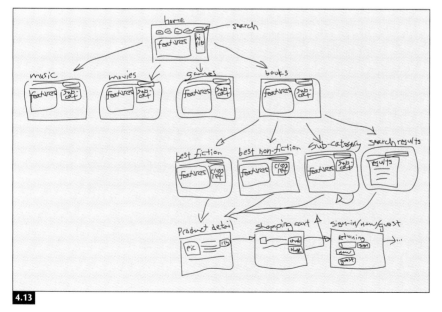

4.13

Figure 4.13

This figure shows a combination of the horizontal and vertical prototypes. Whereas horizontal prototypes illustrate the broad functionality of a design at a high level, vertical prototypes take one feature and detail it in depth. A combination makes a useful demonstration of the broad features in a site (horizontal) and the detailed functionality (vertical) as exemplified by one section.

Limits of Prototyping

There are some downsides to using prototypes. Many people believe that creating prototypes takes time away from building the actual site. Take care to explain the value of creating and testing *rapid* prototypes. In addition, although prototypes are useful for getting some kinds of information, they are not as effective for others, such as estimating download speeds and quality of customer service. Finally, when using medium- and high-fidelity prototypes, you have to manage expectations. Seeing something that looks and feels like it is working can make customers and clients think that the site is almost done. Take the time to explain that the prototypes still represent early stages of design, and that things are still open to change.

4.5 Evaluating Your Web Site

Web site evaluation is the third (and most often overlooked) part of iterative design. Without evaluation you cannot know if you have met your target goals. You can evaluate your Web set by having it reviewed by experts, by informally testing it with a few participants, or by conducting a more formal study with customers. Each of these methods has its pros and cons, as described in the sections that follow.

Expert Reviews

Expert reviews are an effective technique for evaluating sites without the need to involve customers. The most common type of expert review is a **heuristic evaluation**, which was developed by noted Web guru Jakob Nielsen.

The basic idea is have three to five expert judges independently evaluate a site, using a list of usability heuristics or principles. Nielsen's site, www.useit.com, lists ten such heuristics, though the seven design principles we listed earlier in this chapter would work just as well.

In a heuristic evaluation, the judges go through the site, often with a set of sample tasks as a guide, looking for violations of the heuristics. They note each violation and make a suggestion for fixing it. For example, if an expert found that a site used different terminology for the same concept on different pages in the site, the judge would note a "consistency" violation and suggest using one of the terms on each page.

The judges also rate each violation with a level of severity. Severity levels are usually assessed on the basis of the expected customer impact and frequency of the violation.

After each judge has independently evaluated the site, all the judges compare their lists of violations. The point of this step is to merge the lists into one and find agreement on the severity levels. Nielsen's research shows that multiple experts will find different problems, and only by using multiple judges will you have a high probability of finding most of the problems on the site. The more expertise your judges have on human–computer interface design, usability, and heuristic evaluation, the fewer judges you will need. If you can get true experts, we recommend you use three judges. If you are using any team member you can get your hands on, we recommend you involve five or six.

Heuristic evaluation can be an especially effective technique for finding potential usability catastrophes. It also works well for identifying subtle problems that most usability studies might not reveal, such as a poor choice of colors. We have found that heuristic evaluations do not work as well on low-fidelity prototypes as on high-fidelity prototypes. Inexperienced judges tend to focus on the pieces that are missing. We recommend not carrying out a heuristic evaluation until you have a high-fidelity HTML prototype of your site.

There are a couple of caveats to keep in mind with heuristic evaluation. Often experts know too much or not enough. They might be much more sophisticated than your customers and overlook things that will trip up real customers. On the other hand, your site might be designed for customers who have a lot of domain knowledge, such as doctors, and the judges might not have the background necessary to understand the site.

More importantly, heuristic evaluations have a tendency to reveal lots of false positives. **False positives** are violations that are identified by the heuristic evaluation but never found in a usability study of the same interface. In other words, experts often find problems that do not turn out to be problems in practice. Fixing these false positives could end up wasting lots of critical design and engineering resources. Still, a heuristic evaluation is inexpensive, can be carried out in a few hours, and is good at finding possible usability problems. We suggest that you look at Nielsen's site and papers for details on carrying out a heuristic evaluation, and use this technique in tandem with informal and formal usability tests.

Informal Evaluations

Informal evaluations are a natural outgrowth of rapid iteration and low-fidelity prototyping. The idea is quite straightforward: Recruit five to ten people who are representative of your target customers, show them your

Web site prototype, ask them to do some of the tasks from your task analysis, and take good notes. Your goal is to obtain qualitative feedback from customers about what works and what doesn't, both from what they say and from what they actually do.

The prototype does not have to be computer based. It can be as simple as a paper prototype. In this case, have people point and click with their fingers, just as they would do with a mouse.

You might recruit several representative customers to come to your offices and ask them to complete the tasks with the prototype. Alternatively, you might visit customers in their homes or offices and ask them to do the same.

Before you begin, ask participants to "think aloud," to say what's going on in their minds. This is known as a **think-aloud**, or **verbal**, **protocol**. They will probably find doing this a little strange at first, but they will get used to it quickly. You may have to prompt them every so often by asking a question like, "So what are you looking for now?"

The data collected in informal evaluations is qualitative **process data**. This kind of data gives an overall gestalt feeling for what works and what doesn't. While participants are testing, keep an eye out for instances in which they seem confused, say something negative, or even swear. These are called **critical incidents**. Use them as a starting point for places you will redesign. Look for positive incidents, cases in which the customer liked your site or things appeared to be going smoothly. Positive incidents give you a hint about which parts of your design work well, and you might be able to take advantage of some of the same ideas elsewhere.

We do not recommend that you use informal evaluation techniques to show that one site design is better than another, or to say how long certain actions will take. Instead, use the results to identify potential problem areas that need to be improved. After you think you have solved the problems, rerun the tests with a new set of representative customers and see if the problems have been addressed properly.

See the appendixes for more information on how to set up and run usability tests. They lay out the roles the testers assume, scripts for what to do and say during the evaluation, and tips for how to analyze the information you collect.

Formal Usability Studies

As soon as you have a running prototype of your Web site, you can start getting hard numbers on whether the site meets the goals your team has set. For example, one of your goals might be that customers be able to register and create an account in less than two minutes. You can run this study with as few as ten participants, though it generally takes more participants when you want to test numerical goals.

The type of information to collect in this situation is quantitative **bottom-line data**. Bottom-line data consists of hard numerical metrics where you are looking for statistical significance—a serious and reliable difference instead of one due to chance.

Bottom-line data is especially important for simple, repetitive interactions such as, "Are customers completing the task faster when this button is placed on the left or right side of the page?" This type of data is also useful for comparing two different interfaces, such as, "Can more people successfully make purchases and check out using shopping cart interface A or B?"

Online testing makes it easy to test a variety of similar issues. It lets you recruit and test many participants online to achieve statistical accuracy quickly. Several companies offer products to set up and run online tests. These sites can recruit research participants for you, or allow you to enter a list of e-mail addresses from current customers or your own participant pool. The sites then automatically e-mail research participants, lead them to a test site, and ask them to complete tasks that you have defined in advance. Most systems allow you to track the pages the participants go through, as well as ask survey questions.

Some practitioners have developed creative—and potentially controversial—ways to measure usability. One Web site study used "returns to the homepage" as an indication of an error. The inference was that people got lost and had to go back to the homepage. This might be a big assumption without further data to back it up. What if customers *want* to return to the homepage because they are done with a particular section? If you want to measure the number of errors, make sure that you define errors beforehand and that everyone agrees on the definition.

See the appendixes for more details on running formal usability evaluations, both offline and online.

Choosing an Evaluation Technique

When do you use expert reviews, informal evaluations, and formal evaluations? The answer is to use multiple techniques. The techniques should be balanced by your cost constraints, as well as by how early in the process the evaluation is taking place. For example, testing low-fi prototypes is especially effective in very early stages. In later stages, because you have defined more of the site details, you might want to create HTML prototypes instead so that you can evaluate these details.

Always run expert reviews and informal evaluations as you iterate, to work out basic design flaws. Focus especially on qualitative process data in the early stages of design because it helps you figure out where the big problems are. Use the patterns to find solutions to these problems and then iterate. Do a few formal evaluations as your Web site matures, as it gets closer to deployment, or even after it has been deployed. This strategy will help you refine and polish your site.

Sometimes using five to ten test participants will be good enough to convince you and your teammates that the problems found during testing are legitimate design issues that must be resolved. However, it will often be harder to convince management or the marketing organization that you need to make changes, especially on a high-traffic page like the homepage. In that case, use more formal usability studies and techniques, such as online usability testing, which makes it easy to test the site quickly with 50 to 200 customers.

A small number of test participants uncover only a small number of the potential problems, according to recent research by the consulting firm User Interface Engineering. This firm's theory is that many Web sites attract a varied set of customers who have a wide range of goals they are trying to accomplish, so a small number of participants cannot accurately reflect the diversity of customers. Again, this problem can be overcome by testing with a larger number of customers, on a larger variety of tasks. We believe that online usability testing is a necessity because traditional usability testing with 50 to 200 participants would take too long.

4.6 Take-Away Ideas

The key to designing successful Web sites is a customer-centered, iterative process that first identifies the expected customers and their tasks. Following the principles of keep the customers involved, conduct rapid prototyping, and evaluate designs leads to design ideas and prototypes that you evaluate with real customers. The evaluation leads to redesign, and then you iteratively repeat this process until you achieve your usability and business goals. Involving your customers throughout this process will keep your design on track.

Set your team's usability goals early in the design process, and continually evaluate your progress toward these goals. The iterative design process will improve the site design at the lowest cost. When the site launches, continue to monitor ongoing customer metrics to see how you're doing, to inform changes, and to help set your goals for the next version of the site.

Processes for Developing Customer-Centered Sites

This chapter takes the patterns, principles, and techniques of customer-centered design as described in Chapters 2 through 4 and places them in the context of a complete Web site design process. Think of this chapter as a rough guide to designing, implementing, and maintaining a Web site. You probably have a design process that you use today, and you might say that it's good enough. What we offer is not a quick fix, but a program that will make any Web site you design more useful, usable, reliable, and satisfying for customers.[1]

Our goal is to provide a general process that you can use when creating or updating a Web site—something that will help you focus your time and energy on clear goals. A well-defined process is also useful for your clients. It lets them know what they can expect from you and what you need from them to build a Web site that meets their expectations and the needs of their customers.

The design process will not always go as smoothly as described here. It is iterative; that is, it repeats and it jumps back and forth when necessary. Nor will this process solve all your problems. Tailor it to your team, your project, and your organization. Formal procedures that are necessary for large teams may be overkill for small teams. Techniques that work for art-centered design firms are unlikely to work for e-commerce–centered design firms. At a minimum, however, include in your process the major activities discussed in this chapter (that is, the first four steps of development, as defined next).

---

1 Again, we use the term *customer* to mean any person who will use the Web site you are designing, whether it is a business or a government site, whether the person is an end customer, employee, site administrator, or partner. We use the term *clients* to refer to the people for whom you are doing the work, the people providing the funding.

Development Process Overview

5.1

Generally speaking, development of a Web site can be broken down into seven steps (see Figure 5.1):

1. **Discovery.** Understanding the target customers and their needs, and conceptualizing the business and customer goals for the Web site.
2. **Exploration.** Generating several rough initial Web site designs, of which one or more will be chosen for further development.
3. **Refinement.** Polishing the navigation, layout, and flow of the selected design.
4. **Production.** Developing a fully interactive prototype and a design specification.[2]
5. **Implementation.** Developing the code, content, and images for the Web site.
6. **Launch.** Deploying the Web site for actual use.
7. **Maintenance.** Supporting the existing site, gathering and analyzing metrics of success, and preparing for the next redesign.

The first four steps, Discovery through Production, focus on the overall design of a Web site, clarifying what customers can do on the site and how they do it. You might characterize these four steps as *the* design process. Each is characterized by rapid iteration with progressive refinement, moving the design from high-level and general to increasingly specific and detailed. During these stages we have found that the more time you spend up front in the tight iterations, the more likely it is that the Web site will meet customer expectations. In the Discovery phase a team might iterate five to ten times or more on paper. As the team moves into the electronic representations used in the Refinement stage, it might iterate much less, perhaps only three or four times. The exact number of iterations depends on how well the design performs when evaluated.

Punctuate each of the first four steps with a presentation to the client. Hand over any other agreed-upon deliverables at this time, such as a site map, a high-level diagram of a Web site, or a specification document detailing what the Web site will do when it is completed. The main point of the presentation, though, is to obtain approval about the work you performed during that phase.

---

2 Note that *Production* does not mean creating the site but refers instead to creating the "blueprint" for the site so that someone can build it. Some design firms use the term *production* to mean the actual creation of the Web site—that is, what we have termed *implementation*. However, most designers from our interviews used *production* in the same sense that we have defined it here, so we have kept the term.

Figure 5.1

The Web site development process, both as a whole and at each individual phase, uses iterative design.

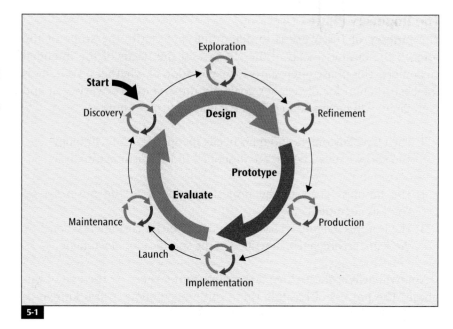

5-1

These presentations should be only one part of what has now become an ongoing dialogue with the client. There are several stakeholders in the design process, including the client and the intended customers. At many points in the process the design team can and should report back to the client to ensure that it is on the right track. For many design consultancies, the client calls the shots, so the client's needs and requirements are considered on a regular basis.

The last three steps, Implementation, Launch, and Maintenance, may not be part of your development process. In fact, many design firms stop at Production, handing off all documentation and interactive prototypes to another team, often in the client's organization but sometimes in a third firm, which goes on to do the rest of the work.

We do not include detailed planning at this stage because each organization has its own way of handling issues such as scheduling, budgets, and risk management. Second, *the process is by no means linear*. A team may be in the Exploration stage and discover that it needs to do more of the activities in Discovery. Another team may be in Production and realize that it needs to go back to Refinement or Exploration to hammer out some details. Such is the nature of design. Although going backward can seem like a defeat of sorts, take heart in the knowledge that time and money are actually being saved if changes are made sooner rather than later.

The Discovery Phase   **5.2**

The purpose of Discovery is to determine and clarify the scope of the project, the business goals of the client, and the needs of the intended customers. This phase often starts by exploration of whether a Web site is the best solution for the client's goals. By the end of Discovery, you and your client will have a shared understanding of three things:

1. The target customers and their needs (people, tasks, technology, and social issues), which are described in the customer analysis document
2. The business goals of the project, described in the business analysis document
3. The features that the Web site should provide for customers when the work is completed, described in the specification document

You will deliver these three documents to the client by the end of this phase. The process of creating these three documents is also known as *requirements gathering*. The sections that follow look at each of these steps in more detail.

Determine the Overall Goals of the Web Site First • You and your client will work together to answer questions before creating a new Web site or redesigning an existing site. These questions might include, What value will the Web site provide to customers? What will it accomplish? Is its goal to sell products online, promote products, educate, inform, provoke, communicate, or provide a community? What will be the focus of the Web site? *Why should the Web site be built at all?*

Other crucial questions that must be asked are, What value will the Web site provide to the client? What role does the Web site play in relation to the rest of the company? How will the site further the client's overall goals? The design team often starts this phase by defining the site together with the client, focusing on the client's goals, the high-level services the client wishes to offer, and preliminary customer categories. These decisions form the basis for the rest of the discovery process.

Some techniques that might be applied at this phase include interviewing or corresponding with clients to clarify what they expect. Discover the needs of the site's target customers by interviewing, running focus groups, and surveying target customers online and offline. These techniques are described in greater detail in Chapter 3—Knowing Your Customers: Principles and Techniques. **3**

This is also a good time to evaluate the existing Web site, as well as to review and evaluate competitors' Web sites for opportunities to improve and differentiate your site from theirs. Techniques for these evaluations are described in Chapter 4—Involving Customers with Iterative Design.

Decide on the Web Site's Value Proposition Next • One of the most essential patterns that come into play here is the UP-FRONT VALUE PROPOSITION (C2). The value proposition states what the Web site offers to the target customers. Your goal is to explain it convincingly to someone on the street, in one sentence. Everything you will put on the Web site draws on this single idea; it is the theme that unifies the site. Figure 5.2 shows compelling value propositions from some existing Web sites.

If you are creating a new Web site, think through the value proposition carefully, making many drafts before you decide on the best one. If you are updating or redesigning an existing Web site, you may need to reconsider the existing value proposition. In either case the UP-FRONT VALUE PROPOSITION (C2) pattern provides steps for hammering out the right one.

You will also consider initial branding ideas at this early design phase. What do you want people to think of when they think of your Web site? What kinds of feelings do you want people to have after visiting your site? Do you want to be thought of as reliable and trustworthy, or maybe exciting and fun? The SITE BRANDING (E1) pattern provides exercises to help you decide what kind of impressions to leave with customers.

At this stage, start thinking about whether personalization is useful for individual customers. The PERSONALIZED CONTENT (D4) pattern provides

Figure 5.2

Many Web sites make their value propositions clear from their tag lines. The goal of the value proposition is to provide a single, powerful idea of what the Web site is all about.

some starting points. For example, if you are working on an e-commerce site, consider how personalization can help your customers find interesting and useful products. Maybe your Web site can recommend products, or maybe it can let people see a list of the most popular items. If you are developing a news site, perhaps your visitors can specify ZIP codes to get local news and weather.

Speaking of ZIP codes, this is a good time to bring up the issue of internationalization because some countries outside of the United States do not use ZIP codes. Again, it comes back to the question of defining your customers. Do you expect people from other countries to use your Web site? If so, there are a host of issues to consider, including currency, color, icons, and layout. We discuss many of these issues in more detail in the INTERNATIONALIZED AND LOCALIZED CONTENT (D10) pattern.   **D10**

Be Firm about Not Skipping Discovery • Some clients may insist on skipping the Discovery phase and jumping straight to Web site development. Unless the scope of the project and the needs of the customers have already been defined, this is usually a bad idea and a likely prescription for failure. It is your job to explain the importance of this phase. (We can help. See Chapter 3—Knowing Your Customers: Principles and Techniques for samples of convincing arguments.)   **3**

Avoid Gold-Plating the Web Site • The term **gold-plating** means trying to get the Web site absolutely perfect before deploying it. You have probably visited other Web sites, seen something cool, and kept saying to yourself, "We should have this on our Web site too!" Usually that cool thing is technically complex (and fun) to design and implement but, frankly, may not be all that helpful to customers.

You can avoid this problem by getting continuous feedback from customers about what is useful and what is not, and prioritizing the features based on that feedback. This strategy will help you cut through the morass of features and keep you focused on what needs to be done. You do not have to develop and deploy all the features simultaneously. Deploy the features in stages, in many small steps instead of one big leap. Plan for future growth, but also plan for the next deployment.

Get the Web Site Fundamentals Right First • The last thing to watch out for is not taking care of the fundamentals first. This becomes an issue when you design things out of order. For example, for e-commerce sites it does

not make sense to design and implement PERSONALIZED RECOMMENDA-
TIONS (G3) or a RECOMMENDATION COMMUNITY (G4) if there are still problems with the SHOPPING CART (F3) and the QUICK-FLOW CHECKOUT (F1).
Take care of the things that the Web site absolutely must have before
adding the icing that makes it look sweeter.

Deliverables

Design teams produce three main documents as an outcome of the Discovery phase: the customer analysis document, the business analysis document, and the specification document. Let's look at each one in turn.

Customer Analysis Document • This document gives the design team and
the client a deep understanding of and empathy for the Web site's
intended customers. It fleshes out the intended customers, describing
their characteristics, their needs, and their tasks. It includes the following:

- The motivation of customers to visit the Web site, or the UP-FRONT
  VALUE PROPOSITION (C2)
- A **task analysis** of the intended customers, describing the people, their
  tasks, the technologies they use, and their social and organizational
  issues. (One increasingly popular way to do this is by creating personas, or highly detailed fictional people, who are representative of
  the customers. Giving the customers names makes it easier to talk
  about them.)

We provide more details about customer analysis in Section 3.2, Techniques for Knowing Your Customers, in Chapter 3—Knowing Your Customers: Principles and Techniques.

Business Analysis Document • This document spells out the business needs
of the client and the business goals of the Web site. It explores how the
goals of the client map to the tasks and customers discovered during the
task analysis. For example, say the client's goal for an intranet site is to be
the primary source of company information. What does this goal mean to
an administrative assistant who is just trying to find the information he
needs to get his job done?

If you are revising an existing Web site, a new business analysis is probably not necessary, but it is still a good idea to check every so often that
the business goals are the right goals, and that the Web site works toward
those goals. A business analysis document usually includes the following:

- **Business plan.** This plan describes the business goals of the Web site and the client's needs. Some goals might be to support existing customers, to bring in new customers by providing information about products, and to increase sales by enabling purchases online.
- **Competitive analysis.** This analysis determines the features that competitors have on their Web sites, and it identifies which features are important to customers and which are not. It also discusses the competitive advantages that the proposed Web site will have over others, and it expresses these advantages as high-level goals.
- **Metrics for success.** How will success be measured for both the business and the competitive goals? For example, how many customers does the site need to draw to stay in business? But just as important as attracting customers is retaining them, keeping them coming back for more. How many are repeat customers? What is the conversion rate, or how many visitors become paying customers? How many become community members?

Specification Document • Also known as a *requirements document,* the specification document describes what the Web site should provide when the work is complete. It describes any functionality the Web site needs, as well as any constraints on the system. At this point you do not have to start thinking about how you'll achieve the needed functionality. Focus instead on what you'll accomplish. A specification document contains the following:

- **Project description**, describing the common purpose and ultimate goals of the project, from both client and customer perspectives.
- **List of tasks**, **scenarios**, **and storyboards**, fleshing out the features (see Chapters 3—Knowing Your Customers: Principles and Techniques and 4—Involving Customers with Iterative Design for more information). These tasks will form the basis of the Web site evaluations. The number of tasks depends on the complexity of the proposed work. Simple projects can make do with ten to twenty complete tasks, but larger projects will need enough to cover all the proposed features. Label tasks as easy, moderate, or difficult. Customers should be able to complete all the easy tasks, most of the moderate ones, and some of the difficult ones.
- **Comprehensive list of proposed features**, classified in importance as "must have," "should have," or "could have." Use competitive comparisons, as well as surveys and other market research techniques, to

obtain this type of information. Decompose features into subfeatures. For example, a Web site that helps manage personal information will likely have a contact manager, which lets people add new contacts, edit existing ones, and search for contacts by name. Each feature also includes a short statement on how it will be evaluated or tested in the final Web site.

- **Overall design goals**, such as reducing the number of mistakes that customers make on the existing site, decreasing the time it takes to make purchases and check out from the shopping cart, or making the site faster to use.
- **Metrics** to measure whether the team has reached these goals and requirements, such as keeping download time to below 20 seconds for 90 percent of the target customers. State how these features will be evaluated in general in the final Web site. (A more precise test specification will be developed later, spelling out more of the details.)

Not writing a specification document is the biggest risk you can take, yet this is the most often skipped step. A specification document does not have to be long or formal, but it is useful because it forces you to think through important details and make sure that they make sense and are realistic. A specification document also makes it easier to communicate with clients and with other team members so that everyone has a shared vision for what the Web site will be like when completed.

Specification documents are often tedious to read. Be brief and concise, and use lots of diagrams to illustrate what you mean. Make it interesting enough that you would take the time to read it yourself.

5.3   The Exploration Phase

During the Exploration phase you will generate and explore several designs. These initial designs often do not reflect ideas about color, imagery, and typography. However, they do reflect ideas about site structure and navigation. By the end of Exploration, you will have several prototypes to present to the client, who will select one for further development and sign off on the work done. Sometimes a client will want to fund continued development of two sites for further refinement before making a final choice. In either case, the selected design is supported by evaluation results that show it is the best at meeting the business, client, and customer goals.

Typically you will generate medium-fidelity site maps, storyboards, and schematics (see Chapter 4—Involving Customers with Iterative Design for details about medium-fidelity prototypes, and about the differences among site maps, storyboards, and schematics). Test all your designs quickly with target customers to ensure usefulness and usability.

4

More design patterns come into play here too. The HOMEPAGE PORTAL (C1) pattern describes some of the ways to structure your homepage, as well as what you'll want on your homepage, such as a PRIVACY POLICY (E4) and a STRAIGHTFORWARD SEARCH FORM (J2).

C1

E4 **J2**

Begin initial work on the information architecture—the overall organization of the Web site's content—at this phase as well. The BROWSABLE CONTENT (B2) pattern has more details on how to design and implement your architecture.

B2

Deliverables

Medium-Fidelity Site Maps, Storyboards, and Schematics • You will present several sets of medium-fidelity site maps, storyboards, and schematics to your client. Each set represents a design alternative that addresses the issues described by the customer analysis document, the business analysis document, and the specification document. In particular, the storyboards will show the initial ideas for how the scenarios in the specification document will be carried out. However, at this phase none of the deliverables will have much detail; rather they will have just enough detail to represent the general idea. See Figure 5.3 for an example of a medium-fidelity site map.

The Refinement Phase

5.4

After you have chosen a design idea from the variations presented in the Exploration phase, you will develop the selected idea further. Polish the navigation, layout, and flow of the selected design more, providing a clearer understanding of how the Web site will look and feel. By the end of Refinement, you will have a highly detailed prototype to present to your client, who you expect will sign off on the work.

During the Refinement phase, iteratively refine, detail, and informally test the design. Determine aspects such as the precise typeface of labels and body text, the exact sizes and appearances of images, and color schemes and palettes. For most sites you will not find it necessary to design every page at this stage because you will break down the site into classes of pages (such as homepage, second-level pages, and pages for

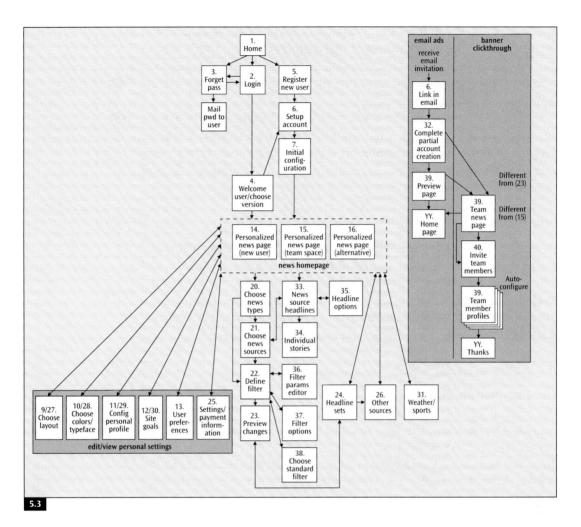

5.3

Figure 5.3

Medium-fidelity site maps such as this one can quickly communicate the flow of a site in an easy-to-read format.

specific types of content). An example, or **template**, can represent each of these classes of pages.

In this phase, site maps are still abstract representations of the entire Web site. On the other hand, storyboards and schematics are no longer drab and dull; instead they are now rich with images, icons, typography, and sophisticated color schemes.

The main difference between Refinement and Exploration is that the design you create in the Refinement phase has more detail than the designs you generated during the Exploration phase. Thus you can apply many of the same patterns in both phases. Some patterns are more useful during Refinement than during Exploration. For example, the pattern CLEAR FIRST READS (I3) takes a concept from graphic design, one intended to give a quick first impression of a visual design. It suggests that you explicitly design the first thing a potential customer sees on a Web page to give an overall feel for the content of the page. A related pattern is GRID LAYOUT (I1), which gives you ways of structuring Web pages in a consistent and understandable manner.

Another pattern to consider is MULTIPLE WAYS TO NAVIGATE (B1). People navigate Web sites in many ways, using a variety of search mechanisms, text links, buttons, and navigation bars. This pattern shows how to provide multiple and sometimes redundant ways of navigating, to make it easier to find the right page.

Deliverables

Medium- to High-Fidelity Site Maps, Storyboards, and Schematics • You will present one set of medium- to high-fidelity site maps, storyboards, and schematics to your client. These deliverables are similar to the ones in the Exploration phase, but they have much greater detail. For example, the site maps flesh out the overall site structure in detail, and the storyboards and schematics make use of more graphical images and color.

The Production Phase   5.5

The goal of Production is to create a detailed set of deliverables that embody and represent the final design idea. The deliverables, including interactive prototypes, written descriptions, guidelines, and specifications, are high-fidelity and contain as much detail as possible about the layout, navigation, visuals, and content for each Web page. Exactly what is delivered at the end of this phase depends on whether you will continue to the next phase (Implementation) or hand off the design to someone else.

If you will hand off the design, then make the interactive prototypes and specifications precise and highly detailed so that there is no ambiguity about what the next team will implement. You may want to call for more evaluation during implementation to ensure that the specification is being implemented correctly. The client should review the ongoing development to catch any problems before the new team does too much work. Ideally, though, the design team will work hand in hand with the engineering, art, marketing, editorial, and management teams so that the site is implemented as designed and tested, and so that the inevitable questions that arise can be answered.

During the Production phase, continue evaluating the product with real customers. Because this will be the first time the new system comes together, often with more complexity than existed in earlier prototypes, new interaction issues may arise.

During Production the patterns become more low-level as the problems become increasingly technical. For example, one pattern that will be used here is ACTION BUTTONS (K4), which explains how to make buttons that look like they can be pressed. Another useful pattern at this stage is OBVIOUS LINKS (K10), which discusses why links must be easy to see and explains how to make them that way.

Deliverables

The deliverables of the Production phase vary from firm to firm. We list the most common ways of describing the design in detail.

Design Document • In contrast to the specification document, the design document describes how the Web site works in great detail. It takes all of the features from the specification document and uses site maps, storyboards, and schematics to describe the flow of interaction.

If your work stops here and you hand the project off to another team, the design document needs to be detailed, descriptive, and unambiguous. If the same design team continues to do Implementation, the design document does not need to be so detailed. Provide just enough information that the client and the team understand precisely how customers will interact with the Web site, and how and when the site is complete.

Interactive Prototypes • Often delivered along with the design document, an **interactive prototype** gives you and your client a better grounding for how the finished Web site will look and behave. Create interactive prototypes using standard Web site production tools, such as Adobe GoLive or Macromedia Dreamweaver, as well as with prototyping tools such as Macromedia Director. The idea is to provide enough detail that everyone can see how the final Web site will look and feel. (For example, not all of the links have to work correctly, as long as it is clear what they do.) Some firms deliver interactive prototypes in lieu of a design document but embed many of the details as annotation to the prototype. For example, moving the mouse over certain sections of the prototype might pop up a specification of the font family and size.

Technical Specifications • Technical details are elucidated in this document, which includes things like the kind of Web server, the kind of programming and scripting languages, the kind of database, and the version of HTML that will be used. Performance metrics can also be included, such as how many people can be supported simultaneously. Optionally, the technical specifications might include some engineering prototypes as a proof-of-concept demonstrating that the difficult parts of the proposed design are technically feasible and can realistically be built.

Design Guidelines • These guidelines are the general rules to be followed on every Web page to minimize inconsistencies between pages. A design guideline could describe which fonts should be used, what color the links should be, when the logo should be used and where it should be positioned, what color scheme to use, what the maximum file size of each Web page is, and so on. The person who will implement and/or maintain the Web site should be able to understand and use the guidelines. Optionally, the guidelines might also include a style guide to ensure that the writing is consistent throughout the Web site, for example, using the term *email* instead of *e-mail*.

Web Page Templates • Web page templates are the HTML files that represent typical Web pages on the site. The goal of using these templates is to avoid inconsistencies between pages. With a minimum of effort you can copy and modify these templates with content specific for a particular page. Six patterns that are useful to consider when you're developing Web page templates are PAGE TEMPLATES (D1), GRID LAYOUT (I1), ABOVE THE FOLD (I2), CLEAR FIRST READS (I3), EXPANDING-WIDTH SCREEN SIZE (I4), and SITE ACCESSIBILITY (B9).

The Implementation Phase   5.6

Your aim is to create the HTML, images, database tables, and software necessary for a polished and fully functional Web site that can be rolled out and used by its target customers. Making sure you reached this goal requires running formal usability tests to ensure that customers can complete the tasks they want to achieve. The quality assurance group, both individually and as a whole, will test all the code, graphics, and HTML thoroughly so that the Web site works as intended and downloads quickly. (See the LOW NUMBER OF FILES (L1) and FAST-DOWNLOADING IMAGES (L2) patterns in Pattern Group L—Speeding Up Your Site.) Check all the content for accuracy at this stage.

Devote more effort to content in the Implementation phase. Two patterns that come in handy here are WRITING FOR SEARCH ENGINES (D6) and

(D9) DISTINCTIVE HTML TITLES (D9), which look at how to improve the internal structure of Web pages for search engines and for customers. Another
(D7) useful pattern is INVERSE-PYRAMID WRITING STYLE (D7), which describes techniques for making text content easier to skim and faster to read. On sites with content that changes frequently, a useful pattern for building a
(D2) content management system is CONTENT MODULES (D2), which puts content in a database to keep production costs down and site reliability high.

Tools useful at this stage include a revision control system for storing and sharing files among a group of people, and a bug database for tracking problems. Choose tools that you already know how to use and that have been proven to work. The Implementation phase of development is a bad time to try out an unknown product. (However, do try out new tools between projects, to keep your skills sharp and up-to-date.)

You also need to determine naming conventions for folders and files. For example, which folder will contain the images? Will there be just one folder or many? If you're selling products, what will the name of each
(F2) product's CLEAN PRODUCT DETAILS (F2) page be? Is the naming set up to make it easy to add new product pages in the future?
(E6) If you're using SECURE CONNECTIONS (E6), you may need to apply for digital certificates at this time. **Digital certificates** are a way for Web servers to prove that they really are who they say they are, and they are issued by a variety of trusted third-party vendors known as **certification authorities**. Keep in mind that digital certificates are often bound to a specific server name, so you may encounter problems if you try to move a digital certificate from a test server to the actual Web server. In this situation, it might not be a bad idea to get multiple certificates, for all the Web servers that you will be using.

The Web site also needs to be rigorously tested in this phase to ensure that it is high-quality and professional. This testing consists of performing more usability tests, doing some editorial spot-checking, and running automated test suites. The following checklist identifies some of the tests that need to be done during Implementation:

- Check that the Web site has all of the features stipulated in the specification document, and that the features are implemented correctly.
- Check that the developed Web pages are compatible with various Web browsers, including text-only browsers used by the blind.
- Test that the developed Web pages can be viewed in different monitor sizes.
- See if the Web pages can be downloaded in a reasonable time by people who have slower Internet connections.

- Stress-test the Web site, by simulating hundreds or even thousands of people using it at the same time, to ensure that it still performs reasonably.
- Check for grammar and spelling errors.

The results of these tests will produce bug reports. Your team will use the bug reports to guide any necessary redesign, code changes, and simple fixes for the problems found during testing.

Deliverables

Completed Web Site • The completed Web site includes all of the HTML Web pages, all of the software, and all of the database tables required for the Web site to work.

Maintenance Document • The maintenance document describes in detail how to maintain the completed Web site. It explains which parts of the Web site will be periodically updated, how often they need to be updated, and who should update them. It should also describe the database tables, showing how they fit together.

Test Plan Document • The test plan spells out what steps will be taken to ensure that the Web site works as intended. At a minimum, it should include checking for performance, spelling, broken links, and the like. It should also explain how each of the features described in the specification document will be tested.

Updates • Any documents that are out of date should be updated at this time (if they have not been already). This includes the specification document, the design document, design guidelines, and Web page templates.

The Launch Phase   5.7

The Launch phase deals with the live deployment of the Web site. At this point, there is time to do only minor polishing on the Web site, such as checking for misspellings, grammatical errors, broken links, and broken images. All of the major checks should have been done in the previous phase, Implementation.

Some design teams choose to roll out the Web site in stages. Instead of developing the entire Web site at once and waiting until the very end to deploy it, selected parts of the Web site are created and deployed incrementally. Develop the most important functions and subsites first, and post them on a beta Web site for early adopters. Use the resulting feedback to drive the immediate design and development of the rest of the Web site. Handle staged development carefully because if the Web site is rolled out too early and shows a lack of content and polish, potential customers may avoid the site later.

Many design teams find a postmortem a useful exercise after launch, to assess what things went right, what did not, why, and how to avoid these problems in the future.

<h2>5.8 The Maintenance Phase</h2>

Maintenance is perhaps the most neglected aspect of Web site design. The objective of the Maintenance phase is to perform all of the activities needed to sustain a Web site. Beyond basic tasks such as updating the site with new content and promptly answering customer e-mail, maintenance includes the following:

- Changing code and fixing bugs
- Collecting usability and satisfaction metrics
- Verifying that all links point to valid pages
- Checking that there are no spelling or grammatical errors
- Ensuring that pages in the Web site follow the design guidelines
- Periodically backing up the entire Web site (to a safe, distant computer)
- Updating the FREQUENTLY ASKED QUESTIONS (H7) pages
- Checking that your team is WRITING FOR SEARCH ENGINES (D6)
- Maintaining server logs that show where people come from, what search terms they use (see ORGANIZED SEARCH RESULTS (J3)), and what they are doing on the site

Maintenance includes assessing the Web site, collecting measurements on how customers use the Web site, analyzing and summarizing the metrics you collect, and making the metrics available to the rest of the team and the company. Metrics are one of the most important parts of maintaining a Web site. They are the heartbeat of a Web site, measuring its overall health. Without them, you cannot tell which aspects are working and which are not.

The Maintenance phase is the longest part of the design cycle. Consequently, it is also the most expensive—an often overlooked factor to consider when you develop the budget. The most important decision in this phase, though, is determining when a revision to the Web site is necessary. A revision can be anything from a minor change to a complete overhaul. In any case, use all of the metrics, wisdom, and experience you gain from developing and maintaining the old Web site to help ensure that the new Web site will succeed.

Small redesigns or additions to the existing site can go through an accelerated development process. In these cases you do not have to revisit such things as the business analysis document. However, pay attention to the specification document, the design document, and the design guidelines, with the goal of keeping the Web site's look and feel the same throughout. (Some design teams insist on making their work look different from the rest of the Web site. Unless there is an extremely compelling reason to the contrary, insist on maintaining a consistent look and feel for the entire Web site to make it easier for customers.)

On the other hand, complete overhauls mean going through the entire Web site development process again. Complete redesigns take place when major changes are needed, such as when customer expectations change, when customer behavior changes, when there are new technology considerations, when fresh content and functionality are necessary, or when the Web site starts looking outdated.

Get customer feedback before making the final switch to a new Web site. The best way is to run usability tests on your new site to verify that customers can complete the essential tasks. Another way is to provide a link on the homepage to let customers try out the new site and to ask them what they do and do not like. If you have a list of e-mail addresses, you can contact your customers to let them know that the Web site will be updated soon.

A third way of getting feedback is through virtual testing. In this case a few select customers will see the updated Web site instead of the regular Web site. You can compare what these customers do on the new Web site to what customers do on the regular Web site to see if any interesting new strengths or weaknesses are evident with the new site. Amazon.com and Google use this method quite successfully. You can use online surveys for this purpose as well.

Deliverables

Periodic Web Site Metrics • Most of your metrics will come from the business analysis document produced in the Discovery phase. They can include such things as the total number of hits, the conversion rate (the number of people who become paying customers), satisfaction metrics, and usability evaluations.

Bug Reports • Customer e-mails, Web site evaluations, and server log file analyses are good ways to find bug reports. Rate each of these in terms of severity (such as must fix, should fix, and could fix), and estimate how long it will take to fix the problem.

Periodic Backups • Back up the entire Web site periodically as protection in case some files are accidentally erased, the Web servers are damaged, or hackers break into the site. Store the backups far away from the building that houses the Web server, in case of an environmental disaster like flood or fire.

5.9 Take-Away Ideas

The process we have described in this chapter gives you a structure to make sure your Web site will meet the needs of your clients and the needs of their customers. The principles and techniques of customer-centered design and iterative prototyping are embedded in every stage. Many firms have similar processes, though the stages and deliverables might have slightly different names. The names are not what is important here. The key is to make sure you have a customer-centered process that is documented, is reproducible, and can be improved by your organization over time.

PART II

Patterns

We have organized the patterns conceptually and divided them into groups, starting with site genres and moving progressively toward particular page elements. This structure gives you a way to navigate the patterns quickly.

You may wish to read each pattern group as a whole or skim from group to group. By using the pattern groups, you can separate the elements you need at each level of your design. Each pattern connects to related patterns in other groups. Once you have chosen one pattern, refer to the related patterns you need to fill out your design. You may also want to read the related material we reference in the Resources section of the book.

If you read patterns outside your core site needs, you may find that at first the patterns do not seem to make sense for your Web site. But you may end up using patterns you did not plan to use because they embody principles or features necessary to complete your vision. We are presenting what we see as the essential elements of customer-centered Web site design.

Keep in mind that this collection of patterns is by no means complete. Patterns are a constantly evolving language that changes as our tools, technologies, practices, and culture change.

Pattern Group A
Site Genres

In this pattern group we have categorized Web sites into types that we refer to as *genres*. Each genre has its own content, needs, and audience.

This pattern group provides the framework you need to construct many different kinds of sites. Each site pattern gives you concrete ways to differentiate your site and explains how to deliver the best experience to your customers. The site genre patterns are high-level and fairly abstract, describing general properties and characteristics of various types of Web sites. Throughout the text of each pattern are many references to other, lower-level patterns, which contain more details for designing and implementing the ideas presented, as well as references to other related patterns.

Not all Web sites have the same customer requirements. STIMULATING ARTS AND ENTERTAINMENT (A9) sites and EDUCATIONAL FORUMS (A8), for example, differ as much in design as they do in content. Arts and entertainment sites engage people by immersing them in new worlds and ideas; educational forums build dialogues around the concerns of the educational community.

That said, you might pull ideas from one genre to another so that each can benefit from elements of the other. Educational forums may benefit from clearly defined areas that purposely break the rules of navigation to encourage exploration and discovery. Stimulating arts and entertainment sites may include educational forums on related topics, to promote a depth of understanding.

Just as there are differences between genres, though, there are also strong similarities. Both sites in the previous example need good navigation cues and searchable pages.

Site Genres

This pattern group is about building sites. It explains the unique aspect of each site genre and helps you choose more detailed patterns. The rest of the book contains patterns that may be specific to a type of site or general to all sites.

A1 PERSONAL E-COMMERCE

A2 NEWS MOSAICS

A3 COMMUNITY CONFERENCE

A4 SELF-SERVICE GOVERNMENT

A5 NONPROFITS AS NETWORKS OF HELP

A6 GRASSROOTS INFORMATION SITES

A7 VALUABLE COMPANY SITES

A8 EDUCATIONAL FORUMS

A9 STIMULATING ARTS AND ENTERTAINMENT

A10 WEB APPS THAT WORK

A11 ENABLING INTRANETS

A1 PERSONAL E-COMMERCE

A1.1

(www.llbean.com, February 2, 2002)

Figure A1.1

L. L. Bean gives customers a sense of familiarity because the categories on the site (left) are similar to what they find in L. L. Bean's physical stores and catalogues. The bright colors, clean layout and navigation, and picture in the center work together to draw people in.

✳ BACKGROUND

This pattern forms the core that makes online shopping possible. Start by using it in its most basic form, then expand and extend it as needed. Use it separately or in conjunction with other site genre patterns, such as NEWS MOSAICS (A2), VALUABLE COMPANY SITES (A7), and STIMULATING ARTS AND ENTERTAINMENT (A9).

✳ PROBLEM

Customers appreciate the convenience of ordering online, but if a site is cumbersome, is veiled about its pricing and policies, or does not seem to provide a personal benefit, they leave.

E-commerce holds the promise of making customers' lives easier and more enjoyable. They can find things that they otherwise would never come across, and they can order anywhere, anytime, and with only a few button clicks (see Figure A1.2). People enjoy the pleasure of the discovery, the simplicity of the process, and the convenience of the delivery. But on many e-commerce sites, customers do not always understand what is being offered and whether it will be of any personal benefit.

Make It Clear Why People Should Purchase from You • You have to make clear from the outset what value you are providing to customers. Why should they purchase anything from your Web site? Do you offer low prices? Fast shipments? Unbiased, high-quality product reviews? A wide selection of products? A specialized set of really hard-to-find products?

Figure A1.2

Amazon.com offers all of the basic features an e-commerce site needs, and many of the advanced features as well. It offers value to customers by showing them items they might want on a homepage customized for them.

A1.2

(www.amazon.com, July 21, 2001)

Ease of use? This is your UP-FRONT VALUE PROPOSITION (C2), the core value that is woven throughout the design and organization of your entire Web site.

Provide Many Ways to Find Products • Web sites must provide customers MULTIPLE WAYS TO NAVIGATE (B1) because they look for products in many different ways. Some customers will know exactly what they're looking for and will want to type the name of the product into a SEARCH ACTION MODULE (J1) and jump straight to that product's page. Others may have only a vague notion of what they want and will want to explore lots of BROWSABLE CONTENT (B2) to get a better sense of what's available.

Searching and browsing are two basic approaches for navigating through Web sites. However, they are often not very effective for revealing the really interesting products—the ones that everyone else is buying, the ones that are on sale, or the ones that are just plain cool. Once you have the basics of e-commerce down, find new ways to help your customers scratch itches they did not even know they had. Tell your customers what new and interesting products you have by showcasing FEATURED PRODUCTS (G1) on your HOMEPAGE PORTAL (C1). Help them find related or more expensive versions of products by CROSS-SELLING AND UP-SELLING (G2). Drive more sales by providing PERSONALIZED RECOMMENDA-TIONS (G3) specially tailored to their individual interests and needs. Finally, offer a RECOMMENDATION COMMUNITY (G4) in which customers can provide feedback and comments on products. By fostering a thriving community, you are partnering with your customers, having them create new content for your Web site, and, in effect, providing everyone with yet another reason for visiting your Web site again in the future.

Keep It Convenient • Customers love to be able to search vast stores of information, see many CLEAN PRODUCT DETAIL (F2) pages that provide detailed descriptions, and compare products. In doing so they can make more educated decisions about the products and services they need. On the flip side, if you do not provide the information in a way that is easy to find, your customers will become frustrated and perhaps even leave.

If customers find one thing they like, it may spur them to find some other things they like. A site that facilitates collecting multiple items together through a SHOPPING CART (F3) can greatly simplify the shopping process.

Keep customers focused on their tasks so that they do not become distracted when they go through the QUICK-FLOW CHECKOUT (F1) process.

Customers might abandon the entire order if they do not find checkout simple and straightforward. Remember, at this point their goal is to finish shopping, and your goal should be to close the sale as smoothly and as quickly as possible (see Figure A1.3).

One common problem of many early Web sites was that they forced potential customers to create a new account through the SIGN-IN/NEW ACCOUNT (H2) process even before the customers could see what the Web site had to offer. Needless to say, many visitors balked. Some e-commerce sites still require customers to sign in or create a new account before going through QUICK-FLOW CHECKOUT (F1). You can avoid the problem by letting customers use a GUEST ACCOUNT (H3) and then create an account after the purchase is completed.

Figure A1.3

Half.com's checkout interface is simple and straightforward: It lets customers purchase items by taking them through a logical sequence of steps. It always shows customers what stage of the process they're in, and what they have to do to finish.

(**www.half.com**, October 1, 2001)

Advanced Features • After you have solved the basic mechanics of shopping and purchasing, you might want to take a look at some of the more advanced issues. For example, many people purchase products as gifts for other people. There are many details involved in GIFT GIVING (G6), such as wrapping, receipts, personalized notes, returns, and buying multiple gifts and sending them to MULTIPLE DESTINATIONS (G5). As another example, some people may be interested in seeing their ORDER TRACKING AND HISTORY (G7) to check the status of their purchases or see what they have bought in the past.

Avoid Surprises • Customers want to know what to expect when they start shopping because it will take at least a few minutes to complete the transaction, and they do not want to have a surprise toward the end. Full disclosure about site policies up front is important to shoppers. They have three areas of concern:

1. **Privacy and security.** Customers value their anonymity because it provides them with a sense of privacy and security from being defrauded or abused by people who gain access to their personal information. Many want to shop in total anonymity and complete their transactions while revealing only what is necessary. Build trust by establishing a set of FAIR INFORMATION PRACTICES (E3) that will be followed throughout your company, and make these practices clear in your PRIVACY POLICY (E4). Furthermore, use a SECURE CONNECTION (E6) whenever personal or financial information is being transmitted.
2. **Additional charges.** Sometimes, given economy of scale, customers find products at a lower price when shopping online, only to discover that the shipping and handling charges erase the savings. Granted, if people factor in the time saved from personally traveling to and from the store, shipping and handling costs can sometimes be justified. However, if the costs of shipping and handling are surprisingly large, shoppers become discouraged. They think the online merchant is trying to trick them, and they become distrustful. Providing information about all the costs involved with a purchase early in the shopping experience will build trust and keep customers from experiencing "sticker shock," one of the reasons that people abandon shopping carts (see Figure A1.4).
3. **Returns.** Many shoppers prefer to see, hear, touch, smell, or taste some products in person before buying. This is one of the major reasons that only 25 percent of all shoppers buy from print catalogs. Although some

Figure A1.4

Netmarket avoids surprises by showing its customers shipping and handling costs, as well as taxes, as soon as they add items to their shopping cart. (© 2001 Trilegiant Corporation.)

A1.4

(www.netmarket.com, August 24, 2001)

people may never shop online, more will shop on a site that provides EASY RETURNS (F9) because they know if what they buy does not work for them, they can return it for a full refund.

✳ SOLUTION

Differentiate your site so that customers know why it is compelling and valuable. Give shoppers browsing and searching tools, and provide rich, detailed information about your products and services. Make your site accessible to everyone. On every page include clear links to your privacy and security policy, shipping and handling policies, return policy, and frequently asked questions. Let customers collect items together and check out quickly, with minimal distraction.

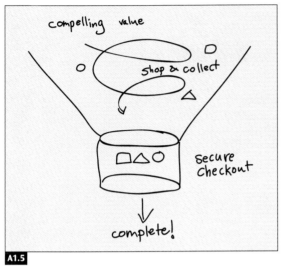

Figure A1.5

E-commerce sites should offer value, let customers shop and collect multiple items, and then quickly check out in a secure manner.

A1.5

✳ CONSIDER THESE OTHER PATTERNS

All E-Commerce Sites

Apply the solutions in Pattern Group F—Basic E-Commerce. Create an UP-FRONT VALUE PROPOSITION (C2) on your HOMEPAGE PORTAL (C1), and provide clear links for everyone for SITE ACCESSIBILITY (B9). Give customers MULTIPLE WAYS TO NAVIGATE (B1), make sure you have BROWSABLE CONTENT (B2), and provide CLEAN PRODUCT DETAILS (F2) so that people can compare different offers, pick the products or services they want by putting them in their SHOPPING CART (F3), move through your QUICK-FLOW CHECKOUT (F1), and if necessary, take advantage of EASY RETURNS (F9).

Provide a FREQUENTLY ASKED QUESTIONS (H7) page that answers common questions about security, privacy, shipping, and returns. Build trust by making your PRIVACY POLICY (E4) always available and using FAIR INFORMATION PRACTICES (E3) throughout your company.

Advanced E-Commerce Sites

Choose options from Pattern Group G—Advanced E-Commerce. You may want to add daily FEATURED PRODUCTS (G1) to keep customers coming back for a glimpse of what your reviewers recommend, and to show them something they may not have seen before.

F
C2 **C1**
B9
B1
B2 **F2**

F3
F1 **F9**
H7

E4
E3

G
G1

Customers like to save time, and sometimes they buy more than one thing. Help people save time, and perhaps show them something they might want but have not seen, by CROSS-SELLING AND UP-SELLING (G2). Shoppers like to hear recommendations from others they trust, but they do not want to be pigeonholed as a particular kind of person. By using PERSONALIZED RECOMMENDATIONS (G3), you can offer ideas on the basis of what you know someone might be looking for, without resorting to a formulaic recommendation. Customers like helping others, too. By offering a RECOMMENDATION COMMUNITY (G4), you allow customers on your site to make their own recommendations.

Sometimes customers who are GIFT GIVING (G6) need to send gifts to people in many places. By using MULTIPLE DESTINATIONS (G5), they can buy and send all the gifts in one order. Sometimes customers need to review their orders to make sure the products they ordered arrived. And if a product that has shipped does not arrive when it should, the ORDER TRACKING AND HISTORY (G7) feature helps customers solve shipping problems.

Figure A2.1

CNN's Web site provides not only the top news of the day, but also archives of reporting from years gone by. It varies the content with diverse topics, in short form and in depth. The site encourages readers to use cnn.com as a resource, and it provides a quick guide to what is important today.

A2.1

(www.cnn.com, July 26, 2001)

❋ BACKGROUND

This pattern forms the core that makes news sites useful. Use it separately or in conjunction with any other site genre pattern, such as PERSONAL E-COMMERCE (A1) if you sell products or services, GRASSROOTS INFORMATION SITES (A6) for expert analysis or content and links to the best sources of information on the Web, or COMMUNITY CONFERENCE (A3) for ways your customers can discuss the topics of the day. No matter which news site you create, it must have this basic capability of news mosaics.

A1
A6
A3

✳ PROBLEM

Many readers come to Web sites to learn about their world through news and history. These sites must deliver the news their readers want, with the depth and breadth of coverage necessary to engage them, and make the historical record available online so that customers can search for older stories.

News on the Web borrows heavily from what has been learned by offline news organizations, but it also poses new problems unique to the online medium. In terms of time and access, form, and audience, there are key differences between the way news is presented in television, radio, and print, and the way news is presented on the Web.

Time and Access • News stories on television, on radio, and in print last only the moment, the day, or sometimes the week (they are called *newspaper piles*), and then they are banished to a library archive. In other words, they appear now and then become mostly inaccessible tomorrow. Web-based news is different in that you can deliver any kind of news—up-to-the-second news, two-week-old news, or five-year-old news—and readers can still access it online. The information in your database remains both newsworthy and historical in value (see Figure A2.2).

Because the Web can deliver the "scoop" faster than other media can, it can create many time pressures. One is with publishing new content. You do not want to be re-creating the page layout and manually copying and pasting in text every time you want to add a new story. Use PAGE TEM-**(D1) (D2)** PLATES (D1) that contain one or more CONTENT MODULES (D2). The content modules can be linked to a database, making publication as simple as adding a new story to the database, and adding the associated HEADLINES **(D3)** AND BLURBS (D3) to other pages.

Another time pressure created by the Web is on checking sources. As with many other businesses, the long-term value of a news organization is based on the continuing quality of its product. This is especially true on the Web, where trust and reputation are closely tied to quality. Make sure your site goes the distance and properly checks the sources of your stories. The Web makes it easy to offer links to attributions and references, further encouraging the trust of your readers. In fact, studies have shown that people perceive news articles as more credible if there are references **(K8)** and EXTERNAL LINKS (K8) to other Web sites.

Figure A2.2

CBS MarketWatch uses embedded links and sidebars to link to stock prices, further research, and stories related to the current article. (Copyright © 1998–2001 MarketWatch.com, Inc.)

(cbs.marketwatch.com, May 9, 2002)

Form • News stories on television have the impact of motion and sound but are usually limited in duration, and therefore depth. Radio has the storytelling and music advantages of audio but is also usually limited in duration and depth. Unlike TV, however, radio travels well and does not consume precious eye time. Print has the benefit of more space, more depth, and mobility. The Web has some of the advantages of all three offline media, but it has other limitations.

One limitation is with how people read online. Many people skim Web pages instead of reading them closely. If something is not interesting, people hit the **Back** button pretty quickly. Draw people in by using a

CLEAR FIRST READ (I3) that sets and unifies the visual and writing style for the article, and by using an INVERSE-PYRAMID WRITING STYLE (D7) that gives them the most important information first.

Another limitation is that online news reading lacks the portability, large format, and legibility of print. It is true that online news can include video, audio, print, hyperlinked text, and historical access to stories. However, online video lacks the quality and screen size of video on television unless the viewer has broadband capability. Web audio is useful for playing live and archived news, but it is not as portable as live news updates on the radio because it often requires a live connection. Furthermore, it is difficult to search on these kinds of media or to make them accessible to people with physical impairments unless a transcript is provided.

Take advantage of the Web's strengths. Provide short and long forms of your news using hyperlinks. Break up the text into manageable chunks to make it easier to read, thereby giving your readers the benefits of both TV's brevity and print's depth. In addition, use EMBEDDED LINKS (K7) or CONSISTENT SIDEBARS OF RELATED CONTENT (I6) to add depth to a story. A text-based news article can link to video footage, audio interviews, or a richer set of images (see Figure A2.3). That way you do not have to fit the different media on a single Web page.

Audience • Web-based news can be tailored to each person, whereas television, radio, and print are limited to targeted demographic groups. The Web creates opportunities, as well as possible limitations. Although readers can specify exactly the kinds of news they would like to read or receive, they also might be limiting their exposure to news outside their immediate areas of interest. As Andrew Shapiro observed in a review of online news, the result can be a further Balkanization of information, where we no longer have communities that share common experiences and sources of information, and we splinter off into small communities that do not fruitfully interact with one another.

Your challenge is to select not only the information your readers want, but also the high-quality information they do not know about that you want them to read. Your decisions are critical because your customers are looking for a guide when they come to a site with lots of information. With virtually unlimited "rack space," the volume of news can be overwhelming. Traditional media provide stories in a hierarchical manner. You need to make similar decisions about how you display the news, on the basis of what you know about your readers and their interests. One way to prioritize the information on a page is by screen placement and type size, as illustrated by cnn.com (see Figures A2.1 and A2.3).

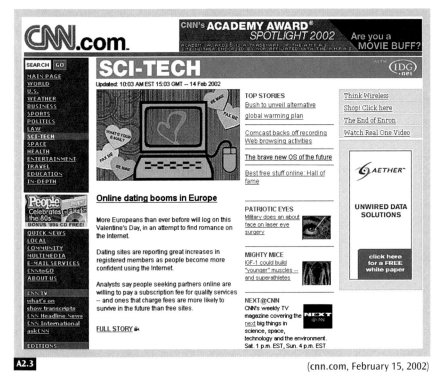

A2.3

(cnn.com, February 15, 2002)

Figure A2.3

CNN's news articles mix text with photo essays, audio, and video clips. CNN also provides a page that shows all of its multimedia in one place.

When readers come to your site, they want to browse for articles on subjects that are important to them. Your challenge is not to bury everything but the most popular news, thereby making it harder for readers to find the more personal topics they seek. Give readers MULTIPLE WAYS TO NAVIGATE (B1). Let them look for topics by category, by keyword, or by historical reference. Also make it easy for people to search for specific content by WRITING FOR SEARCH ENGINES (D6) and providing ORGANIZED SEARCH RESULTS (J3).

Some news sites, such as cnn.com, nytimes.com, and washingtonpost.com, provide archives, but only one of them archives the news in files and directories with permanent addresses: cnn.com. An EXTERNAL LINK (K8) on your site, to a CNN news story today, will always be an unbroken link. Most other news sites do not provide this capability.

Getting news right on the Web is also important for societal reasons. A study by the Pew Research Center for the People & the Press found that 33 percent of online U.S. citizens used the Internet in the year 2000 to inform themselves on politics. This finding shows that the quality of your news site can have a major impact.

✳ SOLUTION

Build a mosaic of news by providing breadth and depth of coverage through a diversity of categories and further refinement through subcategories. Within each category highlight the most important article and lead text, while also providing a breadth of articles that might otherwise be missed. Within each article, provide a high-level summary first, for people who are looking for a quick read, but also provide the more in-depth information in the rest of the article. Link together related news items, whether they are articles, radio stories, or video clips. Archive this information in the same place on your servers for historical reference.

Figure A2.4

Provide a mosaic of news in your article arrangement. Your site organization should give readers quick access to the most important news on various subjects, but it should also allow people to drill down for other articles on a subject, as well as back in time to earlier articles.

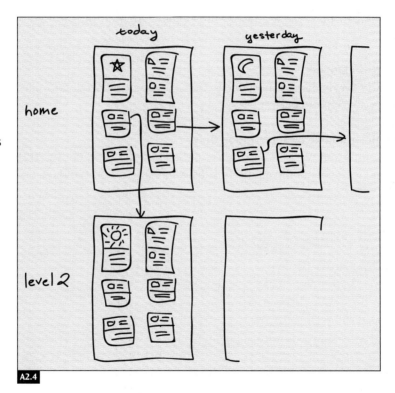

A2.4

✳ CONSIDER THESE OTHER PATTERNS

Basic News Mosaics

Make this information easily accessible by providing top-level navigation to the various topic regions and to historical content through MULTIPLE WAYS TO NAVIGATE (B1). Start every page with a CLEAR FIRST READ (I3) of   the main article. Make links to subcategories available on a NAVIGATION BAR (K2), as well as through article HEADLINES AND BLURBS (D3). Using the INVERSE-PYRAMID WRITING STYLE (D7), write content for quick reads and for more in-depth reads.

Improve your search capabilities by WRITING FOR SEARCH ENGINES (D6) and displaying ORGANIZED SEARCH RESULTS (J3). Lay out topic sections using PAGE TEMPLATES (D1), with each article in CONTENT MODULES (D2) so that they can be created quickly and updated frequently through a database.

Advanced News Mosaics

Provide ways for readers to subscribe to news updates in particular topics with E-MAIL SUBSCRIPTIONS (E2).

News Mosaics Available by Subscription Only

Create accounts and provide sign-in using the SIGN-IN/NEW ACCOUNT (H2) pattern, and give people the ability to subscribe using QUICK-FLOW CHECK-OUT (F1).

Figure A3.1

Beliefnet's community section offers many ways for people to come together: large open discussions, smaller closed groups, and personal groups used on special occasions for families and close friends.

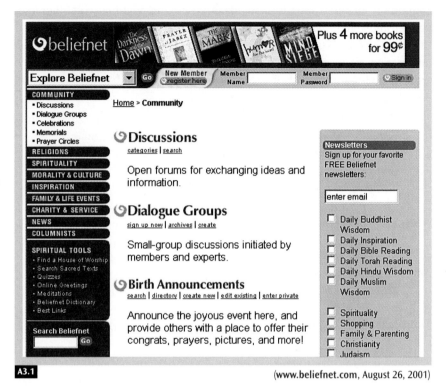

(www.beliefnet.com, August 26, 2001)

✳ BACKGROUND

D5 MESSAGE BOARDS (D5) are only one part in creating an ongoing and thriving community. This pattern endorses responsibility and open discourse. As a place where people can trust one another to speak honestly and intelligently without fear of hooliganism, it can be used in conjunc-
A7 tion with and integrated into VALUABLE COMPANY SITES (A7), PERSONAL
A1 A8 E-COMMERCE (A1), EDUCATIONAL FORUMS (A8), and other site genre patterns.

✳ PROBLEM

Community members want to share ideas, views, and opinions with other like-minded individuals, whether they live across the street or across the planet. However, a host of issues must be resolved, such as community usage policies, moderation of forums, anonymity, archives, interaction, trust, sociability, growth, and sustainability. The challenge is to strike a balance within the online community.

The ability to have ongoing conversations with anyone, anywhere, anytime, is one of the most powerful aspects of the Web. However, many issues that are intrinsic to online communities are very different from our everyday experiences in the real world. In this section we discuss many of the policy issues that have to be resolved for all community conferences.

Community Usage Policies • Managing online communities is not easy. It is far easier to set up MESSAGE BOARDS (D5) and let things just happen. Making any community conference work takes time and effort to organize, invite, give access, monitor, and facilitate. Which rules are important to the community? Should you remove off-topic comments from a discussion thread, or should you archive them to a separate location? What kinds of things are acceptable for people to post? What happens if a member breaks the rules?

Every community must declare its own standards and enforce those standards. Every community must also establish a set of FAIR INFORMATION PRACTICES (E3) on how personal data will be used, and communicate these practices through a clear PRIVACY POLICY (E4). Getting the members of your community to agree on rules can be time-consuming (see Figure A3.2), but once they have done so, our experience shows that their discussion will be more thoughtful and enlightening.

Synchronous or Asynchronous Communication • One immediate question with respect to community conferences is whether people must interact with one another now, or can respond to one another later. The former is an example of **synchronous communication**, meaning that all parties have to be online simultaneously and interaction takes place in real time. Examples of synchronous communication include chat rooms, video conferencing, and shared drawing spaces. The latter is an example of **asynchronous communication**, meaning that members can leave messages that others can respond to later. Examples of asynchronous communication include e-mail, MESSAGE BOARDS (D5), and community-created Web pages.

Figure A3.2

The online community Craigslist sets the ground rules for postings as soon as customers go to the list of forums.

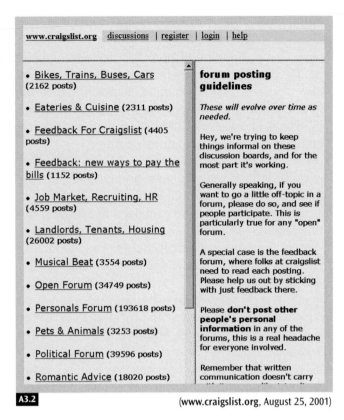

www.craigslist.org   discussions | register | login | help

- Bikes, Trains, Buses, Cars (2162 posts)

- Eateries & Cuisine (2311 posts)

- Feedback For Craigslist (4405 posts)

- Feedback: new ways to pay the bills (1152 posts)

- Job Market, Recruiting, HR (4559 posts)

- Landlords, Tenants, Housing (26002 posts)

- Musical Beat (3554 posts)

- Open Forum (34749 posts)

- Personals Forum (193618 posts)

- Pets & Animals (3253 posts)

- Political Forum (39596 posts)

- Romantic Advice (18020 posts)

forum posting guidelines

These will evolve over time as needed.

Hey, we're trying to keep things informal on these discussion boards, and for the most part it's working.

Generally speaking, if you want to go a little off-topic in a forum, please do so, and see if people participate. This is particularly true for any "open" forum.

A special case is the feedback forum, where folks at craigslist need to read each posting. Please help us out by sticking with just feedback there.

Please **don't post other people's personal information** in any of the forums, this is a real headache for everyone involved.

Remember that written communication doesn't carry

A3.2   (www.craigslist.org, August 25, 2001)

Each approach has pros and cons. Synchronous communication is more spontaneous and often leads to faster decision making. However, people with slow Internet connections suffer enormously, and sometimes it is difficult to keep track of who is saying what. Asynchronous communication can be more thoughtful (though not always!), and participants can reply to posted messages at any later time. However, because of slow turnaround it is sometimes difficult to come to a consensus on issues, and it can be difficult to manage and take part in the many continuing conversations.

You can support both synchronous and asynchronous forums, depending on the interests and needs of your customers. For example, it is not uncommon for Web sites to host MESSAGE BOARDS (D5), as well as several chat rooms. Also note that there is not always a strict separation between synchronous and asynchronous communication. A synchronous chat can be archived for other people to see, at which point it becomes an asynchronous resource.

D5

Moderation • Another question you will need to answer up front is whether your forums are moderated, and if so, to what degree. On **moderated forums**, messages are filtered and processed by one or more moderators that must approve all messages to make sure that they follow the established rules and norms. An example of a moderated forum would be a message board for people coping with cancer. The moderator in this case would approve all messages except for blatant advertisements and trolls (messages intended to inflame and infuriate others).

Unmoderated forums are free-for-all discussions in which anything goes. People can say whatever they want, and it is up to the members of the community to enforce any rules and social norms. An example of an unmoderated forum is an ad hoc chat room set up by a high school student where she and her friends can talk about whatever they want. The only thing keeping people from being viciously rude to one another in this case is the fact that they know each other and have an ongoing relationship, seeing each other in school.

There are many options between these two extremes. For example, an e-mail list could be moderated to the extent that a moderator has to approve the first few messages that everyone posts, but unmoderated in the sense that after someone has had three messages approved, her messages no longer have to be approved to be posted. As another example, a message board could be unmoderated except for a few spot checks to make sure that no one is posting copyrighted material. Furthermore, people can send complaints or notifications of usage violations to the owner of the message board, who can then act reasonably in handling the complaint.

The upshot is that there are many options with respect to moderation. Your choice of the level of moderation all depends on what kind of community and discussion you want.

Anonymous, Pseudonymous, or Identified by Real Name • Anonymity is an extremely important and sometimes contentious issue that you will have to deal with on community conference sites. The online world's capabilities for anonymity can be liberating (see Figure A3.3), freeing people from social norms and pressures. However, they are also highly prone to abuse, as potential sources of false and libelous information. Because anyone can create an anonymous identity, your customers can pretend to be who they're not.

In a positive sense, anonymity means that community members can veil their identity or playact, giving them the opportunity to "try on"

Figure A3.3

Anonymous postings can be important on the Greenpeace Cyberactivist Community site, where visitors might want to participate in environmental activism without alerting their employers.

A3.3

(cybercentre.greenpeace.org/t/s, August 26, 2001)

being a different person, similar to acting in theater or playing make-believe. This freedom is critical for people who need to hide their true identities, such as victims of abuse, who with anonymity can participate in online discussions without fear of reprisal from their abusers.

On the negative side, because it is difficult to trace activities that are completely anonymous online, people abuse complete anonymity for hostile and sometimes illegal purposes. At the annoying but benign level, being completely anonymous is a consequence-free way to digress and ruin an otherwise enlightening conversation. At hostile but not illegal levels, some people use complete anonymity to abuse others with angry comments. Tragically, when adults prey on children in complete anonymity, or commit other crimes online, the whole online community suffers. If you cannot restrict access by requiring participants to verify their true identities, abusive activities can go unchecked.

There is a fair balance between no anonymity, or real names (see Figure A3.4), and complete anonymity. When your customers inform you of their true identity and then assume a different name in the community, they can realize the benefits of partial anonymity. This is known as a **pseudonym**. By restricting access to only those individuals who are willing to divulge their true identities *to the site operators,* an online community fosters more responsible behavior.

Home Join About Conferencing Members Services & Help Enter

The WELL is an online gathering place like no other. Since 1985 this literate watering hole has drawn thinkers from all walks of life -- people who like an intelligent and uninhibited conversation in a members-only environment.

What makes The WELL different from other online communities?

- **You know who you're talking with:** As a WELL member, you use your real name. This leads to real conversations and relationships.

- **Your privacy and intellectual property choices are assured.** You own your own words at The WELL.

- **You can control access to your discussions:** As a Complete Plan member you can set up your own closed-door "private conference" -- open only to other WELL members you select.

A3.4

(www.well.com, August 25, 2001)

Figure A3.4

In the WELL's community, like-minded individuals can share ideas, develop a rapport, and build strong, trusting relationships. Requiring real names and confirmed identities helps build this trust.

Table A3.1 shows what levels of anonymity are reasonable in different circumstances.

Archives • There are three basic questions to answer here. First, will messages be stored? Second, if so, for how long? Third, who has access to see and possibly delete old messages? For example, messages in chat rooms are usually not stored, but message boards often save all posts and make them permanently available for all people to see. On the other hand, it's not unheard of for chat sessions to be archived, or for message board posts older than one month to be automatically deleted.

There are many pros and cons to storing archives of past messages. Some messages represent useful knowledge, and searching for that information can be easier and faster than having someone repeat it over and over. For team projects, a message archive can be a record of design

Table A3.1

Reasonable Levels
of Anonymity
in Community
Conferences

Conference Type	Level of Anonymity Required	Disclosed to Community	Disclosed to Site Operator
Adult educational conference	None	Name and contact	Name and contact
New parent support group	None	Name and contact	Name and contact
K–12 class discussions	Partial	Anonymous or student-created user name	Name and contact
Abuse victim discussions	Partial	None	Name and contact

rationale, helping someone who joins the team later understand why a certain design decision was made. These archives are also useful to researchers, letting them see patterns of communication among community members and changes in those patterns over time.

There are also some potentially serious disadvantages of archiving past messages. Some messages just aren't that valuable. There's not much point in archiving informal chats about computer games or gossip, for example. Also there is the danger that things people write will come back and haunt them many years later. It does seem somewhat unfair that people can search on someone's name and see something that he thoughtlessly posted 12 years ago. As a result, long-term archives might cripple open discussion and lead to potentially embarrassing situations in the future. In fact, it's not unheard of for a company's e-mail archives to be subpoenaed in a legal dispute.

This leads into the next question: How long should archives be kept? Short-lived archives can help people remember recent messages and avoid problems with those messages being taken out of context in the future. Long-lived archives are useful for finding important messages in the past. There is no single answer, unfortunately, and decisions have to be made on a case-by-case basis.

The last question about archives has to do with access. Who should be able to access the archives, and should they be able to delete old messages? For example, one possible policy is to let only the person who posted a message see his or her own messages. Another is to let anyone in the community search for and see all messages, and allow posters to delete their old messages. This decision should be part of your PRIVACY POLICY (E4), as well as your community's usage policy.

Trust and Sociability • It is true that some of the benefits and social cues of in-person contact are lost online. There are many benefits to online conferences, however: Your readers can be geographically dispersed; they do not have to be together at the same time; conversations can last weeks, months, or longer; and newcomers can join and read the history of the conversation so far.

Once involved, moderators must keep conversations on track and turn major digressions into their own discussion threads. Creating an online community is time intensive but well worth the effort when responsibility, respect, and a shared commitment to intelligent conversation are the standards.

Publish and follow these basic rules:

- We seek thoughtful and intelligent people to enrich each conference.
- Newcomers are allowed to visit and listen, and join in when they're ready.
- Each member's view will be respected.
- Personal attacks are not allowed.
- People who are not respectful and thoughtful will be ejected.
- If you ever feel harassed, you can e-mail the moderator and express your concern.
- No single person will run the whole conversation because the community is not a personal soapbox.

Growth and Sustainability • Creating an ongoing and thriving community is a difficult task. The greatest obstacles are attracting people to your community and then getting them to participate. When first starting out, you will probably have to nurture and lead some discussions to get things going.

Ideally, you want your community to exhibit a positive network effect, where newcomers will join your community because there are already a lot of community members, all without much effort on your part. Most communities have a critical mass—that is, a minimum number of participating community members for the community to become self-sustaining, as already described.

Reaching this critical mass is much more important than it may seem at first because it marks the beginning of a fairly successful online community. This milestone has significant benefits for recruiting new community members because new people will come to see what all the hubbub is about. This could attract more visitors to the community and encourage them to stay longer. The longer people try out a community conference, the more they will become accustomed to the forums, discussions, customs, social norms, and people in the community. And most importantly, while it's easy for people to switch to a competing e-commerce site and buy something there, it's much more difficult for people to switch to a competing community conference. They simply can't switch their friends and chat partners as easily.

Additional Information • A great deal of high-quality information about creating, managing, and sustaining an online community is available. Use the sources listed in the Resources section later in the book to find more information about nurturing a community, running a large online community, hosting conversations, free speech, and many, many other issues.

✳ SOLUTION

To make a community conference work, establish a clear community usage policy that specifies behaviors that are acceptable and sanctions that will be imposed on anyone who breaks the rules. Set up a variety of synchronous and asynchronous forums to suit you and your customers. Determine if the community will be moderated, and if so, to what degree. Agree on the level of anonymity your community will support. Decide whether messages will be archived, and if so how they will be archived and who will have access to them. Increase trust and sociability by keeping discussions on track and establishing social norms of behavior (see Figure A3.5). Promote growth by leading discussions and attracting new community members.

Figure A3.5

When you require nonanonymous sign-ins for access to community conferences, your community members will act more respectfully and responsibly. Managed discussions keep conversations on target.

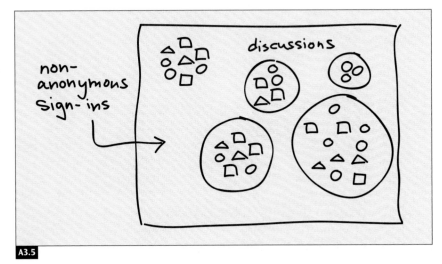

A3.5

✳ CONSIDER THESE OTHER PATTERNS

Basic Community Conference

Make your FAIR INFORMATION PRACTICES (E3) clear to your customers through an understandable PRIVACY POLICY (E4) available on all pages. Ask all potential participants to create nonanonymous accounts using SIGN-IN/NEW ACCOUNT (H2). Verify the addresses of the individuals by sending an e-mail message to which they must respond, and if security needs dictate (and privacy policy allows), call them on the phone as well.

Place BROWSABLE CONTENT (B2) in the MESSAGE BOARDS (D5). Manage these message boards on a daily basis, creating new threads for major digressions.

Advanced Community Conference

Give members a way to understand how their values are being perceived. If you have hundreds or thousands of members, use a RECOMMENDATION COMMUNITY (G4) to let people rate each other on how insightful and help- ful their assessments and views really are to others. This feedback will help newcomers better judge each person and give them the goal of earn- ing respect.

Figure A4.1

The official site of Sydney, Australia, provides access to government information and services from the convenience of each citizen's desk, eliminating bureaucracy and frustration.

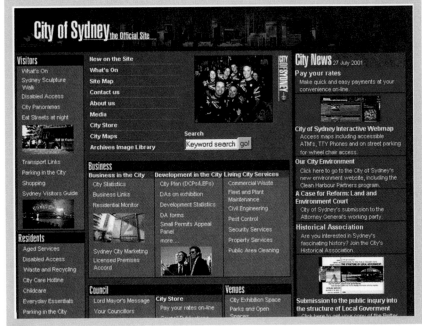

(www.sydney.com, July 27, 2001)

❋ BACKGROUND

This pattern describes how to build an environment that makes government services more available and accessible. You can add other site genre patterns, such as PERSONAL E-COMMERCE (A1) and COMMUNITY CONFERENCE (A3).

✳ PROBLEM

Making a government agency's information available on the Web can be helpful. But if the agency is too large and centrally controlled, its Web site can seem unresponsive, bureaucratic, and impersonal to its customers.

A September 2000, Hart–Teeter study found that the U.S. public believes that online interaction between citizens and their government, or e-government, means better government, and that investing tax dollars in e-government should be a medium to high priority. According to Peter Hart Research, 61 percent of people believe the Internet should be used to make it easier for citizens to interact with government to find the information and services they need, when they need them. If your job is to make e-government a reality, your local, state, or federal government Web site needs to provide this capability while avoiding the problems that citizens currently face in their offline interactions with government agencies: red tape and a faceless bureaucracy.

Red Tape • A preponderance of evidence shows that red tape is a result of government agencies that have grown too large. Whether wasting time waiting in line or battling red tape as they are bounced from one bureaucrat to another, citizens must fight their way through centrally controlled government processes. This red tape can come in many forms. People must submit formal requests and wait until their requests are processed. This process can take a day, a week, or months, and there is little or no feedback about where the request is in the process or what the estimated time to complete it is. In the case of a problem, generalized regulations and centralized control prevent low-level government agents from having the autonomy to make decisions on their own. To a large, centrally controlled agency, local community issues are unmanageable.

Faceless Bureaucracy • When customers come to use your Web-based services, there are more problems. They find that online government agencies are usually even less personable than offline: They are nameless, faceless, and generic, and they provide no feedback. Site visitors might find a government form, but it is usually for printing and submitting offline. If submitted online, such forms are processed as offline forms. If individuals are named on a Web site at all, they are usually so far removed from individual services (such as the mayor) that they are of no help.

Given these issues, we conclude that your government agency Web site can provide better levels of service than offline services alone can if you do the following:

- Provide small, autonomous self-service applications that give feedback as requests are being processed (see Figure A4.2).
- Deliver comprehensive and personalized answers to general and local community questions.
- Connect people to local agents who have the autonomy to solve problems and answer questions (see Figure A4.3).

Figure A4.2

The city of San Jose's site shows how e-government can be done. It has taken much of the hassle out of getting a construction permit by allowing citizens to complete the entire process online.

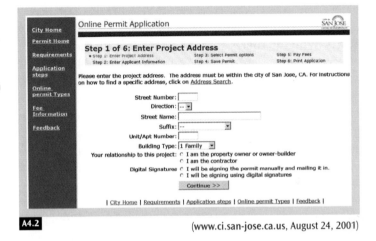

(www.ci.san-jose.ca.us, August 24, 2001)

Figure A4.3

The state of California's Web site offers several useful, though not yet usable, self-service applications. This site allows citizens to make appointments at the Department of Motor Vehicles.

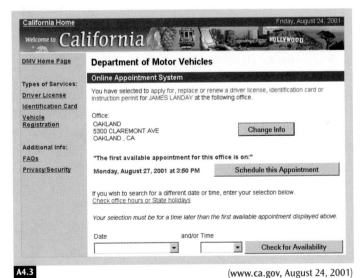

(www.ca.gov, August 24, 2001)

To make a government Web site work most effectively, you must also address the issues of universal access and of privacy and trust.

Universal Access • Any government that attempts to take advantage of the Web to provide government services online needs to give everyone access to the Web, whether this means subsidizing purchases of Internet appliances (à la Minitel in France) or making Web access devices ubiquitous in public spaces, such as libraries and post offices. Web sites should also be built so that people with slow Internet connections, older computers, and older software can still use them. Finally, be sure to build your site for SITE ACCESSIBILITY (B9), to serve citizens who require special assistance in reading, hearing, or navigating Web sites.

B9

Privacy and Trust • When it comes to online services, the government must respect the privacy of each citizen. The entire agency behind the Web site must establish FAIR INFORMATION PRACTICES (E3) that will be respected and followed by everyone involved. These practices must also be clearly explained in a prominently displayed PRIVACY POLICY (E4). In general, avoid the use of IP tracking and cookie-based PERSISTENT CUSTOMER SESSIONS (H5) unless absolutely needed because these can inadvertently create an image of abuse of government power and infringement on the rights of the citizenry. On the other hand, do provide SECURE CONNECTIONS (E6) and a SIGN-IN/NEW ACCOUNT (H2) process for any transactions that contain personal and trusted information.

E3

E4

H5

E6 **H2**

✳ SOLUTION

Provide secure, autonomous self-service applications that report current process status through your site and e-mail after the initial request submission. Give your customers the estimated time to completion, on the basis of the kind of request made. Personalize site information for each citizen by giving direct access to that citizen's agency representative and providing answers to questions posted by local community members.

Figure A4.4

Secure, autonomous applications eliminate the need for people to wait in line, and personalized pages give people direct access to local agents and information.

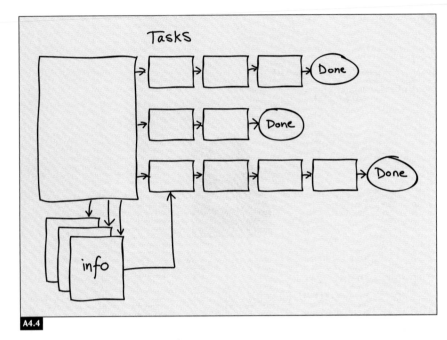

A4.4

✳ CONSIDER THESE OTHER PATTERNS

B1 Develop a site organization using MULTIPLE WAYS TO NAVIGATE (B1) so that citizens can easily find the information and services they need. Determine your FAIR INFORMATION PRACTICES (E3) and state them clearly in **E4** your PRIVACY POLICY (E4) so that people know how their private information will be used. Using SECURE CONNECTIONS (E6) will also build trust. **B9** Give access to all by providing SITE ACCESSIBILITY (B9).

Develop secure, autonomous applications by creating PROCESS FUNNELS **H1 H2** (H1) that require SIGN-IN/NEW ACCOUNT (H2) creation and use noncookie **H5** PERSISTENT CUSTOMER SESSIONS (H5).

Provide local-agent contact information and local-issue question and answer information, as well as general information through PERSONAL-**D4 D2** IZED CONTENT (D4) and CONTENT MODULES (D2). Keep citizens informed **E2** about their pending requests using weekly E-MAIL SUBSCRIPTIONS (E2).

A5 NONPROFITS AS NETWORKS OF HELP

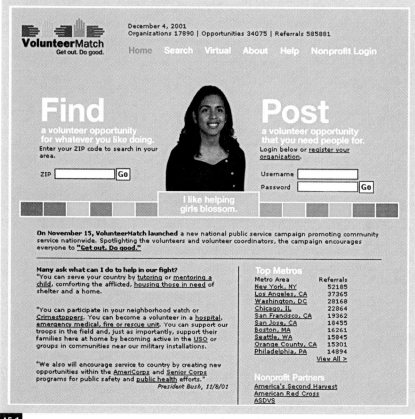

A5.1

(www.volunteermatch.org, December 4, 2001)

Figure A5.1

VolunteerMatch uses the Web to help volunteers and nonprofit organizations find each other.

✳ BACKGROUND

This pattern forms the core of all nonprofit sites. Integrate other site genre patterns into a nonprofit site to expand its capabilities or use this pattern to add a charitable service to a VALUABLE COMPANY SITE (A7), PERSONAL E-COMMERCE (A1) site, NEWS MOSAIC (A2), or EDUCATIONAL FORUM (A8).

A7

A1 **A2**

A8

❋ PROBLEM

Nonprofits rely on financial sponsors, volunteers, and staff members to benefit the needs of a client cause. But if these groups are not brought together in a network, a major benefit of the Web is neglected.

A nonprofit's financial sponsors, volunteers, and staff members are all looking to help its beneficiaries, but each group has its own needs and criteria for participation. Addressing these needs is the first and most basic step of developing a nonprofit Web site. Such a design may provide access to information anytime anywhere and start to build an individual relationship between the nonprofit and each visitor.

A True Network of Help • Providing only "the basics" keeps each visitor isolated and does not leverage the tremendous power of the Web as a network. A Web site can be the nexus of communications that allow people to connect directly to one another.

There are many reasons to connect everyone involved in a nonprofit. Most nonprofits are organized around projects and schedules that bring together volunteers, beneficiaries, and sponsorships from financial contributors—all organized and coordinated by staff members.

Coordinating these projects requires effort and precious staff time, as well as continual updates to the entire team about the project status. Invariably, issues arise that you must address with employees, volunteers, sponsors, beneficiaries, or the entire project team. Individual volunteers and beneficiaries can benefit others by sharing what they have learned. Financial sponsors benefit from seeing the project process in action. Staff members seek to learn and help their systems evolve from one project to the next. Each project becomes a success story to document and publish. Everyone involved becomes a key part of the success story.

 Connecting people on a nonprofit Web site reduces management costs, while improving communication between the players. Tools such as MESSAGE BOARDS (D5), online schedules, and site-publishing tools facilitate the coordination of teams and the sharing of information without costly overhead and administration. By providing these tools on a central project management server, you can create a system in which people communicate more frequently because the tools eliminate time and location constraints. Such a benefit is called a **network effect** because everyone gains more benefit as more individuals use this network of connections.

Providing Specific Solutions • Financial sponsors, volunteers, staff members, and beneficiaries will have different questions, and they will carry out different tasks. These needs form the basis for the solutions shown in Table A5.1.

A basic nonprofit site must entice each group to participate by answering these key questions. An advanced nonprofit network of help provides the means for entire projects to be coordinated online. In such a case the Web site becomes the primary vehicle for connecting groups in a coordinated activity and shared dialogue.

Table A5.1
Sample Questions, Tasks, and Solutions for Nonprofits

Group	Question or Task	What to Provide as a Solution	
Financial sponsors (see Figure A5.2)	Why do I want to fund this nonprofit?	The benefits of funding this nonprofit	
	What does this nonprofit do?	ABOUT US (E5), an overview of the program	
	Who are the beneficiaries?	An overview of beneficiaries and some of their stories	
	How will my money be used?	Statistics on how much of each dollar is used for the cause and how much covers administrative overhead	
	How do I make a donation?	Instructions for making donations offline or online, with the online version providing a SECURE CONNECTION (E6) through a PROCESS FUNNEL (H1)	
Volunteers (see Figures A5.3 and A5.4)	Why is this a worthy cause?	ABOUT US (E5), an overview of the program	
	What do volunteers do?	The benefits for volunteers and some of their stories	
	How do I become involved?	A schedule of events, a volunteer sign-up form, E-MAIL SUBSCRIPTIONS (E2) for newsletters and nearby events	
Staff	Who are the current volunteers, financiers, and beneficiaries?	Secure page listing volunteers, financial sponsors, and beneficiaries	
Beneficiaries	Who are the people helping me?	Offers of gratitude to all the financiers, volunteers, and staff members, and what they contributed (in general)	
Everyone	What are the latest developments with current projects?	MESSAGE BOARDS (D5) with current topics open for discussion, HEADLINES AND BLURBS (D3) of new events	

Figure A5.2

The Rotary Foundation, a division of Rotary International, is the charitable-works arm of Rotary clubs. Its site allows visitors to make gifts to the foundation, manage their gifts, find local sponsors for initiatives, and see what their district has donated.

(**www.rotary.org/foundation**, February 8, 2002)

Figure A5.3

Kiwanis International is dedicated to serving its community and promoting the needs of children worldwide. Its Web site features relevant news headlines and makes it easy for members to join events and discuss issues.

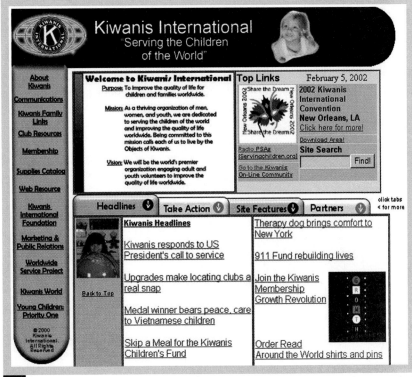

(Reprinted from **www.kiwanis.org**, February 5, 2002)

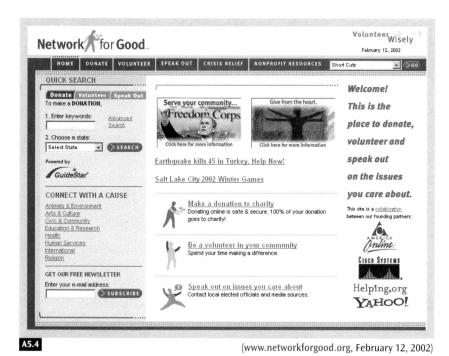

A5.4

Figure A5.4

Network for Good promotes civic participation and philanthropy. Its Web site aggregates content and resources from over 20 nonprofit organizations, making them conveniently available all in one place.

(www.networkforgood.org, February 12, 2002)

✳ SOLUTION

At a minimum, provide information that addresses the questions posed by financial sponsors, volunteers, staff members, and beneficiaries. To harness the power of the Web as a network, give people the ability to sign up for projects in a place where all team members can coordinate, participate, and record project developments for future reference.

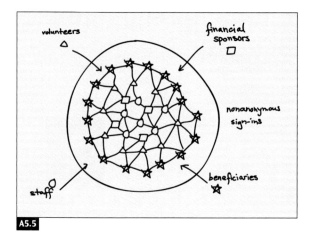

A5.5

Figure A5.5

Basic nonprofit sites provide compelling reasons for people to become financial sponsors, volunteers, staff members, and beneficiaries. To make the most of the network, a nonprofit site must help coordinate people around specific projects.

✻ CONSIDER THESE OTHER PATTERNS

Basic Nonprofit Networks of Help

Build a site that provides program information targeted to your distinct audiences: financial sponsors, volunteers, staff, and beneficiaries. Provide MULTIPLE WAYS TO NAVIGATE (B1) to a CATEGORY PAGE (B8) for each audience, where you publish success stories and past accomplishments in CONTENT MODULES (D2) for easy updating. Keep your project calendar up-to-date.

Provide volunteers with a basic form for them to sign up by using a PROCESS FUNNEL (H1). Also place an E-MAIL SUBSCRIPTION (E2) form on or just off of the HOMEPAGE PORTAL (C1) to make it easy for visitors to remain informed about events.

Make your FAIR INFORMATION PRACTICES (E3) clear through a simple and understandable PRIVACY POLICY (E4).

Advanced Nonprofit Networks of Help

Make it easy for people to contribute by giving visitors the opportunity to make donations online through a QUICK-FLOW CHECKOUT (F1) process.

To take advantage of the Web's network effect, use your project calendar to help volunteers choose a particular project by qualifying their participation online using a PROCESS FUNNEL (H1). Give them a SECURE CONNECTION (E6) to use a SIGN-IN/NEW ACCOUNT (H2) and access a PERSONALIZED CONTENT (D4) area of the site specifically for the project team.

In addition, publish progress reports through CONTENT MODULES (D2) and provide MESSAGE BOARDS (D5) so that otherwise disconnected volunteers and financial sponsors can talk with other volunteers and financial sponsors, as well as with staff members and beneficiaries. On the public site, excerpt and publish the results of each project using CONTENT MODULES (D2).

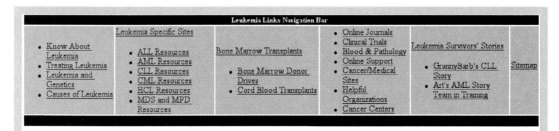

A6.1
(www.acor.org/leukemia, August 27, 2001)

Figure A6.1

The Leukemia Links grassroots information site is one of the best resources on the Web for information about leukemia, consistently ranking in the top five on Google in searches on *leukemia*. Although a modest site, Leukemia Links is valuable because it provides not only basic information about leukemia, but also a well-organized, comprehensive, prequalified list of links to the best leukemia sites on the Web.

✳ BACKGROUND

This pattern forms the core of all information reference sites. You can integrate other site genre patterns to build a resource site, including VALUABLE COMPANY SITES (A7), COMMUNITY CONFERENCE (A3), and EDUCATIONAL FORUMS (A8).

✳ PROBLEM

Sorting through hundreds of search results about a particular topic is time-consuming. Without a guide, visitors become discouraged and give up, or possibly act on partial information.

Customers often search for topical information on the Web, but any complete topic overview is usually buried so deeply that it takes a long time to uncover. Search engines do a good job of finding reams of results sorted by each site's **value ranking**.[1] But even highly ranked sites usually provide only one point of reference, or a piece of the overall picture. Directories like Yahoo! work well to an extent, but the number of librarians required to build comprehensive catalogues for all categories of information on the Web would bankrupt the directories. As a result of seeing only a partial picture, some people act on partial information.

Why a Grassroots Information Site? • People who build grassroots information sites have a deep interest in a particular topic (see Figure A6.2) and

Figure A6.2

Grassroots sites can be one person's attempt to right a wrong in his or her community. This site publicized the disrepair of a set of public staircases and energized the community to pressure the city to repair the damage.

The purpose of this website is to provide the local community with contact information and current status about the unacceptable state of the Merriewood Stairs.

The stairs are dangerous and unusable; barricaded, decaying and overgrown. There are no sidewalks to use as an option to dodging cars on the narrow and winding neighborhood streets.

🔦 **HOT NEWS:**

Demolition and construction have begun on the upper Merriewood stairs!

(updated 7/25/01)

● **Hot News** ● Archives ● City Contacts ● Reports ● Video ● Pictures ● Map ●
Media ● Mailing List ● Home ●

HOT NEWS ARCHIVES:

6/11/01: Initial engineering plans made available at Public Works Engineering Meeting
see report (by Kirk van Druten)

`A6.2` (www.landsharks.net/landsharks/stairs, August 26, 2001)

---

1 Google is such a search engine. Its value rankings are guided by the idea that the best Web sites have the most links pointed to them from other sites. In other words, if many other Web site publishers think a site is worth referencing, it must be a good site.

have scoured the Web to build a comprehensive picture of that topic. Initially they might want a Web site for purely personal reasons, but eventually, realizing the value that their site could provide to others in need, the authors post their pages and let others read the information, reference it, and act on it.

Readers appreciate site authors who answer tough questions, and they respect them for their expertise, commitment, and honesty. To build a grassroots site—one that builds traffic through word of mouth—you need to create value and establish trust and credibility. Building a grassroots site takes time and commitment because the site is continually updated to address new issues and provide better resources.

Answering Questions • When people go to an information site, they hope to have their questions answered quickly and easily. Answers can come in an extensive Web site of self-created or collected knowledge, as an extensive directory to the best resources on the Web, or a combination of the two (see Figure A6.3).

Credibility and Trust • When people trust a site, they trust that the information is accurate. When they trust a site on a particular topic, they believe it will answer most questions they pose. Provide both accurate and comprehensive information to establish trust and build credibility. Also date all of your Web pages, so that people will be able to assess how old the information is and whether it is still relevant to them.

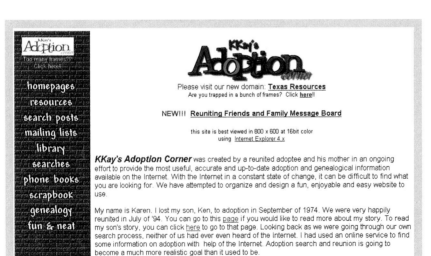

A6.3

(www.koyote.com/personal/hobb, August 26, 2001)

Figure A6.3

Grassroots sites often combine personal expertise on a topic with a good selection of external resources. This adoption site includes addresses of relevant organizations, a discussion board, and the personal history of the site creator.

Writing Style • The most basic rule of writing applies here: Know your audience. In this case there are two audiences to keep in mind. The first is search engines because presumably many people will find your Web site through one of these. (See WRITING FOR SEARCH ENGINES (D6) for more details.)

The other audience is your readers. If your site is fact based and aims to be an authoritative news site, use an INVERSE-PYRAMID WRITING STYLE (D7). Keep in mind, though, that this style of writing does not work well for all kinds of grassroots information sites, such as those with a sarcastic or storytelling bent.

External Resources • When building a grassroots information site, use basic organizational and navigational principles. Avoid long lists of EXTERNAL LINKS (K8) because visitors have no way of knowing which are interesting and which are not. Editorialize by adding a few comments about each link, describing what kind of content the site has and what you thought of the site. This information helps visitors find what interests them and lets them know more about your personality, outlook, and standards.

If there is an especially large number of links, organize them by grouping similar content together and then labeling the group with a high-level name. Try to make the list of external links fit on a single Web page that can be viewed without excessive scrolling. If the list becomes unwieldy, break it up into separate pages with 15 to 20 links per page, and provide a top-level directory of categories so that readers can find the particular information they're looking for quickly, or jump to one of the recommended sites. Keep the number of top-level links leading to categories or external sites to less than 20. Break all lists of 20 or greater into subcategories. See HIERARCHICAL ORGANIZATION (B3) for more information on creating categories.

We chose 15 to 20 as a list limit because long lists are difficult for people to read, and they make it hard to locate a particular item. The high-traffic directory sites we reviewed, such as Yahoo!, Lycos, and Excite, did not exceed this number at any level in their organization. These sites have put a lot of effort into researching how to present this type of information. Take advantage of their findings.

Growing the Site • Grassroots information sites often start out small, with just a few pages of highly focused, interesting content. Over time, they grow, with new pages and resources added every so often, but this goes only so far. To take the site to the next level, the site maintainer will need to add some way for visitors to participate, turning it into both an information site and a COMMUNITY CONFERENCE (A3) site. This step represents a fundamental shift in how the Web site operates. The site will change from a place where only a few site maintainers collect and disseminate information, to a self-sustaining and ongoing conversation where many people contribute, interact with one another, and create new content about the core topic that brings everyone to the site in the first place.

✳ SOLUTION

Establish value by answering potential questions, either by providing content you author yourself or by directing people to Web sites that can answer their questions. On your homepage, create a topic directory of up to 20 categories or external links. Provide contact information if customers have new questions or suggestions, or if they find new sources of information.

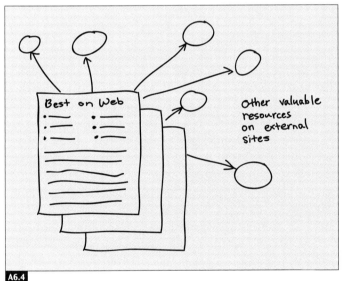

Figure A6.4

Grassroots information sites provide background or specialized information on a topic and organize other valuable resources by offering links to external sites.

A6.4

✳ CONSIDER THESE OTHER PATTERNS

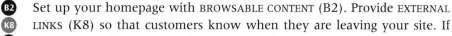

Set up your homepage with BROWSABLE CONTENT (B2). Provide EXTERNAL LINKS (K8) so that customers know when they are leaving your site. If you have many links, try using a HIERARCHICAL ORGANIZATION (B3) to break them into categories. Open the links in POP-UP WINDOWS (H6) if you need people to return to your site after they're done with the linked site.

Use the WRITING FOR SEARCH ENGINES (D6) pattern, and tell your story and research methodology using the INVERSE-PYRAMID WRITING STYLE (D7) if that matches the style of your site.

A7 VALUABLE COMPANY SITES

A7.1   (www.ibm.com, February 5, 2002)

Figure A7.1

IBM's homepage prominently displays links to its products and services, as well as links for specific customer groups (for example, home, small business, and government). Links for less important visitors, such as developers, partners, and investors, are displayed in a less prominent position and in a lighter font at the lower left side of the page.

✳ BACKGROUND

This pattern forms the core of all company sites. Combine it with one or more of the other site genre patterns, especially PERSONAL E-COMMERCE (A1), EDUCATIONAL FORUMS (A8), and WEB APPS THAT WORK (A10).

✳ PROBLEM

Company sites must address the needs of many audiences, but a site that does not balance these needs in proportion to the audience size will not succeed.

Company sites engage, sell to, and support customers and partners. They also promote to media, inform investors, and recruit employees. These audiences have varying needs. If you want your company site to be valuable to its primary visitors, focus on that primary audience and take care of its needs first. Other audiences can be served as well, but in a less directly accessible way.

The visible space on the homepage is a constraint of site design. Because this is the page customers usually visit first, it must direct them to the information they need (see Figure A7.2). To allocate this precious space, classify your site visitors to give the largest groups priority over all others.

Figure A7.2

This site has everything that customers might want to see about Hewlett-Packard. They can look up product information, purchase products, get the latest software drivers, or access support information.

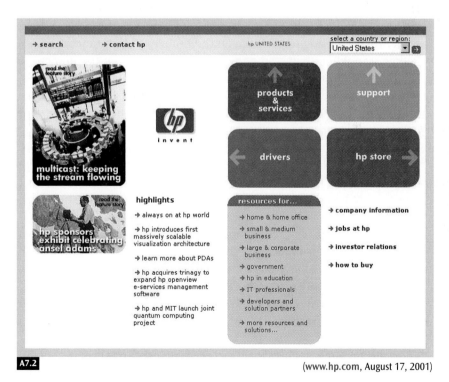

A7.2

(www.hp.com, August 17, 2001)

Potential customers, current customers, partners, press, investors, and potential employees need basic information about a company, from an overview of the company and its policies to details about its products and services. Although these groups ask and need different things, a valuable company site must provide answers to all. The solutions that we derive from these questions and tasks are listed in Table A7.1.

Balance Space for Brand against Space for Navigation • Balance the home-page trade-off between space used for communicating the company's value and differentiation, and space used for giving customers the navigation tools to find what they seek. We have made three observations that provide solutions:

1. Because the CLEAR FIRST READ (I3) on the homepage is often the company's brand in the top left corner (see Figure A7.1), and the second read is often the UP-FRONT VALUE PROPOSITION (C2), most of the company's value and differentiation should be clear from the outset. If they are not, the value proposition and SITE BRANDING (E1) are not executed well enough yet. Have your team focus on improving these two aspects rather than on using more space on the homepage for branding.
2. People scan when they read on the Web, and they scan the homepage for succinct phrases and for links that they recognize and deem potentially valuable (see Figure A7.3). Focus your design on finding the proper wording for these phrases, and on making them easy for your customers to scan.
3. Because every primary audience is really composed of many subgroups, each subgroup needs answers to its specific questions. For example, if the primary audience consists of investors, answer the questions of both institutional investors and direct investors. If the primary audience is a products and services buyer, answer the questions of the decision maker, recommender, and technical reviewer. You can often take these customers to a subsidiary page where you have them select their role to obtain more targeted information (see Figure A7.4). Use the techniques described in Chapter 3—Knowing Your Customers: Principles and Techniques to understand what these roles are for your customers and your site.

From this previous analysis we conclude that a **splash screen**—that is, an opening screen, often heavy with multimedia, that is shown before the homepage—cannot help build a valuable company site. There are

Table A7.1

Sample Questions,
Tasks, and Solutions
for Companies

C2 D8

E5

D3

E2

K8

F2
F3
F1

H7
D5

C2

E5

E5

E5

Group	Question or Task	What to Provide as a Solution
Everyone	What does this company offer?	An UP-FRONT VALUE PROPOSITION (C2), a set of PRINTABLE PAGES (D8) of product and service overviews and details, ABOUT US (E5) to describe company background
	What's new?	HEADLINES AND BLURBS (D3), latest product and service announcements, press releases, E-MAIL SUBSCRIPTIONS (E2) to a free company newsletter
	What products and services do you offer?	Listings and detailed descriptions of all products and services, both current and past, organized in multiple ways based on customer needs
Current and potential customers	Who uses the products and services?	Typical customer profiles and a list of existing customers
	How do people use the products and services?	Case studies and white papers, EXTERNAL LINKS (K8) to reviews, testimonials
	How do I buy the products and services?	Ordering information, CLEAN PRODUCT DETAILS (F2), SHOPPING CART (F3), QUICK-FLOW CHECKOUT (F1)
	What are the support options?	Customer service, training, product specifications, online manuals and support guides, FREQUENTLY ASKED QUESTIONS (H7), MESSAGE BOARDS (D5)
Current and potential partners	What would a partnership offer my company?	An UP-FRONT VALUE PROPOSITION (C2) for partners, partner benefits, and partnership details
	How do I become a partner?	Partnership application form
Press	Who do I contact for more information?	ABOUT US (E5), press contacts page
Current and potential investors	What is the background of this company, including past financial performance?	ABOUT US (E5), company background, management, current investors, current customers, ticker symbol, quarterly and annual reports
Potential employees	Do you have a job for me?	Open job listings and on-line job applications
	Why would I want to work for this company?	ABOUT US (E5), company background, leadership, corporate culture, and benefits

Figure A7.3

The Microsoft home-page provides quick links to all the major parts of its site but emphasizes the product and support areas. Links to information for partners and journalists are less prominent or below the fold.[2]

A7.3

(www.microsoft.com, May 16, 2002)

Figure A7.4

On the NetRaker site we created explicit links for each of our target customers, linking them to a page that discusses each of their specific needs and questions.

A7.4

(www.netraker.com, August 27, 2001)

2   The **fold** is an imaginary line on a Web page that delineates what is visible in a browser without making the visitor scroll down. See ABOVE THE FOLD (I2) for more information.

places for product and service overview animations and presentations, but they should be self-selected destinations by customers, not automatic commercials on the very first page of a site.

Organize for Customers' Convenience • A company's internal organization does not make a good Web site organization. This is a common mistake in the designs of company sites. What makes sense to people internal to a company may not make sense to its customers. Sun's Web site is organized with its customers' needs in mind (see Figure A7.5).

Figure A7.5

Sun Microsystems' homepage provides quick links to all the major parts of its site. The navigation on the left provides resources targeted to specific audiences, such as "Developers" and "Investors."

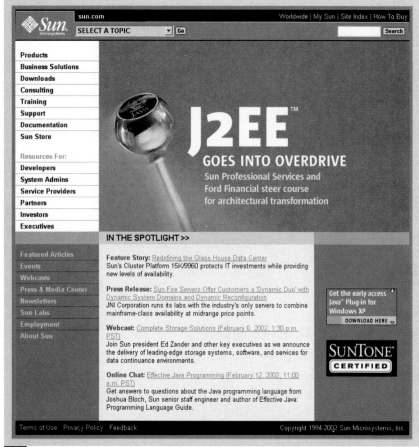

(www.sun.com, February 12, 2002)

✳ SOLUTION

On the company homepage, above the fold, dedicate 95 percent of the area and links to the visitor groups that account for 95 percent of the total visitor population, and keep the remaining area and links for the visitor groups that account for the remaining 5 percent. Use the footer of the homepage to provide explicit links for each group, including those in the 5 percent category. Balance space for your branding against the navigation needs of your target audience. Throughout the site, focus attention on the specific roles of your customers, and use value propositions they will understand. Include in-depth presentations and lists of information to keep visitors engaged if they want to know more.

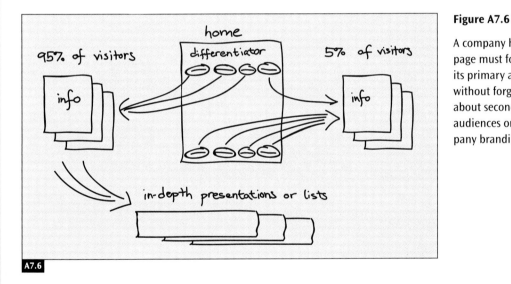

A7.6

Figure A7.6

A company homepage must focus on its primary audience, without forgetting about secondary audiences or company branding.

✳ CONSIDER THESE OTHER PATTERNS

For valuable company sites, using the 95 percent–5 percent solution, create a HOMEPAGE PORTAL (C1) that gives people an UP-FRONT VALUE PROPOSITION (C2) and MULTIPLE WAYS TO NAVIGATE (B1). Use FAMILIAR LANGUAGE (K11) targeted to the role and kind of visitor, including customer, partner, press, investor, or potential employee. Make use of online marketing by offering E-MAIL SUBSCRIPTIONS (E2) to a free company newsletter, to keep ongoing contact with previous site visitors. Post job openings to recruit potential employees.

Figure A8.1

Phillips Academy's Web site provides resources that bring together parents, teachers, and alumni mentors to support student education.

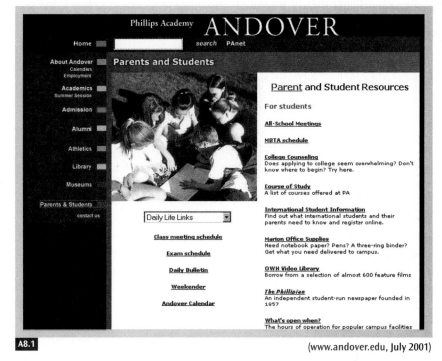

(www.andover.edu, July 2001)

✳ BACKGROUND

Educational sites promote learning by providing schools, universities, and online institutions with a way to publicize using NEWS MOSAICS (A2), to build COMMUNITY CONFERENCES (A3) for student development, to deliver online learning and research tools, and to offer courses online. This pattern describes the keys to making these types of sites succeed.

✳ PROBLEM

Bringing together students, parents, mentors, alumni, and educators is essential to educational sites. If no forum among these groups is created, the students' education suffers, and so does the institution.

The primary goal of any educational institution is student development. But students do not learn just from reading and solving problems. They require interaction with other students, teachers, parents, and mentors. The physical classroom provides student–teacher interaction, but depending on class size, geography, and transportation issues, this interaction can be limited. Furthermore, parents and teachers have limited opportunity to interact, usually only through in-person meetings or phone calls.

An educational site can bring together these groups, across geographic and economic boundaries, for the benefit of students. We have argued in NONPROFITS AS NETWORKS OF HELP (A5) that a network effect[3] cannot occur **A5** unless certain tools and capabilities are part of a site. The same is true for this pattern. An educational forum functions as a valuable resource and support system for students by providing a network for student development through student–teacher, student–student, parent–teacher, student–mentor, and parent–parent relationships.

When an educational site focuses on improving the efficiency of school administration, it leaves the effectiveness of the education behind. *Educational forums can be the conduits, the networks that bring together and help build school communities.* In a primary school, parents, teachers, and classmates need to communicate on an ongoing basis. In a university setting, professors, students, and teaching assistants need ongoing forums of discussion. By making the educational forum the central communication tool, all students benefit from sharing ideas, questions, and problems with classmates, parents, and teachers. The forums enhance intellectual and social life at school when students, faculty, and parents interact and share ideas and values, thereby enhancing students' complete education. An educational forum establishes tight connections that extend beyond the school grounds, where social pressures to conform sometimes outweigh students' genuine desire to learn.

---

3 Person-to-person connections increase as a result of a communication network. The value of a network grows in proportion to the square of the number of people connected.

Different Visitors Have Different Needs • Students, parents, and mentors need basic information about an educational institution—from an overview of the institution's policies, to details about its curriculum and schedules. The same might be true for potential students, potential and current teachers, potential and current employees, and researchers and students at other institutions. Finally, educational institutions need to maintain a lifelong relationship with their alumni. The needs of these groups vary, and an educational site must provide answers (see Figure A8.2). The solutions that we derive from these questions and tasks are listed in Table A8.1.

Figure A8.2

The designers of Carnegie Mellon University's site did a good job of identifying its customers, including prospective students, researchers, alumni, and current students. The designers created clear links to information targeted for these different groups.

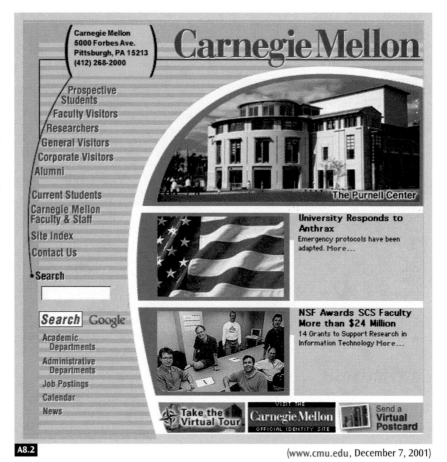

A8.2

(www.cmu.edu, December 7, 2001)

Table A8.1
Sample Questions, Tasks, and Solutions for Educational Forums

Group	Question or Task	What to Provide as a Solution	
Students and prospective students	When are classes?	A searchable, printable table of class schedules with links to teachers, syllabi, and course materials	
	Who are the teachers and how do I contact them?	Teacher profiles, ratings, and links to classes	
	What am I going to learn in class?	Class profiles and syllabi	
	What are the school's policies?	A series of documents showing the school's policies	
Parents and mentors	How do I contact someone in charge, such as the principal, president, or dean?	A page with administration contact information	
	How do I contact a teacher?	A page with teacher contact information	
Teachers	How do I contact a parent?	Secure page of student and parent information	
Potential teachers and employees	Why do I want to work for this school?	School overview, leadership, employment benefits	
Alumni	What is new at the school?	HEADLINES AND BLURBS (D3) to press releases detailing new programs, new buildings, important research, and other activities of interest	**D3**
	How do I make a donation?	SECURE CONNECTIONS (E6) to pages where gifts can be given to the institution or where alumni can leave contact information for follow-up	**E6**
Researchers	What research is a particular professor or department working on?	Easy access to faculty and department directories that link directly to their own Web sites	
Everyone	What does the community think about the new science program?	MESSAGE BOARDS (D5) with current topics open for discussion	**D5**

Taken to an advanced level, an educational forum provides course material online, including teacher- and student-developed training materials, quizzes, exercises, complete courses, and archived or live video (see Figure A8.3).

Figure A8.3

The Math Forum is a valuable resource for both students and educators. The Teacher2Teacher community allows parents and teachers to ask questions, discuss problems, and find ideas for new problems and exercises. At the Student Center, students can ask Dr. Math questions about solving math problems, and they can find fun challenges in mathematics.

| STUDENT CENTER | TEACHERS' PLACE | RESEARCH DIVISION | PARENTS & CITIZENS |

What's New

Regular Tessellations
Future of the Problems of the Week
Nonstandard Analysis & the Hyperreals

Forum Features

Ask Dr. Math
Discussion Groups
Search for Math Forum Showcase
or browse our Internet Newsletter
Internet Problems of the Week
Mathematics Teacher2Teacher
Library Web Units & Lessons

Math Resources by Subject Math Education Key Issues in Math

K-12, College, & Advanced Math Innovations and Concerns

SUGGESTION BOX | MATH LIBRARY | HELP | QUICK REFERENCE | SEARCH OUR SITE

A8.3 (forum.swarthmore.edu, now mathforum.org, August 27, 2001)

Raising the Bar • The education reformer John Holt was once quoted as saying, "I suspect that many children would learn arithmetic—and learn it better—if it were illegal." This sentiment captures many of the problems with education as it exists today. Advanced educational forums need to draw students in, challenging them with real-world problems that everyday people face, not artificial ones commonly found in classroom textbooks. They need to stimulate students' natural interests and foster a social norm of educational excellence and lifelong learning. Internet access alone is not enough. There needs to be an ongoing and thriving community—both online and offline—of enthusiastic experts, local technicians, designers, alumni, parents, teachers, and students to make it happen.

Many attempts at introducing educational technologies into the curricula have failed. There are numerous issues involved with costs of procuring the hardware and developing the software, with making these tools fit into existing work practices, and with training teachers to use these tools effectively. In fact, it is not uncommon to have students who are more comfortable and experienced with using computers than the teachers are.

Basic educational forums need to support all of the routine and ordinary tasks that students, teachers, alumni, and parents face. Advanced educational forums need to look even further, seeking new ways of creating a sustainable and inclusive community of learning and scholarship.

❄ SOLUTION

Provide news and information for students, potential students, parents, mentors, and teachers that help coordinate offline activities such as class schedules, reading lists, exam schedules, and contact and office hour information for teachers and administrators. As a part of student registration, gather parent and student e-mail and phone information for direct updates. Optionally publish curriculum and research for other schools and universities.

To create a forum for online student–parent–teacher–mentor support of student development, create a secure area on the site that provides the following:

- Direct communication between parents and teachers, students and teachers, and students and mentors
- Public communication between students in the same class and the teacher
- Parent–teacher conferences
- Online writing, exhibits, experiments, exercises, projects, and other activities
- Online course material
- Online examinations

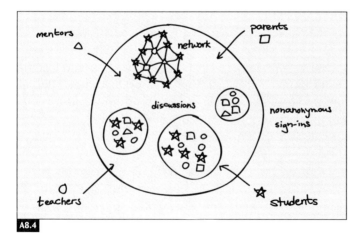

A8.4

Figure A8.4

An educational forum is a secure area where students, parents, teachers, and mentors can share concerns, ideas, and codevelop and share activities.

❋ CONSIDER THESE OTHER PATTERNS

Basic Educational Forums

To address the needs of the different audiences using the site, use a **C1** **B1** HOMEPAGE PORTAL (C1) with MULTIPLE WAYS TO NAVIGATE (B1) to the class information, teacher backgrounds and contact information, department information, and school background. Provide news on the homepage and **D2** category pages with CONTENT MODULES (D2).

If you create an online student application and registration system, use **H1** the PROCESS FUNNEL (H1) to facilitate a smooth process.

Update entire classes, the entire school, and alumni with E-MAIL SUB-**E2** SCRIPTIONS (E2) to school announcements. As an option, publish class **D2** curricula and research on the site using CONTENT MODULES (D2).

Advanced Educational Forums

To create a forum for online student–parent–teacher–mentor support of **E6** student development, create a secure area using SECURE CONNECTIONS (E6) and have people create nonanonymous accounts using SIGN-IN/NEW **H2** ACCOUNT (H2).

D4 Once a person has signed in, show PERSONALIZED CONTENT (D4) on the homepage for each visitor, with class news and links. Within the class information for students, provide a directory of teacher contact information, and e-mail addresses for student–student, and student–mentor communication. Within the class information for parents and mentors, provide only the teacher and single student contact information.

D5 For each class, create a MESSAGE BOARD (D5) for student–teacher–mentor–parent discussions, as well as a separate message board for teacher–parent discussions.

Provide students with Web publishing tools and a directory to upload class projects.

Publish course materials online and keep the material engaging by **A9** using the STIMULATING ARTS AND ENTERTAINMENT (A9) pattern.

To conduct online examinations, bring students into a PROCESS FUNNEL **H1** (H1) to complete questions dynamically generated in CONTENT MODULES **D2** (D2). Alternatively, link to an existing courseware system, such as WebCT or Blackboard, for online exams, grading, and course management.

A9 STIMULATING ARTS AND ENTERTAINMENT

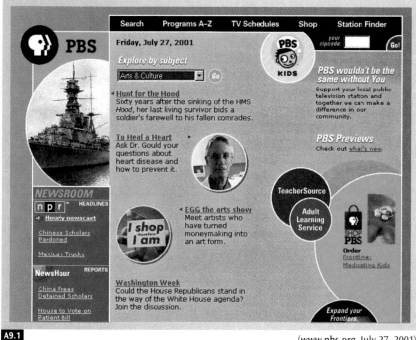

A9.1

(www.pbs.org, July 27, 2001)

Figure A9.1

PBS.org provides a straightforward interface to audio clips, video clips, and games on the site, as well as guides to the many offline programs that PBS produces. If visitors play the games on the site, though, they find that new interface metaphors abound. (The screen shot taken from **www.pbs.org** is used herein with permission from The Public Broadcasting Service.)

✳ BACKGROUND

This pattern forms the core of any site specializing in engaging content. Combine this pattern with other site genre patterns—including PERSONAL E-COMMERCE (A1), VALUABLE COMPANY SITES (A7), and EDUCATIONAL FORUMS (A8)—to make a hybrid.

A1 A7
A8

✳ PROBLEM

Arts and entertainment sites evoke new feelings and thoughts by challenging customers or by offering them an escape. But challenging visitors with a hard-to-use interface too early in their exposure to your site will turn them away.

People do not enjoy being forced to sit through something they're not prepared for. Sites that display animated movies on the first page can be frustrating for this reason; nothing can warn customers before they arrive at a site. Similarly, sites that require complex navigation schemes from the very first page, as part of the "artistic experience," tend to lose visitors who cannot appreciate why the experience is important. Customers like to be challenged with thoughtful, well-executed art and entertainment, but they want to choose for themselves (see Figures A9.2 and A9.3). If they are not given the choice of where to go on a straightforward intro-ductory homepage, and they are immediately dropped into an animation or strange interface, they will most likely choose to leave.

Figure A9.2

Fans of professional basketball can go to nba.com to find out about players, teams, and game schedules, and even to enjoy some of the on-court action through links to audio and video clips. (Reprinted with the permission of NBA Entertainment.)

A9.2

(www.nba.com, August 27, 2001)

A9.3

(www.ifilm.com, February 2, 2002)

Figure A9.3

IFILM is an Internet movie site that contains independent short movies, movie trailers, and quirky but often hilarious "viral" videos that friends email to their friends.

People enjoy arts and entertainment because they are moved and challenged by the experience. Whether it is a movie that evokes strong emotions of fear, sadness, excitement, or romance, or an exhibit of paintings that stimulates thoughts of an era gone by, these are powerful cultural experiences. Online art and entertainment sites are no different.

Online Exhibits Come in Many Forms • When art or entertainment is exhibited online, it can range from pictures of a gallery installation to an online-only animation (see Figure A9.4). The Web provides a low-cost, widely accessible medium for delivery of these different "exhibits."

Set Expectations Before Breaking the Rules • Site designers who break design rules with a purpose, in places where people know to expect it, can use the medium to provoke and challenge in positive ways. Many of the design patterns in this book may no longer make sense in an experimental interface. Perhaps links should not be obvious, and things should not have descriptive names. This kind of interface has its place on art and entertainment sites.

Figure A9.4

Apartment is an interactive exhibit that starts by asking the visitor to select a city. As the visitor types, rooms start to take shape in the form of a blueprint. The layout is based on a semantic analysis of the visitor's words. The apartments are then clustered into buildings and cities according to their linguistic relationships. The site sets clear visitor expectations for large page loads or for the need to download an additional plug-in.

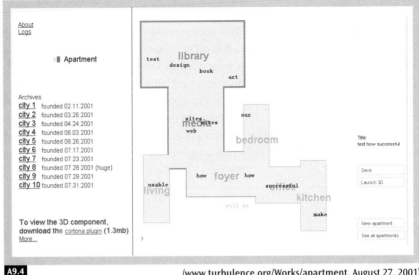

A9.4

(www.turbulence.org/Works/apartment, August 27, 2001)

Setting customer expectations about what they will experience is key. Table A9.1 shows some examples of how you can include a few words in exhibit descriptions to set expectations before launching an exhibit.

Often online content will augment offline content. In addition to using your introductory pages to set people's expectations, you can use it to provide information about accessing offline exhibits, such as exhibit hours, addresses, and driving directions.

Table A9.1
Sample Exhibit
Descriptions for
Setting Customer
Expectations

Exhibit	Included in the Description
Guided tour	Five screens (3 minutes on 56K modem)
Movie	24 minutes on 56K modem
Music	John Cage's 4.33 seconds (6 minutes to download on 56K modem)
Gallery exhibit	17 images (20 seconds to download each on 56K modem)
Interactive exhibit	Experimental interface

✳ SOLUTION

On the first page or pages of the Web site, provide a straightforward interface that describes the exhibits on your site and provides links directly to them. Link from the introduction pages to background information pages that expand on the exhibits. In a separate area provide the actual exhibits and entertainment in whatever formats are required. Once a customer has chosen an art exhibit to view or a movie to play, the interface should conform to whatever is required by the artist or work of art. This is where it is permissible to break the usual rules in order to challenge or entertain your customers.

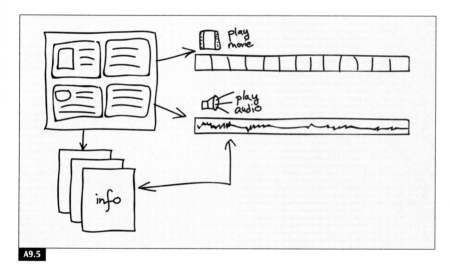

A9.5

Figure A9.5

Easy-to-use homepage and background pages provide familiar navigation cues so that people don't get lost. The actual art exhibits, movies, audio clips, games, or other entertainment are in well-defined areas.

✳ CONSIDER THESE OTHER PATTERNS

Use your HOMEPAGE PORTAL (C1) to provide basic navigation elements that will be familiar to customers immediately, by giving them MULTIPLE WAYS TO NAVIGATE (B1). Within the homepage and the additional background pages, use CONTENT MODULES (D2) to highlight recent additions, and to provide links to archived content through CONSISTENT SIDEBARS OF RELATED CONTENT (I6).

Figure A10.1

Salesforce.com is a sales force automation Web application that lets salespeople see tracking, forecasting, and editing capabilities after they create a customer account.

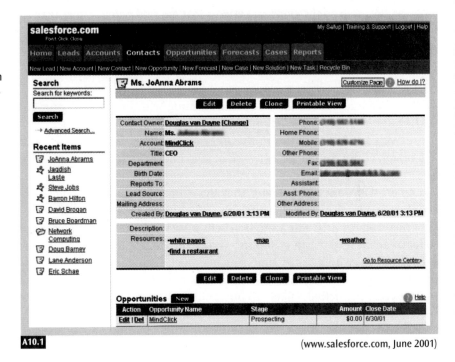

A10.1

(www.salesforce.com, June 2001)

✳ BACKGROUND

Like other site genre patterns, this pattern is flexible enough to add to almost any other, including VALUABLE COMPANY SITES (A7), EDUCATIONAL FORUMS (A8), COMMUNITY CONFERENCES (A3), and STIMULATING ARTS AND ENTERTAINMENT (A9). It can also provide a business focus on its own. This pattern shows you what is at the core of a Web application.

✳ PROBLEM

Web applications are not like software applications that come in a shrink-wrapped box. Web applications are services that are sold online rather than in a store, have simple interfaces compared to desktop applications, and often do not have documentation in printed form. Similarly, customers use Web applications differently from traditional Web sites: They use them for real work, often for hours every day.

Web applications get customers up and running without time-consuming and costly software installation, configuration, and maintenance. Because Web applications run on the Internet, they can immediately take advantage of the connected network of customers.

Customers Will Want to Try Before They Buy • Providing a Web application requires a special approach—one that is centered at the company site. When customers arrive at a site that sells a Web application, they expect to learn about it, see it in action, try it out, buy access to it if they like it, use it from anywhere at any time, and get quick online support and training. If the application cannot meet even one of these expectations, customers will be much less likely to buy and use it.

Help your customers by providing lots of information about your service. Make the UP-FRONT VALUE PROPOSITION (C2) clear on the HOMEPAGE PORTAL (C1), letting customers know what your service does and how it can help them get their work done faster or better. Take customers through a sample task by showing them static or animated screen shots of someone using the Web site. If it is feasible to do so, let customers go through the SIGN-IN/NEW ACCOUNT (H2) process and create a temporary account so that they can try your service and see if they like it. Finally, help convince customers that you offer a high-quality service by providing testimonials from real customers and EXTERNAL LINKS (K8) to positive reviews.

There also needs to be an extremely strong focus on usability. People buy shrink-wrapped software first, often before trying it out. Because they have already made a large financial commitment, they have more of a motivation to spend the time to learn how to use it. With Web applications, however, it is just the opposite. People try the Web application first, and if they don't like it they just hit the **Back** button and go somewhere else. Draw people in by establishing MULTIPLE WAYS TO NAVIGATE (B1) to the various applications and options. For critical tasks, take cus- tomers through a PROCESS FUNNEL (H1), and provide a FREQUENTLY ASKED

H7 **H8** QUESTIONS (H7) page and CONTEXT-SENSITIVE HELP (H8) to assist customers whenever they encounter problems.

Web Apps Rely on Web Principles • If you work for a traditional software company that wants to sell a Web application, be aware that installable software does not quickly convert into a Web application. Nor can it always be converted into a successful Web application. Your company must adopt Web principles for design, development, testing, security, IT, marketing, sales, billing, documentation, support, and training.

From an application design perspective, a Web application requires a relatively simple interface. Standard HTML provides the best cross-platform, cross-browser compatibility (see Figure A10.2). But if you use standard HTML, each page may be limited to only a few atomic actions, and you cannot offer direct manipulation of objects in a page, except for buttons and input fields (see Figure A10.3). If you use Dynamic HTML,

Figure A10.2

The First Internet Bank site lets customers easily transfer funds between accounts, view canceled checks, and manage bill payments. The site follows Web principles: home banking customers often arrive over slow network connections, so the site is light on graphics and performs just fine with a 56K modem.

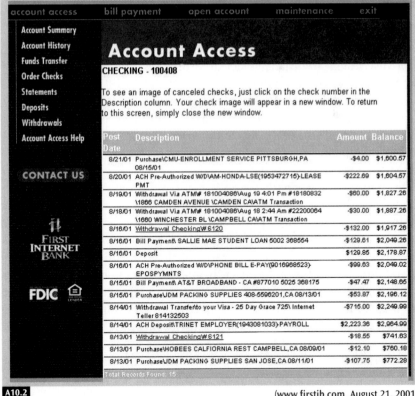

A10.2

(www.firstib.com, August 21, 2001)

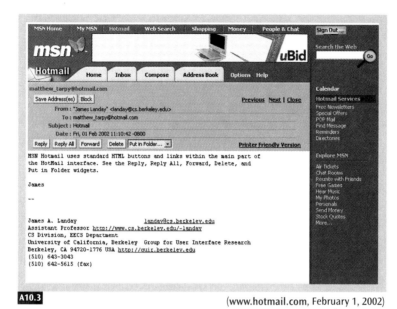

Figure A10.3

Microsoft's Hotmail offers much of the same functionality as a basic, desktop-based e-mail client, such as an address book, folders, and filtering. The site has a clean design, and although it has many tabs and buttons, it has a decidedly Web-based look and feel, evident in the Previous and Next buttons.

(www.hotmail.com, February 1, 2002)

you can add direct manipulation and create applications that look and feel very similar to installable desktop software. But only when a single standard implementation of Dynamic HTML exists will the extra work to make pages work across browsers be eliminated.

Dynamic HTML aside, Web applications typically do not support fine manipulation of images, heavy file processing, or any other customer-side computation-intensive or disk-based activity.

Offer Informative Feedback • Another difference between Web applications and installable desktop software is the inherent **latency** limitations of the Web, even within intranets. Your Web application will not be able to respond to customer actions immediately. Your customers will become impatient and will often commit errors, such as executing the same command multiple times or inadvertently interrupting a command. Although you might want to give your customers more room for their work in your Web application, eliminating the standard browser buttons and controls could cause a problem. This design will eliminate the browser feedback showing that a command is in progress, such as Internet Explorer's spinning globe. However, many designers have found that this feedback is insufficient for Web applications anyway. Following our design principle from Chapter 4—Involving Customers with Iterative Design, offer informative feedback: Include in your PROCESS FUNNEL (H1) a progress bar for any communication or processing that will take longer than ten seconds. Also design your pages so that they will be fast to download, as described in Pattern Group L—Speeding Up Your Site.

Offer Abundant Help • Web applications are often tools that your customers will use every day for several hours. They do not have the same walk-up-and-use requirements that a general consumer-oriented Web site has. Sometimes you have to trade efficiency for learning time. CONTEXT-SENSITIVE HELP (H8) becomes important because at least some tasks in every Web application won't be immediately obvious to your customers. Making this help available via POP-UP WINDOWS (H6) ensures that the customer doesn't lose important work.

If you are designing your Web application for an intranet, you can minimize employees' learning time by making the application consistent with other Web applications already deployed on the intranet. As a result, employees will get up to speed on a new application much more quickly.

Make Security and Privacy Tight • Because Web applications host confidential information for multiple customers, you need to reassure customers of the security and privacy of their data. Use SECURE CONNECTIONS (E6), and inform them of the security precautions and FAIR INFORMATION PRACTICES (E3) you have employed. A reviewer considering the purchase of a Web application will use this information to help make an informed decision.

Support Different Roles • Many Web applications support different customer roles, including application administrator, primary operator of the application, and management. These customers have different views of the applications and varying access to their capabilities. Your Web application must provide the ability to set up and manage these roles, as part of regular application maintenance.

✳ SOLUTION

Provide a public site where potential customers can preview the application, see how it will work, and sign up to try it. Once they have signed up, give them access to their application home through a secure sign-in, and provide a menu of options for their roles. Use standard Web interface widgets for complete cross-platform, cross-browser compatibility. Give effective feedback about communication and processing delays. Provide online documentation, training, and support.

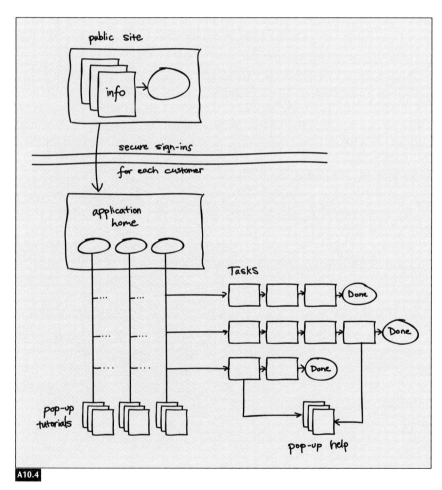

Figure A10.4

A Web application can be sold over the Web through detailed information pages and demonstrations. Once customers have signed up and received secure access to their application home, they see a menu of tasks and associated online help.

❊ CONSIDER THESE OTHER PATTERNS

(B1) On your public homepage, provide MULTIPLE WAYS TO NAVIGATE (B1) to information and demonstrations of the various Web applications you sell. If visitors decide to buy, you can ask them to pay online with QUICK-FLOW **(F1)** **(E6)** CHECKOUT (F1). Create a SECURE CONNECTION (E6) and ask customers to **(H2)** use SIGN-IN/NEW ACCOUNT (H2). Build an application home with PERSON-**(D4)** ALIZED CONTENT (D4) for each customer's role. Again, establish MULTIPLE **(B1)** WAYS TO NAVIGATE (B1) to the various applications and options, where **(H1)** each discrete task a customer may perform is a PROCESS FUNNEL (H1) and **(H8)** has CONTEXT-SENSITIVE HELP (H8).

(H1) Provide informative feedback in your PROCESS FUNNEL (H1) by showing a progress bar for any delays longer than ten seconds.

(A11) If you are designing a Web application for ENABLING INTRANETS (A11), make sure that it is as consistent as possible with other applications already deployed on the intranet.

A11 ENABLING INTRANETS

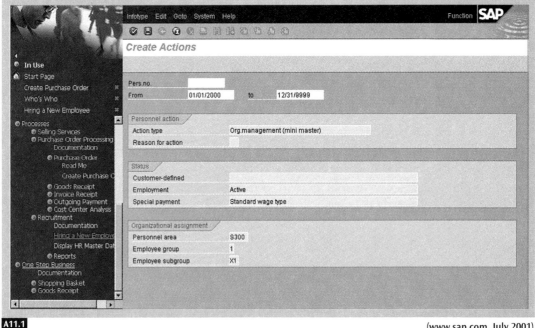

A11.1   (www.sap.com, July 2001)

Figure A11.1

This "intranet in a box" from SAP provides many of the basic applications that a business needs for sales, human resources management, and finance. Customers can find these applications immediately on the left-hand navigation bar.

✳ BACKGROUND

Unlike the other site genre patterns that cater to external customers, intranets support the internal work of an organization. You may employ entire site genre patterns, like NEWS MOSAICS (A2) and WEB APPS THAT WORK (A10), within the intranet, however. This pattern forms the core of what makes an intranet work.

✳ PROBLEM

Companies need employees to be more productive, but each employee has responsibilities that change over time. Employees should not have to constantly learn entirely new computing systems to carry out their new responsibilities.

Developing a corporate intranet has many benefits, from improving internal communications to streamlining processes and reducing costs. To realize the benefits, you will need to build a site or use intranet software that provides the kinds of information and applications that will make employees more productive and satisfied with their jobs. In addition, you will need to update, maintain, and administer your intranet content and applications.

Provide Personalized Views • Employees will not use all the company information or applications. More likely, some information and applications—such as salary information or financial management applications—will be off-limits to some employees but available to others. So an intranet needs to provide capabilities that depend on each employee's roles and responsibilities. These will change over time if an employee is promoted, quits, or changes jobs.

An intranet can provide many pieces of information that employees need. The solutions that we derive from some sample questions and tasks are listed in Table A11.1.

Support Workflows • Because an intranet connects all employees, intranet Web applications can help manage the flow of work through an organization. As Table A11.1 illustrates, employees who fill out an expense report in the expense report Web application will be automatically submitting it to their managers online, thereby reducing the time spent on this regular administrative task. These kinds of automatic workflow management features can be built into any Web application that facilitates work among employees, and even with partners and customers.

You may already have legacy applications to facilitate workflow. The problem is that these applications may not be accessible from the Web. If you think it's worth the time, money, and effort, seriously consider creating bridges between these legacy applications and your intranet, to make it easier for employees to access these applications.

Table A11.1
Sample Questions, Tasks, and Solutions for Intranets

Group	Question or Task	What to Provide as a Solution	
All employees	Who is my HR contact?	Custom resources profile per employee	
	What is Mary's phone number?	Database of employees	
	When are the company holidays?	Holiday information page	
	How do I submit an expense report?	Expense report Web application	
	What is the latest company news?	Updated news page with HEADLINES AND BLURBS (D3) and EXTERNAL LINKS (K8)	
Team manager	How do I write a review?	Employee review Web application, tips, and pointers on what to write about	
	How do I hire someone?	Job requisition Web application	
	What are my employees' expenses this month?	Team manager side of expense report Web application to approve or reject each report	
	How do I become a partner?	Partnership application form	
Financial manager	What are the accounts receivable amounts?	Report over a SECURE CONNECTION (E6) from accounting data	
	What is the sales forecast for this quarter?	Report over a SECURE CONNECTION (E6) from sales data	
	What are the current month's expense reports?	Financial manager side of expense report Web application to review approved reports	
Salesperson	Is this product available right now?	Report over a SECURE CONNECTION (E6) from inventory database	
	Can we customize this product for our customer right now?	Web application for product customization	
	What is the status of this purchase?	Secure report about product fulfillment	
Sales manager	How much business does each sales representative forecast for this month?	Secure forecast report roll-up from sales database	
CEO	What are our production capacity, inventory, and sell-through numbers?	Secure reports pulled from production, warehousing, and sales channel data	

Be Consistent Throughout • This key design principle, discussed in Chapter 4—Involving Customers with Iterative Design, becomes all the more important for intranets. Create a consistent interface in the terminology you use and in the interfaces you design for each Web application. Consistency is the best way to keep employee skills and knowledge up-to-date as employees' roles change in your organization. It will also save your company money because employees will be able to come up to speed quickly on new applications.

Establish Policies on New Content • Who will maintain the intranet? Will any employee be allowed to add a new page, or will there be a dedicated team? Do project teams own a Web space where they can publish proposals, designs, and status reports? How will new pages be added? Are there any checks on the content that is published internally, to make sure that no confidential information is being published? Are there any guidelines on the design of new pages, to make sure that the interfaces are consistent? These are just some of the questions about content that need to be worked out, ideally before the intranet is deployed.

Provide Simple Ways to Add New Content • One way of simplifying the addition of new pages is to use PAGE TEMPLATES (D1) that contain one or more CONTENT MODULES (D2). The content modules can be connected to a database, making it easy to add new pages, serve up new content in existing pages, and search for old information. Also consider creating a special administrator page that makes it easy to add new content, as described in CONTENT MODULES (D2).

Start Simple but Plan for Growth • You don't want to build an entire intranet all at once. It's best to start simple and take many small steps forward. For example, you could begin by focusing on making forms, documents, and news about the company accessible to employees. At the same time, you could devote effort to making sure that security is being maintained properly. After this you could start looking at administrator pages that make it easy to add new content and Web applications for handling workflows (eliminating the need for many of the forms).

❋ SOLUTION

Provide a secure area customized for each employee, where the employee can go to see a list of applications and information. List employees' current pending requests of others and any pending requests made of them. Automatically trigger new requests via an application workflow. Support employee learning by using consistent terminology across the intranet, and by designing consistent interfaces for your Web applications.

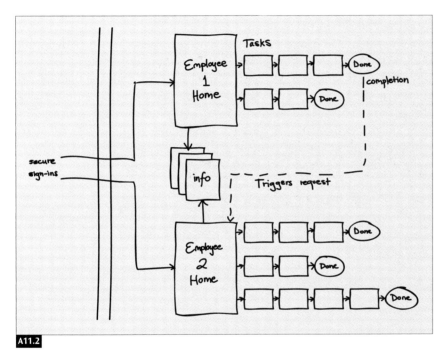

A11.2

Figure A11.2

If provided with customized lists of applications and information, employees need not wade through unnecessary items they will never use. Applications that trigger requests forward a request automatically to the next person in the workflow.

❋ CONSIDER THESE OTHER PATTERNS

All employees must use a SECURE CONNECTION (E6) and go through a secure SIGN-IN/NEW ACCOUNT (H2) to access the intranet from outside the firewall.

Once on their HOMEPAGE PORTAL (C1), employees will see PERSONALIZED CONTENT (D4) and company news. Requests that are pending and requests that require action from the various Web applications are displayed in CONTENT MODULES (D2). Employees can find information about human resource issues, company product and service issues, and project status through MULTIPLE WAYS TO NAVIGATE (B1). Each employee's WEB APPS THAT WORK (A10) are accessible as well.

E6
H2

C1
D4

D2

B1
A10

Creating a Navigation Framework  **B**

One of the challenges in designing for the Web is that customers often come to a site in many different ways. They may not enter at your homepage, and their goals and tasks often vary widely. One of the keys to a satisfying customer experience is your site's ability to support these differences. This pattern group will help you maximize your site's flexibility to accommodate customers' different navigation, browsing, and search habits.

B1 MULTIPLE WAYS TO NAVIGATE

B2 BROWSABLE CONTENT

B3 HIERARCHICAL ORGANIZATION

B4 TASK-BASED ORGANIZATION

B5 ALPHABETICAL ORGANIZATION

B6 CHRONOLOGICAL ORGANIZATION

B7 POPULARITY-BASED ORGANIZATION

B8 CATEGORY PAGES

B9 SITE ACCESSIBILITY

B1.1

(www.amazon.com, August 23, 2001)

Figure B1.1

Amazon.com understands that both intention and impulse are navigation motivators. Customers can look for what they *intend* to buy, using browsing and searching tools. The site also provides links to *impulse* items that customers might not have intended to buy but act on anyway.

✳ BACKGROUND

Used by all the patterns in Pattern Group A—Site Genres, from PERSONAL E-COMMERCE (A1) to ENABLING INTRANETS (A11), this pattern provides schemes that support how customers navigate sites.

✳ PROBLEM

Customers navigate Web sites in many ways. If any of the key navigation tools are hard to find or missing, visitors will find the site tedious to use.

Customers navigate through a site to gather information and to accomplish goals. They may look for information, activities, or products in any number of ways. One customer may have something specific in mind and use the search tool to find it. Another customer may also have something in mind but may prefer to browse the site by following hyperlinks. A third customer may only vaguely know what she or he wants and may wish to look around and see what catches the eye. Because customers want to move through your Web site in different ways of their choosing, the site needs to offer them multiple ways to navigate.

Intention and Impulse Drive Customers to Act • Before you design a navigation framework, it helps to understand what drives customers to take action online. Customers come to a site with a goal: to accomplish a specific task—for example, "to find George's phone number"; to do something more general, such as "to buy the best ski jacket"; or just to look around, perhaps because someone else recommended the site. Once on a site, however, customers also navigate on the basis of things that grab their attention, whether it is a targeted promotion or they simply see a related item of interest.

From these observations we have identified two things that drive customers to action: intention and impulse (these can also be thought of as goal and trigger, or need and desire). Neither intentional or impulsive behavior is inherently good or bad, but a site that omits intention-based navigation might feel shallow and quirky, while one that omits impulse-based navigation might feel boring. You can take advantage of both intention- and impulse-based behavior to help your customers have a satisfying experience. Figure B1.2 diagrams the feedback loop among customer attitudes, intentions, impulses, and behavior.

Different Motivations Lead to Different Styles of Navigation • Familiar navigation helps customers the most, regardless of whether they have a clear idea of how to move forward. Navigation options include the familiar *search* and *browse* styles (see Figure B1.3), as well as the *next-step,* or *wizard,* style. The *relate* and *promote* navigation styles work best with impulsive behavior. Table B1.1 shows how motivations and navigation styles are supported through specific navigation tools.

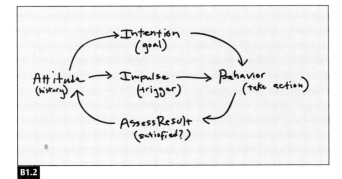

Figure B1.2

Two kinds of motivation drive customers to act: intention and impulse. Your customers' histories and attitudes form their goals and triggers, from which they take action and assess their satisfaction. This experience feeds back into their histories to start the loop all over again.

B1.2

Figure B1.3

The navigation options at the top of this page provide customers' account information in "My Account," as well as multiple ways to search. The navigation options on the left let customers choose from and browse through multiple shopping categories. The main content area showcases the hottest sellers, providing images and links for more details, as well as links to buy the items right on the spot.

B1.3

(www.overstock.com, August 26, 2001)

Put Tools Where Customers Will Find and Use Them • Not only does it make sense for each navigation tool to appear in a specific place so that customers can find it, but on the basis of past experience on the Web, customers have come to expect these tools to be in certain places. Consistent placement of navigation tools is one of the most important ways of making navigation easy.

Table B1.1

Motivators, Styles, and the Tools that Support Them

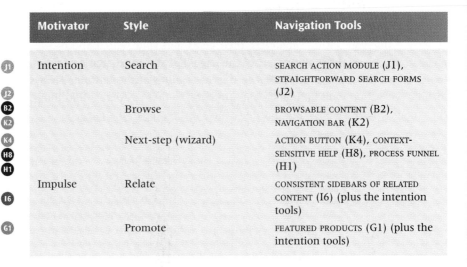

Motivator	Style	Navigation Tools
Intention	Search	SEARCH ACTION MODULE (J1), STRAIGHTFORWARD SEARCH FORMS (J2)
	Browse	BROWSABLE CONTENT (B2), NAVIGATION BAR (K2)
	Next-step (wizard)	ACTION BUTTON (K4), CONTEXT-SENSITIVE HELP (H8), PROCESS FUNNEL (H1)
Impulse	Relate	CONSISTENT SIDEBARS OF RELATED CONTENT (I6) (plus the intention tools)
	Promote	FEATURED PRODUCTS (G1) (plus the intention tools)

Once they have opened the page, customers must find the links that will enable them to complete their goals and intentions. Put the tools that start visitors on the path toward their goals near the point at which they will begin reading. This location ensures that the tools will be found and used. The tools that help customers continue or complete their goals also need to be near the top of the page, so that customers can see them without scrolling. They work best if you place them on the opposite side of the page (top right) from where customers start reading. Customers tend to scan from start to finish, so they also expect the continuation links to lie toward the finish (bottom).

Because you cannot guarantee that your customers will have an impulsive reaction, the impulse navigation tool's screen space is less valuable. You can push it down or to the side of the page opposite where customers start reading (right).

✴ SOLUTION

To ensure that your visitors complete their goals, put your search and browse navigation tools at the top and start of the page. Put your next-step navigation tools toward the top, but opposite the start, as well as at the bottom. Always include navigation tools that relate and promote, so that customers find things they might otherwise miss, but put these tools farther down the page.

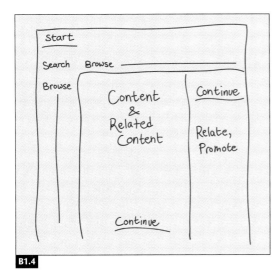

Figure B1.4

By giving your visitors multiple ways to navigate on your site, depending on their goals and desires, you can keep them engaged.

B1.4

✴ CONSIDER THESE OTHER PATTERNS

Give customers multiple ways to navigate by consistently using intention-based navigation: Place a SEARCH ACTION MODULE (J1) or a link to your STRAIGHTFORWARD SEARCH FORMS (J2) at the top of every page, provide a consistent NAVIGATION BAR (K2) on every page, and provide BROWSABLE CONTENT (B2). Make it easier for everyone to navigate your site with SITE ACCESSIBILITY (B9).

Help customers complete their tasks by using ACTION BUTTONS (K4) and links to CONTEXT-SENSITIVE HELP (H8) located at the top right of the page. Use a PROCESS FUNNEL (H1) for tasks where completion is absolutely necessary.

Provide impulse-driven navigation capability by using CONSISTENT SIDE-BARS OF RELATED CONTENT (I6) and promotions that use DESCRIPTIVE, LONGER LINK NAMES (K9).

Figure B2.1

Wal-Mart's site pro-
vides customers with
easy navigation and
clear signals for find-
ing their way back.
They can click on the
Wal-Mart logo to
return to the home-
page, on the tab row
at the top or the nav-
igation bar on the
left to go to another
section, or on the
location bread
crumbs near the top
to backtrack.
(Image courtesy of
Wal-Mart.com, Inc.
Copyright 2000–2002
Wal-Mart.com, Inc.
and Wal-Mart Stores,
Inc.)

B2.1

(www.walmart.com, February 12, 2002)

✳ BACKGROUND

A Used in any pattern of Pattern Group A—Site Genres that allows customers to navigate by browsing, and as a requisite element of MULTIPLE
B1 WAYS TO NAVIGATE (B1), this pattern makes content browsable through a
combination of organization and navigation cues.

✻ PROBLEM

Browsing content on a site can be difficult if the information is not organized, or if there are no clear and consistent navigation cues for finding content and returning to it later.

Customers group and organize information in many ways. Just go to a local library and take a look at how things are organized. In the United States, every library uses either the Dewey decimal system or the Library of Congress system for organizing books. These methods work fairly well for a wide variety of libraries—from small libraries of just thousands of books to national libraries of millions of books. Libraries are organized for searching. If patrons know the system, they can find anything.

Now think about how a bookstore is organized. In contrast to a library, magazines are usually grouped together in the front of the store, recent novels are in another section nearby, children's books are in yet another section, and so on. Often books are organized alphabetically within each group, but sometimes a series is so successful and numerous that it warrants its own subsection. Bookstores are organized for browsing as well as searching. Customers of bookstores and patrons of libraries have slightly different needs. The same is true for content on the Web.

Use an Organizational Scheme • Web sites need architectures that depend on the types of information involved, on the amount of information, and on customer tasks. Finding the best organization schemes for a particular site requires analysis. We have included patterns on HIERARCHICAL ORGANIZATION (B3), TASK-BASED ORGANIZATION (B4), ALPHABETICAL ORGANIZATION (B5), CHRONOLOGICAL ORGANIZATION (B6), and POPULARITY-BASED ORGANIZATION (B7). Other organizational schemes that might make sense for your site include spatial (for example, geographic) or numerical organizations. Use CATEGORY PAGES (B8) as directories to content in subcategories.

Structure Content with Customers in Mind • Use card sorting to group items so that people will be able to find what they're looking for by recognizing the group names (see Chapter 3—Knowing Your Customers: Principles and Techniques). It is best to do this with several customers to see if there is a consensus. If there isn't, try to change the names of the items or groups that are causing confusion. Asking these questions about where to put each item and what to call the categories will make it easier for customers to browse your content, picking the right links each step of the way.

Help Customers Find Their Way Back • While navigating from page to page, customers can go down a path on purpose to explore or go down a path accidentally and find themselves lost. If they cannot find their way back to a place they remember, they will feel less adventurous. Leaving links on TAB ROWS (K3) or as LOCATION BREAD CRUMBS (K6) gives customers the reassurance they need to explore freely and to find their way back (see Figure B2.1). Most customers expect to be able to return to your homepage by clicking on your site logo in the upper left-hand corner of any page, as described in SITE BRANDING (E1).

When Does Content on a Page Become Too Much? • Customers can be overloaded with too much information, and the overload might shut down their ability to read, even though your page could be jam-packed with valuable information. Many factors contribute to the feeling of being overwhelmed—from fonts that are too small, to sections on a page that are indistinguishable, to an unclear hierarchy of content. You do not want customers to concentrate too much on figuring out what's important and what's not. You can mitigate information overload by using techniques that allow customers to scan a page and find what they seek. Lay out each page with a clear GRID LAYOUT (I1), a strong visual hierarchy, consistent content areas, consistent NAVIGATION BAR (K2) and link areas, and a font that customers can read easily, even if it means they will need to scroll (see Figure B2.2).

Figure B2.2

The information on The Knot's Web site is organized clearly and aligned in a clean grid layout. The navigation bar consists of a tab row along the top and links along the left-hand side, making it easy to move through the site.

(www.theknot.com, August 26, 2001)

✳ SOLUTION

Organize your content in several ways, in categories that make sense to your customers and in the intuitive ways they think about doing their tasks. Build navigation tools and cues that let customers know where they are, where they can go, and how to get back. Build each page with its own reading hierarchy so that customers can scan it quickly.

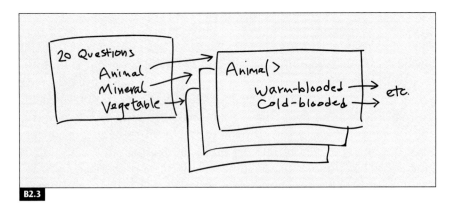

B2.3

Figure B2.3

Present content in a simple, scannable format that leads browsing readers from one page to the next, while giving them clear navigation markers to make their way back.

✳ CONSIDER THESE OTHER PATTERNS

Determine the best organizational schemes for your content by using HIERARCHICAL ORGANIZATION (B3), TASK-BASED ORGANIZATION (B4), ALPHABETICAL ORGANIZATION (B5), CHRONOLOGICAL ORGANIZATION (B6), and POPULARITY-BASED ORGANIZATION (B7) separately or in combination. Use CATEGORY PAGES (B8) as directories to content in subcategories. Make it easier for everyone to navigate your site with SITE ACCESSIBILITY (B9).

Give customers ample opportunity to find their way back, by employing NAVIGATION BARS (K2), TAB ROWS (K3), SITE BRANDING (E1), and LOCATION BREAD CRUMBS (K6).

On every page, make the content browsable by building a hierarchy of content with a clean GRID LAYOUT (I1), CLEAR FIRST READS (I3), and clearly defined areas with CONTENT MODULES (D2).

Figure B3.1

Yahoo! uses hierarchies to categorize thousands of Web sites. Categories range from "Art & Humanities" to "Society & Culture." (Reproduced with permission of Yahoo! © 2000 by Yahoo! Inc. YAHOO! and the YAHOO! logo are trademarks of Yahoo! Inc.)

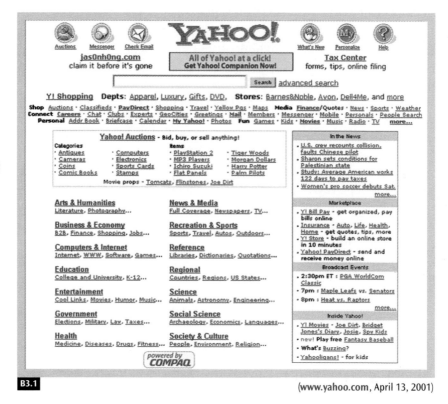

B3.1

(www.yahoo.com, April 13, 2001)

✳ BACKGROUND

 Used as part of MULTIPLE WAYS TO NAVIGATE (B1) and BROWSABLE CONTENT (B2), this pattern provides a way to organize large amounts of content when the content can be structured in a hierarchy.

✳ PROBLEM

Organizing information in a hierarchy of categories can help customers find things. Building an effective hierarchy is not easy.

Hierarchies are a common way of breaking long lists into smaller chunks. But customers think in different ways and may not put the same smaller chunks together in the same categories. What makes good organization depends on your audience, the language that audience uses to describe the subjects you will categorize, and the amount of information you present at a given time.

The best-known example of a hierarchy on the Web is the one created by Yahoo!, which contains several thousand Web sites. Despite the enormous number of categories, customers find things easily because the items are grouped according to a logical scheme. Yahoo! built its directory over time, through serious and thoughtful debate among the information architects and content experts working for the company.

Building a smaller hierarchy is not as daunting but still requires the same dedication to understanding the way your customers think and talk about the topics.

Organize Your Hierarchy to Match the Way Customers Think • This task can be quite a challenge because customers do not all think alike, and because a designer may not think like customers. For example, would most customers expect to find *organic apples* under *groceries, produce, fruits,* or *organic fruits?* Should you cover your bases and create all the categories? Or should you create just one category?

To make this decision requires interviewing customers about where they would expect to find things. Use card sorting, as described in Chapter 3—Knowing Your Customers: Principles and Techniques, to have customers help you organize the content on your site. You can relate the resulting categories by creating links between them. It is also useful to provide a few redundant links to the same information, especially if different customers consistently give different names for the same thing.

3

Use Descriptive and Distinctive Category Names • Customers may choose unexpected names for categories. It is not that customers will not understand the names that a designer chooses, but words that a designer thinks best describe a category may not be the same as those that most customers choose.

One example comes from a health and nutrition site we tested that used the generic label *information* as the link name for a category that included nutrient characteristics and disease information. While *information* made perfect sense to the site designers and to a few of the customers, 70 percent of customers could not find where *disease information* was located when starting at the top of the hierarchy. This seemingly simple name choice had huge consequences when customers could not purchase products because they could not find them.

Category labels need to be descriptive of what that category contains. Avoid labels such as *miscellaneous* and *other*—names that are so ambiguous that customers will not know what they mean. Category labels also need to be distinctive from one another. For example, having the label *nutrition information* by itself is fine. Having both *nutrition information* and *diet information* as labels makes things confusing because they sound too similar. Which link would have information about vitamins? What about vegetarianism?

The key here is to test the categories and category labels. You can use card sorting with one group of customers to help you come up with potential categories and category labels. Then you can test the effectiveness of these names by using category identification and category description with another set of customers. The basic idea behind **category identification** is to give people a list of category names and a list of tasks, and ask them to choose the category that they think would help them complete each task. In **category description**, people are asked to describe what they think a given category contains. Both of these techniques are described in greater detail in FAMILIAR LANGUAGE (K11).

Provide Examples in Each Category • In FindLaw's Web site (see Figure B3.2), there are 14 top-level categories, including "Legal Subjects" and "Legal Organizations." FindLaw also provides some second-level links, describing a few of the items that you would find inside each category. Because customers can thus more easily understand what a category contains, they are more likely to pick the right one.

Keep the Number of Subcategories under Fifty • When subcategory lists are too long, they become cumbersome to read because there is so much information to process on one page. Keeping the number of subcategories to under 50 (two columns of 25) will make your pages easier to read and faster to navigate. If you have more than 50 items, try to make sub-subcategories or to combine similar categories.

B3.2

(www.findlaw.com, August 26, 2001)

Figure B3.2

FindLaw uses a hierarchy to categorize legal information, providing links to top-level categories, as well as examples within each category.

❋ SOLUTION

Build a hierarchy of categories with input from customers or from experts known for good communication skills in the subject area. Use descriptive category names that are distinctive from one another. Use techniques such as card sorting to develop the categories and labels, and use techniques like category identification and category description to test. Repeat the items in multiple categories where it makes sense. Keep the maximum number of subcategories per category to between 20 and 50, and avoid generic terms like *miscellaneous*.

Figure B3.3

Use words that are familiar to your customers without overloading a single category with too many subcategories.

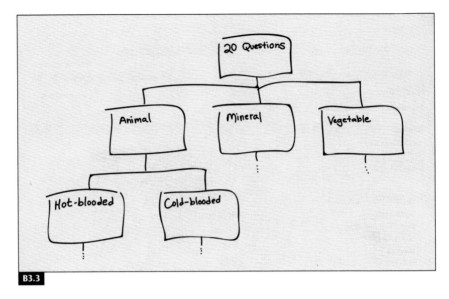

B3.3

✳ CONSIDER THESE OTHER PATTERNS

Use card sorting, category identification, category description, and the techniques in FAMILIAR LANGUAGE (K11) to find the names of your top-level and second-level categories. Use CATEGORY PAGES (B8) as directories to content in subcategories. This pattern can be combined with other organizational patterns, including TASK-BASED ORGANIZATION (B4), ALPHA-BETICAL ORGANIZATION (B5), CHRONOLOGICAL ORGANIZATION (B6), and POPULARITY-BASED ORGANIZATION (B7).

B4 TASK-BASED ORGANIZATION

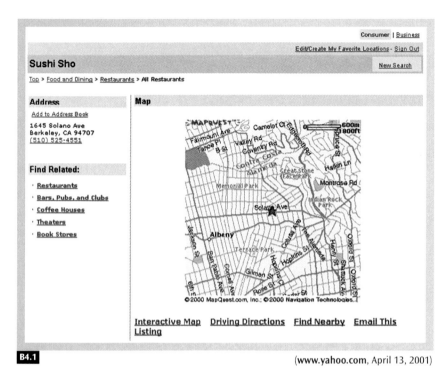

B4.1

(**www.yahoo.com**, April 13, 2001)

✳ BACKGROUND

Used as part of MULTIPLE WAYS TO NAVIGATE (B1) and BROWSABLE CONTENT (B2), this pattern deals with organizing content according to the way customers use it.

B1
B2

✳ PROBLEM

Completing multiple tasks on a site is not fast and easy unless related tasks are linked together.

When customers perform tasks on a site—whether they are searching for information, shopping for a product, or performing a process in a Web application—the task is often the first of many in a bigger project. If related tasks are not linked together, customers are forced to return to a central page to start the next task, making repeated use of the site tedious. By grouping related tasks together, where customers complete one task and immediately link to the next, the site simplifies and speeds the flow of work.

Figure B4.2

Clicking on a task subject on Salesforce.com provides you with space to enter update information and schedule a follow-up task.

Organize content and processes by how customers are likely to use them. For example, if customers search for a restaurant using Yahoo!'s map service, Yahoo! provides not only a map and directions but also task-related links that make it easy to find nearby movie theaters and coffee houses (see Figure B4.1). Similarly, on Salesforce.com's site, salespeople set meeting reminders in their calendars, and while they are recording notes, the site provides links to create follow-up meetings (see Figure B4.2). These shortcuts save customers time.

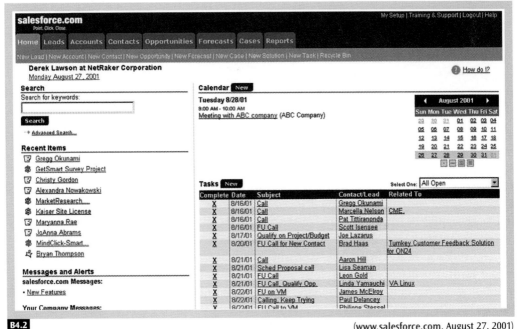

(www.salesforce.com, August 27, 2001)

Study What Your Customers Do • What do your customers do online, offline, and on your Web site? In creating the map example of the preceding section, you could have asked your customers, "What kinds of places do you look up on Web sites that provide maps?" Or you could look at the Web server log files to see which destinations customers are typing in. Or you could approach this research as ethnographic and visit customers. When you observe your customers, they will reveal things they might not even realize they're doing. (See Chapter 3—Knowing Your Customers: Principles and Techniques for an overview of techniques for understanding customer needs, including interviews, ethnographic observations, and surveys.)

3

Build Scenarios of Related Tasks • Once you understand how customers might use your site, you can build scenarios of related tasks, modeling the flow between tasks. From one task, the next available tasks should be the ones that regularly follow the first. For example, if for task A the next logical step is task B, C, or D, but not E or F, then the available options should be B, C, and D (see Figure B4.3).

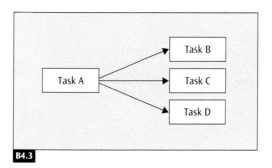

B4.3

Figure B4.3

Link logically related tasks together. For example, if task A can be followed by task B, C, or D, add links to those tasks on completion of task A.

    Once you have built a description of related tasks, create links on task completion pages that will take customers directly into the next task or tasks. As a result, your customers will be able to move more quickly through your application, and their overall experience will be enhanced.

    LowFare.com's Web site lets customers search for and book airplane tickets. Figure B4.4 shows what the Web site looks like after a visitor selects a round-trip ticket. At this point the tasks include buying the ticket, holding the ticket for later purchase, searching for other flights, or canceling the entire transaction and starting over. LowFare.com's Web site supports many other tasks, such as renting a car and booking a hotel, but they are not emphasized on this page because they do not make sense in the context of the current task, which is purchasing an airplane ticket.

Figure B4.4

LowFares.com is a fictitious Web site we have created that is representative of several major travel sites we have seen. On LowFares.com customers search for flights and selected itineraries by schedule or price. Once they have chosen the flight they want, the site takes them directly to the purchasing options. Customers can also search for other flights, which is another common task at this stage of the process.

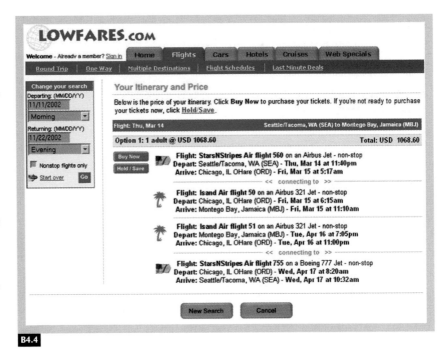

✳ SOLUTION

Study customers, the tasks they do, and the sequence in which they do them. Then build relationships between tasks and link them together so that the completion of one task can immediately precede the start of the next.

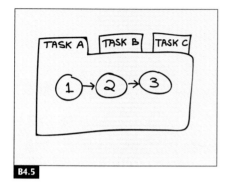

B4.5

Figure B4.5

Link the completion of one group of tasks to the beginning of the next related task or tasks.

✳ CONSIDER THESE OTHER PATTERNS

PROCESS FUNNELS (H1) are similar to task-based organization but are focused on completing an extremely specific task, with few choices at each step. If you have a HIERARCHICAL ORGANIZATION (B3) of different types of tasks, use CATEGORY PAGES (B8) as directories to content in subcategories.

 H1

B3
 B8

Figure B5.1

An alphabetically organized list works well when the list is fairly short and the pieces of information are unrelated to each other, or when their names are well known.

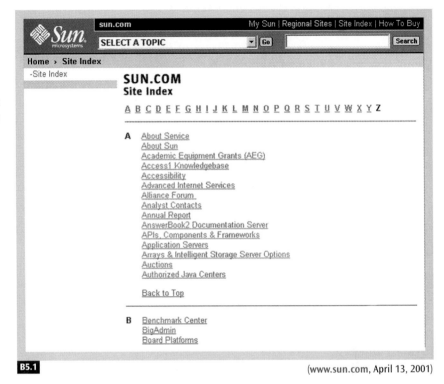

B5.1

(www.sun.com, April 13, 2001)

✳ BACKGROUND

Used as part of MULTIPLE WAYS TO NAVIGATE (B1) and BROWSABLE CONTENT (B2), this pattern provides a way to organize a relatively small amount of content when the content is unrelated or is made up of items with well-known names.

✳ PROBLEM

Alphabetizing a list seems like an obvious way to organize content. Long alphabetical lists on a site, however, are cumbersome to use.

Alphabetical organization is ingrained in the way people remember things. It is effective when the individual pieces of information are known by name more than by what they represent.

When Does an Alphabetical List Work? • As long as customers know the precise word or phrase they are seeking, they can quickly find the items they want in an alphabetical list. Alphabetical lists can be useful for organizing information such as the following:

- Desired items, if known by name
- All documents on a Web site, if the document names are well known
- All of a company's customers
- All products that a company offers

Try to Keep the List on One Page • If an alphabetical list is split into multiple Web pages, customers must click on the first letter of the first word and wait for that letter's page to download. Long waits like this can be frustrating when the desired link is not guaranteed to be on the next page. Imagine looking for a video. Is it listed under *T* for _The Last Tango in Paris_ or under *L* for just _Last Tango in Paris?_ Neither order is right or wrong, but if the entire movie list appears on one page, it is easy to find it in either place. You can create an index at the top of the page that links to each letter group, as illustrated in Figure B5.1. You can also use a TAB ROW (K3) to do the same thing. This will let your customers find the section they want without their having to make a lengthy scroll.

K3

Alphabetical organization may not work well for people who grew up with nonalphabetical languages, such as Japanese and Chinese.

❋ SOLUTION

Provide links to each letter group at the top of your single alphabetical list page of well-known items.

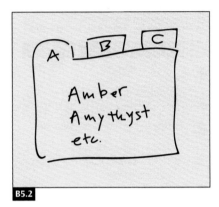

B5.2

Figure B5.2

A page with the entire alphabetical list works best when it has links at the top to jump to each individual letter group.

❋ CONSIDER THESE OTHER PATTERNS

K3 Create an alphabetical TAB ROW (K3) at the top of your page that links to each letter's group farther down on the page.

B6 CHRONOLOGICAL ORGANIZATION

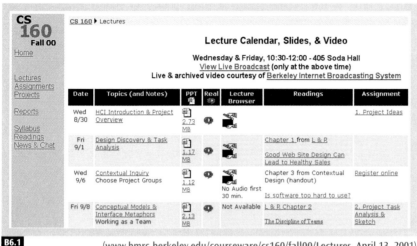

Figure B6.1

This course Web page offers information about an interface design and evaluation class taught by one of the coauthors of this book. It uses chronological ordering to organize the class assignments and materials as they were presented.

B6.1

(www.bmrc.berkeley.edu/courseware/cs160/fall00/Lectures, April 13, 2001)

✳ BACKGROUND

Used as part of MULTIPLE WAYS TO NAVIGATE (B1) and BROWSABLE CONTENT (B2), this pattern provides a way to organize content related by time.

B1
B2

✳ PROBLEM

Chronologically organizing content on a site helps visitors understand the order of content in time, whether past or future. But very long lists of events are difficult to read and use.

Chronological structure makes sense for things that have a strong notion of time, such as historical events, technical reports, plane tickets, and changes on a Web page. But if a list is too long, with no hierarchical breakdown into eras, types, or milestones, it will take too long to read and scroll through, and thus it will become less useful.

Display Chronological Information in Lists or Time Lines • One way of displaying time-related content is by showing it as a vertical list, where the sorted column shows the time. This is the simplest solution because it can be implemented quickly, but it is not as intuitive as a time line, where content appears horizontally from left to right. The latter is how most people visualize time, but its implementation on the Web is more difficult because text is not laid out with much precision. Lists and time lines are useful when you want to display content in relation to well-known dates (such as the 1960s, 1970s, or 1980s) or in chronological relation to other content (such as "event *X* came before event *Y*").

You could also use a calendar to group information, showing events on a daily, monthly, or yearly basis. But this method does not work as well when you have to display large lists because each day, week, or month can show only a fixed number of items.

Keep Chronological Lists under Fifty Items • When sorting items in chronological order, keep them short and easy to use. Chronological lists do not work well when the lists are long because there are too many items to read. If you have to, organize your events into hierarchies based on spans of time, or use another kind of organization. For example, if you had more than 50 items in your chronology, you could break them out as shown in Table B6.1.

Table B6.1

Some Useful Groupings for Dividing Large Chronological Lists

Content	Suggested Group for Breakdown
Musical events this month	Day
The history of the Christian Church	Century
What drives economic boom-and-bust cycles	Decade
The major milestones of World War II	Topic—for example, Nazi invasion of Poland, Pearl Harbor, D-Day

✳ SOLUTION

Display chronological lists in a vertical, horizontal, or calendar format, keeping the total number of items in each list under 50 by dividing the list into smaller groups of time.

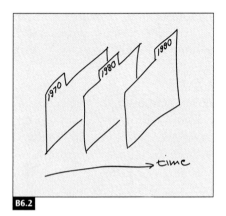

B6.2

Figure B6.2

Organizing content into smaller groups of time makes reading about each era that much easier.

✳ CONSIDER THESE OTHER PATTERNS

Use a PAGE TEMPLATE (D1) to publish your vertical, horizontal, or calendar display in a CONTENT MODULE (D2) to keep it in a well-known place. Organize your list of chronological items in a HIERARCHICAL ORGANIZATION (B3) to keep each list manageable. Use a CATEGORY PAGE (B8) as a directory for each group in the hierarchy.

Figure B7.1

Billboard shows customers the top music hits, from top-selling CDs to singles and airplays. Customers can also view top hits by music genres, as well as by number of hits on the Web.

B7.1

(www.billboard.com, September 1, 2001)

✳ BACKGROUND

Used as part of MULTIPLE WAYS TO NAVIGATE (B1) and BROWSABLE CONTENT (B2), this pattern provides a way to organize content related by popularity.

✳ PROBLEM

Some customers want to see which content or products are the most popular. But without clear labels of how you rated the content, over what period, popularity lists are useless.

Some customers enjoy seeing what other customers think is popular. Whether a list of most-purchased products, a controlled democratic tally, or a popularity contest, these lists are intriguing, no matter how they are displayed. But if the list of rated items does not clearly indicate how others rated the content, it becomes suspicious and ineffective.

How to Create a List • Your ability to find the most popular items on your site can be a fairly straightforward matter, or it can be devilishly complex. Do you buy the list of content ratings from a provider (such as the *New York Times* Best-Seller Lists)? Do you use a RECOMMENDATION COMMUNITY (G4), where you ask customers to rate your content? For example, IFILM asks visitors to rank short films on a scale from 1 to 5. Or do you automatically extract the information from customers' page views or purchases? In the example in Figure B7.2, Yahoo! provides a page where

B7.2

(www.yahoo.com, August 26, 2001)

Figure B7.2

Yahoo! has a popularity-based news Web page that shows the most popular stories and photographs, according to the number of times they were e-mailed by customers. (Reproduced with permission of Yahoo! © 2000 by Yahoo! Inc. YAHOO! and the YAHOO! logo are trademarks of Yahoo! Inc.)

customers can review the most e-mailed news photographs and news stories of the previous six hours.

How to Determine the Time Period for Taking Measurements • Customers will expect the list of content to be interesting news or to have historical value. The most popular content from three months ago will not be interesting, unless three months ago coincided with an important event. The most popular information from this week, compared to last week, might be interesting if enough movement has occurred.

From the information you have gathered, build a rating that changes frequently enough that visitors coming back on a regular basis will see movement. If customers come back daily, you should have enough information to show a daily best. If customers come back every month, monthly or quarterly scores might be more appropriate.

In Figure B7.3, IFILM shows visitors its top-viewed short films for the current week, as well as its top-rated short films of all time. The Lycos 50

Figure B7.3

IFILM's homepage shows an easily read list of the most popular short films.

(www.ifilm.com, December 7, 2001)

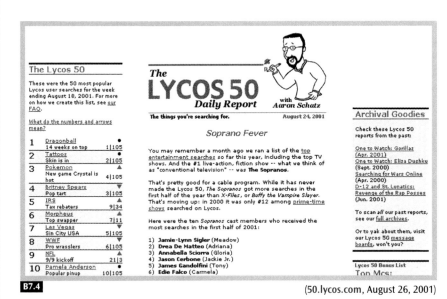

(50.lycos.com, August 26, 2001)

Figure B7.4

The Lycos 50 Daily Report shows visitors the 50 most popular customer search subjects on its search engine. (© 2001 Lycos, Inc. Lycos® is a registered trademark of Carnegie Mellon University. All rights reserved.)

Daily Report shows the 50 most popular search terms for that week (see Figure B7.4). Sometimes, just for fun, Lycos features special categories, such as the most popular teen singers or the most popular actors.

❈ SOLUTION

Build your lists of popular content from customer usage, customer ratings, or acquired outside lists. Label each list with a descriptive title that indicates what you rated and over what period.

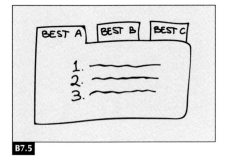

Figure B7.5

Show the most popular content, but be sure to descriptively label how it was rated, and to show the time period that the ratings cover.

✳ CONSIDER THESE OTHER PATTERNS

Integrate multiple popularity-based organization lists into levels of a HIER-
ARCHICAL ORGANIZATION (B3). Use CATEGORY PAGES (B8) as directories to
content in subcategories. Employ customer usage meters, a RECOMMEN-
DATION COMMUNITY (G4), or acquired data to generate your lists. Also
show your customers the time period you used to acquire the data.

B8 CATEGORY PAGES

B8.1

(www.marthastewart.com, February 1, 2002)

Figure B8.1

Categories are labeled well and laid out consistently throughout Martha Stewart's Web site. When visitors travel deeper down the levels, they know where they are by the color scheme, the navigation elements, and the content.

✳ BACKGROUND

This pattern shows how to design different sections of a Web site so that they are distinct but still obviously part of the larger overall site. Category pages are often reached through one of your MULTIPLE WAYS TO NAVIGATE (B1) including any of the organization schemes for BROWSABLE CONTENT (B2), such as HIERARCHICAL ORGANIZATION (B3), TASK-BASED ORGANIZATION (B4), CHRONOLOGICAL ORGANIZATION (B6), and POPULARITY-BASED ORGANIZATION (B7).

B1
B2 **B3**
B4 **B6**
B7

✳ PROBLEM

As customers navigate through a site, if category sections are not introduced through a consistent layout, each section may seem like a new site.

Whether navigating through sections of content, products, or applications, when customers come across a new area, it must be consistent with the rest of the site or they might think they have gone to a new site. Category sections that are consistent in layout and navigation elements reinforce a sense of location (see Figure B8.2). This does not mean that all

Figure B8.2

Consistently colored categories and banner titles show Amazon.com customers that no matter which section they're in, they are still on the same site.

B8.2

(www.amazon.com, August 23, 2001)

categories must look exactly alike, but the basic structure must be the same. With a consistent structure, customers can recognize not only their location, but also the main elements of the section.

Use a Consistent Layout • Customers may become confused if they expect to find a section title in a certain location and it is not there. They might go to another page even if they are actually in the right place. Keep all the content and navigation elements in the same locations on each page so that people recognize the layout and feel secure that they are still on the right site. Keep the name of the section in a consistent place as well so that you can maintain a strong sense of location while introducing customers to a new section. You can do this by using the same or similar GRID LAYOUTS (I1) throughout your Web site and consistently placing these key elements in the same place.

(I1)

Maintain Consistent Navigation • Make your navigation system the same throughout your site. You can change the color of a TAB ROW (K3), for example, and the subsection search element of a SEARCH ACTION MODULE (J1), to give it a sense of place, but avoid radical changes to other elements.

(K3)

(J1)

Provide Strong Feedback That Visitors Have "Arrived" • When you drive into a new town, it helps to see a big sign that says, "Welcome to Woebegone"; you know you have arrived. The same is true on the Web and within sections of your site. Provide a large sign or just a page title that indicates the category page section name the way it appears in navigation elements throughout the site.

✳ SOLUTION

Use a section category layout consistently throughout your site, with the same navigation elements, giving customers a strong sense that they have "arrived" at a new section and a clear idea of how to get back.

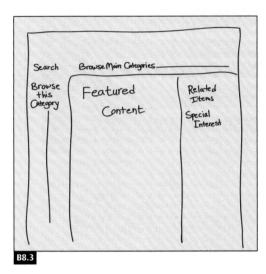

Figure B8.3

Focus category pages on the featured content, while using consistent navigation.

✳ CONSIDER THESE OTHER PATTERNS

Build a consistent category page layout using a PAGE TEMPLATE (D1) and CONTENT MODULES (D2), with consistent GRID LAYOUT (I1), NAVIGATION BARS (K2), and LOCATION BREAD CRUMBS (K6) to indicate where the customer is on the site. If you're using TAB ROWS (K3), you might change the color of the tab for each category section. If you're using a subsection element in a SEARCH ACTION MODULE (J1), make the default the current section. Use the CLEAR FIRST READ (I3) to indicate the section name so that visitors know they have "arrived" at a new category.

B9 SITE ACCESSIBILITY

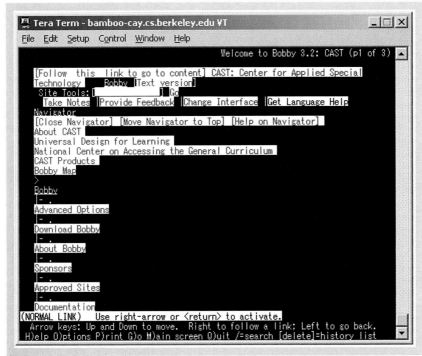

Figure B9.1

Web sites need to be designed for access and use by everyone, regardless of physical ability or computer capability. This example shows a screen shot from the text-based Lynx Web browser, which gives a flavor of what the Web is like for people who are blind.

B9.1 (**universalusability.org**, October 31, 2001)

✳ BACKGROUND

People with disabilities find it difficult to use many Web sites. By law, you must make SELF-SERVICE GOVERNMENT (A4) and other sites that are provided by, purchased by, or used by the U.S. government universally accessible. Used in any pattern of Pattern Group A—Site Genres, this pattern describes how to structure your Web site to improve navigation accessibility for people with disabilities.

✳ PROBLEM

People with audio, visual, motor, or cognitive disabilities find it difficult to use Web sites that are not explicitly designed with their accessibility in mind.

A significant portion of the population has problems accessing and using the Web. People who are blind, have poor vision, are deaf, or have physical disabilities find it difficult—sometimes even impossible—to navigate through Web sites designed without their accessibility in mind.

Age is also an important factor to consider. On one end of the spectrum, young children have not fully developed their motor skills. On the other end, senior citizens may have impaired vision and hearing. These are two potential customer segments to consider when designing your Web sites.

More and more mobile Internet devices, from cell phones to personal digital assistants (PDAs), are Internet enabled. Clearly these devices do not have the same screen size, input capabilities, and processing power of desktop computers. People who use these kinds of devices form another potential customer segment to consider when you're creating your Web site.

If you have the U.S. government as a customer, a legal requirement also affects your accessibility design. Section 508 of the Rehabilitation Act requires all electronic and information technologies purchased by the U.S. government to be accessible. This stipulation explicitly includes services such as Web sites used by the federal government.

Accessibility helps more than just its intended audience. *Accessibility helps everyone.* Curb cuts meant to help people with wheelchairs also make things easier for people traveling on roller blades, pushing baby strollers, and lugging around luggage on wheels. Closed captions on television programs help not only people with hearing deficiencies but also people in loud sports bars, people in exercise centers, people trying to learn English, and spouses quietly watching television in bed at night.

The same is true for Web site accessibility. Offering captions and transcripts of audio and video, using clearer link names, and providing alternative text for images will improve the usefulness and usability not just for customers with disabilities, but for everyone else as well. It is a win–win situation.

Whether you're designing a new Web site or revising an existing site, here are some issues to think about. The ideas outlined in the sections that follow are not meant to be exhaustive, but they should give you an idea of the range of possibilities.

People with Physical Difficulties Use the Web • Although there is a wide range of physical difficulties, focus your efforts on keyboard and mouse input because these are the primary input modes for computers for the near future. A customer with a physical disability might not be able to use a keyboard effectively, or even at all. The same is true for use of a mouse. Here's how to address these problems:

- Test if your Web site can be used without a mouse. Determine whether a visitor could use just the keyboard to navigate through your Web pages.
- Minimize the amount of typing a visitor has to do. For example, a common technique in QUICK-FLOW CHECKOUT (F1) is to have customers enter their shipping address and then be able to indicate that this is also the billing address just by clicking a button with the mouse. This is much simpler than having a customer type in the same thing twice. Another way to minimize the input required of customers is to save the information that they typed in on a previous visit to the site, providing them with a QUICK ADDRESS SELECTION (F4), a QUICK SHIPPING METHOD SELECTION (F5), and a streamlined PAYMENT METHOD (F6) the next time they purchase something.
- Make sure that your navigation elements are large enough to see clearly. Avoid links that are in small fonts and links that use small images. These elements are just too difficult to click on with a mouse. This caution applies to NAVIGATION BARS (K2), ACTION BUTTONS (K4), and OBVIOUS LINKS (K10).

People with Auditory Disabilities Use the Web • Currently, most Web sites do not make heavy use of audio and video. However, if your site relies heavily on audio, provide text descriptions of audio sound files. For sites that provide video, provide text transcripts and video captioning so that customers with auditory disabilities will know what is being said.

People with Visual Disabilities Use the Web • This segment of the population includes people who are blind, have impaired vision, or have color deficiencies. The relevant issues are basic readability of text and links. Here are some tips for ensuring the readability of your Web site for people with visual disabilities:

- Provide sufficient contrast between the text and the background. Use either dark text on a light background or light text on a dark background. Also avoid complex background patterns because they can make reading text extremely difficult. Use simple patterns or solid background colors instead.

- Use a sufficiently large font. Cramming in more information by shrinking the font merely forces customers to move closer to the monitor and squint. Web browsers have a default font size, and people with visual disabilities often increase this default size, so if you use relative font sizes, the text will usually be the right size. Make sure that your page layout still looks right when the font sizes change.

- Avoid using ALL CAPS for text because the letter forms of capitals are more difficult to read. It is OK to use this technique sparingly to bring attention to something, such as "NEW" features or a "SALE." Capitalizing whole words is a good way of bringing attention, but doing it excessively can slow down reading.

- Avoid animations and blinking text. These kinds of distractions can make reading difficult.

- Avoid creating text that runs all the way from the left of the page to the right. This format makes it difficult for people's eyes to pick up the start of the next line. It also makes the text feel tight, as if it were being crammed in. A little white space on both sides of a Web page will make text easier to read. Using a FIXED-WIDTH SCREEN SIZE (I5) will help you easily achieve this effect.

- Stay away from link color combinations that people with color deficiencies will not be able to differentiate. In particular, avoid green for unvisited links and red for visited links because those colors are hard for people with red–green color deficiency to distinguish.

(I5)

Good readability by itself is not sufficient, however. You also need to ensure that people with visual disabilities can navigate your Web site. One way of doing this is to underline links and use a distinct color, as described in the OBVIOUS LINKS (K10) pattern. This pattern also describes how to use the TITLE attribute in hyperlinks to describe where the link goes.

(K10)

So far in this section we have talked just about issues affecting people with poor vision. What about people who are completely blind? People who are blind use a special hardware device or software program, called a **screen reader**, which takes all the text on a page and uses computer-based speech synthesis to read it out.

You can help blind customers by making sure your links make sense when taken out of context. People who are blind often skip text and go straight to the links (on most Web browsers they can do so by hitting the **Tab** button). Pressing **Tab** causes the screen reader to jump over most of the surrounding text and just read out the text of the link, making short link names like *Click Here* useless. Using DESCRIPTIVE, LONGER LINK NAMES (K9) will help significantly.

People who are blind will not want to use images as the only way to navigate your Web site. You could have both a regular Web page and a text-only copy of the Web page to remedy this situation, or you could create redundant navigation links—that is, text and image links that go to the same place.

Provide text descriptions for images by using the ALT attribute to describe images. Here's an example of how to use the ALT attribute:

```
<IMG SRC="img.jpg" ALT="Text describing the image">
```

Here's how ALT attributes are used in the Weather Channel's Web site:

```
<IMG SRC="http://image.weather.com/pics/banners/banner_general.jpg"
BORDER=0 ALT="click on banner to return to Home Page">
```

Screen readers read out the ALT attribute to describe an image. And there are other advantages to using ALT attributes. Figure B9.2 shows how visitors with normal vision can get text descriptions of images in the form of tool tips.

Figure B9.2

The ALT attribute on the Weather Channel's site is displayed as a tool tip when a customer moves the mouse over the image. It is also useful for people who are blind because their screen readers can read out the description of the image.

B9.2 (www.weather.com, July 17, 2000)

ALT attributes are also useful if you have a broken link to an image. Figure B9.3 shows what a person with normal vision would see if the Weather Channel's banner were missing. Interestingly, this is also what a person sees *before* the image is loaded, making it a FAST-DOWNLOADING IMAGE (L2). Thus ALT attributes let customers with slow network connections navigate through a Web page without waiting for all its contents to load!

Figure B9.3

Another advantage of the ALT attribute is that it is shown if the image cannot be displayed.

B9.3 (www.weather.com, July 17, 2000)

People with Cognitive Disabilities Use the Web • A cognitive disability can make it hard for people to write, read, and navigate. Here are four ways you can make these tasks easier:

1. Provide a consistent navigation scheme throughout your Web site. Place navigation elements in a standard GRID LAYOUT (I1), and place the most important content ABOVE THE FOLD (I2).
2. Use OBVIOUS LINKS (K10) and ACTION BUTTONS (K4) to ensure clarity (see Figure B9.4).
3. Avoid distracting elements, such as animations and blinking text.
4. Use recognition over recall. In other words, minimize the amount of information that visitors have to remember to use your Web site. Search engines, for example, display not only search results, but also the search terms that the visitor typed in, making it easier for a visitor to remember a past action.

People May Use the Web with Mobile Internet Devices • Although more and more mobile Internet devices are coming out on the market, there are still significant challenges in making Web sites usable on them. Compared to a desktop computer, these kinds of devices are poor in terms of screen size, processing power, battery life, and input.

Currently only a few standards are in place for small devices, including the Handheld Device Markup Language (HDML), the Wireless Application Protocol (WAP), Compact HTML (cHTML), and XHTML Basic.

Figure B9.4

Microsoft uses a simple organizational scheme, good link labels, and clear text labels for all of its images, making it easier for customers with disabilities to access its Web pages.

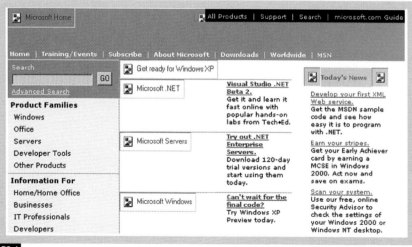

(www.microsoft.com, August 26, 2001)

The field is very young and is still subject to rapid changes. In the meantime, here are a few suggestions for how to improve your Web pages for small devices today:

- Minimize the amount of text input required of customers. Text input is quite difficult on small devices, even if they include a keyboard. You could help people by letting them enter personal information on a desktop computer, for example, and then associate that information with the device they are using.
- Do not rely exclusively on images for navigation. When you do use images, include the ALT attribute for them.
- Use the TITLE attribute for links, as discussed in OBVIOUS LINKS (K10). Doing so provides an alternative name for links that some devices and browsers can use.
- Use DISTINCTIVE HTML TITLES (D9) on each Web page. These titles are likely to be at the top of the device, describing the page. They need to be short enough to fit on a small display, but descriptive.
- Put the most important information at the top of a page. Because portable-device screens are so small, important information should be placed ABOVE THE FOLD (I2). And in this case the fold is quite limiting.
- Provide alternatives for scripts, applets, and plug-ins. Not all devices and Web browsers will be able to run Java applets, play sound files, and show Macromedia Flash content. Providing alternative but similar content will let more customers use your Web site.

✳ SOLUTION

In designing your Web site, keep in mind accessibility for people with audio, visual, motor, and cognitive disabilities. Make the navigation and content both understandable and usable by employing good layout, clean visual design, straightforward text descriptions for all images and links, and alternative text-based formats for rich multimedia. Use features built into HTML that simplify accessibility.

Figure B9.5

Making your site accessible to people with disabilities will make your site more accessible to everyone.

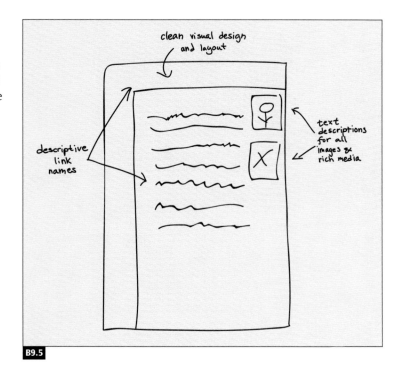

B9.5

✳ CONSIDER THESE OTHER PATTERNS

Focus first on making accessible the most important pages, including the   HOMEPAGE PORTAL (C1) and QUICK-FLOW CHECKOUT (F1). In terms of navigation, concentrate first on improving the accessibility of key navigation   elements, including NAVIGATION BARS (K2), OBVIOUS LINKS (K10), and ACTION BUTTONS (K4). Use DESCRIPTIVE, LONGER LINK NAMES (K9) and FAMILIAR LANGUAGE (K11) for all links. Also use DISTINCTIVE HTML TITLES (D9) for every page.

Using the ALT attribute for all images also improves responsiveness because people can click on linked images even before the image has downloaded. This feature is emphasized in FAST-DOWNLOADING IMAGES (L2).

Align the content and navigation in a consistent GRID LAYOUT (I1). The most important content should always be near the top, ABOVE THE FOLD (I2). Pages with lots of text should use a FIXED-WIDTH SCREEN SIZE (I5) to make it easier for customers to read and skim.

Creating a Powerful Homepage

The homepage is the most visited page on any Web site, and its design deserves serious attention so that it can accommodate the rich diversity of customers and their needs. This pattern group describes how to design a powerful homepage to fit the needs of your customers.

 C1   HOMEPAGE PORTAL

C2   UP-FRONT VALUE PROPOSITION

Figure C1.1

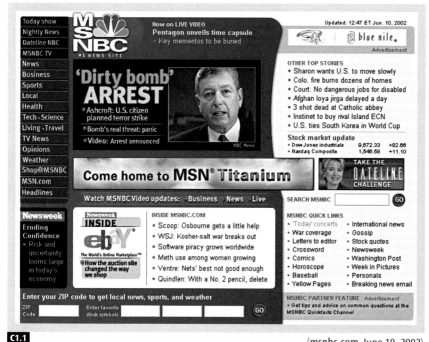

(msnbc.com, June 10, 2002)

MSNBC gives readers a breadth of topics to delve into, while highlighting news of general interest. With its clearly distinguished links, customers need only a quick glance to see how to navigate the site. Subsections highlighted in the navigation bar show more detailed areas of interest. Readers can customize the news by entering their ZIP codes to get local news.

❋ BACKGROUND

Used by almost every site and site genre, a homepage must satisfy the needs of all potential and current customers by establishing the company's identity, while providing MULTIPLE WAYS TO NAVIGATE (B1). This pattern forms the core for homepage designs.

✳ PROBLEM

Homepages are the portal through which most visitors pass. They must seduce visitors while simultaneously balancing many issues, including branding, navigation, content, and the ability to download quickly.

The homepage is usually the first thing customers see on your site. This page is critical because not only is it seen 10 to 1,000+ times more than any other page, but it must also provide an exceptional customer experience to seduce visitors to continue.

Yet the space on the page, especially above the fold, is limited. It must be divided among the following goals: creating the right look and feel, building site brand and identity, providing valuable content, making navigation easy to use, establishing a cohesive and logical page layout, and delivering high performance. Creating a seductive page, while striking a balance with all these elements, requires iterating and refining your page through testing. It also requires that you focus on building trust and providing value and options to your customer population.

Build Site Identity and Brand • Customers need to know that your site holds a valuable promise. They also need to know it is a promise they can trust you to fulfill. And if the site is valuable, they will want to remember it for later, to use for themselves or to tell friends about. This is what it means to build a positive identity and a valuable brand. Building a site brand requires presenting a promise of what your site offers, with the goal of attracting customers to come in, and earning their trust and respect by continually fulfilling that promise.

 This means focusing on the company's UP-FRONT VALUE PROPOSITION (C2), SITE BRANDING (E1), and PRIVACY POLICIES (E4) using text, logos, photos, and illustrations to convey that you are trustworthy and professional. But the site itself must reinforce the brand by fulfilling the promise and building trust on every page.

Make a Positive First Impression with the Right Look and Feel • Visitors can be turned off by style alone, or by a homepage look and feel that says, "This site is not for me." Whether a site uses inappropriate colors and graphics, or the writing is unfamiliar or grating, customers respond negatively to a style that is not targeted for them. Neon green screaming graphics and a skateboarding illustration might appeal to teens, but if you use it to represent a serious family issue or a conservative business, visitors will immediately question if they have come to the right place.

When you design for your target customers, you will get a positive response to your look and feel. Tune the site by showing it repeatedly to a dozen or more members of your intended audience. Conduct further testing to determine how *useful* your customers perceive it to be, as well as how *usable* it is. Although it takes time to conduct tests, avoiding early feedback will cost more in the long run when you have to redesign the site because it is not working.

Seduce with Content • Each customer makes a judgment within just a few seconds of entering a site. This is the time you have to get the visitor's attention and keep it. Lively writing and visuals are essential, as is bringing compelling and timely content to the front page. This content can be news, enticing imagery, seductive navigation text, and/or personalization.

Organize content into headlines, summaries, and body. Entice visitors with a catchy HEADLINE AND BLURB (D3), and follow through on the article page with the content body. To make your design cost-effective, establishing a publishing system can help you update and rotate CONTENT MODULES (D2) automatically. Several commercial tools make this easier to do for larger Web sites.

Personalize Content If Possible • Visitors appreciate coming to a site tailored to their needs because it makes the site feel more useful, faster to use, and more personal. As a result, customers feel more important. However, a personalized site requires additional effort for visitors to use. This is especially true if customers are required to enter personalization information to use the site at all. Personalized sites, also known as *customized sites,* are also more difficult to design and develop, and they require more Web server and database resources, not to mention support for logins or cookies. But if the content is varied enough, personalization can help customers find what they care about and use the site more effectively.

A personalized homepage will contain CONTENT MODULES (D2) and use PERSONALIZED CONTENT (D4) to tailor the homepage to individual customers (see Figures C1.2 and C1.3). To be willing to provide this personal information, visitors need to trust you enough to directly or indirectly tell you about their desires and requests. You must use the information they provide ethically, for their benefit only, and they must trust that you will do so.

Balance Space for Brand against Space for Navigation • There is a trade-off between space used for communicating the site's value and differentiation, and space used for giving customers navigation tools to find what they seek. We have made three observations that provide solutions:

Figure C1.2

My Yahoo! shows how to build customer loyalty by personalizing everything from news and stock quotes to calendars. (Reproduced with permission of Yahoo! © 2000 by Yahoo! Inc. YAHOO! and the YAHOO! logo are trademarks of Yahoo! Inc.)

C1.2

(my.yahoo.com, November 14, 2001)

1. Because the first read on the homepage is often the SITE BRANDING (E1) in the top left corner, and the second read is the UP-FRONT VALUE PROPOSITION (C2), both parts must be instantly clear to customers. If they aren't, customers may become doubtful, confused, or irritated enough to go elsewhere. Have your team focus on designing these two parts well, rather than on using more space on the homepage for branding.

2. Customers skim when they read on the Web, and they will skim your homepage as well, looking for succinct phrases and links they recognize and deem potentially valuable. Focus your design on finding the proper wording for these phrases, and on making them easy to skim. Be sure to use DESCRIPTIVE, LONGER LINK NAMES (K9).

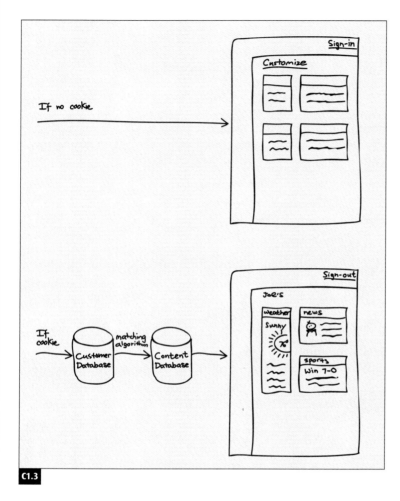

Figure C1.3

Personalized homepages are customized for each customer. This sketch shows how to return a default page for new customers (top), and a personalized page for a returning customer (bottom).

C1.3

3. Every primary audience is really composed of many subgroups, and each subgroup needs answers to its specific questions. For example, if the primary audience consists of investors, you must answer the questions of both institutional investors and direct investors. Dedicate 95 percent of the area and links above the fold to the primary audience. Keep the remaining area and links for secondary groups. If the primary audience is a products and services buyer, answer the questions of the decision maker, recommender, and technical reviewer. You can often take these customers to a subsidiary page where they can select their role to obtain more targeted information. Use the techniques described in Chapter 3—Knowing Your Customers: Principles and Practices to understand these roles for your customers and your site. **3**

Make Navigation Easy to Use • The only way people can find their way around a site is by understanding the navigation. This means that all levels of visitors—with varying degrees of computer skills, domain expertise, and experience with your Web site—must quickly comprehend how to get around. Give your customers MULTIPLE WAYS TO NAVIGATE (B1) so that each customer has a way that fits his or her previous Web experience.

There are two essential rules to navigation. First, people know that some things on a Web page can be clicked on. *Do not make them guess what is clickable and what is not.* Second, people know that when they click on something, an action will take place. *Make those actions clear and predictable.*

Provide a Cohesive and Logical Page Layout • A disorganized page layout can confuse site visitors. They need to be able to identify the most important objects to view immediately so that they know they're in the right place.

Create a homepage that makes it easy to understand what the Web site is about and where things are located. Implement a clean GRID LAYOUT (I1) in a PAGE TEMPLATE (D1) that organizes the entire page cohesively. Apply the CLEAR FIRST READS (I3) pattern. The **first read**, a concept from graphic design, is the single element that pulls the Web page together. Having a first read on your homepage helps give customers a place for their eyes to go first, and it provides a design focus for the page.

Place the most important navigation tools and content ABOVE THE FOLD (I2), making them visible so that the customer will not have to scroll down. People do not always realize that they can scroll down for more information, and they might miss out on things you want them to see right away if those things are below the fold.

Make the Homepage Download Quickly • You know all about this. You go to a new site, and it takes so long to load the homepage that you back out to another site.

Test your site to ensure that your homepage does not take more than a few seconds to download and appear in a browser. Here are some strategies for faster downloads:

- The images on your homepage are guaranteed to be the slowest the first time a visitor comes to your site because at that point the images are not cached yet. To combat this problem, take advantage of HTML POWER (L4) and use text as much as possible instead of graphics. HTML text is the first thing that downloads, so the visitor gets all the necessary text information without waiting for image downloads.

- People will tell you that HTML text is ugly. Make the best of it by working with a Web-savvy graphic artist who can move your site to the next design level. This professional can choose the right complementary font colors, background colors, and font styles and make an exciting and dynamic homepage design.
- Use FAST-DOWNLOADING IMAGES (L2) to improve the speed of your site. Crop, shrink, reduce colors, and increase compression to make images smaller and faster to download.
- Use SEPARATE TABLES (L3) for page layout instead of one large HTML table. The problem with using a single large table is that it forces customers to wait until all of the images are loaded before they can see anything. If you separate your Web page into multiple tables, people can see some parts of the page as it is loading.
- On the main homepage avoid slow-loading content such as sounds, splash screens, Flash animations, and Java applets. If you include features such as these, not only will you make your main homepage slower to load, but you will risk having it look like Figure C1.4 to visitors who do not have the latest technologies installed on their computers.

C1.4

Figure C1.4

Don't let this be your homepage. Unless there is an extremely compelling reason, keep Java applets, browser plug-ins, and other "bleeding-edge" technologies off of your main homepage.

✳ SOLUTION

On your homepage portal, establish and reinforce the value of your site with a strong, clearly stated promise that is fulfilled on every page of the site. Dedicate 95 percent of the area and links above the fold to the visitor groups that comprise 95 percent of the total visitor population. Keep the remaining area and links for visitor groups that make up the remaining 5 percent. Use additional links in the footer of the homepage to make explicit links for each group, including those in the 5 percent category. Build a homepage layout that provides strong cues to define navigation and content, and that downloads quickly. Test your homepage design to ensure that you have created the right look and feel—one that seduces visitors with content, regardless of whether it is personalized.

Figure C1.5

Sketch out strong first impressions of your homepage with compelling titles and logos, and simple navigation.

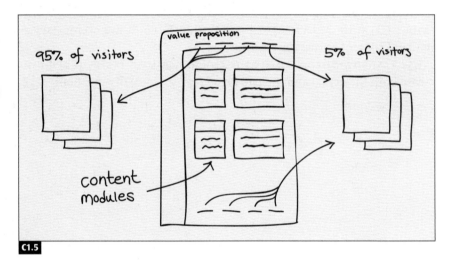

C1.5

❋ CONSIDER THESE OTHER PATTERNS

On the homepage, clearly state the site's UP-FRONT VALUE PROPOSITION (C2), show the SITE BRANDING (E1), and provide links to the site's PRIVACY POLICIES (E4).

C2 **E1**
E4

Use a publishing system to automatically update and rotate CONTENT MODULES (D2) on the homepage. A personalized homepage will contain CONTENT MODULES (D2) and use PERSONALIZED CONTENT (D4) to tailor the homepage to individuals.

D2
D2 **D4**

Make navigation easier by creating consistent MULTIPLE WAYS TO NAVIGATE (B1) and by establishing your navigation design on the homepage. Create BROWSABLE CONTENT (B2) and use NAVIGATION BARS (K2), OBVIOUS LINKS (K10), ACTION BUTTONS (K4), DESCRIPTIVE, LONGER LINK NAMES (K9), and EMBEDDED LINKS (K7).

B1
B2 **K2**
K10 **K4** **K9**
K7

Create an easy-to-read homepage using a PAGE TEMPLATE (D1) and GRID LAYOUT (I1) with CLEAR FIRST READS (I3). Put the most important navigation and content ABOVE THE FOLD (I2).

D1
I1 **I3**
I2

Use FAST-DOWNLOADING IMAGES (L2) and SEPARATE TABLES (L3) to increase both the actual and the perceived performance of your homepage.

L2 **L3**

Figure C2.1

Epicurious offers "The World's Greatest Recipe Collection." Epicurious's value proposition is reinforced by the images, navigation, and text on its homepage. (Epicurious.com © 2002 CondéNet. All rights reserved. Reprinted by permission.)

C2.1

(www.epicurious.com, February 6, 2002)

✳ BACKGROUND

C1 The HOMEPAGE PORTAL (C1) must communicate the purpose of the site immediately and clearly. This pattern describes how to come up with that message.

✳ PROBLEM

On many Web sites, people often cannot tell when they arrive what the company or site offers.

When customers come to your site for the first time and don't see a clear, persuasive promise about what your company or site has to offer, they must figure it out on their own. Sometimes they will leave the site right then and there because they cannot be bothered or they don't have time. Sometimes they surf around your site to find the answer, and sometimes they never do understand the site or company's full value, even if you have stated it on the homepage. This miscommunication can lead customers to undervalue your site or, worse, your entire company, in their critical first moments of using a site. Changing a customer's initial impression later can cost you substantial money and time because you will have to earn their trust in order to reeducate them.

Even if you get it right, a value proposition alone will not make a site valuable. You must fulfill your promise on every page and reinforce it offline through your business practices. A compelling value proposition, along with these other elements, will create a positive impression with customers. This in turn will build trust and goodwill that you can enhance and build on over time. This pattern focuses on offering you a proven way to articulate a powerful promise.

To get there, you will need to work through many ideas and iterations until you create the strongest statement possible. Our solution provides a framework to make this development easier.

Requirements • The homepage is an advertisement for the rest of the site. It must sell customers on continuing their journey to explore, use, possibly purchase, and return again and again. As David Ogilvy reveals in his book *Ogilvy on Advertising*, an advertisement is much more effective when it persuasively promises a unique benefit. Not only are customers more likely to read it, but they are more likely to purchase the product. For a Web site, that means visitors are more likely to explore and use your site.

Here's what you need (see Figure C2.2):

- A persuasive promise
- A unique offering
- Descriptive wording and images that are easily and quickly understood

Creating a persuasive and unique statement about what your company provides can be difficult without the right processes, people, and tools. To write and select the best promise, use creativity and brainstorming exercises to pull together an initial list of candidates. You can also use customer research to shape your promise; it has been proven to help select the most persuasive offer.

Exercise 1: Articulate the Value

Develop an initial list of value propositions. Invite everyone on the site design team to a brainstorming session, especially the most visionary, imaginative, and vocal members of the team. Seat everyone in a comfortable space that has a whiteboard on the wall. Ask this question: In ten

Figure C2.2

These value propositions quickly communicate the types of services the companies behind them offer. They speak broadly to the overall benefit, instead of one particular benefit, and they are easy to understand and quick to read. Read each and rate for yourself how persuasive and unique they are.

C2.2 (www.snapfish.com, February 11, 2002; www.techbargains.com, www.culturefinder.com, February 5, 2002)

words or less, what do we promise to our visitors that is persuasive and unique?

In a brainstorming session, no one passes judgment. Every statement is equally valuable, and no statement is wrong. Everything goes. Write down all suggestions, even if you do not like them, they are longer than your target number of words, or they are not as unique or persuasive as you would like. Continue for half an hour or more, if time permits. Then copy all the ideas on a piece of paper or onto a computer for later review (this is not the final step).

Exercise 2: Select the Strongest Candidates

Distribute the list developed in the brainstorming session to a core group of marketing and business visionaries on the site design team. Ask them to identify the ten most persuasively articulated value propositions that make a unique offer. Tell them to be prepared to defend their choices. Convene a meeting to choose the ten best promises. To determine the best, ask these questions: Is this promise consistent with our strategic direction? Is it persuasive? Is it unique? If not, why not? Can it be improved? This meeting could easily take longer than the initial brainstorming session, so limit the time to a couple of hours to make the process manageable.

Research Project 1: Have Customers Nominate the Best

Now turn to your customer base and ask a sample of 100 customers to participate in a research survey to rate each of the team's ten chosen value propositions (for an overview of customer research methods, see Appendix A—Running Usability Evaluations). Ask customers to rate the promises for *importance,* from not important at all (0) to very important (10); and for *uniqueness,* from not unique at all (0) to very unique (10). From the results, identify the value propositions that averaged a 7 or higher in both importance and uniqueness. If none of the value propositions rates this high, go back to Exercise 1 and start over.

Research Project 2: Have Customers Select the Top Value Proposition

Turn to your customer base one more time (coordinate this test with other research to reduce time and costs) and ask a sample of 100 customers to choose their top choice from the highly rated value propositions found in the previous test, again based on its importance and uniqueness. The winner is the one that most appeals to your customers. Congratulations! You've got your value proposition.

Integrate Your Value Proposition into the Site • Now develop some sample designs that emphasize this new value proposition. Think about the different ways you can get your message across to your customers in a quick, simple fashion (see Figure C2.3). Some other patterns that will help you are SITE BRANDING (E1) and CLEAR FIRST READS (I3).

C2.3

(www.ciena.com, July 2001)

Figure C2.3

These value propositions are integrated directly into the main logo and are some of the first things visitors will read. (The CIENA logo and the CIENA.com Web site have been reprinted with permission from CIENA Corporation. "CIENA" is a trademark or registered trademark of CIENA Corporation in the United States and other countries and is being used with the permission of CIENA Corporation.)

✳ SOLUTION

Your value proposition is a site advertisement that must persuasively articulate your company's uniqueness. Use team brainstorming to develop ideas, and refine the best ideas into a list of top ten candidates. To determine the very best value proposition, ask your customers to rate each promise on importance and uniqueness. Place the value proposition next to your homepage's logo for quick scanning and maximum exposure.

Figure C2.4

A customer's positive impression starts with a clear value proposition in the form of a persuasive and unique promise. By fulfilling the promise through a valuable Web site and trustworthy business practices, you can continue to build customer loyalty and word of mouth.

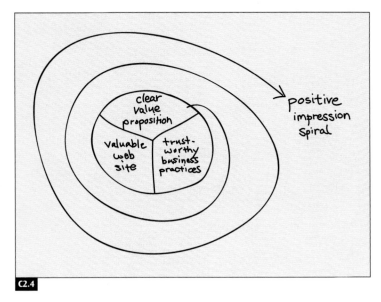

C2.4

✳ CONSIDER THESE OTHER PATTERNS

E1 Integrate your value proposition with your SITE BRANDING (E1), making it
I3 a CLEAR FIRST READ (I3).

Writing and Managing Content

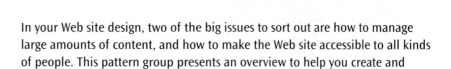

In your Web site design, two of the big issues to sort out are how to manage large amounts of content, and how to make the Web site accessible to all kinds of people. This pattern group presents an overview to help you create and manage your content effectively.

D1 PAGE TEMPLATES

D2 CONTENT MODULES

D3 HEADLINES AND BLURBS

D4 PERSONALIZED CONTENT

D5 MESSAGE BOARDS

D6 WRITING FOR SEARCH ENGINES

D7 INVERSE-PYRAMID WRITING STYLE

D8 PRINTABLE PAGES

D9 DISTINCTIVE HTML TITLES

D10 INTERNATIONALIZED AND LOCALIZED CONTENT

D1.1

(news.yahoo.com, October 29, 2001)

Figure D1.1

This page template from the Yahoo! News homepage targets its database content to specific locations on the page. (Reproduced with permission of Yahoo! © 2000 by Yahoo! Inc. YAHOO! and the YAHOO! logo are trademarks of Yahoo! Inc.)

✱ BACKGROUND

Many of the patterns in Pattern Group A—Site Genres are based on database content, which allows information to be published dynamically to the site without files having to be moved to the server. The result is a streamlined publishing process and enhanced productivity. Even if a site is not database driven, customers come to expect images and text to be in the same place when they are moving around a site or returning to a particular page. You can organize your information into BROWSABLE CONTENT (B2), with CATEGORY PAGES (B8) and content pages. Each of these pages requires a template to describe its content. This pattern provides the solution.

❋ PROBLEM

A site that is not consistent from page to page is difficult for customers to navigate and hard for site managers to maintain. However, it is challenging to design Web pages to be consistent because not all pages are the same, and many will need some way to be updated.

Your homepage implicitly establishes a pattern for layout and design of your entire Web site, and from then on customers expect to find key elements of the page in the same places on other pages. You can build a system that takes advantage of the HOMEPAGE PORTAL (C1) design by creating a family of page templates that all relate to one another but have their own variations.

Designing, editing, and publishing unique pages can be time-consuming and tedious. Even if content does not come from a database, a standard design benefits the site team by giving everyone a system to work within, and therefore less work. Often page designers are not the same people who write the content. Separating the design from the writing helps the process by letting each team focus on its strong suit. This pattern provides the solution that addresses the needs of the site team and the customers.

Build a Page Template by Using Grids • People read along vertical and horizontal lines. If you use implied lines on your page designs, as described in GRID LAYOUT (I1), customers can skim and read more quickly than when objects and text are not aligned. Help your visitors read more easily by using grids as the backbone of every template you build.

Define Global and Individual Page Templates • Keep your basic graphic design structure the same throughout your site. Customers remember where navigation tools and content appear from page to page, so keeping these places consistent will make the site easier to use. Create a page template by setting aside areas of every page for navigation, content, and CONSISTENT SIDEBARS OF RELATED CONTENT (I6) (see Figure D1.2). Each area needs rules about what to put in that space. The template becomes especially important when multiple teams are updating different parts of a site.

Global page templates describe the overall page structure and layout of every page on a Web site. This would include things like SITE BRANDING (E1), NAVIGATION BARS (K2), and SEARCH ACTION MODULES (J1). Individual page templates build on global page templates, describing specific types of pages. For example, you might have individual page templates for your CATEGORY PAGES (B8) (see Figure D1.3), CLEAN PRODUCT DETAIL (F2) pages, and news articles.

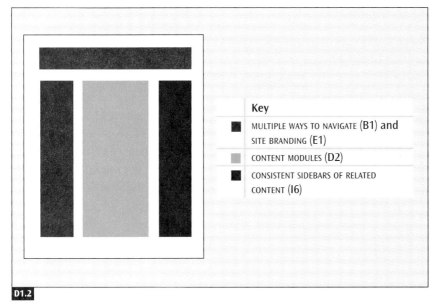

Key

■	MULTIPLE WAYS TO NAVIGATE (B1) and SITE BRANDING (E1)
▨	CONTENT MODULES (D2)
■	CONSISTENT SIDEBARS OF RELATED CONTENT (I6)

Figure D1.2

Page templates define areas for navigation, branding, content, and related links on every page.

Be consistent with how you adjust your layout-to-browser window resizing, using either EXPANDING-WIDTH SCREEN SIZE (I4) or FIXED-WIDTH SCREEN SIZE (I5). Key items must be ABOVE THE FOLD (I2), just as in the HOMEPAGE PORTAL (C1) pattern.

CONTENT MODULES (D2) will form the basis of new content in your templates. Either new content will appear as you publish it, or more sophisticated personalization will target special content to each customer. The page template is the skeleton that holds everything together, and the content modules are the muscles and flesh that bring life to a page.

Content modules also need to be part of the basic graphic design of the page. However, the length of a content module can range from a few lines to several pages because content modules can be retrieved dynamically from files or from a database. Because of the way HTML works, if one content module has too much information, it will become extremely long and lead to an unbalanced visual design.

Set standards for the length of the content or the length of every page. For text-based articles you can use multiple pages, which let you break up a long piece of writing into more readable chunks. If your site is supported by advertising, readable chunks of text broken into pieces across several pages will also provide more ad impressions. Also provide a method for customers to view all of the pages at once in a PRINTABLE PAGE (D8) so that it is easier for them to print if they want.

Figure D1.3

Amazon.com uses a global page template to maintain consistency across the entire site, and individual page templates to maintain consistency for categories of pages. The global page template is first designed to have the site branding, tab row, search action module, and sidebars appear in the same locations. Individual page templates are then created from the global page template. Both (a) and (b) show examples of category pages created from the same individual page template.

D1.3a

(www.amazon.com, October 15, 2001)

D1.3b

(www.amazon.com, October 15, 2001)

Figure D1.4

At Sun.com, the basic template remains the same in each section. Small variations address particular visitor needs, yet reinforce the overall design.

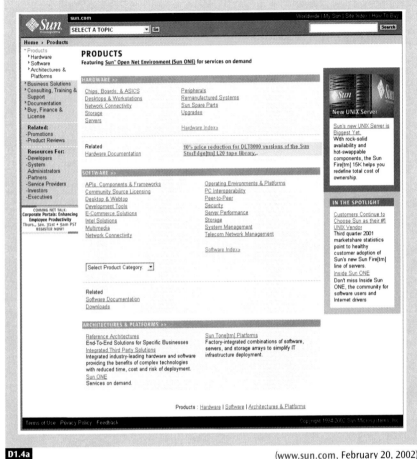

`D1.4a`

(www.sun.com, February 20, 2002)

Use Other Patterns to Build Templates • Different global and individual page templates will show some variation. The goal is to design for small multiples of differences, by creating templates that are basically the same but with small differences, to suit particular customer and business needs.

For example, Figure D1.4 shows two different pages from Sun's Web site. The pages are essentially the same in terms of color, layout, and navigation structure, but they are slightly different in terms of the NAVIGATION BAR (K2) and REUSABLE IMAGES (L5).

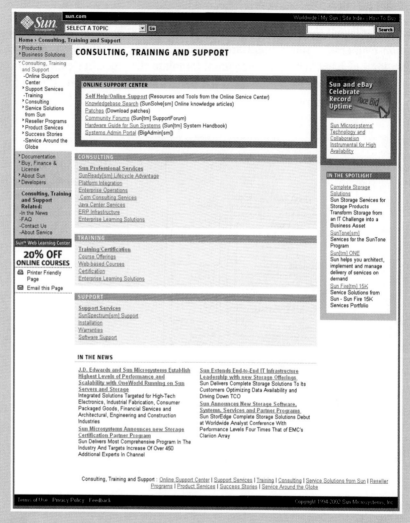

D1.4b

(www.sun.com, February 20, 2002)

✳ SOLUTION

Use a grid layout to help define a global template that includes the basic navigation elements, major content areas, and any areas for related content. For each kind of page, define an individual template that specifies content limits for images and text. Each individual template should use the global template as part of its structure.

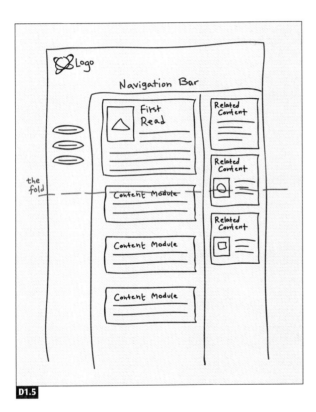

D1.5

Figure D1.5

Use a grid layout to align content modules in your templates.

✳ CONSIDER THESE OTHER PATTERNS

In the global page template, make the GRID LAYOUT (I1), as well as CLEAR FIRST READS (I3) and the NAVIGATION BAR (K2), consistent. Choose between EXPANDING-WIDTH SCREEN SIZE (I4) and FIXED-WIDTH SCREEN SIZE (I5). Employ templates that use REUSABLE IMAGES (L5), SEPARATE TABLES (L3), and a LOW NUMBER OF FILES (L1).

    Within each individual page template file, create section-specific CONTENT MODULES (D2), and use CONSISTENT SIDEBARS OF RELATED CONTENT (I6) and FAST-DOWNLOADING IMAGES (L2).

Figure D2.1

Content modules make it easy to update and display content. On the My Sun homepage, visitors can select which content modules they wish to display. Not all sites will need this level of personalization, though.

D2.1

(my.sun.com, November 15, 2001)

❋ BACKGROUND

In BROWSABLE CONTENT (B2) we provided a solution for finding content on a site, and in PAGE TEMPLATES (D1) we described how to present page elements in a consistent and easy-to-use manner. This pattern describes content modules, a key component of every page template and a way of managing the publishing process.

❄ PROBLEM

Without a good system, publishing and managing large volumes of content are time-consuming and error-prone processes.

When customers visit your site and find that the homepage is the same as it was a week ago, or maybe a month ago, they might say, "Nothing new here!" and leave. If you don't keep the site updated, it is probably not worth revisiting. Customers will find a better site, one that has the latest information. Fresh content keeps customers coming back.

You might be tempted to let your site go stale because updating and publishing information by hand is tedious, slow, and error prone. It takes time to create or acquire content, but the rest of the publishing process can take even longer for large Web sites. You have to recode a Web page, upload it, test it, revise it, and check it again, before finally publishing the final page. By the time the page is published, the news may no longer be news. Without a publishing system, updating a site is a time-consuming and error-prone process.

A publishing system can simplify the process if you're willing to plan ahead. You might build a simple publishing system from content files and then push the data from these files into your Web pages. A more robust and sophisticated system might store content in a database, have the data, such as the date, automatically trigger updates, and then push new content through. Either way, a publishing system can save large amounts of time.

When you create a publishing system, you will want to include content modules. These are the active areas on a page that change whenever new content comes online. Designing content modules into a site's pages makes updates quick and easy. Content modules and their component pieces deliver the power to integrate new content pages into an existing browsing structure. They can also be used to promote new related content, as well as to provide highly PERSONALIZED CONTENT (D4) tailored for each individual site visitor.

Define Where You Want to Position Content on a Page • Creating a PAGE TEMPLATE (D1) with content modules makes it easy to add new pages and plug in new content, saving you the trouble of trying to figure out how to lay out the document every time.

To give customers potentially useful information that is related to the current item, make space on the side for CONSISTENT SIDEBARS OF RELATED CONTENT (I6). These items can be directly related to the current article, or indirectly related through the current content category. Related links can also help keep customers engaged longer, clicking on related articles or products.

To hook visitors into related articles, use the headline from the related content and perhaps a short description or blurb to explain the content of the related article. These HEADLINES AND BLURBS (D3) entice customers to click through to the full article. Related links can be grouped by subject or by whether they are EXTERNAL LINKS (K8) to other Web sites. Or if there are only a few of them, related links can just be thrown together in no particular order.

Organize Content with Files or with a Content Database • Use a content database to publish content. This way you can avoid recoding each page on which content appears. The content database can use the file system or a real database. Different levels of engineering are required for each, but the net effect is the same. It all depends on the amount of content on your site and the kinds of features you want to provide to your customers. Smaller sites can use files to store articles, whereas more sophisticated and larger sites should use a database, especially if PERSONALIZED CONTENT (D4) is provided.

To create an article for a content module, define its content HEADLINES AND BLURBS (D3), body copy, reference information, byline, related content, related products, and related links (see Figures D2.2 and D2.3). These pieces can then be connected to a specific content module in a specific page, which reassembles the content on demand (see Figure D2.4).

Figure D2.2

Store this information in all your content files or content database records. Program your publication system to use the information to publish content pages and related links on other content pages.

Figure D2.3

Here's how information might look in a content file or record.

```
ArticleNumber:
Headline:
Blurb:
PubDate:
Author:
Copyright:
ContentHome:
ContentPosition:
NumPages:
PageTitle1:
Body1:
Image1:
PageTitle2:
Body2:
Image2:
PageTitle3:
Body3:
Image3:
RelatedArticles:
```
D2.2

```
ArticleNumber: 12345
Headline: For Whom Pacific Bell
Tolls
Blurb: Long derided for poor serv…
PubDate: 20010511
Author: Alexander Graham
Copyright: 2001 NewArch Media, Inc.
ContentHome: Utilities
ContentPosition: Middle
NumPages: 3
PageTitle1: Once for the Money
Body1: Ipso facto decorum unum…
Image1: http://www.newarch.com/img…
PageTitle2: Two for the Show
Body2: Ipso facto decorum unum…
Image2: http://www.newarch.com/img…
PageTitle3: Three to Get Ready
Body3: Ipso facto decorum unum…
Image3: http://www.newarch.com/img…
RelatedArticles: 56789, 98765
```
D2.3

D2.4

(my.yahoo.com, October 31, 2001)

Figure D2.4

My Yahoo! provides many types of content modules, including news, stocks, and weather. Weather always appears in a content module on the left, and news appears in the middle. Short headlines entice customers to click through to read more. (Reproduced with permission of Yahoo! © 2000 by Yahoo! Inc. YAHOO! and the YAHOO! logo are trademarks of Yahoo! Inc.)

Create an Administration Page • Building a content module publishing tool reduces the time and effort it takes to publish content. All you need is a Web-based form that includes all the content fields plus publication date and their location in the site. This form lets you publish faster and more often (see Figure D2.5).

Figure D2.5

eDealFinder.com helps people find special deals and coupons. These two administration pages show how new advertisements are added to the site (a) and how affiliate Web pages, logos, descriptions, search keywords, and so on are managed (b).

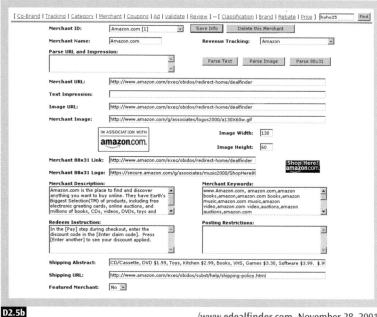

(www.edealfinder.com, November 28, 2001)

✳ SOLUTION

Define content locations in page templates. Organize all content into the file system or into a content database. Manage content from an administration page.

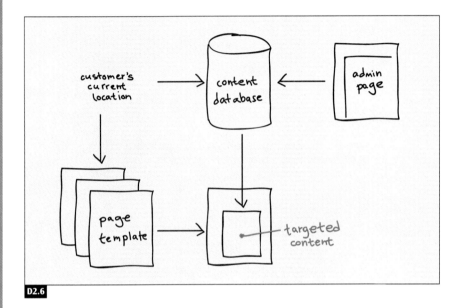

Figure D2.6

The customer's location in a site is used to target content to content modules in a page template.

✳ CONSIDER THESE OTHER PATTERNS

Define locations where content is targeted on each PAGE TEMPLATE (D1). These content modules can be articles, CONSISTENT SIDEBARS OF RELATED CONTENT (I6), or EXTERNAL LINKS (K8). Give visitors a hook into related articles by defining HEADLINES AND BLURBS (D3) for each piece of content, and put those HEADLINES AND BLURBS (D3) on related pages. Organize content in a content database, and use it to publish general visitor content, as well as PERSONALIZED CONTENT (D4) if personalization is part of the site.

Figure D3.1

The World News site uses database-driven headlines and blurbs to draw readers' attention to the full article on a page deeper in the site.

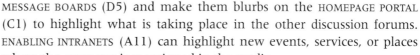

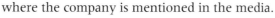

D3.1

(www.worldnews.com, October 31, 2001)

✳ BACKGROUND

For NEWS MOSAICS (A2), headlines and blurbs are critical ways to drive reader interest. COMMUNITY CONFERENCE (A3) sites can take excerpts from MESSAGE BOARDS (D5) and make them blurbs on the HOMEPAGE PORTAL (C1) to highlight what is taking place in the other discussion forums. ENABLING INTRANETS (A11) can highlight new events, services, or places where the company is mentioned in the media.

   In PAGE TEMPLATES (D1), we defined the structure of each page and how CONTENT MODULES (D2) can be used to publish new content. To draw people into these detailed pages, though, each piece of content needs a hook in the form of a headline. This pattern forms the core of the content hook.

✳ PROBLEM

Content pages need short, descriptive headlines and blurbs to hook customers into clicking for more content deeper on a site. These hooks also need to be published elsewhere on a site so that visitors will be able to see them.

On most sites, visible content is only the tip of the iceberg. A site's content cannot be revealed in its entirety on just one page. Finding all the content that is buried in a site is a challenge. Customers need MULTIPLE WAYS TO NAVIGATE (B1) to find their way around. In addition, from their experience with newspapers and magazines, people are accustomed to seeing headlines and blurbs to introduce every story when they scan for content.

In fact, headlines and introductory paragraphs provide tantalizing leads to pull visitors into the text. According to INVERSE-PYRAMID WRITING STYLE (D7), when an article's conclusion is put in its headline, and the main conclusions are put in the beginning paragraphs, the reader is pulled in to read more.

The style of writing a headline and a short introduction, with each piece hooking the reader further into the story, is what we call *headlines and blurbs.* Use blurbs to give customers a quick grasp of the content. These blurbs can consist of the first few lines of an article, placed on an opening page to tantalize readers about what lies ahead. Or they can be sentences that stand on their own and provide a complete thought.

The sections that follow present some guidelines for writing headlines and blurbs.

Write a Hook • For both headline and blurb, think about what makes the content *important, unique,* and *valuable* to the reader. Think about why visitors would want to read your content. Will they learn something new? Get a bargain? Have a good laugh? Meet people with the same hobbies? Look at your subject matter from the readers' perspective, and then write directly to the reader, with a promise of value.

Headlines and blurbs have a particular structure on Web pages. **Headlines** are typically a sentence fragment, roughly ten words or less so that they can appear in large type in a small space. A headline articulates the hook in the shortest form possible. The **blurb** is a continuation of the headline, providing details of the customer benefit, reinforcing what is important and unique about the content. Blurbs have to be short and precise, not more than one or two sentences.

Using a DISTINCTIVE HTML TITLE (D9) as the headline is possible if the title is descriptive enough. By employing the INVERSE-PYRAMID WRITING STYLE

(D7) (D7) when writing articles, you can pull a blurb from the first paragraph of the article, which is also the conclusion.

Try the following exercise: Write out three to five sets of headlines and blurbs and test them with your team and, if possible, with real customers. They will tell you if you have hit upon what's valuable to them. Continue shaping your message until you can succinctly articulate what customers find important and unique. Now you have created a reason for visitors to click through and experience more of your Web site. The final step is to formulate the hook as a finished headline and blurb.

Put Headlines and Blurbs in the Content Database • Writing one headline and blurb for each longer piece of text gives you the capability to place a reference to the text anywhere on your site, especially on the HOMEPAGE **(C1) (D1)** PORTAL (C1) and other PAGE TEMPLATES (D1). Referencing content on other pages becomes as simple as referencing the article number. The code on related pages looks up the article number and places the headline, blurb, and content link in the page. Figure D3.2 shows an example of how the content for a piece of text might be broken up into a database-compatible form.

Figure D3.2

A content file or record might show information in this way in a database.

```
ArticleNumber: 12345
Headline: For Whom Pacific Bell
Tolls
Blurb: Long derided for poor
customer service by its DSL
subscribers, Pacific Bell has
continued to over-commit on DSL
installations as it tries to beat
the cable industry in the broadband
Internet services business. So why
is Pacific Bell still a good
investment?
PubDate: 20010511
Author: Alexander Graham
Copyright: 2001 NewArch Media, Inc.
ContentHome: Utilities
...
```

D3.2

Put Headlines and Blurbs into Various Content Modules throughout the Site • To bring content to the fore, you must highlight it throughout the site, as headlines and as sidebars. Promote content pages using headlines and **(D2) (C1)** blurbs in CONTENT MODULES (D2) on the HOMEPAGE PORTAL (C1) (see Figure D3.3). Put headlines and blurbs in related content articles in CONSISTENT **(I6)** SIDEBARS OF RELATED CONTENT (I6) (see Figure D3.4).

If there are only a few headlines and blurbs, just use a CHRONOLOGICAL **(B6)** ORGANIZATION (B6). A chronological structure makes it easier to find what's new, on the basis of the date.

Figure D3.3

Giga Information Group highlights recent research results in a series of headlines and blurbs. In fact, this whole page is an enticement to go deeper into the site.

(www.gigaweb.com, October 28, 2001)

If there are lots of headlines, organize them by related topic. Newspapers, for example, have categories such as national news, local news, sports, and entertainment. Some companies have categories such as new products, company information, and a contact section. Within each section, use a CHRONOLOGICAL ORGANIZATION (B6).

B6

Figure D3.4

Lands' End promotes products on its Web site with headlines and blurbs in content modules, providing a way to highlight new products easily.

D3.4

(www.landsend.com, February 12, 2002)

✳ SOLUTION

Write a hook in the form of a headline and blurb that articulates why the content is important and unique to the visitor. Store these headlines and blurbs in the content database, along with the longer text, so that they can be targeted to content modules on different pages.

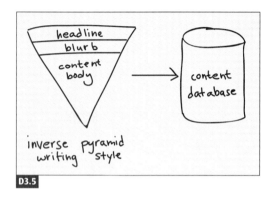

Figure D3.5

Use the inverse-pyramid writing style to write your headlines and blurbs.

✳ CONSIDER THESE OTHER PATTERNS

Use the headline you create for the content as the DISTINCTIVE HTML TITLE (D9) for the target page containing the longer text. You might also use the blurb as the first paragraph in an article, as part of the INVERSE-PYRAMID WRITING STYLE (D7). Put headlines and blurbs of related content in CONSISTENT SIDEBARS OF RELATED CONTENT (I6).

Figure D4.1

One of the first sites to personalize content for each visitor, My Yahoo! provides news, weather, stock quotes, e-mail, and many other customizable options. (Reproduced with permission of Yahoo! © 2000 by Yahoo! Inc. YAHOO! and the YAHOO! logo are trademarks of Yahoo! Inc.)

(my.yahoo.com, October 31, 2001)

✳ BACKGROUND

 PERSONAL E-COMMERCE (A1), NEWS MOSAICS (A2), and all the other site genres can benefit from personalized content. PAGE TEMPLATES (D1) provide the framework for CONTENT MODULES (D2) and HEADLINES AND BLURBS (D3), two of several mechanisms for displaying personalized content. This pattern provides the solution for personalizing content to individual visitors.

✳ PROBLEM

Personalized information can be more useful to people than generic informa-tion. However, engineering a dynamic site can produce less-than-satisfactory results if the basic structures and designs are not in place first.

Dynamic content targeting is a powerful way to provide individualized content. In contrast to a one-size-fits-all approach, dynamic content tar-geting gives customers a site tailored specifically to their needs. However, designing and implementing a system to manage all the content types for all customers can be daunting, requiring significant database and algo-rithm development. Yet it can also be of great value to customers, giving them another reason to return to your Web site. If done well, a dynamic, personalized site can be a significant competitive advantage. The frame-work we provide here, used in conjunction with other patterns in the book, makes personalization a more manageable development process.

This pattern describes two forms of dynamic content targeting. The first uses information that customers enter explicitly to dynamically create targeted content. We call this *intentional personalization*. The second form uses information about where visitors go and what they do on a site to target content to their needs. We call this *automatic personalization*. These approaches can be used separately or together.

By targeting content using the methods we describe, in conjunction with other content management techniques like PAGE TEMPLATES (D1) and CONTENT MODULES (D2), you can make personalized content an integral part of your site.

Create a Site with Intentional Personalization

Personalization gives customers the power and satisfaction of building their own environment. To make this possible, a site needs categorized and scored content. Using a targeting engine, you can target relevant content to each customer profile. See Figures D4.2 and D4.3 for examples before and after targeting is applied.

Or Create a Site That Requires Little Personalization Up Front • Visitors often do not know that they can personalize a site until after they have spent some time on it. If your site requires visitors to enter personal informa-tion before they are comfortable with the site, they will shy away alto-gether. Before you find out anything about your visitors, give them a sampling of what the site has to offer. For example, many e-commerce sites list top-selling FEATURED PRODUCTS (G1), thereby letting visitors know what other customers are purchasing.

Figure D4.2

Before targeting your content to people, categorize it and decide which profile format you will use for each customer. If visitors say they are interested in art, for example, the system will show them content that is categorized under the heading *Art*.

Figure D4.3

Once customers have completed their profiles, you can target content to each person, creating a personalized site.

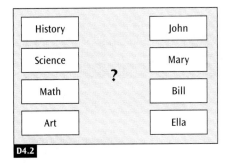

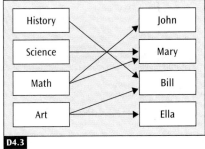

Figure D4.4 shows a more sophisticated example. My Yahoo! provides newcomers with basic content, such as stock prices and headline news. It also places a large notice in the center that tells people they can create personalized content whenever they want to.

The upshot of all this is this: Do not force people to personalize your site before they're ready because they may not want to spend the time if they cannot see what's in it for them.

Invite Visitors to Personalize • People need a simple and enticing offer that invites them to click through to the personalization menu. The invitation must be obvious and clear so that they cannot miss it. Entice them by giving them an idea of what they will be able to do once they personalize the

Figure D4.4

First-time visitors to My Yahoo! will see a simple page that offers basic content, as well as a note to let them know that they can personalize what they see. (Reproduced with permission of Yahoo! © 2000 by Yahoo! Inc. YAHOO! and the YAHOO! logo are trademarks of Yahoo! Inc.)

(my.yahoo.com, November 28, 2001)

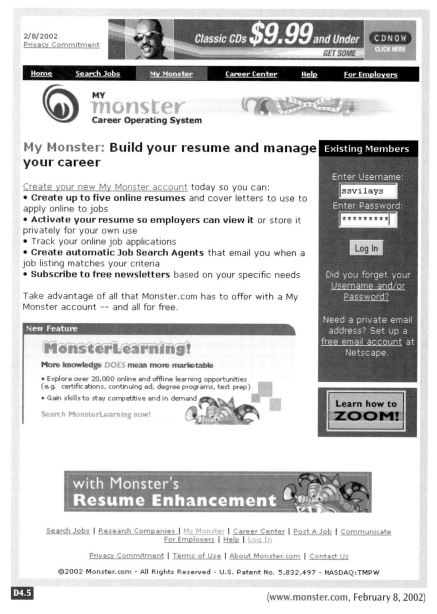

Figure D4.5

Monster.com makes clear the benefits people will get if they do the work it takes to personalize the site.

(www.monster.com, February 8, 2002)

site. For example, Figure D4.5 shows how Monster.com takes a different approach from that of Yahoo!. The site has little value for individual visitors until they go through the personalization process, so it tells them up front what the benefits will be. Lands' End invites people to personalize

Figure D4.6

Customers are invited to create a virtual model at this fun part of the Lands' End site. The model gives visitors a sophisticated and personalized shopping experience.

D4.6

(www.landsend.com, February 18, 2002)

its site by creating a fun and interactive experience with a virtual model (see Figure D4.6).

Categorize Content • Let customers choose the content they want to see on their personalized pages so that there is no ambiguity about what information interests them. Organize content by subject, date, or task, depending on how it is organized. Use the same information architecture designed for BROWSABLE CONTENT (B2) to lay out the options because this structure will make sense to customers and provide consistency with the information structure of the site. Keep in mind that not all content needs to be strictly related to one category in a site. For example, news about technology could be categorized under "news" or "technology."

B2

Use People's Background Information • If customers are willing to tell who they are, where they live, how old they are, what they have done in life, and/or what type of business they're in, you can use this information to make inferences about their interests. This level of detail can be much more enlightening and useful to you than the information gathered from their surfing habits. For example, you can provide a great deal of local information for visitors in the United States—such as weather, news, and traffic conditions—just on the basis of their ZIP codes (see Figure D4.7).

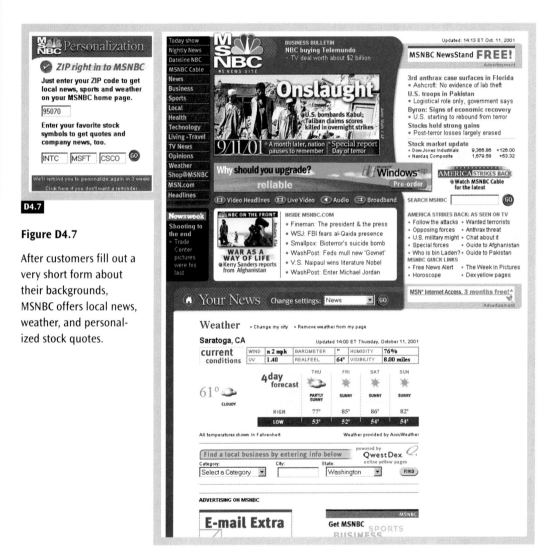

Figure D4.7

After customers fill out a very short form about their backgrounds, MSNBC offers local news, weather, and personalized stock quotes.

(www.msnbc.com, October 11, 2001)

Map Content to Each Visitor • Establish the fundamental selection criteria for how people receive personalized content. To map people's interests to content, devise a schema showing the relationships between the two. The schema can be as simple as a map between areas of a site and areas of expressed interest (see Figure D4.3). Or the schema can use a map of content zones and personality profile vectors (see Figure D4.8).

Create a Site with Automatic Personalization

With automatic personalization, people's interests are inferred on the basis of the actions they take, such as pages they visit, links they click on, and products they buy. Such inferences can lead to erroneous assumptions about visitors' interests, however, because people's intentions may be different from the actions they perform. For example, if a visitor looking for recipes mistakenly navigates to cooking classes, hoping to find links to recipes, her profile will indicate an interest in cooking classes, which may not be true.

Create a Scoring System • Devise a system that automatically matches the needs of the audience to the content you have available. The basic idea here is to divide customers into groups, on the basis of a shared characteristic, and to look for trends within those groups. The assumption is that because customers within a group are similar in one way, they may be similar in other ways. For example, if Victoria is placed in a group with 20 other people, 15 of whom really like the novel *The Scarlet Letter*, the odds are that she will like it too.

Figure D4.8

Another alternative is to make a schema based on a mapping algorithm that uses personality vectors and content regions. This example shows Bill is a beginner with computers, but more advanced in finance.

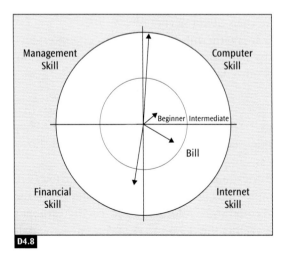

Use one or more of the following scoring methods to automatically divide customers into groups:

- **Rank.** An ordered list of how the students in a class ranked on an exam, for example.
- **Top rank.** A list of the top three scores only.
- **Threshold score.** A list of only those students who scored over 80 percent on the exam.
- **Required attributes.** A list of all students who answered a particular question correctly.

Here's how a scoring system would work. Say you offer 500 products on your site. Instead of making visitors sort through all 500 products to determine which one is best for them, you want to present only those that best fit their needs. If you have initially rated each product for speed, power, ease of use, and price, you can now have visitors score or rate these same criteria through a quick online interview. Store each customer's scores in a database. To determine which products to present to visitors, reference each customer profile by looking up the person's account using the account ID that you stored in that customer's cookie (cookies will be discussed shortly), and show only those products that meet the guest profile threshold scores.

Use Personalized Content-Matching Schemes

You can create personalized pages by matching a customer to the highest-rated content in an area and by pushing the content to CONTENT MODULES (D2) in PAGE TEMPLATES (D1). Include a list of all the related content by publishing links to CONSISTENT SIDEBARS OF RELATED CONTENT (I6) so that visitors can browse and make their own selections.

Here are four techniques for gathering information: edit, interview, deduce, and filter. The first two are forms of intentional personalization, and the last two are forms of automatic personalization.

1. **Edit.** Visitors click on buttons to make selections. They edit and configure each CONTENT MODULE (D2) area, choosing which modules they most desire. For an example, see the top of Figure D4.4, which shows My Yahoo!'s editing process.
2. **Interview.** Visitors answer questions by clicking on multiple choices in an interview. For an example, see Figure D4.6, a screen shot from the virtual model at landsend.com. Store information in each customer's database profile, and offer visitors the option to continue the personalization process over time.

3. **Deduce.** "Watch" visitors' behavior preferences, record them, and offer them personalized results later. Amazon.com tracks the products that visitors order, for example, and later offers them a list of PERSONALIZED RECOMMENDATIONS (G3) of similar or related products they might like to buy. Store this kind of information in each customer's database profile.

4. **Filter.** Build a list of customer preferences and display the recommended items to visitors. Amazon.com does this when it tracks the books that all its readers buy most and displays them as FEATURED PRODUCTS (G1). Provide CONTENT MODULES (D2) based on similar customer profiles. To determine areas of interest, analyze the correlation of all the guest profiles. This is also known as collaborative filtering.

Employ these techniques singly or in combination. By providing initial personalization from filtering, customers do not need to enter any special information up front. Over time, implicit and explicit information voluntarily offered by a customer can be added, allowing you to target customer needs more directly.

Use Predefined Content Locations • Follow the pattern of CONTENT MODULES (D2) to display content in predefined areas on each page. This way you can code each page in a uniform template.

Track Customer Visits and History with Cookies • Use cookies to track and remember what visitors found valuable on your site. A **cookie** is a way of storing uniquely identifying information in a customer's computer. A site can store anything in a visitor's cookie: an account ID, user name, even historical information, like the number of times each customer visits a different area of the site. For security reasons, the cookie is accessible only by the site that created it. What makes cookies especially useful is that they enable a site to remember visitors automatically when they come back. Cookies are discussed in greater detail in PERSISTENT CUSTOMER SESSIONS (H5).

If you want to use cookies, make sure you offer a way to let people move from machine to machine, such as from home to office. Create a personalization recovery scheme, in case the cookie is deleted, by providing ACCOUNT MANAGEMENT (H4) tools for customers to create and manage their user name and password.

There are also several legal and privacy issues with respect to cookies and to the kinds of information that may and may not be collected about

minors under a certain age. See FAIR INFORMATION PRACTICES (E3) and
PRIVACY POLICY (E4) for more details.

E3
E4

✳ SOLUTION

It is best not to force people to personalize your site before they can use it.
Draw customers in by providing basic but valuable content to new customers
that, later, can be personalized. Next invite customers to personalize the site
from a menu of options, using information that can be gathered quickly, such
as their backgrounds and areas of interest. Gather this information by conducting interviews or by giving people the ability to edit their interests. Deduce
what other things might interest your customers by tracking the areas of your
site that they visit and scoring the information. Categorize the content and map
it to the people who find such content useful. Structure the site into page templates and content modules that receive content from the targeting engine.

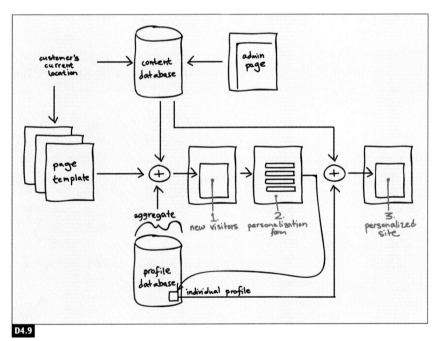

Figure D4.9

A personalized site
uses page templates
and customer infor-
mation to target con-
tent modules.

✳ CONSIDER THESE OTHER PATTERNS

(D1) (D2)
(I6)
Target content to PAGE TEMPLATES (D1), CONTENT MODULES (D2), and CON-
SISTENT SIDEBARS OF RELATED CONTENT (I6) from information in each cus-
tomer's database profile. Use the same information architecture designed
(B2)
for BROWSABLE CONTENT (B2) to lay out the options consistently with
(H4)
other pages. Provide ACCOUNT MANAGEMENT (H4) tools to let people see
and edit their profile data.

(E3) (E4)
FAIR INFORMATION PRACTICES (E3) and PRIVACY POLICY (E4) describe several legal issues that must be addressed when data about individuals is
collected and stored.

(G3)
PERSONALIZED RECOMMENDATIONS (G3) are one form of personalized
content tailored specifically for e-commerce.

Figure D5.1

Craigslist provides a broad spectrum of message board topics and organizes them into hierarchical categories.

D5.1

(www.craigslist.org, August 26, 2001)

✴ BACKGROUND

Used by COMMUNITY CONFERENCE (A3), NONPROFITS AS NETWORKS OF HELP (A5), and EDUCATIONAL FORUMS (A8), message boards are a tested way for people to communicate with one another. Whereas these site genres provide the framework for building respectful communities, this pattern forms the core of posting and storing messages on message boards. This pattern can also be applied to e-commerce through RECOMMENDATION COMMUNITIES (G3).

A3
A5 **A8**

G3

✳ PROBLEM

Message boards can engage customers if they are easy to find and use. But managing boards to keep them from becoming unruly requires administrative tools and manual labor.

Giving people the ability to communicate directly with one another is one of the great benefits of online communication. People can carry on conversations with communities around the clock and around the world. If customers can find their favorite boards time and again, and use them with ease, the communities that form around these message boards can grow.

If your target visitors want anonymity, you can choose to let them use your message board without revealing their complete names and personal information. Even without complete anonymity, however, some people might act irresponsibly. To prepare, you must build in systems to ensure that your boards do not become overrun with off-topic, off-color, and perhaps even illegal conversations.

Some communities have no anonymity because administrators know that if a name is attached to a message, the person is likely to act more responsibly when posting. Other communities have rules that visitors cannot have complete anonymity. These kinds of rules are important because in cases of criminal activity such as fraud, libel or corruption, law enforcement officials must be able to investigate. This requirement forces site administrators to track more information about people who post, and **E4** it potentially changes the site's PRIVACY POLICY (E4).

You should start with one or two message boards, but eventually you will add more as your community grows. It's best to start simple, but keep the potential for expansion in mind when you're designing message boards.

Decide Whether to Make Your Board Moderated or Unmoderated • On moderated message boards, a site administrator filters messages before they are posted to make sure that everyone is conforming to the rules of the community. On unmoderated message boards, if one person posts a message and another visitor complains, the administrator can choose to remove the message, but otherwise it's a no-holds-barred, free-for-all forum where anything goes.

Moderated boards can be kept organized and on topic, but they require more administrative work and they can slow down conversations. Although unmoderated boards offer freedom and speed, they are also more unruly, and certain individuals can sidetrack or dominate conversations.

Both kinds of boards must be monitored at some level, either by customers who call other customers on their behavior, or by site management.

Both kinds of boards require tools to delete messages, but only moderated boards require tools to review posts before they appear on the site.

Make It Easy to Find Your Message Boards • People need to find your message boards to take advantage of them. If you put the boards in a separate area from the rest of the related content on the site, they become harder to find. Also people want to return to the boards they are most interested in and see replies to posts they have written.

Build a UNIFIED BROWSING HIERARCHY (K1) to include content, commerce, and community message boards, and link content through CONSISTENT SIDEBARS OF RELATED CONTENT (I6) to give customers MULTIPLE WAYS TO NAVIGATE (B1).

K1

I6

B1

Store your visitors' lists of favorite boards, and let them edit those lists through an ACCOUNT MANAGEMENT (H4) page so that it is easier for them to find the message boards they visited before (see Figure D5.2). This feature requires customers to sign in with SIGN-IN/NEW ACCOUNT (H2) before saving a favorites list. At a minimum, add LOCATION BREAD CRUMBS (K6) on pages and give them DISTINCTIVE HTML TITLES (D9) so that people can bookmark them in their list of favorites.

H4

H2
K6
D9

Once inside a message board, customers might want to search for keywords, scan the latest messages, follow the thread of one conversation, or scan posts by authors they like. A SEARCH ACTION MODULE (J1) that

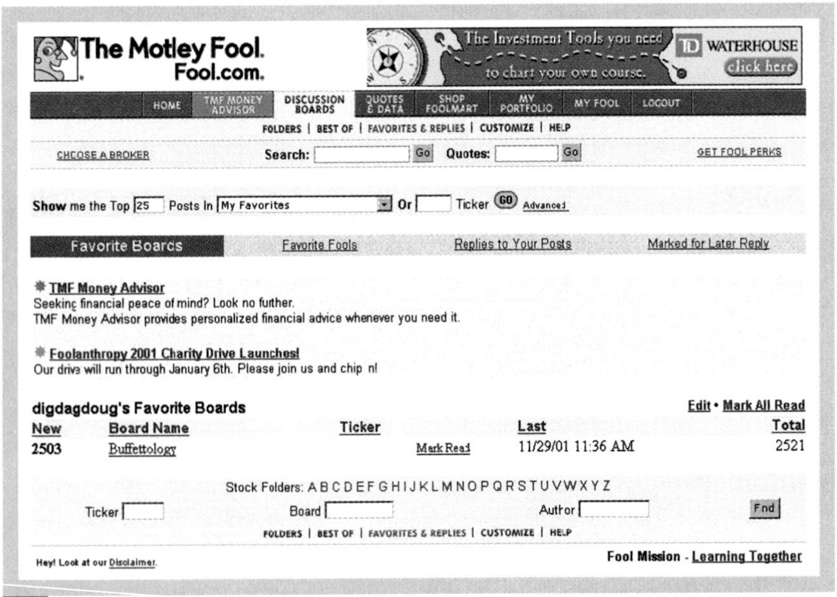

J1

Figure D5.2

The Motley Fool gives customers the ability to save a list of favorite message boards for the next time they sign in.

D5.2

(www.fool.com, November 29, 2001)

searches the posts gives customers consistent access to keyword search capability, while a filter that supplies a CHRONOLOGICAL ORGANIZATION (B6) makes it easy to look for the latest messages. A POPULARITY-BASED ORGANIZATION (B7) scheme can also be used to let visitors know which posts were most read or most highly rated by other visitors.

Unlike an unthreaded view (see Figure D5.3), a threaded view lets people follow conversations very quickly (see Figure D5.4). On the other hand, a column sort that provides ALPHABETICAL ORGANIZATION (B5) of page contents provides quick access by author.

Figure D5.3

The Motley Fool site provides the ability to search, filter by date, view each thread, and sort alphabetically. This screen shot shows an unthreaded view.

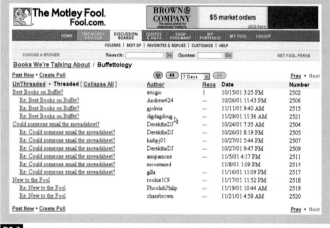

(www.fool.com, November 28, 2001)

Figure D5.4

This screen shot shows a threaded view of the same message board that is shown in Figure D5.3.

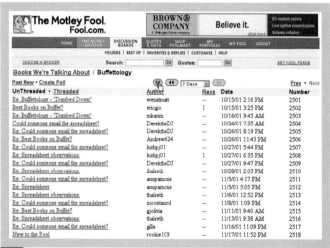

(www.fool.com, November 28, 2001)

Require Newcomers to Sign In after Reading Posts • Some sites let newcomers read message boards without going through SIGN-IN/NEW ACCOUNT (H2), but newcomers cannot post until they have registered. This approach lets people see what a community is like before joining it. Once a visitor has decided to become a community member, offer him or her PERSONALIZED CONTENT (D4), in the form of favorite message boards and favorite community members.

Other sites require newcomers to go through SIGN-IN/NEW ACCOUNT (H2) before they can even read any posts, thereby ensuring that only reg- istered community members can read and post messages. However, this approach will turn off people who do not like to create an account before they can see what the message boards offer.

In stricter communities where true identity is important, or where content is of an adult nature, you may want to ask for a credit card number to validate a customer's identity and age.

Present Clear Rules • Each site must establish rules of behavior for its message boards. Customers will not want to waste their time writing posts that won't be accepted or must be removed. If customers are malicious, the rules might dissuade them from posting at all, making site management easier.

The first area to address is a site's FAIR INFORMATION PRACTICES (E3). What kind of information is collected about community members? For what purposes? For how long? And are there any legal requirements, such as content that cannot be viewed by international audiences or by minors? This kind of information needs to be made clear through the site's PRIVACY POLICY (E4).

To help visitors remember specific rules, present the rules before they post a message. Use a POP-UP WINDOW (H6) or put the rules directly on the page (see Figure D5.5). Specifically, message board rules must address the following:

- Whether the site is moderated
- The fact that your site will terminate site privileges and possibly pursue legal action against people who post copyrighted, hateful, threatening, illegal, racist, or other undesirable information, such as spam
- Whether the site allows hyperlinks in messages
- Whether the site allows images in messages
- How long posts are retained
- Whether people can delete their posts

Figure D5.5

Yahoo! News makes its message board rules clear right on the posting page. (Reproduced with permission of Yahoo! © 2000 by Yahoo! Inc. YAHOO! and the YAHOO! logo are trademarks of Yahoo! Inc.)

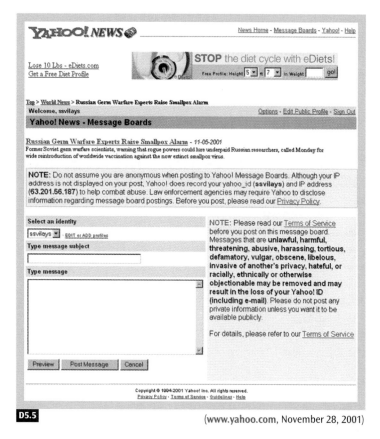

D5.5

(**www.yahoo.com**, November 28, 2001)

Make Posting Painless • People can create new messages or reply to a current message. Place ACTION BUTTONS (K4) that lead customers to these two options on every message, to let them continue conversations. Also provide just the **New Message** ACTION BUTTON (K4) in strategically placed locations to let community members start new conversations.

Place the message to which visitors are replying on the same page where they are composing their new message because they may be responding to one or several points. Create a form so that customers can edit their messages. Customers creating new messages need fields, one for the title and one for the body. When replying to a message, automatically create the title on the basis of the original message by using the term *re*, as in "Re: What is the best book to buy on cooking pasta?" Community members can change the title if they want to. Also be sure to have a **Submit Message** ACTION BUTTON (K4) at the bottom of the form.

A preview capability helps customers visualize what their messages will look like to others. If the site allows images or HTML in posts, the preview capability is an essential function to help people verify the links and look of their posts. Create a **Preview Message** or a **Preview Reply** ACTION BUTTON (K4) below the form (see Figure D5.6).

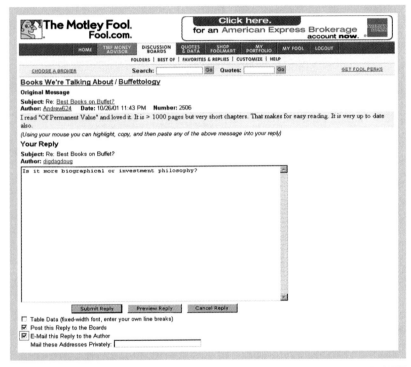

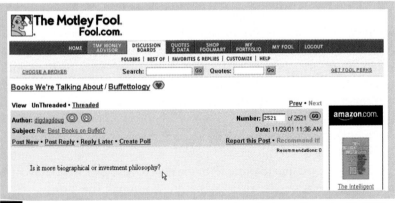

D5.6   (www.fool.com, November 29, 2001)

Figure D5.6

The Motley Fool has a straightforward interface for entering new posts and replies, and it lets customers e-mail replies directly to the original poster, making it much easier for the original poster to respond.

Create an Administrative Back End • On moderated boards an administrator must review all new posts. This interface provides the ability to preview each post and accept or reject it. Create a CHRONOLOGICAL ORGANIZATION (B6) of posts that takes an administrator to a preview page, with ACTION BUTTONS (K4) for accepting posts that follow community standards and rejecting posts that violate any rules.

For all boards, administrators need the ability to remove posts, and to remove access for customers who violate the rules. The administrator's view of the message boards, accessed through a special SIGN-IN/NEW ACCOUNT (H2), gives him or her the capability to click a **Remove Post** ACTION BUTTON (K4) on the post pages and remove undesirable content.

❋ SOLUTION

To make message boards easy to find and use, build them into your navigation hierarchy and link to the boards from related content. Provide the means for people to save their favorite boards in their customer profile, and save board links in the browser favorites. Let visitors search for keywords in posts, filter posts by date, view threaded and unthreaded conversations, and sort posts by the name of the person posting. Give people the ability to read posts before signing in or registering. Make sure they know the board rules so that they are not surprised if their messages are removed. Provide a simple form to post a new message or a reply. Enable administrators to approve or reject posts before posting if the site is moderated, and give them the ability to remove messages on both moderated and unmoderated boards.

Figure D5.7

Build your message boards into your navigation hierarchy, and provide a simple way for people to reply to posts.

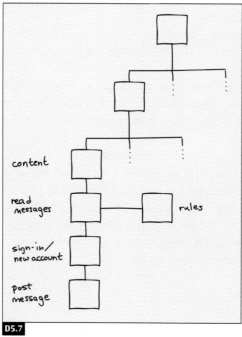

✳ CONSIDER THESE OTHER PATTERNS

Build message boards into your UNIFIED BROWSING HIERARCHY (K1) and
link to content through CONSISTENT SIDEBARS OF RELATED CONTENT (I6), giving customers MULTIPLE WAYS TO NAVIGATE (B1). Message boards can also
form the basis for RECOMMENDATION COMMUNITIES (G4) on e-commerce
sites.

Store customers' lists of favorite boards in their database profiles, and
let them edit their profiles through ACCOUNT MANAGEMENT (H4). These
features require customers to go through the SIGN-IN/NEW ACCOUNT (H2)
process. At a minimum, provide LOCATION BREAD CRUMBS (K6) on pages
and give pages DISTINCTIVE HTML TITLES (D9) so that people can save them
in their browser favorites.

Provide a SEARCH ACTION MODULE (J1) on every page so that people can
search for keywords in posts. Allow people to filter posts through a
CHRONOLOGICAL ORGANIZATION (B6) so that they can see the latest messages. Provide an ALPHABETICAL ORGANIZATION (B5) of page contents to
give people quick access to authors they like, and a POPULARITY-BASED
ORGANIZATION (B7) to see what others liked.

Require people to sign in with SIGN-IN/NEW ACCOUNT (H2) before posting new messages. Verifying that people are signed in requires checking
before each post, and before the selection of any PERSONALIZED CONTENT
(D4), such as favorite message boards.

Address message board FAIR INFORMATION PRACTICES (E3) and community rules in a site's PRIVACY POLICY (E4), in a POP-UP WINDOW (H6), or
directly on the post message page.

Give people **Reply to Message** and **New Message** ACTION BUTTONS
(K4) on existing posts, and a **New Message** ACTION BUTTON (K4) on every
page. Create a **Submit Message** ACTION BUTTON (K4) at the bottom of the
post message form.

For moderated message boards, give board administrators a CHRONO-
LOGICAL ORGANIZATION (B6) of posts that takes them to a post preview
page with ACTION BUTTONS (K4) for accepting and rejecting posts.

For all board administrators, provide a view of the message boards,
accessed through a special SIGN-IN/NEW ACCOUNT (H2), that gives administrators the capability to remove undesirable content by clicking a **Remove Post** ACTION BUTTON (K4) on the post pages.

Figure D6.1

E-LOAN keeps most of its keyword-filled content high on the homepage, which helps it score high on search engine rankings.

D6.1

(www.eloan.com, November 2001)

✳ BACKGROUND

When searching the Internet, or an intranet, people cannot find your site if it appears too many pages away from the front of the search results list. Your site needs as high a ranking as possible on the list so that customers can find it quickly and regularly. The writing on a site becomes critical for a high listing because most search engines index words to build a database of search results. This pattern provides the solution for writing pages that will be highly ranked by search engines.

✳ PROBLEM

It is difficult to find a site on a list of search engine results if it is too far down the list. Making a site appear toward the top of any search requires writing site content in customized ways.

Search engines are one of the primary tools people use to find sites,[1] just as they are one of the most popular ways people find pages within a site. But one of the biggest problems people face on search engines is that they have to wade through page after page of results to find a site that meets their needs. Because your potential visitors start at the top of the first page and read down, your site needs to be near the top of the first page of search results, before readers lose interest or find your competitors.

Some search engines rank sites purely on their relevance to searchers' keywords, and each search engine has its own way of calculating relevance. Other search engines rank sites that have paid for top listings first, but they also list all other sites with relevant results. Understanding how relevance is ranked on various search engines is the key to building a site that returns high rankings because rankings are built from the content of sites. This pattern provides the solution for writing content that ranks sites higher and is clicked on more frequently in search result pages.

Remember That Search Engines Crawl and Index Web Sites • Search engines have such a vast and widespread index of the Internet (or an intranet) because half of their job is to crawl every page they can find and index every distinctive word. These programs, called **crawlers** or **spiders**, start from a list of a few sites, and go from link to link, opening pages and indexing the words on those pages. The other half of a search engine's job is to generate results for every search query, whether a query consists of one word or many.

Some search engines calculate relevance scores on the basis of the frequency of word occurrences in a page or site; others rank sites on the basis of their importance. Either way, the words and content on your site (see Figure D6.2) must match the keywords that searchers use when they type in the search form. And the results that search engines display depend on the words and content of your pages as well.

---

1 According to information gathered from the Media Metrix U.S. Top 50 ranking for Web sites (www.jmm.com/xp/jmm/press/mediaMetrixTop50.xml), search engines consistently ranked as the most popular sites on the Web from May 2000 through November 2001.

Figure D6.2

CancerNet uses key-words in the body of its homepage to help improve its search engine rankings.

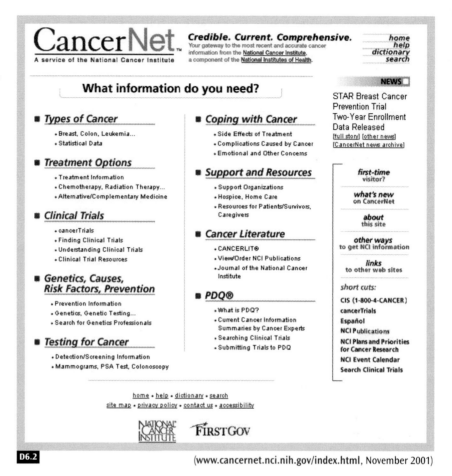

(www.cancernet.nci.nih.gov/index.html, November 2001)

Strategies That Work

Here are the content writing strategies we use to improve site rankings and make search results easier to use overall.

Write Distinctive Titles for Every Page • DISTINCTIVE HTML TITLES (D9) are important to search engines for two reasons. First, many search engines rank Web pages higher if one of the search terms is in the title. Second, search engine designers often make HTML titles the leading description for each search hit in the ORGANIZED SEARCH RESULTS (J3) page. If a page does not have an HTML title, the search engine will have to fall back on the **anchor text** for a link—namely, the hypertext label used to link to the page—or in the worst case, the URL of the Web page, as the title of a search result.

Write Keyword-Filled Descriptive Text near the Top of Each Page • Some search engines give text near the top of a page more weight than text near the bottom. If you place your site's most often used keywords ABOVE THE FOLD (I2), search engines are sure to include those words as part of a site's index. Simply put, **keywords** are significant and descriptive words that describe the content and services offered by a site. For example, a site designed for parents might have keywords like *parents, parenting, children, baby, babies, adoption, family,* and *marriage.*

Write keyword-filled descriptive text so that the customer's search results include the keywords in context and so that the links from the search engine to the site will make sense to the customer (see Figure D6.3).

Use META Tags • Most search engines recognize keyword **META tags.** These are markers in files that indicate to software applications, including search engine crawlers, what a site and page contain. Use keyword META

⑫

D6.3

(www.yahoo.com, November 2001)

Figure D6.3

To help customers scan for the most relevant site, Yahoo!'s search results include each keyword as it is used in context on each site. Including keywords in context is one of the most important strategies for improving site rankings and click-through. (Reproduced with permission of Yahoo! © 2000 by Yahoo! Inc. YAHOO! and the YAHOO! logo are trademarks of Yahoo! Inc.)

tags on all pages to provide additional keywords not included in the text, including synonyms, phrases, and language translations. A keyword META tag looks like this:

```
<HTML>
<HEAD>
        <TITLE>Acme Corporation - Homepage</TITLE>
        <META name="keywords" content="best widgets available,
        gadgets, electronics, machinery">
</HEAD>
```

Strong content for META tags includes the following:

- Terms that customers use most frequently (found in the log of a site's own search engine requests)
- Main site themes
- Synonyms
- Common misspellings
- Foreign-language translations of keywords if your site's audience is international

Make Your Site Accessible to Web Crawlers • People who have impaired vision are some of the best customers of the Internet, and they often use text-only browsers and text-to-speech converters to navigate through Web sites. However, many SITE ACCESSIBILITY (B9) barriers make it difficult for them to enjoy a Web site as much as people with normal vision do.

Interestingly, the same kinds of barriers that stop people with impaired vision also stop Web crawlers. You can address both issues at the same time by making sure that there is always at least one full version of content in a form that people with visual impairments can read. Label pictures clearly with ALT text to explain what a person with normal vision would see. Also be sure to have text versions of multimedia files, such as images, image maps, movie files, sound files, and Flash presentations.

Finally, be judicious with frames. Many Web crawlers are easily confused by frames, and some crawlers avoid framed pages altogether. Having a PRINTABLE PAGE (D8) version of content helps here.

Specify in a Robots File the Content You Do Not Want Crawled • The robots exclusion standard is a convention used by search engines, telling a crawler what it can and cannot crawl. It is a file called *robots.txt* that can be found off the root of a site. For example, the robots file for *The New York Times* can be found at www.nytimes.com/robots.txt.

The robots file is a convenient way of telling crawlers to avoid database-backed pages, pages that are likely to change quickly, pages that require sign-in through SIGN-IN/NEW ACCOUNT (H2), and multimedia files. Do not use the robots.txt file to specify the location of confidential information because anybody can look at the robots.txt file. For a humorous example, check out www.sun.com/robots.txt.

H2

Counterproductive Strategies

Writing for search engines is a black art. Most search engines closely guard the secret of their relevance-ranking algorithm because of competition from other search engines and because of deceptive tricks used by some site developers. One such trick is to add popular but nonrepresentative search keywords, such as *sex* and *MP3,* to drive traffic to the site. The logic is that such a Web site will be more likely to appear in search results because so many people search for these keywords, even though the Web site has nothing to do with sex or MP3s.

Another trick is to present one set of fake pages for search engines while presenting another for site visitors. In other words, the search engine crawler indexes a page that does not actually contain any of the content it says it does.

We consider many of these schemes for improving rankings in search engines unethical. Furthermore, the managers who run search engine services are constantly watching out for these kinds of behavior. In fact, some of these strategies may decrease a site's ranking because the search engine algorithms may think that the site is cheating. Here's our list of search engine strategies to avoid:

- Repeated keywords
- Keywords that do not describe the content of the site
- Keywords owned by other sites
- Colored text that is the same color as the background, used to hide words that are not really content on the site or to repeat keywords
- Repeated URL submissions to search engines
- Fake pages for search engines

There are also nonmalicious design choices that may adversely affect search engine ratings. These include the following:

- Slow connections that take too long to download pages
- Pages with the same HTML title
- Pages with the same content but different URLs

- A META refresh tag that repeatedly loads a page
- Content hidden in CGI (Common Gateway Interface), Java, or JavaScript

- Content hidden behind SIGN-IN/NEW ACCOUNT (H2) forms
- Content hidden within databases, behind SEARCH ACTION MODULES (J1)
- Content believed to be dynamically generated, such as Active Server Pages (ASP) and JavaServer Pages (JSP) or pages that have URLs with special characters, such as & and %
- Content from disreputable Internet service providers (ISPs) known to host pornographic Web sites or to send unwanted spam

❋ SOLUTION

Begin by writing distinctive HTML titles for every page because they are used as the page title in search results and sometimes search engines rank pages higher if search terms are contained in titles. Use keywords, those you would use most frequently to describe the site's purpose and offering to customers, at the top of each page and in the body of the text. Include descriptive META tags representative of the content contained in each page. Make your site accessible to people with impaired vision because doing so also helps search engines. Avoid rigging the system with bogus keywords and text—an approach that is often counterproductive.

Figure D6.4

Use the page title, keywords, and descriptive text in your Web pages to help ensure high rankings in Web search results.

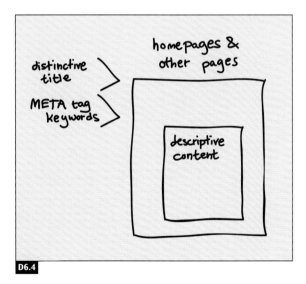

✳ CONSIDER THESE OTHER PATTERNS

DISTINCTIVE HTML TITLES (D9) are important to search engines because programmers often use HTML titles as the leading description for each search hit in the ORGANIZED SEARCH RESULTS (J3) page, and because they are often favorably weighted if they contain search keywords. If you include the most often used keywords about the category of service your site provides ABOVE THE FOLD (I2), search engines are sure to include those words. Make your site accessible. SITE ACCESSIBILITY (B9) also helps search engines by making the nontextual content textual, such as by giving images ALT text descriptions. When these descriptions contain keywords, they become part of a search engine's index.

Figure D7.1

A concise yet descriptive headline, an engaging blurb, and simple, clear writing make the first paragraphs on the Yahoo! Internet Life site a prime example of the inverse-pyramid writing style. (Reproduced with permission of Yahoo! © 2000 by Yahoo! Inc. YAHOO! and the YAHOO! logo are trademarks of Yahoo! Inc.)

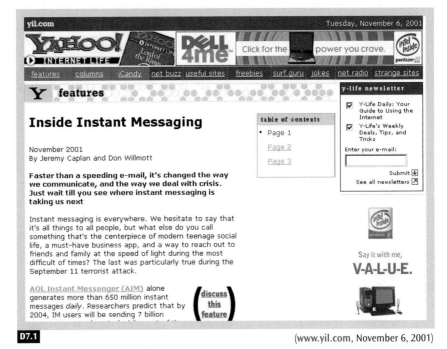

D7.1

(www.yil.com, November 6, 2001)

✳ BACKGROUND

Whether you write text based on MULTIPLE WAYS TO NAVIGATE (B1), by HIERARCHICAL ORGANIZATION (B3), as BROWSABLE CONTENT (B2), or for better SITE ACCESSIBILITY (B9), there is no escaping the written word on the Web. This pattern forms the core for all site writing.

✳ PROBLEM

People move about quickly on the Web, skimming for information or key words. If a site's writing is not quick and easy to grasp, it is usually not read.

Your customers want Web pages to be fast to download, easy to use, and quick to skim. They do not want to wade through self-promoting propaganda or scroll through pages of text to get to the point. Although customers will be more tolerant if they know of no alternative site, you cannot count on their good nature. If a page does not deliver, your visitors will be gone in a single click.

Often customers find a lot to read on sites, but all this text can be tedious for people who are skimming or looking for specific pieces of information. To help them you can employ a common journalistic style called **inverse-pyramid writing**. Newspapers and magazines excel at this style because they know readers tend to scan and skim until they reach a particular item of interest, and even then they may not read past the headline or first paragraph. This pattern provides the solution for writing in this style.

Create a Concise but Descriptive Headline • A descriptive headline tells readers what to expect in the following text. People can read a concise title quickly. As we said in HEADLINES AND BLURBS (D3), you must articulate in the headline why the content is *important* and *unique*. Implicit in the headline is a promise about what the content offers.

The headline is typically a sentence fragment, roughly ten words or less so that it can appear in large type in a small space.

What makes a good headline? A good headline does all of the following:

- It contains keywords, most importantly subject and verb. The best headlines indicate action, such as *Buy or Sell Anything Here*.
- It confirms the information that follows in the blurb.
- It does not reveal the whole story, so the reader is compelled to continue.
- If it is news based, it states the most important aspect of the relevant news.
- It is clean, simple, and specific. The headline "Inside Instant Messaging" on Figure D7.1 is a good example.
- It is not a boring label, such as "Blue Slacks."
- It is humorous without injuring or perplexing its readers.

A powerful headline is important for many reasons. When implementing a page, take care to put the title in *two* places: in the HTML TITLE tag, as described in DISTINCTIVE HTML TITLES (D9); and in the body of the text itself. HTML titles are used by search engines (see WRITING FOR SEARCH ENGINES (D6)), and in favorites, bookmarks, and desktop shortcuts. Also a descriptive title makes it easy to create a DESCRIPTIVE, LONGER LINK NAME (K9).

Continue with the Most Important Points in the Blurb or Lead • If you're writing a short list of blurbs, focus on the point you want to make. Keep your target customer in mind at all times.

It is difficult to write short, succinct blurbs, so write something longer first and edit it down to its essence. If you want your page to show a list of blurbs, place the most important ones ABOVE THE FOLD (I2) so that readers can quickly determine whether they are on the right page. The blurb in Figure D7.1 begins with the words "Faster than a speeding e-mail."

The term **lead** refers to the first few paragraphs of a story or longer text. It reinforces the headline and entices the visitor to read more (see Figure D7.2). Following the inverse-pyramid style, state the most important idea first and continue to the least important.

Use Less Text • Text on computer monitors is harder to read than on paper, so people read less online than they do on paper. This means that online articles must be shorter than those in print (see Figure D7.3). Instructions for using a Web application must be kept especially short to keep reader attention on the navigation items and the other application objects.

Write Short Sentences and Check Your Work • Write in a straightforward manner, avoiding complex sentences. Use simpler words and FAMILIAR LANGUAGE (K11) to ensure that readers can understand what you're communicating.

Just like short sentences, short blocks of text are easier to read than long blocks. If you break up long paragraphs into shorter ones, readers can skim more quickly. Finally, to avoid confusion and mistakes, run the text through a spell checker and a grammar checker, and then completely proofread it before publishing. These kinds of errors are the easiest to correct, but they are embarrassing if they make it to the site.

Avoid Hype • Do not underestimate your customers. They can become frustrated and annoyed easily when presented with self-promoting hype and blatant advertising. By avoiding hype, you raise your site's credibility. Present facts clearly and concisely, without sounding self-promoting.

D7.2

(cnn.com, February 15, 2002)

Figure D7.2

The most important paragraph in this news article is at the top and in boldface. The following paragraphs continue the story and draw readers in.

Concise Title

Short summary paragraph

Short, easy-to-read bulleted list

Simple follow-up paragraphs

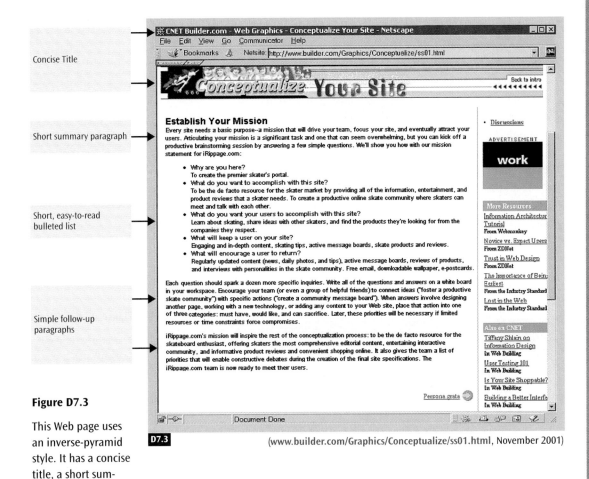

D7.3

Figure D7.3

This Web page uses an inverse-pyramid style. It has a concise title, a short summary paragraph, and supporting paragraphs. However, it's not necessary to read the supporting paragraphs in order to understand what the page is about.

(www.builder.com/Graphics/Conceptualize/ss01.html, November 2001)

Hype can backfire if you say that your product is the best. Visitors might have found your site in a search engine list, so they can research your competitors' sites as easily as they found yours, just by clicking the **Back** button.

Use Bullets and Numbered Lists • Readers appreciate bulleted lists for the following reasons:

- They draw people's attention.
- They are conducive to rapid skimming.
- They highlight information quickly.
- They identify the most important information.

However, follow these guidelines when you use bulleted lists:

- Use them when the order of the items is not important. Use *numbered* lists if the ordering matters.
- Use HTML bullets, instead of fancy images, to improve download time.
- Apply bullets sparingly, or they will lose their effectiveness.
- Avoid having too many bullets in the list. Seven is usually the most you should have.

Use Embedded Links • EMBEDDED LINKS (K7) help visitors find more information about a topic that is mentioned in an article. **Embedded links** are contained in the body of a text (as opposed to being listed at the end of an article; see Figure D7.4 for an example). Embedded links make text easier to skim because people can scan for them. However, EMBEDDED LINKS (K7) may also distract readers.

Figure D7.4

This article from CBS MarketWatch uses an embedded link ("Read the statement") to give readers immediate access to another article mentioned in the text of this article. (Copyright ©1998–2001 MarketWatch.com Inc.)

(cbs.marketwatch.com, November 2001)

Experiment with Different Writing Styles for Entertainment Purposes • If your Web site centers on fun over usability, figure out how to use humor, but carefully. Stories and humor do not need to be written in the inverse-pyramid style. Tailor your presentation to your specific audience.

✳ SOLUTION

Start with a concise but descriptive headline, and continue with the most important points. Use less text than you would for print, in a simple writing style that uses bullets and numbered lists to call out information. Place embedded links in your text to help visitors find more information about a related topic. Experiment with different writing styles for entertainment purposes.

Figure D7.5

For inverse pyramids, start with a good title, continue with a few blurbs, and follow up with supporting information.

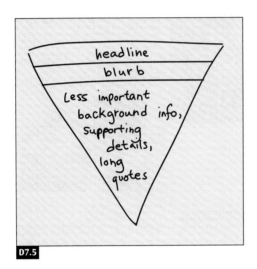

✳ CONSIDER THESE OTHER PATTERNS

(D3) (D9) (D6) (K11) (K9) (I2) (K7) Articulate in HEADLINES AND BLURBS (D3) why each page is *important, unique,* and *valuable* to visitors. Write DISTINCTIVE HTML TITLES (D9) and integrate them with WRITING FOR SEARCH ENGINES (D6) to improve search engine results. Use FAMILIAR LANGUAGE (K11) that your target visitors will understand. Provide DESCRIPTIVE, LONGER LINK NAMES (K9) for other articles to reference. Place the most important information ABOVE THE FOLD (I2) so that readers can quickly determine whether or not this is a page they want. EMBEDDED LINKS (K7) make text easier to skim because people can easily spot them as they scan text.

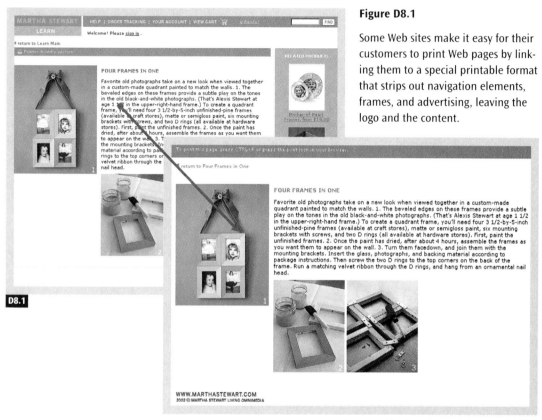

Figure D8.1

Some Web sites make it easy for their customers to print Web pages by linking them to a special printable format that strips out navigation elements, frames, and advertising, leaving the logo and the content.

(www.marthastewart.com, February 20, 2002)

✳ BACKGROUND

Every site genre has pages that could be useful to print, especially the HOMEPAGE PORTAL (C1), CATEGORY PAGES (B8), CLEAN PRODUCT DETAIL (F2) pages, and ORDER CONFIRMATION AND THANK-YOU (F8) page. This pattern provides the solution to print any Web page.

C1 B8 F2
F8

✳ PROBLEM

Sometimes customers want to print what's on their screen. Customers become frustrated if a printed Web page chops off content, goes on and on with pages of irrelevant data, or does not offer a "printer-friendly" version.

When people are on a site and they need to print a page, they might hit the **Print** button on the browser and see what comes out. Sometimes the results are too short, with chopped off key content, such as the last lines of text or important images. Or it might be too long, with pages and pages of irrelevant data. Visitors with advanced knowledge of computers might be able to save the HTML and edit it, or take a screen shot. But novice computer users are more likely to abandon the process, and perhaps abandon the site. This is unfortunate because creating a separate printer-friendly version of most pages is easy.

Modifying any existing page to make a printer-friendly version re-quires numerous changes that restrict your design options for images and layout. For this reason it is better to create an alternate page with the same content that is more appropriate for printing. You can do this by creating a printer-friendly PAGE TEMPLATE (D1) and then loading the content from the original page into the template.

Remove Extraneous Navigation and Content from the Printable Template • To convert a PAGE TEMPLATE (D1) to a printer-friendly version, remove all frames, CONSISTENT SIDEBARS OF RELATED CONTENT (I6), and side-running NAVIGATION BARS (K2) that run vertically down a page because these are not very useful in a printed form. Sometimes articles are split across multiple Web pages, making it difficult to print them out in their entirety. For your printer-friendly version, join split-page articles into one page each (see Figure D8.2).

Add Labels to Help People Find the Article Online Again • Creating a printer-friendly version of your Web page gives you a chance to pass on useful information to customers. List the title, the author, the date, and the URL of the page. Some Web sites sneak in an advertisement or two here as well.

Take the Main Content Out of Any HTML Tables • Tables and GRID LAYOUTS (I1) are one of the main sources of problems in printing. Unless it needs to be formatted as such, make sure that the main content is not placed within a table in the printer-friendly PAGE TEMPLATE (D1).

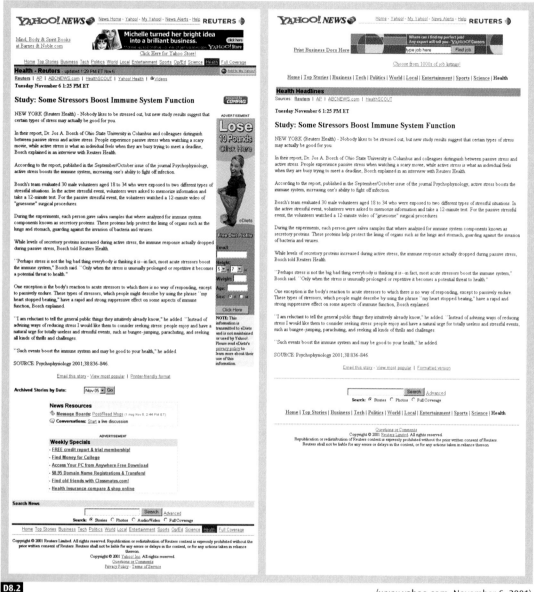

D8.2

(www.yahoo.com, November 6, 2001)

Figure D8.2

Yahoo! chose to create a single-column format for its printer-friendly version
(on the right) of Yahoo! News. They also removed the sidebar of related content
from the bottom of the page. (Reproduced with permission of Yahoo! © 2000
by Yahoo! Inc. YAHOO! and the YAHOO! logo are trademarks of Yahoo! Inc.)

✳ SOLUTION

Create a printer-friendly page template by removing frames, additional columns, navigation bars, and sidebars. Label the page with the page title, author, and URL. Finally, be sure that the main content is not placed within a table as this can cause serious printing problems.

Figure D8.3

To make your pages more printable, simplify them by removing extra columns.

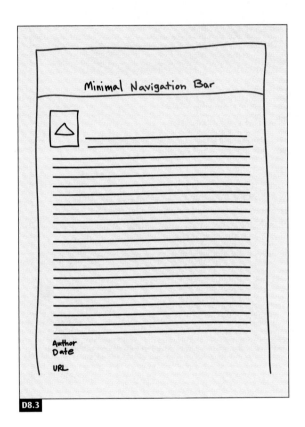

✳ CONSIDER THESE OTHER PATTERNS

Create a printer-friendly page template by removing frames, CONSISTENT **I6** **K2** SIDEBARS OF RELATED CONTENT (I6), and NAVIGATION BARS (K2) that run next to the content going down a page.

Creating printable versions of your content can help with SITE ACCESSI- **B9** **D6** BILITY (B9), as well as with WRITING FOR SEARCH ENGINES (D6).

D9 DISTINCTIVE HTML TITLES

Figure D9.1

This screen shot shows an article from MSNBC about a Harry Potter book. Note the exceptional title in the Web browser window title bar (top arrow). The bottom window shows how to create the HTML title (bottom arrow). You need good, distinctive HTML titles for bookmarks and favorites, shortcuts, search engines, and mobile Internet devices.

D9.1

(www.msnbc.com, July 23, 2001)

✳ BACKGROUND

In HEADLINES AND BLURBS (D3), WRITING FOR SEARCH ENGINES (D6), and INVERSE-PYRAMID WRITING STYLE (D7) we maintained that well-written HTML titles add to a site's value. This pattern provides the foundation of a distinctive HTML title.

✳ PROBLEM

HTML page titles are used as browser bookmarks or favorites and as desktop shortcuts. They are also used by search engines when displaying search results. Often, however, page titles do not provide useful reminders of page contents.

Word-processing documents and spreadsheets with ambiguous file names are confusing. People are forced to open up documents with names like *foo.doc* and *misc-calculations.xls* just to see what they actually contain, and they are justifiably annoyed if there are dozens of poorly named files.

The same is true for Web pages. Customers need to remember the content of a page, whether on or off the Web. HTML titles are used as the default names for Web pages if they are saved to a local drive, or stored as bookmarks or favorites in the Web browser. In addition, some search engines use HTML titles to index site pages and present search results. In this case, people use the HTML title to make an educated guess about whether this is the page they want. However, vague titles make it difficult for people to distinguish one Web page from another. You can address all of these issues at once by writing distinctive HTML titles.

HTML Titles Are Used for Headlines and Blurbs • The key here is to understand how these titles are seen by customers. Figure D9.1 shows how HTML titles are displayed by Web browsers. It also shows how good headlines are resources for well-written HTML titles. Figure D9.2 shows how an HTML title can be reused as the name of a link to a page. See

D3 HEADLINES AND BLURBS (D3) for hints on writing these well.

HTML Titles Are Used by Search Engines • Search engines use HTML titles

J3 when presenting ORGANIZED SEARCH RESULTS (J3). Figure D9.3 shows the results of MSNBC's site search. The first hit looks like an automatically generated title, which is not very useful when customers are trying to understand the search results. Look at the fourth search hit. It uses the HTML title to display the name of the page. Figure D9.4 shows what the same search result looks like in an Internet-wide search engine.

HTML Titles Are Used by Desktop Computers • HTML titles are also used as desktop shortcuts (see Figure D9.5), as well as bookmarks and favorites in Web browsers (see Figure D9.6).

Distinctive HTML titles make it easier for customers to find the right page. They also provide useful link names that can be used on other

Good HTML titles provide a good link name that can be used on other pages.

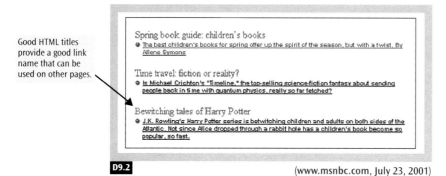

D9.2

(www.msnbc.com, July 23, 2001)

Figure D9.2

These headlines and blurbs come from an MSNBC page.

This is what happens when HTML titles are not set correctly.

Note that the HTML title is used as the name of the search hit here.

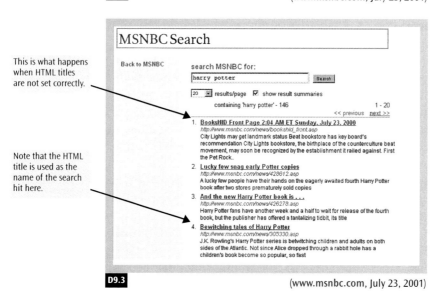

D9.3

(www.msnbc.com, July 23, 2001)

Figure D9.3

This result comes from an MSNBC search on the term *Harry Potter.*

Again, the page title presents the search hit.

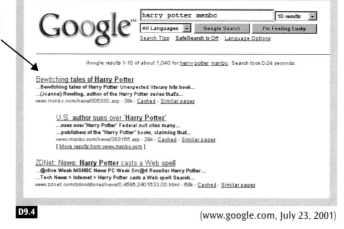

D9.4

(www.google.com, July 23, 2001)

Figure D9.4

This sample result from Google, based on a search for the term *Harry Potter,* uses the HTML title of the page as the name of the hit.

Figure D9.5

Desktop shortcuts use HTML titles as names.

Figure D9.6

Web browsers use HTML titles as the names of bookmarks.

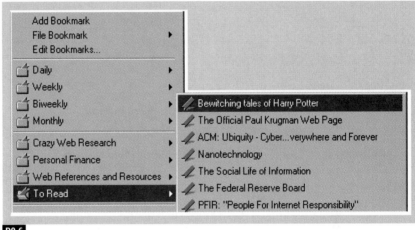

pages. A poorly chosen title, or worse yet, no title, can be confusing, and it looks unprofessional. Figure D9.7 shows some examples of bad HTML titles.

Vary Titles from Page to Page • It would be easy to make all the titles on a site the same, but then visitors would not know which page to choose, or which page they were on. You may do this accidentally if you use a PAGE TEMPLATE (D1) and forget to change the title for each page.

Use Titles and Bread Crumbs • When you add a new page to your site, you have to write a new title. Using a system similar to LOCATION BREAD CRUMBS (K6), base the title of the page on the path that a customer would take to get there. This helps customers locate the page again later, while providing some important context about the page.

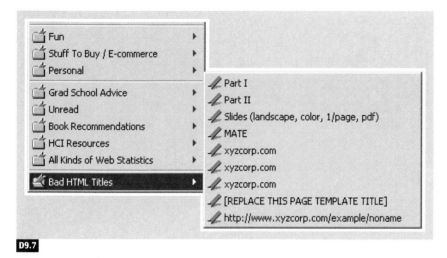

D9.7

Figure D9.7

These examples illustrate bad HTML titles. Titles like *Part I* and *Part II* are vague. One bookmark, of the fictional xyzcorp.com, is listed three times because all of the page titles on its site are the same. The last bookmark, the URL, is listed that way because the page has no HTML title.

CNN uses an approach like this on its site, by using its Web site name, the article type, the article name, and the date to title its Web pages. Here are two page title samples:

- CNN.com—Technology—Study Retail sites fall short on customer service—December 13 2000
- Technology—Global Web sites prove challenging—August 22 2000

CNET uses a similar approach, with titles such as the following:

- CNET.com—News—E-Business—How to build that elusive customer loyalty
- CNET Builder.com—Web Graphics—Conceptualize Your Site

✳ SOLUTION

Create distinct names for each page, even if your pages are generated from page templates. Consider using the site's organizational hierarchy as the basis for titles that describe the categories and subcategories of each page.

Figure D9.8

Use a different name for each page on your site.

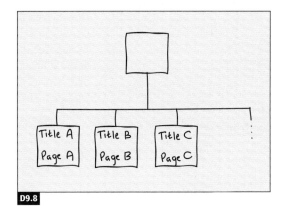

D9.8

✳ CONSIDER THESE OTHER PATTERNS

The titles of pages can be the same as the paths created for LOCATION BREAD CRUMBS (K6). It is easier to create an ORGANIZED SEARCH RESULTS (J3) page if each Web page has a distinctive HTML title because titles are displayed as the name for each page. A distinctive HTML title also makes it easier to create DESCRIPTIVE, LONGER LINK NAMES (K9) to a page because you can often just take the title of the page and use it as the link itself. Having good HTML titles also improves SITE ACCESSIBILITY (B9) for people using mobile Internet devices to access your Web site.

K6
J3
K9
B9

Figure D10.1

Web sites need to be internationalized and localized for a worldwide audience. These screen shots show Yahoo!'s U.S. Web site (background), compared to its Taiwan Web site (foreground). (Reproduced with permission of Yahoo! © 2000 by Yahoo! Inc. YAHOO! and the YAHOO! logo are trademarks of Yahoo! Inc.)

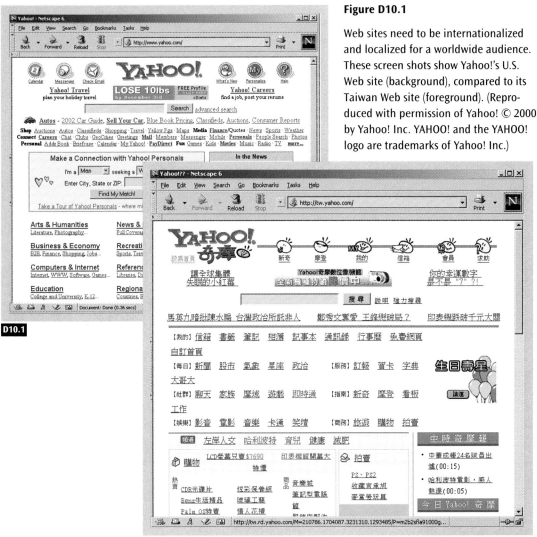

D10.1

(yahoo.com and tw.yahoo.com, November 3, 2001)

✳ BACKGROUND

All site genres can be created for an international audience. This pattern provides the foundation for building sites that are localized to different audiences around the world.

❋ PROBLEM

The Web is a global medium, but many sites do nothing for international and nonnative audiences. People from all over the world can visit a site, but they will find the experience frustrating if language, cultural, and economic transactional issues are not handled well.

Internationalization and localization are becoming an increasingly important factor as Web sites start crossing national borders.[2] Internationalization and localization range from simple issues, such as how information like a phone number is represented, to extremely complex issues, such as political and religious beliefs. **Internationalization** refers to the software changes required to support different languages, dates and times, currencies, weights and measures, and number formats. **Localization** is the process of redesigning the human–computer interface and translating content to support a local culture.

The best solution calls for designing internationalization into a site during initial site design, and then localizing for specific audiences on the basis of need. Because most sites are not originally designed with a global audience in mind, they are not often easily localized when the time comes.

Store Strings Separately from Code • How flexible for localization a Web site is depends on how well the underlying code is designed to support internationalization. This means that strings of text should be stored as separate resources from site code, to make translation easier and simplify the process when text changes are necessary. A modular approach to page layout will allow for flexibility and substitution of elements. Many commercial localization tools exist to help manage the external assets for sites. However, you need to decide how you intend to manage locale specific assets internally.

Do Not Rely Exclusively on Machine Translation • Although software programs for translating from one language to another have come a long way in recent years, a lot of research still needs to be done before text can be translated in a meaningful way. Computers simply do not understand context.[3] For example, if you use the word *cook* as a navigation element

---

2 Note that the terms *internationalization* and *localization* are often abbreviated to *I18N* and *L10N*, respectively, because of the large number of letters in each word.
3 A researcher at Microsoft once commented that computers are idiots—just really fast idiots.

in your Web site, which form of the word do you mean? Do you mean the verb *to cook*, the noun *cook* (as in *chef*), or someone who has the name *Cook*, as in *Captain Cook*? A machine will translate the word only one way, and that may not be the way it was intended. Without an experienced human translator distinguishing the many meanings of various words, the result will be a shoddy translation.

Hire Competent Translators • The common adage "you get what you pay for" holds true for translators. Although most translators have the best intentions, if they do not devote significant time during translation to understanding the specific needs and cultural differences of your customers, as well as the specific requirements of your particular domain and application, they may make embarrassing mistakes. No one wants to appear amateurish with poor word choices, bad grammar, or nonsense statements.

Choose Centralized or Decentralized Localization Management • There is much to be said for both approaches. *Centralized* localization management provides translation services to the entire site team but does not usually have the domain expertise of each of the areas. *Decentralized* localization management has domain expertise spread throughout the organization, but it lacks the localization organization to help manage the process most effectively. It is also more difficult to achieve consistency with decentralized teams because they may not know what other teams around the world are doing. Evaluate the capabilities of the organization's resources and financial investment to decide what approach works best. In many cases, a hybrid approach, using some aspects of centralized management, along with local expertise, is the best solution.

Be Aware of Terms and Concepts That May Not Be Widely Known • Terms like *IRS* and *ESPN* may be familiar to people in the United States, but they are not as recognizable in other nations. In fact, most acronyms, except the most international ones, such as *SCUBA*, will not be known. Things like government agencies, government policies, and local laws and practices often have different names and responsibilities in other countries. See if more universal concepts can convey the same point.

Recognize Holidays, Customs, and Nonverbal Communication • Not every holiday in one country is a holiday abroad. That means you will need staff for vital services like customer support on holidays, or staff who reside in the regions that you support.

Other local customs to be aware of include color use. For example, sites targeted toward China or Taiwan should be careful of how white is used because it is the color of mourning there. Colors, images, and icons that have one meaning in one cultural context may be offensive in another. Do not discount the existence of these attributes as unsophisticated design foibles of the uninitiated. Take the time to understand the value of specific color choices and icons. In some cases those colors and icons contribute a great deal to brand identity and add a local feel. There will be a fine balance between global structure and local appeal.

Transform Your Representation of Dates, Currencies, Weights, and Measures •
A great deal of confusion can arise if special care is not taken here. For example, the date format 1/3/01 can mean either March 1, 2001, or January 3, 2001, depending on whether dates are represented as day/month/year or month/day/year. In cases like this, it is better to spell out the name of the month so that there is no room for ambiguity.

Time zones add more complexity to sites if you are executing time-sensitive functions and updates. Most contact databases do not track the time zone of the resident. If a site allows people to schedule appointments with someone in another time zone, the invitation should account for both participants' time zones.

Currencies represent a unique challenge. In the simplest case, a site must support the representation of the local currency. In more complex cases, when you're selling across national borders, your site must handle representation of the currency and the exchange rate fluctuation.

Table D10.1 lists the types of information that must be represented differently in different locales.

Table D10.1

Information That Must Be Represented Differently in Different Locales

Type of Information	Global Format Examples
Numbers	100,000.00 or 100.000,00
Dates	March 3, 2005, or 3 Mar 2005
Times	6:04 PM or 18:04 or 18.04
Time zone	GMT −08:00 or FMT +02:00
Currency	$1, ¥1, £1, €1, or ₣1
Units of measure	lb or kg
Phone numbers	(415) 555-1212 or 098-88-1234
Address	two lines or four lines
Postal codes	90210 or BYT 123
Punctuation	Hello?, ¿Hola?, "Hello," or <<Hallo>>
Character sets	Hello! or привет!

Prepare for the Varying Devices People Use to Surf Web Sites • In many countries, mobile Web access is very popular—sometimes more popular than desktop computers. You might need to make your site accessible from mobile devices as they become popular in new locales. The page description format for mobile devices varies from region to region. Where one country might have mostly WAP devices, another country might use mostly HDML. In addition, instant messaging protocols are sometimes popular. You might need gateways to these protocols to enhance your site's value in local markets. Some of the issues involved in designing for mobile devices are discussed in more detail in SITE ACCESSIBILITY (B9).   **B9**

Understand the Local Legal Issues • Legal issues may become important when customers start accessing your site from abroad. If your site sells products, foreign trade laws and customs might apply. These can affect what you can sell, what you can send, when it is sent, and how long it will take to get there. Tax laws change from country to country as well, and when products are sold overseas, international sales tax may also apply.

Your site may also need to support different privacy laws and offer more ACCOUNT MANAGEMENT (H4) tools to manage customer profiles. For   **H4** example, the privacy laws in the European Union are more comprehensive than the ones in the United States, stating that individuals must be able to access and manage all information stored about them where reasonable. Privacy issues are discussed in depth in FAIR INFORMATION PRACTICES (E3) and PRIVACY POLICY (E4).   **E3** **E4**

Finally, there may be issues with the legality of content. Some countries restrict content that might be on your site. For example, France restricts the sale of any Nazi-related material within its borders. Research each country before opening for business, and avoid having to remove content.

Provide Tailored Services • Translation is not always enough; sometimes you must personalize a service to the desires and tastes of your audience. What are the local food preferences? What do customers there do for fun? How many times a week do your customers go shopping? These questions might have different answers, depending on where customers live. Do the research to find out. Online marketing and usability research can help, providing concrete answers without the expense and time of travel (for more information about how to do this, see Appendix E— Online Research).

✷ SOLUTION

Store strings separately from code so that text can be sent to your translation team easily. Do not rely on machine translation. Hire competent translators. Manage internationalization and localization processes through either a centralized or decentralized system. Understand that certain local terms and concepts may not be widely known, and that holidays, customs, and nonverbal communication in other cultures can affect a site's design. Transform how you represent certain information, such as dates and currencies. Be aware of the devices people use to surf Web sites because mobile customers may be a large audience for your services. Understand which legal issues might affect your business. Consider providing tailored services to locales that do not have the same practices as those you are addressing domestically.

Figure D10.2

Store strings for different languages in separate files.

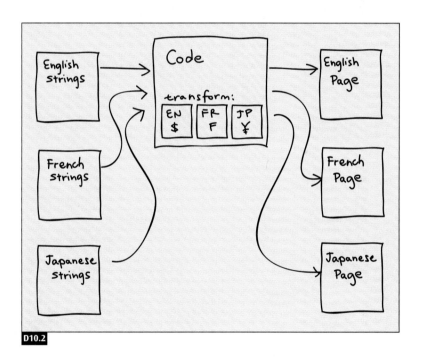

D10.2

✷ CONSIDER THESE OTHER PATTERNS

Local representations for dates, times, currencies, taxes, addresses, and shipping requirements should be reflected in the site's SHOPPING CART (F3) and QUICK-FLOW CHECKOUT (F1). Certain countries may have stricter privacy laws, which should be reflected in your site's FAIR INFORMATION PRACTICES (E3) and PRIVACY POLICY (E4).

F3
F1

E3 **E4**

Building Trust and Credibility

Trust and credibility are essential to establishing a relationship with customers. Without them, people have no reason to believe (or purchase) anything on your Web site. This pattern group gives an overview of issues related to trust and credibility.

E1 SITE BRANDING

E2 E-MAIL SUBSCRIPTIONS

E3 FAIR INFORMATION PRACTICES

E4 PRIVACY POLICY

E5 ABOUT US

E6 SECURE CONNECTIONS

E1 SITE BRANDING

E1.1

(www.msn.com, February 12, 2002)

Figure E1.1

MSN uses its brand very consistently throughout its site.

✳ BACKGROUND

In all the site genres (see Pattern Group A) it is important to build a site brand to help visitors identify where they are on the Web, and to help build an identity for the company. In HOMEPAGE PORTAL (C1) we showed how to balance the various elements on that page and how to provide a strong UP-FRONT VALUE PROPOSITION (C2). This pattern provides the solu- tion for successful branding throughout a site.

✳ PROBLEM

Brand is more than image. Customers need to know where they are and whether they can trust that place to provide something important and unique.

The identity created on a site, through advertising and in interactions with people at a company, persists even after customers leave their computers, close their magazines, or hang up their phones. Some may suggest that **brand** is the image, the graphic look, or even the logo of a company. But it is more than that. It is what people remember. And like the cattle brand of cowboys, a company brand cannot be taken off once it has been created with customers.

People are bombarded with facts and opinions suggesting what is important for them to think, feel, and do. These messages permeate almost every aspect of our lives, from print and television ads to endorsements by famous people, traveling even by the word of mouth of friends and peers. People respond to these suggestions in different ways, depending on their background and what they value. Some people may value getting the best price on a purchase; others may value getting the highest-quality product. The brand a company builds depends on the audience it hopes to reach and the values that audience deems important.

Our research has shown that a Web site is assessed in five areas:

1. **Content quality.** Does the site have what I want?
2. **Ease of use.** Is it simple and efficient to find what I want?
3. **Performance.** Is the site fast?
4. **Satisfaction.** Is the overall experience satisfactory?
5. **Brand value.** Does the site provide something important and unique?

To build a trusted brand requires creating a positive assessment in these five areas. The rest of the book helps in the first four areas. This solution provides insight into building brand value through differentiation and a Web brand identity program.

Differentiating a Brand • Customers will try to discern the differences between one company and its competitors, particularly the promises they make and their abilities to fulfill promises. Figure E1.2 illustrates many of the factors that will have an impact on your brand. A company can dominate only one area of business: price, access, product, service, or experience (as many well-respected businesspeople have said). A company may excel at one or more other areas, but because of human limitations it cannot dominate all the areas. If you establish an important and unique brand value, customers are more likely to remember that value when they need it.

What assessment does the company want to trigger? The first thing customers will do is evaluate your purpose. Perhaps the company offers something less expensive or more entertaining than what its competitors offer. Whatever the differentiation, it must translate into a message people will remember. What is the branding message you want visitors on your site to come away with? As you would when "dressing for success," consider the kind of impression you wish to make. By running research in the exercises that follow, you can find out more about your audience's likes and dislikes and hone a brand identity plan.

Exercise 1

Write a one-page narrative about why your Web site is different. Specifically, explain how the idea for the Web site came about, and what problems the site solves. Take about a half hour, and write at least 350 words.

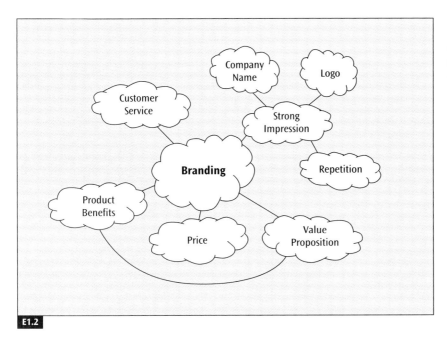

E1.2

Figure E1.2

A good branding statement results from the intertwining of many factors.

Exercise 2

Pick from the following list of adjectives, or from your own list, the words that best describe the identity you plan to create:

- Sincere
- Trustworthy
- Reliable
- Competent
- Accessible
- Friendly
- Functional
- Smart
- Expensive
- Inexpensive
- Fun
- Techno-savvy
- Fashionable

Now sort your list by picking the top three adjectives that describe your site.

Exercise 3

Write site **scenarios**, one-page narratives about what it feels like for different customers to use the Web site. Put yourself in the shoes of at least three kinds of customers. Write at least 250 words about each. For an example of a scenario, see the discussion on building scenarios in Section 3.2 of Chapter 3—Knowing Your Customers: Principles and Techniques.

Exercise 4

Write ten short "what we do" sentences that accurately describe the purpose of your Web site. If you like, use the same list that you created in the UP-FRONT VALUE PROPOSITION (C2) pattern. Test these statements with customers to identify the single most powerful description.

Exercise 5

It is not all about words. If you have a logo and color treatments in place for your homepage, test them through research. Customer research is the best way to discover which treatment best matches the identity you wish to create. Survey your customers or run focus groups, as described in Section 3.2 of Chapter 3—Knowing Your Customers: Principles and Techniques. You can also do this type of research online (for details, see Appendix E—Online Research).

Basic E-Commerce

The ability to find and buy products online is one of the most compelling reasons to use the Web, but for customers to be successful, your design must have clean, simple interfaces and support for common tasks. This pattern group discusses how to create the best possible customer experience on your e-commerce Web site. You will notice numerous examples from Amazon.com in this pattern group. We have looked far and wide for good examples but have often come back to Amazon.com because it makes e-commerce work well for the customer—better than any other site we have seen.

F1 QUICK-FLOW CHECKOUT

F2 CLEAN PRODUCT DETAILS

F3 SHOPPING CART

F4 QUICK ADDRESS SELECTION

F5 QUICK SHIPPING METHOD SELECTION

F6 PAYMENT METHOD

F7 ORDER SUMMARY

F8 ORDER CONFIRMATION AND THANK-YOU

F9 EASY RETURNS

Brand Identity • Customers identify a Web site by the brand image. If visitors arrive at a Web site and do not know where they are, the brand must not be prominent enough on the homepage, perhaps being overwhelmed by other elements. Once customers leave the homepage to visit other pages of a site, they can become confused about where they are if the company brand is not visible. If too big, however, the brand can adversely minimize the many other important things on the site. Site designers must quickly convey the brand, but keep it from overpowering a page (see CLEAR FIRST READS (I3)).

Here are the four main graphic design considerations for every Web brand treatment:

1. **Consistency.** Use the exact same fonts, colors, graphics, relative positions, and proportions for the brand image wherever it appears. Studies show that repetition helps customers recall information.
2. **Size.** Make the logo large enough to be the second or third item that will be read on the page.
3. **Position.** The established location is the upper left; people already know to look there to identify the site.
4. **Reuse of graphics to make it fast.** Reusing graphics helps ensure that each page is fast. You may also want to use a logo that is integrated into the NAVIGATION BAR (K2), and keep a LOW NUMBER OF FILES (L1).

Involve your team in the branding design process. Consider hiring a consultant with expertise in strategic marketing. Once the branding process is complete, the editorial and graphic design teams will have a clear understanding of the identity to convey and reinforce.

❋ SOLUTION

Build a strong site brand by differentiating your company from other companies through the promise that you make and through the actions your company takes to satisfy customers. Keep your graphical elements (1) consistent in style, (2) moderate in size, (3) in the upper left corner, and (4) reusable from page to page.

Figure E1.3

Make the brand the first read in the upper left corner of every page on your site.

E1.3

❋ CONSIDER THESE OTHER PATTERNS

I3 Take advantage of CLEAR FIRST READS (I3) to quickly convey your brand. A
K2 logo that is integrated into the NAVIGATION BAR (K2) will load faster and
L1 help you keep a LOW NUMBER OF FILES (L1).

E2 E-MAIL SUBSCRIPTIONS

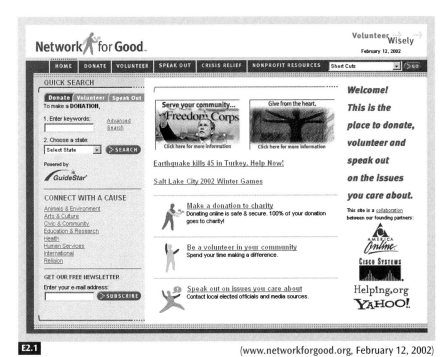

Figure E2.1

Network for Good has a text entry field on the bottom left portion of its home-page that makes it easy for people to subscribe to news about upcoming events and new Web site features.

E2.1
(www.networkforgood.org, February 12, 2002)

✳ BACKGROUND

Maintaining contact with visitors to your site can be difficult. E-mail sub-scriptions are one way of informing interested and self-selected visitors of new and interesting content, such as upcoming events, sales, or news. This pattern looks at different kinds of e-mail subscriptions and ways that e-mail newsletters should be written for greatest impact.

✳ PROBLEM

Companies need a way of maintaining contact with customers who are interested in what their Web site has to offer.

E-mail subscriptions are an inexpensive way of maintaining a connection with customers, and they are especially effective if customers are interested in what a Web site can offer. Providing customers with fresh, timely, and relevant information is a great way of giving them another reason to visit your Web site again.

There are three kinds of e-mail subscriptions: newsletters, focused advertisements, and alerts. **Newsletters** are periodic bulletins that provide useful information, such as interesting tidbits and links, tips and tricks, and descriptions of new services and content. **Focused advertisements** draw attention to new promotions, special offers, and new products. **Alerts** are brief messages that notify a customer of special events that may be of interest, such as that a library book is due soon or that the price of a stock has dropped below a certain mark.

Make It Easy to Sign Up for an E-Mail Subscription • Offering a subscription on your HOMEPAGE PORTAL (C1) is a simple way of getting people to give you their e-mail addresses. Network for Good has a link off of its homepage that allows visitors to easily subscribe to its newsletter (see Figure E2.1). Figure E2.2 shows part of the Women.com Web site, which lets people sign up to be notified when the site redesign is deployed.

Another good place to set up a subscription is the SIGN-IN/NEW ACCOUNT (H2) page, when a customer is creating a new account. One Web site that does this is yahoo.com, as Figure E2.3 shows. A third place is the ORGANIZED SEARCH RESULTS (J3) page, notifying customers when new information matching their search criteria is found. Figure E2.4 shows how Amazon.com does this with product searches.

Figure E2.2

Many Web sites let people sign up to be notified when major new features or site redesigns are deployed.

(www.women.com, September 22, 2001)

Figure E2.3

Yahoo! lets people sign up for newsletters when they create an account. (Reproduced with permission of Yahoo! © 2000 by Yahoo! Inc. YAHOO! and the YAHOO! logo are trademarks of Yahoo! Inc.)

My YAHOO!

Help - Yahoo!

Sign up for your Yahoo! ID   Already have an ID? Sign In

Get a Yahoo! ID and password for access to My Yahoo! and all other personalized Yahoo! services.

Yahoo! ID: [   ]

(examples: "lildude56" or "goody2shoes")

Password: [   ]

Re-type Password: [   ]

Choosing your ID
You will use this information to access Yahoo! each time. Capitalization matters for your password!

If you forget your password, we would identify you with this information.

Security Question: [select a question to answer ▼]

Your Answer: [   ]

Birthday: [select one ▼] [ ] , [ ] (Month Day, Year)

Alternate Email: [   ]

Recalling your password
This is our only way to verify your identity. To protect your account, make sure "your answer" is **memorable for you** but **hard for others** to guess!

First Name: [   ]   Last Name: [   ]

Language & Content: [English - United States ▼]

Zip/Postal Code: [   ]   Gender: [--- ▼]

Occupation: [select occupation ▼]

Industry: [select industry ▼]

Customizing Yahoo!
Yahoo! will try to provide more relevant content and advertising based on the information collected on this page and on the Yahoo! products and services you use.

☑ Contact me occasionally about special offers, promotions and Yahoo! features.

Interests (optional):

☐ Entertainment   ☐ Business   ☐ Shopping
☐ Home & Family   ☐ Computers & Technology ☐ Sports & Outdoors
☐ Health   ☐ Personal Finance   ☐ Travel
☐ Music   ☐ Small Business   ☐ Sweepstakes & Free Stuff

E2.3

(www.yahoo.com, October 6, 2001)

E2.4

(www.amazon.com, September 23, 2001)

Figure E2.4

Amazon.com has a feature on its search results page that notifies customers when new products matching their search criteria come out.

Figure E2.5

TVEyes uses e-mail subscriptions to notify customers when any of the key-words they have selected are spoken on television.

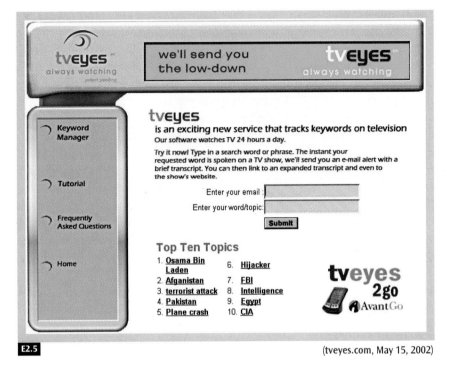

E2.5

(tveyes.com, May 15, 2002)

Some Web sites use e-mail subscriptions in very novel ways. For example, TVEyes alerts people whenever a preset keyword is spoken on television. Figure E2.5 shows how easy TVEyes makes it to start an e-mail subscription.

The fewer barriers there are to creating a subscription, the more subscribers you will have. Make it easy to find the subscription request, and make it clear what you are offering. If it is a newsletter, provide a few samples to help set expectations. Finally, keep the information you need from your customers short. The more information you require, the less likely it is that people will bother subscribing.

Write Newsletters, Focused Advertisements, and Alerts in Inverse-Pyramid Style • Using an INVERSE-PYRAMID WRITING STYLE (D7) for your e-mail subscriptions will make it easier to get your message across, especially to people who receive 70 or more e-mails every day. Have specific e-mail subject lines, and use short, concise paragraphs. Put the most important information or a summary at the top of the e-mail, and use headings and bulleted lists to call out information.

Use Text E-Mail Messages • Unless you have a compelling need for graphics, you should avoid HTML e-mail and use text messages only. Some people cannot read HTML e-mail, and they end up seeing a lot of junk. This is not the impression of your Web site that you want to convey. This caveat may not be necessary in the future as the programs and devices we rely on begin to use HTML e-mail exclusively.

Text e-mail messages should be at most 70 characters wide and word-wrapped. Long lines do not always appear correctly in some e-mail readers, and they make e-mails look amateurish. Be careful of smart curly quotes. Some word processors will automatically convert straight quotes (") to curly quotes (" "). However, curly quotes sometimes appear as numbers. It's best to avoid word processors and use text editors when composing e-mail subscriptions. Finally, be sure to run the e-mail message through a spell checker and a grammar checker to avoid simple typos.

Include Information on How to Subscribe and Unsubscribe in Each E-Mail • Each e-mail message should also have information about how to subscribe and unsubscribe. The subscribe information is included in case your customers forward the message to their friends. You want their friends to be able to sign up easily too! The unsubscribe information is included in case the customer is simply not interested and does not want to receive any more messages. Sometimes customers unsubscribe by sending an e-mail to a certain address or by clicking a link in the e-mail. Clicking a link is usually easier for the customer, so support this option if you can. The same information should also be included on your FREQUENTLY ASKED QUESTIONS (H7) page.

Use Your Customers' E-Mail Addresses Only for What You Say You Will • One of the FAIR INFORMATION PRACTICES (E3) is *choice*. Your customers' e-mail addresses should be used only for the e-mail subscriptions they signed up for, and nothing more. Remember, the way you treat your customers will affect their perception of your brand. If you develop a new feature for your customers, they should be given a choice of opting in rather than having to opt out.

✳ SOLUTION

Make it easy for people who are interested to set up an e-mail subscription. Write newsletters, focused advertisements, and alerts in inverse-pyramid style. Use text e-mail messages unless you know recipients can read HTML e-mail. Include information about how to subscribe and unsubscribe in each e-mail message. Be sure to use your customers' e-mail addresses only for what you say you will.

Figure E2.6

E-mail subscriptions can be used to send newsletters, focused advertisements, and alerts to interested and self-selected customers.

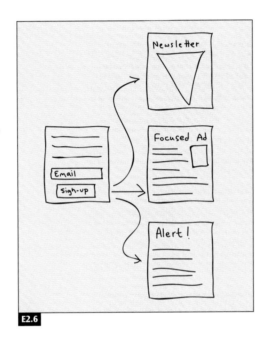

E2.6

✳ CONSIDER THESE OTHER PATTERNS

C1
H2
J3
Three places to offer e-mail subscriptions are the HOMEPAGE PORTAL (C1), the SIGN-IN/NEW ACCOUNT (H2) page, and the ORGANIZED SEARCH RESULTS (J3) page.

D7
H7
Newsletters, focused advertisements, and alerts should be written in INVERSE-PYRAMID WRITING STYLE (D7). Information about subscribing and unsubscribing should be included in each message, as well as on a FREQUENTLY ASKED QUESTIONS (H7) page.

E3
E4
Your customers' e-mail addresses should be collected and handled according to the FAIR INFORMATION PRACTICES (E3). Furthermore, these policies should be communicated to your customers through a PRIVACY POLICY (E4).

E3 FAIR INFORMATION PRACTICES

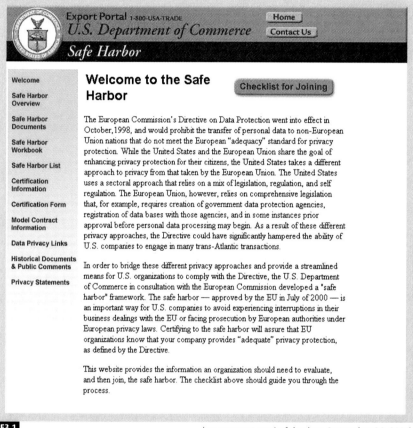

Figure E3.1

The safe harbor Web site provides a great deal of information about the safe harbor privacy agreement between the United States and the European Union. Safe harbor compliance is crucial for companies wishing to do business with citizens and companies in the European Union.

E3.1

(www.export.gov/safeharbor, September 26, 2001)

✳ BACKGROUND

It's not always clear how a company should handle and manage the personal information of its customers. Web companies often collect this information on SIGN-IN/NEW ACCOUNT (H2) and E-MAIL SUBSCRIPTION (E2) pages. This pattern describes fair information practices, which provide guidelines for what kinds of policies and procedures Web sites should have to ensure that customers' personal information is collected and handled equitably and securely.

✳ PROBLEM

Privacy is a serious concern for many people using the Web. However, it is not always clear what policies and procedures a Web site should have to collect and handle personal information in a fair and secure manner.

Privacy is moving to the fore as more and more people come online. A myriad of complex issues have to be handled, such as what information can be collected, as well as how and from whom. The best thing to do here is to get legal expertise to help guide you through this rapidly changing area. This pattern is meant simply to give you a flavor of what's required.

The U.S. Privacy Act of 1974 created the notion of fair information practices. Although this act applies only to U.S. government agencies, it has significantly influenced privacy policies worldwide. So far, the most important of these has been the European Union's Directive 95/46/EC (commonly shortened to *the Directive*) on the protection of individuals with regard to the processing of personal data and on the free movement of such data. Effective as of October 1998, this directive has served as a framework to help European Union (EU) nations create legislation that enforces fair information practices.

The Directive has already had significant impact on e-commerce because one of its articles stipulates that EU countries may prohibit data transfers from EU citizens or companies to non-EU countries that do not ensure "an adequate level of protection." Currently the United States has no national laws guaranteeing such protection. To address this issue, the U.S. Department of Commerce and the European Commission have drawn up a safe harbor framework as a means of having companies based in the United States regulate themselves. Companies can be certified as being compliant with safe harbor, which in turn makes them compliant with the Directive.

The seven safe harbor principles are as follows:[1]

1. **Notice.** Organizations must notify individuals about the purposes for which they collect and use information about them. They must provide information about how individuals can contact the organization with any inquiries or complaints, the types of third parties to which it discloses the information and the choices and means the organization offers for limiting its use and disclosure.

---

1 These descriptions of the safe harbor principles come directly from www.export.gov/safeharbor/sh_overview.html.

2. **Choice.** Organizations must give individuals the opportunity to choose (opt out) whether their personal information will be disclosed to a third party or used for a purpose incompatible with the purpose for which it was originally collected or subsequently authorized by the individual. For sensitive information, affirmative or explicit (opt in) choice must be given if the information is to be disclosed to a third party or used for a purpose other than its original purpose or the purpose authorized subsequently by the individual.

3. **Onward transfer (transfers to third parties).** To disclose information to a third party, organizations must apply the notice and choice principles. Where an organization wishes to transfer information to a third party that is acting as an agent, it may do so if it makes sure that the third party subscribes to the safe harbor principles or is subject to the Directive or another adequacy finding. As an alternative, the organization can enter into a written agreement with such third party requiring that the third party provide at least the same level of privacy protection as is required by the relevant principles.

4. **Access.** Individuals must have access to personal information about them that an organization holds and be able to correct, amend, or delete that information where it is inaccurate, except where the burden or expense of providing access would be disproportionate to the risks to the individual's privacy in the case in question, or where the rights of persons other than the individual would be violated.

5. **Security.** Organizations must take reasonable precautions to protect personal information from loss, misuse and unauthorized access, disclosure, alteration and destruction.

6. **Data integrity.** Personal information must be relevant for the purposes for which it is to be used. An organization should take reasonable steps to ensure that data is reliable for its intended use, accurate, complete, and current.

7. **Enforcement.** In order to ensure compliance with the safe harbor principles, there must be (a) readily available and affordable independent recourse mechanisms so that each individual's complaints and disputes can be investigated and resolved and damages awarded where the applicable law or private sector initiatives so provide; (b) procedures for verifying that the commitments companies make to adhere to the safe harbor principles have been implemented; and (c) obligations to remedy problems arising out of a failure to comply with the principles. Sanctions must be sufficiently rigorous to ensure compliance by the

organization. Organizations that fail to provide annual self-certification letters will no longer appear in the list of participants and safe harbor benefits will no longer be assured.

The safe harbor principles apply only for U.S. companies that want to do business with citizens and companies in the European Union. The landscape for Web sites that operate entirely in the United States is much more chaotic. There has not been a lot of legislation in this regard, but the safe harbor principles still provide a good starting point. In fact, in May 2000, the U.S. Federal Trade Commission (FTC) issued a report on privacy online. This report recommended legislation of four practices that Web sites should have for collecting and handling personal information. Although these practices are currently not legally required in the United States, they offer a reasonable guideline for Web sites. The practices are:

1. **Have a Clear and Conspicuous Privacy Policy.** Provide a clear and understandable PRIVACY POLICY (E4). Typically, the link to a Web site's privacy policy is posted in the footer of each Web page. However, this link should be made especially conspicuous on key Web pages, such as the HOMEPAGE PORTAL (C1), QUICK-FLOW CHECKOUT (F1), and SIGN-IN/NEW ACCOUNT (H2) Web pages. The privacy policy should contain a description of what information is being collected, how it is used, and how it is shared with others. See PRIVACY POLICY (E4) for more details.

2. **Let People Choose How Their Personal Information Is Used**. If personal information is to be used for purposes beyond the primary intent, let people choose how it will be used. For example, e-commerce sites need mailing addresses to ship products. However, this information can also be used for marketing back to consumers. This is an example of a secondary intent. In these cases, customers should be offered a choice of whether their personal information is used in this manner.

   Choice is especially important for E-MAIL SUBSCRIPTIONS (E2). Some Web sites ask for a valid e-mail address and then start sending people unwanted e-mail advertisements. When customers create a new account with your Web site, make it clear up front how their e-mail addresses will be used. As an alternative, make it possible for customers to use a one-time GUEST ACCOUNT (H3) on your Web site.

3. **Tell People What Information the Web Site Has about Them.** Web sites should provide an ACCOUNT MANAGEMENT (H4) facility to let people review and in some cases change the information the Web site has

collected about them. The information a Web site has about a person may be inaccurate or simply out of date, making an account management system a practical necessity.

4. **Take Reasonable Precautions to Protect Personal Information.** Web sites should take reasonable steps to protect all of the information about their customers. Such steps include using SECURE CONNECTIONS (E6), testing any custom software for potential security flaws, keeping up to date with security-related software updates, having clear policies on how customer information is to be handled internally, and periodically auditing the entire process to ensure that procedures are being followed properly.

❊ SOLUTION

Have a clear privacy policy, and make it conspicuous on key Web pages. Let your customers choose how their information is used. Provide account management tools to let them review and correct their information. Protect your customers' personal information. Be certified as a safe harbor Web site if you are doing business with customers or companies in European Union nations.

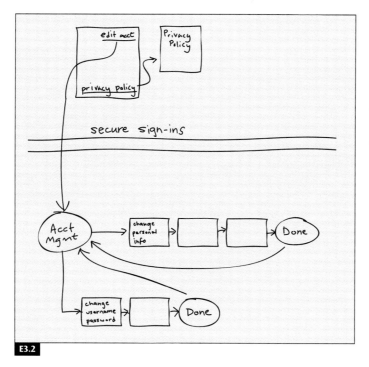

Figure E3.2

Make your privacy policy clear, keep your customers' information secure, and make it easy for customers to manage and update their information.

✳ CONSIDER THESE OTHER PATTERNS

One way of maintaining openness and transparency is by stating a PRIVACY POLICY (E4) on all Web pages. At a minimum, privacy policies should be posted on key Web pages, such as the HOMEPAGE PORTAL (C1) and other major entry points, the QUICK-FLOW CHECKOUT (F1) page, and any Web page where substantial personal information is collected, such as SIGN-IN/NEW ACCOUNT (H2).

People should be given the choice of how their e-mail addresses are used, especially for E-MAIL SUBSCRIPTIONS (E2). An alternative is to let customers use one-time GUEST ACCOUNTS (H3).

SECURE CONNECTIONS (E6) should be used for any transactions involving sensitive information, including passwords, personal finances, and e-commerce purchases.

Web sites should also provide an ACCOUNT MANAGEMENT (H4) facility, letting people see what information the Web site currently has about them.

E4 PRIVACY POLICY

FEDERAL TRADE COMMISSION

Privacy Policy

This is how we handle information we learn about you from your visit to our website. The information we receive depends on what you do when you visit our site.

If you visit our site to browse, or to read or download information like consumer brochures or press releases:

> We collect and store: the name of the domain and host from which you access the Internet (for example, aol.com or princeton.edu); the Internet protocol (IP) address of the computer you are using; the browser software you use and your operating system; the date and time you access our site; and the Internet address of the website from which you linked directly to our site.

> We use this information to measure the number of visitors to the different sections of our site, and to help us make our site more useful. Generally, we delete this information after one year.

> We do *not* use "**cookies**" on this site.

If you choose to identify yourself by sending us an email or when using our secure online forms (e.g., Bureau of Consumer Protection, Project Know Fraud, or Identity Theft complaint forms, or our FOIA Request Form):

> We use personally-identifying information from consumers in various ways to further our consumer protection and competition activities. We collect this information under the authority of the Federal Trade Commission Act and other laws we enforce or administer. We may enter the information you send into our database to make it available to our attorneys and investigators involved in law enforcement. We also may share it with a wide variety of other government agencies enforcing consumer protection, competition, and other laws. If you contact us because you have been the victim of *Identity Theft*, we also may share some

E4.1

(www.ftc.gov, September 22, 2001)

Figure E4.1

Web sites need to provide privacy policies that make it clear what kind of information is being collected and how that information will be used.

✻ BACKGROUND

The FAIR INFORMATION PRACTICES (E3) pattern described what kinds of policies and procedures Web sites should have when dealing with customers' personal information. This pattern describes how to communicate these policies and procedures to your customers through a privacy policy.

✳ PROBLEM

Many customers are concerned about their privacy online. Web sites need a way of telling their customers the kinds of information they are collecting and how that information is used to provide value, as well as the conditions under which that information is disclosed to others.

Surveys and interviews have repeatedly shown that most people are concerned about their privacy online. According to a study by the Pew Internet & American Life Project, privacy concerns are especially high among Internet novices, parents, older Americans, and women. One way of directly addressing these concerns is to have a clear and reasonable privacy policy.

Privacy is a complex and rapidly changing issue. Legislation, regulation, and self-regulation will certainly change while the issues are worked out. The best thing to do here is to get legal expertise to help guide you through this rapidly changing area. This pattern is meant simply to give you a flavor of what's required.

Make the Privacy Policy Available on Each Web Page • Most Web sites place their privacy policy at the footer of each page and make it more conspicuous on key pages, such as the SIGN-IN/NEW ACCOUNT (H2) and QUICK-FLOW CHECKOUT (F1) pages.

(H2)
(F1)

Address the Fair Information Practices in the Privacy Policy • The privacy policy should address how the FAIR INFORMATION PRACTICES (E3) are implemented. This means including what information is collected, how it is collected (for example, with cookies for PERSISTENT CUSTOMER SESSIONS (H5)), how the information is used, and with whom the information is shared. It should also identify the security precautions used, such as SECURE CONNECTIONS (E6). Netflix uses bullets to make it easy to access the details on each of these issues (see Figure E4.2).

(E3)
(H5)
(E6)

Be Aware of Special Privacy Policies for Children • On April 21, 2000, the Children's Online Privacy Protection Act (COPPA) was put into effect in the U.S., limiting the information that Web sites can collect about children. The key provisions stipulate that sites must do the following:

- Provide parents with notice of their information practices.
- Obtain verifiable parental consent before collecting a child's personal information, with certain limited exceptions (see Figure E4.3).

Figure E4.2

This sample privacy policy comes from Netflix, a Web site that offers DVD rentals.

E4.2

(www.netflix.com, September 26, 2001)

- Give parents a choice of whether their child's information will be disclosed to third parties.
- Provide parents access to their child's personal information and allow them to review it and/or have it deleted.
- Give parents the opportunity to prevent further use or collection of information.
- Do not require a child to provide more information than is reasonably necessary to participate in an activity.
- Maintain the confidentiality, security, and integrity of information collected from children.

The FTC has created a Web site with additional details and resources, at www.ftc.gov/bcp/conline/edcams/kidzprivacy.

Keep in Mind That U.S. Government Web Sites Must Have Clear and Conspicuous Privacy Policies • All federal SELF-SERVICE GOVERNMENT (A4) Web sites in the United States are required by law and policy to establish clear privacy policies and to comply with those policies. In June 1999, the Office of Management and Budget published a memorandum directing every U.S. federal agency to post a PRIVACY POLICY (E4) on all major entry points of its Web site, as well as on Web pages where substantial personal information is collected.[2] The memorandum also stated that the privacy policy must inform Web site visitors of three things: what information the agency collects about individuals, why it is collected, and how it is used.

Consider Special Exceptions for Valid Legal Procedures • Figure E4.3 shows part of the Exploratorium's privacy policy, describing how its Web site will comply with well-established and valid legal procedures, such as search warrants or court orders. Detailing these kinds of exception conditions will help smooth out any potential problems with criminal investigations.

Provide Tangible Value for Personal Information • One of the missteps many early Web sites made was collecting too much information about people. Like a nosy neighbor, these Web sites intrusively asked for information that had no bearing on the current task. Many people simply balked and left those Web sites, perhaps for good.

Figure E4.3

The Exploratorium is a hands-on children's science and art museum in San Francisco. Its Web site has a short and simple privacy policy, explaining the kind of information that is collected, how that information is used, the exception conditions, and the fact that personally identifiable information from children is not requested.

Exception

One exception to this policy is that we will release specific information about you or your account to comply with any valid legal process such as a search warrant, subpoena, statute or court order.

Privacy of Minors

The Exploratorium does not solicit personal information from minors. Consistent with the Children's Online Privacy Protection Act of 1998, we will never knowingly request personally identifiable information from anyone under the age of thirteen (13) without prior verifiable parental consent.

If we become aware that a subscriber is under the age of thirteen (13) and has registered without prior verifiable parental consent, we will remove his or her personally identifiable registration information from our files. Please note: we may nevertheless maintain a record of that person's name and address in a "do not register" file to avoid subsequent registration by a child under the age of thirteen (13).

E4.3

(www.exploratorium.edu, September 22, 2001)

2 OMB Memorandum 99-18, June 1999.

However, it is clear that people are willing to trade some privacy for convenience and value. For example, credit card companies keep a record of purchases, providing a trail of what purchases are made, and when and where they are made. Likewise, cellular phones provide a rough level of location tracking, providing information about where a person is. But the point is that people still use credit cards and cell phones, precisely because of the value they provide.

When collecting personal information, state why you are collecting it and how it benefits the consumer. For example, if your Web site requires a visitor to create an account, make it clear that the reason is to provide PERSONALIZED CONTENT (D4), PERSONALIZED RECOMMENDATIONS (G3), or E-MAIL SUBSCRIPTIONS (E2). If your Web site keeps track of people's addresses, let them know that the reason is to streamline the checkout with QUICK ADDRESS SELECTION (F4) and QUICK SHIPPING METHOD SELECTION (F5).

✳ SOLUTION

Make the privacy policy available on each Web page. Address the fair information practices in the privacy policy. Be aware of special privacy policies for children. Keep in mind that U.S. government Web sites must have a clear and conspicuous privacy policy. Communicate special exceptions for valid legal procedures in your privacy policies. Provide tangible value for personal information.

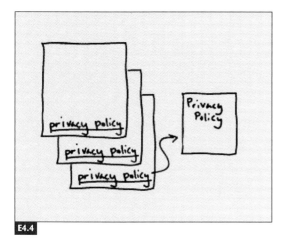

Figure E4.4

Make the privacy policy available on each Web page of your site.

❋ CONSIDER THESE OTHER PATTERNS

The privacy policy is part of the FAIR INFORMATION PRACTICES (E3) pattern, which describes reasonable rules that should be followed when you're collecting and handling personal information. The privacy policy should be available on most pages on a Web site, and it should be especially prominent on key pages like SIGN-IN/NEW ACCOUNT (H2) and QUICK-FLOW CHECKOUT (F1).

SECURE CONNECTIONS (E6) are one way of helping to provide security for personal information transmitted over the Web.

Personal information can be used for such things as PERSONALIZED CONTENT (D4), PERSONALIZED RECOMMENDATIONS (G3), E-MAIL SUBSCRIPTIONS (E2), QUICK ADDRESS SELECTION (F4), QUICK SHIPPING METHOD SELECTION (F5), and PERSISTENT CUSTOMER SESSIONS (H5).

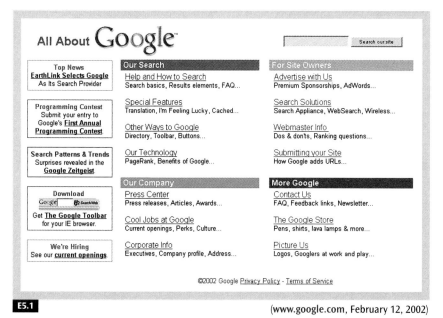

E5.1

(www.google.com, February 12, 2002)

Figure E5.1

Google's **About Us** Web page targets several customer groups, including people interested in learning more about search engines, site owners interested in advertising and improving their ranking in search results, and prospective employees.

✱ BACKGROUND

Another way of building trust is to provide information about the company or the people behind the Web site, including basic real-world information, such as a mailing address, phone number, and fax number, as well as background information on the company and the people in the company. This pattern describes how to organize this information in the **About Us** pages.

✳ PROBLEM

Many Web sites have a great deal of useful background information that is distinct from the main focus of the Web site, such as contact information and public relations. You need a way of organizing all of this information.

When people encounter your Web site for the first time, they have three questions in mind:

- Who are you?
- What do you do?
- Why should I trust you?

The **About Us** pages are one way the Web site can help answer these questions. **About Us** pages collect assorted background information about a Web site, providing information about the people, the organization, and/or the company behind the HTML. **About Us** pages are also important for establishing trust because they let customers know that there are real people and a real organization behind an otherwise virtual world.

The **About Us** pages should provide information tailored to customer demographics, interests, and needs. The list that follows identifies some of the things often found on **About Us** pages. The list is by no means definitive, and you will have to tailor it for your specific Web site genre, but it should give you a flavor of what you should have:

1. Organizational profile
2. Contact information
3. Disclaimers and legal information
4. Customers and partners
5. Employment opportunities
6. Public relations
7. Investor relations
8. Community relations
9. Site credits
10. Frequently asked questions

1. Organizational Profile • The profile describes who you are and what you do. It might include a description of the team behind the Web site, a brief history of the company, an overview of products and services, and a mission statement that communicates your UP-FRONT VALUE PROPOSITION (C2). However, the profile should be written from a customer-centered perspective. You may know what your company does, but visitors might not (see Figure E5.2). For example, if you're a law firm, it makes sense to identify the general types of law you practice. If you're a consulting firm, it makes sense to list your strengths and specialties.

2. Contact Information • Contact information is information that every business must have, such as a physical mailing address, phone numbers, fax numbers, and e-mail addresses. Having a physical address is more important than it may seem on the surface. It is sometimes difficult to tell if the company behind a Web site is a real company or a fly-by-night company. Listing a street address and directions to your company can help allay some of your customers' fears.

Phone and fax numbers are important for the same reason. Maybe a customer is having a problem late at night. Maybe a customer's order is wrong. Maybe someone needs immediate help, or just prefers phone and fax over e-mail. For these reasons it's crucial to have numbers that your customers can use.

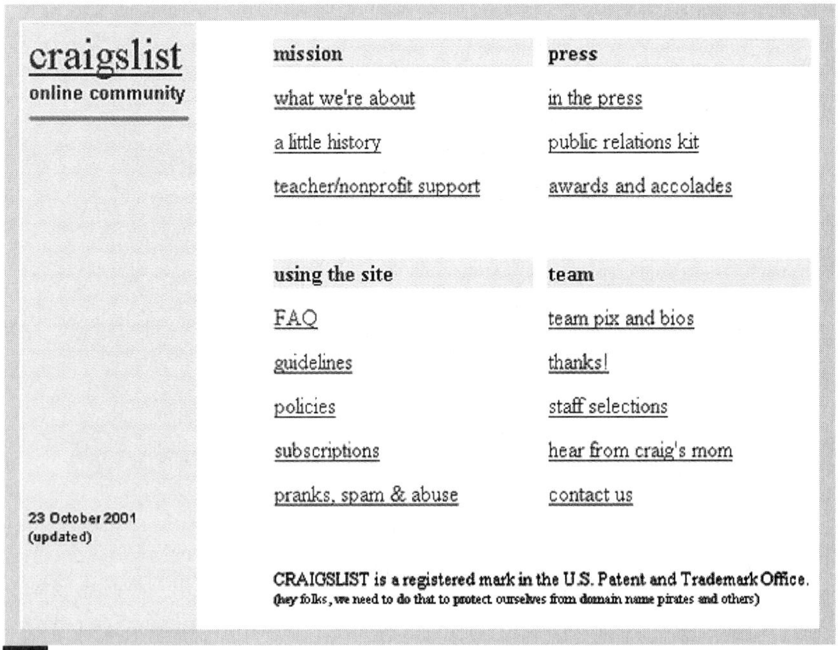

Figure E5.2

Craigslist has a simple, down-to-earth **About Us** page. The "mission" section describes the values and history of the site. The "press" section has links to where the site is mentioned in mainstream media, as well as a public relations kit for journalists. The "using the site" section describes what is acceptable behavior in the community forums. The "team" section describes the people behind the site and includes a charming minibiography about the founder by his mother.

craigslist
online community

mission	press
what we're about	in the press
a little history	public relations kit
teacher/nonprofit support	awards and accolades

using the site	team
FAQ	team pix and bios
guidelines	thanks!
policies	staff selections
subscriptions	hear from craig's mom
pranks, spam & abuse	contact us

23 October 2001 (updated)

CRAIGSLIST is a registered mark in the U.S. Patent and Trademark Office. (hey folks, we need to do that to protect ourselves from domain name pirates and others)

E5.2

(www.craigslist.org, February 14, 2002)

On the other hand, some people prefer e-mail. Your customers may want to report a PAGE NOT FOUND (K14) error. Or maybe they need some tech support. Or maybe they want to compliment you on how cool and usable your Web site is. Again, whatever the reason, make sure you have e-mail addresses to which your customers can send questions and comments.

3. Disclaimers and Legal Information • Many Web sites have a link to their PRIVACY POLICY (E4) and to their **Terms of Use** page from their **About Us** page. Some Web sites also list rules about the right way to link to the site and provide images that people can use. In addition, some Web sites have disclaimers about the content on the Web site, as well as fair use policies. For example, the LEGO Web site (see Figure E5.3) has a page describing how fans of the toy can create their own Web sites in a way that does not infringe on any copyrighted materials or trademarks.

Figure E5.3

The LEGO **About Us** Web pages include a page about fair play, describing why LEGO has to protect its trademarks, and what fans may and may not do when creating their own Web sites about the toy. (Lego is a trademark of the LEGO Group © 2001 The LEGO Group. The LEGO® trademarks and products are used with permission. The LEGO Group does not sponsor or endorse *The Design of Sites*.)

(www.lego.com, February 1, 2002)

4. Customers and Partners • Listing some of your customers and partners helps establish your credibility. A list of links to past and present customers and partners is like a list of references that other people can check. It also makes it look like you have been reliable in the past and are likely to be reliable in the future. Be sure to ask for permission from any customers and partners before listing them.

5. Employment Opportunities • This page simply describes what kinds of job openings and internships your company or organization has available. Large companies often provide very advanced database searches, describing positions, responsibilities, and geographic locations. Smaller companies do not need to be as sophisticated, and they often just list all of the open positions.

6. Public Relations • The public relations page contains information published by, as well as for, media outlets. Included are such things as

- Press releases about new products, new partners, changes in management, and so on
- Links to or excerpts of media coverage about the Web site
- Awards won
- Contact information for interviews (see Figure E5.4)

7. Investor Relations • The investor relations page contains relevant financial literature about the company. Common items included here are annual reports, Securities and Exchange Commission (SEC) filings, analyst coverage, and positive media coverage.

8. Community Relations • The community relations page describes how the company gives back to the local community, including past charitable events, as well as what the company can provide for future events, such as software, hardware, services, time, people, or money. It is also useful to explain how people can contact your company to request help.

9. Site Credits • The site credits page gives credit to the Web teams that helped develop the Web site. This is often useful for Web design firms because it gives them a little bit of free advertising.

10. Frequently Asked Questions • Some Web sites collect questions that customers often ask and create a FREQUENTLY ASKED QUESTIONS (H7), or **FAQ**, page that answers them.

Figure E5.4

The LexisNexis **About Us** page contains many of the features described in this section, including an organizational profile, contact information, and disclaimers and legal information.

(www.lexis-nexis.com, October 6, 2001)

✳ SOLUTION

Collect background information in About Us **pages. These pages should help people learn more about who you are, what you do, and why they can trust you. You should include things like an organizational profile, contact information, disclaimers and legal information, customers and partners, employment opportunities, public relations, investor relations, community relations, site credits, and frequently asked questions.**

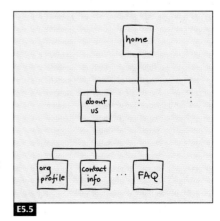

Figure E5.5

Although the specific content for the **About Us** pages will vary from site to site, they should be easily accessible from the home-page portal.

✳ CONSIDER THESE OTHER PATTERNS

The **About Us** page should help reinforce the Web site's UP-FRONT VALUE PROPOSITION (C2). It should also have a link to the Web site's PRIVACY POLICY (E4) and FREQUENTLY ASKED QUESTIONS (H7) pages.

Contact information should be included in the **About Us** pages, as well as on the PAGE NOT FOUND (K14) error page.

Figure E6.1

At Half.com, the checkout process is conducted over a secure connection. Half.com reinforces this fact by placing a "Secure Shopping" icon at the top right of the checkout pages.

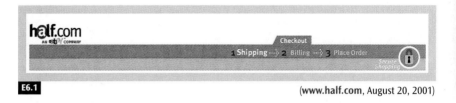

E6.1 (**www.half.com**, August 20, 2001)

✳ BACKGROUND

E3 One of the requirements of FAIR INFORMATION PRACTICES (E3) is collecting and handling sensitive personal information in a secure manner. One way of doing this is with secure connections. This pattern deals with interface issues for letting people know that they are entering a secure area.

✳ PROBLEM

People are often uncomfortable transmitting sensitive personal information over the Web.

Many people are uncomfortable sending sensitive information online. There are still many worries that credit card numbers and passwords can be stolen by hackers. One of the ways of tackling this problem is to use secure connections.

You can establish a secure connection using Secure Sockets Layer (SSL). SSL uses a sophisticated encryption scheme to scramble data sent over the Web, making it very difficult for snoopers to look at the data. You can tell you are using SSL if the Web address begins with *https* instead of just *http*. Most Web browsers also provide feedback that you are using a secure connection, as Figures E6.2 and E6.3 show. (A full discussion of the technical details involved in setting up SSL is beyond the scope of this book. See the Resources section later in the book for more information.)

The problem is that this feedback is extremely minimal and easily overlooked. One way of reassuring your customers is by providing better feedback. For example, Figures E6.4 and E6.5 show how an ACTION BUTTON **K4** (K4) can be used to make it clear that a secure connection is being used.

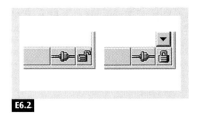

E6.2

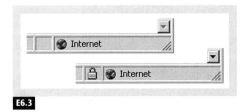

E6.3

Figure E6.2

The screen shot on the left shows an insecure connection in Netscape 6.1. The one on the right shows a secure connection.

Figure E6.3

The screen shot on the top shows an insecure connection in Microsoft Internet Explorer 6.0. The one on the bottom shows a secure connection.

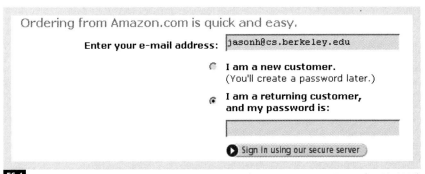

E6.4

(www.amazon.com, September 22, 2001)

Figure E6.4

Amazon.com uses a labeled button to let customers know that the login information will be secure.

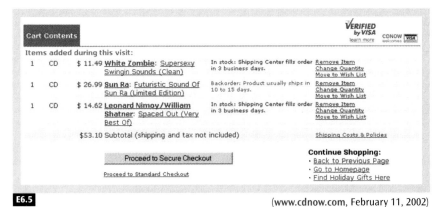

E6.5

(www.cdnow.com, February 11, 2002)

Figure E6.5

CDNOW uses secure connections for its shopping cart. An action button labeled **Proceed to Secure Checkout** reinforces this point.

Some Web sites provide further assurances about their security. For example, Figure E6.6 shows L. L. Bean's guarantee that all orders placed on its Web site will be safe and secure.

Figure E6.6

In addition to using secure connections, L. L. Bean provides assurances that all orders taken on its Web site will be safe and secure.

E6.6

(www.llbean.com, September 22, 2001)

✳ SOLUTION

Use a labeled icon or a labeled action button to let customers know that they are transmitting information securely. If needed, provide a Web page describing the security practices you use to reassure customers that their personal information will be kept safe.

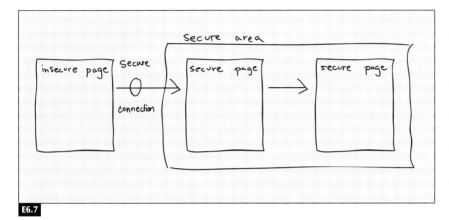

E6.7

Figure E6.7

Web pages should provide feedback to let customers know when information is being transmitted securely. Special care should be taken that the secure connection is maintained for as long as necessary.

✳ CONSIDER THESE OTHER PATTERNS

Secure connections help safeguard sensitive personal information that your customers send you, partially addressing the security requirements in FAIR INFORMATION PRACTICES (E3).

Secure connections should be used in all Web pages where sensitive information is entered by the customer or displayed for the customer. This stipulation includes places such as SIGN-IN/NEW ACCOUNT (H2), QUICK-FLOW CHECKOUT (F1), important PROCESS FUNNELS (H1), ACCOUNT MANAGEMENT (H4), and any Web page dealing with financial information. Specially labeled ACTION BUTTONS (K4) can be used to let customers know that the transaction is secure.

F1 QUICK-FLOW CHECKOUT

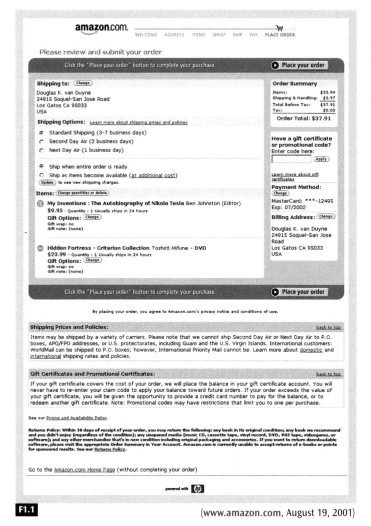

F1.1

Figure F1.1

Amazon.com's checkout lets the customer specify what is necessary, see the important details, and finish quickly.

✳ BACKGROUND

PERSONAL E-COMMERCE (A1) calls for an easy shopping experience for customers, with personal benefits. Once shoppers have collected all the items they wish to purchase in a SHOPPING CART (F3), this pattern shows how to have them check out, using a quick and simple PROCESS FUNNEL (H1).

A1

F3

H1

✳ PROBLEM

An e-commerce shopping experience will not be enjoyable, or worse, a purchase might not be completed, if the checkout process is cumbersome, confusing, or error prone.

By the time your customers get to the checkout process on your site, they may be impatient to finish the order and get out the door. Online shoppers do not want surprises, such as hidden charges, unavailable items, tedious text entries, confusing links, or broken pages. These can only frustrate and even scare customers away. Only a straightforward process that is streamlined to include minimal navigation and data entry can make the process feel easy.

Eliminate Distractions • It is easy to complicate the checkout. Shoppers can become distracted during a purchase by following extra links on a page, or by clicking on buttons that don't do what they expect.

People who want to make a purchase do not like long or complicated instructions. When looking for the next ACTION BUTTON (K4), people tend to look at what is immediately visible on the page. They will go back to the instructions only when the buttons fail to do what they expect. Likewise, to keep distracting links to a minimum, this is a good time to stop CROSS-SELLING AND UP-SELLING (G2). In addition, customers want to go through a minimum of pages because each page takes time to download and understand. So each page is critical. The entire checkout sequence should use a PROCESS FUNNEL (H1) to eliminate these distractions (see Figure F1.2).

Address Potential Deal Breakers • When customers are about to place an order, they may have questions about shipping or return policies, and they will want answers even before they begin to check out. They might wonder any of the following:

- When will my order be shipped?
- Are the products in stock?
- What are my shipping options?
- How much will shipping my order cost?
- If not all the products are in stock, will you ship what you have?
- What is your return policy?
- Will I be charged tax?
- Do you ship internationally?
- Do you offer gift wrapping?
- Can I ship to multiple addresses?

F1.2

(www.half.com, August 20, 2001)

Figure F1.2

By the last page of the checkout process, Half.com stops cross-selling and up-selling to customers to ensure that they will complete their orders.

Your ability to answer these questions can help improve sales. Provide this information before customers add items to their SHOPPING CARTS (F3) or during checkout, depending on their needs (see Figure F1.3).

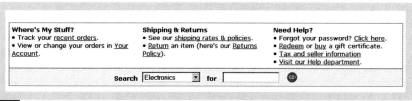

F1.3

(www.amazon.com, August 19, 2001)

Figure F1.3

Amazon.com provides answers to deal breakers on key pages so that customers can have their questions answered quickly.

Build Trust throughout the Process • Customers are sensitive to the order and amount of information you ask. Personal information is just that, and people do not want to reveal more than they need to, until they need to. If a Web site asks for too much information up front—personal or otherwise—customers become suspicious or negative. Remember that in a physical store, customers are not asked for any personal information until they check out.

This problem is even worse if you do not provide a clear PRIVACY POLICY (E4). Some site visitors may not want their personal information stored at all, and they will continue with the order only if they know that the information will be used for just the single transaction, as with a GUEST ACCOUNT (H3). For example, at united.com, customers who do not want their personal information stored can create an itinerary and check out as guests. The site explicitly informs them that "guest information is not stored online." Other customers may want their personal information stored for convenience because they do not want to reenter it all every time they place an order.

Customers are often not comfortable entering personal information if the Web site is not secure or does not provide a SECURE CONNECTION (E6). And no one wants to try to remember yet another unique user name and password to yet another Web site.

Recap the Order • Shoppers want to make sure all the details of their orders are correct. An ORDER SUMMARY (F7) lets them review the products that have been selected, the total cost, and the shipping information. If any information is incorrect, customers should be able to edit the order summary by changing their orders or any of the delivery or billing information. Customers want to see that the information they entered will be used correctly so that they don't find out later, for example, that the shipping and billing addresses were reversed. Give them an ORDER CONFIRMATION AND THANK-YOU (F8) that confirms their order, gives the order number, and says how to contact the company, all on one page so that they can print it out for their records (see Figure F1.4).

Retailers need to make sure that funds are available in customer accounts before they process orders because sometimes criminals use stolen credit cards or a customer tries to use a card that has insufficient funds. Verifying the availability of funds at checkout increases the likelihood that a transaction will be completed with sufficient funds. Several commercial services offer systems that plug into your server to carry out verification and credit card processing.

(www.snapfish.com, January 30, 2002)

Figure F1.4

A good order confirmation page includes an order number, the order date, shipping and billing details, and an itemized list of all products ordered. Customers can print this page and use it for reference later.

☀ SOLUTION

Follow a simple four-step approach so that customers can complete their orders:

1. In a secure area of the site, allow customers to check out without storing their information, or let them create or use a customer identifier so that they do not need to reenter information. Set expectations by giving an overview of the process and providing answers to common questions.
2. Gather shipping and handling information and shipping methods so that you can tabulate the total cost of the order, including taxes, at the next step.
3. Show the total cost of the order along with the order summary so that customers can verify that the information is correct. Ask for payment information, and ease any concerns about the security and privacy of your customers' financial information.

4. Confirm that funds for the order are currently available, and give the customer a final opportunity to confirm the order. When the order is complete, provide a printable receipt and invite the customer to return.

On all pages, keep action links visible at all times, and remove all links that do not direct customers to closing the sale.

Figure F1.5

Checking out should be a simple four-step process that funnels customers toward completion of an order.

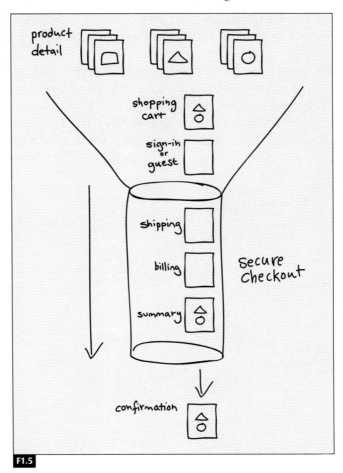

✴ CONSIDER THESE OTHER PATTERNS

E6
H3
H2

Make a SECURE CONNECTION (E6) with the customer before providing a GUEST ACCOUNT (H3) or asking the customer to register on a SIGN-IN/NEW ACCOUNT (H2) page. Allay concerns about the process that your customers are entering, or answer questions they may have about particular policies.

Give an overview of the process and provide your PRIVACY POLICY (E4), CONTEXT-SENSITIVE HELP (H8), and answers to FREQUENTLY ASKED QUESTIONS (H7). Provide links to your return policy for EASY RETURNS (F9).

Use HIGH-VISIBILITY ACTION BUTTONS (K5) because probably you will have more information than will fit on a single screen. Provide a progress bar on each page so that shoppers know where they are in the process.

Allow customers to use QUICK ADDRESS SELECTION (F4) or MULTIPLE DESTINATIONS (G5), and provide a means of GIFT GIVING (G6) if appropriate. Let customers choose a QUICK SHIPPING METHOD SELECTION (F5) on the same page.

On the next page, provide an ORDER SUMMARY (F7), as well as links so that people can make changes before you ask for their preferred PAYMENT METHODS (F6). Finally, give customers one last chance to verify their orders with an ORDER CONFIRMATION AND THANK-YOU (F8) page. To reduce your customer support calls, direct people to ORDER TRACKING AND HISTORY (G7), if you provide this facility.

Figure F2.1

Dell's product details page highlights the most important information high on the page to make sure it appears above the fold. In-depth information appears below the fold and on separate tabs. The site also provides some unique features, such as the product configuration button **Customize it**, because each product has many options.

F2.1

❋ BACKGROUND

Every PERSONAL E-COMMERCE (A1) site must allow customers to view details about the products it sells because customers will demand that information before they feel comfortable to proceed with a QUICK-FLOW CHECKOUT (F1). This pattern provides the framework for all product pages.

✳ PROBLEM

When shopping, customers want to see product details to help inform their buying decisions. They must also trust a seller before deciding to make a purchase. Many sites do not provide enough in-depth information about their products, or they project an untrustworthy image.

Having plentiful, well-organized, helpful information about your site's products or services helps customers make better and more frequent purchasing decisions. Shoppers need to scan for basic, valuable blocks of information, including product photos, thorough descriptions, features, prices, and even benefits. When this information is sparse or hard to find, one of the big advantages of online shopping is lost.

Web sites have nearly unlimited space to describe, show, and even critique products. If your customers are unfamiliar with a product, detailed information including images and demonstrations can give them what they need to make decisions.

When information is poorly organized, valuable content is not enough. If the presentation is poor, visitors may not find the information that will close the deal, or they may judge a site untrustworthy because of a lack of attention to basics.

Which site are customers more likely to purchase from in Figure F2.2? Figure F2.2a shows a product shot with other items in the picture, obscure terms like *Western Wear* and *14.75 oz. Denim,* unaligned text and navigation tools, and poor spelling. Figure F2.2b shows a clean product shot, suitable product details, an easy-to-read GRID LAYOUT (I1), sizing assistance, and color examples.

Figure F2.2

(a) Small improvements, such as a better product shot and corrected spelling, will improve this product detail page. (b) This product detail page shows the fabric colors up close, helps with sizing, and has a clean product shot.

I1

TOMBSTONE JACKET

High grade Western Wear, five button front with adjustable side tabs. 100% cotton 14.75 oz. Denim.

Pendleton leather jean patch, Jacquard wool under collar and back panel, dry clea.

Double click on photo to enlarge - hit back button to return.

DK414   Regular price: $100.00   Sale price: **$90.00**   Size:: [S ▾]
[Order]

F2.2a

clean jean jacket
PRICE: $58.00
SIZE: XS - XXL

ITEM: #174409

Choose the classic indigo wash or the hip, dark rinsed wash. Classic fit. Falls to waist, two side pockets, two front button pocket, durable reinforced seams, front copper button closure, adjustable waist, button cuffs. 100% Cotton. Machine wash. Imported.

[▶ PURCHASE THIS ITEM]

AVAILABLE COLORS:

indigo blue   rinsed

SHOPPING TOOLS:
[Size Charts]

WISHLIST:
[Add Item To Wish List]

We currently deliver orders within the United States and U.S.territories only.

F2.2b

Create a Clean, Standard Template • A product detail page that is quick to scan and read helps customers find the information they need on a conceptual level, and gives them a satisfying experience on an emotional level. A standardized product template helps customers find the details they need as they move from one product page to the next.

On the emotional level, some customers become intrigued with the way a product looks or sounds (if it makes a sound), and the image it portrays.[1] For some people, the first impression of the product can be the most important. Portraying the image that your customers respond to the most—one consistent with your SITE BRANDING (E1)—helps to positively reinforce your company's identity and your brand.

General information is useful to every customer, so providing it at the top of the page is helpful. Some things, like price, are important for almost every customer. Learning what else is useful can take trial and error. You might evaluate one design versus another through an active test online (see Appendix E—Online Research) to see which page works best on a live site, or more deliberately, through usability research on a page design (see Appendix A—Running Usability Evaluations). Both methods require time and effort by different team members in your organization. Investing in evaluating these subtle nuances offers a strategic value to your company because a more effective product page can easily translate into higher sales.

A clean design in a GRID LAYOUT (I1) lets customers scan a page to find information by reading along a line instead of forcing their eyes to jump around the page. Create a PAGE TEMPLATE (D1) that takes into account these elements and the factors described in the sections that follow.

Keep Key Elements above the Fold • The exact information shown ABOVE THE FOLD (I2) depends on what customers need to see first. If you hide crucial facts too far down the page, customers may never see them. The key e-commerce elements to keep above the fold include the following:

---

1 Direct references to other emotional factors, such as touch, taste, and smell, may be important to your product line, but they are difficult to portray online. Usually companies forgo direct references to these emotional factors for more indirect ones, by portraying a compelling image. For example, perfume ads generally must sell a scent with an image. Wine merchants have developed a special language to help describe their products, using metaphors of fruits and other flavors. Although this is a far cry from the emotional response of actually tasting a wine, it can often be as close as the customer gets without going to the winery for a taste.

- **Standard navigation and shopping tools.** Customers want to use the standard navigation bars, shopping tools, and search tools right away if the current product is not the one they want. Forcing customers to backtrack to find a different product only frustrates them.
- **A small product thumbnail that is clickable.** Unless all your customers have fast Internet access, use FAST-DOWNLOADING IMAGES (L2). To keep the initial product detail page fast and simple, keep your product shot small and in JPEG or GIF format. Provide a higher-resolution, more finely detailed image of each product so that customers can examine it for important particulars that help them make a purchase decision. Whereas the product shot on the first page must work on the lowest-bandwidth connections with browsers that do not have special visualization plug-ins for the detailed shot,[2] you could use a high-resolution image that can pan, if the product encompasses a room or an outdoor space. For some products, the back side might be as important as the front, in which case you can make the link go to a product image that customers can rotate.
- **A needs-oriented description that goes along with the product title.** This description can be just enough to show customers the major differences between this product and others. Make sure the description answers customers' needs, such as how a jacket "keeps out the cold." This brief description may also be used elsewhere on the site.
- **The product price and currency** (unless options change the price greatly). Because nine times out of ten the price is a part of the decision-making process, your customers expect to find this information quickly and easily. Price gives customers a quick understanding of the relative costs of similar products. In some cases, when the product's price varies by 50 percent or more, showing a low price might mislead customers, and showing a high price might turn them away. In these cases, show either a range of prices or a base price and a typically configured price.
- **Product option quick picks or a configuration button.** If a product has several options—whether configuration, style, or something else— quick picks and configuration buttons are easy ways to let customers select their options while they are in the context of the current product, so that they can browse and choose. Implement this feature with a pick list when short textual descriptions are sufficiently descriptive,

---

2 Visualization plug-ins, like QuickTime, that provide panning and rotating, are not always included with Web browsers. Most customers will not download and install these plug-ins to use your Web site.

Figure F2.3

Nordstrom shows the options for this product. The red arrow directs customers to choose size first and then color. The color pick list is generated according to the size chosen.

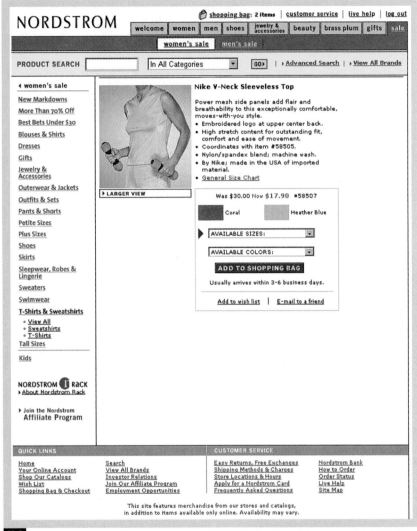

F2.3   (www.nordstrom.com, October 3, 2001)

 or with a pop-up window that takes customers through a configuration PROCESS FUNNEL (H1) that returns the choice to the parent product detail window (see Figure F2.3).

In some cases, showing product availability on an option-by-option basis may be difficult. Unfortunately, customers who want the blue version of a product, for example, will be frustrated and might cancel a purchase if they find out later in the process that the blue version is not available after all. The best solution is to show only the options that are currently in stock. See SHOPPING CART (F3) for ideas on how to do this.

- **Overall ratings of your product, if appropriate.** To help your customers understand how the current product stacks up against similar ones, give them a summary of how the company rates it, how outside experts (magazine reviews or awards) rate it, and how customers rate it. Ratings should use standard scales of either five stars or an industry-specific standard.

- **An idea of when the product will arrive so that the customer can plan for its arrival.** This estimate might come from your inventory system, your production system, or your typical deployment schedule. Failing to include this information, or providing inaccurate information, will greatly increase your support costs.

- **A product item number (if the site is a sales channel).** If customers use the site to order items by phone or in person, a product part number greatly simplifies the task of locating the exact product desired.

- **The Add to Cart ACTION BUTTON (K4).** Customers might be sold by the title, description, photo, ratings, and price alone. Make it easy to order the product by keeping a visible **Add to Cart** action button high on the page. If applicable to your site, a **Wish List** link, used for storing products for future purchase or for purchase by friends and family as a gift, works well when it is near the **Add to Cart** button.

- **Links to more detailed information.** Let customers know that more information exists and is only a click away, by making links to these resources visible above the fold. If customers want more in-depth reviews, for example, they should be able to click right to **Reviews**. If customers are concerned about the product's physical dimensions, they should be able to link to **Product Specs.** Both bits of additional information could be on the same page, below the fold, but the links will make customers aware that more information exists and will provide quick routes to it.

You could also supply more detailed information through direct product comparison tools. Comparators, recommenders, and selection guides can help make the selection process easier. For complex products with similar features, such tools might even be required for customers to make selections online, without a human attendant to help.

Figure F2.4 shows examples of how two different Web sites manage to keep this information above the fold.

Put Less Crucial Information below the Fold • Place secondary elements that are not crucial to customers below the fold. These elements include the following:

- **Full product description.** This description will answer questions about the product's usefulness, its target buyer, and its positive characteristics. Customers are looking to fulfill a need—whether functionality, features, or style. The full product description fills in the blank for customers when they think, "I need something that can do _____."
- **In-depth expert and customer reviews.** License the content or highlight product reviews. Provide a way for customers to add ratings and content directly to your product detail page. Highlight the best products with special markings, such as "The best in the category" or "Five stars." Ratings like "G100" are not very useful.
- **Related products and accessories.** List accessories that might be useful, and show related products that complement the current product. Link directly to these products. Or if they do not require much explanation (such as batteries), creating a separate **Add to Cart** button will make customer purchases even simpler, provided that the customer does not lose the context of the current page.
- **Similar products with numerous features.** Sometimes it is difficult to pick the right product among many. If you have many similar products, provide a means to compare and contrast. Include expert ratings, customer ratings, popularity scores, and feature-by-feature comparisons.

F2.4a

(www.netflix.com, December 3, 2001)

Figure F2.4

(a) Above the fold (the red dashed line), these product detail pages include a brief movie description, a small product shot, the price, links to more detailed information farther down the page, and obvious action buttons to purchase the movie. Below the fold, Netflix provides a detailed synopsis of each movie and lists similar movies and customer reviews. (b) Cooking.com gives product descriptions and detailed characteristics below the fold.

F2.4b   (www.cooking.com, December 3, 2001)

✳ SOLUTION

Provide in-depth information in a grid layout. Keep important items that every customer will need above the fold, such as general navigation, product thumbnails, needs-based descriptions, prices, an options pick list or a link to a configuration page, product ratings and delivery time frame, the Add to Cart **action button, and links to more detailed information, even if the information is farther down on the page. Put secondary items, such as a full product description, reviews, related products, and a product comparator if possible, below the fold.**

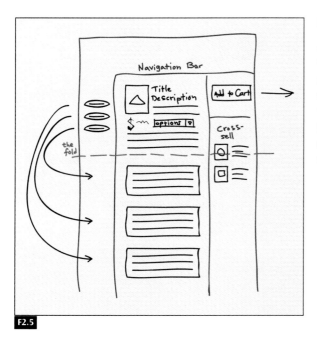

Figure F2.5

A good product description page puts the key product details—such as the description, a thumbnail, and the price—above the fold and additional information below the fold.

F2.5

✳ CONSIDER THESE OTHER PATTERNS

Keep the product details page consistent with other SITE BRANDING (E1), and build it with a PAGE TEMPLATE (D1) in a GRID LAYOUT (I1). Make sure the key elements are ABOVE THE FOLD (I2), and put them in CONTENT MODULES (D2) for database updates. Show links to your return policy to ensure EASY RETURNS (F9) and to assure your customers that they can change their minds if they are not satisfied. Provide **Add to Cart** ACTION BUTTONS (K4) to keep the shopping experience moving through the PROCESS FUNNEL (H1). For all product detail information, make a PRINTABLE PAGE (D8).

E1

D1 I1

I2

D2

F9

K4

H1

D8

Figure F3.1

Amazon.com's shopping cart keeps navigation to the rest of the site clearly indicated at the top of the page, but it makes checking out even more abundantly clear. For a business that makes money online through sales, it is critical that customers find their way through to checkout.

(www.amazon.com, October 26, 2000)

✳ BACKGROUND

 After customers select products from a CLEAN PRODUCT DETAIL (F2) page, a successful PERSONAL E-COMMERCE (A1) site will use a well-designed shopping cart to lead the customer to the start of a QUICK-FLOW CHECKOUT (F1), removing any barriers to making the purchase.

✳ PROBLEM

Customers want to collect and purchase several items in one transaction. Online shopping carts can provide much more than their offline namesakes, such as making it easy to change the quantity of an item in the cart. However, making shopping carts simple and useful requires restraint.

The shopping cart is a common way to let customers keep track of what they want before they finalize a purchase. Clear ACTION BUTTONS (K4) throughout the site must indicate how to get to the shopping cart and how to put items in it. Let customers use your shopping cart without having to enter personal information. This will encourage them to browse. Once customers arrive at the critical shopping cart page, the existence of too many options can distract them into wandering off without completing their orders. Give shoppers the opportunity to continue shopping at this stage, but encourage them to check out too.

A clear path to the QUICK-FLOW CHECKOUT (F1) is important for shoppers who are ready to buy. Strike a balance between providing navigation to continue shopping and navigation to check out.

Provide Easy Access to the Shopping Cart • Customers may decide to check out from any page on the Web site. They start the checkout by reviewing items in their cart to verify products, quantities, and subtotals.

On every page, include a **Go to Shopping Cart** button so that people know how to proceed whenever they're finally ready to say, "I'm done shopping for now." Not everyone understands the shopping cart icon (see the small icon at the top of Figure F3.2), so a text label helps.

Make it easy to add items to the shopping cart from product pages. You might think this is obvious, but you would be surprised at how many Web sites make this a difficult task. Amazon.com does this right, as Figure F3.2 shows. On the right-hand side of the page is a yellow HIGH-VISIBILITY ACTION BUTTON (K5) that draws the eye. Also note the label. Besides saying, **Add to Shopping Cart**, it even provides reassurance, saying, "You can always remove it later."

Let Customers Continue to Shop • One common source of confusion for online shoppers is what to do after adding a product to a shopping cart. Help customers by making their options clear (beyond hitting the **Back** button, of course). In the Amazon.com example in Figure F3.1, an ACTION BUTTON (K4) labeled **Continue Shopping** lets customers go back to the last product category page.

Figure F3.2

Each product page should give a clear way to add the product to the shopping cart. Note how Amazon.com uses action buttons to make it look like customers can push down on the **Add to Shopping Cart** button.

(www.amazon.com, October 26, 2000)

 Help Customers Proceed to Checkout • Use ACTION BUTTONS (K4) labeled **Proceed to Checkout** to lead customers to a QUICK-FLOW CHECKOUT (F1) that allows them to finish their order without distraction. Eliminate distractions on the shopping cart page itself by maintaining the main navigation bar, while eliminating any subnavigation.

Give Details in the Cart • Each item description in the shopping cart needs to remind the shopper what it is. Provide the following information:

- The name of the item to be purchased and a link to a detailed description
- A short description of the item, such as "book," "CD," or "software"
- The size, color, and other details as appropriate
- The availability and delivery time frame of the item (*especially* important during the holiday season)
- The price of each item
- The quantity to be purchased and a way to modify the quantity
- A way to remove the item from the shopping cart by clicking on a remove button or by unchecking a check box (you might ask people to set the quantity to zero, but not everyone notices these instructions)

A shopping cart must also inform the customer of other charges and offer links to additional information about the purchase:

- Shipping and handling costs if known, or how they will be calculated
- Any applicable taxes (again, if known)

- Any other charges that contribute to the total cost
- Subtotals for the items in the cart
- Link to the return policy
- Link to shipping information, including costs, acceptable destinations, order processing times, and shipping times

Set Expectations about Availability • Customers become frustrated when they add products to their shopping carts and find out later that the items are not available. For a Web site to reflect product availability in the shopping cart, however, inventory management software must be integrated with the Web server software. Set up business rules to automatically remove products from the Web servers when stock on hand drops below a certain level. Include a buffer in case multiple customers pick the same option at the same time. Keep track of products and product option availability.

Set customers' expectations as well as you can, either with high precision, such as "Ships in 24 hours," or with less precision, such as "Usually ships in 3–6 days." The precision factor depends on the amount of volume your business does and the inventory kept on hand.

Provide this information as early as possible, on the CLEAN PRODUCT DETAIL (F2) page, as well as in the shopping cart.

F2

Store Carts for Later • One serious problem on some e-commerce sites is that the shopping cart disappears if a customer does not do anything on the site for a while. There are dozens of plausible explanations beyond "the customer abandoned the shopping cart." Customers might be comparison shopping on other Web sites, taking a lunch break, or talking to someone next to them. At a minimum, save customer shopping carts for *24 hours* or more. However, a saved cart must be merged with a new cart when a shopper logs in and collects a new cart full of other products. In such cases be sure to communicate that a customer already has items in the cart as soon as you can. In addition, you must tell customers about items in the saved carts that are no longer in stock.

Another option to give customers is the ability to store items for later purchase. This option can be provided in one of two ways: as a private list for each customer or as a public list for customers to share with friends and family, also known as a *wish list*. CDNOW has such a wish list (see Figure F3.3). Clearly wish lists are not useful if they are retained for only 90 days. The best approach is to retain an item in a wish list until it has been purchased or explicitly removed.

Figure F3.3

CDNOW lets customers save items in a wish list, helping them to remember the products they would like to purchase. It also makes it easy to move items from the wish list to the shopping cart.

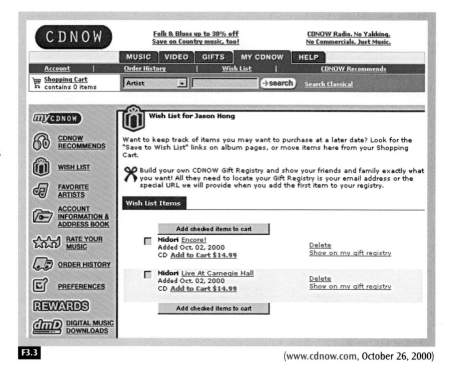

F3.3   (www.cdnow.com, October 26, 2000)

Cross-Sell and Up-Sell • Help your customers and your business by promoting products related to ones the customer already wants to purchase (see Figure F3.4). For example, printers also need paper and toner. Promoting related products in this way is **cross-selling. Up-selling** highlights products that have more features and benefits than the one the customer wants to purchase. Products highlighted through up-selling cost more too. For example, if customers select cell phones, a site could recommend phones with more features in the next price level. Highlight these cross-selling and up-selling opportunities at points in the purchase process, including in the shopping cart.

Be careful when cross-selling and up-selling, though, because it is possible to lose your customer by complicating the purchase. Keep the center of attention on the products your customer wants, and make the cross-selling and up-selling recommendations secondary. The CROSS-SELLING AND UP-SELLING (G2) pattern offers more specifics.

F3.4

(www.us.buy.com, February 13, 2002)

Figure F3.4

Buy.com cross-sells additional products on the shopping cart page. Because these products are well known, customers generally do not need to research them and may simply click the check box to add them to their orders. This strategy is similar to what supermarkets do when they put magazines and candy next to the checkout stand.

Show Cart Contents on Every Page • Every page can provide shopping cart item information so that customers remember what they selected without going back to the cart. Figure F3.5 shows how CDNOW displays the number of items in a customer's shopping cart. The Staples site takes a different approach by providing a mini-shopping cart (see Figure F3.6).

These approaches give constant feedback about cart contents, but they also take up precious screen real estate and can cause problems when customers use the **Back** button. In addition, they might curb enthusiasm if the shopper is constantly monitoring how many items are in the cart. Showing a list on every page may help when tens of products are needed and shoppers cannot remember what they have in their carts, but for sites with only a few items in a typical order, this approach needs testing with customers.

Observe Local Customs • Sometimes the shopping cart metaphor is not the best. In England, the term *shopping basket* is more appropriate, and this term is used by Amazon.co.uk, for instance. Other metaphors make more sense on particular types of sites. We have seen *shopping bag* on clothing and cosmetics sites, for example.

Figure F3.5

CDNOW's shopping cart tells customers how many items are in it.

F3.5

(www.cdnow.com, October 26, 2000)

F3.6

(www.staples.com, October 26, 2000)

Figure F3.6

On the right-hand side of each page of its Web site, Staples shows a mini-shopping cart that has a link to the full shopping cart.

✳ SOLUTION

Give customers easy access to the shopping cart from every page of your site. On product detail pages, make the Add to Cart **buttons hard to miss. On the shopping cart page itself, provide highly visible action buttons leading to checkout and action buttons to continue shopping, along with the top-level navigation elements and search features. In the detail of the contents, include product name, a short description, a link to the product page, availability time frame, price, quantity, a button to delete each item, shipping, tax, and subtotal information or links. Display a link to your return policy. Optionally, you might also cross-sell and up-sell other products on the cart page, and put a summary of the cart contents on every site page.**

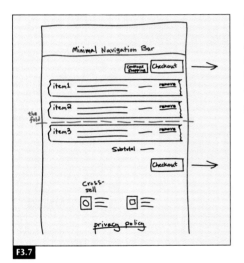

F3.7

Figure F3.7

A good shopping cart shows customers details about what they have bought, including how much the order is going to cost, and then makes it easy to check out without being distracted.

✳ CONSIDER THESE OTHER PATTERNS

One common feature on CLEAN PRODUCT DETAIL (F2) pages is to let people add items to the shopping cart. Shopping carts should have HIGH-VISIBILITY ACTION BUTTONS (K5) to let people start the QUICK-FLOW CHECKOUT (F1). Shopping carts are a good place for CROSS-SELLING AND UP-SELLING (G2), recommending products that may be useful, given the current items in the shopping cart. Issues of INTERNATIONALIZED AND LOCALIZED CONTENT (D10) are becoming important as more people worldwide use the Web. This means that you need to make sure the title of your shopping cart makes sense for the culture or country using your site. Provide links to your return policy to enable EASY RETURNS (F9) and to assure your customers that they can change their minds if they're not satisfied.

Figure F4.1

Half.com employs an address book and provides a simple, clean, single-column form for entering a new address.

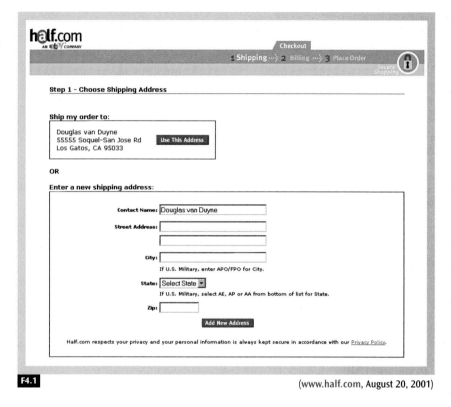

F4.1

(www.half.com, August 20, 2001)

✳ BACKGROUND

For QUICK-FLOW CHECKOUT (F1) on a PERSONAL E-COMMERCE (A1) site, each step must be simple and clearly defined. In the SHOPPING CART (F3) pattern, items are collected and summarized. This pattern provides the mechanism for choosing and entering addresses for shipping and billing.

✳ PROBLEM

Entering addresses need not be cumbersome, especially if customers are ordering from a site for a second time.

Customers must always enter their shipping and billing information if they are using a site for the first time. However, long, complicated, or poorly labeled forms intimidate people. Confusing forms also lead to errors. Furthermore, if customers return, they will likely need the previously entered address, but they might also need to enter an address of a friend (if it is a consumer e-commerce site) or another business location (if it is a business e-commerce site). In fact, customers may need to enter multiple addresses over time. Providing a list of previously entered addresses, as well as a clean, simple form with a space to enter new addresses, gives customers speed and flexibility.

This pattern provides a design solution for simple shipping and billing address pages. In Pattern Group G—Advanced E-Commerce, the MULTIPLE DESTINATIONS (G5) pattern covers sending one order to multiple locations.

Ⓖ
G5

Store Addresses • Customers who are returning to a site will likely use a previous address for shipping and billing. Putting the list of stored addresses at the top of the page ensures that they will immediately see one or more of their earlier addresses. To select a certain address, all they have to do is click on the button next to it. Putting an ACTION BUTTON (K4) labeled **Use this address** next to each address takes the customer to the next step of the order process (see Figure F4.2).

K4

Place a link at the top of the page for entering a new address, which the customer will do in an area beside or below the stored addresses. Even when many addresses are already stored, the link will be visible to the shopper.

Create a Clear Form for New Addresses • If customers are ordering from a site for the first time, the new address form should appear at the top of the page. If the customer has stored addresses, the link at the top of the page will scroll the customer to the right place on the page. To make the form for entering a new address easy to use, do the following:

- Build a simple GRID LAYOUT (I1) with all of the field labels right-aligned along a single grid line, and all of the text entry fields in a single column left-aligned along the same grid line. This arrangement helps people scan the labels and fields (see the new shipping address form in Figure F4.1).
- Keep the number of fields to a minimum to simplify data entry.

I1

Figure F4.2

To help people check out quickly, Nordstrom stores customer addresses for quick reuse (left) and provides space for a new destination (right).

F4.2

(www.nordstrom.com, October 3, 2001)

- Keep labels and instructions short because customers tend to skim forms and resort to reading only when necessary.

Figure F4.3 shows an example of a form that does not follow these conventions. You can immediately see several reasons why it would be hard for customers to use.

Use only the following few fields:

- Full Name
- Address Line 1 (or company name)
- Address Line 2 (optional)
- City
- State/Province/Region
- ZIP/Postal Code
- Country
- Phone

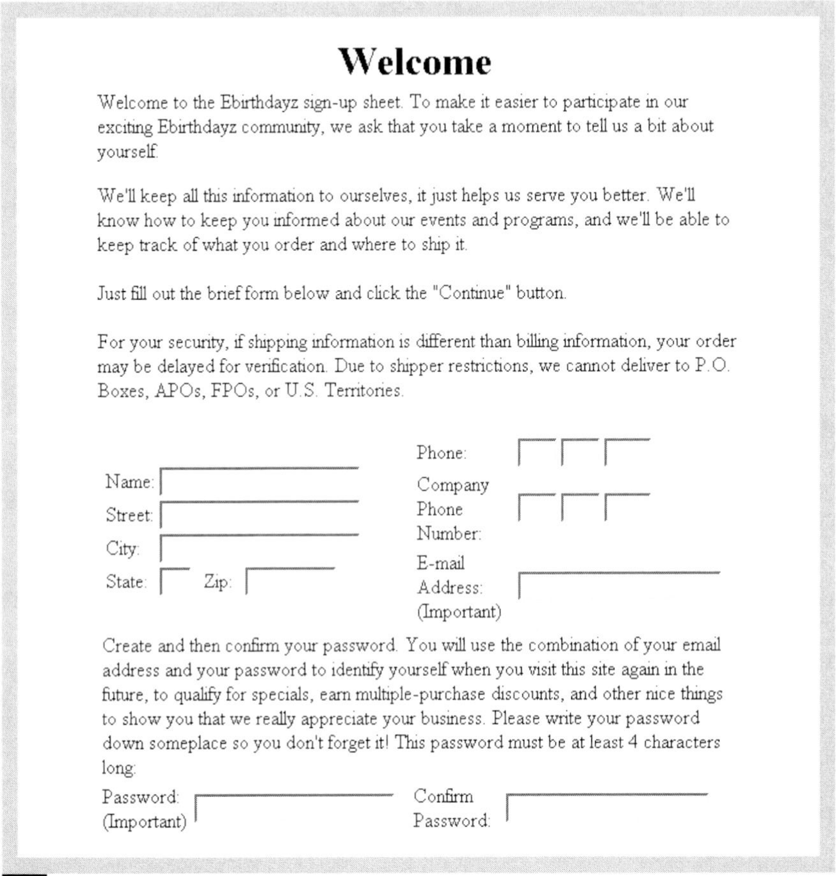

Welcome

Welcome to the Ebirthdayz sign-up sheet. To make it easier to participate in our exciting Ebirthdayz community, we ask that you take a moment to tell us a bit about yourself.

We'll keep all this information to ourselves, it just helps us serve you better. We'll know how to keep you informed about our events and programs, and we'll be able to keep track of what you order and where to ship it.

Just fill out the brief form below and click the "Continue" button.

For your security, if shipping information is different than billing information, your order may be delayed for verification. Due to shipper restrictions, we cannot deliver to P.O. Boxes, APOs, FPOs, or U.S. Territories.

Name:
Street:
City:
State: Zip:

Phone:
Company Phone Number:
E-mail Address: (Important)

Create and then confirm your password. You will use the combination of your email address and your password to identify yourself when you visit this site again in the future, to qualify for specials, earn multiple-purchase discounts, and other nice things to show you that we really appreciate your business. Please write your password down someplace so you don't forget it! This password must be at least 4 characters long:

Password: (Important)
Confirm Password:

F4.3

Figure F4.3

This address form is hard to read and use. There are too many instructions, labels appear inconsistently and are unaligned with the corresponding text entry field, and the text entry fields are not aligned with one another.

Typically, separate fields for first name and last name complicate matters for the customer. On the other hand, having both fields in your database might make other data-processing tasks easier, such as a customer service representative's search for a customer's account. This is a trade-off that you should work through with your software development team.

Use two more fields to handle the address and company name because a company name can be automatically separated (parsed out) later if you need it. A country pick list ensures that country names are not misspelled or spelled in more than one way. You might want to require a phone number for overnight shipments, so provide a single input field for it. Field labels that work in any country help international customers understand how to use the fields (such as ZIP/Postal Code).

Next to the form, put a **Use this new address** ACTION BUTTON (K4). Pressing this button will validate the fields, store the address, and set it as the current address. Figure F4.4 shows how Snapfish uses a POP-UP WIN-

DOW (H6) to add new addresses so that customers will not lose the context of their work.

Validate Fields • Help customers enter correct information by using software to validate their input. Check required fields to ensure that they contain data. Because there are so many formats for addresses and city names, it is difficult to verify the actual content of these fields. For the State field, if all commerce must be conducted within the United States, the field could be restricted to a pick list of states. For international ordering, a pick list for country can guarantee the integrity of the information customers submit. One trade-off is that pick lists this large can be difficult to navigate. You may want to verify that the phone number contains only numbers and legal punctuation, but if you allow international phone numbers, the formats may be very different. Your goal should be PREVENTING ERRORS (K12), but when they do occur, you can use field validation and MEANINGFUL ERROR MESSAGES (K13) to help your customer recover.

Figure F4.4

To keep the customer from forgetting the context of the order, Snapfish uses a pop-up window for its address form.

(www.snapfish.com, January 30, 2002)

❉ SOLUTION

At the top of the page, provide a link to the area where a new address can be entered. Place all previously stored addresses next, with a Use this address **action button next to each one. Create a new address form that is quick and easy to read: with labels right-aligned and input fields left-aligned along the same vertical grid line, using a minimum of fields, minimal instructions, and a** Use this address **action button.**

Figure F4.5

Customers should be able to use addresses they have entered before, and to add new addresses easily.

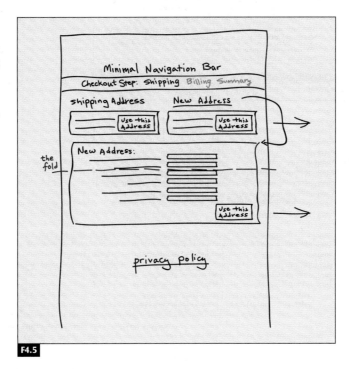

F4.5

❉ CONSIDER THESE OTHER PATTERNS

Answer potential questions about your site security by linking directly to your PRIVACY POLICY (E4). Help customers fill out the information form by PREVENTING ERRORS (K12) and providing MEANINGFUL ERROR MESSAGES (K13) for errors that do occur. Use ACTION BUTTONS (K4) to lead customers to the next step in the checkout process. Organize the text fields in a GRID LAYOUT (I1). If the customer wants to ship to MULTIPLE DESTINATIONS (G5), provide a way to enter multiple addresses. Provide links to your return policy to enable EASY RETURNS (F9) and to assure your customers that they can change their minds if they are not satisfied.

F5 QUICK SHIPPING METHOD SELECTION

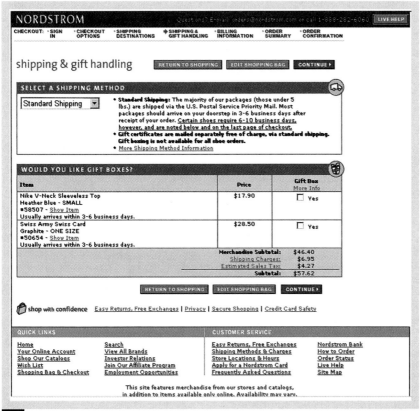

(www.nordstrom.com, October 3, 2001)

Figure F5.1

Nordstrom provides a pick list right next to the shipping details so that customers can quickly select the best shipping method and see how it affects the price.

✳ BACKGROUND

For QUICK-FLOW CHECKOUT (F1) on a PERSONAL E-COMMERCE (A1) site, each step must be simple and clearly defined. In the SHOPPING CART (F3) pattern, items are collected and summarized. This pattern provides the mechanism for choosing a shipping method.

✳ PROBLEM

Customers resent hidden shipping and handling charges, and they want to pick the best shipping option for their situation.

If shoppers encounter previously undisclosed, expensive shipping charges when they reach the checkout phase of an order, they can be quite shocked. With regard to shipping, immediately communicate two things: (1) how long it will take before the items arrive and (2) how much it will add to the cost to speed things up. Other issues, such as customs and insurance for precious cargo, may depend on the particular products that customers purchase.

Show Delivery Options • Most sites that ship items small enough to be handled by one of the major carriers, such as the U.S. Postal Service, UPS, or FedEx, offer several options for delivery. When you must ship with a carrier that handles large items, you may not be able to offer any shipping choices. But customers still need to know shipping times and costs. Set their expectations for each delivery option with a pick list or radio buttons so that they can choose what's best for them (see Figure F5.2).

Figure F5.2

Customers use Amazon.com's radio buttons to select the shipping method. Clicking on **Update** shows the cost of the selected shipping method in the order summary on the right. It would be even better to show the costs right next to the radio buttons as well.

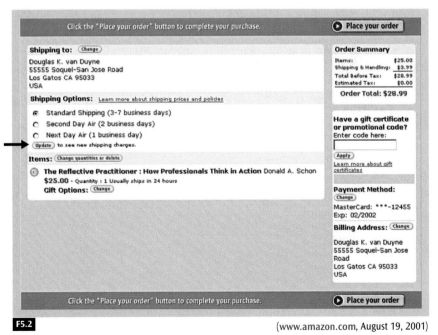

F5.2

(www.amazon.com, August 19, 2001)

Explain Shipping Times • Even when precise estimates are not possible, providing a range of days it will take for the customer to receive the goods is better than giving no information at all. Customers appreciate knowing what to expect. Indicate when to expect each item—for example, by saying something like, "Usually ships in 3–5 days."

If an item will take longer to arrive than the time indicated in the order, update the customer with an e-mail explaining the delay and giving the new time estimate. Because the original estimated time frame may have been important (for it to arrive before a birthday or project start day, for example), give the customer an opportunity to update or cancel the order immediately.

International orders may take longer to arrive than estimates indicate, and this information is also important to include on the shipping page. But it is perhaps too much detail if most customers are local. Putting this information behind a link that refers to international shipping keeps it from overwhelming the majority of shoppers.

Give Costs • The costs of shipping can vary depending on the size and weight of the goods shipped, the time frame the customer requires, insurance for expensive items, and possibly international charges. The specific costs then must be calculated for the items in the cart and the shipping destination. If shipping outside the country is not standard on the site, you can calculate the shipping on the shopping cart page using the products' size, weight, and insurance requirements. Figure F5.3 shows how Buy.com displays shipping type and costs at the same time.

Figure F5.3

Buy.com includes the shipping method as a pick list item in the shopping cart, so customers can select it along with the price.

F5.3

(www.us.buy.com, February 13, 2002)

✳ SOLUTION

Provide a pick list or radio buttons for selecting shipping options. Give a high-level description of the delivery time frames and the associated costs. Calculate the shipping costs on the basis of size and weight of the products being shipped. Provide links to more in-depth information about shipping issues, including international requirements and insurance.

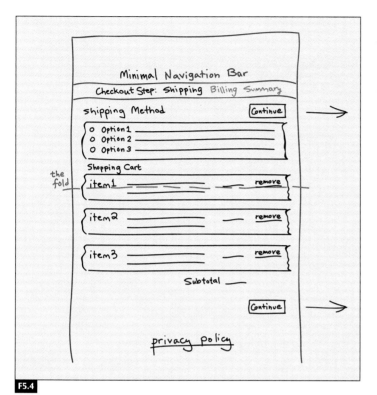

Figure F5.4

The shipping page informs customers of their options and costs for shipping, while moving them through the checkout process with little distraction.

✳ CONSIDER THESE OTHER PATTERNS

Help customers fill out the form by PREVENTING ERRORS (K12) and providing MEANINGFUL ERROR MESSAGES (K13) when errors do occur. Use ACTION BUTTONS (K4) to lead customers to the next step in the checkout process. Display the shipping information in a GRID LAYOUT (I1), in CONTENT MODULES (D2). Provide links to your return policy to enable EASY RETURNS (F9) and to assure your customers that they can change their minds if they are not satisfied.

Figure F6.1

Half.com provides the ability to use previous billing information or quickly enter new billing information. With only a minimum of fields for the credit card details, the address can be quickly copied from the shipping address.

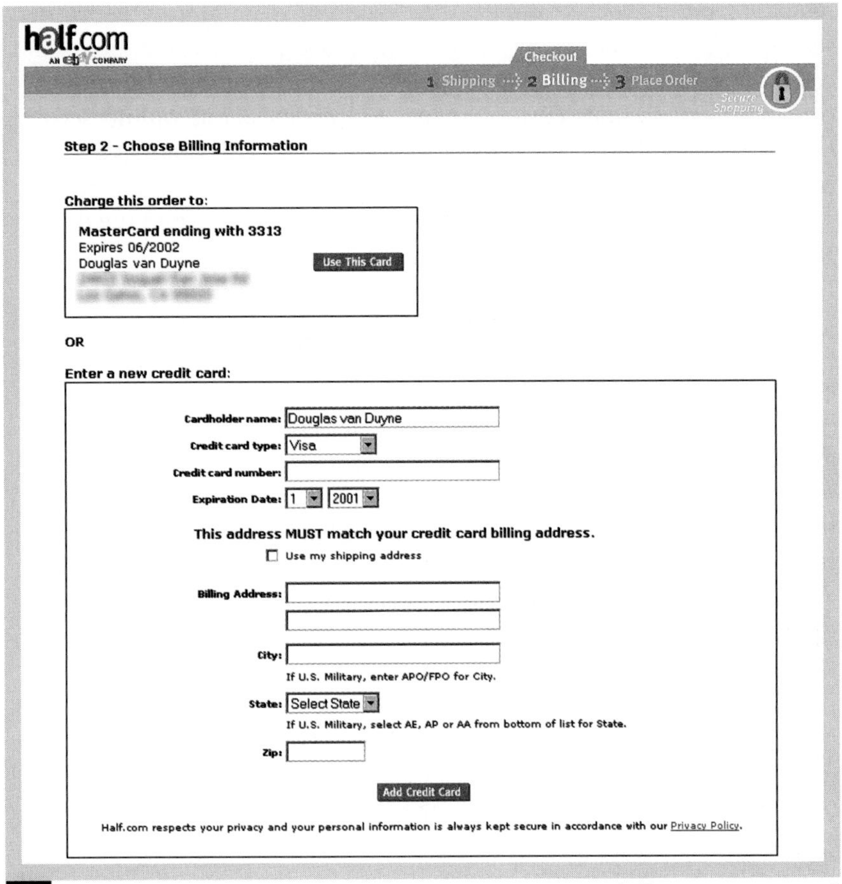

half.com
AN eBay COMPANY

Checkout

1 Shipping ···▷ 2 Billing ···▷ 3 Place Order

Secure Shopping

Step 2 - Choose Billing Information

Charge this order to:

MasterCard ending with 3313
Expires 06/2002
Douglas van Duyne

[Use This Card]

OR

Enter a new credit card:

Cardholder name: Douglas van Duyne

Credit card type: Visa

Credit card number:

Expiration Date: 1 ▾ 2001 ▾

This address MUST match your credit card billing address.

☐ Use my shipping address

Billing Address:

City:

If U.S. Military, enter APO/FPO for City.

State: Select State ▾

If U.S. Military, select AE, AP or AA from bottom of list for State.

Zip:

[Add Credit Card]

Half.com respects your privacy and your personal information is always kept secure in accordance with our Privacy Policy.

F6.1

(www.half.com, August 19, 2001)

❋ BACKGROUND

For QUICK-FLOW CHECKOUT (F1) on a PERSONAL E-COMMERCE (A1) site, each step must be simple and clearly defined. In the SHOPPING CART (F3) pattern, items are collected and summarized. The QUICK ADDRESS SELECTION (F4) and the QUICK SHIPPING METHOD SELECTION (F5) patterns allow the customer to specify where and how to ship the order. This pattern provides the mechanism for specifying how to pay for the order.

✳ PROBLEM

When it comes to paying for an order, people demand security and simplicity.

As with every other part of the online shopping experience, the payment section of the checkout process must be quick and easy. But other concerns are specific to the payment page. Whether making a business or a consumer transaction, customers are concerned about online security because they have heard stories about credit card theft and worse. Although it may be easier for someone to steal a credit card in a real store, people perceive online purchases to be less secure, and the dangers are not well understood.

Take steps to help people overcome their security concerns. Show the lock icon to indicate that the contents of the page have been encrypted. However, the lock icon cannot be the full solution because only savvy customers know to look for it. In addition to showing the lock icon, you must dispel security concerns and provide a simple mechanism for choosing payment options and entering billing details.

Dispel Concerns about Security • Customers will want to know that your site is secure, and that their information will not be accessible to outsiders. Dispel concerns by linking to a security or PRIVACY POLICY (E4) page that covers issues about how the information that customers enter is used, how it is stored on site servers, and who has access to it.

When passing credit card information to or from the browser, be sure to encrypt all the checkout pages with a SECURE CONNECTION (E6) (the lock icon will show it). Minimize the risk of credit card theft by referring to a customer's credit card by only the last four digits of the card and the expiration date.

Provide Easy Payment Choices • On consumer sites, customers may be ordering with credit cards or gift certificates. They may be using one of many credit cards, and they may have old information in the system, such as expired credit cards or old billing addresses. Business customers might also be ordering with credit cards, but they will probably need to be billed, perhaps against a purchase order. A pick list or radio buttons let customers choose easily among these different payment options.

Make an Uncomplicated Form for Billing Information • If customers are ordering from a site for the first time, put the billing form at the top of the page, where they can easily see it. If shoppers have stored credit cards, include areas on the page where customers can choose a stored card or input a new one (see Figure F6.1). To make the form for entering new billing information easy to use, do the following:

- Build a simple GRID LAYOUT (I1) with all of the field labels right-aligned along a single grid line, and all of the text entry fields in a single column left-aligned along the same grid line. This arrangement helps people scan the labels and fields (see the new credit card form in Figure F6.1).
- Keep the number of fields to a minimum to simplify data entry.
- Keep labels and instructions short so that customers can skim forms and resort to reading only when necessary.

Use only the following few fields:

- Full Name
- Address Line 1 (or company name)
- Address Line 2 (optional)
- City
- State/Province/Region
- ZIP/Postal Code
- Country
- Phone

For business orders, add the following fields:

- Billing Contact E-Mail
- Choice to Be Billed or Pay by Credit Card
- Purchase Order

For support of credit cards, add the following:

- Name on Credit Card
- Credit Card Number (allow multiple formats, as described in PREVENTING ERRORS (K12))
- Expiration Date

Typically, separate fields for first name and last name complicate matters for the customer. On the other hand, having both fields in your database might make other data-processing tasks easier, such as a customer service representative's search for a customer's account. This is a trade-off that you should work through with your software development team.

A country pick list ensures that country names are not misspelled or spelled in many different ways. Providing labels that work in any country helps international customers use the fields.

Next to the form, put a **Save Billing Info** or **Continue** button. Pressing this button will validate the fields, store the address, and set it to be the current address.

Figure F6.2 shows a simple and straightforward form for billing.

Store Credit Card Information • Customers who are returning to a site will likely use a previously entered credit card. Put the list of stored credit cards at the top of the page to ensure that they will be seen. Use an ACTION BUTTON (K4) labeled **Use this card** next to each credit card to take the customer quickly to the next step of the order process (see Figure 6.1).

At the top of the page, include a link to a place where the customer can enter new credit card information, which will appear below the stored cards. Even if the customer has already stored many credit cards, the link

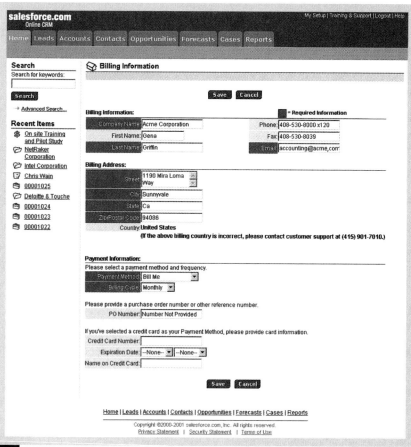

Figure F6.2

The billing information page on Salesforce.com's Web site shows how few fields are required to process business billing. This Salesforce.com process funnel then asks whether to bill by purchase order or credit card.

(www.salesforce.com, October 20, 2001)

will be visible. Another approach to this problem is to separate the card selection mechanism from the billing address specification. This way there will always be room to see the new card fields (see Figure F6.3). This approach has the drawback of requiring an additional page to load, and it separates the context of the chosen credit card and the associated billing address, which may lead to errors.

Redeem Gift Certificates • Though they are payment related, gift certificates are not stored as a recurring payment option. Customers use promotion codes and gift certificates once, and then they are gone (any extra money may be stored as credit). Customers want to see a place to enter their certificate information early in the checkout process. If they become concerned that they will not be given the opportunity to use their certificate or promotion code, they might think the promotion and site are misleading or a scam. Customers are reassured if you put the certificate redemption or promotion redemption at the point where a payment option must be selected (see Figure F6.3a).

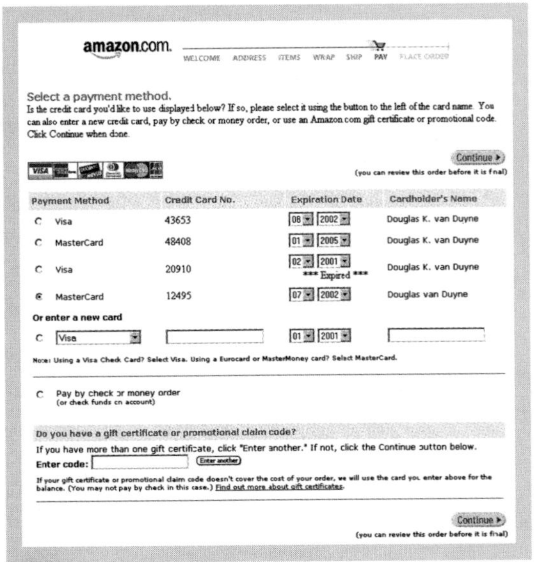

Figure F6.3

Amazon.com has customers select credit cards and the associated billing address on two pages. (a) On the first page customers pick a stored card or enter a promotion code. (b) On the second page customers select one of the existing billing addresses in their Amazon.com address book or enter a new one.

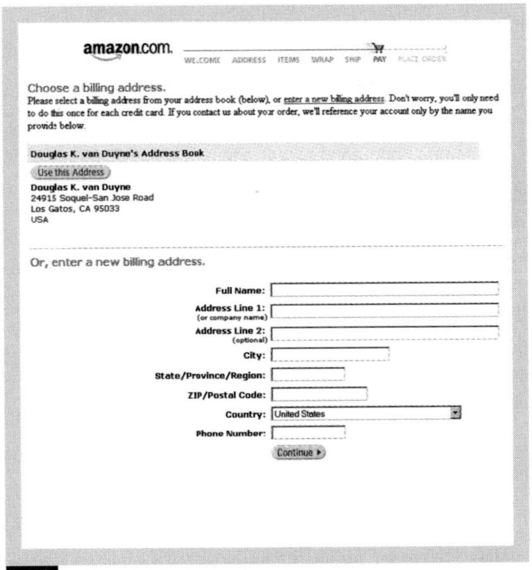

(www.amazon.com, October 21, 2001)

✳ SOLUTION

Dispel any concerns that customers might have about security by addressing them up front with a link to your security or privacy policy. A pick list or radio buttons help customers select the billing options. Create a new credit card form that is quick and easy to read: with labels right-aligned and input fields left-aligned along the same vertical grid line, using a minimum of fields, minimal instructions, and a Use this card action button. If storing multiple billing addresses, above the new address form include a list of all previously stored addresses with a Use this address action button next to each one.

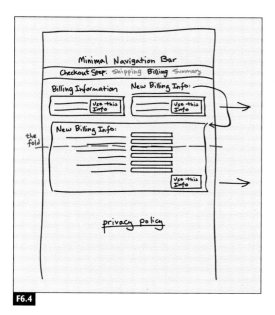

F6.4

Figure F6.4

Customers can specify how to pay for their orders, whether by selecting from previously used billing information or by entering new information.

✳ CONSIDER THESE OTHER PATTERNS

Answer questions that people might have about your site security by linking directly to your PRIVACY POLICY (E4). Link to your return policy to enable EASY RETURNS (F9) and to assure your customers that they can change their minds if they are not satisfied.

Help customers fill out the form by PREVENTING ERRORS (K12) and providing MEANINGFUL ERROR MESSAGES (K13) when errors do occur. Use ACTION BUTTONS (K4) to lead customers to the next step in the checkout process. Display the rows of items in a GRID LAYOUT (I1), in CONTENT MODULES (D2).

Figure F7.1

Amazon.com offers a single, organized page that summarizes a complete order and provides links to edit the individual elements.

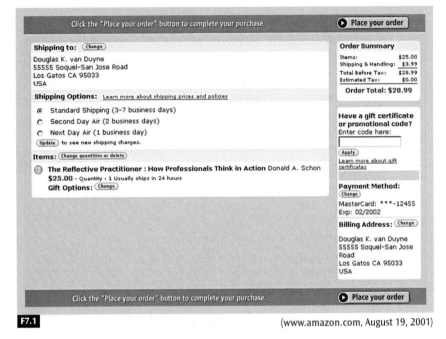

F7.1

(www.amazon.com, August 19, 2001)

✳ BACKGROUND

For QUICK-FLOW CHECKOUT (F1) on a PERSONAL E-COMMERCE (A1) site, customers must double-check orders before finalizing them. In the SHOPPING CART (F3) pattern, items are collected and summarized. Then a QUICK ADDRESS SELECTION (F4) and a QUICK SHIPPING METHOD SELECTION (F5) are made, and a PAYMENT METHOD (F6) is selected. This pattern presents the information entered in these other patterns for final review by the customer.

✳ PROBLEM

When finalizing orders, customers want to see everything related to what they're ordering: the specific products, all the charges, and the billing methods, as well as where, how, and approximately when packages will be delivered. If any one of these elements is missing from an order summary, customers might abandon their purchases.

If the proper information is missing from an order summary, people might wonder whether they entered all the correct information, or they might suspect that the company did not heed the information they entered on previous pages. In any case, it does not engender further trust to ignore one of the critical elements of e-commerce: People want to review their orders. If you include every item, customers will be able to review their progress and check out with confidence.

Confirm That the Order Is Ready to Complete • Customers might arrive at the order summary page and think that their order has been submitted already. But if they close the browser, they will never receive their order and your company will not receive a completed transaction. At the top of the page, highlight the fact that the order is not complete. Make HIGH-VISIBILITY ACTION BUTTONS (K5) that indicate this by labeling them **Complete your order**. See Figures F7.1 and F7.2 for a sample order summary page.

Show Key Elements • The elements to show on the order summary page include everything entered on the site for the specific order, except for customer passwords and their full credit card numbers. For shipping information, show the key fields described in QUICK ADDRESS SELECTION (F4), along with an ACTION BUTTON (K4) to change this element.

For shopping cart items, show the key details discussed in the SHOPPING CART (F3) pattern. Again, include an ACTION BUTTON (K4) to change this element.

For billing information, show the same name and address related fields for the billing address, as well as the PAYMENT METHOD (F6) details. Include an ACTION BUTTON (K4) to permit the customer to make changes to any of the billing information.

Figure F7.2

This order summary from Nordstrom notifies the customer that the order is not yet complete and provides high-visibility action buttons above and below the fold so that the customer will see what to click to complete the order, even if scrolling is necessary. This page would work better if it made it easy for customers to change the shipping or billing information.

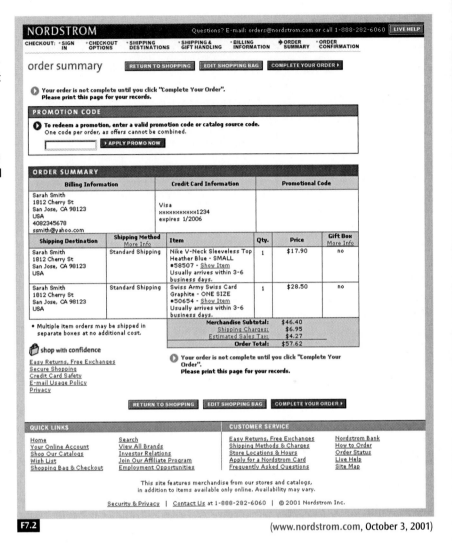

F7.2 (www.nordstrom.com, October 3, 2001)

Finally, be sure to include all other charges and the total:

- Shipping and handling costs
- Any other charges that contribute to the total cost
- Subtotals
- Tax
- Total

Figure F7.3 shows an example of a simple, straightforward order summary page.

Figure F7.3

Once customers have entered their billing and shipping information at snapfish.com, an online photo service, a summary of the order verifies all the items, costs, and taxes.

(www.snapfish.com, January 30, 2002)

❈ SOLUTION

First, let the customer know that the order still has not been placed, and provide high-visibility action buttons for completing the order. Second, show the items being purchased and all the information that the customer entered: address, payment method, and shipping selections. Provide action buttons to edit these items in case they are incorrect. Third, calculate and present the total costs, including shipping and taxes.

Figure F7.4

Summarize all information that the customer has entered: the items being purchased, the shipping and billing information, and all the costs. Make it easy for the customer to change any of this information and to see whether the order still needs to be updated.

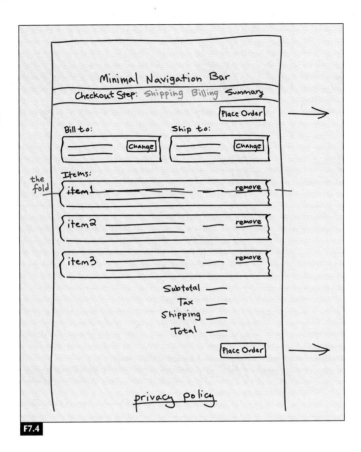

F7.4

✳ CONSIDER THESE OTHER PATTERNS

(K5) (K4) Create HIGH-VISIBILITY ACTION BUTTONS (K5) to encourage shoppers to complete their orders. Provide ACTION BUTTONS (K4) on each of the element sections for editing, including shipping address, shipping method, billing method and address, and the items ordered. Display the rows of **(I1) (D2)** items in a GRID LAYOUT (I1), in CONTENT MODULES (D2). Link to your PRI- **(E4)** VACY POLICY (E4) to help answer any final questions that customers might have about your information use policies. Link to your return policy to **(F9)** enable EASY RETURNS (F9) and to assure your customers that they can change their minds if they are not satisfied.

F8 ORDER CONFIRMATION AND THANK-YOU

F8.1

(www.snapfish.com, January 30, 2002)

Figure F8.1

The order confirmation and thank-you page makes it clear to the customer that the order has gone through. It also shows the date of the order, the order number, and all items in the order. This is a printable page from snapfish.com.

✳ BACKGROUND

Once customers have completed the QUICK-FLOW CHECKOUT (F1) on a PER-SONAL E-COMMERCE (A1) site, they like to have a receipt for their order. In the SHOPPING CART (F3) pattern, items are collected and summarized. Then a QUICK ADDRESS SELECTION (F4), a QUICK SHIPPING METHOD SELECTION (F5), and a PAYMENT METHOD (F6) selection follow. In the ORDER SUMMARY (F7), customers review their order and decide to finalize it. This pattern confirms the order and items entered in these other patterns.

✳ PROBLEM

After they complete their orders, if customers do not get confirmation or a receipt indicating that the order has gone through, they will be unsure of their order status and have to work to find confirmation evidence.

Online orders are not tangible; that is, customers cannot walk out with goods in their hands. Yet they must trust the online company that their money is not being stolen. What reassures people is a confirmation that shows everything in their order, and an order number to reference in case there is a problem. Without all this detailed information, customers might wonder what they ordered, and they might second-guess the company. If you include every element of an order, the customer can review the details and print out the confirmation for later reference. Suddenly an order becomes somewhat tangible.

Thank Your Customers • After their order is completed, thank your customers for shopping with you. It's just a very simple courtesy.

Highlight the Order Number and Date • To help customers organize their various orders, made on various days, display the order number and the date of the order on the confirmation (see Figure F8.2). If they want to go back later, they can look up the order by number or date.

Figure F8.2

This confirmation highlights the order number and date, but it is missing several key elements. The confirmation should display all of the product items, as well as the shipping and billing information.

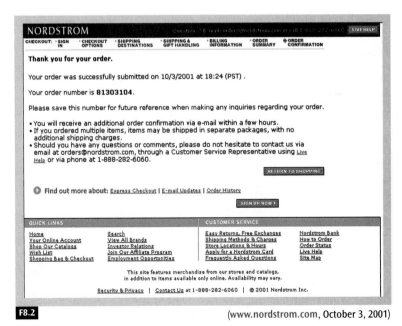

(www.nordstrom.com, October 3, 2001)

Show All Key Elements • The elements to show on the confirmation page include everything on the ORDER SUMMARY (F7).

F7

Send an E-mail Confirmation • Send customers an e-mail confirming that their purchase was completed. This message should have all of the key elements found in the ORDER SUMMARY (F7), and it will make it easier for customers to remember what they purchased and to track the status of their order.

F7

Make the Page Printable • Customers may want to reference an order later. They can go online to do it, but they may not know where to find this information, or a computer with a network connection might not be within easy reach. Plus, some people like the artifact of a paper receipt for their files. By making the order confirmation and thank-you a PRINTABLE PAGE (D8), you can satisfy both of these needs.

D8

Encourage Customers to Continue Shopping • Customers may remember an item that they did not order and thus might like to return to shopping. Some shoppers might want to place a separate order for someone else. Make sure your customers can return to your site quickly and easily after placing an order. Use CROSS-SELLING AND UP-SELLING (G2) to highlight other products that might interest them, given the items they just purchased (see Figure F8.3). Use a HIGH-VISIBILITY ACTION BUTTON (K5) labeled **Continue Shopping** to take them back.

G2

K5

F8.3

(www.us.buy.com, February 13, 2002)

Figure F8.3

Buy.com does a good job of cross-selling products after customers have completed purchases. The trade-off here is that the space at the bottom is gained by forcing the customer to click on a button to view a detailed receipt that contains the shipping and billing information.

✳ SOLUTION

Provide a thank-you on a printable page that displays the order number, the order date, and all the order information, including items purchased, quantities, prices, shipping prices, tax, total, and shipping and billing information. Give customers an action button to continue shopping, and cross-sell them on other products they might be interested in purchasing.

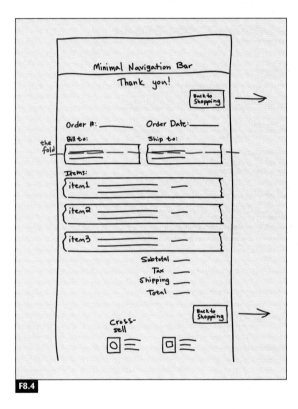

Figure F8.4

An order confirmation page lets customers know that their orders have gone through. It gives them summary information to record what they bought and the specifics of the billing and shipping for future reference.

✳ CONSIDER THESE OTHER PATTERNS

Provide a PRINTABLE PAGE (D8) that displays all the elements from the previous ORDER SUMMARY (F7) page. Include on the page a HIGH-VISIBILITY ACTION BUTTON (K5) to encourage people to continue shopping, in case they forgot something. Suggest other products they might be interested in by CROSS-SELLING AND UP-SELLING (G2). Link to your return policy to enable EASY RETURNS (F9) and to assure your customers that they can change their minds if they are not satisfied.

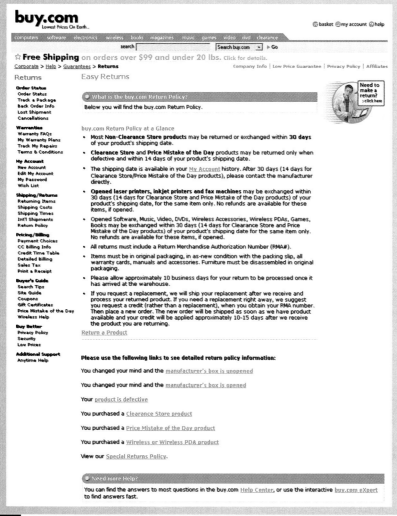

F9.1

(www.us.buy.com, February 13, 2002)

Figure F9.1

A site can help close sales by letting customers know that returns are not only possible, but also easy. It requires trust for shoppers to buy items sight unseen. Knowing that they can make a mistake and not be charged for it is reassuring. Buy.com clearly states its return policy and provides a clear link to make a return.

✳ BACKGROUND

To build trust on a PERSONAL E-COMMERCE (A1) site, each policy and process must center on satisfying the customer. In QUICK-FLOW CHECKOUT (F1), items are purchased. This pattern provides the mechanism for returning goods for replacement or refund.

✳ PROBLEM

When items that are accidentally ordered, damaged during delivery, or just not wanted can be returned quickly and easily, customers are more likely to order. But making returns easy is not simple.

Customers may become tentative during a checkout process if they are not sure the product fits them or their needs. Customers who have not placed an order yet need to know that the site where they are shopping makes the return process easy.

Place Return Policy Links Prominently on All Product and Checkout Pages • For customers to know that the company policy allows returns, they must be able to find the return policy (see Figure F9.2). They want to know things like the following:

- Does the company have a return policy?
- If there is a return policy, can I return an item for any reason?
- What condition must the products be in?
- Will I be charged return shipping?

A return policy answers all these questions, as well as more specific details about where to send something or how to use an online return process. Put a link to the return policy on all QUICK-FLOW CHECKOUT (F1) pages, on every CLEAN PRODUCT DETAIL (F2) page, on all CATEGORY PAGES (B8), and on the HOMEPAGE PORTAL (C1).

Provide a Return Process Funnel • After receiving a shipment, opening it, and finding that one or more of the items ordered are incorrect, broken, or unwanted, a customer might put the items back in the box and return them immediately. Some customers, however, might not put the items right back in the box because they do not realize they have a problem. These customers might throw away the return label or the box itself. By providing a way to generate a label on the site, a company can help customers through the process of returning an item and getting their money

Figure F9.2

Putting a link to the return policy on every page helps ensure that people know they can return items. This is the first step in educating customers about your return policy, and giving them quick access to the return process. Amazon.com puts these links on every product page.

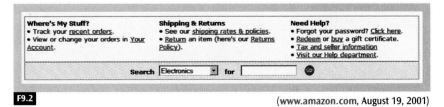

Where's My Stuff?	Shipping & Returns	Need Help?
• Track your recent orders.	• See our shipping rates & policies.	• Forgot your password? Click here.
• View or change your orders in Your Account.	• Return an item (here's our Returns Policy).	• Redeem or buy a gift certificate.
		• Tax and seller information
		• Visit our Help department.

Search [Electronics ▼] for [ ] ⊚

F9.2 (www.amazon.com, August 19, 2001)

back, and helping itself sort through the returned merchandise. A PRO-
CESS FUNNEL (H1) can simplify returns to a few clicks and a page print. **H1**

Have customers find the previous order containing the item that needs
to be returned. There might be many orders, so provide a list and the
order contents. Make the order easy to find, even if customers do not
know the order number or exact date, or if the order was a gift from
someone else.

Display the items in the order, and provide a list of reasons why a customer might legitimately make a return for each item (see Figure F9.3).

Once customers have selected the items to return and the reasons for
the return, offer to print a label for the package, or tell customers to use
the return shipping label that was included with the original order (see
Figure F9.4). By tagging your order database with the return, the returns
department will know what to expect in the box.

If customers elect to print labels, generate a tracking code that will tie
into the order database when the package returns (see Figure F9.5). This

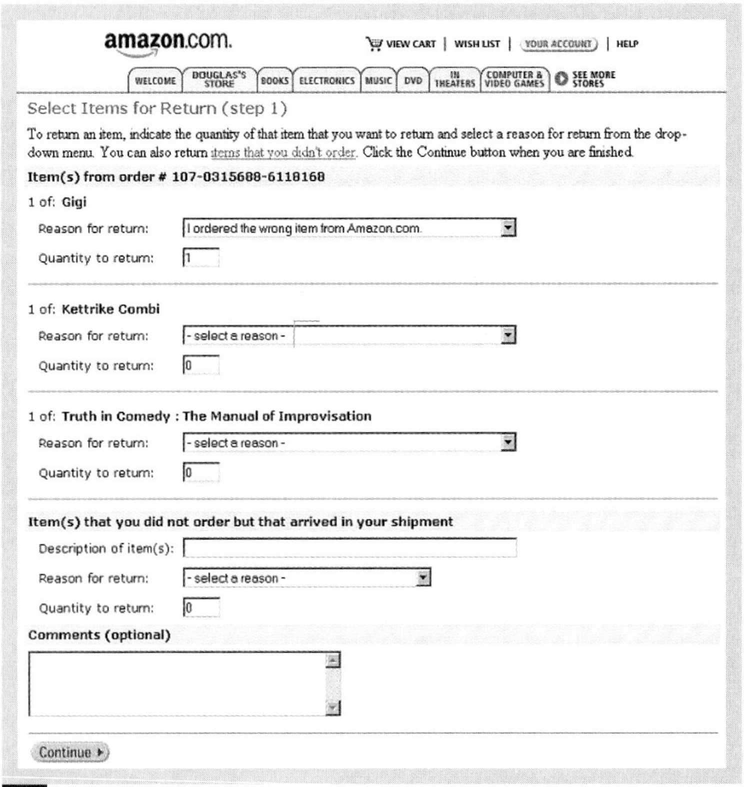

Figure F9.3

Amazon.com pro-
vides a form for
selecting the reason
to return every item
in an order.

(www.amazon.com, August 19, 2001)

Figure F9.4

Amazon.com asks customers if they would like to print a return label.

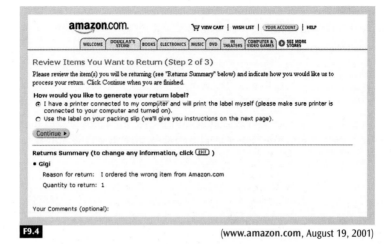

(www.amazon.com, August 19, 2001)

Figure F9.5

If the customer elects to print a return label, Amazon.com automatically generates this label and gives instructions for how to use it.

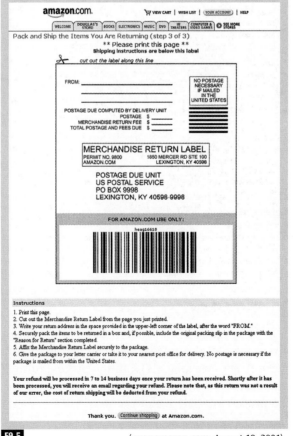

(www.amazon.com, August 19, 2001)

will make it easier for your company to credit customer accounts. The faster you can do this, the happier customers will be with your site, and the more likely they will be to place another order later.

✳ SOLUTION

Put the return policy on all product and checkout pages, including a link to a return process. If customers throw away a return label, give them the ability to print another one, and use the label to track returns as they arrive.

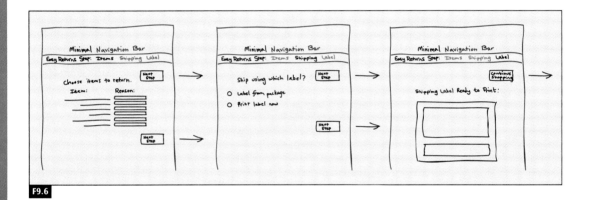

F9.6

Figure F9.6

Make the return process easy by using a process funnel that takes customers step-by-step through identifying the order, specifying the items to return and the reasons why, and finally printing a shipping label if necessary.

✳ CONSIDER THESE OTHER PATTERNS

On QUICK-FLOW CHECKOUT (F1) pages, CLEAN PRODUCT DETAIL (F2) pages, CATEGORY PAGES (B8), and the HOMEPAGE PORTAL (C1), include a link to the return policy and the return PROCESS FUNNEL (H1). In the process funnel, ask customers to select the order, and the items and reasons for the return. At the end of the process, display a PRINTABLE PAGE (D8) with a label to affix to the package for return purposes.

Advanced E-Commerce

Pattern Group F—Basic E-Commerce established the basic framework for e-commerce. This pattern group discusses advanced and optional features that you may wish to include on your site, such as promoting products, sending gifts, and tracking orders.

G1 FEATURED PRODUCTS

G2 CROSS-SELLING AND UP-SELLING

G3 PERSONALIZED RECOMMENDATIONS

G4 RECOMMENDATION COMMUNITY

G5 MULTIPLE DESTINATIONS

G6 GIFT GIVING

G7 ORDER TRACKING AND HISTORY

Figure G1.1

CDNOW highlights several kinds of featured products, including "Recommendations," "Recent Reviews," and "Today's Picks." It also editorializes about the items, giving them a seductive quality.

G1.1

(www.cdnow.com, October 8, 2001)

✳ BACKGROUND

In PERSONAL E-COMMERCE (A1) we provided a solution for building sites and promoting sales within those sites. Recommendations can make customers more confident in their choices and help close more sales. This pattern, along with CROSS-SELLING AND UP-SELLING (G2), PERSONALIZED RECOMMENDATIONS (G3), and RECOMMENDATION COMMUNITY (G4), describes how to provide useful recommendations. Specifically, this pattern describes the featured product page, which provides recommendations on or near the homepage.

✳ PROBLEM

Customers find value when sites identify specific products as recommended or featured. Otherwise product lists can appear bland and tedious.

Having tens, hundreds, thousands, even millions of products on a Web site gives customers a wide selection of choices. But if they can get to those products only through long lists or search engines, they will find it difficult to browse through your site, and you will make fewer sales. If your site presumes that visitors already know what they want and gives them no easy way to explore the site, people who like to browse will be at a loss. The site will not be a place to gather information before making a buying decision.

One way to make it easy for your customers to explore your products is by showing them a list of featured products. This gives them an opportunity to window-shop and lets them know that there is always something new to look at. On the downside, the site must be set up so that it can be quickly updated either manually or automatically.

Editorialize in Your Product Recommendations • For some customers, simply having the product name, a picture, and the price is not enough. These customers are accustomed to getting personal recommendations from salespeople and friends when they shop in a store. On the Web, however, there is no direct connection, and people are usually alone at their computers. You can minimize their feelings of isolation by editorializing in your recommendations, giving the site a personality and a human touch (see Figure G1.2).

Adopting a consistent editorial voice gives the site personality, and it gives customers the sense that they're interacting with a real person instead of a large, faceless company. Decide on your voice and make the copy match. Do you want your site to be friendly? Wisecracking? Authoritative? Avuncular? Whatever you choose, be consistent to avoid confusion.

Provide Different Kinds of Recommendations • Shoppers have diverse needs and different values. On a site that sells jewelry, for example, a shopper who likes to see the latest styles may decide to go elsewhere if she cannot see what's new. Fashionable shoppers want to see what's popular; cost-conscious customers may want to see what's on sale. Those who need help with a purchase will want to see a buyer's guide. Featuring products from all of these different slants can dramatically improve your customers' ability to find the desired items. Categories to use for featuring products might include things like best-sellers, editor's choice,

Figure G1.2

Electronics Boutique's homepage lists several product recommendations with editorial comments that seduce customers much more effectively than a simple list would.

G1.2   (www.ebgames.com, October 8, 2001)

rare finds, and new releases. Figure G1.3 shows two examples, of top-selling products and rare finds.

Table G1.1 shows another way of thinking about featured products. Any of the questions shown in the table can be used as the basis for categorizing featured products. Start with the most relevant and appropriate products for your customers' needs. Keep in mind that each of these tools takes time to build and that some will be more important than others, depending on how your shopper looks for products. For example, shopping by brand might be very important on a clothing site.

Figure G1.3

Here are two different kinds of recommendations. (a) Barnes&Noble.com's recommendation shows top-selling books. (b) Eziba shows rare finds for people looking for exotic pieces for their homes.

G1.3a

(www.bn.com, February 1, 2002)

G1.3b

(www.eziba.com, October 6, 2001)

	Choose One		Choose One		
I'm interested in	+	all of	+	a product type.	→ Where is it?
		the best of		a product.	
		the least expensive of		a brand.	
		the best for this price of		anything.	
		what's new of		anything on sale.	
				something new.	
				something for a friend.	

Table G1.1

Questions customers commonly ask can be used as the basis for categorizing featured products.

So that your customers can find . . .		Provide These Tools	Patterns to Apply
all of / the best of	a product type	Product type CATEGORY PAGES (B8), SEARCH ACTION MODULE (J1)	B8 J1
all of / the best of	a brand	Brand CATEGORY PAGES (B8)	B8
all of / the best of	anything	SEARCH ACTION MODULE (J1)	J1
all of / the best of	anything on sale	"On Sale" CATEGORY PAGES (B8)	B8
all of / the best of	something new	"What's New" CATEGORY PAGES (B8)	B8
all of / the best of	something for a friend	"Gift Finder" PROCESS FUNNEL (H1) and GIFT GIVING (G6)	H1 G6
the least expensive of	a product type	Price sort on Product type CATEGORY PAGES (B8)	B8
the least expensive of	a brand	Price sort on Brand CATEGORY PAGES (B8)	B8
the least expensive of	anything	Price sort after SEARCH ACTION MODULE (J1)	J1
the least expensive of	anything on sale	Price sort in "On Sale" CATEGORY PAGES (B8)	B8
the least expensive of	something new	Price sort on "What's New" CATEGORY PAGES (B8)	B8
the least expensive of	something for a friend	Price criteria in "Gift Finder" PROCESS FUNNEL (H1) and GIFT GIVING (G6)	H1 G6

Table G1.2

Patterns to Apply

Table G1.2 is more extensive than what you can provide on your site. Pare it down according to your customers' needs, and customize it for your site by naming the appropriate products and categories.

To implement these featured products, you can also refer to the patterns for MULTIPLE WAYS TO NAVIGATE (B1), BROWSABLE CONTENT (B2), ORGANIZED SEARCH RESULTS (J3), PERSONALIZED CONTENT (D4), and RECOMMENDATION COMMUNITY (G4).

B1 B2
J3 D4
G4

Give Chances to Explore • Not everyone will come to your site with a specific question, goal, or product in mind. Yet visitors will not browse through thousands of products over a slow connection. Like a virtual window dresser, you have to give your customers chances to explore your products by highlighting imagery and detail that will compel them to click for more information. By featuring several different ways for people to experience your products, you will draw people in according to their varying interests (see Figure G1.4).

Figure G1.4

Amazon.com starts editorializing right on its homepage, which can be customized for visitors. Note the enticing use of titles in the middle of the Web page, such as "Top Sellers" and "Get the Best."

(www.amazon.com, October 6, 2001)

✳ SOLUTION

To give people a better sense of what's on your site, build category pages that highlight special featured products and editorialize in the product recommendations. Provide different kinds of recommendations, choosing different categories, such as top sellers, editor's choice, and so on. Let visitors explore by highlighting as many areas of interest as possible.

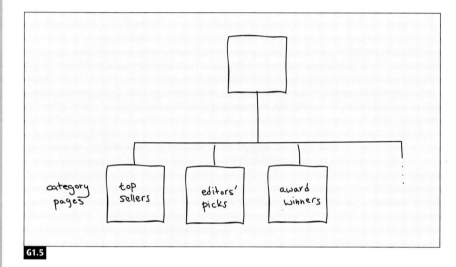

Figure G1.5

Feature products in a variety of ways to recommend and promote sales.

G1.5

✳ CONSIDER THESE OTHER PATTERNS

Provide MULTIPLE WAYS TO NAVIGATE (B1) to the best products on your site, including a SEARCH ACTION MODULE (J1) and BROWSABLE CONTENT (B2). Use PERSONALIZED CONTENT (D4) in a PAGE TEMPLATE (D1), as well as the reviews of a RECOMMENDATION COMMUNITY (G4). Different sets of featured products can be thought of as different CATEGORY PAGES (B8).

Figure G2.1

Cross-selling and up-selling mean promoting products and services that are highly related to the current product. Here the assumption is that people who are interested in wine goblets might also be interested in place cards, champagne glasses, and nicer goblets. These cross-selling and up-selling links reduce people's shopping time by helping them complete a transaction.

G2.1

(www.theknot.com, November 27, 2001)

✳ BACKGROUND

(A1) In PERSONAL E-COMMERCE (A1) we provided a solution for building sites and promoting sales within those sites. Recommendations can make customers more confident in their choices and help close more sales. This pattern, along with FEATURED PRODUCTS (G1), PERSONALIZED RECOMMEN-DATIONS (G3), and RECOMMENDATION COMMUNITY (G4), describes how to provide useful recommendations. Specifically, this pattern describes cross-selling and up-selling—that is, recommending additional products according to what the customer has already expressed an interest in.

⁂ PROBLEM

When choosing a product in stores, people appreciate hearing about related products that are complementary to or better than the products they have chosen. Doing the same thing online requires prudence and planning.

People often come to a site looking for something, whether they have a specific idea of what they need or only a vague notion. Once they're looking around, however, they find pleasure in finding something useful they didn't know about. Cross-selling and up-selling are two techniques for providing related products and services right when the customer is making a purchase. These strategies make more on each sale by enticing customers to buy items related to what they're planning to purchase anyway.

Cross-selling is promoting accessories related to the current choice. For example, someone who buys a cell phone may be interested in buying extra travel chargers and spare batteries. **Up-selling** is promoting a better (and more expensive!) version of the current choice. For example, a person interested in one product line of cell phones may be interested in more upscale versions or in an extended warranty covering any damages. From a fast-food restaurant perspective, cross-selling is "Do you want fries with that?" and up-selling is "Do you want to supersize that?"

Although cross-selling and up-selling have specific meanings in sales, the distinction between the two can sometimes become blurry. In fact, we think it's easier and better to think of both approaches as promoting products and services that are highly related to the current products that interest the customer. The goals in both cases, though, are the same. For customers, the goal is to get help finding useful items and completing purchases more quickly. For the company, the goal is to increase sales and revenue. This pattern describes how to use cross-selling and up-selling on your Web site, and how to implement these techniques without being too assertive.

Cross-Sell and Up-Sell Related Products • What will customers find useful if they are already looking at a specific product? Such items might include accessories, complementary products, better versions of the current product, or similar products with slight differences (see Figures G2.2 and G2.3). You can offer all these related products, depending on customer needs. Not all customers will find all of the related products useful, but if enough of them do, your efforts will have been worth the trouble.

Figure G2.2

RedEnvelope makes it easy for gift givers to add batteries to their orders so that there will be no disappointed recipients of electronic gifts.

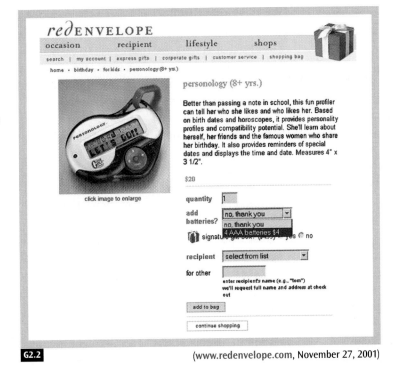

G2.2

(www.redenvelope.com, November 27, 2001)

Figure G2.3

Buy.com relates products to each other to help its customers make the most useful connections. Here, people thinking of purchasing this DVD are shown, on the right-hand side, a related audio CD.

G2.3

(www.buy.com, February 13, 2002)

Related products are connected in the product database, as well as in the customers' mind. The product database must implement the connection to automatically sell related products on the main product pages. In your product database, list all the products that are related to a given product. You can have your Web site update these relationships automatically on the basis of previous customer purchases so that the recommendations change over time.

To create automatic product relationships, do the following:

1. Group together all products that customers purchased with the current product.
2. Rank the products by how many times they were purchased together.

These two steps will tell you which products sell best together, so you will also know exactly which top three to five related products to show on your current product page.

On the other hand, you can manage these relationships by hand, updating them once a month or quarter. Hand-merchandising is much more time-consuming but also gives you the opportunity to give customers some unique insights about the products you sell, such as why two products go well with each other.

Cordon Off and Minimize the Screen Real Estate Devoted to Related Products •
Customers must be able to differentiate between related products and current products. A visual distinction that puts the related products to the side, or in a special area, helps when people scan the page. Set off the related products in separate CONTENT MODULES (D2), each with its own title showing how the products are related. The titles give customers a quick way to scan the boxes and items. Provide a brief description or picture to help customers identify the value of the items.

At the same time, be sure to minimize the amount of screen space used to advertise related products. In physical stores, customers appreciate salespeople who graciously provide help in finding a product. But salespeople can cross a line when their suggestions become too pushy and annoy customers. You can cross the same line online. The graphics and text promoting related products can make the page look too busy and distract customers from reading about the main product. Make sure that more space is devoted to the main product than to related products. Keep the main product in the center of the screen, and push related products to the bottom or to the side.

F2

Editorialize about Related Products • Customers want to know something about a product before they leave their current Web page to explore it. Giving them a descriptive preview helps them judge whether it is worth checking out that product's CLEAN PRODUCT DETAIL (F2) page. Images can take up valuable screen real estate, so unless the product name is very descriptive, add one or two sentences of editorial description.

Allow Quick Purchase of Related Products • When you take customers to a separate page to purchase a related product, they might get lost on their way back or be sidetracked and forget about the original product. Make it easy for customers to buy related products without losing the original product. Give customers enough information about a related product so that they can decide on the product's value without having to jump to another page (see Figure G2.4).

Figure G2.4

Netflix highlights related movies (under "Members Also Enjoyed") on its product page. To select one of these options, customers click on the **Rent** button, which pops up a window without taking them off the product page. Customers can then close the pop-up window and continue along the main product page.

G2.4

(www.netflix.com, October 28, 2001)

You can also provide quick-purchase ACTION BUTTONS (K4) or check
boxes to make it easy to add related products to the SHOPPING CART (F3)
without leaving the current page. For example, let's say the customer is
buying a toy that requires batteries. A quick-purchase ACTION BUTTON
(K4) can let the customer add batteries to the shopping cart and then
refresh the page or show a POP-UP WINDOW (H6) to indicate that the batteries have been added.

Sell Related Products during Checkout • If there are important related
products that the customer has forgotten to purchase, you can suggest
them again from the SHOPPING CART (F3), the ORDER SUMMARY (F7), and
the ORDER CONFIRMATION AND THANK-YOU (F8) pages (see Figures G2.5 and

Figure G2.5

On the basis of
what the customer
has placed in the
shopping cart,
Amazon.com pro-
vides links (at the
bottom) to related
products.

G2.5

(www.amazon.com, December 3, 2001)

Figure G2.6

After completing a checkout, Amazon.com provides links to products that the customer might have missed.

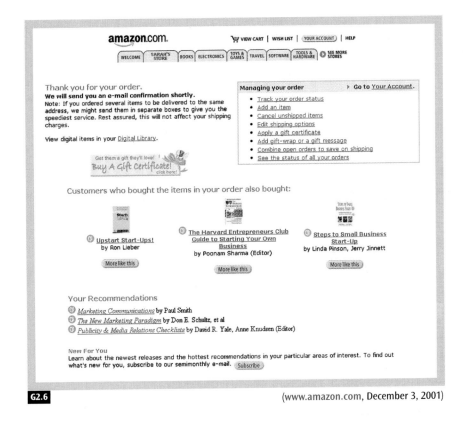

G2.6

(www.amazon.com, December 3, 2001)

G2.6). This is similar to what grocers do with impulse buys at the checkout stand, but you can provide much more relevant products because you already know what is in your customer's shopping cart and what will be of additional value. Again, you must make it simple and quick to add these related items because your first priority is to close the primary sale.

☀ SOLUTION

In a subtle and careful way, cross-sell and up-sell related products by indicating the benefit they provide to your customers. Customers will be seduced and will not need to go far to make a purchase if you make it quick and easy to add a related product to a shopping cart without leaving the context of the current page. Make a visual distinction between these promotions and the other content on the page. Sell the related products again later in the checkout process, in case customers missed them the first time.

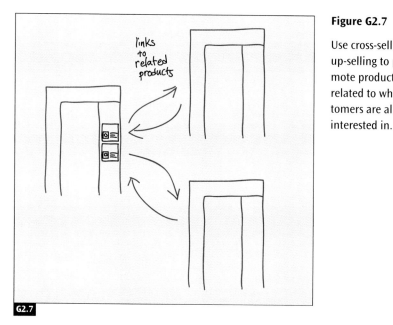

Figure G2.7

Use cross-selling and up-selling to promote products related to what customers are already interested in.

✳ CONSIDER THESE OTHER PATTERNS

Editorialize about related products so that customers get a preview of the CLEAN PRODUCT DETAIL (F2) page. For accessories and other related items, add a quick-purchase ACTION BUTTON (K4) to the SHOPPING CART (F3).

Highlight related products in separate CONTENT MODULES (D2), each with its own title showing how the products are related. The titles give customers a quick way to scan the boxes and items in the list. Customers may want to purchase related products after they have already purchased a product. Adding products to a SHOPPING CART (F3) always takes customers forward in the QUICK-FLOW CHECKOUT (F1), and if they want a product that was promoted on an earlier page, they can hit the **Back** button. If the customer has not purchased important related products, suggest them again from the SHOPPING CART (F3), the ORDER SUMMARY (F7), and the ORDER CONFIRMATION AND THANK-YOU (F8) pages.

Figure G3.1

Amazon.com makes available a personalized area that has all its recommended products.

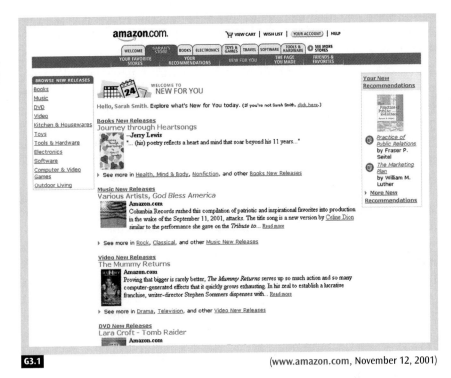

G3.1

(www.amazon.com, November 12, 2001)

✳ BACKGROUND

(A1) The core of PERSONAL E-COMMERCE (A1) is to provide an experience that satisfies each customer's unique needs. Making the shopping experience personal requires tailoring it to the customer. This pattern forms the core (D4) of personalized recommendations, a form of PERSONALIZED CONTENT (D4) that provides recommendations based on past purchases and on information that customers reveal about themselves. This pattern can be used in (G1) conjunction with FEATURED PRODUCTS (G1), CROSS-SELLING AND UP-SELLING (G2) (G4) (G2), and RECOMMENDATION COMMUNITY (G4) to provide useful recommendations and streamline purchases for customers.

✳ PROBLEM

Personalized recommendations can provide customers with a better sense of what's useful and what isn't. But if they require too much effort on the customer's part, or if they are based on what customers perceive as scant evidence, they will fail.

When shopping online, customers can benefit from personalized recommendations. These suggestions can make shopping easier and more enjoyable, helping customers to choose between products and to find new products that they did not even know might interest them. Unfortunately, personalized recommendations require significant design and engineering, and priming the pump with enough information to make useful comments requires detailed customer information.

When visitors go to your site for the first time, there is very little the site can tell about them. Over time, the site can learn what customers are interested in on the basis of where they go, what they click on, and what they search for. However, basic path and search information is not enough to make strong conclusions about visitor interests because they might have clicked on a link to a product page but found it was not the one they were looking for, or typed in a search word but did not use the expected words. Recommendations that come from such information, which can be false or misleading, will not always deliver the kinds of personalized recommendations that customers will find useful.

More deliberate expressions of interest, such as actual purchase behavior, make reliable indicators. But requiring customers to purchase something before you can recommend other products does not provide any value to first-time shoppers, the people whom a site wishes to attract to become long-term, repeat customers. Instead, try alternatives such as providing easy-to-perform ratings of products, carrying out recommendation interviews, and using the purchase behavior of other customers. This solution provides you with the framework to create each of these alternatives.

Avoid Using Pure Inference Data • Server logs, referrer information from Web browsers stating the page a customer just came from, and other information about other sites that customers have visited can be used to infer customer needs. But such inferences are not always accurate because navigation errors may have led customers to the wrong locations. Product recommendations that are based on false leads can ring hollow.

Recommending products on the basis of inference data is different from making recommendations about products that this customer or

Figure G3.2

Amazon.com bases its category recommendations on customer purchases.

other customers bought (see Figure G3.2). In both of these other cases, customers vouch for their interest in a particular product by buying it. By itself, visiting a product category or a specific product page does not provide enough information to say it was the right product for someone.

Make It Easy for Customers to Choose Preferred Products • Customers do not want to fill out forms to get product recommendations unless there is a clear and tangible benefit. Give customers a way to rate preferred products without having to purchase them. However, keep in mind that this scheme works only if people are familiar with the products you sell, or if they can provide assessments based on information on your site.

Provide customers with a rating scheme on CLEAN PRODUCT DETAIL (F2) pages, letting them rate how much they liked something. Keep the rating scheme on the current page and reflect the selection made by the customer. Ideally, the page will not even reload, making the ratings instantaneous and more likely to be used (see Figure G3.3). **F2**

Once customers have rated a few products, the Web site can start recommending related products that may interest them.

Invite Customers to State Their Needs • Another way to provide recommendations for customers is through an interview. For example, on

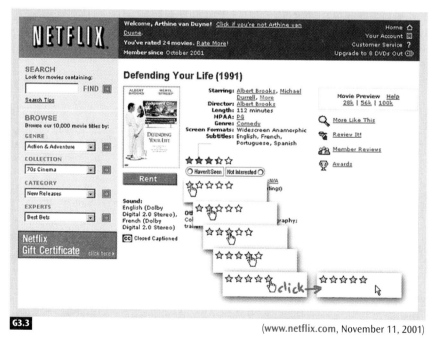

Figure G3.3

Netflix lets customers rate movies they have not rented but know about. Here red stars identify the average rating by other customers, and yellow stars the current customer's ratings. When visitors choose their ratings for a movie, the yellow stars "stick" to what they select. After a customer has rated a movie, the Web site can recommend related movies that may be of interest.

G3.3

(www.netflix.com, November 11, 2001)

a health and nutrition site, an offer of personalized nutrition recommendations might lead to a short series of questions, asking about the customer's family medical history, eating, and exercise habits. After answering the questions, the customer receives expert health and nutrition tips, and personalized product recommendations.

The same method could be employed on almost any site where the products are complicated and customers' needs vary widely. Employ a **H1** PROCESS FUNNEL (H1) that takes a customer through a short sequence of choices. Be sure to keep the process funnel short, and to indicate how long the process will take because customers may balk if there is too much work involved with little perceived benefit. Figure G3.4 shows how Lands' End has customers answer a few simple questions before it provides personalized recommendations.

Provide Different Levels of Recommendations • Often multiple data points on each customer's interests can yield useful personalization recommendations. Here are the basic schemes for personalizing recommendations and the information required to generate them:

- Tracking the most popular purchases of customers who like the same things requires the following:
  - A database of product ratings by customers (this is different from just using product purchases because that approach assumes that customers really liked everything they purchased)
  - The current customer's product ratings
- Tracking the best products, according to information provided by the customer, requires the following:
  - Specific information about customer needs, such as interest in new sports products or in kid's toys
  - Expert recommendations for targeting people with specific interests

Provide Feedback about Why a Recommendation Was Made • One of the biggest problems with personalized recommendation schemes is that customers do not know how reliable the recommendations are. One way of addressing this concern is by providing some sort of feedback as to why a certain recommendation was made. It can be as simple as telling customers that the reason was that they also liked three other similar products. The key here is to avoid describing how the algorithm works at a highly technical level because that will simply confuse customers.

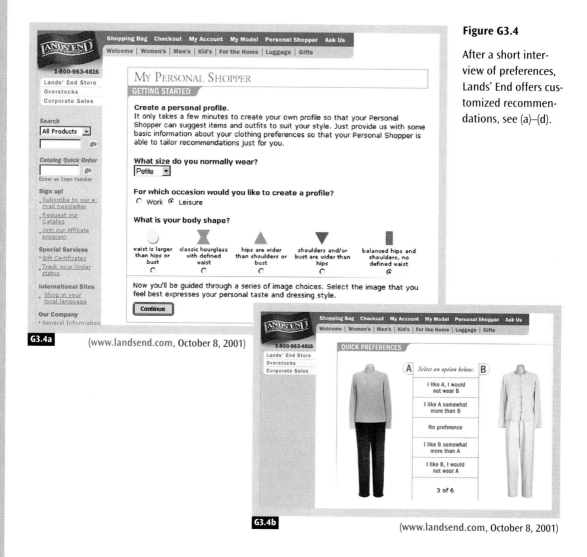

Figure G3.4

After a short interview of preferences, Lands' End offers customized recommendations, see (a)–(d).

G3.4a (www.landsend.com, October 8, 2001)

G3.4b (www.landsend.com, October 8, 2001)

Provide Multiple and Repeated Recommendations • Another way of providing feedback on the reliability of a recommendation is to give several (five to seven) recommendations, and to include items that customers have seen before and liked. This last part is especially important because it gives customers a way of knowing whether or not the system is working. From customers' perspectives, if the Web site is recommending things that they already like, then it is probably working correctly, and the other choices are probably things that they will also like. On the other hand, if the Web site is recommending things that they do not like, they will think that the site is "broken" and will ignore any personalized recommendations.

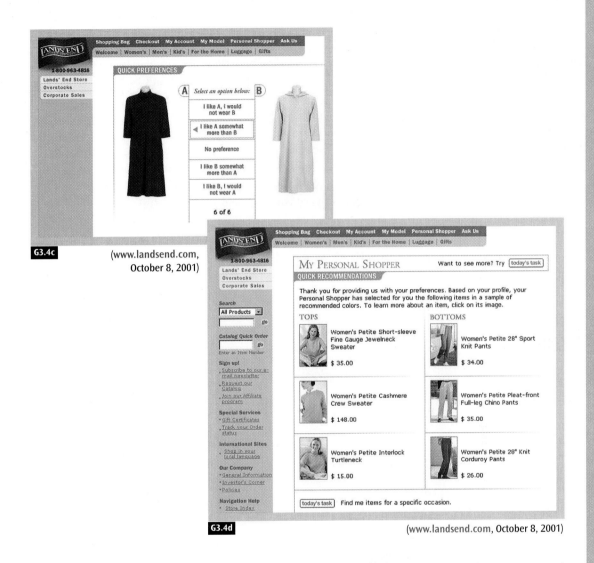

G3.4c

(www.landsend.com,
October 8, 2001)

G3.4d

(www.landsend.com, October 8, 2001)

Address Privacy Concerns • In an era of ever more targeted marketing and database recording of personal information, privacy is a primary concern for customers. But personalized recommendations can help customers find items of interest and value. If your company does not abuse customer information, and discloses clearly and simply how it will use the information, customers are more likely to trust you. Make sure your PRIVACY POLICY (E4) identifies the kinds of information collected and explains how the information is used.

❊ SOLUTION

Avoid using pure inference data to make product recommendations because it will not necessarily reflect real customer choices. Start by offering product and category recommendations based on previous purchases by other customers. Then add recommendations based on past purchases, ratings, and interviews completed by the customer. Integrate this data into your site on product pages, category pages, and personalized recommendation pages. Provide feedback about why a recommendation was made. Provide multiple recommendations, including those that customers have seen before, to help people gauge the quality of the recommendations. Address privacy concerns and how the personalization data will be used.

Figure G3.5

Page templates can be used in conjunction with individual preferences and the product database to present recommendations to new visitors (1). Visitors have their individual preferences stored whenever they explicitly personalize their preferences or purchase something (2). Individual preferences can be combined with the product database to provide personalized recommendations (3). Web site managers can manage the product database through an administrative page that makes it easy to add, remove, and edit content.

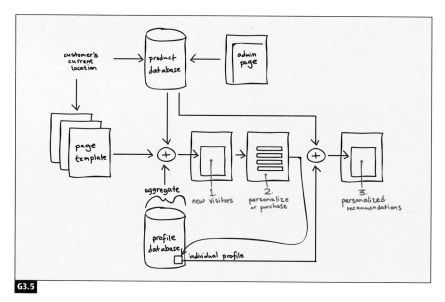

G3.5

❊ CONSIDER THESE OTHER PATTERNS

To give customers a way to explicitly state their needs, invite them to participate in a "needs assessment" interview that leads them through a PROCESS FUNNEL (H1). Provide PERSONALIZED CONTENT (D4) based on customer profiles to build product CATEGORY PAGES (B8) and CLEAN PRODUCT DETAILS (F2) pages.

Figure G4.1

Amazon.com's recommendation community provides content for customers. This review content comes from other customers and it gives the site research value, thereby making it a destination as well as a shopping site.

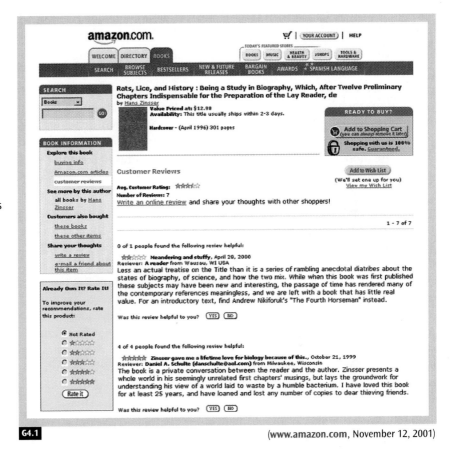

G4.1

(www.amazon.com, November 12, 2001)

✳ BACKGROUND

In PERSONAL E-COMMERCE (A1) we discussed how COMMUNITY CONFERENCE (A3) tools could augment the shopping experience. This pattern provides the core for giving customers a voice on an e-commerce site and describes how customers' opinions can be used to provide recommendations for other customers. This pattern can be used in conjunction with FEATURED PRODUCTS (G1), CROSS-SELLING AND UP-SELLING (G2), and PERSONALIZED RECOMMENDATIONS (G3) to provide useful recommendations and streamline purchases for customers.

✳ PROBLEM

Recommendations from other customers are valuable, but the process of making sure the community system is not abused is time-consuming and littered with obstacles.

Within the Web lies a powerful potential for building lasting and sustainable online communities. You can take advantage of this potential on e-commerce sites by creating recommendation communities, letting your community members help each other. The goal of a recommendation community is to empower customers to make informed decisions and thus encourage e-commerce transactions. It is a win–win situation: Customers are more satisfied with their purchases, and sites make more sales and thus improve their bottom line.

Customers like recommendations so much that even strangers, especially those who seem knowledgeable, influence them. A past customer's rave review of a product or service is a very strong selling point. Conversely, customers avoid products if they have heard bad things. If we multiply all of the written conversations exchanged by hundreds, even thousands, of customers, we begin to get a small inkling of the power of online communities.

Some of the major obstacles to overcome with recommendation communities are how to deal with obscenities, copyrighted material, abusive writers, and negative reviews. Your site needs to make sure customer-written comments do not include profanity and do not promote competitors' sites. It also needs to be able to remove reviews that make it past your profanity filters: those that are libelous and those that make use of copyrighted material.

For sites that sell a variety of equivalent products, negative reviews are not a crucial problem, as long as customers eventually make a purchase. For sites that sell their own products, though, negative reviews can have a serious adverse effect on sales. The problem is that customers will keep looking for reviews, beyond your site, even if you do not provide them.

According to statistics from the Pew Internet & American Life Project, 73 percent of people research a product or service before buying it.[1] If customers cannot do the research on your site, they will do so on a competitor's site, especially one that has a recommendation community containing an abundance of reviews. In the worst case, customers will make

---

1   Internet Activities, May–June 2000 poll, www.pewinternet.org/reports/chart.asp?img =4_summary3.gif.

Figure G4.2

The Yahoo! Video site provides review guidelines on the same page as the input form (a), and it shows reviewers their work so that they can proofread what they have written before posting it (b). (Reproduced with permission of Yahoo! © 2000 by Yahoo! Inc. YAHOO! and the YAHOO! logo are trademarks of Yahoo! Inc.)

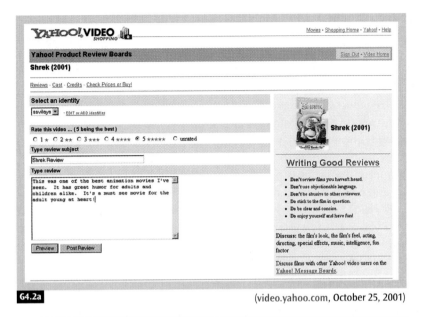

G4.2a   (video.yahoo.com, October 25, 2001)

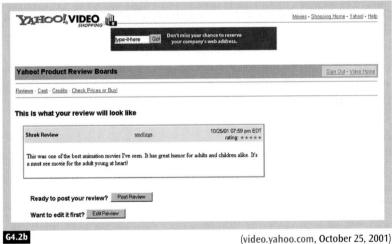

G4.2b   (video.yahoo.com, October 25, 2001)

the purchase on a competitor's site! This is a difficult issue, but it is something that the management of a company has to face head-on.

This pattern creates the framework for all recommendation communities.

Help Community Members Write Their Reviews • It can be quite difficult to write reviews, especially for a customer who has never done it before. Help your customers by providing some structure (see Figure G4.2). Having a customer write a review is a two-step PROCESS FUNNEL (H1):

1. Let the customer write a title for the review, and provide a separate area for the text of the review. Include a section to give the product a numerical rating. Provide writing guidelines that specify what to say and how to say it. For example, book reviews should focus on the content of the book and describe why the reader liked or disliked it. However, reviews should avoid giving away book and movie endings, should refrain from profanity, and should not attack the authors personally (although attacking their skills as authors is legitimate).

2. Let the customer review what he or she has written, and show how it will appear, before it is posted. Give customers the opportunity to go back and edit if they choose.

Provide Policies of Use • Allowing customers to post text or links on a site opens the door to abuses. What if someone posts copyrighted material in a review? If a review allows images, what if someone points to something obscene? What if someone posts an obviously fake review, or an insider such as a restaurant owner gives his or her own establishment a positive review? In addition, who owns the reviews? What about minors under a certain age? For example, as discussed in PRIVACY POLICY (E4), the U.S. government restricts the kinds of information that can be collected about minors.

These are all issues that the site management team must address in its FAIR INFORMATION PRACTICES (E3). Many of these issues have potentially serious legal ramifications, so consult legal counsel to develop the best policy. Figure G4.3 shows an example of such a policy.

A site also needs an editor to check reviews, to ensure that any obscene or possibly libelous material is removed from the review prior to posting. However, it is practically impossible to read and edit every review in a timely manner. One way of managing this responsibility is to randomly spot-check new customer reviews. Another way is to provide a feedback form that lets your customers identify problematic reviews so that they can be sent to the editor.

Equip Your Site with Meta-ratings • People need a way of knowing which reviews are good and which reviews are not. One way of providing this information is with meta-ratings, or reviews of recommendations. Figure G4.4 shows Amazon.com's system. It asks, "Was this review helpful to you?" Reviews with many yes votes are seen as more useful than those with many no votes.

Figure G4.3

Amazon.com provides links to policies and writing guidelines on the same page as the review form. You can write your review (a), check your review (b), and submit your review (c)

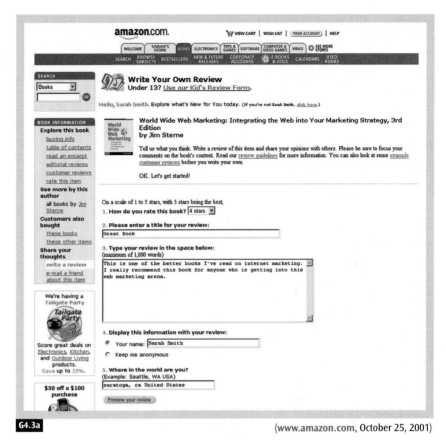

G4.3a

(www.amazon.com, October 25, 2001)

G4.3b

(www.amazon.com, October 25, 2001)

(continued)

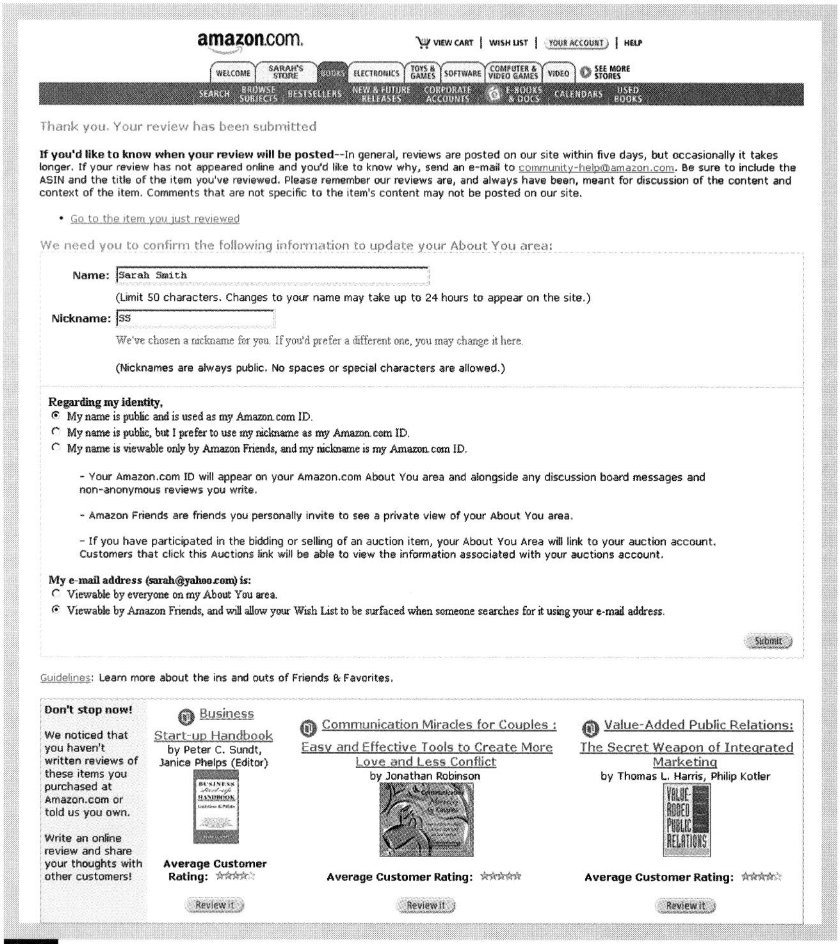

Figure G4.3
(continued)

G4.3c

(www.amazon.com, October 25, 2001)

The online auction site eBay uses a similar system for providing feedback about buyers and sellers (see Figure G4.5). The scoring is simpler: −1 for a negative comment, 0 for a neutral comment, and +1 for a positive comment. This approach is novel because it rates not the quality of a product, but the trustworthiness and reliability of people who buy and sell. However, the general theme is still the same: Provide information to empower future customers to make informed decisions.

Implement your meta-rating system with ACTION BUTTONS (K4) that give customers the power to rate each recommendation.

Figure G4.4

Amazon.com lets customers comment on reviews in a meta-review.

All Customer Reviews
Avg. Customer Rating: ★★★★☆
Write an online review and share your thoughts with other shoppers!

7 of 9 people found the following review helpful:

★★★★☆ **A useful text for computer scientists**, November 8, 1998
Reviewer: **landay@cs.berkeley.edu** from Berkeley, CA USA
Most existing UI/HCI books ignore the details on how to implement user interfaces and are thus inappropriate for courses in many computer science departments. Olsen's book steps into this vacuum and provides a text that covers how to go about determining the tasks an interface should support as well as how to implement the resulting design. The bulk of the book is on the implementation side and thus students will also come to understand how toolkits, which practitioners generally use, work internally.

This text can be used in a quarter long course on UI development or in a more comprehensive semester long HCI course when supplemented with additional material on human abilities, design, and evaluation. We have found this book quite valuable in three offerings of our course on UI Design, Prototyping, and Evaluation here in the EECS Department at UC Berkeley.

Was this review helpful to you? (YES) (NO)

G4.4

(www.amazon.com, September 30, 2001)

Figure G4.5

eBay shows numerical ratings and comments on sellers and buyers.

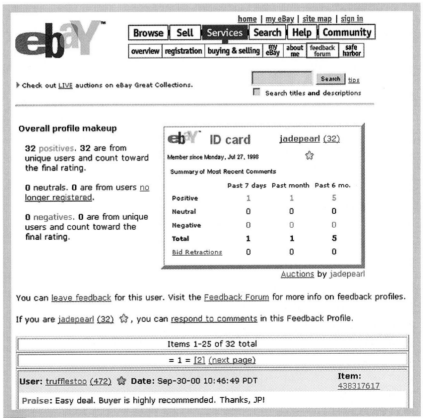

G4.5

(www.ebay.com, September 30, 2001)

Prime the Pump • Customers will follow the example of a few early adopters, and recommendation communities are no different. Before your site can gain popularity, it must be perceived as having useful recommendations. Use a UNIFIED BROWSING HIERARCHY (K1) to integrate content, commerce, and customer reviews. Put customer reviews on the CLEAN PRODUCT DETAILS (F2) page, and add links to make it easy for visitors to add reviews. Also consider providing motivation to write a review, perhaps entering customers who write their first review into a contest in which they could win a $50 (U.S.) gift certificate.

Remember, the most important resource in a recommendation community consists of the members themselves. Involve them in the development of their community by testing new ideas with those who are active in the community.

✳ SOLUTION

Provide a two-step process to write a review: (1) Have customers enter review title and text of the review, and any numerical rating. The text must follow the guidelines of the site. (2) Let customers see the recommendation as it will appear in the site, and allow them to edit it. Filter the title and text for profanity and HTML that might link to another site. Staff an editor to review customer-written recommendations and remove them if they are offensive or libelous. Once the review has been posted, provide a mechanism for other customers to rate the review, giving it a meta-rating. Finally, offer an incentive for customers to write the first review, to get people to use the community features.

Figure G4.6

Provide a two-step process funnel to help customers write reviews. Let them write the review (1), and check that their review is formatted correctly before submission (2). After the publisher makes sure that the review conforms to all stated rules, other customers can see the published review (3).

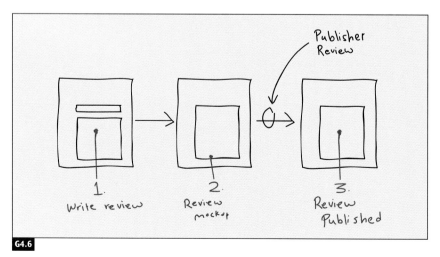

❊ CONSIDER THESE OTHER PATTERNS

Provide a UNIFIED BROWSING HIERARCHY (K1) to integrate content, commerce, and community in your Web site. Build a two-step PROCESS FUNNEL (H1) for people to write reviews and enter numerical ratings, then review and edit what they wrote. Publish the review guidelines, as well as your FAIR INFORMATION PRACTICES (E3). Integrate the reviews into the CLEAN PRODUCT DETAILS (F2) pages. Once reviews have been posted, let other customers rate them by clicking rating ACTION BUTTONS (K4).

G5 MULTIPLE DESTINATIONS

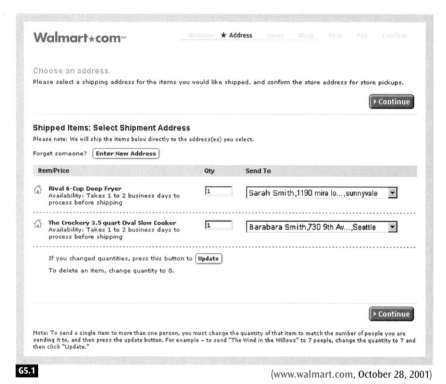

Figure G5.1

Walmart.com provides a quick and easy way to ship items to multiple addresses. (Image courtesy of Wal-Mart.com, Inc. Copyright 2000–2002 Wal-Mart.com, Inc. and Wal-Mart Stores, Inc.)

G5.1 (www.walmart.com, October 28, 2001)

✳ BACKGROUND

Sometimes customers fill their SHOPPING CARTS (F3) and indicate in QUICK ADDRESS SELECTION (F4) that they want to send items to multiple addresses. This pattern gives the framework for shipping to multiple destinations.

✳ PROBLEM

Customers sometimes want to ship to multiple addresses once they have chosen their items to purchase. Making this process simple requires changes throughout the checkout process.

Shoppers need to assign items to particular addresses when shipping them as gifts or to multiple destinations. To do this, they have to fill out multiple destination addresses. With QUICK ADDRESS SELECTION (F4), we formulated the pattern for shipping to a single address, but we did not offer a means to assign each product to a particular destination. Once shoppers have assigned products to destinations, they will want to review which items are going to each address to verify the completeness and correctness of each order. Once they have finished placing the order, they will want a printable confirmation. This pattern provides the solution.

Let Customers Choose Multiple Destinations • When customers are shopping and selecting items, they leave the specifics of shipping for later, during checkout. On the QUICK ADDRESS SELECTION (F4) page of QUICK-FLOW CHECKOUT (F1), provide a **Ship to multiple addresses** ACTION BUTTON (K4), as Walmart.com does (see Figure G5.2).

Figure G5.2

Walmart.com asks shoppers, during quick address selection, if they would like to ship to multiple addresses. (Image courtesy of Wal-Mart.com, Inc. Copyright 2000–2002 Wal-Mart.com, Inc. and Wal-Mart Stores, Inc.)

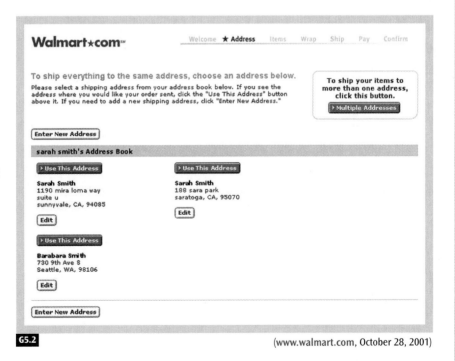

(www.walmart.com, October 28, 2001)

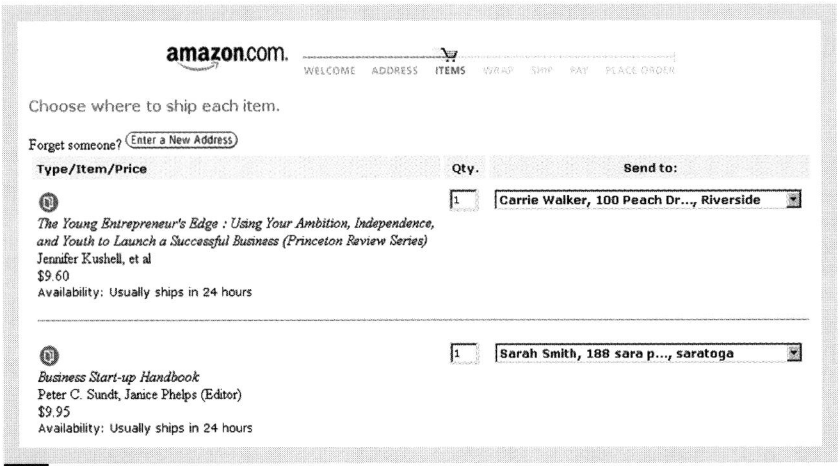

(www.amazon.com, October 28, 2001)

Figure G5.3

An address assignment page on Amazon.com shows each product and provides a pick list of prior addresses with each. Customers can also enter a new address.

Let Customers Choose Addresses from Their Existing Address Book • If customers have purchased products in the past, they will already have an address book with the Web site. On a page listing all the products to be purchased, have a pick list next to each product, listing all of the possible destinations available from the address book (see Figure G5.3).

On the other hand, if the customer is new to the site (and thus has an empty address book), or if returning customers need to add a new shipping address, present them with a page that is essentially the same as the shipping address entry form from QUICK ADDRESS SELECTION (F4).

Confirm the Order • Before checking out, customers need to review their orders and confirm their correctness and completeness. An ORDER SUMMARY (F7) page that categorizes items by destination gives customers a way to quickly review the order before completing it. And if they need to correct anything, an **Edit** ACTION BUTTON (K4) on each address section of the order takes them back to the address assignment screen. Figure G5.4 shows an example of an order summary that displays multiple addresses.

Finally, an ORDER CONFIRMATION AND THANK-YOU (F8) page that includes the items ordered and their destinations in a printable format gives customers a tangible order record that they can print out.

Figure G5.4

The order summary page needs to be modified to show multiple shipping addresses. This is how Amazon.com does it.

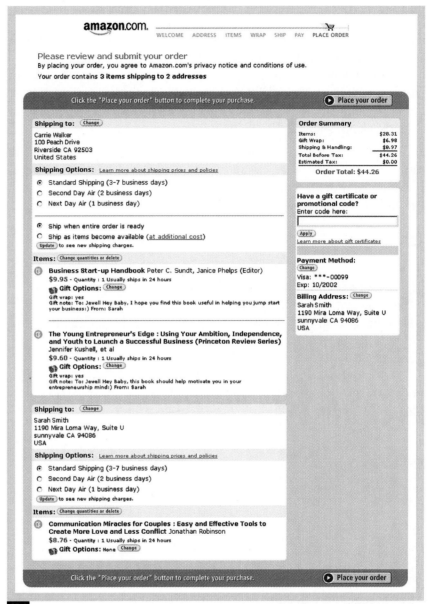

G5.4

(www.amazon.com, October 28, 2001)

✳ SOLUTION

Provide a Send to multiple addresses **action button at the top of the quick address selection page. If the customer clicks it, show a new page with an** Add new address **action button, a list of all the products in the order, and a pick list next to each product. The pick list provides all the destination options. If there are no existing addresses, as in the case of first-time customers, immediately go to a new-address page.**

On the new-address page, have a new-address form that is quick and easy to read. On the order summary page, separate orders by their destinations, and provide a link to change the items in a destination's order. On the confirmation and thank-you page, separate items by destination.

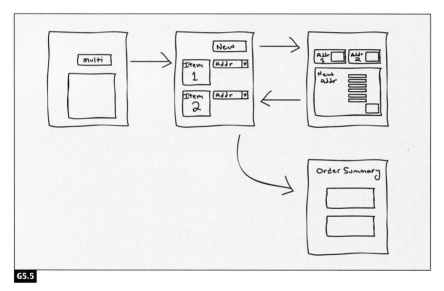

G5.5

Figure G5.5

Give customers the option to send products to multiple addresses. Let customers choose which items will be shipped where, and provide a way for them to add new addresses. Before the order is finalized, provide a concise order summary that shows where all of the items will be shipped.

✳ CONSIDER THESE OTHER PATTERNS

Answer questions that customers might have about your site security by providing a direct link to your PRIVACY POLICY (E4). Help customers fill out the form by PREVENTING ERRORS (K12) and providing MEANINGFUL ERROR MESSAGES (K13). Use ACTION BUTTONS (K4) to lead customers to the next stage in the checkout, and to edit a destination's order on the ORDER SUMMARY (F7) page. Display the rows of items in a GRID LAYOUT (I1), in CONTENT MODULES (D2).

Figure G6.1

Martha Stewart's Web site makes it easy to find gifts for loved ones for a variety of special occasions. The Web site also offers gift wrapping and a gift message on every order. These features, combined with the site's clean design and navigation, make it a good service-based gift-giving site.

G6.1

(www.marthastewart.com, February 12, 2002)

✳ BACKGROUND

PERSONAL E-COMMERCE (A1) establishes how people can order online and complete their orders through the QUICK-FLOW CHECKOUT (F1) process. Enabling customers to purchase and send gifts online requires a few changes to the standard checkout process. This pattern describes some requirements for gift giving online.

✳ PROBLEM

When ordering gifts online, customers want to write notes to the recipients and to be assured that the price will not be disclosed. If a site does not offer these conveniences, customers will be less likely to order gifts.

If your site offers consumer items, shoppers will want to send them as gifts to family, friends, associates, and customers. Gifts sent online are especially convenient because all the wrapping and mailing is handled by the online store, and because customers can shop for multiple people and send to MULTIPLE DESTINATIONS (G5) with one order. But there are variables. Customers will not want their recipients to see an item's price, might want to send gift-wrapped presents, and probably will want to include a personal note. Making the process simple and clear, especially for different items going to different people, is key if you want your site to be a resource for gift giving.

Not all items will necessarily be going to the same person, even if they are being sent to the same location. Especially on holidays, when whole families are celebrating, customers will send gifts to different people at one address. Making the notes customized for each gift ensures that the right person gets the right gift, and that the customer is able to convey any special messages.

Some products may be too big for gift wrapping, but a note could still be attached. Larger products might require more gift-wrapping paper and therefore understandably might cost more to gift-wrap. By providing separate prices for gift-wrapping each item, you can charge the right amount for both large and small products.

You will need to make changes to the QUICK-FLOW CHECKOUT (F1) PROCESS FUNNEL (H1) to create a gift-giving site (see Figure G6.2). Once

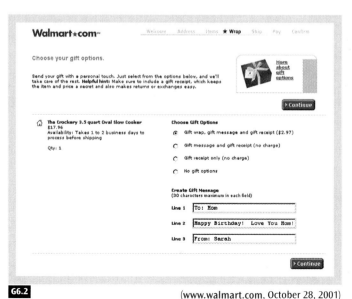

Figure G6.2

In this example of the gift-giving process funnel, Walmart.com makes it easy to add gift wrapping and personalized notes to each gift. (Images courtesy of Wal-Mart.com, Inc. Copyright 2000–2002 Wal-Mart.com, Inc. and Wal-Mart Stores, Inc.)

G6.2

(www.walmart.com, October 28, 2001)

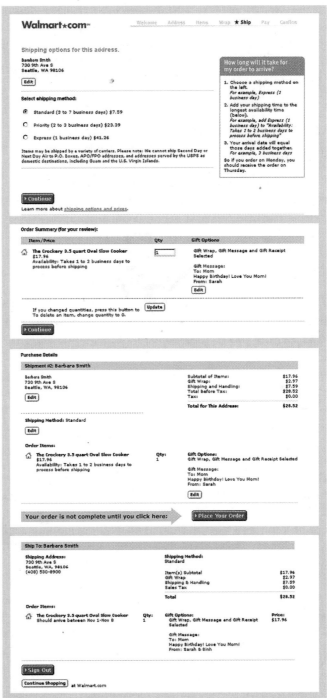

customers have selected their gifts by putting them in their SHOPPING CARTS (F3), the QUICK-FLOW CHECKOUT (F1) process needs to indicate that items can be gift-wrapped and gift notes can be attached. It is best to disclose these prices at this point so that customers are not surprised later. Including the price right next to the option means that your customers won't have to bother looking elsewhere.

State That There Will Be No Price or Item List on the Packing Slip • The packing slip that ships with products usually includes prices of the respective items. When giving gifts, however, people do not want the recipients to see or know the prices. People receiving gifts that are gift-wrapped should not know what's inside before opening the wrap, but recipients do need instructions on how to return items if necessary. If the packing slip for a gift order includes the sender information, the recipient information, the order number, and the return instructions, recipients can make exchanges if they like.

Select and Edit Gifts • After customers have placed items in their SHOPPING CARTS (F3), but before they have completed QUICK-FLOW CHECKOUT (F1), they will need to identify the recipients of the gifts by attaching notes. Provide a form so that gift givers can enter a personal note per package, to help ensure that the individual items go to the right person, and to give gift givers the chance to say something intimate. Use a **Save gift options** ACTION BUTTON (K4) to save the edits and take customers back to the ORDER SUMMARY (F7) page.

Summarize and Confirm the Order • Once customers have made their selections, have decided which items are gifts, have written personal notes, and have selected items to wrap, they will want to see a summary before confirming the entire order. On the ORDER SUMMARY (F7) page, show each item and indicate any additional costs for wrapping so that there are no surprises later.

Provide an **Edit gift options** ACTION BUTTON (K4) on the ORDER SUMMARY (F7) page to take customers back to the gift selection and editing page if there are any problems with the order. If the order is satisfactory, the **Place this order** ACTION BUTTON (K4) takes customers to the ORDER CONFIRMATION AND THANK-YOU (F8) page, where the details are reported again for confirmation, and possible printing.

Provide Other Gift-Giving Features • Sometimes customers want help choosing gifts. To provide help, create a PERSONALIZED RECOMMENDATIONS (G3) system for selecting gifts. Such a system takes customers through the process of identifying appropriate gift ideas, and makes recommendations based on editorialized product selections that are currently in stock. Figure G6.3 shows how Amazon.com helps customers find gifts for friends and family.

Figure G6.3

Providing gift ideas can help customers find the right gift.

G6.3

(www.amazon.com, May 15, 2002)

✳ SOLUTION

Give customers clear indications early in the shopping process that the site has gift-giving options, so that they can shop for that reason. On the checkout page, provide a button that takes customers to a form where they can enter notes and select gift-wrapping options. And on this form, provide a button that takes customers back to the order summary page, where they can review their whole order, including gift options. When they're done, the order confirmation page will list the entire order, including gifts, in case customers want the information for their records.

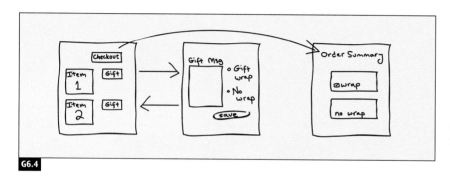

Figure G6.4

Let customers choose which purchases are meant as gifts. Give customers the option of wrapping each gift and typing in a personal message.

✳ CONSIDER THESE OTHER PATTERNS

Indicate in the SHOPPING CART (F3) that gift options are available so that customers can plan to send items directly to the gift recipients. Modify the QUICK-FLOW CHECKOUT (F1) PROCESS FUNNEL (H1) by inserting an ACTION BUTTON (K4) that allows customers to change gift options in the ORDER SUMMARY (F7) page. Provide a form with note text input fields and gift-wrapping options for each item, and an ACTION BUTTON (K4) to save gift options. Once they have confirmed their gift options on the ORDER SUMMARY (F7) page, customers can click the **Place order** ACTION BUTTON (K4) and receive the ORDER CONFIRMATION AND THANK-YOU (F8) page. For other gift-giving features, consider offering a gift wizard PROCESS FUNNEL (H1) that provides PERSONALIZED RECOMMENDATIONS (G3).

Figure G7.1

Nordstrom's Web site shows clear order detail, including product shipping destination, product detail, quantity, price, gift options, shipping methods and charges, tax, and totals.

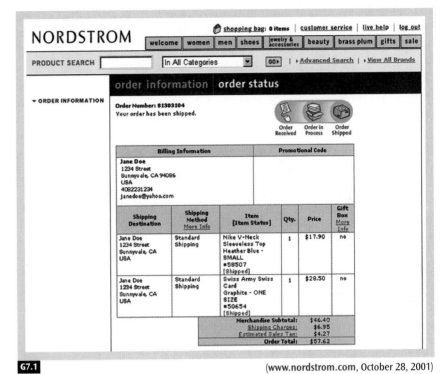

G7.1   (www.nordstrom.com, October 28, 2001)

✳ BACKGROUND

PERSONAL E-COMMERCE (A1) establishes how people can order online and complete their orders through the QUICK-FLOW CHECKOUT (F1) process. Once customers have completed their orders, they receive ORDER CONFIRMATION AND THANK-YOU (F8) message pages. Some customers might also like to receive shipping information. This pattern provides the core for tracking e-commerce orders.

✳ PROBLEM

When customers place online orders, the details about order status and shipping become important. If this information is not easily available online, the cost of processing customer inquiries increases dramatically.

Shoppers sometimes need to receive packages by a certain date. As a result, they often have questions about the status of their orders and would like to get that information quickly and easily. Usually they can call customer service to get this information. However, because phone centers require significant budgets to manage and operate, companies have looked for cheaper alternatives. On the Web, customers can track more information than is typically available over the phone. A site can link directly to the shipper, for example.

Building an order-tracking system on the Web requires integrating the site with the order fulfillment department, the part of the company that makes sure products are shipped on time. The customer experience must be smooth, and it must provide the information customers need to make decisions if items are delayed. This pattern provides the solution.

Provide Access to Orders • Customers sometimes need to modify orders that are still pending. Perhaps the shipping address needs to change, the contents of the order need to be updated, or the billing information is not correct. In all of these cases, the ability to update an order online, in the same manner that the order was placed, improves the customer's experience, as long as the process is simple.

To gain access to this information, secure account information by requiring returning customers to sign in on the SIGN-IN/NEW ACCOUNT (H2) page. A customer who created an account can sign in with his or her user name and password. A customer who used a GUEST ACCOUNT (H3) must reference the order number together with other secure information, such as a billing ZIP code.

Once they are in the system, customers may not remember the orders they have placed, and they may wish to review their order history to find a particular order. Give customers a list of their orders organized by the processing stage of each order. For example, let customers review orders by the following categories:

- Pending shipment
- Recently shipped
- Shipped and received

People need a way to skim through the results of these order histories. A logical way to sort order histories is with a CHRONOLOGICAL ORGANIZATION (B6) so that customers can see the order of their purchases. List all the orders by date, and if the list of items is not too long, indicate the contents as well. Figure G7.2 shows how Shutterfly organizes its order tracking and history page.

Figure G7.2

Shutterfly's site provides a convenient order history with status and order detail.

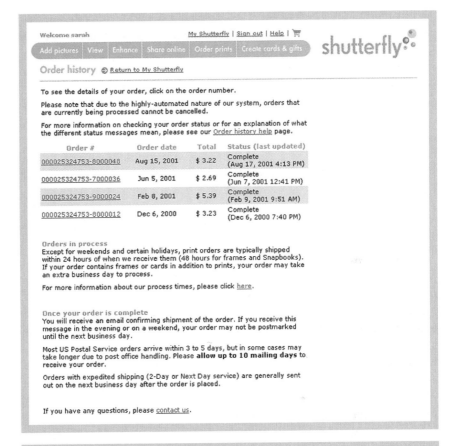

G7.2

(www.shutterfly.com, November 20, 2001)

For Pending Orders, Indicate Product Availability • When products have not been shipped yet, it helps to tell the customer how far along the fulfillment process is for each product. Especially for time-sensitive orders, the knowledge that a product has not been shipped, or is not in stock, can set a customer's expectations.

While checking out, customers assume that a product is in stock. If it is not in stock, and customers need the product by a certain time, they need to know so that they can order something else. In fact, if the product or order changes status in any significant way, you should notify customers so that they can take action accordingly. Even though it might be bad news, customers appreciate knowing as soon as possible. It is worse to set expectations and not deliver than to adjust expectations along the way.

Table G7.1 shows the different actions to take when there are changes in the order status.

Allow Order Modification, If Possible • Customers might need to change an order in some way if there is a negative change in the status of an order, such as a shipping delay. If customers cannot change orders on the site, they will need to call customer service. If customer service is not available, they will need to send e-mail, which does not provide an immediate resolution to a potentially time-sensitive issue. Providing the means to solve the problem on the site reduces customer service costs but requires complete integration of back-end fulfillment systems with the site. Provide ACTION BUTTONS (K4) to edit different parts of the order. Table G7.2 lists the parts of the order that might need modification, and the respective patterns that address changes to the order. Figure G7.3 shows how Amazon.com handles order tracking and modification.

Order Status	Automated Action
Product in stock	None
Product out of stock	Inform customer through e-mail
Product discontinued	Inform customer through e-mail
Product delayed	Inform customer through e-mail
Product in stock, processing order	None
Order shipped	Inform customer through e-mail
Order delivered	None

Table G7.1

Actions to Take on Order Status Changes

Table G7.2

Potential Changes to
Orders

Order Changes	Navigation Tools
Shipping address(es)	QUICK ADDRESS SELECTION (F4), MULTIPLE DESTINATIONS (G5)
Shipping method	QUICK SHIPPING METHOD SELECTION (F5)
Billing address	PAYMENT METHOD (F6)
Payment method	PAYMENT METHOD (F6)
Product items	CLEAN PRODUCT DETAILS (F2), SHOPPING CART (F3)
Product quantities	SHOPPING CART (F3)
Gift options	GIFT GIVING (G6)

Sometimes orders cannot be canceled after processing begins. If customers know this, they might have time to change the order before processing begins.

Allow Order Tracking • If an order becomes delayed, or if the customer needs the package on a precise day, as in the case of a priority delivery gift or a business-critical item, order tracking provides the information customers need to locate the package.

Order tracking provides a direct link to the shipper's database and displays information, such as date and time of receipt, at various way stations. To provide this type of information, your site must store a shipper's tracking number and interface with the shipping database.

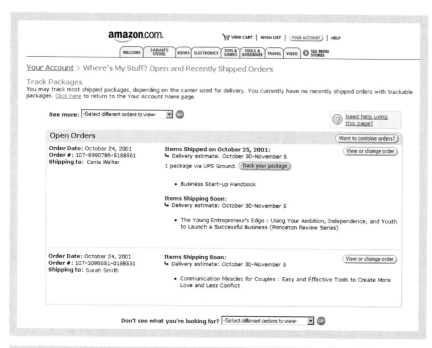

Figure G7.3

Amazon.com offers order histories and modifiable orders (top). Once an order has shipped, the site provides order tracking.

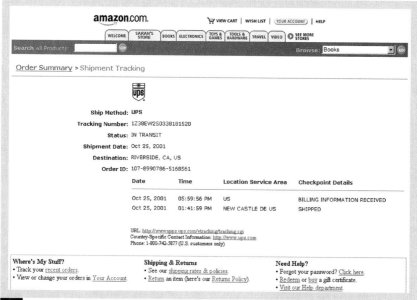

(www.amazon.com, October 27, 2001)

✳ SOLUTION

Require customers to sign in to review their orders and modify them. Give them access to an order history that categorizes orders as pending, shipped, or completed. Display the selected orders chronologically, listing the order number, as well as the contents of the order if the list is not too long. For pending orders, indicate each item's availability, and allow modification of everything from shipping and billing to products and options. For orders you have already shipped, allow order tracking by interfacing with the shipper's database and displaying the shipment way-station history.

Figure G7.4

Provide a secure order tracking and history system to let customers check on their past and pending orders.

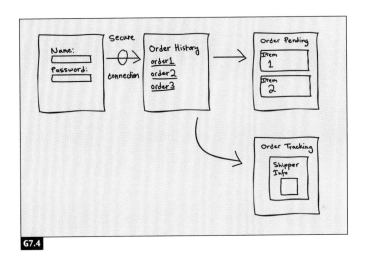

G7.4

✳ CONSIDER THESE OTHER PATTERNS

To gain access to their account information, returning customers must use the SIGN-IN/NEW ACCOUNT (H2) page. Once they are in their accounts, give them access to view their order history sorted by CHRONOLOGICAL ORGANIZATION (B6). If the list of items in an order is not too long, indicate the contents of the order. If a customer wishes to change an order, provide ACTION BUTTONS (K4) to edit different parts of the order. For modifying shipping address and method, use QUICK ADDRESS SELECTION (F4) and MULTIPLE DESTINATIONS (G5). For customers modifying billing information, access the PAYMENT METHOD (F6) page. Allow customers to change items using CLEAN PRODUCT DETAIL (F2) pages and the SHOPPING CART (F3). To update gift options, use GIFT GIVING (G6).

Helping Customers Complete Tasks

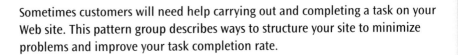

Sometimes customers will need help carrying out and completing a task on your Web site. This pattern group describes ways to structure your site to minimize problems and improve your task completion rate.

H1 PROCESS FUNNEL

H2 SIGN-IN/NEW ACCOUNT

H3 GUEST ACCOUNT

H4 ACCOUNT MANAGEMENT

H5 PERSISTENT CUSTOMER SESSIONS

H6 POP-UP WINDOWS

H7 FREQUENTLY ASKED QUESTIONS

H8 CONTEXT-SENSITIVE HELP

H1 PROCESS FUNNEL

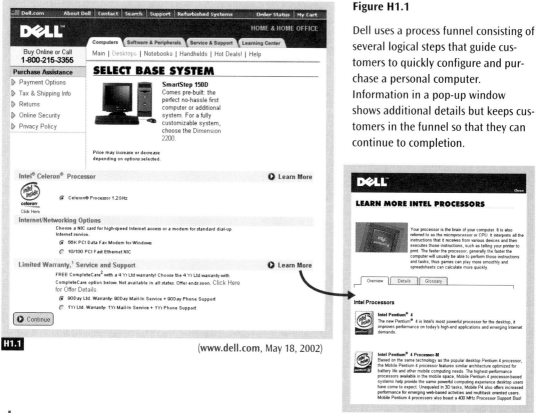

Figure H1.1

Dell uses a process funnel consisting of several logical steps that guide customers to quickly configure and purchase a personal computer. Information in a pop-up window shows additional details but keeps customers in the funnel so that they can continue to completion.

(www.dell.com, May 18, 2002)

✳ BACKGROUND

All Web applications that lead visitors through stepped tasks—PERSONAL E-COMMERCE (A1), SELF-SERVICE GOVERNMENT (A4), WEB APPS THAT WORK (A10), and ENABLING INTRANETS (A11)—need ways to help people succeed at completing the tasks.

✳ PROBLEM

Customers often need to complete highly specific tasks on Web sites, but pages with tangential links and many questions can prevent them from carrying out these tasks successfully.

People enjoy completing the tasks they start. Yet all kinds of distractions—including links that lead off the critical path, extra steps, and extra content—can inadvertently lead them away from accomplishing their goals. These diversions can have legitimate purposes, however, such as providing continuity, giving visitors opportunities to explore, providing instructions, or providing extra details. Striking a balance between these various forces and the actual task can be challenging.

Minimize the Number of Steps Required to Complete a Task • Customers find tasks daunting if there are too many steps. A process funnel should have just two to eight discrete steps. Anything less than two steps is not a process, and a process of more than eight steps is unmanageable. If there are more than eight steps, try to split the process into two or more separate process funnels, or try combining multiple steps into one page. However, this is not always a viable solution because one choice may precede another, and not every page can hold all the information that customers might need at certain points.

Provide a Progress Bar to Let Customers Know Where They Are in the Process Funnel • Showing a progress bar at each step lets your customers know how much farther they need to go to complete the task (see Figure H1.2). It is often not worth your time to make the individual steps on the progress bar clickable because doing so adds more complexity but little benefit for customers.

Remove Unnecessary Links and Content While Reinforcing the Brand • Removing links and content unrelated to the task at hand will reduce the number of distractions, making it more likely that your customers will successfully complete their tasks. Remove all NAVIGATION BARS (K2), TAB ROWS (K3), LOCATION BREAD CRUMBS (K6), and EMBEDDED LINKS (K7), leaving only the links and ACTION BUTTONS (K4) that help visitors reach their goals. Take out any content that is superfluous to the task.

Reinforce the Web site brand to minimize any disorientation customers might feel from sudden changes in navigation options. Use the same fonts, images, colors, layout, and logo throughout the Web site so that no matter where they are, people know they're still on the same site.

Figure H1.2

Many Web sites use a progress bar to let customers know where they are in the process funnel and how much farther they have to go.

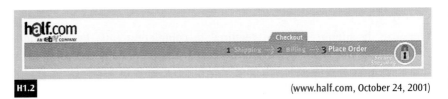

(www.half.com, October 24, 2001)

Use Pop-Up Windows to Provide Extra Information, without Leading Visitors Out of the Process Funnel • Sometimes customers need additional information that you have not provided on a page, such as extra help or product details. Provide a link to a POP-UP WINDOW (H6) containing CLEAN PRODUCT DETAILS (F2) (see Figure H1.1), CONTEXT-SENSITIVE HELP (H8), or information from the FREQUENTLY ASKED QUESTIONS (H7) page, to make the extra information less intrusive. Your challenge is to implement this extra content without detracting from the main purpose.

Make Sure the Back Button Always Works • Customers often use the **Back** button on browsers to modify answers they have typed in on previous pages. However, if the Web site is not implemented correctly, the information they have already entered may be lost when they hit the **Back** button, forcing them to type everything again. In the worst case, people get a cryptic error message saying that the posted information was lost. You can address this annoying problem by temporarily storing the information they type in on each page, redisplaying this information if customers hit the **Back** button, and then overriding the temporarily stored information on the page if it is changed.

Always Make It Clear How to Proceed to the Next Step • Some Web pages are longer than can be displayed on a customer's Web browser. The problem is that people sometimes get lost if the critical ACTION BUTTON (K4), the one that takes them to the next step, is hidden below the fold. Place HIGH-VISIBILITY ACTION BUTTONS (K5) both high *and* low on the page, ensuring that at least one of the critical action buttons will always be visible without scrolling.

Prevent Errors Where Possible, and Provide Error Messages Whenever Errors Do Occur • People will always make mistakes, even with the best of designs. You can provide good customer service if you use structured fields and sample input to help PREVENT ERRORS (K12). At the same time, provide MEANINGFUL ERROR MESSAGES (K13) whenever errors do occur.

✳ SOLUTION

Minimize the number of steps required to complete a task, keeping them between two and eight. Remove unnecessary and potentially confusing links and content from each page, while reinforcing the brand to maintain a sense of place. Use pop-up windows to provide extra information, without leading people out of the process funnel. Make sure the Back button always works so that customers can correct errors. Make it clear how to proceed to the next step with high-visibility action buttons. Prevent errors where possible, and provide error messages whenever errors do occur.

Figure H1.3

A process funnel lets people complete their goals by breaking down complicated tasks into a small number of steps, using pop-up windows for detailed information, and reducing the number of links to only the critical ones, so that people are never distracted.

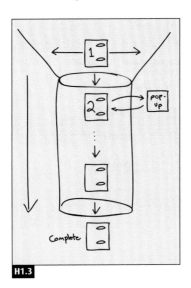

H1.3

✳ CONSIDER THESE OTHER PATTERNS

Many kinds of Web sites use process funnels, including sites for PERSONAL E-COMMERCE (A1), SELF-SERVICE GOVERNMENT (A4), WEB APPS THAT WORK (A10), and ENABLING INTRANETS (A11). Customers use process funnels when they finalize purchases through QUICK-FLOW CHECKOUT (F1), when they create new accounts through SIGN-IN/NEW ACCOUNT (H2), and when they post new messages to a RECOMMENDATION COMMUNITY (G4), to name some examples.

Remove NAVIGATION BARS (K2), TAB ROWS (K3), irrelevant ACTION BUTTONS (K4), LOCATION BREAD CRUMBS (K6), and EMBEDDED LINKS (K7) to ensure that customers stay on their paths. However, keep strong SITE BRANDING (E1) so that customers still know where they are.

Design process funnels to PREVENT ERRORS (K12), and provide MEANINGFUL ERROR MESSAGES (K13) when errors do occur.

Track your customers through PERSISTENT CUSTOMER SESSIONS (H5) to avoid problems with the **Back** button, and to save customer-entered information.

Move extra content, such as CONTEXT-SENSITIVE HELP (H8) and FREQUENTLY ASKED QUESTIONS (H7), to POP-UP WINDOWS (H6) to keep the main task page on the screen. Make the next action visible by keeping it ABOVE THE FOLD (I2) and by using HIGH-VISIBILITY ACTION BUTTONS (K5).

H2 SIGN-IN/NEW ACCOUNT

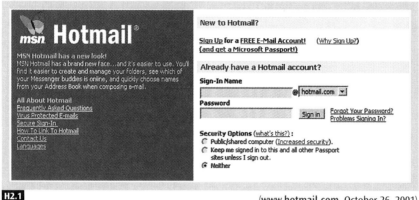

H2.1

(www.hotmail.com, October 26, 2001)

Figure H2.1

MSN Hotmail has an easy sign-in if customers already have an account, or if visitors create a new account on the spot.

✳ BACKGROUND

To provide PERSONALIZED CONTENT (D4), PERSONALIZED RECOMMENDATIONS (G3), and other individualized services, Web sites need a way for both returning customers and new customers to identify themselves. This pattern covers the sign-in and new account processes, describing how to structure the design of these pages, as well as common mistakes to avoid.

✳ PROBLEM

One process has to handle both returning customers, who sign in and identify themselves to get personalized content, and new customers, who need to create an account before going further on the site.

The sign-in/new account pattern solves this problem by using a variation of the PROCESS FUNNEL (H1) to achieve its goals: an easy way for customers to sign in if they already have accounts, and an easy way for visitors to create new accounts. The sections that follow identify some things you should consider when creating a sign-in mechanism.

Collect the Minimum Amount of Information for Creating New Accounts •
You risk alienating potential customers if creating a new account takes
too long, if you ask for too much personal information, or if the process
doesn't run smoothly. If creating a new account is simple and painless,
more customers will do it (see Figure H2.2).

Make Clear Which Fields Are Required and Which Are Optional • Splitting
the information into required and optional fields can help keep account
creation short. Many Web sites flag required fields with bold type or asterisks so that customers are clear on what is optional.

Figure H2.2

If you want visitors
to create a new
account, make the
process simple and
painless by minimiz-
ing the number of
possible mistakes
and by keeping it as
short as possible.

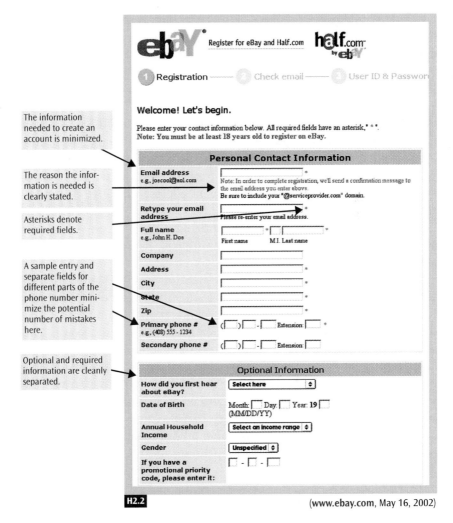

The information
needed to create an
account is minimized.

The reason the infor-
mation is needed is
clearly stated.

Asterisks denote
required fields.

A sample entry and
separate fields for
different parts of the
phone number mini-
mize the potential
number of mistakes
here.

Optional and required
information are cleanly
separated.

(www.ebay.com, May 16, 2002)

Prevent Errors • Smooth the account creation process by PREVENTING
ERRORS (K12), and by providing examples of the data you expect. For
example, if you need a phone number, should it be shown in the format
(510) 555-5555 or 510 555 5555? Or do you need an international
phone number, such as +1 510 555 5555? Develop software that accepts
any possible format so that any number typed in can be translated into
the format that your databases use.

Provide Your Web Site's Privacy Information • Include a link to your
PRIVACY POLICY (E4) on the account creation page, to explain your FAIR
INFORMATION PRACTICES (E3). Have explanatory text describing why you
need certain pieces of information, and how that information will be
used. For example, e-commerce sites need to make it clear that they need
their customers' e-mail addresses and phone numbers in case there are
delays in shipping or problems with the order, and that these pieces of
information will not be used for spamming with promotional e-mail or
phone calls unless the customers choose those options.

Have a Process for Handling Forgotten Passwords • People often forget their
passwords, especially if they have many accounts on different Web sites.
Web sites need mechanisms for helping people remember their passwords. One approach is to send the password to a customer's e-mail
address. You will already have the e-mail address from the customer's
sign-up.

However, there are several potential dangers. E-mail systems are not
always secure, and although doing so is difficult, hackers could break in
and get your visitor's password.

Avoid sending passwords through e-mail if your Web site provides
access to sensitive information, such as a student's grades or a customer's
bank account. For special cases like these, one partial solution is to have
customers create a security question when they open a new account. This
security question requests a piece of personal information, such as a
favorite pet's name, the person's city of birth, or a mother's maiden name
(see Figure H2.3). If customers forget their passwords but can answer the
security question, they either get a hint to what their password is, or they
can reset it. Have your software check that the answer to the security
question is not the same as the password. If it is the same, then provide a
MEANINGFUL ERROR MESSAGE (K13) explaining the point of the security
question and how it works.

Figure H2.3

(a) eBay asks a security question in case a customer forgets his or her password.
(b) The security question is used to reset the password if the customer forgets what it is.

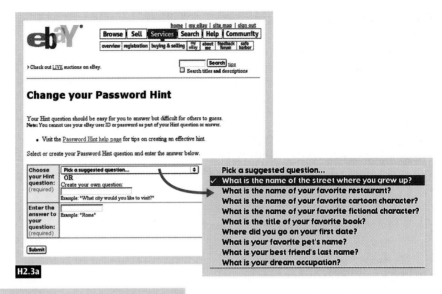

(www.ebay.com, May 16, 2002)

Another solution is to create a one-time URL and e-mail that to your customers. When they click on the link, the URL will take them to a unique page on the site where they can change their password. That way, the password is never transmitted, and the ability to change the password is given only once with that URL.

Another partial solution is to have customers go to a physical location and bring pieces of identification so that someone on your staff can reset the password. This approach makes sense for Web sites that serve a local area, such as a school or a university. It provides more security, but it is still not foolproof because people can fake identification and it can be time-consuming for the customer.

Don't Force First-Time Customers to Sign In Too Early • There are two reasons not to hide all your content behind a sign-in screen. First, you could reduce traffic. Pages that require a sign-in will cause most search engines to fail. This means that none of those pages will ever appear when people search sites like Google or Yahoo!. Second, visitors dislike having to create a new account just to see the content of a site, particularly when it is a shopping site. Tempt people with enough content to persuade them to stay around a little longer.

You can address both of these issues by dividing your Web site into a public portion that is accessible to everyone and a private part that requires people to sign in. The public part is a sampler, which might provide headlines, a few paragraphs of fresh content, or complete access to a few pages.

❉ SOLUTION

Collect the minimum amount of information you need to create new accounts. Make it clear which fields are required and which are optional. Prevent errors where possible. Provide your Web site's privacy information. Have a process for handling forgotten passwords. Do not force first-time customers to sign in too early.

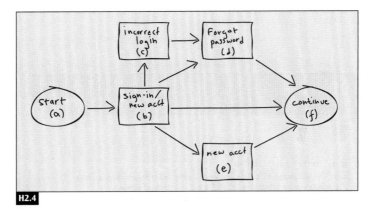

H2.4

Figure H2.4

In general, the process of signing into a Web site should go as follows: Visitors come to an entry point (a) that requires them to sign in (b). Customers who already have an account and remember the password can sign in and continue (f). Visitors who want to create an account do so (e) and then continue (f). Returning customers who enter the wrong account information or password are blocked from continuing (c). A returning customer can ask to receive help remembering the password or to have the password reset (d).

✳ CONSIDER THESE OTHER PATTERNS

The sign-in/new account pattern is actually a version of PROCESS FUNNEL (H1), which covers techniques to help customers complete highly specific tasks.

Sign-in/new account should be designed to PREVENT ERRORS (K12) and to provide MEANINGFUL ERROR MESSAGES (K13) whenever errors do occur.

Make your PRIVACY POLICY (E4), which explains your FAIR INFORMATION PRACTICES (E3), prominent when visitors sign in, or when they're creating a new account. Use a SECURE CONNECTION (E6) if sensitive personal information is involved.

Content that requires people to sign in cannot be indexed by search engines. See WRITING FOR SEARCH ENGINES (D6) for more information.

H3 GUEST ACCOUNT

Figure H3.1

HealthGiant lets its customers make purchases as either guests or registered members. When purchasing as a guest, customers are assured that their personal information will be used for only processing the order and will not be kept in the company's database.

H3.1

(www.healthgiant.com, February 27, 2002)

☀ BACKGROUND

Some customers prefer just to use a Web site instead of having to create an account first. An example would be going through the QUICK-FLOW CHECKOUT (F1) without having to go through SIGN-IN/NEW ACCOUNT (H2). This pattern describes guest accounts in detail.

✳ PROBLEM

Many customers will be put off and possibly leave the site if they have to create an account to use the Web site. However, you need information from customers in order to support them in their tasks.

Customers may become annoyed if they have to create yet another account and password just to make a purchase on PERSONAL E-COMMERCE (A1) sites. This is especially frustrating for customers who intend to make only a single purchase and have no plans to return in the future.

Forcing customers to create an account is just another barrier to entry, and it may cause some people to leave your site. Requiring your customers to give you personal information before making a purchase violates the standard "sales script" that people are familiar with when they shop in regular stores (see QUICK-FLOW CHECKOUT (F1)). On the other hand, you need shipping and billing information to complete a purchase. healthgiant.com makes a nice compromise by assuring its customers that their shipping and billing information will be used only for the current transaction (see Figure H3.1). The U.S. Mint's Web site makes similar assurances to its customers (see Figure H3.2).

This is one instance where guest accounts make sense. In this case the guest account lets customers make purchases first. Once they have completed the QUICK-FLOW CHECKOUT (F1), they are given the option of creating a new account, thus saving all of the information about shipping and billing that they have just typed (see Figure H3.3). It can be helpful to inform your customers up front that they will not need to create an account before checking out (see Figure H3.4).

WEB APPS THAT WORK (A10) are another place where guest accounts make sense. For example, you might let first-time customers try out the service, and only when they want to save their information ask them to create a new account.

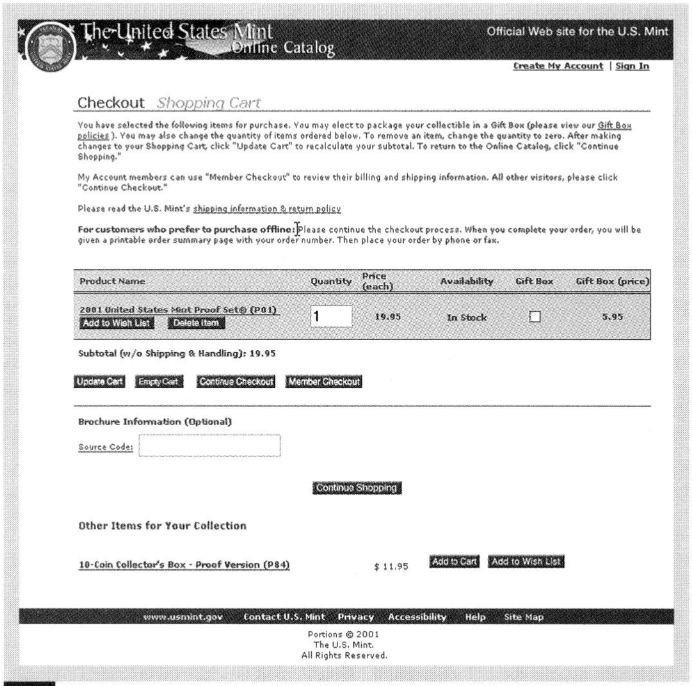

H3.2a

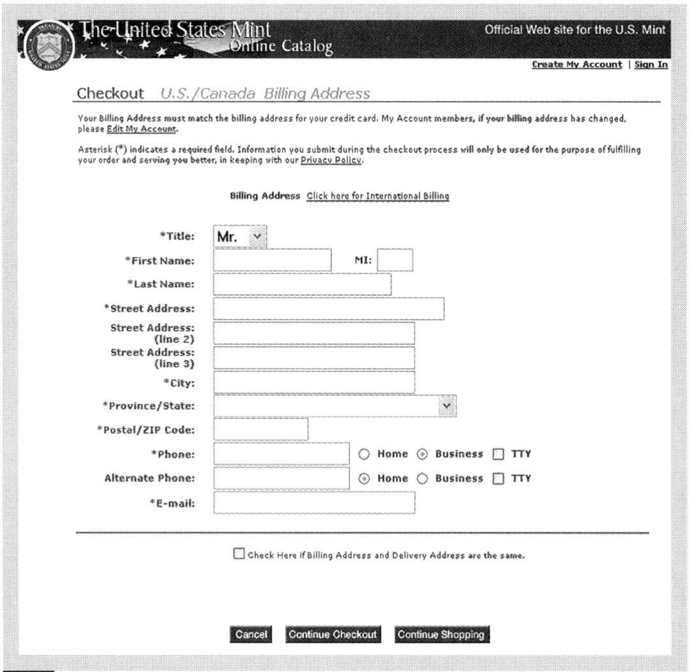

H3.2b

(www.usmint.gov, February 27, 2002)

Figure H3.2

(a) The U.S. Mint's checkout gives customers an option between **Continue Checkout** and **Member Checkout.** (b) The first option leads to the **Billing Address** page, which assures customers that the information submitted will be used only for the purpose of fulfilling the order.

Figure H3.3

Outpost.com lets people without accounts make purchases first and then create an account, if they choose. It also provides an expedited checkout process for customers who already have an account.

H3.3

(www.outpost.com, October 26, 2001)

Figure H3.4

Taxpayers Australia's Web site makes it very clear to its customers that they do not need to be members of the site before purchasing tax information there.

H3.4

(www.taxpayer.com.au, February 27, 2002)

❋ SOLUTION

Give new visitors the option of creating an account at the end of a process, rather than forcing them to create one at the beginning.

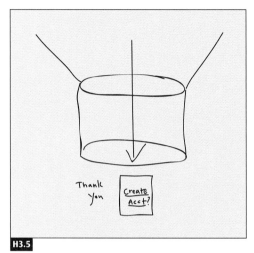

Figure H3.5

Make account creation optional, and put it at the end of the process.

H3.5

❋ CONSIDER THESE OTHER PATTERNS

Guest accounts are an alternative to requiring customers to go through the SIGN-IN/NEW ACCOUNT (H2) process at the beginning of QUICK-FLOW CHECKOUT (F1).

To implement guest accounts, use temporary session IDs, as discussed in PERSISTENT CUSTOMER SESSIONS (H5).

Figure H4.1

This account management page lets customers see and update all the information that Buy.com manages for them. Customers can update their e-mail address, payment information, and shipping details, as well as see the status of their past and current orders.

H4.1

(www.buy.com, February 20, 2002)

✳ BACKGROUND

All Web applications that provide personalization, such as PERSONAL E-COMMERCE (A1), NEWS MOSAICS (A2), and COMMUNITY CONFERENCE (A3), need a way to let customers manage personal data.

✳ PROBLEM

Customers need to see and manage the information a Web site keeps about them.

Web sites need to keep track of a great deal of information about their customers to create highly PERSONALIZED CONTENT (D4) for them. For example, a PERSONAL E-COMMERCE (A1) site might store shipping address, billing address, and credit card information to streamline the checkout process. A NEWS MOSAIC (A2) might store the kinds of news articles that a specific customer likes, presenting a high-value news site tailored for that individual. A COMMUNITY CONFERENCE (A3) site might store a customer's favorite message boards and favorite participants, making it easy to find new and relevant discussions. A STIMULATING ARTS AND ENTERTAINMENT (A9) site might store a customer's movie and music preferences and provide recommendations.

When you're developing a personalized Web site, remember that one of the FAIR INFORMATION PRACTICES (E3) is *access*. Individuals should be able to see the information that a Web site has about them, correct inaccurate data, and delete undesired data. This is not just a matter of fairness; it is also a matter of practicality. If customers give you their mailing addresses when creating new accounts, it makes sense to let them change them if they move.

We call any kind of system designed to help people manage their personal information an **account management system.** Account management systems are essential to any Web site that offers personalized content. In the sections that follow we offer some ideas about how to design these systems.

Provide a Single Page That Gathers All the Account Information in One Place • Your Web site can store a great deal of information about individuals. Consolidating all the information in one place makes it easy for people to see and manage their information. Figure H4.2 shows how the U.S. Mint Web site lets customers manage their address books, wish lists, ORDER TRACKING AND HISTORY (G7), and other information.

As another example, Figure H4.3 shows how CDNOW, a music site, groups all of the information related to an account on a profile page. This page lets customers check whether their contact information, preferences, and financial information are correct and up-to-date.

Figure H4.2

The U.S. Mint Web site lets customers manage all their account information in one convenient place.

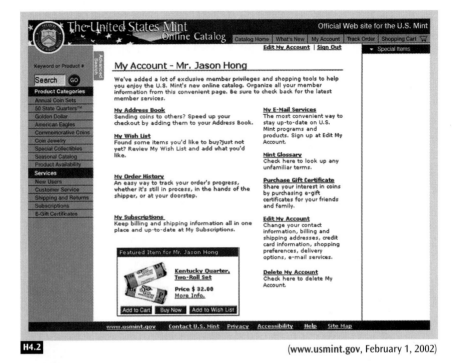

(www.usmint.gov, February 1, 2002)

Figure H4.3

CDNOW consolidates all of a customer's account information on a single page.

(www.cdnow.com, February 11, 2002)

Provide a Task-Based Organization Scheme to Let Customers Modify Their Information • Use a TASK-BASED ORGANIZATION (B4) scheme that lets visitors access their account information while they are in the middle of a task, without having to go back to the account information page to add or update information. For example, Figure H4.4 shows how CDNOW provides links to let customers change their credit card information while they are checking out.

Figure H4.4

CDNOW shows customers their account information in context, when they need it for a specific task. For example, customers can change their credit card information at the checkout instead of having to go back to the account information page.

3. Payment Information	
Payment Method:	Bill To:
Visa Card ending with 123.	**JASON HONG**
Change Payment Method	
Redeem Your CDNOW Gift Certificate	

4. Submit Your Order

Please make sure that all of the information above is correct.
You must click on the "Place Order" button to submit your order.

Place Order

H4.4

(**www.cdnow.com**, February 11, 2002)

✷ SOLUTION

Provide a single page that gathers all the customer's account information in one place. Use a task-based organization scheme to let people see and modify their information in the context of specific tasks.

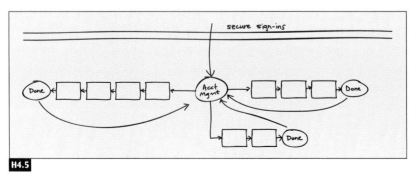

H4.5

Figure H4.5

An account management system should use a secure connection to protect each customer's personal information and should guide customers through the steps needed to see and change their information.

✳ CONSIDER THESE OTHER PATTERNS

As part of the FAIR INFORMATION PRACTICES (E3), every Web site that provides PERSONALIZED CONTENT (D4) must also provide an account management system to let customers manage their personal information. Such information might include customers' favorite MESSAGE BOARDS (D5), E-MAIL SUBSCRIPTIONS (E2), address books for QUICK ADDRESS SELECTION (F4), shipping preferences for QUICK SHIPPING METHOD SELECTION (F5), PAYMENT METHOD (F6) information, and ORDER TRACKING AND HISTORY (G7).

Use a centralized organization scheme, with all the information in one place, as well as TASK-BASED ORGANIZATION (B4), where the information is spread out according to task.

The more sensitive the data is, the more protection customers need. If the account management system contains sensitive personal or financial information, use a SECURE CONNECTION (E6) with extremely strong encryption to protect the data.

H5 PERSISTENT CUSTOMER SESSIONS

The Unofficial Cookie FAQ
Version 2.54

Contributed to Cookie Central by David Whalen

- A Note from the Author

- 1. INTRODUCTION
  - 1.1 What is a cookie?
  - 1.2 Where did the term cookies come from?
  - 1.3 Why do sites use cookies?
  - 1.4 Where can I get more information?
- 2. GENERAL QUESTIONS/MISCELLANEOUS
  - 2.1 Introduction
  - 2.2 Can I delete cookies?
  - 2.3 How do I set my browser to reject cookies?
  - 2.4 Are cookies dangerous to my computer?
  - 2.5 Will cookies fill up my hard drive?
  - 2.6 Are cookies a threat to my privacy?
  - 2.7 Sites are telling me I need to turn on cookies, but they *are* on. What's wrong?
  - 2.8 I deleted my cookies, and I can't log-on to my favorite site anymore. What can I do?
  - 2.9 How did I get a cookie from doubleclick.net? I've never been there!
  - 2.10 I looked at my Internet Explorer cookies, and they had my *username* on them! Can servers see my username?
- 3. COOKIE FUNDAMENTALS
  - 3.1 Introduction
  - 3.2 How does a cookie *really* work?
  - 3.3 Breakdown of Cookie Parameters

H5.1

(**www.cookiecentral.com**, November 28, 2001)

Figure H5.1

Cookies are the most common way of implementing persistent customer sessions, which are necessary to provide personalized services. However, cookies pose several implementation and privacy problems.

✳ BACKGROUND

All Web applications that provide any degree of PERSONALIZED CONTENT (D4), such as PERSONAL E-COMMERCE (A1), COMMUNITY CONFERENCE (A3), and WEB APPS THAT WORK (A10), need a way to identify and track customers.

✳ PROBLEM

To provide personalized services, Web sites need to identify and track their customers while the customers are on the site.

HyperText Transfer Protocol (HTTP) is the means by which pages are downloaded from a Web server to a Web browser. When HTTP was first invented, it was designed to be stateless, meaning that Web servers had no memory of who was requesting pages or which pages customer had seen. All customers saw exactly the same Web pages.

 This limitation made it difficult for designers to provide personalized services, such as SHOPPING CARTS (F3), PROCESS FUNNELS (H1), and PERSONALIZED CONTENT (D4). It also made it impractical to provide fee-based services, such as an online news site that customers would pay monthly subscription fees to view. Customers would have to enter their identity and password for *every* page they downloaded. What was needed was a way of providing **customer sessions** so that Web servers could keep track of who their customers were and what they were doing on-site.

Cookies were invented to solve this problem. **Cookies** are small pieces of data used by Web servers to uniquely identify customers. However, it is more useful to think of this problem in terms of *temporary* and *persistent* customer sessions.

Temporary Customer Sessions • Sometimes Web servers remember customers for a short period of time, usually until the customer closes the Web browser. **Temporary customer sessions** are useful when a Web site needs to maintain only short-lived information about customers, such as what items are in the customers' SHOPPING CART (F3) or which part of the QUICK-FLOW CHECKOUT (F1) they're in.

There are two ways of implementing temporary customer sessions. **Session IDs** temporarily store the identity of a customer in Web addresses. The session ID is usually a long, nonsensical string, such as *http://www.website.com?sessionid=$qoijlgsk185794q$*. This string is passed along in every page the customer sees, but it is discarded when the customer leaves the site. **Session cookies** also temporarily store the identity of a person. When a customer closes his or her Web browser, however, the session cookie is deleted, making it impossible to track people over long periods of time. The chief difference between session IDs and session cookies is that session cookies are sent to Web servers through HTTP, instead of through the Web address. For all practical purposes, though, the two are equivalent when used to implement temporary customer sessions.

Persistent Customer Sessions • Compared to temporary sessions, **persistent customer sessions** let Web servers remember customers for longer periods of time. Persistent customer sessions are useful when you want to maintain permanent information about a customer, such as when your site generates PERSONALIZED RECOMMENDATIONS (G3) or shows customers their ORDER TRACKING AND HISTORY (G7) information. A good rule of thumb is that if your customers ever need to go through the SIGN-IN/NEW ACCOUNT (H2) pattern, you probably need to use persistent customer sessions.

Persistent customer sessions are implemented with **persistent cookies**, which are similar to session cookies but are stored on customers' hard drives, allowing your Web site to track customers over longer periods of time.

Differences between Temporary and Persistent Customer Sessions • Table H5.1 not only shows the differences between the two kinds of customer sessions, but also describes when one should be used over the other, as well as which patterns require use of a particular type of customer session.

Most of the patterns you can implement through temporary customer sessions can also be implemented with persistent customer sessions. For example, you can implement INTERNATIONALIZED AND LOCALIZED CONTENT (D10) with temporary customer sessions, by having each customer select a specific language on the homepage. All of the subsequent pages will be displayed in that language, as long as the customer's Web browser remains open. However, once the Web browser is closed, that information is lost. If you used persistent customer sessions, the Web site could store customers' language preferences so that they would not have to select the language every time they visited.

The only pattern unique to temporary customer sessions is GUEST ACCOUNTS (H3), which describes how to implement temporary accounts. This pattern applies when customers are certain they want to purchase something now, but they do not plan to return. A guest account would let customers add items to their SHOPPING CARTS (F3) and proceed through the QUICK-FLOW CHECKOUT (F1) without having to go through the SIGN-IN/NEW ACCOUNT (H2) process of creating a new account and a password.

Choosing between Temporary and Persistent Customer Sessions • Two factors to consider when you're choosing between temporary and persistent customer sessions are complexity and privacy. Temporary customer sessions are easier to implement because you do not need to store most of

Table H5.1

Temporary and Permanent Customer Sessions Compared

	Temporary Customer Sessions	**Persistent Customer Sessions**
Mode of implementation	Session IDs, session cookies	Persistent cookies
Context for use	You want to keep track of and use temporary information, or privacy concerns are important.	You want to keep track of and use permanently stored information, such as the customer's identity, to provide personalized content.
Patterns involved	• INTERNATIONALIZED AND LOCALIZED CONTENT (D10) • PROCESS FUNNELS (H1) • GUEST ACCOUNT (H3) (which implies SHOPPING CARTS (F3) and QUICK-FLOW CHECKOUT (F1) as well)	• PERSONALIZED CONTENT (D4) • MESSAGE BOARDS (D5) • INTERNATIONALIZED AND LOCALIZED CONTENT (D10) • QUICK-FLOW CHECKOUT (F1) • SHOPPING CARTS (F3) • PERSONALIZED RECOMMENDATIONS (G3) • RECOMMENDATION COMMUNITY (G4) • ORDER TRACKING AND HISTORY (G7) • PROCESS FUNNELS (H1) • SIGN-IN/NEW ACCOUNT (H2) • ACCOUNT MANAGEMENT (H4)

the information permanently. With persistent customer sessions, however, the customer's preferences and customized information need to be stored in a database, and this data must be retrieved every time the customer returns.

Temporary customer sessions are also better for consumer privacy because lots of data is thrown away after customers close their Web browsers, making it difficult to track a customer's browsing habits over an extended period of time. On the other hand, persistent customer sessions make it easier not only to track customers, but also to provide streamlined, personalized services.

 Because of privacy concerns, SELF-SERVICE GOVERNMENT (A4) Web sites are restricted in their use of customer sessions. In June of 2000, the Office of Management and Budget published a memorandum establishing U.S.

federal policy on the use of cookies.[1] In general, the OMB stated, a self-service government Web site should not use cookies unless it

- Provides clear and conspicuous notice of their use
- Has a compelling need to gather the data on the Web site
- Has appropriate and publicly disclosed privacy safeguards for handling information derived from cookies
- Has the personal approval of the head of your organization

Although the memorandum does not explicitly say so, the government is more concerned about the use of persistent cookies than session cookies on government Web sites. Here, use session cookies rather than persistent cookies because session cookies do not pose the same privacy concerns.

Two Warnings about Customer Sessions • Avoid putting any sensitive data in session IDs. Occasionally customers will see a URL like this:

```
http://www.xyzzyz.com/index.html?user=jhong
```

or worse:

```
http://www.xyzzyz.com/index.html?user=jhong&password=xyzzyz
```

making it easy for snoopers to see the password.

Similarly, cookies are not securely transmitted, meaning that clever hackers can see the cookie data being passed back and forth. If you designed your Web site improperly, a hacker would be able record a customer's cookie data as it was sent, and then could impersonate that individual.

The first step in solving this problem is to understand the difference between **identification** and **authentication**. A user name is an example of identification, stating who someone is. Passwords are examples of authentication, proving that customers really are who they say they are. Cookies help streamline identification, but they should not be used for authentication unless there is nothing sensitive to protect.

If sensitive information is involved, divide the Web site into secure pages (those that require authentication) and insecure pages (those that customers can always view). Many e-commerce sites are designed so that customers can browse the site and add items to the SHOPPING CART (F3), but so that to start the QUICK-FLOW CHECKOUT (F1), they must have a SECURE CONNECTION (E6) and go through the SIGN-IN/NEW ACCOUNT (H2) process.

---

1 OMB Memorandum 00-13, June 2000.

✳ SOLUTION

Use customer sessions to provide personalized services. Use temporary customer sessions for short-lived temporary data or when privacy concerns dictate, such as on self-service government Web sites. Use persistent customer sessions for long-lived data, or when the customer's identity needs to be known. Avoid placing any sensitive data in session IDs. Use cookies for identification, but not for authentication.

Figure H5.2

Persistent customer sessions are maintained by a small piece of information passed between the Web browser and the Web server. This information can be used to create personalized content and services.

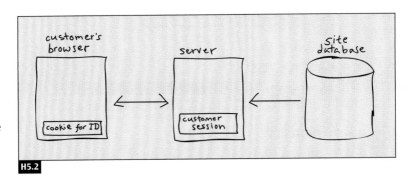

H5.2

✳ CONSIDER THESE OTHER PATTERNS

Any Web site that requires visitors to go through the SIGN-IN/NEW ACCOUNT (H2) pattern, or that provides any form of PERSONALIZED CONTENT (D4), requires persistent customer sessions.

Every Web site needs a clear and well-thought-out PRIVACY POLICY (E4) that explains the FAIR INFORMATION PRACTICES (E3) and how your site uses persistent customer sessions.

Consider using SECURE CONNECTIONS (E6) when you use persistent customer sessions, especially if potentially sensitive data is involved. Financial information, the authority to make purchases, and personal data are examples of sensitive data.

H6 POP-UP WINDOWS

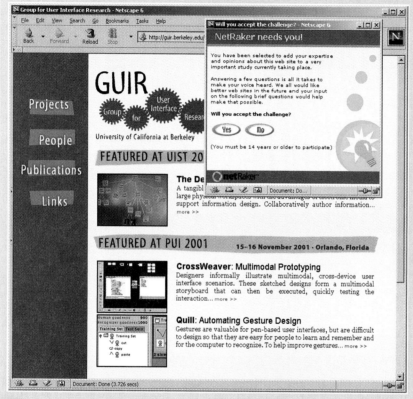

H6.1

(guir.berkeley.edu, May 18, 2002)

Figure H6.1

Use pop-up windows to keep the main browser window visible while displaying another page. Pop-up windows are useful for surveys and advertisements, and for showing extra information while maintaining a specific context. In this example, a survey window asks visitors to evaluate the usefulness and usability of the Web site.

✳ BACKGROUND

Some PROCESS FUNNELS (H1), CONTEXT-SENSITIVE HELP (H8), and EMBEDDED LINKS (K7) need to display information in addition to the current page, without taking visitors to another Web page. This pattern describes how pop-up windows can be used for this purpose.

H1 **H8** **K7**

✳ PROBLEM

You need to show the customer extra information, while maintaining context and keeping the customer's Web browser on the same page.

Sometimes customers need additional information that is not on the current Web page, but at the same time they need to stay there. For example, you want customers to remain on the main path of a PROCESS FUNNEL (H1), but you also want them to read extra information that might be useful.

As another example, you want to use EMBEDDED LINKS (K7) to let your customers see potentially useful and interesting content on other sites. At the same time, however, you want to keep your customers on the same page, to maintain coherence in the text and to keep them on your site.

One solution is to use pop-up windows to create new browser windows, letting customers see other Web pages while keeping their original browser windows on the same page. However, too many pop-up windows can be confusing and overwhelming. In this section we describe some ideas for using pop-up windows.

Use Automatic Pop-Up Windows for Showing Unrelated Information When People Enter or Exit a Web Site • There are two kinds of pop-up windows: automatic and link based. **Automatic pop-ups** appear simply as a result of a customer's arrival at or departure from a Web site. These kinds of pop-up windows usually contain advertisements or surveys for improving the quality of a Web site.

Many people find advertisements in automatic pop-up windows annoying, but some Web sites have found success with them. One recent innovation is the **pop-*under*** advertisement, which places an advertisement pop-up window under the customer's browser window so that customers will not see the window until they close their browsers. If you want to show pop-up advertisements, there are many factors to consider, including usability, customer satisfaction, and business revenues. We cannot say for sure whether pop-up windows are good or bad for a Web site. This is something that has to be judged on a case-by-case basis.

Another use of pop-up windows is for surveying your customers, a powerful tool for understanding the needs of customers and how well the Web site is meeting those needs. Using a bit of JavaScript, you can randomly select customers so that only a few will be shown the pop-up survey. Figure H6.1 shows an example of a pop-up survey.

Use Link-Based Pop-Up Windows to Show Related Information in a New Window, While Maintaining Context • A **link-based pop-up** appears when customers click on a link designed to open a new window. Use link-based pop-ups with EMBEDDED LINKS (K7), EXTERNAL LINKS (K8), and PROCESS FUNNELS (H1) to display information related to the current page.

Figure H6.2 shows an example of how to use pop-up windows with EMBEDDED LINKS (K7). Clicking on the link opens a new window to the specified Web page, letting customers see and explore related information without having to leave the original Web site.

Pop-up windows are especially useful for PROCESS FUNNELS (H1), like QUICK-FLOW CHECKOUT (F1) and SIGN-IN/NEW ACCOUNT (H2). Pop-up windows let customers see extra information, such as CONTEXT-SENSITIVE HELP (H8) or an answer to a FREQUENTLY ASKED QUESTION (H7), while keeping them in the funnel. Figure H6.3 shows how Dell uses pop-up windows to show extra details about a laptop computer, while not leading customers off the Web page where purchases are made.

Use Pop-Up Windows Sparingly • Minimize the number of automatic and link-based pop-up windows your Web site creates because they can quickly overwhelm and frustrate visitors.

Use automatic pop-ups when visitors first come to your site and when they leave. Also consider using cookies and PERSISTENT CUSTOMER SESSIONS (H5) so that people see your pop-up windows only once.

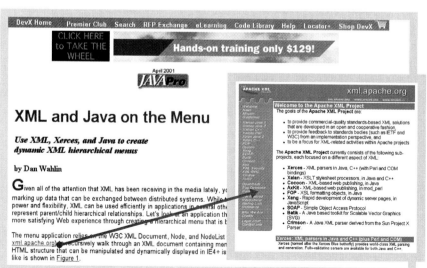

H6.2

(www.java-pro.com, xml.apache.org, May 17, 2002)

Figure H6.2

This magazine article has an embedded link to another Web site. The site opens a new Web browser window rather than going directly to that Web site, letting visitors continue reading the main article.

Figure H6.3

Dell uses pop-up windows to show context-sensitive help in a process funnel, while maintaining context.

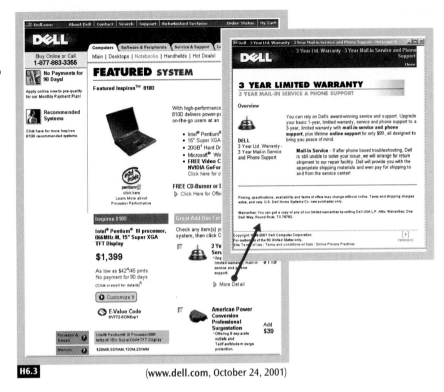

H6.3   (www.dell.com, October 24, 2001)

If you're using link-based pop-ups, you can reuse previously opened pop-up windows. This makes it easier for customers because only two browser windows are open at a time. You can do this with both Java-Script and plain links. The following JavaScript fragment is an example of how to create a new pop-up window, in this case a window from this book's Web site:

```
window.open ('http://designofsites.com', 'wnd')
```

The part labeled 'wnd' is the internal name of this window. You can make this new pop-up window go to another site with the following fragment:

```
<A TARGET="wnd" HREF="http://anothersite.com">link</a>
```

Alternatively, if the pop-up window 'wnd' does not already exist, this link will create a new pop-up window for you.

✳ SOLUTION

Use automatic pop-up windows for showing unrelated information when customers enter or exit your Web site. Use link-based pop-up windows to show related information in a new window, while maintaining context. Minimize the use of pop-up windows.

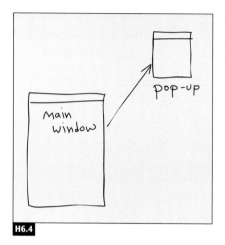

Figure H6.4

Use pop-up windows to display extra information while still maintaining context.

✳ CONSIDER THESE OTHER PATTERNS

Use link-based pop-up windows whenever you need to display information related to the current page, such as a FREQUENTLY ASKED QUESTION (H7) or CONTEXT-SENSITIVE HELP (H8), but do not want visitors to leave the current page. This is an issue in the PROCESS FUNNEL (H1), EMBEDDED LINKS (K7), and EXTERNAL LINKS (K8) patterns.

Figure H7.1

Snapfish has extensive help that offers a FAQ page and several categories of answers to common questions. The categories and a "top 10 list" make it easier for customers to find their question in a large set. Snapfish also offers a page for customers who need more help.

H7.1

(www.snapfish.com, February 11, 2002)

✳ BACKGROUND

Customers often have the same questions when browsing through a Web site, whether they are on a PERSONAL E-COMMERCE (A1) or a COMMUNITY CONFERENCE (A3) site. A good way to answer these repeated questions is through a **frequently asked questions** (**FAQ**) page. This pattern describes how to gather the questions, what the basic structure of a FAQ page is, and where to place the FAQ page so that it is easy to find.

✴ PROBLEM

Customers often ask the same questions on a Web site, and it can be expensive and time-consuming to answer the same questions over and over.

Whether on a PERSONAL E-COMMERCE (A1) site, a GRASSROOTS INFORMATION SITE (A6), or an EDUCATIONAL FORUM (A8), visitors usually ask the same kinds of questions. Although Web sites must answer these questions, it can be expensive to answer the same questions repeatedly.

Let your visitors help themselves by providing a frequently asked questions (FAQ) page, a list of common questions and their answers. A FAQ page makes it easier for people to search for answers themselves, while reducing help desk or response time costs for you.

First Identify Some Frequently Asked Questions • Start with a list of questions from your design team. Get everyone on the design team—from business and marketing, to design and usability, to programmers—involved in brainstorming. Draft a list of questions, but don't spend too much time organizing and grouping the questions yet.

Examine Your Competitors' FAQ Pages • Ask yourself which questions on your competitors' Web sites apply to your Web site, and see if their answers have better solutions than yours. Keep these in mind for the next iteration of your Web site.

Collect competitors' questions that are relevant for your Web site, but don't copy the answers. Provide answers that are relevant and appropriate for your Web site instead.

Supplement Your Questions with Those Collected from People in Close Contact with Customers • Collect questions and answers from people who have a great deal of contact with your customers. One such source is the people who conduct usability tests. What questions did customers ask when they were using your Web site? Were they unfamiliar with certain concepts? For example, if you have an auction site, did the testers understand how bidding works? If you offer wish lists, did people understand how they work? What were their concerns? Were they worried about having their credit card information stolen? Were they worried about returning products?

Another source of questions is the help desk staff. Find out which questions customers repeatedly ask by phone or by e-mail. Does the help desk already have a database to help answer questions? Can you get a copy of the help desk's e-mails and replies so that you can see what questions people asked and what answers were sent back?

Also talk to the marketing and sales staff. Inquire about the questions customers ask about the products. What features interest them? What concerns do they have?

3 See Chapter 3—Knowing Your Customers: Principles and Techniques for more information about understanding the needs of your customers.

Group Related Questions Together • After collecting questions and answers, decide how to organize the questions. If there are more than 40, use an organization scheme. For example, Figure H7.1 shows how Snapfish uses a combination of POPULARITY-BASED ORGANIZATION (B7) (see the "top 10" list on the right) and HIERARCHICAL ORGANIZATION (B3) to group frequently asked questions.

On the other hand, if there are only a few questions, the easiest thing to do is to put all of them on one Web page, at the top, and then link the questions to the answers below (see Figure H7.2).

If There Are Many Questions, Add a Search Feature • Browsing through a long list of questions can be dull. Adding a SEARCH ACTION MODULE (J1) makes it easier to find answers to common questions quickly.

Use Redundant Navigation to Make It Easy to Find Your FAQ Page • Have multiple links to your FAQ page, including one from the NAVIGATION BAR (K2) to the FAQ page, labeled **FAQ** or **Help**. You can also locate the FAQ page under ABOUT US (E5) and on the PAGE NOT FOUND (K14) page.

Use a TASK-BASED ORGANIZATION (B4) scheme to link to specific questions on the FAQ page. For example, if the FAQ page contains information about shipping policies, make this information easily accessible on the QUICK-FLOW CHECKOUT (F1) pages, where customers are more likely to need it.

Use the FAQ Page Only as a Temporary Fix for Usability Problems • Do not rely on the FAQ page to help your customers overcome usability problems. Design the Web site to help customers successfully accomplish their tasks. Consider the FAQ page a redundant source of information. Your customers' goal is not to browse through the FAQ page, but to accomplish a particular task, and the FAQ page is just one way of helping them do it.

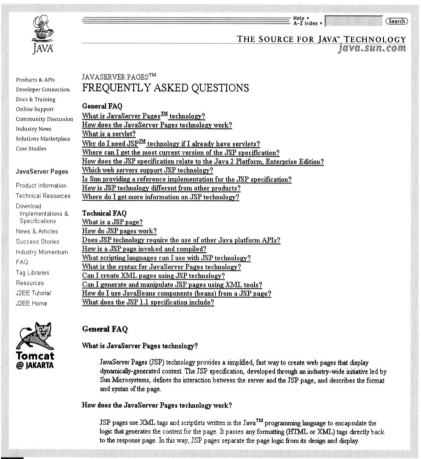

H7.2

(java.sun.com, October 20, 2001)

Figure H7.2

In many FAQ pages, questions are grouped together at the top and linked to the answers below or on separate pages.

Encourage Your Community Site to Create a FAQ Page • The FAQ page can be a significant community-building effort for COMMUNITY CONFERENCE (A3) sites. Usually a few people take the initiative to create the first version of the FAQ page, and they post it to the community site. They collect comments, new questions, and new answers from other members of the community and then iteratively improve the FAQ page (giving due credit to the contributors, of course). Figure H7.3 shows an example of a community conference FAQ page.

Figure H7.3

Many community conference sites feature a FAQ page. This example shows a portion of the rec.birds newsgroup FAQ page, developed with the help of many members of the community.

```
Archive-name: birds-faq/wild-birds/part1
Last-modified: May 30, 2001
Posting-frequency: Every 37 days

rec.birds Frequently Asked Questions (FAQ) (Part 1/2)

This is part 1 (of 2) of the Frequently Asked Questions list for the Usenet
newsgroup rec.birds.  The FAQ is posted every five weeks.  Its current editor
is Lanny Chambers; send suggestions for new questions and other comments to
him. Remember the FAQ is intended as a living document about rec.birds,
constant updating is welcome!

This section of the FAQ contains information about rec.birds and about
wild birds.  The other section of the FAQ contains pointers to more
information about wild birds.

Do not send articles to the FAQ editor for posting.  rec.birds is an
unmoderated newsgroup, so you may post articles yourself.  If you are a
newcomer to Usenet, please read the official articles about etiquette
in the newsgroup news.announce.newusers before you post.

Contents:

1.0.    All-purpose rec.birds etiquette
1.1.    I have a question about pet birds.
1.2.    Are domestic cats Satan?  --A Non-judgmental Attempt at Consensus.
1.3a.   Can I "count" this bird?
1.3b.   What are "listers"?
1.4.    I found an injured bird; what can I do?
1.5.    I found an abandoned nestling; what can I do?
1.6.    A wild bird is annoying me; what can I do?
1.7.    What is the Migratory Bird Treaty?
1.8.    I saw a rare bird!  What do I do?
1.9.    Why does everybody seem to hate Starlings and House Sparrows so much?
1.10.   Why does everybody seem to hate Cowbirds so much?
1.11.   I saw a bird which I can't identify.  Can someone help me?
1.12.   How do I keep squirrels out of my feeders?
1.13.   How can I make homemade hummingbird nectar?
1.14a.  What kind of binoculars should I buy?
1.14b.  What kind of scope should I buy?
1.15a.  I found a dead bird with a band.  What do I do?
1.15b.  I saw a banded or marked bird.  What do I do?
1.16.   If we throw rice at our wedding, will birds eat it and explode?
1.17.   Does providing food at feeders during summer keep birds from migrating?
1.18.   If I stop feeding birds, will they die?
1.19.   Does anyone archive rec.birds?
1.20.   ETHICS FOR BIRDERS
1.21.   Acknowledgements
```

H7.3

(news://rec.birds, August 24, 2001)

✳ SOLUTION

Start by identifying some frequently asked questions with the entire design team. Review the questions and answers in your competitors' FAQ pages to identify any questions your team might have missed. Supplement your questions with those collected from people in close contact with target customers. Use an organizational scheme to group related questions. Add a search feature if there are many questions. Use redundant navigation to make it easy to find the FAQ page on your site. Use the FAQ page only as a temporary fix if there are usability problems.

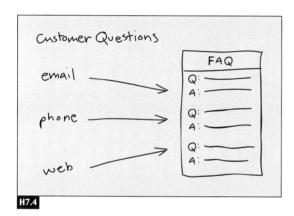

Figure H7.4

A FAQ page contains commonly asked questions and answers, helping customers help themselves.

✳ CONSIDER THESE OTHER PATTERNS

FAQ pages are useful for all kinds of Web sites, including PERSONAL E-COMMERCE (A1) sites, GRASSROOTS INFORMATION SITES (A6), EDUCATIONAL FORUMS (A8), and COMMUNITY CONFERENCE (A3) sites.

Short FAQ lists are usually organized on a single page; longer ones might use HIERARCHICAL ORGANIZATION (B3) and possibly POPULARITY-BASED ORGANIZATION (B7). Large FAQ lists should have a SEARCH ACTION MODULE (J1) to let people quickly search through the FAQ page.

Link the FAQ page from the main NAVIGATION BAR (K2) as **Help** or **FAQ**, or put it on the ABOUT US (E5) and PAGE NOT FOUND (K14) pages. Use TASK-BASED ORGANIZATION (B4), with pages linking to a specific question and answer on the FAQ page, depending on the task.

Figure H8.1

Dell provides links to context-sensitive help to give customers detailed descriptions of features. This context-sensitive help is contained in a pop-up window, letting customers maintain the context of the task while seeing the information they need.

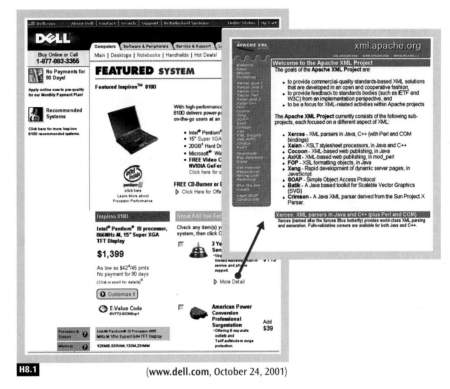

H8.1   (www.dell.com, October 24, 2001)

✳ BACKGROUND

People will always encounter problems, finding that they need more information to complete a task. This may even occur when they are trying to complete a task in a PROCESS FUNNEL (H1). Help your customers by offering context-sensitive help that provides additional information related to the current task. This pattern describes context-sensitive help in general, presenting guidelines for how to use it most effectively.

H1

❊ PROBLEM

Customers sometimes need highly specific help to complete a task.

Sometimes, in the middle of a task, customers have questions that cannot be answered on the current page. Your Web site might already have a help page, but it does not make sense to force your customers to go to that page and lose the context of their work.

Address this problem by providing context-sensitive help. This means providing appropriate answers, both in text and links, near where customers are likely to have questions. The content might include any of the following:

- An example of what is expected, helping to PREVENT ERRORS (K12)
- A MEANINGFUL ERROR MESSAGE (K13) describing the problem and how to solve it
- Detailed descriptions (such as the POP-UP WINDOW (H6) in Figure H8.1 describing a feature in great detail)
- Steps describing how to do the task
- Part of the FREQUENTLY ASKED QUESTIONS (H7) page

In this section we describe some ways of using context-sensitive help on your Web site.

Place Context-Sensitive Help near Where It Is Needed • Place links and text to help your customers spatially. As Figure H8.2 shows, MSN Hotmail puts a "Why Sign Up?" link right next to links letting customers sign up for an e-mail account on its SIGN IN/NEW ACCOUNT (H2) page. MSN Hotmail also has "Forgot Your Password?" and "Problems Signing In?" links right next to where customers can sign in and check their e-mail.

H8.2

(www.hotmail.com, October 26, 2001)

Figure H8.2

MSN Hotmail offers a great deal of context-sensitive help on its sign-in/new account page. Help appears in the form of friendly questions, such as "Why Sign Up?" "Forgot Your Password?" and "Problems Signing In?"

Consider Using Pop-Up Windows to Let Customers Maintain Context • Use a

POP-UP WINDOW (H6) to display help when people need to see the help
page and stay on the same page. The résumé builder service provided by
Monster.com, shown in Figure H8.3, has links to sample titles and objec-
tives. Clicking on one of these links opens a pop-up window that contains
examples, letting people see the information and still type in their information in the text fields.

Figure H8.3

Monster.com, a Web
site that matches
job seekers with
employers, provides
a service where
prospective job
hunters build online
résumés. This screen
shot shows the step
of the résumé
builder in which job
hunters are expected
to enter in a title and
objective. To help,
Monster.com pro-
vides links to exam-
ples, which appear in
pop-up windows.

(www.monster.com, October 26, 2001)

✳ SOLUTION

Help your customers by placing context-sensitive text and links near where they are needed on a page. Consider using pop-up windows to display the help, letting people continue with their tasks.

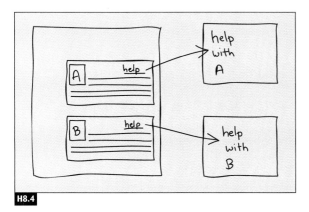

Figure H8.4

Context-sensitive help should be placed near the content that needs it.

H8.4

✳ CONSIDER THESE OTHER PATTERNS

Use context-sensitive help to PREVENT ERRORS (K12) and to provide MEANINGFUL ERROR MESSAGES (K13). Link context-sensitive help to a specific FREQUENTLY ASKED QUESTION (H7), or display it in a POP-UP WINDOW (H6) to let people maintain the context of a task.

Designing Effective Page Layouts

It can be difficult to design structured, ordered layouts for Web pages. This pattern group describes how to create layouts that your customers will find clear, predictable, and easy to understand.

11 GRID LAYOUT

12 ABOVE THE FOLD

13 CLEAR FIRST READS

14 EXPANDING-WIDTH SCREEN SIZE

15 FIXED-WIDTH SCREEN SIZE

16 CONSISTENT SIDEBARS OF RELATED CONTENT

I1 GRID LAYOUT

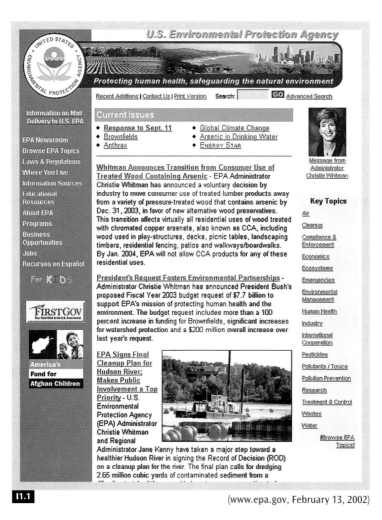

I1.1

(www.epa.gov, February 13, 2002)

Figure I1.1

The Environmental Protection Agency's Web site has a strong grid layout. The navigation bar runs along the left side, with features like "Recent Additions" and "Search" running along the top. The main content is in the center, and relevant side content on the right.

✳ BACKGROUND

A major step in creating a PAGE TEMPLATE (D1) is designing a clean grid layout, one that will give your Web pages structure and coherence. This pattern describes grid layouts and how to create one. You can use it in conjunction with ABOVE THE FOLD (I2), CLEAR FIRST READS (I3), EXPANDING-WIDTH SCREEN SIZE (I4), and FIXED-WIDTH SCREEN SIZE (I5) when you're designing a page template.

✳ PROBLEM

It is difficult to organize the many competing elements of a Web page in a cohesive manner without creating clutter and overwhelming the reader.

Grid layout is a technique from graphic design used for organizing page layouts for newspapers, magazines, and other documents. Grid layout can also be used to organize the content of your Web pages. In a grid layout, a page is divided into rows and columns, and every element is made to fit within this grid. Constant design elements, such as titles and logos, always appear in the same place, giving a consistent theme to every page.

There are three advantages to using a grid layout:

1. It gives your entire Web site a coherent visual structure, making it easier for your customers to predict where they will be able to find elements such as page titles, NAVIGATION BARS (K2), and CONTENT MODULES (D2).
2. It reduces clutter and gives your site visitors strong visual cues to follow, making things easier to find and text quicker to read.
3. Once it has been designed, your design team can reuse it, giving them more time to focus on content development instead of reinventing the wheel. They can place new content into the right place in the grid every time.

The sections that follow present some guidelines for making grid layouts.

Identify the Elements That Are Common throughout Your Web Site • Decide which elements are essential and which are common to the majority of your pages, such as the logo, NAVIGATION BARS (K2), SEARCH ACTION MODULES (J1), PRIVACY POLICY (E4), and CONTENT MODULES (D2) containing news items, stock quotes, travel information, and sports scores. Use these elements to anchor the structure of your Web pages.

Sketch Out Grid Layouts That Incorporate the Common Elements • Rough out several grids that combine the basic elements of your Web site in a design that you can use consistently. Group related items together; keep unrelated items apart.

Create Sample Web Pages and Get Feedback • Use your sketches to create rough Web pages, and test them for usability with your customers. See if the placement of your elements makes sense to them. "Greek" the text by changing it to nonsense words, and see if your customers can still guess the basic elements of the Web site on the basis of position and layout.[1] Use this feedback to fix potential errors early in the process, when they are still easy to correct. (For more information on getting feedback in usability tests, see Appendix A—Running Usability Evaluations.)

Make related elements look similar, either by grouping them near each other or by making them the same in size, color, and font. Leave proper spacing between unrelated elements. For example, keep your navigation visually separated from other images and the main text. Thin lines can also be used to emphasize elements.

Study How Other Web Pages Implement Their Grids • If you understand how other Web sites use and implement their grid layouts, you will find it easier to implement your own. Practically all Web pages use HTML tables for grids, making them quite easy to reverse-engineer. Go to a Web site and save one of the Web pages to your computer. Then open the Web page in a text editor. Find every instance of *BORDER=0* and change it to *BORDER=5*. Now you're ready to open the local copy of the Web page in your Web browser. You should be able to see the overall grid and how each individual element fits in.

✷ SOLUTION

Create a grid layout that you can use to organize all of the elements on a Web page. Sketch out multiple grid layouts to see if they can accommodate the most important navigation and content elements. Run usability tests on the grid layouts by greeking the navigation and content, and determine if customers can guess the elements solely on the basis of position and layout.

---

1 Most Web designers use a variation of a poem for greeking. It starts with "Lorem ipsum dolor sit amet." Oddly enough, the poem was written in Latin and historically has always been misquoted!

Figure I1.2

Align the navigation
and content on your
Web pages in a grid
layout.

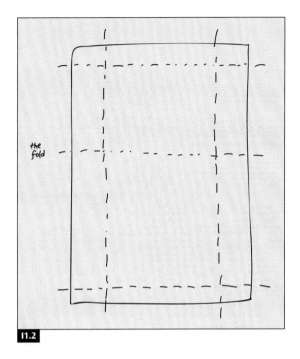

the
fold

I1.2

✳ CONSIDER THESE OTHER PATTERNS

D1   Grid layout is one part of the PAGE TEMPLATE (D1) pattern. The three most
K2   important elements of a grid layout are NAVIGATION BARS (K2), SEARCH
J1 D2   ACTION MODULES (J1), and CONTENT MODULES (D2).

I2   Grid layouts need to take into consideration which elements will be
ABOVE THE FOLD (I2)—that is, which elements customers will be able to see
without having to scroll. Design your layout to emphasize a CLEAR FIRST
I3   READ (I3)—that is, the first element that visitors typically see on a page.

D2   Many of the items you place in the grid will be CONTENT MODULES (D2),
dynamically retrieved content. One issue to consider is that these modules will have variable length, making it more difficult to have precise
control over the layout of a Web page.

Designers often implement grid layouts using HTML tables, but these
L3   can be slow to load on older Web browsers. SEPARATE TABLES (L3) looks at
one trick for speeding up the load time: splitting large tables into smaller
separate tables.

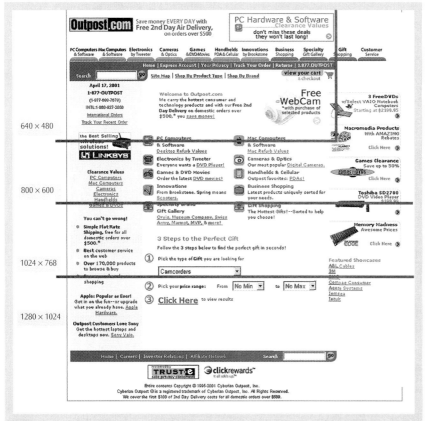

12.1

(www.outpost.com, April 17, 2001)

Figure 12.1

Each of the solid red lines here represents a different fold, or the imaginary line marking the bottom of the area that customers with different screen sizes would see when viewing a Web page without having to scroll. The most important things should go at the top, where they are visible to all visitors and easy to access.

✳ BACKGROUND

Site visitors do not always scroll down, and they can miss important information if it is not positioned well. This pattern describes why you should have your most important information at the top of a Web page, and how to design your Web site accordingly. This pattern is part of the PAGE TEMPLATE (D1) pattern, and you can use it with GRID LAYOUT (I1), CLEAR FIRST READS (I3), EXPANDING-WIDTH SCREEN SIZE (I4), and FIXED-WIDTH SCREEN SIZE (I5) when you're designing a page template.

D1 **I1**
I3 **I4**
I5

✳ PROBLEM

Customers often miss navigation elements and content if they have to scroll down to see them.

The term *above the fold* comes from the newspaper business because newspapers are folded in half when they are sold on the street. Newspapers know to put the most important stories above the fold of the front page to draw attention and drive sales. On the Web, *above the fold* refers to what your customers can see on your Web page without having to scroll down. Visitors do not always realize that they can scroll down, or that there is more information below. Therefore it makes sense to put all the vital links and content at the top.

The difference between designing for the fold on print and on the Web is that on the Web, you don't always know the size of the customer's screen. Consequently, you cannot be sure of what a customer who visits your site will see.

Figure I2.1 shows what visitors with screens of different sizes would see on Outpost.com's Web site. The designers have done a good job of positioning the most important elements toward the top left of the page, making these the first things that everyone will see. A common mistake of Web sites is to have too much unimportant information at the top of a page, while pushing more important content below the fold. This problem is common on sites with large logos or advertising banners.

Because what goes above the fold constitutes the most important real estate on the page, marketing people will want to place their ads and featured products there, programmers will want to display the functionality they just implemented, and artists will want to show off their graphic design skills. You will have to combine business needs, usability needs, customer experience needs, and aesthetics to find a design that everyone can agree on.

The sections that follow describe our solution for designing above the fold.

Choose a Minimum Screen Resolution That the Web Site Will Support • The first step is to survey your customers to determine their screen resolutions and how many customers you want to support. How many view Web pages at a resolution of 640 × 480 pixels? How many at 800 × 600? How many have something better? Ultimately, you will have to decide on the minimum size that your Web site will support. This minimum will not cut out visitors with smaller screens entirely, but it will make reading and navigating your Web pages a little more difficult for these customers.

Determine the Elements That Must Be above the Fold • Consider the page title, the CLEAR FIRST READ (I3), NAVIGATION BARS (K2), advertisements, and CONTENT MODULES (D2). Try out various layouts and rank them with your clients and customers to see which one works best for everyone.

✳ SOLUTION

Make sure that the most important material is at the top of the Web page, easily visible and easily accessible. Test the page to see how it looks on various screen sizes and to make sure that the important navigation elements and content are always visible.

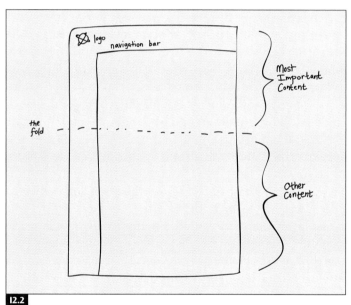

I2.2

Figure I2.2

Put the most important navigation elements and content above the fold, where people can see them immediately.

✳ CONSIDER THESE OTHER PATTERNS

Page elements that should be above the fold include NAVIGATION BARS (K2), SEARCH ACTION MODULES (J1), and CLEAR FIRST READS (I3). Other page elements to consider include LOCATION BREAD CRUMBS (K6), HEADLINES

AND BLURBS (D3), FEATURED PRODUCTS (G1), and PERSONALIZED RECOMMENDATIONS (G3).

Above the fold is especially important for PROCESS FUNNELS (H1) such as QUICK-FLOW CHECKOUT (F1) and SIGN-IN/NEW ACCOUNT (H2). These kinds of processes often use HIGH-VISIBILITY ACTION BUTTONS (K5) to help guide people through a task.

The CLEAR FIRST READS (I3) pattern stresses the use of font, size, color, and position of a single element to give your Web page something that most people will see first. However, first reads need to be balanced with the above the fold pattern, since first reads may take up precious screen real estate and reduce the number of items that can be added. The clear first reads pattern also emphasizes designing for a specific screen resolution, and points out that you have to design at a slightly lower resolution than the screen resolutions that your customers have.

I3.1

(www.landsend.com, February 13, 2002)

Figure I3.1

What's the first thing you see when you look at this page? Through a combination of position, font, color, size, and graphic design, the image of the shoes and the headline "Slip into the shoe that's taking America by storm" are the items that pop out best. The first read helps to set expectations and conveys a wealth of subtle information to your customers. This first read tells the visitor that these shoes are featured and popular with other customers.

✳ BACKGROUND

Although your Web page may contain many elements, your customers must be able to easily find the most important item on the page. This pattern covers first reads, a technique from graphic design that helps focus Web pages and gives readers a clear first impression. You can apply this pattern to the creation of a PAGE TEMPLATE (D1), and you can use it with GRID LAYOUT (I1), ABOVE THE FOLD (I2), EXPANDING-WIDTH SCREEN SIZE (I4), and FIXED-WIDTH SCREEN SIZE (I5) when you're designing a page template.

D1

I1 I2 I4

I5

✳ PROBLEM

How can a Web page be designed with a single unifying focus when there are so many visual elements competing for attention?

As a Web designer, you have many goals for each page on your Web site. However, these goals often conflict and could cause you to lose focus. With all of the information on each page vying for a customer's attention, you need something that unifies the entire page.

The **first read** is one technique that brings order to your Web pages. Think of it as an overall first impression, a gestalt feeling that sets the theme for the entire Web page. The first read is the dominant visual element that fuses all of the disparate elements of the Web page.

In this section we describe some approaches for making effective first reads on every page.

Determine the Most Important Element on Each Page • For each group of pages, find a focus. Some common choices include the following:

- A company logo
- The page title
- A news headline
- An advertisement
- A product name
- A product image

Use Multiple Features to Differentiate the First Read • By coordinating features such as color, size, font, weight (i.e., boldface), and position, you can make an effective first read that stands out. With color, for example, you want to make the first read contrast well with the page background. Picking complementary colors, such as purple text on yellow, or colors that have good contrast, such as black text on white, works well here.

In terms of size, it is a good idea to make the first read larger than the surrounding elements. In Figure I3.1 note that the first-read text and the image of the shoes are larger than any other text or image on the entire page. Similarly, the first-read image in Figure I3.2 dominates the page, and the first-read text is larger than any other text on the page, save the brand "L.L. Bean" in the upper left corner.

Clean, easy-to-read sans serif fonts, such as Arial or Verdana, work well. On the first read, these fonts will not look cluttered. (These fonts make clean text headers for the same reason.) Stay away from hard-to-read, overly ornate faces, such as MS Comic Sans.

(www.llbean.com, February 5, 2002)

Figure 13.2

The large colorful image centered at the top of L.L. Bean's homepage immediately draws people's eyes.

For position, place your first read near the top left of the page for two reasons. First, many sites use a page layout that naturally converges at the top left corner. They use "inverse L" NAVIGATION BARS (K2)—that is, navigation bars positioned along the top and left side. Visitors tend to look at the top left first because these navigation bars come together there. Second, most of your customers will be reading from left to right and top to bottom, so it is natural to have the first read at the top left. This is not a hard rule, though. Other constraints may make it necessary to place the first read elsewhere.

This placement strategy also came from newspapers. Readers go to the top of the page, where the designer placed the first read. Then the design lures them through the page to the bottom right, where they turn the page because that's all that's left to do.

Design for Lower-Resolution Displays • One quirk about the Web is that you do not necessarily know what kind of display size your customers will have. Some people still have displays with only 640×480 resolution. Most will have at least 800×600 resolution, and a few will have better resolution. Survey your customers and gather the statistics for your target customers so that you can create the most effective design for them.

Design your Web pages to work at a slightly lower resolution than the resolution of your customers' monitors. Remember that Web browsers, with the browser buttons and scroll bar, take up space themselves. In addition, not all of your customers will have their Web browsers maximized to fit the entire screen.

Test Your First Reads • Create a high-fidelity mock-up of a sample Web page. The mock-up can be anything from an image to an HTML page. Bring in some representative customers and show them the mock-up for a few seconds. Ask them what they remember about the page and what they think the page is about. Revise your first read if a majority of these test customers did not understand the point of the page, and keep doing quick tests until you come up with a design that satisfies both you and your customers.

Also try out the first reads on a range of screen resolutions that are different from the one on which you designed it to see how they work.

✷ SOLUTION

Use a first read to give each page a unifying focus on the most important message, and to emphasize the most important element of that page. Use color, size, font, weight, and position to differentiate and highlight the first read. Design for lower-resolution displays, and test your first reads with your customers to see if they are effective.

Figure 13.3

Use color, size, font, weight, and position to create a first read that unifies your Web pages.

13.3

✳ CONSIDER THESE OTHER PATTERNS

Clear first reads should be applied when you create PAGE TEMPLATES (D1).
Clear first reads can also be used with the GRID LAYOUT (I1), ABOVE THE
FOLD (I2), EXPANDING-WIDTH SCREEN SIZE (I4), and FIXED-WIDTH SCREEN SIZE
(I5) patterns.

First reads are often located in the top left corner of a Web page, affecting the layout and placement of NAVIGATION BARS (K2).

If you use an image as the first read, make it a FAST-DOWNLOADING
IMAGE (L2). First reads should be placed in SEPARATE TABLES (L3) for faster
loading.

Figure I4.1

iWon uses an expanding-width screen—one that looks good on varying screen sizes. Note that the left and right columns remain constantly sized, while the center column expands.

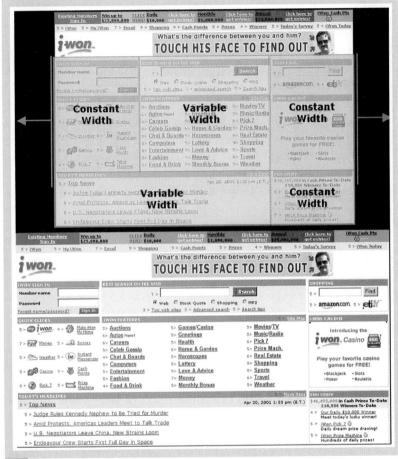

I4.1

(www.iwon.com, April 20, 2001)

✳ BACKGROUND

Designers often create a site for one screen size. In general, this strategy works, but sometimes designers leave Web pages, especially those with lots of navigation elements and content, with a great deal of wasted empty space. This pattern describes how to design your Web pages for a full screen size. You can apply it when creating a PAGE TEMPLATE (D1), and you can use it together with GRID LAYOUT (I1) and ABOVE THE FOLD (I2).

✳ PROBLEM

Many Web pages are packed with navigation elements and content but do not take advantage of extra space when visitors resize the browser to make it larger.

Web sites often do not take advantage of the extra space that results when customers make their browsers bigger, keeping the layout and content of the page the same. But the empty space resulting from such expansion of the screen offers the opportunity for displaying more content.

Use expanding-width screen size to make Web pages adapt to different widths. Expanding-width screen size uses a feature in HTML tables to adjust to the size of the Web browser as it shrinks and grows. In the sections that follow, we describe some techniques for implementing it.

Use Relative Table Widths to Create Expanding-Width Web Pages • Create expanding-width screen sizes by using relative-width HTML tables. In HTML you can specify table widths as either absolute or relative values. Absolute widths are expressed in terms of pixel sizes and are calculated only once by the Web browser. For example, the expression *<TABLE WIDTH=60>* would create a table exactly 60 pixels wide.

Relative widths are expressed in terms of percentages and are recalculated dynamically, so they expand properly every time the customer resizes a Web browser window. For example, the expression *<TABLE WIDTH=80%>* would create a table that is exactly 80 percent of the current width of the Web browser window.

Mix Absolute and Relative Widths to Fix the Width of Some Parts of a Web Page • You can make specific columns within a table fixed width or relative width. Many Web site designs take advantage of this feature by making the navigation and side content on the left and right sides fixed, while letting the center content expand. Here's an example of how to do this in HTML:

```
<HTML>
<BODY>

<!– this makes the entire table expanding width –>
<TABLE WIDTH=100% BORDER=1>
   <TR>
      <!– the left column is fixed at 170 pixels –>
      <TD WIDTH=170>
```

```
        Fixed width left
    </TD>

    <!- the browser puts any leftover space here ->
    <!- making this column expand to fill up space ->
    <TD>
        Expanding-width content goes over here. This
        sentence is extra long just to underscore this
        point.
    </TD>

    <!- the right column is fixed at 170 pixels ->
    <TD WIDTH=170>
        Fixed width right
    </TD>
  </TR>
</TABLE>

</BODY>
</HTML>
```

Figure I4.2 shows what this sample looks like in a Web browser set at three different browser sizes.

Figure I4.2

A common approach to fitting content on a page that will be viewed in browsers with different resolutions is to keep the outer columns fixed width and let the content in the center column expand to fit the size of the individual customer's browser window. The three variations shown here are of the same page at three different resolutions.

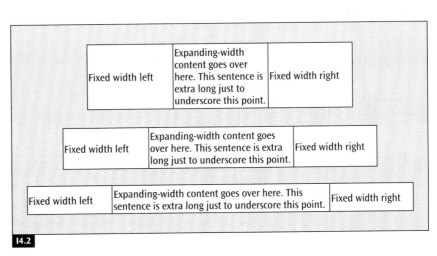

Design Your Web Page with a Minimum Width in Mind • Expanding-width screen sizes work well, up to a point. You will find it relatively easy to create Web pages that still look good when the width is expanded, but not when the width is shrunk beyond a certain size. Currently, there are no good solutions to this problem. The best way to deal with it is to survey the computer platforms and Web browsers used by your target customers and make sure you support all the groups you care about. (This point is described in more detail in ABOVE THE FOLD (I2).)

✳ SOLUTION

Design your Web pages to use an expanding-width screen size that you create using relative-width HTML tables. Keep the basic navigation elements at fixed width, and let the center area containing the main content expand.

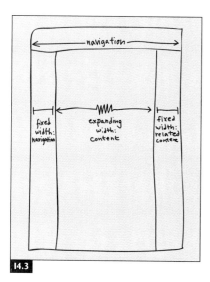

Figure 14.3

Expanding-width screen sizes grow to fill the entire Web browser.

✳ CONSIDER THESE OTHER PATTERNS

Contrasting with expanding-width screen size is FIXED-WIDTH SCREEN SIZE (I5). It is useful to make pages fixed width if there are few navigation elements and the main portion of the page emphasizes a single passage of text. A Web page should also be made fixed width if you need strong control over its layout and appearance.

Use expanding-width screen sizes in conjunction with GRID LAYOUT (I1) and ABOVE THE FOLD (I2) when creating PAGE TEMPLATES (D1) that can be reused throughout the Web site.

Figure I5.1

CNET News.com
keeps its Web pages
fixed width so that
the content stays
in the center of
the page.

I5.1   (news.cnet.com, August 21, 2001)

✷ BACKGROUND

Articles, essays, and other forms of online writing need to be designed for
comfortable reading on computer screens. Text width is a factor that
influences readability. Text that is too wide can be awkward to read. This
pattern describes how to keep the text at a fixed size for easy reading. You
can apply this pattern when creating a PAGE TEMPLATE (D1), and you can
use it together with GRID LAYOUT (I1) and ABOVE THE FOLD (I2).

✳ PROBLEM

Customers' browser sizes affect the amount of text they can see on the screen. When people make their browsers too large, each line of text becomes too long to read comfortably.

When text is too wide, it is difficult to skim and to find the next line of text. Use fixed-width screen sizes to correct this problem. In contrast to EXPANDING-WIDTH SCREEN SIZES (I4), fixed-width screen sizes keep a Web page at exactly the same width, regardless of the size of your customer's Web browser (see Figure I5.2). This is a useful technique for news and magazine articles, essays, and other long passages of text.

Usually you can implement fixed-width screen sizes by making the table containing the main content a fixed width. Place the main content of your page either in the center of the page or on the left.

I5.2

(www.ifilm.com, February 2, 2002)

Figure I5.2

IFILM keeps its Web pages at a fixed width, choosing to keep the content on the left side of the page when the Web browser window is expanded.

Here's an example of how to place the content in the center:

```
<HTML>
<BODY>

<!- this makes the entire table 600 pixels wide ->
<!- and puts it in the center of the page ->
<TABLE WIDTH=600 BORDER=1 ALIGN=CENTER>
   <TR>
      <!- the left column is fixed at 170 pixels ->
      <TD WIDTH=170>
         Fixed width left
      </TD>

      <!- the browser puts any leftover space here ->
      <!- in this case, this is 430 pixels ->
      <TD>
         Fixed-width content goes over here. This
         column is not resized.
      </TD>
   </TR>
</TABLE>

</BODY>
</HTML>
```

Some Web sites keep the content on the left. This is the default if the designer does not set the ALIGN=CENTER attribute in the main table. There is no real difference between having the content on the left or in the center. It is simply a matter of style.

✳ SOLUTION

Use a fixed-width screen size to make the long tracts of text more readable by constraining the width of the text column. Create fixed-width screen sizes by using absolute widths in your HTML tables.

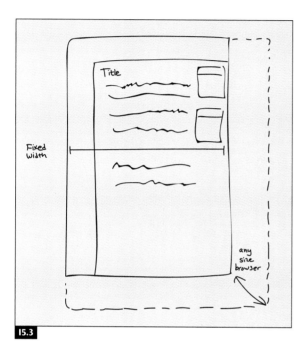

Figure 15.3

Fixed-width screen sizes keep a constant width regardless of the size of the Web browser.

✳ CONSIDER THESE OTHER PATTERNS

Contrasting with fixed-width screen size is EXPANDING-WIDTH SCREEN SIZE (I4). Using expanding width for a page is useful if there are many navigation elements or a wide variety of content instead of a single passage of text. However, making a Web page expanding width reduces the amount of control you have over its overall layout and appearance.

Use fixed-width screen sizes in conjunction with GRID LAYOUT (I1) and ABOVE THE FOLD (I2) when creating a PAGE TEMPLATE (D1) that can be reused throughout the Web site.

Figure I6.1

Beliefnet, a multi-faith community Web site, uses sidebars to highlight special content. This example shows "news" and "Today's Top Picks" sidebars.

I6.1

(www.beliefnet.com, January 16, 2002)

✳ BACKGROUND

In CROSS-SELLING AND UP-SELLING (G2), we discuss how it can be useful to showcase accessories and more expensive versions of the current product, to entice customers to spend more money. In UNIFIED BROWSING HIERARCHY (K1), we discuss reasons why community, content, and commerce should be combined instead of being separated into distinct categories. In HEADLINES AND BLURBS (D3), we look at ways of promoting content found on other parts of your Web site. This pattern discusses how to use a sidebar to feature these kinds of related BROWSABLE CONTENT (B2) on a Web page.

✳ PROBLEM

Finding related content on a page can be frustrating.

On content pages, such as news articles or CLEAN PRODUCT DETAILS (F2)
pages, people often want to see related items—things like similar products, PERSONALIZED RECOMMENDATIONS (G3), other news articles on similar
topics, or MESSAGE BOARDS (D5) for further discussion. The key idea here
is to encourage customers to explore more content. The main problem is
presenting these related links to visitors in a clear and obvious manner,
without distracting them from the main content and without taking up
too much valuable page space.

One way of doing this is by placing related content at the bottom of
the Web page. A potential problem is that some visitors might not see the
content, especially if they have to scroll down to get to the bottom of the
page. Another way is by using consistent sidebars of related content.
These sidebars feature the related content but are placed near the top of a
Web page on the side (see Figure 16.2). This kind of layout makes the
related links easy to see and visually distinct from the main content.

The sections that follow give some tips on using sidebars of related
content.

Make the Location of Sidebars Consistent • Because NAVIGATION BARS (K2)
generally run along the top and the left of a page, and because the main
content is generally placed in the center, sidebars of related content usually lie on the right side of a page. The easiest way of making sidebars
appear in a consistent location is by creating a GRID LAYOUT (I1) for your
page, partitioning some space for sidebars, creating a PAGE TEMPLATE (D1)
that reflects the layout, and then using this page template for new pages.

Determine a Maximum Length for Sidebars • As discussed in CONTENT MOD-
ULES (D2), one potential problem with sidebars is that they might be
longer than the main content, making the page layout look awkward.
One solution is to impose a maximum number of lines for each sidebar,
which can be enforced manually by editors or automatically if the content in the sidebar is retrieved from a database.

Figure 16.2

CNN places related news stories, photo essays, and video clips in sidebars. Note how the sidebar is visually segmented from the rest of the page.

(cnn.com, February 15, 2002)

✳ SOLUTION

Make the location of sidebars consistent by using a grid layout and page templates. Also determine a maximum length for sidebars so that the page layout will be balanced.

Figure 16.3

Consistent sidebars of related content appear in the same place on every page so that customers know where to find them.

16.3

✳ CONSIDER THESE OTHER PATTERNS

Consistent sidebars of related content are often used for HEADLINES AND BLURBS (D3), CROSS-SELLING AND UP-SELLING (G2), UNIFIED BROWSING HIER-ARCHY (K1), and EXTERNAL LINKS (K8). EMBEDDED LINKS (K7) are sometimes used instead of sidebars.

Sidebars are often implemented as CONTENT MODULES (D2) to make it easier to automatically serve up related content. Sidebars are sometimes used to feature PERSONALIZED CONTENT (D4). A PAGE TEMPLATE (D1) can be used to make it easy to include sidebars on new pages. PRINTABLE PAGES (D8) are often stripped of sidebars to make them easier to print.

Making Site Search Fast and Relevant

Search is an essential feature for all Web sites. Make sure you have search features that are useful and usable. Pay special attention to which words customers type in, how you present the results, how customers interact with the results, and what happens if they cannot find what they're looking for. This pattern group deals with designing the interaction so that your customers' searches are more effective.

J1   SEARCH ACTION MODULE

J2   STRAIGHTFORWARD SEARCH FORMS

J3   ORGANIZED SEARCH RESULTS

Figure J1.1

Amazon.com's Web site provides an effective search feature, one that is simple and powerful at the same time.

(**www.amazon.com**, August 27, 2001)

✳ BACKGROUND

As a standard element of MULTIPLE WAYS TO NAVIGATE (B1) and a counterpart to BROWSABLE CONTENT (B2), this pattern explains the search half of the search and browse combination.

B1
B2

❋ PROBLEM

Customers sometimes want to quickly jump from one location to another, but search pages are too complex for this.

When entering your site, customers sometimes know exactly what they're looking for. A quick and simple search function on the homepage is critical to win these visitors' confidence. Other visitors may browse through a site and then perform a search. If they do not spot a search tool immediately, or they have to go through a complex search page, they are less likely to spend the time. Building a simple search action module into every page serves the needs of all customers best.

Create a Simple Search Tool • A simple tool for searching, when possible, is much easier to understand than a complicated search page. Although advanced search tools might allow customers to look for words near another word, to search for specific words and not others, and to enter other complex search expressions, most customers would rather have a simpler tool that works well and returns ORGANIZED SEARCH RESULTS (J3). Use simple phrasing to indicate the search field and an ACTION BUTTON (K4) for starting the search.

Some large Web sites use a search selector to help narrow the focus of the search. Figure J1.2 shows the search selector on Barnes & Noble.com. There are two issues for search selectors. The first is to make sure that the search selector has the right default, in case someone does not notice it. For example, the default for Barnes & Noble.com is to search on Books. Anyone who types in something without changing the default and expects to find music will only find books. The second issue is one of size. Smaller sites that have less than a couple hundred pages in various

Figure J1.2

Barnes & Noble.com provides a search selector that lets people search on specific categories, such as Books and Music.

(**www.bn.com**, January 30, 2002)

categories will not have enough results to warrant a subsection search selector.

We advocate starting simply, using a straightforward search mechanism that lets people type in whatever terms they want. However, when your site becomes large and produces dozens of results to common searches, it's time to add a search selector to let people narrow their searches.

Put the Search Tool in a Consistent Place • People expect to find the search tool in the same place on every page. Because search is something that people might use from any page, include your search action module ABOVE THE FOLD (I2) either in the top left, middle, or right, and keep it there on every page.

✳ SOLUTION

Build a search action module into every page, using simple phrasing that indicates the search space for typing in words or phrases and an action button for starting the search. If you have a large site and want to give customers the ability to search a subsection, add a list of subsections and the word *for* to indicate the string to look for.

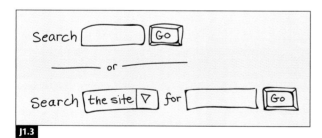

J1.3

Figure J1.3

Customers will readily use the search action module if it is kept simple and appears on every page.

✳ CONSIDER THESE OTHER PATTERNS

Keep your search tool in a consistent place on every page, ABOVE THE FOLD (I2) at the top left, middle, or right.

If you are WRITING FOR SEARCH ENGINES (D6) when you develop your site's search facility, customers will use your site's content more readily because the search action module exists on every page.

The button that starts the search, often labeled **Search** or **Go**, should be an ACTION BUTTON (K4).

When necessary, customers can fill out more detailed STRAIGHTFOR-WARD SEARCH FORMS (J2). Results will always be returned on an ORGAN-IZED SEARCH RESULTS (J3) page.

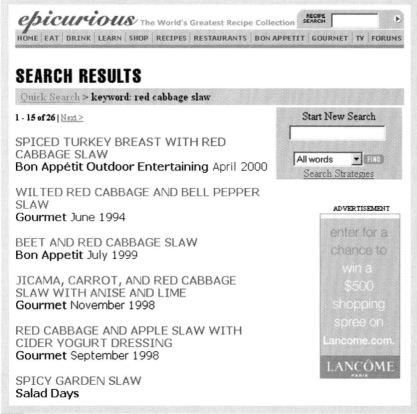

Figure J2.1

The search form at Epicurious does not require much precision from the customer. Searching for "red cabbage slaws" results in recipes with the singular *slaw,* as well as slaw recipes without *red cabbage* at all.

(www.epicurious.com, February 6, 2002)

✳ BACKGROUND

SEARCH ACTION MODULES (J1) make it easy for your customers to find the search feature on your site. However, the way search terms are specified can be confusing to customers. This pattern describes how to avoid common errors with search entry forms.

✳ PROBLEM

Search forms are often ineffective because they require too much precision.

Search is an essential feature for all Web sites. However, most search facilities have limited value because they are designed to make searches easy for the computer to process, instead of being useful and usable for customers.

Boolean Expressions Are Hard to Understand • Boolean searches are searches that use the terms *and* and *or*. For example, the search "computer and monitor" would find all Web pages containing both *computer* and *monitor,* whereas "computer or monitor" would find all Web pages containing either *computer* or *monitor.*

It is easy to add Boolean searches to a search engine. However, many studies show that customers find Boolean searches difficult to understand. The basic problem stems from how we use *and* and *or* in everyday conversation. For example, whereas a person would say, "I want to search for information about cats *and* dogs," the correct search term for computers is actually "cats *or* dogs." Help your customers by providing a search engine that does not use these Boolean operators at all, or by providing a search form that has explicit phrasing, such as Google's "with **all** of the words" and "with **any** of the words."

Exact Matches Mean No Matches • Some searches require exact matches. For example, if a customer is searching for "presentation," she will not get any results if she types in the plural "presentations" or misspells it as "presentatino." Getting the response "no matches were found" may make customers think that there are no results at all. Web search engines can help compensate by using a dictionary to check for plurals and for misspellings.

Another place where exact matches crop up is with product names. For example, is it a *laptop* or a *notebook* computer? Is it *apparel* or *clothes*? Your customers will use different terms to mean the same thing, and the development team should design the search engine to take synonyms into consideration.

Category Searches Should Have Defaults • Some search forms require visitors to specify a category to search in. For example, a music Web site might let people search on categories such as Artist Name or Album Title. But it is easy for customers to end up with no matches because they did not notice the category field. To ensure that your customers will get some results, set the default action to be a search on all categories.

✴ SOLUTION

Use a search engine that does not require extreme precision. Avoid Boolean searches and exact matches. Compensate for different terms for the same thing. Set the search to look across all categories by default.

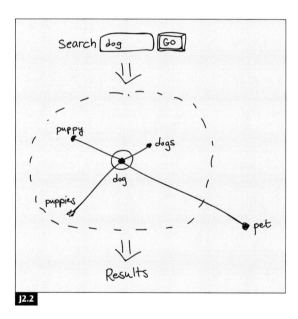

Figure J2.2

Search results should include words that are closely related.

J2.2

✴ CONSIDER THESE OTHER PATTERNS

Straightforward search forms need to be part of a visible SEARCH ACTION MODULE (J1) that visitors can easily find on a Web page. ORGANIZED SEARCH RESULTS (J3) will make it easier for your customers to understand what your search has found for them.

Figure J3.1

In its extensive online restaurant guide, Zagat lets its customers sort by name, cuisine, area, food, décor, service, and cost. It also shows a restaurant's address and phone number, as well as a short excerpt from the review.

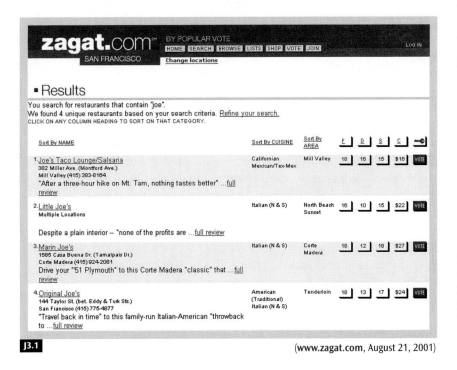

J3.1

(www.zagat.com, August 21, 2001)

✳ BACKGROUND

A visible SEARCH ACTION MODULE (J1) and a STRAIGHTFORWARD SEARCH FORM (J2) address some of the common problems that site visitors have using search engines. However, it might still be difficult for your customers to comprehend search results, especially when there are a large number of them. Structuring and organizing search results can make them much easier to understand. This pattern covers ways of arranging and categorizing search results to make them more valuable to your customers. It applies to both local searches on your site and Web-wide search engines.

✳ PROBLEM

It can be difficult for site visitors to understand search results if there are too few or too many results.

A search engine is only as good as the results it presents. It does not matter if it is fast and can simultaneously support thousands of queries per second if people cannot understand the results.

Provide Relevant Summaries with the Search Results • The Zagat restaurant guides are indispensable for many city dwellers, providing an overview of all the major restaurants in a metropolitan area. Zagat provides a high-quality online version of its popular restaurant guidebooks. Figure J3.1 shows how zagat.com provides useful, domain-specific information in its search results, including a short excerpt from the full review, as well as ratings of the food, décor, service, and cost of the restaurant.

There are no hard rules here, though. You have to determine what should be shown in search results on a per Web site basis. On e-commerce sites, for example, it makes sense to show the price and availability of products. And search results on community message boards could show the author and date of posting.

Offer Clear Organization of the Search Results • No one likes sifting through hundreds of hits to find the right one. One way of addressing this problem is to group the hits according to a coherent, logical scheme, such as alphabetically or chronologically. For example, Figure J3.2 shows how Amazon.com groups related search results together. This is one way to make sure your search results present customers with BROWSABLE CONTENT (B2).

Provide Good Hyperlinked Titles for Each Hit • Search engines typically display a Web page's HTML title as the name of the search result. Because these titles are what visitors see, it is crucial to give your Web page a DISTINCTIVE HTML TITLE (D9).

Use Log Files to Tailor Results for the Most Common Search Terms • Search engines by themselves do not always provide the best results. The key to better results for your customers lies in your analysis of the log files, which keep track of the terms your customers use to search.

Find the most common terms, and make sure that search results using those terms point to the right place. This approach solves two problems.

Figure J3.2

Amazon.com groups search results together by category. On a search for "addison wesley computer," the various hits are grouped by Books and zShops.

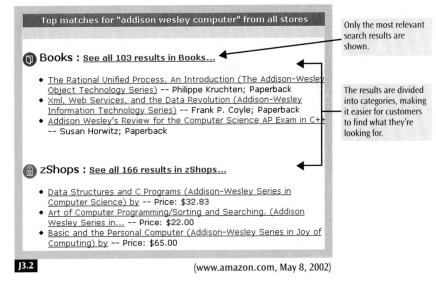

Top matches for "addison wesley computer" from all stores

Books : See all 103 results in Books...

- The Rational Unified Process, An Introduction (The Addison-Wesley Object Technology Series) -- Philippe Kruchten; Paperback
- Xml, Web Services, and the Data Revolution (Addison-Wesley Information Technology Series) -- Frank P. Coyle; Paperback
- Addison Wesley's Review for the Computer Science AP Exam in C++ -- Susan Horwitz; Paperback

zShops : See all 166 results in zShops...

- Data Structures and C Programs (Addison-Wesley Series in Computer Science) by -- Price: $32.83
- Art of Computer Programming/Sorting and Searching. (Addison Wesley Series in... -- Price: $22.00
- Basic and the Personal Computer (Addison-Wesley Series in Joy of Computing) by -- Price: $65.00

Only the most relevant search results are shown.

The results are divided into categories, making it easier for customers to find what they're looking for.

J3.2   (www.amazon.com, May 8, 2002)

First, it compensates for the fact that customers use different words to mean the same thing. Figure J3.3 shows how IBM does this on its Web site. The search terms "notebook," "laptop," and "ThinkPad" all point to the same page, greatly increasing the chance that a customer will find the right page.

Second, this approach lets you create the best possible hit for search terms. Look at Figure J3.3 again, and you will notice a special area for tailored search results. Whenever a customer searches on "notebook," "laptop," or "ThinkPad," the search page shows a special promotion for selling these computers. However, the regular searches on the site show only ordinary search results. IBM keeps these ordinary search results in case their customers' "best" hits are not what they're looking for.

Compensate for Common Misspellings • Figure J3.4 shows how Amazon.com handles misspelled search terms. At the top of the Web page, it notes that there are no search results for the exact search terms entered, but then it corrects the spelling and searches on the new terms. It is likely that customers will not notice that they misspelled the terms, nor will they see the message at the top of the Web page stating that they misspelled the terms, but Amazon.com does the right thing and shows them the results anyway! This is a customer-savvy, elegant design.

Is it a "notebook," a "laptop," or a "ThinkPad" computer? On IBM's Web site, it doesn't matter; they all work correctly!

Also, a special search result appears that lets people get to the right page more quickly.

These are the standard search results.

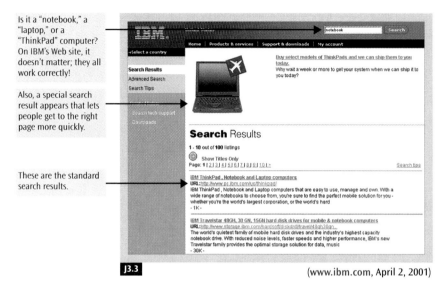

J3.3

(www.ibm.com, April 2, 2001)

Figure J3.3

IBM presents specially tailored search results for common searches, such as "notebook" and "laptop," in addition to the standard search results.

States that it couldn't find any results.

Does the next search, what a person would do anyway, instead of presenting "No results."

J3.4

(www.amazon.com, April 14, 2001)

Figure J3.4

Amazon.com automatically corrects certain misspellings. In this case, it corrects the search "crossing cashm" to read "crossing chasm."

Compensating for spelling mistakes means you have to tailor the spell checker's dictionary to your specific domain. An ordinary spell checker dictionary will not be useful for Web sites dealing with legal matters, for example, because it will not have legal terms in it.

Another way to compensate is to go through the log files to find the most commonly misspelled search terms. You will have to manually enter these misspellings into the search engine to make them point to the right terms (see Figure J3.4). This is clearly a tedious proposition, especially if there are a huge number of search terms. Concentrate on finding the most popular terms, perhaps by limiting your corrections to the top 100 or 500.

Provide Support for Common Search Tasks • Common search tasks include things like going to the next page of results, starting a new search, and refining a current search. Figure J3.5 shows a good example of how the Google search engine handles these tasks. The top of the page provides a search entry form, letting visitors quickly create a new search if they did not get the results they wanted. In addition, the new-search form includes the search terms that the customer originally typed in, making it easy for them to remember what they entered and to edit it if necessary.

Figure J3.5

Google has a clean, minimalist design for displaying search results and supporting common tasks.

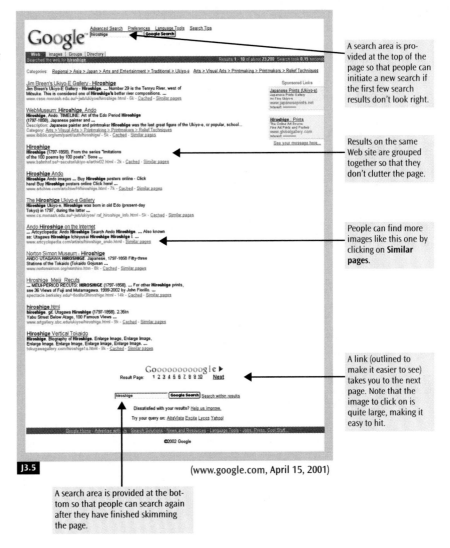

A search area is provided at the top of the page so that people can initiate a new search if the first few search results don't look right.

Results on the same Web site are grouped together so that they don't clutter the page.

People can find more images like this one by clicking on **Similar pages.**

A link (outlined to make it easier to see) takes you to the next page. Note that the image to click on is quite large, making it easy to hit.

J3.5   (www.google.com, April 15, 2001)

A search area is provided at the bottom so that people can search again after they have finished skimming the page.

The bottom of the page has a second search entry form because the customer may look through all of the search results for a page, reach the bottom, and then decide to start a new search or refine the existing one. This design is more considerate than forcing the customer to scroll back to the top of the page.

The bottom of the page also contains links to the next set of search results. One subtle but very useful thing that designers have done here is to make the "gle" part above the **Next** button a link to the next search results. The upshot is that there is a fairly large target to click on that will take customers to the next page of search results. Incidentally, designs with large targets are also good for improving SITE ACCESSIBILITY (B9) for customers with poor motor control.   **B9**

At first glance the controls at the bottom might seem to argue against designing for ABOVE THE FOLD (I2). But visitors tend to read the page from top to bottom. If they have not found what they want by the time they reach the bottom, *then* they can go to the next page of results.   **I2**

✳ SOLUTION

Provide your customers with relevant summaries in their search results. Offer a clear organization of the search results. Provide hyperlinked titles for each hit on the search result page. Use log files to tailor the search engine for the most common search terms. Compensate for common misspellings. Provide support for your customers' common search tasks.

Figure J3.6

Organize search results, and continue to update the search database with common synonyms.

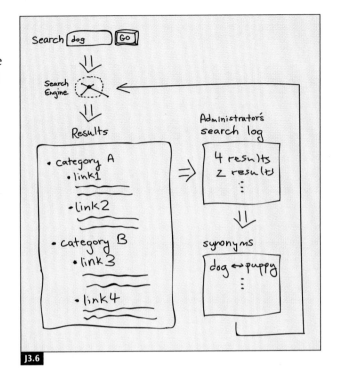

J3.6

❈ CONSIDER THESE OTHER PATTERNS

3 You can also use the card-sorting techniques described in Chapter 3— Knowing Your Customers: Principles and Techniques to find common search terms, but do this before launching the site and before performing a log file analysis. This strategy can help you prevent errors, instead of waiting for them to happen and then fixing the problems after the fact.

B9 Use the SITE ACCESSIBILITY (B9) pattern to ensure that the results you return can be used by all of your potential customers, including those with disabilities.

D6 When writing for SEARCH ENGINES (D6), you need to give your Web
D9 pages DISTINCTIVE HTML TITLES (D9), as well as simple HTML that search engines can understand.

Making Navigation Easy

Navigation is an integral part of every Web site, but customers cannot always find links and don't always know where links will take them. This pattern group describes several well-known techniques for organizing and displaying navigation elements to make them easy to find and easy to understand.

K1   UNIFIED BROWSING HIERARCHY

K2   NAVIGATION BAR

K3   TAB ROWS

K4   ACTION BUTTONS

K5   HIGH-VISIBILITY ACTION BUTTONS

K6   LOCATION BREAD CRUMBS

K7   EMBEDDED LINKS

K8   EXTERNAL LINKS

K9   DESCRIPTIVE, LONGER LINK NAMES

K10   OBVIOUS LINKS

K11   FAMILIAR LANGUAGE

K12   PREVENTING ERRORS

K13   MEANINGFUL ERROR MESSAGES

K14   PAGE NOT FOUND

K1 UNIFIED BROWSING HIERARCHY

Figure K1.1

Yahoo! brings together content, community, and commerce in its site directory, creating a unified browsing hierarchy. (Reproduced with permission of Yahoo! © 2000 by Yahoo! Inc. YAHOO! and the YAHOO! logo are trademarks of Yahoo! Inc.)

K1.1

(www.yahoo.com, September 2001)

❋ BACKGROUND

We have considered designing for MULTIPLE WAYS TO NAVIGATE (B1) and BROWSABLE CONTENT (B2), but what about cases in which a site offers content, commerce, and community all around the same topic or topics? This pattern provides a navigable design for sites that have these features.

B1
B2

❋ PROBLEM

When Web sites have distinct community, content, and commerce sections, it is hard for people to find related topics in each of these sections, and the community areas can grow stale.

When you put content, commerce, and community about the same topics on different pages, you create a challenge for your customers. What if they are interested in all three sections? You are forcing them to go to three separate sections, requiring them to do more work. To avoid this situation, you can link separate elements from the three sections or even combine them into one unified whole.

Your customers want quick access to all your site's benefits. Forcing them to navigate back to the homepage, only to navigate down another branch, is cumbersome, especially when the branches could be connected.

Why Always Force Visitors to Go Home? • Many designs require customers to go from the content section to the homepage before going to the commerce or community sections. Some visitors will miss the related areas entirely because they do not know the areas are there or do not have the energy to go and find them. Such a design might look like this:

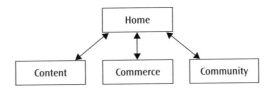

But site information is related through the unified purpose of the site. Even if these sections are written by different people, making the site a unified whole reinforces the value of all the sections.

Granted, unifying the sections requires making someone responsible for the unification process—someone who has the time and capability to add mechanisms to link from one section to the next—but your customers benefit by having full use of your site.

Create Links for Easier Navigation • Link the related content, commerce, and community categories so that customers have easier access. You could keep the sections separate and accessible from the homepage but connect related content through special links in each area. Your design might look something like this:

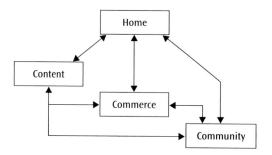

Another approach is to connect sections directly within one page, providing two or three of the different types of elements on a single page, something like this:

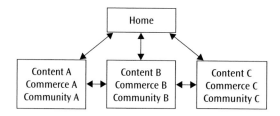

Either of these solutions will work. As long as the content, commerce, and community sections are related by cross-linking in one unified browsing hierarchy, you benefit from CROSS-SELLING AND UP-SELLING (G2) content and products, providing more value to your customers.

✳ SOLUTION

If your site offers content, community, and commerce on the same topics, integrate the three elements into one unified browsing hierarchy, either by directly linking the three elements, or by integrating the elements into one page.

Figure K1.2

Provide links among your content, commerce, and community Web pages, integrating them into a unified whole.

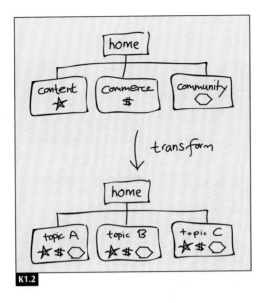

❋ CONSIDER THESE OTHER PATTERNS

If content, community, and commerce are not integrated on one page, give customers immediate access to the separate elements of the site through your NAVIGATION BAR (K2) or through CONSISTENT SIDEBARS OF RELATED CONTENT (I6). Provide strong feedback on the customer's location with LOCATION BREAD CRUMBS (K6).

K2 NAVIGATION BAR

K2.1

(www.epicurious.com, February 6, 2002)

Figure K2.1

Epicurious has a top-running navigation bar—one that runs across the top of the page—on its Web site.

❋ BACKGROUND

From MULTIPLE WAYS TO NAVIGATE (B1) we know we need a consistent interface for browsing and searching a site. BROWSABLE CONTENT (B2) and SEARCH ACTION MODULE (J1) provide the fundamentals for building a browsable structure and straightforward search. Navigation bars are a common way to provide access to the main parts of your Web site. This pattern describes how to make navigation bars that your customers will find useful.

B1
B2
J1

✳ PROBLEM

Customers need a structured, organized way of reaching the most important parts of your Web site that is easy to understand and use.

Large-scale Web sites need a clear and systematic scheme to make it easy for visitors to navigate them. Web sites on this scale are usually organized into subsites that focus on a specific topic, or into categories that focus on a specific product or type of information.

One common pattern that has emerged for helping people move across subsites and categories is the navigation bar. There are three types of navigation bars. The first type, the *top-running* navigation bar, stretches across the top of a Web page (see Figure K2.1). Top-running navigation bars often act as top-level navigation—that is, navigation linking directly to different subsites or categories.[1]

The second type is the *side-running* navigation bar. Side-running bars often are positioned along the left side of a Web page. It is fairly rare to see a navigation bar on the right, even on sites designed for languages that read from right to left. Side-running navigation bars have more space to work with than top-running navigation bars. They usually show more categories, too, often providing second-level navigation that provides links within a subsite.

The third type of navigation bar is the *top-and-left* navigation bar, which resembles an upside-down letter *L*. This bar runs across the top and along the left side of a Web page. Often the top-running portion provides broad navigation across subsites, and the side-running portion provides deep navigation within the current subsite (see Figure K2.2).

Navigation bars link to the most important portions of a Web site either through text links or through icons and text. Icons by themselves are usually not effective because they are not always universally understood across cultures or even within a culture. It helps to have a text description to augment an icon (see Figure K2.3).

---

1 Here the word *top* is being used in two different ways. *Top-running* refers to the fact that the navigation bar is positioned across the top of a Web page. *Top-level* means that the navigation bar provides access to all of the major portions of a site.

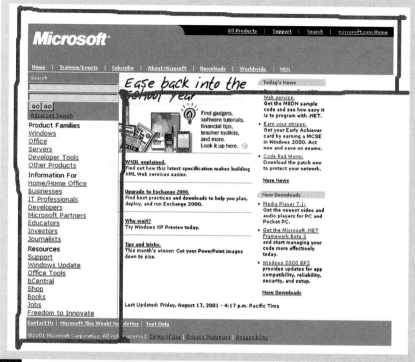

(www.microsoft.com, August 21, 2001)

Figure K2.2

Microsoft's Web site has a navigation bar that runs across both the top and the left. The links along the top represent fairly broad topics; the links on the left point to more specific topics.

(www.yahoo.com, November 12, 2000)

Figure K2.3

Note how the text under the icons here makes it clear what the images represent. Interestingly, the blue hyperlinked text is actually part of the image.

✳ SOLUTION

Coordinate top-level and second-level navigation in a navigation bar along the top and/or left side of each Web page. Use text or both icons and text as links inside the navigation bar.

Figure K2.4

Create a navigation bar that runs along the top and/or left side.

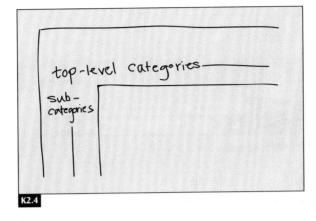

K2.4

✳ CONSIDER THESE OTHER PATTERNS

If your navigation bar uses images, make sure that they are FAST-DOWNLOADING IMAGES (L2). Navigation bars that use OBVIOUS LINKS (K10) achieve maximum clarity. Alternatively, by using HTML POWER (L4) to create a background color that is distinct from the body copy background color, and by keeping the navigation bar to the left or the top, you can bend the rules of OBVIOUS LINKS (K10) and remove the underlines or change the link color to something other than blue.

TAB ROWS (K3) are often used for top-level navigation. One advantage of tab rows is that they clearly show customers which category they are currently viewing.

CLEAR FIRST READS (I3) are sometimes placed at the top left corner of a Web page, affecting the placement of navigation bars.

K3 TAB ROWS

Figure K3.1

Well-designed tab rows provide visual cues that help customers recognize and use them more effectively. On BabyCenter's site they look just like file folders (top), an image that is instantly familiar.

K3.1

(www.babycenter.com, August 2001)

✳ BACKGROUND

MULTIPLE WAYS TO NAVIGATE (B1), BROWSABLE CONTENT (B2), and NAVIGATION BARS (K2) show the value of providing clear and consistent navigation indicators. One type of NAVIGATION BAR (K2) is a tab row, which offers clear visual cues about what your customer can click on, as well as straightforward feedback about the currently selected item.

✳ PROBLEM

Sites need to let customers navigate through categories of content and give them feedback on where they are. But to make tab rows work well requires including specific details in the visuals.

Tab rows are cues that people find familiar. They are reminiscent of tabs on file folders at the office and in school. When implemented well, they clearly indicate what is active and open, while showing customers which other sections they can access. This design provides a simple but powerful navigation aid to quickly orient visitors and give added visual appeal to a site. Making tab rows work on the Web, though, involves creating some specific graphical devices.

Clearly Identify the Active Tab • Customers need to be able to see which tab is active. Make the active tab stand out from the nonactive tab by giving it a different color and accentuating the contrast in brightness for visitors who cannot distinguish by color differences alone. Making a tab active, even when customers first come to a site, will be another visual clue that the row of rectangles is a collection of tabs. Use color, contrast, and preselection to make your active tabs stand out (see Figure K3.2).

Figure K3.2

Nolo's Web site differentiates the active tab by color and contrast, and the tab is preselected when a customer comes to the site.

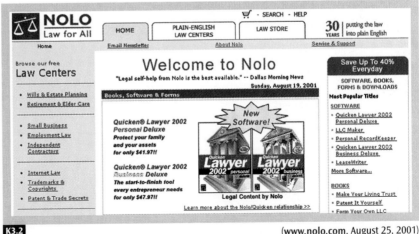

(www.nolo.com, August 25, 2001)

Create an Indicator Line • To reinforce the illusion that the row of tabs is just that, and to bring content to the foreground, give visitors an indicator showing that the content of the page is controlled by tabs. Showing a line below the active tab in the same color—one that extends from left to right over all the content—indicates that the tab is not only a switch, but also a control over the content that customers see (see Figure K3.3).

Tab Rows Have Limitations • Tab rows can do only so much. The number of categories that a tab row can effectively manage on one line is somewhere between 10 and 15, and when you use multiple rows of tabs the screen begins to look cluttered, where too much of it is consumed by tabs (see Figure K3.4).

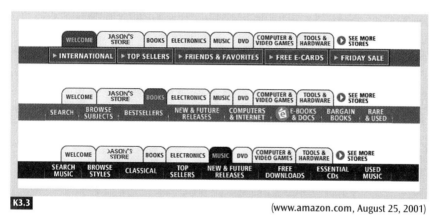

K3.3

(www.amazon.com, August 25, 2001)

Figure K3.3

On Amazon.com's site, the indicator line covers the width of the page, giving the impression that all content on the page belongs to that tab.

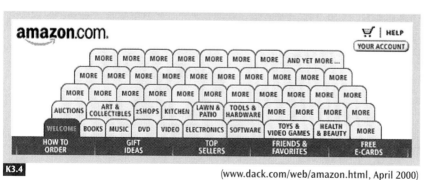

K3.4

(www.dack.com/web/amazon.html, April 2000)

Figure K3.4

This is an extreme (and fictional) example, but it makes a point: Too many tabs clutter the screen.

✳ SOLUTION

Create tab rows using an active tab and indicator line, but with no more than 10 to 15 items, or whatever can fit on one line of tabs. Differentiate an active tab by color and contrast, as well as through preselection. Create an indicator line that extends across the page to create the impression that the whole page below the line belongs to the active tab.

Figure K3.5

Use tab rows to let customers navigate through different categories of information.

K3.5

✳ CONSIDER THESE OTHER PATTERNS

L1
L2 L4

L3

Create your tab rows graphically with a LOW NUMBER OF FILES (L1) and FAST-DOWNLOADING IMAGES (L2), or use HTML POWER (L4) to build them with HTML. To make downloading the page even faster, use SEPARATE TABLES (L3) to download through the tab row portion of the page first, giving the impression that the page is faster than it really is.

K4 ACTION BUTTONS

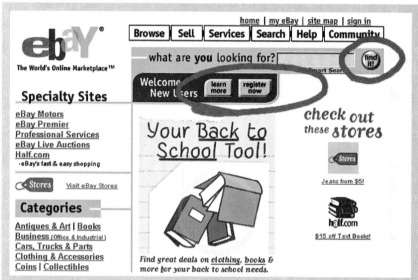

Figure K4.1

Action buttons
highlight the most
important actions
you want customers
to take.

K4.1

(www.ebay.com, August 25, 2001)

✳ BACKGROUND

As described in MULTIPLE WAYS TO NAVIGATE (B1), a navigation framework
needs to support both impulse- and intention-based activity. Most links
on a Web page simply take you to another page. Some links, however,
represent actions that cause other actions to happen. In a PROCESS FUNNEL
(H1) we know that moving from step to step requires a clear call to
action. This pattern looks at how to differentiate ordinary links from
action links through the use of buttons.

B1

H1

✳ PROBLEM

Text hyperlinks are good for moving from one page to another, but they are not quite right for representing actions that do something important, such as authorizing a purchase or submitting a message to a message board.

Text hyperlinks are well understood as words that customers can click on to bring up another page. There are no side effects or consequences. However, text hyperlinks are not quite right for representing *transactions,* where you are sending important information back to a Web server for processing.

For cases like these, buttons make more sense than text links because in the physical world, buttons cause action. Pushing a button on a remote control causes the television to change channels. Pushing an elevator button causes the elevator to come to your floor. Pushing the power button on a computer turns the computer on.

There are two kinds of buttons on the Web: graphical action buttons and HTML action buttons.

Graphical Action Buttons • Graphical action buttons are made from images, but they are modified to look like they can be pressed. A common problem with many great-looking Web pages is that it is not clear to customers what can be clicked on. They end up moving the mouse all over the page trying to figure out what to click on next. By adding slight lighting touches around the border of an image, you can make the image look like it is raised, providing a visual cue that customers can click on it (see Figure K4.2).

Graphical action buttons should have supporting text or labels where possible, to help explain their purpose. The text can be part of the graphical image (as in Figure K4.3). The text can also be part of the HTML, but in this case it is a little harder to align the image and the text correctly.

Figure K4.2

These two images illustrate the difference between flat images (left) and graphical action buttons (right). Graphical action buttons are tailored to look like real buttons, making them appear as if they could be physically pressed.

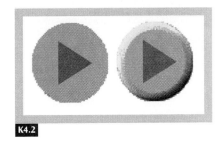

K4.2

K4.3

(www.amazon.com, www.geocaching.com)

Figure K4.3

Buttons should be accompanied by text describing what they do.

Graphical action buttons should not be too small, or they will be hard to see and hard to click on. On the other hand, if they are too large, they will take up too much screen space. As we mentioned in Chapter 3— Knowing Your Customers: Principles and Techniques, human motor skills are predicted by what is known as Fitts's Law, which says that it takes customers a lot longer to hit objects that are far away or small. You will have to decide the size of your buttons on a case-by-case basis, but we recommend a minimum of 20 × 20 pixels.

3

HTML Action Buttons • HTML action buttons are encoded directly in HTML, and on most Web browsers they are represented as gray buttons (see Figure K4.4).

HTML action buttons are faster to download than graphical action buttons, but they do not provide as much control over layout and appearance beyond the text inside of the button. One consequence of this lower amount of control is that HTML action buttons with a lot of text become very wide, making them visually unattractive. Another consequence is that the Web browser may make wide buttons wrap to the next line if there is not enough space. The best solution is to keep the text of an HTML action button short so that the button will be small and will be more likely to be positioned where you want it.

Search for: Search

K4.4

Figure K4.4

The button on the right, labeled **Search**, is an example of an HTML action button. HTML action buttons are created directly in HTML.

✳ SOLUTION

Use buttons to represent actions. If you use images, make them look like they can be clicked on by giving them a three-dimensional appearance. Also provide clear, concise labels to explain what the buttons will do.

Figure K4.5

Use buttons for actions, and make it clear that these buttons can be clicked on.

✳ CONSIDER THESE OTHER PATTERNS

For important action buttons that are critical to completing a task, use HIGH-VISIBILITY ACTION BUTTONS (K5), which are placed in redundant locations above and below the fold.

You can use buttons in NAVIGATION BARS (K2). However, these buttons do not represent actions, but just navigation. The same techniques for making images look three-dimensional can be applied to images in navigation bars. However, you should avoid using HTML action buttons in these bars because of the lack of control you have over layout and appearance.

Graphical action buttons work against achieving a LOW NUMBER OF FILES (L1) unless the images are combined. Having many of these buttons can make your Web pages slower to download. To compensate, make graphical action buttons into FAST-DOWNLOADING IMAGES (L2). Shrink images by reducing the number of colors, combining many nearby images in a single image, and using a different file format. You will want to make most graphical action buttons in the GIF image format so that they can have transparent backgrounds.

SITE ACCESSIBILITY (B9) is an important factor to consider for action buttons. Making graphical action buttons universally accessible entails adding ALT attributes to all of them describing what they will do when selected.

K5 HIGH-VISIBILITY ACTION BUTTONS

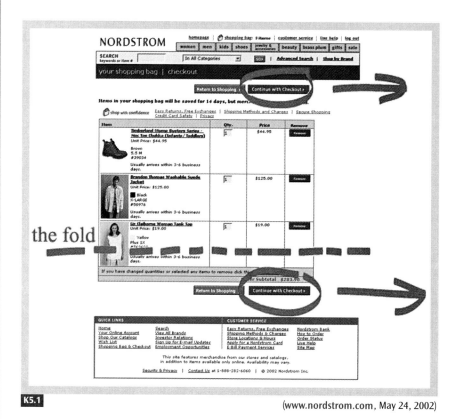

K5.1

(www.nordstrom.com, May 24, 2002)

Figure K5.1

Nordstrom's key checkout button is always visible above and below the fold, so customers can always see how to proceed to checkout.

✳ BACKGROUND

This pattern helps complete PROCESS FUNNELS (H1) and QUICK-FLOW CHECK-OUT (F1). To help customers finish tasks, put ACTION BUTTONS (K4) and other critical information ABOVE THE FOLD (I2) and create OBVIOUS LINKS (K10). If pages are longer than a screen, this pattern tells you how to handle ACTION BUTTONS (K4) in a way that makes sense for your customers.

H1

F1 K4

I2

K10

K4

❊ PROBLEM

People can easily be derailed from completing a task if the next step is not obvious.

When working on a task, customers become frustrated when they reach a roadblock because they cannot figure out the next step. If all the buttons are the same size, shape, and color, or are ambiguously named, people have a tough time deciding which button they should care about more. If the link they think should be next is not visible on the page, some people will not have the patience to scroll down to look for it. On certain pages, customers need to scroll to make selections or verify information. On other pages, they can see that the information at the top is correct, and they will assume that the rest of the page is correct.

Mind the Fold • Designing pages for different Web browsers and configurations has challenges too. Web pages "fold" in different places, depending on the browser type, the browser's window size, and optional configurations, such as the default font size. Some people set their browser windows to the maximum window size; others shrink their windows so that they can see multiple windows at once. Customers who shrink their browser windows see less of what's on your Web page. The maximum browser window size depends on a computer screen's resolution. A large window on one machine could be a medium window on another, and a small window on a third. But putting the critical buttons at the very top of a page can confuse customers if the buttons are the first thing to draw the eye. If customers do not scan the site brand and recognize the site they're on, they might feel lost.

To be obvious, the critical buttons that take people to the next step in a process must follow these rules: Because browser size cannot be controlled, critical buttons must be as close to the top of a page as possible, without being at the absolute top. Including duplicate critical buttons below the fold, at the bottom of critical content, makes it easier for customers to move forward after reading the content, and it does not increase page download time. Action buttons must be differentiated from other buttons so that customers notice them right away.

✳ SOLUTION

On every page that is part of a process

1. Provide your action button or buttons right below the top navigation bar, tab row, or progress bar.
2. If critical content cannot be placed above the fold, repeat the same buttons at the bottom of the content.
3. Make action buttons larger than all other buttons on the screen, and give them a color that contrasts well with the background color. Choose button labels that are descriptive and different from the names of other buttons
on the page. Make the buttons that move a task forward the largest ones on the page.

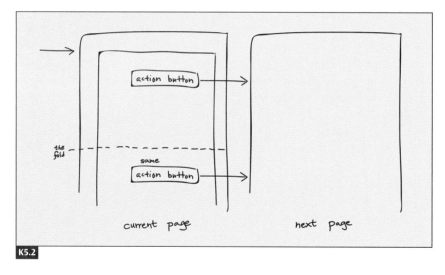

Figure K5.2

Task-critical action buttons should be distinct and appear near the top of the page, as well as below the fold, so that customers always know how to complete their tasks.

✳ CONSIDER THESE OTHER PATTERNS

Use ACTION BUTTONS (K4) to make highly visible buttons. Place these buttons both ABOVE THE FOLD (I2) and below the fold. The button at the top should be near the NAVIGATION BAR (K2) or TAB ROW (K3).

Use FAMILIAR LANGUAGE (K11) and DESCRIPTIVE, LONGER LINK NAMES (K9) for button names, and make sure each is different from other links on the same page. Use the same image at the top and bottom of a page so that you have a LOW NUMBER OF FILES (L1).

Figure K6.1

The bar at the top of this Web page shows location bread crumbs, which identify where customers are on the Web site. Bread crumbs also provide a quick way of backtracking to previously seen pages.

K6.1
(www.bmrc.berkeley.edu/courseware/cs160/fall00/, December 1, 2000)

✳ BACKGROUND

Part of providing BROWSABLE CONTENT (B2) is including a feedback mechanism that lets people know where they are. NAVIGATION BARS (K2) and TAB ROWS (K3) provide feedback on their own, but other navigation schemes do not. It can be quite a challenge for customers to know where they are on some Web sites, and how to get back to where they came from, especially on large sites. Location bread crumbs, also known as trail markers, provide location indicators that customers can also use as navigation. This pattern describes ways of using location bread crumbs effectively.

✳ PROBLEM

It is easy for customers to get lost on Web sites, losing track of where they are in relation to other pages on the site.

In the traditional fairy tale, a wicked stepmother leads a young Hansel and Gretel into a dark forest. Hansel leaves a trail of bread crumbs to mark their path so that they can return home to their father.[2] So what does this fairy tale have to do with the Web? Every Web site's navigation design must answer these three questions for the customer:

- Where am I now?
- Where did I come from?
- Where can I go from here?

The term **bread crumbs** refers to the bar at the top of a Web page showing the trail of pages that a customer took from the homepage to the current page (see Figure K6.1). Showing this trail helps visitors answer the first two questions. NAVIGATION BARS (K2), EMBEDDED LINKS (K7), EXTERNAL LINKS (K8), and other links on a page help answer the third question.

Provide Bread Crumbs to Link Visitors Back to Where They've Been • Each page in the bread crumb bar is hyperlinked, letting customers quickly backtrack through the site. Bread crumbs also let people see where they are in relation to the homepage, providing information about the Web site structure in the process. Visitors who jump directly into a Web page through a bookmark, an e-mailed link, or a search engine, may find bread crumbs extremely helpful to orient themselves.

Use Separators to Show Relationships among Categories • There are many implementation variations of location bread crumbs. To show how each category leads from one to the other, designers use symbols such as >, /, and |. While each of these symbols has a different meaning in another context, we recommend > as the best separator because it suggests that one category "points" to the next level of detail. Also this symbol is widely understood in the most popular directories, such as Yahoo!. Here's an example of how this symbol might be used:

Home > Arts > Performing Arts > Acting

---

2 Unfortunately for the children, some birds eat the bread crumbs, leaving the children lost in the woods.

✳ SOLUTION

Provide bread crumb links that show how to get from the homepage to the current page and back. Use a string of back links and separate them by a "pointing" (>) character.

Figure K6.2

Use bread crumbs to show people where they are on the Web site.

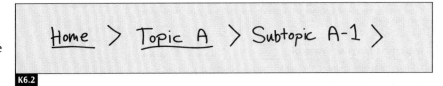

K6.2

✳ CONSIDER THESE OTHER PATTERNS

Bread crumbs should use OBVIOUS LINKS (K10) to make them easy to see and understand. Bread crumbs are usually placed at the top of a page's GRID LAYOUT (I1). They can interfere with NAVIGATION BARS (K2) that run across the top. In these cases it is usually better to place the bread crumbs underneath the navigation bar.

K7.1

(www.whatis.com, August 17, 2001)

Figure K7.1

On this page from Whatis.com, a site that explains in simple language what technical terms mean, note how many of the links appear in the middle of the text. These kinds of embedded links encourage visitor exploration and help provide more context for identifying where a link goes.

✳ BACKGROUND

As we claimed in MULTIPLE WAYS TO NAVIGATE (B1) and BROWSABLE CONTENT (B2), customers need more than one way to find things on a site. When you're reading, it can be tedious to go elsewhere on the page for additional information. One way around this problem is to embed OBVIOUS LINKS (K10) in the body of the text. In this pattern we discuss the pros and cons of using embedded links, and ways of maximizing their effectiveness.

✳ PROBLEM

Sometimes visitors want to delve deeper into a certain subject that appears in the text, or they need an explanation but don't want to go searching for it. Links off to the side or at the end of the text may lack the context necessary for readers to understand how they relate to specific portions of the content.

One of the most common approaches to using hypertext links is to place them in the body of the text, letting customers jump to other pages if they're interested. This approach allows people to explore more about a topic if they choose. Embedded links also stand out from the rest of the text, making them easy for people to find while skimming.

However, one disadvantage of embedded links is that it is difficult to create a coherent experience. People might leave the original page and never return. Furthermore, if you embed too many links in the text, the text becomes hard to read and hard to skim because everything looks important. So where is the balance? In this section we present our solution for getting the most out of embedded links.

Use Helpful Link Names • Take more words from the surrounding text and use them to create DESCRIPTIVE, LONGER LINK NAMES (K9). For example, suppose we had the following (somewhat) fictitious paragraph:

> Although the number of Web pages is increasing dramatically with every passing month, it is quite clear to any Web surfer that the overall Web experience has not improved at the same fast-paced rate. In fact, a recent Web usability survey revealed that most customers do not return to sites that they consider hard to use.

Now suppose we wanted to make a link to the survey page. Here are three good ways to do it:

1. In fact, a recent <u>Web usability survey</u> revealed that most customers do not return to sites that they consider hard to use.
2. In fact, <u>a recent Web usability survey</u> revealed that most customers do not return to sites that they consider hard to use.
3. In fact, a recent Web usability survey revealed that <u>most customers do not return to sites that they consider hard to use</u>.

Which is the best choice? It depends. Link 1 sounds like it might go to the actual survey, which is good if you want to send people there. Link 2 sounds like it could go to the survey or an article about the survey. Link 3 sounds like it will go to a specific part of the results or to an article about the survey, which is good for impatient Web surfers who like to read summaries only.

How Many Links Are Too Many? • A page with too many links feels cluttered, and visitors cannot tell what is important. Avoid linking to arbitrary things that do not really matter. <u>We once saw a Web page that looked like this sentence, which had every word in its text linked to an online dictionary</u>. This is an extreme case, but it illustrates the minimalist philosophy quite well: Less is more.

Consider Pop-Up Windows for Some Embedded Links • Maintain coherence on a page by making the links open up POP-UP WINDOWS (H6). The benefit to this approach is that customers can view the linked material in the new window, without losing track of the original page. This technique is useful, for example, when a visitor needs to see extra information, such as a definition, or when a visitor is going through a PROCESS FUNNEL (H1).

In considering pop-up windows for your links, remember that having a lot of new windows can quickly become confusing. Also no patterns have emerged for representing links that open up new windows. For now, use this technique sparingly and only in places where it really makes sense.

❊ SOLUTION

Embed links within a text passage to allow more free-form exploration. Use descriptive, longer link names to let customers know where the links will take them. Keep the number of embedded links per page of text low, so as not to overwhelm readers. Use pop-up windows for some embedded links, to provide additional information while maintaining the context, and to keep visitors from jumping to other pages.

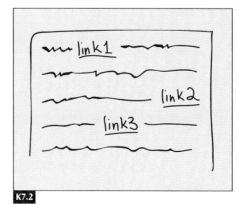

Figure K7.2

Use embedded links to let people explore.

✳ CONSIDER THESE OTHER PATTERNS

K10 Use OBVIOUS LINKS (K10) with embedded links to make it easier for customers to skim through the text. Embedded links need DESCRIPTIVE,
K9 LONGER LINK NAMES (K9) to help visitors understand where the links will take them.

H6 POP-UP WINDOWS (H6) help keep people from losing the context of the existing page. Embedded links often go to other Web sites. Use EXTERNAL
K8 LINKS (K8) to label and group these kinds of links to maintain coherence.

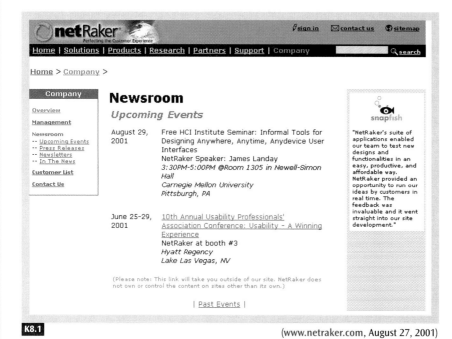

K8.1

Figure K8.1

External links point
to other Web sites
and let people see
how your Web site is
connected with other
people, places, and
things.

(www.netraker.com, August 27, 2001)

✳ BACKGROUND

It can be difficult for customers to know if a link points to something in
your Web site or goes to an outside site. Including links to external Web
sites can improve credibility, as in GRASSROOTS INFORMATION SITES (A6),
but it also makes it easy for customers to leave your Web site unintentionally. This pattern explains some techniques for organizing your external links so that there are no surprises for your customers.

❋ PROBLEM

Most sites have links to other Web sites. These external links need to be treated in a special manner so that customers understand that they lead to other Web sites that are not managed by the current Web site.

Providing external links is important for a site because it helps build trust and credibility. Visitors appreciate a site owner who is willing to reference another site to keep customers better informed and satisfied. But site owners are rightly concerned that customers will leave their sites to follow an external link. And visitors are sometimes surprised when they click on a link and unexpectedly leave a site. You can address these concerns by building in some safeguards, as described in the sections that follow.

Consider Having Links That Go to External Web Sites • Help your customers by providing additional useful information that you do not have on your site. Links might go to partner Web sites, client Web sites, press releases, articles, reviews, products, and services that complement your own.

Minimize Link Rot by Getting Permissions • A site operator could change the content of a page or decommission a page address, and you would never know about it until you tested your external links. This problem is often called **link rot.** If your site has many external links, testing the links can be time-consuming. In addition, the external site you link to may not want you to link to it. It is best to get permission from the external site for several reasons:

- External site operators can give you their conditions for linking to their sites, perhaps agreeing to link to you as well.
- You can inform the external site operators that your site relies on their current link structure, thereby hopefully reducing link rot.
- Talking to another site operator helps you understand how to link to other sites so that the same page addresses will contain the content you wish to reference, again reducing link rot

Receiving permission does not guarantee that the external links will continue to work in the future, but you will be much better informed as a result.

Set Expectations, Mark External References • News sites that reference other news sites often put all their external references together in one area that is clearly marked. For example, the CNN Web site places external links at the bottom of each news article. Other news aggregators, like Yahoo!, put a marker—such as *[external]*—before each link to another site. These strategies inform customers that if they click the link, they will no longer be on the current site, so that they will not be surprised to be transported away. You can use similar strategies by putting external content in specific areas or clearly marking an external reference on the link itself.

Consider Combining Embedded Links with External Links • One technique that the *New York Times* uses for its news articles is to merge embedded links with external links. If customers click on an embedded link, they jump to the bottom of the page, where there is a section labeled as external links.

The advantage of this approach is that it makes it easy for the reader to see all of the external links after they have finished reading a news article. It also lets customers go to external Web sites, making clear which links point to those sites.

Open New Windows for External Links • Open a new window for an external link when you want customers to maintain the context of the original site, especially when they are in the middle of a process. Pop-up windows are problematic, as explained in POP-UP WINDOWS (H6), but if used judiciously, they can work well. Keep in mind that too many open windows can be annoying, and because not every link comes in the middle of a process, not all external links need to open new windows.

✳ SOLUTION

External links can help build trust and credibility among your customers, while reducing the amount of work required to create new content. Take special care to ask permission from external site operators, and learn their policies on page addresses and dynamic content creation so that you can avoid most link rot. Let your customers know that they are about to be sent to an external site by explicitly marking each link, or by putting external links in a well-marked area on your page. Use pop-up windows for external links only when the context of your site must be maintained so that customers do not lose their place in a process.

Figure K8.2

Group external links at the end of a page (left) or in a module separated from the actual content (right).

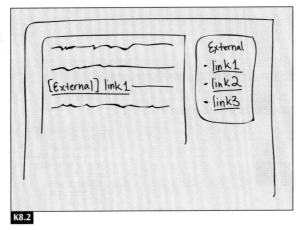

✳ CONSIDER THESE OTHER PATTERNS

Use DESCRIPTIVE, LONGER LINK NAMES (K9) so that customers will know that they're going to another site, or put all external links in their own CONTENT MODULES (D2). Use POP-UP WINDOWS (H6) for external links if customers need to maintain their place in a PROCESS FUNNEL (H1).

K9 DESCRIPTIVE, LONGER LINK NAMES

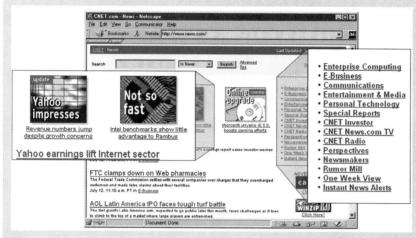

K9.1

Figure K9.1

CNET News.com's links on the left clearly describe where customers will go if they click on them.

(www.cnet.com, July 2001)

✳ BACKGROUND

From MULTIPLE WAYS TO NAVIGATE (B1) we know that customers will be navigating your site using NAVIGATION BARS (K2), BROWSABLE CONTENT (B2), EXTERNAL LINKS (K8), and CONSISTENT SIDEBARS OF RELATED CONTENT (I6). Poorly worded text links can confuse them. This pattern describes how descriptive and longer link names can guide visitors to the right place easily.

✳ PROBLEM

Text hyperlinks must be made predictable and understandable in terms of the Web pages to which they link. Otherwise, when browsing, customers will repeatedly follow links, arrive at something that doesn't interest them, and continually "pogo" back and forth in frustration.

The text of a link is a preview of the linked page. Your customers should be able to guess the content of the linked page before they click on a link. In fact, researchers at PARC[3] have developed a notion of how people follow links called **information scent**. The basic idea is that given a link, its text, its location, and the previous pages they have seen, people should be able to tell if the link will take them closer to the desired information.

Generic Terms Make Poor Link Names • Many Web sites have generic links like <u>click here</u> or <u>download</u> or even <u>http://www.click-this-link.com</u>. "Click here" for what? "Download" what? What is http://www.click-this-link.com and why should anyone go there? Compare these link names to the ones in the CNET News.com example (see Figure K9.1). Take one of its links at random, and guess what kinds of things you would see if you clicked on it. In most cases, you will guess correctly. That's the mark of a good link name.

Longer Link Names Improve Site Accessibility • Descriptive, longer link names can also foster SITE ACCESSIBILITY (B9) in three ways. First, longer link names are easier to click on than short ones, making your Web site easier to use for people with poor motor skills, such as senior citizens and children. Second, descriptive link names are more useful to people who are blind because they often skip over content and listen to just the links on a Web page. Longer link names, such as <u>three recent articles on e-commerce</u> will be more useful to customers with impaired vision than short ones, such as <u>articles</u>. Third, a new page has to be downloaded every time customers click on a link. However, many people still have slow Internet connections. A good link name will help customers feel confident that they are downloading the right page.

Longer Link Names Make a Page Easier to Skim • Longer link names make long passages of text easier to skim. Customers often browse through text, looking for EMBEDDED LINKS (K7). More descriptive link names can help them understand what the text is about and find the right link.

---

3 Formerly Xerox PARC.

Summarize the Linked Page with a Few Choice Words • Remember the five Ws: who, what, when, where, and why. Answering these questions will help you create a descriptive link name. If you're using an INVERSE-PYRAMID WRITING STYLE (D7), a good link name will come straight from the title of the page.

D7

Use Familiar Language • Avoid jargon. If your site customers are consumer car buyers, for example, avoid technical details that they won't understand. Instead of a link name such as <u>Torque and traction to avoid hydroplaning</u>, use something like <u>Driving safely on wet roads</u>.

A corollary of this rule is to use link names that everyone else is using. For example, nearly everyone calls the area where you can see what you plan to purchase a *Shopping Cart* or a *Shopping Bag*. Other common names include *Home* for the homepage, *Search* or *Find* for the search page, and *My* for a personalized Web page. Stick to names your customers already know.

The reverse of this corollary is also true: Avoid using these terms when they don't mean what people expect. For example, some e-commerce sites have Home departments and use the term *Home* to point there. *Home* on a Web site means the homepage, so a Home department needs a link name like *Home Department* or *Household*.

Differentiate or Eliminate Links That Have Similar Names • If customers see links that sound similar, they may become confused. For example, which link would you click on for help: <u>Service</u>, <u>Tech Support</u>, or <u>Help</u>? As another example, what is the difference between <u>Shopping Cart</u>, <u>Checkout</u>, and <u>Order List</u>? FAMILIAR LANGUAGE (K11) describes some techniques for addressing this problem.

K11

This problem also crops up on large Web sites, which often name the same thing differently in different places. Is it *email* or *e-mail?* Is it *notebook computer* or *laptop computer?* Overcome the problem of inconsistent terminology by establishing a style guide that all your site designers follow. As we discussed in Chapter 4—Involving Customers with Iterative Design, strive for consistency by choosing a consistent vocabulary and stick with it throughout the Web site. In addition, be consistent with standard terminology that your customers will see elsewhere.

4

Separate Links That Word-Wrap • Because of the way HTML works, sometimes your link names will word-wrap, making a single link look like multiple links (see Figure K9.2). Use the layout of the Web page to give hints about the number of links you have. CNET News.com avoids the problem

The Rise of the Network
Society
How to Win Friends and
Influence People
The Trouble with
Computers
The Media Equation
Radical Equations
Galileo's Daughter

K9.2

Figure K9.2

How many links does this list
contain? If you guessed six,
you're correct, but why use a
design that makes your customers guess?

- The Rise of the
  Network Society
- How to Win Friends
  and Influence
  People
- The Trouble with
  Computers
- The Media Equation
- Radical Equations
- Galileo's Daughter

The Rise of the Network
Society
_____

How to Win Friends and
Influence People
_____

The Trouble with
Computers
_____

The Media Equation
_____

Radical Equations
_____

Galileo's Daughter

K9.3

Figure K9.3

Bullets and dividing bars can be used to separate links that word-wrap.

of word wrapping well (see Figure K9.1). Headlines are in larger fonts and
thus are visually separated from the text below. Figure K9.3 demonstrates
how you can use bulleted lists and dividing bars to separate links.

✳ SOLUTION

**Use descriptive, longer link names that act as a preview of the linked page. Cre-
ate the link name by summarizing the linked page in a few words. Use familiar
language, and be sure to differentiate links that have similar names. Finally,
make sure that any links with long names that word-wrap are clearly differentiated from other links.**

Figure K9.4

Use descriptive, longer
link names to link to
other content pages.

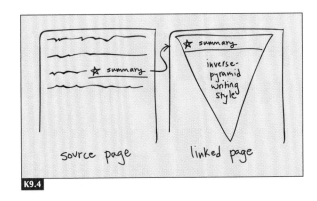

K9.4

✳ CONSIDER THESE OTHER PATTERNS

Write descriptive, longer link names in FAMILIAR LANGUAGE (K11). Use them with OBVIOUS LINKS (K10) to make it clear that they are links customers can click on. EMBEDDED LINKS (K7) also benefit from descriptive, longer link names. It's easy to create link names for pages with content written in an INVERSE-PYRAMID WRITING STYLE (D7) because the title is usu- ally a good summary of the content.

Improve SITE ACCESSIBILITY (B9) with better link names so that cus- tomers with limited access can jump over and navigate through links without having to move slowly through an entire page.

Figure K10.1

Note how quickly you can determine on LUGNET's site which links have already been visited and which have not. Pages that use colors other than blue for links can be confusing because visitors have to learn new rules.

K10.1

(www.lugnet.com, May 23, 2002)

✳ BACKGROUND

Text links can come in the form of NAVIGATION BARS (K2), LOCATION BREAD CRUMBS (K6), EMBEDDED LINKS (K7), and EXTERNAL LINKS (K8). However, it is not always clear which text on a Web page is a link. Most of your customers know that a blue underlined link is an unvisited link. It is possible to change this color or remove the underline, but doing so comes with the risk of confusing some of your customers. This pattern describes the advantages of sticking with blue underlined links and discusses some of the trade-offs.

✳ PROBLEM

It is not always clear which bits of text are links for customers to click.

As you undoubtedly know, most Web sites normally use <u>blue underlined text</u> for unvisited links. You might think that blue links are ugly, are hard to read, and clutter the page, but there is an advantage to using blue underlined text.

Blue links have been part of the Web experience from the very beginning, and customers expect unvisited links to be blue and underlined. Most Web sites still follow this convention. In fact, we took a look at Jupiter Media Metrix's March 2002 25 most-visited Web sites worldwide, at www.jmm.com. Sixteen of the 25 used blue links for a significant portion of their Web site.

Changing your link colors might help differentiate you from the crowd, but Web sites have to provide as many reasons as possible to keep customers coming back. Research shows that ease of use is a critical factor, and because your visitors will spend far more time on other Web sites than on yours, it makes sense to do what everyone else is doing. Blue links may not be the best design, but you have to remember that your Web site is just one of several million out there.

We are not saying that every Web site should have only blue links. You have to balance the trade-offs. Here are some tips for making the most of your link colors.

Avoid Using Blue Text for Anything Other than Web Links • Blue is harder to see than other colors because of the basic physiological structure of the human eye. More important, though, blue text looks like a Web link, and customers will be misled by what appears to be something they can click on. For these reasons, avoid blue text.

Avoid Underlining Anything Other than Web Links • Underlined text often looks like a link and can confuse your customers. Underline nonhyperlinked text sparingly, if at all.

Make Links More Attractive by Using Different Font Sizes and Styles • If you are building a menu, experiment with blue links in a sans serif font like Verdana, Geneva, Arial, or Helvetica. If you have a headline, try making the headline link a little larger and in a sans serif font, to make it look less busy.[4] Figure K10.2 shows how CNET News.com uses larger, sans serif fonts for headlines.

Figure K10.2

CNET News.com uses Arial and a larger font size to differentiate headlines from other text.

Ticketmaster dives headfirst into baseball
Baseball's Seattle Mariners and Ticketmaster Online-Citysearch have a pitch for fans: name your own price for tickets to the ballgame.
July 16, 8:00 p.m. PT in <u>E-Business</u>

Napster founder gets copyright-friendly with new firm
AppleSoup, a new company started by one of Napster's original founders, aims to allow fast, cheap distribution for entertainment products--but with the copyright holders' permission.
July 16, 5:00 p.m. PT in <u>Entertainment & Media</u>

Verizon To launch mobile Net service
Verizon Wireless plans to unveil its version of the wireless Internet tomorrow with a new service for cell phones named Mobile Web.
July 16, 4:20 p.m. PT in <u>Communications</u>

K10.2

(www.news.cnet.com, July 2001)

Use the TITLE Attribute with Text Links • If you use text-based HTML links using the *<a href='...'>* tag, familiarize yourself with the TITLE attribute. The new TITLE attribute in HTML 4.0 allows you to annotate links with a description, in a way similar to how the ALT attribute works for the IMG tag. Currently, Microsoft's Internet Explorer (version 4.0 and up) and Netscape Navigator (6.0 and up) are the only widely used Web browsers that supports this attribute, displaying it as a tool tip. However, future Web browsers may use it as well. For example, audio browsers could read the TITLE attribute to know where a link goes, providing better SITE **(B9)** ACCESSIBILITY (B9). Although this feature is not widely supported yet, we highly recommend using it because it prepares your Web site for the future.

Here's an example of the TITLE attribute:

```
<A HREF="http://www.site.com" TITLE="Your comment">Link text</A>
```

And here's how this TITLE attribute looks in Microsoft's Internet Explorer 5.0:

---

4 A general rule of thumb is to use sans serif fonts for titles and headers and serif fonts for text.

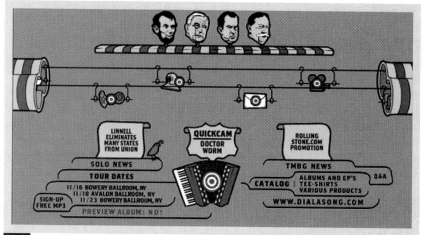

(www.tmbg.com, February 1, 2001)

Figure K10.3

The primary goal of this Web site is fun, not ease of use. In cases like this, things like blue links may not necessarily make sense.

Avoid Using Colors Associated with Color Deficiency • Color deficiency (commonly known as *color blindness*) is a common problem among males (see Chapter 3—Knowing Your Customers: Principles and Techniques). For this reason, if you choose to change your link colors, avoid red and green as a color pair for unvisited and visited links.

3

Use Different Colors for Links If You're Designing a Web Site as a Puzzle, as an Art Piece, or for Fun • If you intend an interface for deliberate exploration or artistic purposes, a site can break the rules we have established in the preceding sections because visitors are there for fun. Figure K10.3 shows the Web site for the quirky band They Might Be Giants. The strange design of the Web site successfully reflects the personality of the band.

✴ SOLUTION

Use blue underlined text for hyperlinks. Avoid using blue or underlines for anything other than Web links. Make links more attractive by using different font sizes and styles. Use the TITLE attribute with text links, and to improve site accessibility, avoid using colors associated with color deficiency. Try different colors or links if you're designing a Web site as a puzzle, as an art piece, or for fun.

Figure K10.4

Stick with blue underlined text for hyperlinks.

✳ CONSIDER THESE OTHER PATTERNS

(K2) NAVIGATION BARS (K2) are one place where blue underlined links do not always make sense. People know they can click on some things on a Web page, and navigation bars have become so common that it is not always necessary to make such text blue and underlined.

(K7) (K8)
(K6)
(K11)
(K9) Use obvious links with EMBEDDED LINKS (K7), EXTERNAL LINKS (K8), and LOCATION BREAD CRUMBS (K6) to make them all easier to see. Use obvious links with FAMILIAR LANGUAGE (K11) and DESCRIPTIVE, LONGER LINK NAMES (K9) to make them easier to understand.

(K4) Use ACTION BUTTONS (K4) as an alternative to obvious links. However, use buttons sparingly and only when you need customers to take a specific action. Graphical buttons take up more space and can take longer to download.

(B9) Using obvious links can make access to your Web site easier for people who are blind and people who use mobile phones to connect to the Internet. For these reasons, obvious links improve your SITE ACCESSIBILITY (B9).

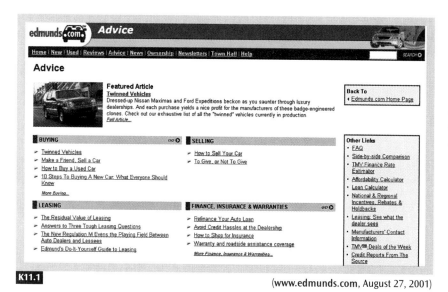

Figure K11.1

Edmunds.com has a friendly site that provides detailed information about automobiles using simple, understandable language.

(**www.edmunds.com**, August 27, 2001)

✳ BACKGROUND

BROWSABLE CONTENT (B2) discussed techniques for structuring the entire Web site in a way that customers understand. This pattern is an extension of that one, continuing the process of naming links on individual pages, and extending it to all text on the site, including CLEAR FIRST READS (I3) and INVERSE-PYRAMID WRITING STYLE (D7). This pattern describes why you should use language familiar to your customers throughout your site, and how you can identify which terms to use to simplify the task of navigation.

✳ PROBLEM

Unfamiliar terms and link names make understanding and navigating a Web site difficult.

Sometimes Web sites are hard to use because there is a chasm between how you see the world and how your customers see the world. One cause of this rift is the mismatch in the language used. Words familiar to you may not be familiar to your customers. Customers often get confused when faced with unfamiliar terms, and this confusion can lead them to become lost in your Web site.

The key to bridging this chasm is understanding the target customers from their point of view. What terms and concepts are familiar? What words do they use to describe things? What expressions and idioms do they use to talk about the world? Understanding how customers think is crucial for writing content and creating link names that they will find understandable and predictable.

Observe and Interview Your Customers • Understand the customer's perspective by ethnographically observing how your customers go about doing things. To do this you will have to follow some people around for a few days to see who they communicate with, what kinds of forms they use, what kinds of tools they use, and what kinds of things they do. Another approach is to interview customers in their workplaces. Have them take you through the steps of their work. These two techniques—ethnographic observation and interviewing—are described in greater detail in Chapter 3—Knowing Your Customers: Principles and Techniques. Note the types of terminology and language your customers use. Also pay special attention to writing at a ninth- or tenth-grade reading level unless your audience is highly sophisticated or much less sophisticated.

Use Card Sorting to Help Structure the Information on Your Web Site • The purpose of card sorting is to give you a better idea of how customers organize information. Give participants a stack of cards, each of which has a label representing a Web page or a set of Web pages, and have participants organize the cards in a way that is meaningful to them, grouping the cards and explaining the reasons for their grouping choices. See what names they use for the groups. These might be good names to use on your site. This technique is also used for creating BROWSABLE CONTENT (B2) and is described in more detail in Chapter 3—Knowing Your Customers: Principles and Techniques.

Test Link Names through Category Identification and Description • Use two related techniques—category identification and category description—to test the usefulness and usability of your link names, independent of visual design and layout.

In **category identification**, present recruited participants with a list of link names that would appear on a page. The links might be grouped together as they would on the Web page, but there is no other content or layout. Also give participants a set of tasks. For each task, ask them to select the link that they think will take them to the right page, and to rate the confidence of their choice on a scale of 1 to 3. This technique provides useful feedback about how well potential customers can map from a given task to the navigation provided on your Web page to complete the task. It also checks if potential customers can differentiate link names. Link names that are too similar will cause people to choose the wrong link. Category identification will help you spot this problem early in the design process.

Category description is the flip side of category identification. In category description, ask participants to examine the same list of links and describe what they expect to find by clicking on each. This technique helps identify unfamiliar or potentially ambiguous link names. It also checks if other people's expectations of page content match yours.

✳ SOLUTION

Use language that your target customers understand. Observe and interview representative customers so that you can empathize with the way they see and understand the world. Use techniques such as card sorting, category identification, and category description to get a better feel for how they organize, structure, and describe things. Use all of this information to create content and links that your customers will find understandable and predictable.

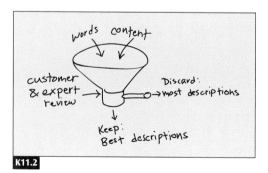

K11.2

Figure K11.2

Ask your customers to review the language you intend to use on your site.

❊ CONSIDER THESE OTHER PATTERNS

B2 Whereas BROWSABLE CONTENT (B2) addresses issues dealing with the entire site structure, this pattern deals more with the names of links on specific pages.

K2 **K10** Apply this pattern when you're developing names for links in NAVIGATION BARS (K2) and OBVIOUS LINKS (K10). This pattern is key for developing DESCRIPTIVE, LONGER LINK NAMES (K9).
K9

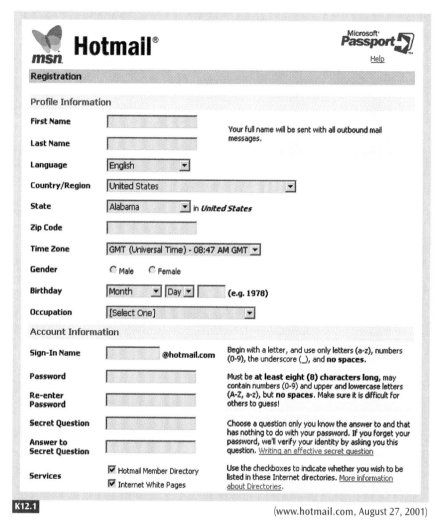

Figure K12.1

MSN Hotmail makes it clear what kinds of information and formatting are required for creating a new account.

K12.1

(www.hotmail.com, August 27, 2001)

❋ BACKGROUND

Web sites need to be engineered for errors, minimizing the number that can occur and providing MEANINGFUL ERROR MESSAGES (K13) when they inevitably happen. This pattern focuses on minimizing the errors for a common source of errors: online forms.

✳ PROBLEM

Customers will make errors and generate erroneous data when faced with online forms that have little structure, include no formatting directions, and are not designed to account for errors from the start.

Errors cause frustration, result in poor performance, and lead to a lack of trust in your site. Errors are common when customers are asked to fill out online forms. Some text input fields require a specific kind of data, such as a name or a phone number, but give very few hints as to what exactly is needed. Often site visitors will try to fill out these forms with what they think is the right data, only to get obscure error messages saying that they did something wrong.

Use Structured Fields, Examples, or Explanatory Text to Provide Hints about the Expected Format • Minimize errors by providing fields to clarify the required format. Figure K12.2 shows two text input fields asking for a customer's phone number. The first one is error-prone. Is "555.5555" acceptable? Is "(510) 555 5555" acceptable? What about "510-555-5555"? It simply is not clear, and it is likely that whatever the person types in will be wrong. Now look at the second example. It has separate fields for the area code and the phone number, leaving no chance for error.

However, structured text input fields can also be misleading. In Figure K12.3, for example, the three input fields, from left to right, are supposed to be for area code, phone number, and extension. However, people might mistakenly think that the extension field is for the last four digits of the phone number.

You can also minimize errors by providing sample values. Figure K12.4 shows a text field with a sample phone number to show customers the format you expect. Providing explanatory text is a third way of helping to prevent errors (see Figure K12.5).

Make Sure the Software Accepts Multiple Formats • A fourth approach to preventing errors in text input fields—slightly more complex from a programming standpoint—is to allow multiple kinds of formatting and have

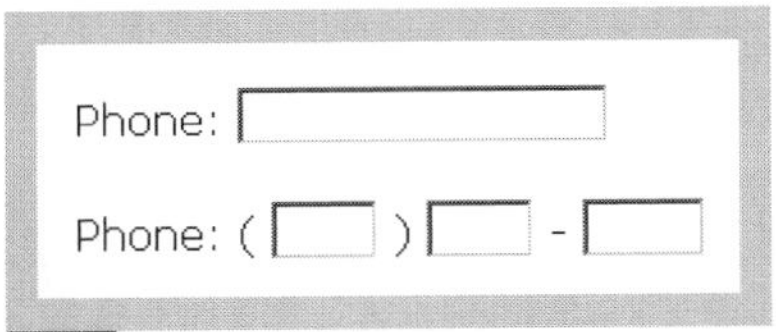

Figure K12.2

Here are two text input fields for a customer's phone number. The first one gives no hint as to how the visitor should format the phone number. The second one makes the required formatting clear.

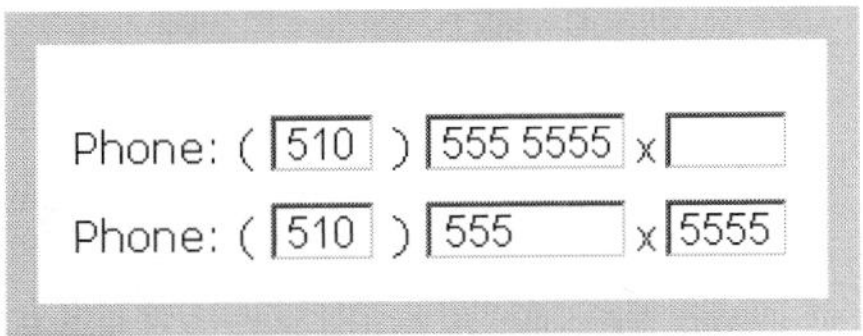

Figure K12.3

These two examples show how even structured text input fields can sometimes be misleading.

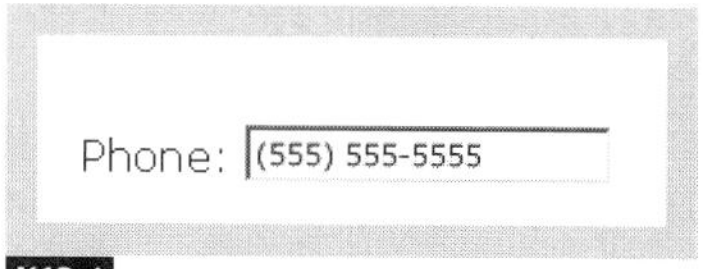

Phone: (555) 555-5555

K12.4

Ex. (510) 555-5555

Phone:

K12.5

Figure K12.4

Providing a default value of how the data should look helps to prevent errors.

Figure K12.5

The example showing how the data should look can also be given in the form of explanatory text.

the computer figure out what the value should be. For example, a credit card field could let people type in credit card numbers with or without spaces. A phone field could allow all the different kinds of formatting for phone numbers. When the processing is straightforward and unambiguous, as with credit card numbers, you should allow flexible formatting.

Make Clear Which Fields Are Required and Which Are Optional • A fifth approach to error prevention informs customers which fields are required so that they can concern themselves with the important information. These fields must be clearly marked with a symbol that is explained in a footnote (see Figure K12.6) or a text label such as *required*.

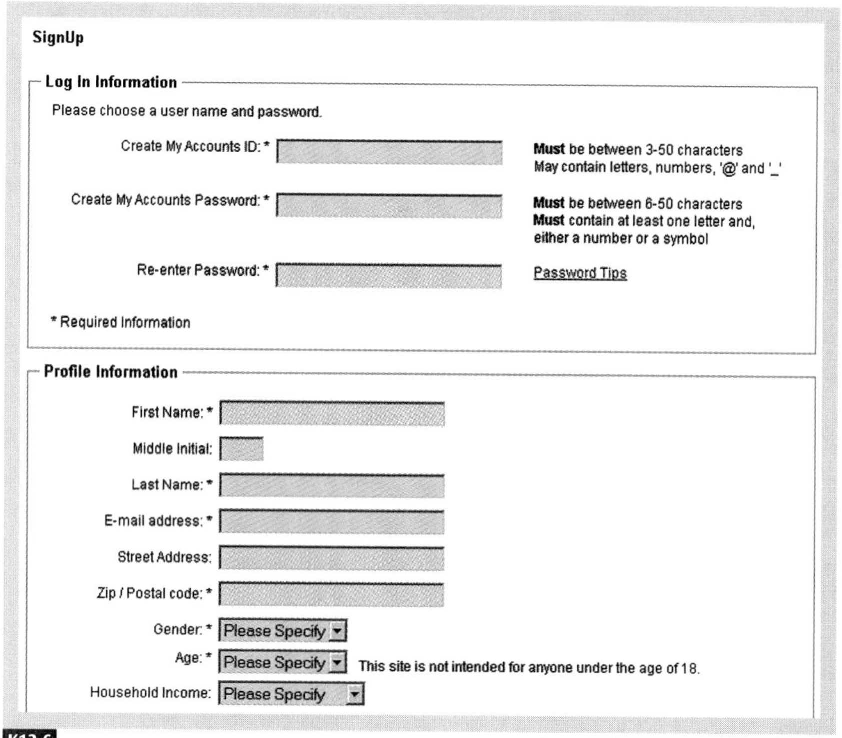

Figure K12.6

Prevent errors by indicating which fields are required. The site pictured here uses the asterisk for this purpose. It is important to explain the required symbol in a place where it will be read.

SignUp

Log In Information

Please choose a user name and password.

Create My Accounts ID: *   **Must** be between 3-50 characters
May contain letters, numbers, '@' and '_'

Create My Accounts Password: *   **Must** be between 6-50 characters
Must contain at least one letter and,
either a number or a symbol

Re-enter Password: *   Password Tips

* Required Information

Profile Information

First Name: *

Middle Initial:

Last Name: *

E-mail address: *

Street Address:

Zip / Postal code: *

Gender: * Please Specify

Age: * Please Specify   This site is not intended for anyone under the age of 18.

Household Income: Please Specify

K12.6

(**www.myciti.com**, August 21, 2000)

✳ SOLUTION

Provide hints about what kind of text input you expect from your customers. You can do this by providing fields showing formatting, by providing sample values in the fields, or by providing explanatory text. Whenever it is simple to do so, allow flexible formatting and have the computer determine the correct format. Also make clear which fields are required and which are optional so that customers will not have to guess.

Figure K12.7

Prevent errors by providing sample formatting and differentiating between required fields and optional fields.

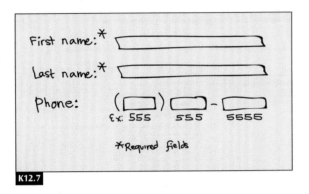

K12.7

✳ CONSIDER THESE OTHER PATTERNS

No matter how well a site is designed to prevent errors, some errors will still occur. In these situations, present MEANINGFUL ERROR MESSAGES (K13) to help people recover. Preventing errors is especially important for PROCESS FUNNELS (H1), such as SIGN-IN/NEW ACCOUNT (H2) and QUICK-FLOW CHECKOUT (F1).

K13

H1 H2
F1

K13 MEANINGFUL ERROR MESSAGES

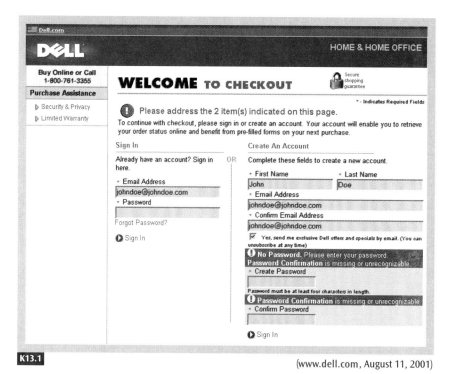

Figure K13.1

Dell's Web page handles errors in the checkout with two error messages, which are positioned near the problem area. These error messages state the problem and what customers must do to fix it.

K13.1

(www.dell.com, August 11, 2001)

✳ BACKGROUND

Web sites need to be engineered for PREVENTING ERRORS (K12), as well as making it easy to recover from errors. This pattern focuses on providing meaningful error messages that smooth the recovery process.

✳ PROBLEM

When customers make mistakes, they need to be gently informed of the problem and how to gracefully recover, or the error condition may persist.

No matter how well a site is designed, people will make occasional errors —some accidental and some because of misunderstanding. In both cases, your Web site needs to provide meaningful error messages designed to help your customers recover from errors. Meaningful error messages have four characteristics in common:

1. Clear statement of the problem
2. Avoidance of humor
3. Explanation of how to recover
4. Positioning near the problem

Provide Clear Error Messages without Assigning Blame • A meaningful error message clearly states the problem in FAMILIAR LANGUAGE (K11) and without blame. Examples of poor error messages include "Error code 15," "Invalid syntax," and "You entered bad data." The first two messages provide no useful information about the problem. The third message places blame on the person by using a you statement, as in "You did this wrong." These kinds of statements can usually be rewritten to avoid placing any blame.

Avoid Injecting Humor into Error Messages • Humor should also be avoided in error messages. Errors can be frustrating, and although humor may help some people, it may also aggravate others. Furthermore, what is funny in one language, culture, or mood may not be funny in another.

Explain How to Recover from the Error • Meaningful error messages provide steps that people can take to recover from the problem. Some examples include offering instructions on what went wrong and how to recover, listing an e-mail address for questions, and providing a phone number that people can call for more information.

In the case of providing instructions, it is better to tell people how to use the system instead of describing the system. For example, the message, "Items can be removed from the shopping cart by clicking on the **Remove** button," can be rephrased as, "To remove an item from the shopping cart, click on the **Remove** button."

Place the Error Message near the Problem It Identifies • Good error messages are presented spatially near the problem area in a visually apparent manner. A common design mistake is to put error messages on a completely separate page, with no context. This approach forces people to remember the problem, hit the **Back** button, wait for the previous page to load, find the problem area, and then try to fix it. Figure K13.1 shows a better design: re-creating the page where the error occurred and placing error messages near the problem areas. This approach makes it easy to find and fix problems.

Another common design mistake is to make error messages look like the rest of the Web page. These kinds of error messages are hard to find because they do not stand out and often leave customers puzzled about why they're still on the same page. Use fonts, icons, and colors that are distinct from the rest of the Web page to highlight the error message and direct your visitors' attention to the right place.

✴ SOLUTION

Provide meaningful error messages in familiar language without assigning blame and without trivializing the problem with humor. State the severity of the problem and provide steps that customers can take to recover. Display the error message near the problem area, and highlight it to make it stand out visually.

K13.2

Figure K13.2

Provide simple, blame-free error messages that let people know what's wrong and what to do.

✳ CONSIDER THESE OTHER PATTERNS

K12 A Web site design should focus first on PREVENTING ERRORS (K12), resorting to error messages only as a fallback. Error messages should always use
K11 FAMILIAR LANGUAGE (K11).

Meaningful error messages are especially important for PROCESS FUNNELS
H1 H2 F1 (H1), such as SIGN-IN/NEW ACCOUNT (H2) and QUICK-FLOW CHECKOUT (F1).

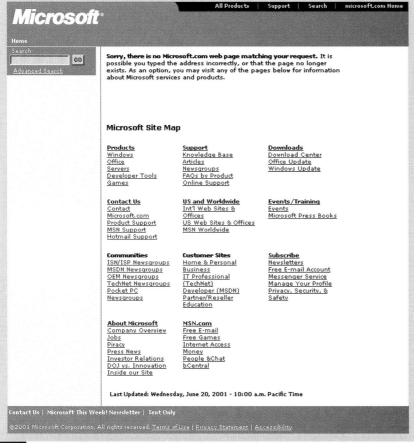

K14.1

(www.microsoft.com, August 24, 2001)

Figure K14.1

Microsoft has a special page that it displays if it cannot find a page. This page helps customers who may be lost by providing a meaningful error message, a site map with an overview, a search form, and basic navigation to the main portions of the Web site.

✳ BACKGROUND

Because pages are moved around as a Web site evolves, invariably some customers will get a "Page not found" error. This pattern looks at customizing the error message to make it easier for visitors to recover from this error.

✳ PROBLEM

Sometimes customers click on links, type in URLs, or have bookmarks for pages that no longer exist, resulting in the dreaded "Page not found" error message or, even worse, "Error 404."

Customers might try to access a page that does not exist. Perhaps the page they came from had a bad link, perhaps the page was moved, or perhaps they typed in the link incorrectly. In any case, you need to inform visitors that the page they're looking for cannot be found, and give them some ways of recovering.

Fortunately, most Web servers let you customize the "Page not found" page. You can make this page display an error message saying that the page cannot be found. You can also add a SEARCH ACTION MODULE (J1) and a NAVIGATION BAR (K2), making it easy for customers to continue browsing and searching (see Figure K14.1). Providing a site map along with the most common links can help your customers see the overall structure of the Web site and direct them to the right place. Finally, including a link to the maintainers of the Web site makes it easy for visitors to send e-mail describing any problems with the site.

Check your Web log files to find out where people are encountering "Page not found" errors. If they are coming from a specific Web site, send a message to the maintainers at that Web site, stating what the old link was and requesting that they update it with the new link. Also create a Web page at the old location that will take visitors to the new location. You can do this using the REFRESH META tag as follows:

```
<meta http-equiv=Refresh
content="0;url=http://www.yoursite.com/newlocation.html">
```

✳ SOLUTION

Create a custom "Page not found" Web page that makes it easy for customers to browse or search for the content they were expecting to find.

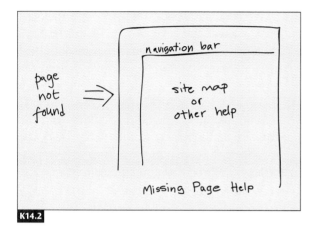

K14.2

Figure K14.2

A "Page not found" page should let customers know that the page is missing and help them find their way back into the Web site.

✳ CONSIDER THESE OTHER PATTERNS

A "Page not found" page needs to have a MEANINGFUL ERROR MESSAGE (K13) explaining that the page could not be found. It should also provide some ways for customers to continue navigating the Web site, such as a NAVIGATION BAR (K2) and a SEARCH ACTION MODULE (J1).

Speeding Up Your Site

Slow Web sites are frustrating to use. A slow homepage can have a major impact on customers' first experience with a site. They might not wait around to find out what you have to offer. Remember, most customers are still connecting to the Web using slow, analog modems. Even if you're designing a business site, many of your customers will be accessing your site from home, after work hours, or from a laptop on the road.

We have done some research on the techniques you can apply to speed up your Web site. It is just as important to speed up the *perceived* speed of your site. This pattern group describes ways to make your Web site look and feel fast.

L1 LOW NUMBER OF FILES

L2 FAST-DOWNLOADING IMAGES

L3 SEPARATE TABLES

L4 HTML POWER

L5 REUSABLE IMAGES

L1 LOW NUMBER OF FILES

L1.1

(www.yahoo.com, August 26, 2001)

Figure L1.1

Yahoo's homepage has a minimalist design with very few images, making it fast to download. (Reproduced with permission of Yahoo! © 2000 by Yahoo! Inc. YAHOO! and the YAHOO! logo are trademarks of Yahoo! Inc.)

✳ BACKGROUND

You can make your Web site pages faster to download by minimizing the number of files contained in those pages. This pattern can be used by itself, or in conjunction with other patterns for making fast-downloading Web pages, such as FAST-DOWNLOADING IMAGES (L2), SEPARATE TABLES (L3), and HTML POWER (L4).

❄ PROBLEM

Web pages that have many images, audio files, applets, and plug-ins are slow to download.

Web surfers are an impatient bunch. It's not called the "World Wide Wait" for nothing. As a Web designer, you face a dilemma. You want your customer to see many items, such as the company logo, navigation bars, a good-looking background, maybe an ad or two, a few images, and lots of text. However, the more image, audio, applet, and plug-in files you put on a Web page, the longer it takes for visitors to download it, and the more frustrated they become.

The key is to minimize the number of files that absolutely must be transferred. Fewer files equals shorter download time because there are fewer bytes to transfer, and because the Web browser does not have to communicate as often with the Web server.

Four approaches minimize the number of files that must be downloaded:

1. Removing unnecessary image, audio, applet, and plug-in files
2. Using HTML features instead of images, where it makes sense
3. Reusing images
4. Moving slow, large files off of pages that need to be fast

Remove Unnecessary Image, Audio, Applet, and Plug-in Files • This approach applies our aesthetic and minimalist design principle (see Chapter 4—Involving Customers with Iterative Design). If removing the file does no harm to the site, take it out. Every extra element draws attention away from the elements that really matter. Removing the extra elements means that Web pages download faster.

Use HTML Features Instead of Images, Where It Makes Sense • This approach takes advantage of the fact that HTML supports buttons, lines, and backgrounds, so you do not have to use images. The features you implement using HTML POWER (L4) in HTML will load much faster.

Reuse Images • This approach makes use of how Web browsers cache to temporarily store files that it has already downloaded. Images that are reused do not have to be downloaded again.

Move Slow, Large Files Off of Pages That Need to Be Fast • This approach advocates moving large image, audio, applet, and plug-in files to a separate, linked page. That way customers get a fast response, and they can preview the large file and decide whether they want it without having to download the whole thing. A good way to create FAST-DOWNLOADING IMAGES (L2) is to present a page of **thumbnails**, or small versions of the original image, each linked to larger versions.

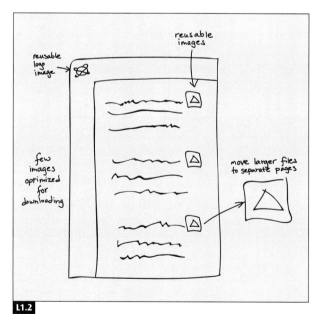

The number of files that require transfer must be reduced on a page-by-page basis. Prioritize your site's pages, and then focus your efforts on making the most important pages faster. If your site has not yet been deployed, you will have to make an educated guess as to which pages are the most important. Likely candidates are the homepage and the pages supporting the most common tasks you expect visitors to want to do. If you already have a live site, analyze your server logs to find your most popular pages.

❋ SOLUTION

Determine your most important pages and focus your efforts on tuning those pages for download performance. Minimize the number of files that absolutely must be downloaded for each page. Take advantage of features in HTML and in Web browsers that minimize the number of images customers have to download. In addition, move slow-loading objects from the most important pages to other pages, and provide links to and previews of them instead.

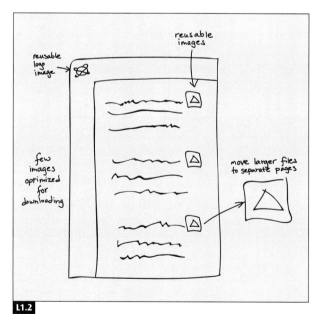

Figure L1.2

Use a variety of techniques to minimize the number of files that are downloaded with each Web page.

L1.2

❋ CONSIDER THESE OTHER PATTERNS

L4
L5
Apply HTML POWER (L4) to use HTML in place of images. Use REUSABLE IMAGES (L5) throughout your site so that you can amortize the download cost.

L2 **L3**
Use a low number of files in conjunction with FAST-DOWNLOADING IMAGES (L2) and SEPARATE TABLES (L3) to greatly improve the download time of individual Web pages.

C1 **F1**
Two important pages you can optimize for a low number of files are the HOMEPAGE PORTAL (C1) and the QUICK-FLOW CHECKOUT (F1).

L2 FAST-DOWNLOADING IMAGES

L2.1

(www.geocaching.com, February 1, 2002)

Figure L2.1

The Geocaching Web site uses small images that are optimized for download.

✳ BACKGROUND

Images are often the slowest-loading part of a Web page. Reducing the size of an image can have significant impact on how visitors perceive your Web site. This pattern describes techniques for reducing the sizes of images, and it can be applied to images you already use or to images you are about to deploy. This pattern can be used by itself or in conjunction with other patterns for making fast-downloading Web pages, such as LOW NUMBER OF FILES (L1), SEPARATE TABLES (L3), and HTML POWER (L4).

✳ PROBLEM

Large images are slow to download.

Reducing the sizes of images can significantly speed up your customers' experience on your Web site. However, reducing the size of an image can also reduce the quality of that image. There are trade-offs you must consider when balancing image quality and image size. Three main approaches to reducing the file size of images are **cropping** (reducing the file size of an image by trimming unneeded portions of the image), **shrinking** (scaling down the entire image), and **compressing** (reducing the number of colors used in an image or intentionally degrading the overall quality of an image, thereby reducing the amount of information required to encode the image).

Understand the Strengths and Weaknesses of the Different Image File Formats • At this writing, the two most popular file formats for images are GIF and JPEG. GIF images are good for small icons. The GIF file format can have up to 256 colors. It supports transparency and can compress the image file size without losing any information. JPEG images are good for photograph-quality images. The JPEG file format can have several million colors, but it does not support transparency, and it throws away some data to get better compression.

A new file format that has recently emerged is PNG (Portable Network Graphics). Developed by the World Wide Web Consortium (W3C), PNG is an improvement on GIF and JPEG. PNG was created as an alternative to GIF because Unisys Corporation decided to enforce its patent on GIF, specifically on software tools that output it. The problem is that only the most recent Web browsers support PNG. Wait until more people have Web browsers that support PNG before switching to it.

Reduce the Number of Colors • Reducing color depth works only in certain cases. For GIF and PNG files, it can help reduce file sizes. For JPEG images, though, reducing color depth can sometimes make file sizes *bigger,* and it will have a significant impact on image quality. You will have to experiment to find what works for your images. Do not employ gradients because they will require a much larger color palette.

Crop and Shrink Images • Cropping and shrinking are two common techniques for making images smaller. **Cropping** means cutting the edges of an image out; **shrinking** means resizing the entire image (see Figure L2.2).

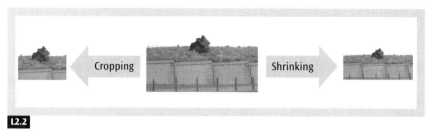

L2.2

Figure L2.2

Cropping makes an image smaller by removing a portion of it; shrinking resizes the entire image.

Cropping and shrinking are often used to create thumbnails, the small images we mentioned earlier. Thumbnails are fast to download, but they also provide access, by their links, to the larger images. A smart way to make small yet legible thumbnails is to first crop the image to the relevant portion of the material, and then shrink the cropped image.

A common way of presenting a large number of images is the thumbnail page (see Figure L2.3). This design allows customers to browse through a large set of images quickly. You can also provide the file size or a download time estimate for the larger image so that people will know if it will take a long time to download.

Use Higher Compression Ratios on Images • A common technique for reducing image file sizes, compression, is done automatically for you with GIF and PNG files. GIF and PNG use **lossless compression**, meaning that image file sizes are reduced without any loss in image quality.

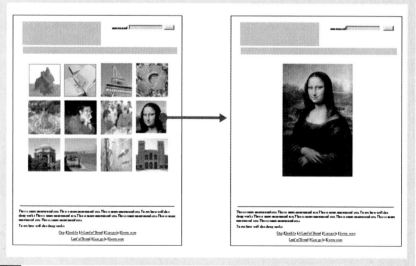

L2.3

Figure L2.3

Clicking on a thumbnail image brings up the full-sized version.

In contrast, you must choose a compression rate with JPEG. The problem is that JPEG uses **lossy compression**, meaning that some of the image quality is sacrificed for smaller file sizes. In other words, the higher the compression rate, the smaller the file size but the lower the image quality. When you're dealing with JPEG files, you have to be careful because you can lose a lot of image quality as you keep working with it. One workaround is to save your image in a different file format and convert it to a JPEG when you're ready. Another is to keep older versions of your JPEG images so that you can always revert to one of higher quality.

Figure L2.4 compares techniques that reduce image sizes. Note the degradation in the image quality as higher levels of compression are used.

Use Progressive-Scan and Interlaced Images • The key idea here is that **progressive-scan** and **interlaced images** let visitors see the image as it is loading, making the Web page feel more responsive. Figure L2.5 shows a progressive-scan JPEG image as it is loading. Figure L2.6 shows an interlaced GIF image as it is loading.

Figure L2.4

Various techniques can be used to reduce the sizes of images. Higher levels of compression yield images of lower quality.

Original photo is a progressive JPEG with low compression. The size of the image is 34K.

Original photo, shrunk by 50%. The size is now 11K.

Original photo, cropped by 50%. The size is now 10K.

Original image, medium compression. The size is now 12K.

Original image, high compression. The size is now 8K.

Original photo with very high compression. Size is now 5K.

L2.4

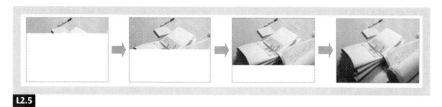

Figure L2.5

When a progressive-scan JPEG image is loading, visitors see the image load from top to bottom.

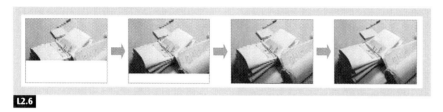

Figure L2.6

When an interlaced GIF image is loading, visitors see first a blurry image, then progressive refinement. Note the graininess in the third image and compare it to the cleaner lines in the fourth. Also compare the quality of the final image to that of the example shown in Figure L2.5.

With progressive-scan JPEG images, the files are usually smaller than regular JPEG files. The opposite is true of interlaced GIF. It can cost a few extra kilobytes to make an interlaced GIF file, but in many cases the faster response time is worth the extra storage space.

Use the Height and Width Attributes for Images • Specifying a height and width makes it easier for older Web browsers to lay out the entire page. The browser does not have to wait for all the images to be downloaded before displaying content. Your customers will think that the page is loading faster, especially if some of the images are below the fold.

Use the ALT Attribute with All Images • Using the ALT attribute with all images (on IMG tags) lets customers with slow network connections see the names of images even before they have loaded (see Figure L2.7). More details on how to use the ALT attribute are provided in the SITE ACCESSIBILITY (B9) pattern.

Consider Combining Small Images That Are Close Together • If you design a page with lots of small images, it can take a long time to download because of the communication overhead of requesting and sending each image. Reduce the overall number of bytes that are downloaded by combining small images into a larger image (see Figure L2.8). If you use the small images as links, the larger image can be made clickable by the use of client-side image maps in the HTML. One trick to be aware of is entering the text name of the link as part of the image. See ACTION BUTTONS (K4) for an example.

Figure L2.7

The first screen shot here shows what a customer sees on a Web page that uses image ALT attributes as it loads. Customers can click on the links without waiting for the images to load. The second screen shot shows the same Web page without ALT attributes.

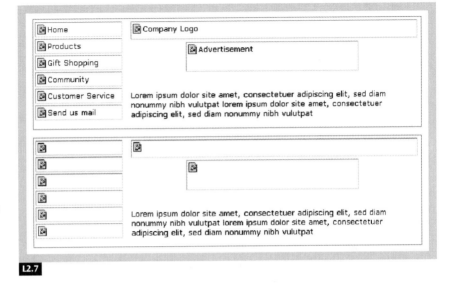

L2.7

Figure L2.8

Combining small images into one larger image speeds up the download. Place an image map on top of the larger image to make it clickable.

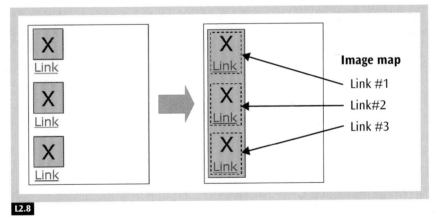

L2.8

One trade-off of combining small images is that you lose the ability to display ALT text for each individual image (see Figure L2.9). You can still label each active region in an HTML image with ALT text, but currently Web browsers do not display these labels.

Focus Your Effort on the Main Web Pages First • Consider shrinking, cropping, compressing, or moving large images off of your homepage and other heavy-traffic Web pages first. These are the pages that customers use the most, so make them fast first.

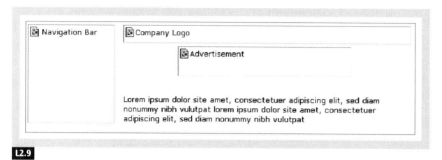

L2.9

Figure L2.9

If you combine small images, visitors can no longer see each individual bit of ALT text.

✳ SOLUTION

Use a combination of techniques to speed up the downloading of images. Apply these techniques—changing the image file format, reducing colors, cropping and shrinking, using higher compression, and using progressive-scan or interlaced images—to the image itself. Other techniques apply to how the image is used on a Web page and help improve the perceived speed of loading the image, such as including the height and width attributes in the HTML, using the ALT attribute for the IMG tag, and combining small images that are near each other into larger images.

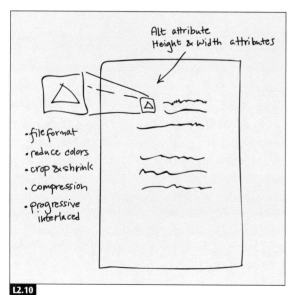

L2.10

Figure L2.10

Apply a variety of techniques, both on the image itself and in how the image is used in the Web page, to make images faster to download.

❊ CONSIDER THESE OTHER PATTERNS

L5 REUSABLE IMAGES (L5) appear to download very quickly, in the eyes of the customer.

K4 K2   ACTION BUTTONS (K4) and NAVIGATION BARS (K2) often contain images that you can tune for download speeds.

(L3) SEPARATE TABLES

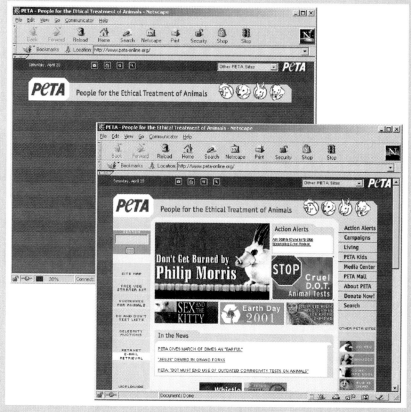

L3.1

(www.petaonline.org, April 20, 2001)

Figure L3.1

This example from the People for the Ethical Treatment of Animals (PETA) site shows separate tables in action. At the top is what a customer sees while the Web page is loading. Note that the logo and some navigation elements are already displayed. At the bottom is what the customer sees after the page has finished loading.

✳ BACKGROUND

This pattern describes ways of simplifying tables and dividing them into smaller tables to make them display faster on Web browsers. This pattern can be applied to Web sites at any stage—whether the sites are about to be developed, or already developed and deployed. Use this pattern alone or in conjunction with other patterns for making fast-downloading Web pages, such as LOW NUMBER OF FILES (L1), FAST-DOWNLOADING IMAGES (L2), REUSABLE IMAGES (L5), and HTML POWER (L4).

✳ PROBLEM

Web pages with long, complex HTML tables take a long time to be displayed in Web browsers.

HTML tables are often used to control the layout of a page. The problem, though, is how much time it takes for Web browsers, especially older browsers, to load these tables. The browser has to calculate height and width of all the text, images, and plug-ins before anything is displayed. The end result is that the Web page feels sluggish.[1]

To make navigation bars and advertisements appear quickly while the rest of the page is still loading, you can split the page into separate tables instead of using one large table. In this approach, the images, text, and tables near the top are displayed first, while the rest of the Web page loads.

The main thing to consider when using separate tables is what should be at the top of the page (see Figure L3.2). Include things like NAVIGATION BARS (K2), and, if possible, CLEAR FIRST READS (I3), and advertisements. Also keep in mind that not everything has to be in an HTML table. See if you can move elements out of a table while maintaining the BASIC GRID LAYOUT (I1) you desire. It will be a little harder to align things in a grid. In

Figure L3.2

Because the top of this page is a separate table, customers can get immediate feedback while the bottom table is loading.

(www.babycenter.com, November 16, 2001)

---

1 Newer Web browsers minimize this problem by recalculating how the table should look as text and images are downloading, instead of all at once at the end. However, until you are sure that the majority of your customers have the latest Web browsers, we recommend dividing long tables into shorter ones.

some cases, the alignment is more important, but this is a trade-off you have to consider on a case-by-case basis.

✳ SOLUTION

Split large HTML tables into completely separate, smaller tables so that each table can be downloaded and displayed independently.

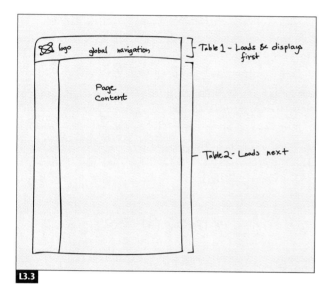

L3.3

Figure L3.3

Use separate tables to let things at the top be loaded first. Put important navigation elements and content in the first table so that people will see them first, while the rest of the page is loading.

✳ CONSIDER THESE OTHER PATTERNS

Consider separate tables when implementing a GRID LAYOUT (I1) in HTML. In some cases, separating the tables or moving things out may make it harder to implement a clear grid.

Decide what will go into the table along the top. Some things to consider include a CLEAR FIRST READ (I3) and NAVIGATION BARS (K2).

Figure L4.1

Craigslist provides a clean, functional, and popular Web site without using any images.

L4.1

(**www.craigslist.org**, August 26, 2001)

✳ BACKGROUND

This pattern describes features built into HTML that help you reduce the number of images on a page so that Web pages have a LOW NUMBER OF FILES (L1) to be transferred. This pattern can be applied to Web sites that you are about to develop or sites you have already developed and deployed. This pattern can be used alone or in conjunction with other patterns for making fast-downloading Web pages, such as FAST-DOWNLOADING IMAGES (L2), SEPARATE TABLES (L3), and REUSABLE IMAGES (L5).

❊ PROBLEM

Images are critical to good Web site design because they provide visual clues about interaction and how the page is organized. Web pages with too many images, however, are slow to download.

Great graphic design is an important part of a customer's experience on a Web site. But the more images you put on your site, the longer the pages take to download. Some designers advocate extreme minimalist design as a solution, with few or no images, but such Web sites are often boring.

HTML has many features built into it that you can use in place of images. For example, you might do any of the following:

- Use the BGCOLOR attribute in the BODY tag in place of an image to set the color of a solid background. Use the same technique in tables so that columns or rows have different colors, making the various areas of your page more obvious.
- Choose text for NAVIGATION BARS (K2).
- Use the UL tag to create the bullets for bulleted lists.
- Choose an HTML button for action buttons.
- Create horizontal lines with the HR tag.

K2

Although you can consider all these alternatives as functional replacements for images, you will have to think through an important trade-off. By using built-in features of HTML to achieve faster-downloading pages, you give up some control over the appearance of a Web page. In some cases this is an acceptable trade-off, but if your Web site relies on a unique look and feel, it can have a serious impact. The solution is to strike a balance between using images and using HTML (see Figure L4.2).

Figure L4.2

The Lincoln Highway site uses HTML features instead of images to handle layout, background colors, and bullets. The result is a simple and clean design that is fast to load.

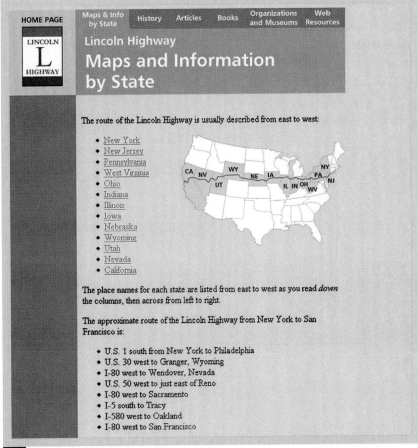

L4.2

(www.ugcs.caltech.edu/~jlin/lincoln, February 11, 2002)

☀ SOLUTION

In places where it is still functional and aesthetically pleasing to do so, use built-in HTML features instead of images.

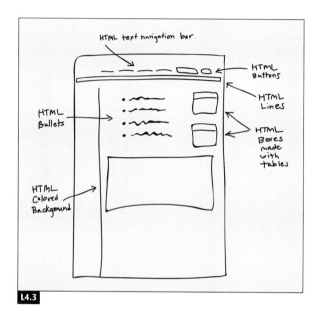

Figure L4.3

Often HTML features, including navigation bars, action buttons, dividing lines, bullets, and backgrounds, can be used in place of images for faster downloading.

L4.3

☀ CONSIDER THESE OTHER PATTERNS

Use this pattern along with REUSABLE IMAGES (L5) to achieve a LOW NUM-BER OF FILES (L1).

If you need ACTION BUTTONS (K4), use HTML as a faster alternative to a custom image. Pure HTML and text can also be used in place of images for NAVIGATION BARS (K2).

Figure L5.1

MP3.com uses many small, reusable graphics to accent its Web pages, including its logo, small question marks for getting help, small plus signs for adding music to a personalized Web site, and small chevrons for playing the music.

L5.1

(www.mp3.com, August 26, 2001)

✳ BACKGROUND

This pattern expands on the ideas in LOW NUMBER OF FILES (L1) and focuses on how you can improve the download speed of your Web site using a special feature found in most Web browsers. Apply this pattern if you are about to develop your site, or if you have already developed and deployed a site. This pattern can be used alone or in conjunction with other patterns for making fast-downloading Web pages, such as FAST-DOWNLOADING IMAGES (L2), SEPARATE TABLES (L3), and HTML POWER (L4).

✳ PROBLEM

A Web browser must download every image that it has not encountered before.

Every well-designed Web browser has the notion of a **cache**, where Web pages and images that have already been downloaded are stored. The basic idea is that if customers go back to a Web page they have seen before, it will be faster to display because it does not have to be downloaded again.

Images are also cached. In fact, if you design your Web pages to reuse the same images, they will seem to display faster (see Figure L5.2). Make sure the images you want to reuse have the same URL. Here's a list of the most reused images on Web sites:

- Accent graphics, such as "New" or "Hot"
- Logos
- Navigation bars
- Stylistic images, such as dividing lines
- Icons, such as those representing mail or shopping carts

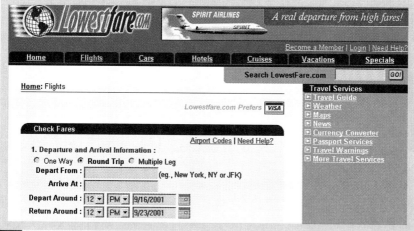

L5.2

(www.lowestfare.com, August 26, 2001)

Figure L5.2

Lowestfare.com makes use of many reusable images for stylistic purposes, such as the small images used to make curved tabs in the tab row and the small white arrows to mark different travel services offered.

✳ SOLUTION

Design your Web pages to use a core set of reusable images. These images will be cached by Web browsers and will be faster to display the next time they're viewed because they will have already been downloaded.

Figure L5.3

Reusable images include logos, navigation bar images, stylistic images, and accent graphics.

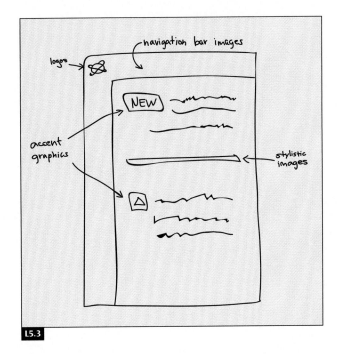

✳ CONSIDER THESE OTHER PATTERNS

Customers will not have to download reused images again. Use this pattern along with HTML POWER (L4) to achieve a LOW NUMBER OF FILES (L1). One trade-off is that in some cases it is easier to reuse many smaller images than to use one large image that contains the smaller images.

Use this pattern in conjunction with other techniques for creating fast Web pages, such as FAST-DOWNLOADING IMAGES (L2) and SEPARATE TABLES (L3).

NAVIGATION BARS (K2) that use images can also be designed to use only text labels, reducing the number of images downloaded.

PART

III

Appendixes

Running Usability Evaluations

Running a usability test with real customers is essential to good design. You may know a lot about your customers, but it is hard to predict how people will react to and interact with a Web site. Usability tests are also effective in ending those endless opinion wars in which members of the design team argue about what people like and don't like. The best way to answer this question is to recruit some participants,[1] run a quick test, and see what they say and do. This appendix lays out the steps for running both formal and informal usability tests, from setting up the test to running the test to analyzing and presenting the results.

Our assumption here is that you want to run a usability test in which both you and the participant are in the same place. You should also be aware that an alternative approach is **remote usability testing**—that is, recruiting and testing many participants online without your having to be there. We discuss how to do this in Appendix E—Online Research.

A.1 Setting Target Goals

What Do You Want to Learn from the Test? • The first thing you have to do is decide what you want to get out of the test. Do you want to find out if people are having problems with a specific part of the Web site? Do you want to see how well a proposed design works? Or do you just want to get general feedback about the existing Web site?

How Will You Get the Information You Want? • After deciding what you want to learn, think about how you will get this information. If people

---

1 In psychology and other fields, the term *subjects* is used instead of *participants*, but we have always felt that the term *subjects* has a slightly sinister tone.

are having problems with a portion of the Web site, the straightforward thing to do is to test tasks that rely on that part and see what the problems are. If you want to test a new design, it is useful to compare it to the old design or to a competitor's Web site. This approach is also useful for getting general feedback about an existing Web site.

Process Data versus Bottom-Line Data • There are two kinds of data that you can get from a usability test: process data and bottom-line data. **Process data** consists of informal, qualitative observations of what people are thinking and doing—an overall feeling of what works and what does not on a Web site. The key things to look for here are **critical incidents**, places on your Web site where participants are confused, frustrated, or even swear. Critical incidents also include cases in which people are pleasantly surprised or say something positive about the site.

In contrast, **bottom-line data** consists of formal, quantitative measurements of what happened, such as the time it takes to complete a task, the number of errors that occur, or the time it takes to learn a task.

In general, you should focus on getting process data first because it gives a good overview of where the problems in a Web site are and because it is easier to get. Process data can also be obtained from low-fidelity paper prototypes, making it a handy technique for the early stages of design.

It takes more work to get and make use of bottom-line data. One reason is that you need to have lots of participants to get statistically reliable results. Another is that bottom-line data does not always tell you what problems need to be fixed, it just tells you that people are going too slowly or are making too many errors. Bottom-line data is better for later phases of design, when you're tuning the performance of an existing Web site. It is also better for comparing two Web site designs, to show that one is superior to another in a particular measurable aspect. Such a comparison can be especially important when you're trying to convince management to make either a major change or a change on an important page, such as the homepage of a high traffic site.

Setting Up the Tasks   A.2

The next step is to choose several representative tasks. By this we mean realistic tasks that your target customers are likely to do on your Web site. Choose some tasks that are simple, some that are of medium difficulty, and some that are hard. Ideally, these tasks will have already been

3

worked out in the task analysis you carried out when learning to know your customers and can just be taken from there (see Chapter 3—Knowing Your Customers: Principles and Techniques).

Simple Tasks Are Short and Performed Often • Simple tasks include things like "Find the latest news article about parenting" or "Find the phone number and e-mail address of the help desk." Success on simple tasks is a binary result: The person either succeeds or fails.

Tasks of Medium Difficulty Are a Little Longer and Harder than Simple Tasks • Examples of medium-difficulty tasks include "Purchase the cheapest printer you can find," "Print out a list of all your previous purchases," and "Add a message to the gourmet cooking community board." These tasks span a few Web pages, but they are reasonable things that people would do. Some medium-difficulty tasks will have binary success metrics; that is, they will either succeed or they will fail. The results of other medium-difficulty tasks will be more open-ended and require further interpretation of the results.

Hard Tasks Span Many Web Pages and Are Fairly Involved • Examples of hard tasks include "Make the Web site show you only the stocks you are interested in," "Buy a digital camera for a friend that he or she will like," and "Buy a toy for your friend's one-year-old child." Most hard tasks are free-form, so it will take some judgment to determine how successful participants are.

Tasks Should Be about What People Want to Do • Be careful not to tell people *how* to do the task. For example, instead of saying, "Go to 'My profile' and find your previous purchases," you should say something like, "Find all of your previous purchases." Again, the task should be worded in the way people would ordinarily think about the problem—that is, *what,* not *how*. Another example of careful wording is, "Make the Web site show you only the stocks that interest you." Not as realistic would be a task like "Customize your profile to show you the stocks that interest you," because the words *customize* and *profile* are not likely to be part of people's regular vocabulary. Another reason is that it might lead people on, especially if there are links labeled "customize" or "profile."

Tasks Should Be Realistic • For example, "Create a new customer account" is something that many people do on a Web site, but not because they

want to. People create an account only because they have to, to get something else done. In other words, creating an account is more of a secondary task that people do to accomplish a primary task.

"Buy a digital camera for a friend that he or she will like" is very open-ended, but it is likely to be the way people approach the problem. It is important that tasks be realistic because you want to find out what people are thinking and see if the design provides the right cues to support them.

Tasks Should Form a Complete Story • Taken as a whole, the tasks should be complete, forming a cohesive and believable story. For example, it does not really make sense if the tasks are given in the following order: "Find previous purchases," "Add a message to a community board," and then "Find the privacy policy." The tasks need to flow together. For example, the following order makes more sense: "Find the privacy policy," "Purchase a printer," and then "Purchase additional ink toner cartridges."

Also be careful not to fragment tasks: "Purchase the best printer for under $300" makes more sense than (1) "Create an account," (2) "Find and compare printers for under $300," and (3) "Purchase the printer you found." Testing fragmented tasks may show that customers can complete the subtasks just fine, but when they are put together in a more realistic situation, the results may not be nearly as good.

The number of tasks to test depends on how extensively you want to test your Web site. Five to ten tasks is about right for most cases—enough to cover a lot of functionality without taking a lot of time for each participant.

Recruiting Participants A.3

After defining some tasks, you should begin recruiting participants. These participants need to be representative of eventual customers in terms of vocabulary, general knowledge, and desired tasks. If the Web site is aimed toward college students, then advertise at a nearby college. If the Web site is for mothers of young children, then get friends of friends who are also mothers or advertise with local mom's groups.

Avoid Friends and Family • One thing to avoid is getting close friends or family to help out unless you're sure that they will give honest feedback. They may be reluctant to criticize something that you have worked so hard on. Also do not get coworkers from down the hall. They are likely to know too much about what you are doing. It's OK to use people like this for a first pass, as a way of getting quick comments on a design and piloting your experimental procedures, but do not rely solely on feedback from these tests. Again, get people who would realistically use the Web site.

Buy Participants' Time with Gifts and Prizes • One way to recruit people is to compensate them for their time. You might be surprised what some people will do for a free T-shirt.[2] Some other ways of drawing in people include giving small toys, coffee mugs, gift certificates, or some money, or giving a large cash prize of $200 to $300 to the participant who "does the best." This last type of compensation works well for experiments where creative performance is important. For straight cash payments, we normally offer about $20 per hour for university students and about $50 per hour for other participants.

If you don't have the time to recruit participants, several market research firms can recruit participants who meet the profile you need for about $100/participant, not including the compensation you must pay each participant. Many usability practitioners and designers go this route, although this approach may double your direct costs for running the tests.

Getting the Right Number of Participants • You do not need many participants to get process data. If you are in the early stages of design, five or six people will be fine, especially for paper prototypes. You will need more people—often about 10 to 20 participants—in the later stages of design to evaluate the site. However, you will need to increase these numbers if you have a large and diverse audience to cover, or if your Web site is very large. Getting so many people right at the outset might seem expensive, but consider how much trouble this investment will save you later when you have created a more useful and usable Web site for your customers.

Getting bottom-line data requires a lot more people. Ten to 20 people can provide initial data, but most tasks will still have a large amount of variability. Section A.5, Analyzing the Data, will give more details about the relationship between the number of people and variability in the data.

When you're recruiting participants, get a few more people than are really needed. The first few tests you run may be a little rough, and you may have to make some changes to make the evaluation flow smoothly. In addition, not everyone remembers to show up.

---

2 Then again, if you've been working in the computer industry, you might not!

There are two things you should do when recruiting people. First, give them a general overview of the experiment, describing what the Web site is about, what they will do, and approximately how long the whole thing will take. Do not provide too many details because you do not want to bias the test. Second, tell them about any prizes or compensation that will be given for participating. If a person agrees to be a participant, schedule a time and place for the test, and then get his or her name and either a phone number or an e-mail address so that you can provide a reminder before the test.

Choosing Between-Groups versus Within-Groups Experimental Design • One important consideration in experimental design is whether each participant participates in more than one experimental condition. Say, for example, that you're testing two versions of a Web site to compare them. In this scenario, there are two experimental conditions. In a **between-groups experiment**, you break your pool of test participants into two groups and each group uses only one of the Web sites. In contrast, in a **within-groups experiment** you have only one group of test participants, and each participant uses both sites.

These two types of experimental design have trade-offs. For example, a within-groups experiment may not require as many test participants before producing statistically significant results. If you're after bottom-line data, the within-groups approach can save you considerable time and money. On the other hand, a within-groups experiment can raise issues of validity if learning effects are involved. For example, if you test the same tasks on two versions of the same Web site, your participants might be quicker completing a task the second time because they learned how to do it on the first site. You can alleviate some of these problems by randomizing or counterbalancing the order of sites tested and other experimental conditions.

In general, within-groups experiments work better when a low-level interaction technique is being tested, such as finding the best position for a particular button on the page. Use between-groups experiments when you want to compare tasks on two versions of a site or between two competitive sites. Try to make sure that the participants in the two groups match as well as possible in terms of demographics, Internet experience, and familiarity with the problem domain.

A.4 Running the Test

Several considerations about the test itself are important—from where you run it to what you say to the participants. In this section we look at these issues.

Setting Up the Test Location

If you are evaluating a paper prototype, you can conduct the test practically anywhere. All you need is a large table and places for everyone to sit. For online prototypes, the testing location just needs to be a quiet place with a networked computer.

Video cameras and audio recorders are useful to have in both cases, but they are not required. You can accomplish some tests simply by taking notes on paper, though audio and video recordings make it easy to clarify specific issues later. In contrast, some companies have special rooms for testing, complete with expensive recording equipment, eye-tracking devices, and one-way mirrors for observers. These kinds of setups are useful for gathering bottom-line data but are not necessary for process data.

Ethical Considerations

Tests can be a grueling experience for some people. Participants have been known to leave in tears, embarrassed by their mistakes or their inability to complete the tasks successfully. You have a responsibility to alleviate these kinds of problems. One way is to avoid pressuring people to participate. You need to get participants' informed consent regarding the subject matter of the test, and then make it clear that the test is voluntary and that participants can stop the test at any time for any reason (see Appendix C—Sample Consent Form). You also need to stress that you're testing the Web site and not the participants themselves, and that they are really helping you by finding problems with the site. If they are having problems, then it is the Web site's fault, not theirs.

If other people will see the collected data, then the data should also be made as anonymous as possible. Names and other pieces of identifying information should be removed, and people's faces should be blurred out in any pictures and video footage. In some cases a videotape of a person struggling with a human–computer interface has been played for an audience that included that very person! Making the data anonymous will help prevent any potentially awkward situations in the future.

Test Roles

The key role in running a usability test is the facilitator. The facilitator greets participants, introduces any other people in the room, explains the procedure for the test, and answers participants' questions.

The other people act simply as observers, watching what participants do. Their role is to take notes and keep quiet. Observers can also be remote if the setup allows them to view things from another location or through a two-way mirror.

If you're running a test on a paper prototype, another role you'll need is the computer. The job of the person playing computer is to run the interface, updating the paper interface as needed.[3]

Running a Pilot Test

Before running the tests with actual participants, you should carry out a pilot test with two or three people. In this case, coworkers and friends are OK. The key is to get used to the procedure of running a test and to work out any bugs in your procedure. A pilot also helps you figure out how long the test will take so that you know whether you need to cut or possibly add more tasks.

After you have finished the pilot tests, try analyzing the collected data. This data should not be used in the final analysis, but you should do the analysis to make sure that you are collecting the right data. For example, once when we were evaluating a Web site, we asked people to sort a list of features according to importance. Although the exercise was useful, it turned out that the data we had gathered was extremely difficult to analyze properly. One person mentioned that only the top two things in the list were really important to her; another identified the top four items as important. In retrospect, a better way of gathering this information would have been to ask people to rate the importance of each feature from 1 (not important) to 7 (very important). If we had tried analyzing data from the pilot test, we would have caught the problem before conducting the real test.

Testing Paper Prototypes

Paper prototypes are useful for obtaining data early in the process, but you should not use them for bottom-line data because they are too far removed from the final implementation. Most people have not seen

---

3 A secondary job is to just smile at all the bad jokes about being slow and needing to upgrade the computer.

Figure AppA.1

It is easier to run usability tests with oversized paper prototypes because everyone can see what's happening.

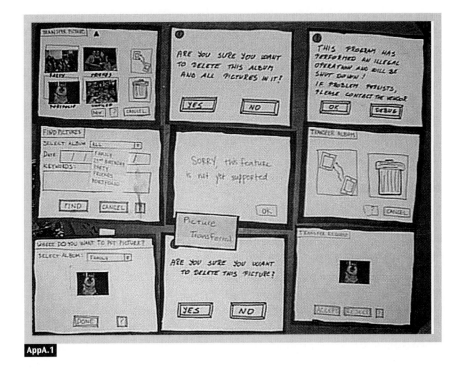

AppA.1

paper prototypes before. You will have to explain the concept, but the majority of people catch on pretty quickly.

Ask participants to point at things with their finger, using it as a mouse. If they click on a link, the person playing the computer just switches to another piece of paper representing the next page. If they click on a drop-down menu, the computer can place an index card with the choices on top. Note that having a paper prototype that is larger than it would be in reality makes it easier for everyone to see what the participant is pointing at (see Figure AppA.1).

It is difficult to simulate highly interactive elements such as mouse roll-overs and animations with paper prototypes. In most cases, this is a good thing because it forces design teams to focus on the core issues first. Be aware that this is a limitation of paper prototypes, and plan accordingly.

Testing Online Prototypes

Online computer–based prototypes can be used for obtaining either process data or bottom-line data. If you're testing a high-fidelity prototype, you need to make it clear to the participants that they will be testing an

early design and not the final Web site. They might mistakenly believe that the Web site is nearly done when it is really in the early stages of design. Setting their expectations properly will help them give you the type of high-level feedback you need at this stage, rather than comments on the visuals, such as colors and fonts. Later you can test again to evaluate these details.

Before starting a test, be sure to clear the Web browser's history and cache so that it will be as if the person had never been to the Web site before, making all the links unvisited.

Starting and Carrying Out the Test

Greet the Participant • Tests are generally broken into three major phases: preliminary instructions and paperwork, performing the task, and a debriefing. Start by introducing yourself and the rest of the team. Then describe the purpose of the test at a high level, and be sure to emphasize that you're testing the Web site and that you're not testing them in any way. Say something like, "We're asking you to help us improve the Web site by helping us find problems with it. We're testing the Web site and not you."

Also make it clear that you will not provide help as they go through the tasks because you want to see how they would go through the Web site normally. However, emphasize that it's all right for them to stop the test at any time for any reason.

This is also a good time to put a "Do Not Disturb" sign on the door saying that there is a customer research study in progress. You do not want any interruptions (unless this is one of the things you want to observe).

Fill Out the Paperwork • After greeting the participants, have them fill out any paperwork you may have. The paperwork may request such things as basic demographic information, a name and address to which you can send a check if you're paying them, and consent. Any consent forms should explain what the test is, what kinds of data will be collected, and how the data will be used. Make sure you have two copies of the consent forms—one for you and one for the participant to keep.

Ask Participants to Think Aloud • If you're gathering process data, ask the participants to think aloud, to say what they're looking for and what they're trying to do. Although some people are really good at this, others find it a little awkward. The facilitator should prompt participants every so often if they stop talking, asking things like, "So what are you looking for now?" or "What are you trying to do now?"

Do not do this if you are collecting bottom-line data because thinking aloud may cause participants to make more errors or to go through the Web site more slowly.

Instruct the Participants How to Start • Ask the participants if they have any questions before starting. Then hand them any instructions you may have, any special information, such as a fake credit card number to use, and the first task to complete. Ask them to read the task aloud. Doing this will help them start thinking aloud.

You may want to have participants fill out a very short survey after completing each task. You can ask questions like how easy or hard they thought the task was. You can also ask questions to make sure that they found the right piece of information. For example, if the task is to find and add a specific item to the shopping cart, you can ask them how much the item cost. This is just a redundant check, to make sure that they really did complete the task successfully.

Take Good Notes during Each Task • The observers should be taking notes about what each participant says and does during the test. It also helps to record audio and video if possible. Use a digital watch or a clock to keep track of time, too. If a certain task takes far too long, tell the participant that it's OK to move on to the next task.

If you're measuring bottom-line data, make sure everyone knows what to measure. For example, is it an error if someone hits the **Back** button on the browser? Is it an error if someone goes back to the homepage? The criteria need to be agreed on beforehand. And what happens if someone

Some Common Mistakes in Running Usability Tests

- Testing a Web site using unrealistic tasks
- Using significantly leading or biased tasks when comparing Web sites
- Recruiting participants who do not represent your expected customers
- Forgetting to clear out the Web browser file cache and history list before starting
- Using only a computer that has a fast network connection, a high resolution monitor, and a fast processor (unless all or most of your customers really do have these)

does not finish a task? There are no hard rules here, but a common technique is to throw out the data for that participant with a clarifying note in the final report or to assign a very large time and a large number of errors, just to keep everything numerical.

Watch Closely • Yes, it will be frustrating to watch people struggle with something you put so much time into, clicking on the wrong link or not seeing the text right in front of them. But bite your lip and keep your mouth closed: You are here to watch and to learn how to improve the Web site. Make sure that none of the observers laugh, groan, or make any other inappropriate response. These are the types of things that can unnerve your participants.

If a participant does something really interesting, ask a follow-up question. Ask open-ended questions, such as, "What are you looking for?" Let the participants know that things are going all right. Prompt them to keep speaking and tell you what they're thinking. Also look out for nonverbal cues, such as a furrowed brow or a puzzled look.

Answer any general questions that participants may have, but do not help them with the tasks. Also do not help some participants more than others. Plan in advance what you will and will not help with. For example, it is common to decide that you will help participants when they run into known bugs or functionality that has not been implemented yet. Simply get them back on track.

Follow Up with a Quick Survey • After all the tasks have been completed, follow up with a short survey. You want to get your participants' overall impressions and comments about the Web site, seeing what they liked and disliked about the Web site. Also ask them where they felt they had problems with the site and where they thought it worked well.

Debrief the Participants after the Test • Wrap up by debriefing each participant, telling them what you were looking for, as well as discussing any interesting behavior the participant had. People often do not remember specific actions, so it may be useful to go through the Web site again or to show video segments to help prompt their memory.

Ask participants if they have any thoughts on how to fix any problems they encountered. Take these comments with a grain of salt because participants usually do not have an understanding of design or the underlying technology. Nevertheless, these comments are useful to hear. Afterward, finish up by asking if they have any final questions, and then thank them for their time.

A.5 Analyzing the Data

Analyzing Process Data • Think about what you saw and what the participants said. Did they understand the things you thought they would? Were they confused by any terms or concepts? If so, maybe things need to be renamed to use FAMILIAR LANGUAGE (K11) or explained in greater detail. If the concept in question is a concept fundamental to the Web site, be sure to make that fact clear on the homepage because otherwise people might leave without ever bothering to figure it out.

What errors could they recover from? For example, did they click on a link but then quickly realize that it was the wrong one? It is important to minimize these kinds of problems, but these are usually just minor annoyances. A bigger problem would be indicated by systematic "ping-ponging"—that is, repeated back and forth attempts from one page down unfruitful paths. Such behavior would suggest a need for more DESCRIPTIVE, LONGER LINK NAMES (K9), which would give the participants more "information scent" to find the page they're looking for.

Focus first on the errors from which participants could not recover. Did participants have problems finding items on the Web site? Did they have trouble understanding the overall structure of the Web site? What about navigation? Could they make their way through the site adequately? Did they make any errors and not even notice that there was a problem?[4] These could be fundamental problems of the site and should be addressed first when you're fixing the site.

The most important question to ask is why the error occurred. Was the navigation too confusing, making it difficult to go to other pages? Was the information disorganized, making it hard to find things across pages? Was the Web page too cluttered, making it hard to find anything on a page? Was the site too slow, causing participants to lose track of what they wanted to do? Just like a doctor, you get to see only the symptoms, but you need to keep asking yourself if any fundamental issues are causing all of these problems.

Another thing to keep in mind is that people do not give up in usability tests as easily as they would in the real world. You have to realize that no matter what you do, you are still putting an implicit amount of pressure on participants to try their best to successfully complete the task. People

---

4 A perfect example of this is the infamous butterfly ballot used in the 2000 U.S. presidential election. Statistical analysis of neighboring counties suggests that at least several thousand citizens unintentionally voted for the wrong candidate, but the voting process lacked a verification process that would let people check their votes.

are more attentive and willing to go through a few more pages when they know they are being observed.

Analyzing Bottom-Line Data • Be careful when analyzing bottom-line data. For example, suppose the target goal is to ensure that a person new to a Web site can find and purchase an item in 20 minutes or less. When running our test, we get times of 20, 15, 45, 10, 5, and 25 for our six participants. The mean or average time for this is 20 minutes. Looks pretty good! The median for this set of numbers is 17.5—even better!

However, the problem is that there is very little certainty here because there are only six participants and the results are highly variable. If you calculate the standard deviation, a measure of how variable the numbers in this set are, you will find that the value is approximately 14. If we divide the standard deviation by the square root of the number of samples we have (6), we get 5.8. This is the *standard error of the mean,* and it tells us how much variation we can expect in the typical value. It is plausible that the typical value is as small as the mean minus twice the standard error of the mean, resulting in a lower bound of 8.5, or as large as the mean plus twice the standard error of the mean, or 32. This latter value would clearly be far from our stated goal of 20 minutes!

We can say more precisely what we mean by *plausible.* The best thing to do here is to use statistical techniques. Cranking through basic statistical methods, you can calculate with 95 percent confidence that the actual average time will be 20, plus or minus 11, minutes. In other words, you are 95 percent likely to be correct in saying that the actual time will be in this range, but 5 percent of the time you'll be wrong.[5]

Usability test data is often quite variable, which means that you need lots of participants to get good estimates of typical values. In addition, the breadth of range depends on the square root of the number of participants. In other words, if you have 4 times as many participants, you narrow the range by an average factor of only 2. Continuing the example, in general, quadrupling the number of participants from 6 to 24 will narrow the spread of the average time from 20, plus or minus 11, minutes to 20, plus or minus 6, minutes (assuming that the mean and the standard deviation stay about the same). This is where online usability evaluation methods, as described in Appendix E—Online Research, become useful

---

5 If you use Microsoft Excel, you can calculate this range using the CONFIDENCE function. If you use a more advanced tool, like SPSS, you probably already know how to calculate this.

because they make it easier to scale up the number of participants and thus tighten your confidence intervals.

Basic statistics is beyond the scope of this book, but a great introduction on the topic is *The Cartoon Guide to Statistics* by Larry Gonick, Jr., and Woolcott Smith. This book covers the main concepts that you will want to be familiar with when doing basic statistical analyses, including mean, variance, standard deviation, correlation, regression, *t*-test, and ANOVA.

A.6 Presenting the Results

After the data has been collected and analyzed, the results need to be presented to the design team or to the clients. Results can be reported in the form of a written report or an oral presentation. Here's a short outline of the sections your report should include:

- Executive Summary
- Tasks
- Participants
- Problems Found
- Participant Feedback
- Suggested Improvements
- Appendices

Start with the Executive Summary, which gives a quick overview of what you did in the test, a summary of the results, and a rundown of the recommendations for improvement. Next, in Tasks, talk about the tasks that you had participants carry out, describing why these tasks were chosen. Continue with Participants, a short description of the number of participants, general demographics, and any defining characteristics.

In the next section, Problems Found, list the problems encountered, prioritized by severity. Use screen shots of problem Web pages, using circles and arrows to point out critical incidents. Graphs showing the success rates of participants at completing tasks will also help people understand the results. If you're presenting the results orally, this is a good time to show video clips to help convey your message. Video is extremely valuable for convincing skeptical programmers and management that there are problems with the Web site. You can also include video clips in written reports that you plan to put online.

The Participant Feedback section contains both positive and negative feedback from participants. This section can include summaries of surveys taken by participants after they finished the test, or direct quotes from them during the test.

The next section, Suggested Improvements, outlines what needs to be changed to improve the Web site. The improvements should be triaged into "must do," "should do," and "could do" categories. The "must do" improvements are the show stoppers, the ones that caused serious problems from which people could not recover. They also include really simple improvements that take only a short time to fix, such as misspellings or broken links. The "should do" improvements represent problems that are annoying but tolerable—problems that most people can figure out. The "could do" improvements are changes that will take too much effort to implement for the resulting benefits. Keep these ideas on the back burner for the next iteration.

The last section, Appendixes, contains any test materials used during the experiment, such as demo scripts and instructions, as well as all of the raw data in a cleaned-up form.

Your evaluation plan can often be used as the basis for your usability test report. See Appendix B—Sample Web Site Evaluation Plan.

Sample Web Site Evaluation Plan[1]

Roles

- **Facilitator.** The facilitator's responsibilities are to read instructions, handle transitions from one section of the test to another, field participants' questions, and if necessary help participants recover from software bugs or places where they are clearly stuck for far too long.
- **Observers.** Observers record times and on-screen events, and they tally tracked metrics.

Introduction

Thank you very much for helping us evaluate two Web sites. We are testing people's perceptions of Web sites that are in the early stages of design. Here's what we have planned for the next [insert time frame here]:

1. *First we will start a Web browser, open up a start page, and ask you to read through the introductory text.*
2. *Next we will ask you to perform some tasks on the first Web site. Interspersed will be some survey questions asking you about your perceptions of the tasks and of the Web site.*
3. *Steps 1 and 2 will be repeated for the second Web site.*
4. *At the end, we will ask you for any comments you have overall.*

We're asking you to help us improve the Web site by finding problems with it. We would like to stress that we are testing the Web site, not you. If you have

---

1   Throughout Appendix B, italic typeface indicates text that is meant to be spoken to participants.

trouble with some of the tasks we ask you to perform, it is the Web site's fault, not yours. Don't feel bad; trouble spots are exactly what we're looking for. And please remember that this is totally voluntary. Although we don't know any reason why this should happen, if you become uncomfortable or find this evaluation objectionable in any way, feel free to quit at any time.

Hand them two consent forms—one for our files, one for them as a copy—as well as any forms for obtaining demographic information or contact information to receive any prizes or checks.

This consent form just says that you understand what this test is about, that you understand we will respect your privacy wishes, and that you will allow us to publish any results from this study.

Wait until the participant completes the forms.

Before we begin, I'd like to ask you to say what comes to your mind as you work. We have found that we get a great deal of information from these informal observations if we ask people to think aloud as they work through the exercises. It may be a bit awkward at first, but it's really very easy once you get used to it. All you have to do is speak your thoughts as you work. If you forget to think aloud, I'll remind you to keep talking.

Do you have any questions for us before you start?

Tasks

Be sure to do the following for each participant:

1. Give them scrap paper and a pen.
2. Give them a sample address and sample credit card number, if necessary for the tasks. *(The two Web sites we will be asking you to test are e-commerce Web sites. Here is an address and fake credit card number to use. No actual purchases will be made.)*[2]
3. Start the Web browser.
4. Clear out the browser cache and history.
5. Maximize the Web browser size.
6. Hand them the first task on a sheet of paper.

---

2 Be sure also to do tests in which you do give your participants money to complete purchases all the way through. Otherwise you won't know if the entire checkout process works.

7. Ask them to read the first task aloud.

8. After they complete each task, ask them what they thought was hard and what was easy about the task. Ask them to rate the difficulty of the task on a scale of 1 to 10.

9. Repeat steps 6 through 8 for each task.

Debriefing

Do you have any final comments about the Web sites, this study, or anything else?

Sample Consent Form

Our names are [*insert your names here*], and we are [*describe your position and the organization you work for here*]. We would like you to participate in our research by evaluating two e-commerce Web sites. Your participation in this study should take about [*insert time frame here*] and poses no risks to you other than those normally encountered in daily life.

All of the information that we obtain from your session will be kept confidential. The information obtained from your session will be tagged with a code number. The correspondence between your name and number will be treated with the same care as our own confidential information. We will not use your name or identifying information in any reports of our research (unless you allow it by signing the second line below).

Your participation in this research is voluntary. You are free to refuse to participate. Whether or not you choose to participate will have no bearing on your standing in relation to [*insert organization name here*].

If you have any questions about the research, you may call [*insert contact person here*] at [*insert contact phone number here*], or send electronic mail to [*insert contact e-mail here*]. You may keep the copy of this form for future reference.

By signing this form you accept the following statements:

I agree to participate in the evaluation of two Web sites. I know that the researchers are studying [*insert description here*]. I realize that I will be asked to test the Web sites and discuss perceptions of those two Web sites over [*insert time frame here*].

I understand that any information obtained during this study will be kept confidential.

I give [*insert your names here*] and their associates permission to present the results of this work in written or oral form, without further permission from me.

_____   _____
Signature   Date

I also agree to allow my name or other identifying information, such as a picture or video, to be included in all final reports and publications resulting from my participation in this research.

_____   _____
Signature   Date

Sample Observer Form

Participant ID: _____

Date: _____

Time started: _____   Time ended: _____

Tallies (make a mark for each incident)

Site A	Site B	Incident
		Could not figure out what to do next for more than 30 seconds
		Was visibly lost in the Web site
		Was visibly frustrated with the Web site
		Said something clearly negative about the Web site
		Said something clearly positive about the Web site
		Cursed out loud

Tasks Completed (mark whether successfully completed or not)

Site A	Site B	Task
❏	❏	1. Find the Web site's privacy policy.
❏	❏	2. Find the two cheapest MP3 players on the Web site.
❏	❏	3. Find a gift for a friend and add it to the shopping cart.
❏	❏	4. Find a gift for yourself and add it to the shopping cart.
❏	❏	5. Check out and finalize the purchase.
❏	❏	6. Check the status of the purchase.
❏	❏	7. Subscribe yourself to the Web site's newsletter.

Notes

Online Research

You can use online research to gather valid data in a short period of time. We have found that this type of research is especially valuable when you're trying to convince management of major changes that must be made on a site or when you're making subtle changes to an important page, such as the homepage. The validity of the data is important because people will make major decisions based on it.

Online research can reduce or eliminate problems typically associated with traditional research—problems such as the following:

- **Sample bias,** in which research participants do not accurately reflect the demographics or psychographics of your target customers
- **Undersampling bias,** in which there are not enough people to have a statistically valid sample
- **Question bias,** in which the questions are worded such that they lead people to answer in a certain way

The benefit of understanding the customer experience on a site is enormous. Web sites are not like physical businesses or stores, where managers can easily ask customers direct questions about their needs and wants. Most sites are set up to be self-service, with a "call to action" that brings customers in contact with the enterprise either through completely automated means, like searching for information or purchasing a product; or through less automated means, such as "for more information, call" offers.

Given the pace of business, running research quickly can be critical to your Web site's success. Data that in the past has traditionally taken months to generate can now be collected online in only hours or days. This speed can provide a competitive advantage.

The quality of the data and the speed with which it is collected are the main reasons for using online methodologies. These are also areas you

need to be careful about, especially with respect to data quality. Make sure that your online methodology collects valid data.

Goals

E.1

Web sites and Web-based applications require a new level of understanding of customer retention to achieve business revenue and savings goals.

Understand Customer Retention • In many cases you can answer the question, "What will make a site more successful?" by asking, "What will make customers come back?"

Online research provides many solutions to this question, as well as to other issues facing site developers, specifically why customers abandon sites and whether customers can complete tasks.

Learn Why Customers Abandon Sites • The reasons that visitors leave a Web site become particularly important when you evaluate which redesign improvements to make and their impact on overall site retention. For any site that attempts to lead customers through a process, whether it is from the homepage to a product page or from start to completion of a transaction, understanding why customers leave a Web site becomes critical.

Find Out Whether Customers Can Complete Tasks • When a customer cannot find information on a site, yet the information *is* there, the customer has just experienced a failure of design and a failure to test the design. Task testing provides a view into the customer's experience on a site, as customers attempt to complete specific tasks. You see where they go, what they try to do, and what works and doesn't work on the site. The success or failure of each customer helps the researcher and designer to understand the customer experience better and to build a better Web site.

Research by Design Phase

E.2

The goal of every Web site, regardless of its stage of development, is to be the best—a site to which customers return regularly. In this section we present suggestions for each development phase.

The Discovery and Exploration Phases • Even when your site is in the conceptual phase, you need to evaluate the needs of the customer to validate or invalidate site goals, messages, and rough designs. Proper testing at this phase helps guarantee that a bigger, more expensive reworking will not be required later. Online research is especially valuable for quickly testing goals and messages with large numbers of prospective customers. Online research can also let you test your rough designs with a diverse population, rather than with only the customers you can find locally. The better online research solutions (see Section E.6, Comparison of Commercial Tools) can provide both the market research capability to validate product concepts, priorities, and goals, and the usability research capability to help you refine design roughs.

The Refinement, Production, and Implementation Phases • When you're developing a site, invariably issues arise that cause the design to change, such as software issues or a change due to a better understanding of the flow of the customer through your site. Whenever you make a change, and as the dynamics of a site evolve, you need additional testing to analyze the customer response. Bringing participants to your company for in-person testing might be too time-consuming for every change. Online solutions (see Section E.6, Comparison of Commercial Tools) that let you test a live site work very well in this phase and can make it easy to rerun the same tests as you have done previously and see how your changes have affected the results.

The Launch and Maintenance Phases • Once a site has been launched and real customers are visiting and experiencing it, you must continue customer analysis. You will probably add new features and designs while the customer mix changes, so you may need alternative methods of accomplishing the same tasks. All these factors lead to new problems in production. Online site satisfaction indices (see Section E.6, Comparison of Commercial Tools) provide ways to understand and improve a site in production. These tools can help alert you to changes in your audience or in your customers' perception of how well your site works. You can use these alerts to follow up with more in-depth research, using traditional laboratory methods or deeper online analyses.

Site Redesign • When your site undergoes a major redesign, you have the opportunity to fix many existing problems. Find the biggest problems and quantify them. Decide what will have the biggest impact on customer retention. Research your existing site and your new ideas with online usability, audience identification surveys, and competitive comparisons.

Your site development team also needs to know whether their new designs will really work for customers. Online solutions (see Section E.6, Comparison of Commercial Tools) can provide ways to analyze, understand, and recommend design improvement.

Types of Research

There are several kinds of research you might want to conduct on your site. Traditionally, two kinds of research have been used to improve the understanding of customers and how they use computer interfaces: market research and usability research.

Market Research • The types of marketing analyses that online research tools can provide include the following:

- **Segmentation analysis,** to see which segments of the population respond best to different product or services
- **Cross-category analysis,** to see which customer groups are alike and which are different
- **Ongoing site assessments and benchmarked competitive comparisons,** to see how well the site is perceived in general and how well it is perceived with respect to competitors' sites
- **In-depth comparisons with competitors' sites,** to identify which features of your site are better and how to improve your site with respect to your competitors
- **Online usage analysis,** to find out where customers are going on your site and why

Usability Research • Online research tools enhance traditional usability processes by conducting remote usability tests anywhere, anytime. With more advanced systems, you can conduct these tests using screen sharing and recording technology, or click-path recording, also known as *clickstream recording.*

Using online research tools allows you to increase the number of participants you include, thereby increasing the validity of data and the breadth of issues covered. You also spend more time *observing* the test participants' actions and less time *capturing and recording* their answers and actions.

The types of usability testing that online research tools can provide include the following:

- **Quantitative remote usability task completion analysis,** including clickstream analysis, to see whether or not customers can complete tasks on your site
- **Qualitative remote usability task completion analysis,** including remote screen viewing and clickstream analysis, to see where and why customers are being tripped up when they try to complete tasks on your site
- **Ongoing site assessments and benchmarked competitive comparisons,** to see how well customers perceive the usability of your site in general and how well they perceive it with respect to competitors' sites
- **In-depth comparisons with competitors' sites,** to identify tasks that are easier to accomplish or more efficient on your site and ways to improve task completion and efficiency on your site with respect to your competitors
- **Site exit analysis,** to see where customers are leaving your site and why
- **Online usage analysis,** to see how customers are using certain pages on your site and why

Here are some key questions you can answer with online research:

- Who is visiting my site, specifically
  - What are my visitors' ages?
  - What percentage of my visitors are female? Male?
  - How much computer experience do they have?
  - How much online experience do they have?
  - What are their occupations?
  - What specialized experience do they have?
  - What specialized products do they own?

- When visiting my Web site, what are visitors' attitudes and impressions about the following?
  - The company
  - The company's products and services
  - The look and feel of the site
  - The messages on the site

- What behavior do visitors exhibit on the Web site?
  - Can they complete tasks and transactions?
  - Can they do the things they need to do so that the site and the company that owns it can be successful?
  - What does not work on the Web site?
  - What can I do to improve the Web site?

- Compared with how they interact on competitors' sites, what do visitors think and exhibit as behavior about the following?
  - The company
  - Site messaging
  - Site content
  - Ease of use
  - Task completion rates

Online research can also generate recommendations to improve your site. Data collected from real customers through online research can reveal trends, usability issues, and design improvement opportunities.

Running the Test   E.4

The first step is to create your research plan, choose how it is to be delivered, and select the type of research you wish to run. Online tools use templates to give you a set of prewritten questions and tasks based on the type of research and characteristics of your site. Next you can edit the questions, manage the layout of the questionnaire, add a nondisclosure agreement, and specify a reward for participation in the research. The last step is to add a list of participants to your research (if you have selected e-mail delivery), edit the messages to participants, and then review the research one last time before you start it. In this section we will describe these areas in more detail.

The Participants' View • An important aspect of any product is how it looks to the end customer. Figures AppE.1 through AppE.3 provide some guidelines for how to design the research for your participants.

Online research should always start with disclosures about the research and assurance to the test participants, as well as a chance for them to decline to participate (see Figure AppE.1).

Online research often takes one of two forms. In the first type of research, you might ask participants to complete tasks on the site or to give you their impressions of the site. In this case you will want to show them the site in one window while asking them questions in another (see Figure AppE.2). In the second type of research, you might simply be asking questions of the participants about themselves or their experience, without tying in directly to a particular Web site (see Figure AppE.3).

Setting Up Your Research • A question editor (see Figure AppE.4) lets you edit your research questions before launching them. This is where you

Figure AppE.1

NetRaker's introduction screen invites visitors to participate in research and makes it clear that the test is not evaluating them, but the site. Any plan to use a video recording of the test must also be divulged in the consent agreement. And nondisclosure agreements are also included at this time.

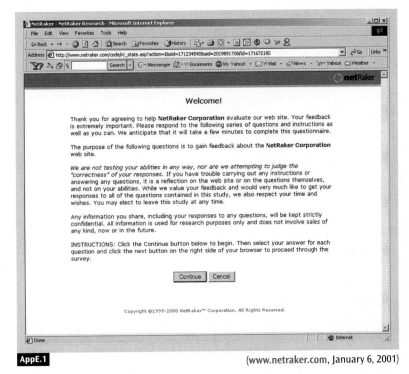

(www.netraker.com, January 6, 2001)

Figure AppE.2

Two-window testing lets you test tasks and concepts simultaneously. The system you use must present the site in question in one window (right) and the tasks or questions in another (left).

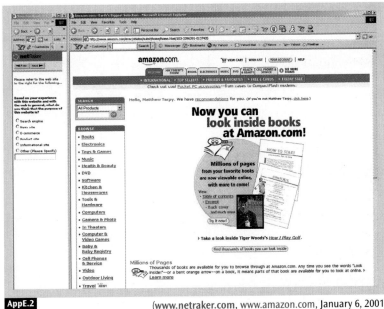

(www.netraker.com, www.amazon.com, January 6, 2001)

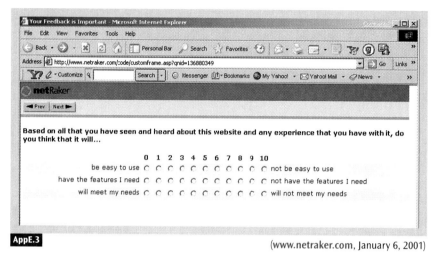

Figure AppE.3

For sections of research that do not need to show a Web site, a full-screen survey is useful.

(www.netraker.com, January 6, 2001)

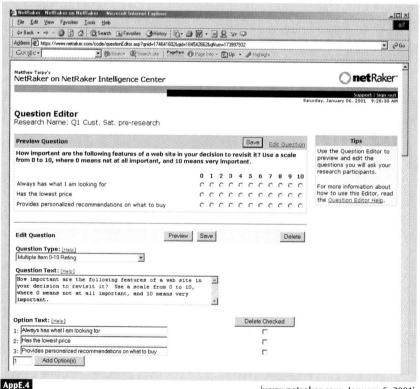

Figure AppE.4

This Web-based question editor gives a preview of how the question will look to your research participants. It also makes it easy to select the question type, text, and options, as well as the Web page to show your participants.

(www.netraker.com, January 6, 2001)

can change the question text, option text, question types, and Web page you show as research participants view and complete the questions (as illustrated in Figure AppE.2).

Choose the correct question types for the information you need during analysis. Better systems offer a range of question types:

1. **Single choice.** Participants choose one option using radio buttons or drop-down pick lists.
2. **Multiple choice.** Participants choose one or more options using check boxes or a list box.
3. **Select button and move on.** Participants click the button representing their choice and immediately go to the next question.
4. **Rank.** Participants type in a numerical value for each option.
5. **Rate: Yes/No.** For each option, participants select "Yes" or "No" using radio buttons.
6. **Rate: Agree/Disagree.** For each option, participants select one of five levels of agreement, ranging from "Strongly Agree" to "Strongly Disagree."
7. **Rate: Would Not/Would.** For each option, participants select one of four levels of likelihood that they would take action, ranging from "Definitely Would Not" to "Definitely Would."
8. **Rate: 0–10.** For each option, participants select a value between 0 and 10 using radio buttons.
9. **Semantic differential.** Participants choose a point on a scale between two extremes. For each option of the form "phrase one: phrase two," a scale is displayed.
10. **Customized ratings.** The researcher defines any sort of scale, from 1 to 5, 1 to 6, 1 to 7, and so on to "Never, Rarely, Sometimes, Often, Always."
11. **Instruction.** Question text is treated as an instruction. No options are displayed.
12. **Free-form.** Participants type responses in a text box. No options are displayed.
13. **Scale 0–10.** Participants select a value between 0 and 10 using buttons. No options are displayed.
14. **Task.** Participants are asked to carry out instructions and are given a fixed set of options asking whether the task was completed.

Other options that some online research systems offer are

- Nondisclosure agreements for beta sites and confidential information
- Flexible reward systems
- Customizable e-mail messages
- Customizable welcome messages and thank-you messages
- Cobranding of the survey presentation to reflect the logo and color scheme of your site

If the sequence of questions in a piece of research must change depending on responses, the research can be programmed to handle that situation. Programming gives you the ability to rotate blocks of questions to control for answer bias, to send participants to various questions on the basis of responses, and to show different options to respondents depending on certain criteria. For example, you might want the questionnaire to branch to different questions depending on the participant's previous use of the site being tested. Not all systems have these capabilities, but research programming logic can greatly improve the quality of data captured.

When setting up online research, choose whether you need videos and **clickstreams**—the paths people take through sites—to be captured during the research. Some clickstream tools provide visualization tools that allow you to quickly analyze many participants' clickstreams in one graph (see Figure AppE.9). Use clickstreams to pinpoint problem pages on a site. Use videos when participant behavior on a page needs further analysis. Because clickstreams identify only problem pages, videos captured during online research can be valuable for revealing exactly what went wrong.

Recruiting the Right Participants • One of the most important parts of successful online and offline research is recruiting the right participants. Procure your participant base through existing customer lists, partner lists, or site intercept research, or contract with an online research company to find your audience.

To pull existing customers from a customer database, all you need are e-mail addresses. If you need specific participants, such as customers who have bought a product multiple times before on your site, or customers who spend less than 15 minutes during each session on your site, your databases need to store this information. If you do not have this second level of information, use **intercept research**; that is, pop up a short questionnaire to a random sample of visitors to your site, to qualify participants.

Online research companies can help by selecting a group of participants tailored to your specific needs. If you contract with them, they will do the following:

- Meet with you to determine which audience the research needs to reach, and how to identify the audience with a screening questionnaire
- Once the screening questionnaire exists, acquire participants from specific pools of potential participants
- Once the customized list of participants has been created, send you the list of e-mail addresses for inclusion in your research participant invitations

E.5   Analyzing the Data

Most online research tools have multiple ways to analyze the resulting data. Typically, online analysis tools provide cross-tabulations (commonly referred to as *cross-tabs*), set analysis and filtering, video playback, click-stream analysis, and raw data reporting.

One of the best ways to delve deeper into your data is to have it **cross-tabulated**. Tabulating respondent answers against the key questions in your research, and viewing the results side by side, is the essence of a cross-tab (see Figure AppE.5). Cross-tabs help you find the similarities, trends, and distinctions between groups of research participants. In the example shown in Figure AppE.5, the site was ranked very low (0) in terms of visual design by 12 respondents (this is the number at the bottom of the first column), but of those 12, 10 respondents ranked the company high on the scale of leadership (1 gave a ranking of 7, 4 a ranking of 8, 2 a ranking of 9, and 3 a ranking of 10). This analysis shows that for the site in question, a strong visual Web design is not necessary for the company to be considered a leader. Cross-tabs allow researchers to discover interesting relationships in their data that would not normally be obvious upon casual inspection.

Another useful technique is to filter all of your data according to participant responses to a particular question. For example, maybe you want to look at data of only the participants who said that the site looked attractive (see Figure AppE.6). You can filter all of the data according to the responses to this question and then see what this group of participants said or did for other questions and tasks.

Similarly, you might use filters to view only the participants who thought they had successfully completed a task and then look at the video of them completing the task (see Figure AppE.7).

Cross Tab: Results

Matthew Tarpy's
eShopping Intelligence Center   **net**Raker™

Support | Sign-out
NetRaker Home > My NetRaker Home > IC Home >   Friday, March 16, 2001   11:53:43 AM

Predictor: Rank your impression of this site's visual design in terms of:
Option: You don't want to continue on this site: You want to explore further

		0	1	2	3	4	5	6	7	8	9	10	Totals
Respondent: For each of the following descriptions, rank your impression of what this site conveys to you about the company it represents. **Option:** Follower: Leader	0												
	1	1											1
	2					1	1						2
	3							1	1				2
	4												
	5	1			1		1	1	4				8
	6						2	1	1				4
	7	1					5	3	3	2			14
	8	4			4		1	3	4	5	2	2	25
	9	2	1				1	2	2	1	3		12
	10	3				1		1	1	5	1	5	17
	Totals	12	1		5	2	11	12	16	13	6	7	85

Key

Predictor: Rank your impression of this site's visual design in terms of:

Respondent: For each of the following descriptions, rank your impression of what this site

AppE.5   (www.netraker.com, March 16, 2001)

Figure AppE.5

A cross-tabulation tool can show correlations between two sets of responses. On this chart the question represented along the horizontal axis is a rating of the quality of the site's visual design. Responses are on a scale of 0 ("You don't want to continue on this site") to 10 ("You want to explore further"); these are the numbers running across the top of the chart. The question represented along the vertical axis is a rating of the overall impression of the company that the site conveys. Again, responses are on a scale of 0 (in this case meaning "Follower") to 10 ("Leader"); these are the numbers running down the left-hand side. In this study there were a total of 85 respondents. Each number in the body of the chart represents the number of respondents whose response to the first question matched the ranking shown at the top of that column and whose response to the second question matched the ranking shown on the left-hand side of that row.

Figure AppE.6

This Web-based reporting tool has a graph of all the respondent answers to each question. This tool also provides buttons for choosing filters to show only responses from individuals who answered a certain way, such as everyone who answered "8 or above" on the same scale.

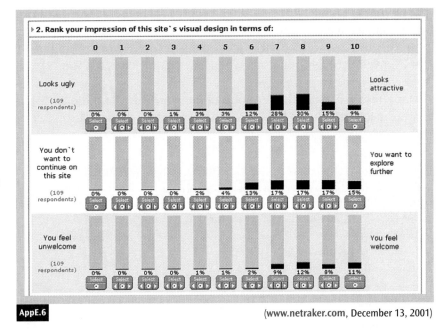

AppE.6 (www.netraker.com, December 13, 2001)

Figure AppE.7

Videos of participant actions are vital in online research when you're looking for site design problems. Individual videos are captured online and recorded for later playback. In this report, only videos of people who were able to complete a specific task are shown.

Filtering of Respondents and Experience Recordings

Filters:

Question	Option	Value
Find the cheapest flight from the Chicago, Illinois area to the Washington D.C. Area leaving on May 2, 2001 and returning May 11, 2001.	I was able to complete the task	is true

(Remove all Question Filters)

Research Participants in this Filter:
RP2 RP4 RP5 RP6 RP7

If a NetRaker Experience Recorder Video is available for a Research Participant, the RP link above will appear with a button.

AppE.7 (www.netraker.com, December 13, 2001)

Sometimes you might be interested simply in whether research participants completed a task and how long it took them (see Figure AppE.8).

You might also want to view a clickstream to see how the different users moved through your site when attempting the task (see Figure AppE.9).

Many research tools also let you import your raw data into software analysis packages like SPSS, SAS, WinCross, Minitab, and Excel. Once

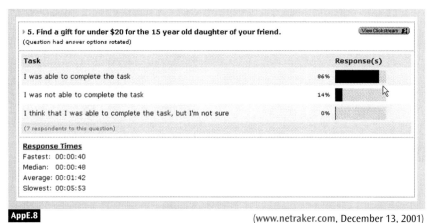

AppE.8   (www.netraker.com, December 13, 2001)

Figure AppE.8

This task report shows the completion rate for a particular task, as well as the response times. Clicking on the **View Clickstream** button displays the clickstream graph for this task (see Figure AppE.9).

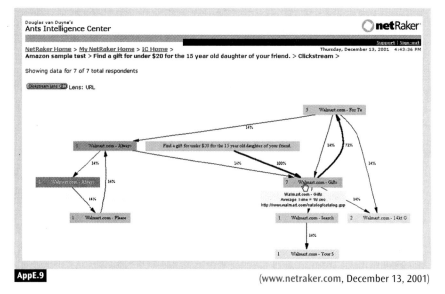

AppE.9   (www.netraker.com, December 13, 2001)

Figure AppE.9

This Web-based clickstream visualization tool shows the paths people took when given a specific task. Pages are color-coded according to the amount of time spent on each page. Pages that show many incoming and outgoing links, like the one the cursor points to in this graph, may be problematic. Videos of visitor interactions on that page will help show any problems they had.

you have done so, you can cross-tabulate the data and perform other statistical analyses (such as regression analysis) on your data.

If you decide to use online research, you can make the capture, analysis, and reporting of quantifiable results quick and affordable.

E.6 Comparison of Research Methods

This section offers a brief comparison of features of online Web research tools from NetRaker[1] and traditional research methods. Depending on your project, certain methods might be more appropriate than others.

Table AppE.1

Research Methods Compared

Features/Benefits	NetRaker	Usability Lab	Market Research
FLEXIBILITY			
Usability Research			
Task testing	✓	✓	–
Competitive comparison	✓	✓	–
Random customer task analysis	✓	–	–
Wireless testing	✓	✓	–
Market Research			
Concept testing	✓	–	✓
Brand value	✓	–	✓
Price elasticity	✓	–	✓
Invitation Methods			
Link invitation	✓	–	✓
Multiple intercept invitation methods	✓	–	✓
Site exit intercepts	✓	–	–
E-mail invitation	✓	✓	✓
Easy-to-change welcome and invitation text	✓	✓	✓
Research Scripting			
Branching	✓	✓	✓
Quotas	✓	✓	✓
Block rotation	✓	✓	✓
Automatic validation of task completion	✓	–	–

(continued)

---

1 Note that two of this book's authors, Doug van Duyne and James Landay, are the founders of NetRaker.

Features/Benefits	NetRaker	Usability Lab	Market Research
Question Types			
Over 20 question types	✓	✓	✓
Customized ratings (for example, 1–10, 1–7, 1–6, 1–5, Hot/Warm/Cold)	✓	✓	✓
Reporting			
Real time	✓	–	–
Cross-tabs	✓	✓	✓
Filtering	✓	–	–
Online videos	✓	–	–
Video archives	✓	✓	✓
DATA ACCESS			
Client ownership of data	✓	✓	✓
Collaborative work environment	✓	✓	✓
REAL CUSTOMER FEEDBACK			
Online view and playback of customer mouse movements, clicks, and typing	✓	–	–
Evaluation of your Web site by real people	✓	✓	✓
Insights into customers' subjective thoughts	✓	✓	✓
REAL-TIME CUSTOMER OBSERVATION			
Capture of participant actions on video	✓	✓	–
Tracking of behavior of real site users	✓	✓	–
REMOTE SITE EVALUATION			
No complex software download	✓	–	✓
Platform independent	✓	–	✓
Browser independent	✓	–	✓
Flexibility to participate anywhere, anytime	✓	–	–
Evaluation of users in their own environment	✓	–	–
Clickstream path analysis of pages visited	✓	–	–
Automatic clickstream page aggregation	✓	–	–

Table AppE.1
(continued)

Table AppE.1
(continued)

Features/Benefits	NetRaker	Usability Lab	Market Research
DATA ACCURACY AND INTEGRITY			
Large sample used	✓	–	✓
Findings based on geographically dispersed, statistically reliable data	✓	–	✓
Depth of information			
Video	✓	✓	–
Clickstream	✓	–	–
Self-report	✓	✓	✓
BENCHMARK DATA			
Ongoing customer satisfaction metrics 24/7	✓	–	–
Inexpensive competitive comparisons	✓	–	–
Tracking against historical data, industries, and best of the best	✓	–	✓
Comparison to national norms	✓	–	–
Determination of customer retention factors in five categories	✓	–	–
PANEL OPTIONS			
Panel recruitment tools	✓	–	–
Probability panel	✓	–	–
Nonprobability panel	✓	–	–
No cost for using client panel	✓	✓	✓
Specialized panels	✓	–	–
Flexible panel screening	✓	–	✓
REPORTING			
Automated real-time online reporting	✓	–	–
Drill-down and filtering capability	✓	–	–
Raw data reports	✓	✓	✓
CONFIGURATIONS			
Research cobranding	✓	–	–
Full service	✓	✓	✓
Self-service	✓	–	✓
Research participant recruitment	✓	✓	✓

24/7 • Twenty-four hours a day, seven days a week. Usually this term refers to the reliability of a system, one that cannot fail under any circumstances. Sometimes found as *24/7/365,* meaning 365 days a year as well. Also found as *24/7/360,* meaning 360 degrees around the globe.

accelerator • A way to speed up a task for the customer, such as a keyboard shortcut, a macro, or automatic storage of information.

access provider • See *Internet service provider.*

account management system • Any system designed to help people manage the personal information stored by a Web site.

acquisition cost • The cost to acquire a new customer.

Active Server Page • See *ASP* (definition 1).

Adobe Illustrator • A graphic design software tool that is useful for the creation of high-fidelity prototypes.

affinity diagramming • A way of organizing data in which all the individual points and concepts that have been gathered are arranged on a wall-sized, hierarchical diagram. For an example, see Figure 3.4 in Chapter 3—Knowing Your Customers: Principles and Techniques.

affordance • A clue, often visual, to how an object works. For example, most door handles provide an affordance for grasping. Buttons in modern graphical user interfaces, such as action buttons, look three-dimensional, providing affordances for pushing. For more information, see ACTION BUTTONS (K4).

alert • A brief message that notifies a customer of special events that may be of interest, such as that a library book is due soon or that the price of a stock has dropped below a certain mark. Compare *focused advertisement* and *newsletter.* For more information, see E-MAIL SUBSCRIPTIONS (E2).

alpha • Referring to the first cut of a Web site created in the Implementation phase of Web development. An alpha version of a site contains basic functionality and major page types but is not yet polished or ready to be deployed. Compare *beta.*

anchor text • The hypertext label that is used to link to a particular page.

antialiasing • Smoothing out jagged edges in images or fonts, creating gradual transitions instead of sharp transitions on the borders of images. Antialiased images usually look more professional, but they take a little more time to produce than unantialiased images.

Apache • One of the most popular Web servers. Apache is an example of open-source software.

API • Application programming interface, the means for using an existing piece of software in the source code for a new piece of software.

application programming interface • See *API*.

application service provider • Sometimes abbreviated *ASP*, a Web site or company that provides individuals or enterprises access over the Internet to applications and related services that would otherwise have to be located in their own personal or enterprise computers. Some ASPs focus on providing highly specific services that can be integrated into another Web site, such as search engines or providers of stock information. You can use an ASP to outsource certain functions of a Web site, such as local search functionality, thereby making it easier to add the search function to a Web site.

ASP • (pronounced by speaking each letter individually) 1. Active Server Page, a technology created by Microsoft that mixes HTML and software code. The code is executed when a client Web browser makes a request, enabling the creation of dynamically generated HTML. Compare *JSP*, a competing Java-based technology, and *PHP*, a competing Perl-based technology. 2. See *application service provider*.

asynchronous communication • A communications setup in which customers can leave messages that others can respond to later, such as in e-mail or on a message board. Compare *synchronous communication*. For more information, see COMMUNITY CONFERENCE (A3). **(A3)**

authentication • A process that proves a person really is who he or she claims to be. One example of an authentication process is the use of passwords. Compare *identification*. For more information, see PERSISTENT CUSTOMER SESSIONS (H5). **(H5)**

automatic pop-up • A pop-up window that appears simply as a result of a customer's arrival at or departure from a Web site. Automatic pop-up windows usually contain advertisements or surveys for improving the quality of a Web site. Compare *link-based pop-up*. For more information, see POP-UP WINDOWS (H6). **(H6)**

b2b • Business-to-business. In e-commerce, a b2b business sells products or services to another business.

b2c • Business-to-customer. In e-commerce, a b2c business sells products or services to end customers or consumers.

b2e • Business-to-employee. In e-commerce, a b2e business provides services and productivity applications online to employees.

b2g • Business-to-government. In e-commerce, a b2g business sells products or services to the government.

back-end cost • A cost incurred as a result of responding to customer needs not addressed by the basic Web site—for example, through support calls, returns, and the like. For more information, see Chapter 1—Customer-Centered Web Design. **1**

bandwidth • A measure of data transmission speeds over a network connection. Bandwidth is often measured in kilobits per second (kbps) or megabits per second (mbps). Typical modem speeds are 28.8 kbps and 56 kbps. Bandwidth should not be confused with *latency,* which refers to the amount of time it takes to transfer data from one point to another. See also *broadband, cable modem, DSL,* and *latency.*

banner ad • A small horizontal advertisement, usually at the top of a homepage. Visitors click it to link to a Web site. Banner ads are often animated and have standard sizes. Most advertisements on Web pages are banner ads.

beta • Referring to the second version of a Web site, created in the Implementation phase of Web development. It contains nearly all of the desired functionality and is more polished than the *alpha* release.

between-groups experiment • An experiment in which the pool of test participants is divided into two groups and each group is assigned to a different condition. For example, if there are two different Web sites to test, each participant uses only one of the two sites. Compare *within-groups experiment.* For more information, see Appendix A—Running Usability Evaluations.

bits per second (bps) • A measure of bandwidth. See *bandwidth* and *latency.*

(D3) **blurb** • A continuation of the headline on a Web page. A blurb provides details of the customer benefit, reinforcing what is important and unique about the content. Blurbs must be short and precise, not more than one or two sentences. Compare *headline.* For more information, see HEADLINES AND BLURBS (D3).

(D9) **bookmark** • A mechanism built into most Web browsers that saves the location of a Web page so that the customer will not need to type in the address each time. Also known as a *favorite.* For more information, see DISTINCTIVE HTML TITLES (D9).

(J2) **Boolean search** • A search that uses the term *and* or *or.* For example, the search "computer and monitor" would find all Web pages containing both *computer* and *monitor,* whereas "computer or monitor" would find all Web pages containing either *computer* or *monitor.* For more information, see STRAIGHTFORWARD SEARCH FORMS (J2).

(4) **bottom-line data** • Quantitative usability data, often collected in later stages of design, that could include time to complete a task, number of errors made, rate of learning, and retention of learned material over time. Compare *process data.* For more information, see Chapter 4—Involving Customers with Iterative Design and Appendix A—Running Usability Evaluations.

bps • See *bits per second.*

(E1) **brand** • What customers remember or feel about a Web site or the company behind it. Brand can be shaped by images, graphic look, or logo of a company. For more information, see SITE BRANDING (E1).

(K6) **bread crumb** • A small navigation cue giving some indication of where a visitor is currently located on a Web site and where he or she came from. For more information, see LOCATION BREAD CRUMBS (K6).

brick-and-mortar • Referring to a company that has a strong real-world presence but weak or no Web presence. Compare *click-and-mortar* and *e-tailer.*

broadband • Referring to a network connection with high bandwidth, such as DSL or cable modem. Typical speeds range from 256 kbps to 2 mbps.

brochureware • A derisive term for a simple Web site that does no more than promote a company and its products.

browser • See *Web browser.*

browsing • One of two major strategies visitors use to find information on a Web site, in which they examine pages and click on links that seem to take them closer to their goal Web page (regardless of whether that page actually exists). Compare *searching*. For more information, see BROWSABLE CONTENT (B2).

bug report • A report of a problem that is provided in a customer e-mail, a Web site evaluation, quality assurance testing, or server log file analysis.

business analysis document • A document, produced during the Discovery phase of Web development, that spells out the business needs of both the client and the customers. For more information, see Chapter 5—Processes for Developing Customer-Centered Sites.

business plan • A high-level proposal that spells out a company's business model, the basic strategy for how a company will make money.

cable modem • A form of broadband communication that transfers data across a cable television network. Compare *DSL*.

cache • (v) To store information nearby. (n) The space used to store cached information. Web browsers cache Web pages that visitors have already seen so that the pages will load more quickly if viewed again. For more information, see REUSABLE IMAGES (L5).

card sorting • A method of categorization by which customers help you organize and label large groups of content. For more information, see Chapter 3—Knowing Your Customers: Principles and Techniques.

category description • A technique for testing the usefulness and usability of link names, independent of visual design and layout, in which participants are asked to describe what they think a given category contains. Compare *category identification*. For more information, see HIERARCHICAL ORGANIZATION (B3) and FAMILIAR LANGUAGE (K11).

category identification • A technique for testing the usefulness and usability of link names, independent of visual design and layout, in which participants are given a list of category names and a list of tasks, and asked to choose the category that they think would help them complete each task. Compare *category description*. For more information, see FAMILIAR LANGUAGE (K11).

certification authority • A trusted third-party vendor that issues digital certificates for Web servers. For more information, see Chapter 5—Processes for Developing Customer-Centered Sites.

CGI • See *Common Gateway Interface.*

click-and-mortar • Referring to a company that has a strong Web presence as well as a strong real-world presence. Compare *brick-and-mortar* and *e-tailer*.

click-through • The number of visitors who click on a banner ad. Click-through is usually expressed as a percentage. To calculate it, we divide the total number of banner ads clicked on by the total number of banner ads displayed. See also *CPM*.

clickstream • The click path or page path that visitors take when they go through a site. Some server log tools and online usability research applications provide clickstream analysis tools. For more information, see Appendix E—Online Research.

client • 1. The specific computer or software that requests information, or any other resource, from a server. Web browsers are the most common clients. Compare *server*. See also *client–server architecture* and *Web browser*. 2. A person or company for whom you are doing Web design and development work; the person (company) providing the funding. Compare *customer*.

client–server architecture • A common form of software architecture, in which a server contains information or other resources, and clients request the information or resources. The Web is an example of client–server architecture. Compare *peer-to-peer architecture*.

Common Gateway Interface (CGI) • The standard way of processing Web-based forms. CGI is also used to create dynamically generated HTML. Programming languages used for CGI include Perl, Python, and Java. Alternatives to CGI are the ASP, JSP, and PHP technologies.

 **community** • A group of people tied together by shared interests or common values. For more information, see COMMUNITY CONFERENCE (A3), MESSAGE BOARDS (D5), and RECOMMENDATION COMMUNITY (G4).

company-centered design • A design strategy in which the needs and interests of the company dominate the structure and content of the Web site. Compare *customer-centered design, designer-centered design,* and *technology-centered design*. For more information, see Chapter 1—Customer-Centered Web Design.

competitive analysis • An analysis that evaluates competitors' Web sites, including the features they offer, as well as which features are important to customers and which are not.

compression • An approach to reducing the file size of an image in which redundant information is encoded more compactly. Alternatively, the number of colors can be reduced, thereby reducing the amount of information required to encode the image. Compare *cropping* and *shrinking*. For more information, see FAST-DOWNLOADING IMAGES (L2).

conversion rate • A value representing the number of visitors who become buying customers on a Web site. This value is usually expressed as a percentage. To calculate it, we divide the total number of unique customers by the total number of unique visitors. Higher conversion rates are better than low ones.

cookie • A browser feature that allows Web sites to keep information on a visitor's computer. Typically, cookies would be used for personalization, but they can also be used for tracking a customer's movements through the Web. For this reason, cookies are at the center of a growing privacy debate. For more information, see   PERSONALIZED CONTENT (D4), PERSISTENT CUSTOMER SESSIONS (H5), FAIR INFORMATION PRACTICES (E3), and PRIVACY POLICY (E4).

CPM • Cost per thousand impressions. CPM is the cost per 1,000 people delivered by a medium or media schedule. For banner ads, CPM is the cost per thousand ads seen by visitors. See also *click-through*.

crawler • A program that gathers and processes content for later use by starting from a list of a few sites and going from link to link, opening pages and indexing the words on those pages. Crawlers make use of meta-information about the content, as well as the content itself, to create a search index. Also known as a *spider*. For more information, see WRITING FOR SEARCH ENGINES (D6).

critical incident • An incident during a usability test, in which the participant has either a positive or a negative reaction. Negative reactions include frustration, anger, or confusion during a task. Expletives can be strong indicators of negative critical incidents. Positive reactions include cases in which people are pleasantly surprised or say something positive about the site. For more information, see Chapter 4—Involving Customers with Iterative Design and Appendix A—Running Usability Evaluations.

CRM • Customer relationship management, methods and software to manage the long-term relationship between a company and a customer.

cropping • An approach to reducing the file size of an image in which unneeded portions of the image are trimmed. Compare *compression* and *shrinking*. For more information, see FAST-DOWNLOADING IMAGES (L2).

cross-selling • Promoting products related to ones the customer already wants to purchase. Compare *up-selling*. For more information, see SHOPPING CART (F3) and CROSS-SELLING AND UP-SELLING (G2).

cross-tabulation • A method of evaluating research results in which respondent answers are compared with the key questions in the research, and the results are viewed side by side. For more information, see Appendix E—Online Research.

customer • A person who will use the Web site you are designing. Also called *target customer.* Compare *client* (definition 2).

customer analysis document • A document, developed during the Discovery phase of Web development, that provides a deep understanding of the needs, tools, and existing practices of the Web site's target customers. For more information, see Chapter 5—Processes for Developing Customer-Centered Sites.

customer-centered design • A design strategy that (1) focuses on understanding people, their tasks, the technology available, and the larger social and organizational context of where they live, work, and play; (2) keeps the customer involved in the design process; and (3) elicits from visitors to your Web site consistently high marks for content, ease of use, performance, trustworthiness, and overall satisfaction—that is, it provides a positive experience for all customers, whether they are there to find information, to be part of a community, to purchase items, or to be entertained. Compare *company-centered design, designer-centered design,* and *technology-centered design.* For more information, see Chapter 1—Customer-Centered Web Design.

customer-centered Web site • A Web site that provides real value and delivers a positive customer experience. Customer-centered Web sites receive consistently high marks for content, ease of use, performance, trustworthiness, and overall satisfaction from visitors.

customer experience • A broad term referring to the whole experience a customer feels when using a Web site, both online and offline. Customer experience includes such online factors as ease of use and content, as well as offline factors such as fulfillment and customer service.

customer relationship management • See *CRM*.

customer session • A set of interactions by a customer with a Web site during one sitting. Web servers typically use cookies to track who the customer is and what he or she did on-site during the session. For more information, see PERSONALIZED CONTENT (D4) and PERSISTENT CUSTOMER SESSIONS (H5).

customization • A customer-driven process in which customers enter data and change the layout of the Web site to fit their tastes and interests. Customization is one way of achieving *personalization*. For more information, see PERSONALIZED CONTENT (D4).

default setting • The normal setting for something, before a customer changes it.

deliverable • The artifact created at the end of a milestone phase (Discovery, Exploration, Refinement, Production, Implementation, Launch, or Maintenance) of Web development. Common deliverables include interactive prototypes and specification documents.

demographics • Detailed characteristics of customers, such as age, education, income, and hobbies.

design document • A document, created during the Production phase of Web development, that describes how a Web site works in great detail and uses site maps, storyboards, and schematics to describe the flow of interaction. For more information, see Chapter 5—Processes for Developing Customer-Centered Sites.

design style guide • General rules for site design to be followed on every Web page to minimize inconsistencies.

designer-centered design • A Web site built to reflect the needs and desires of the designer, not necessarily of the customers. Compare *company-centered design, customer-centered design,* and *technology-centered design.* For more information, see Chapter 1—Customer-Centered Web Design.

desktop metaphor • The conceptual model around which modern computer interfaces are organized, consisting of files, folders, trash cans, and so on. See also *GUI*.

DHTML • See *Dynamic HTML.*

digital certificate • Proof that a Web server is who it says it is. Digital certificates are issued by a variety of certification authorities. For more information, see Chapter 5—Processes for Developing Customer-Centered Sites.

Digital Subscriber Line • See *DSL.*

directory • A form of organizing information, in which content appears in categories, usually alphabetically, sequentially, or hierarchically. The best known example of a directory is Yahoo! Also called *index.* For more information, see HIERARCHICAL ORGANIZATION (B3).

Discovery phase • The first phase of Web development, in which you define the design problem and you and your client come to an agreement about the Web site's overall goals. For more information, see Chapter 5—Processes for Developing Customer-Centered Sites. See also *Exploration phase, Refinement phase, Production phase, Implementation phase, Launch phase,* and *Maintenance phase.*

disintermediation • The removal of middlemen. For example, e-commerce can simplify ordering and distribution of products by giving customers a direct line to the manufacturer. All the people who distributed the product to local stores, and all of the local stores, are removed.

Document Object Model (DOM) • A standard way of representing HTML and XML documents as objects that can be manipulated in programming languages. Developed by W3C as an open standard.

document type definition • See *DTD.*

DOM • See *Document Object Model.*

domain name • Technically, a way to name computers on the Internet. It is more common to use the domain name to identify a Web site, such as www.berkeley .edu, than to use its numerical IP address.

DSL • Digital Subscriber Line, a form of broadband network connection for the home that uses existing telephone lines. Compare *cable modem.*

DTD • Document type definition, a specification that accompanies a document and identifies the codes that separate paragraphs, identify topic headings, and so forth, as well as how each is to be processed. For example, a DTD is used by HTML and XML to define tags such as <HTML> and <B>, and to define any tag ordering constraints.

Dynamic HTML (DHTML) • Not to be confused with *dynamically generated HTML,* DHTML uses the Document Object Model to dynamically change Web pages after they have been downloaded to a customer's browser.

dynamically generated HTML • A Web page that is generated on the fly when a visitor requests it. The HTML in the Web page does not fully exist until the request is made. A simple use of dynamically generated HTML is to include the last time the HTML file was updated. A more sophisticated use is to provide personalization. Usually you would create dynamically generated HTML through CGI, ASP, JSP, or PHP. Dynamically generated HTML should not be confused with *Dynamic HTML,* a Web standard that is being developed by W3C.

e-commerce • The business of selling products or services online. The two major forms of e-commerce are business-to-business (b2b) and business-to-consumer (b2c). For more information, see PERSONAL E-COMMERCE (A1).

e-tailer • An electronic retailer that sells products online exclusively. Compare *brick-and-mortar* and *click-and-mortar.*

embedded link • A link that is contained in the body of a text (as opposed to being listed at the end of an article). For more information, see INVERSE-PYRAMID WRITING STYLE (D7) and EMBEDDED LINKS (K7).

encryption • Translation of data into a secret form so that unauthorized people cannot easily understand it. SSL is a way of encrypting information transferred over the Web. For more information, see SECURE CONNECTIONS (E6).

ethnography • A formal technique used in sociology and anthropology to observe and interact with people. See also *field observation*.

Exploration phase • The second phase of Web development, following Discovery, in which you generate multiple designs. For more information, see Chapter 5—Processes for Developing Customer-Centered Sites. See also *Discovery phase, Refinement phase, Production phase, Implementation phase, Launch phase*, and *Maintenance phase*.

Extensible Markup Language • See *XML*.

extranet • A private portion of a company's Web site intended for suppliers, vendors, partners, and customers. An extranet can also be an extension of a company's intranet. Compare *intranet*.

false positive • A problem with a Web site interface that is identified by heuristic evaluation but never found to exist in a usability study of the same interface.

FAQ • Literally, frequently asked questions. A FAQ page provides answers to questions commonly asked by visitors to a Web site. For more information, see FREQUENTLY ASKED QUESTIONS (H7).

favorite • See *bookmark*.

field observation • An experimental technique in which you watch people in their own environment, at home or at work, to see how they use your Web site and other tools, as well as how they interact with other people in their environment.

firewall • A proxy that limits the kind of information transferred over a network. Companies often use firewalls to protect their computers from unauthorized external access.

first read • The dominant visual element of a Web page that draws the customer's eyes. For more information, see HOMEPAGE PORTAL (C1), UP-FRONT VALUE PROPOSITION (C2), and CLEAR FIRST READS (I3).

Fitts's Law • An empirically determined law used to calculate the time it takes to move from a given point to a target object. Intuitively, the law states that objects that are far away or small take longer to point to than objects that are close or large. Fitts's Law has implications for the size of clickable links and images. For more information, see Chapter 3—Knowing Your Customers: Principles and Techniques and ACTION BUTTONS (K4).

Flash • The tool and the browser plug-in, developed by Macromedia, for creating and viewing interactive multimedia presentations.

flow • 1. An interaction sequence through or navigation structure of a Web site, often illustrated with a storyboard. 2. Natural and easy movement of a customer on your Web site from goals to fulfillment of those goals.

focus group • A group of representative target customers who are gathered to provide feedback on their motivation for visiting a Web site, describe their response to it, and identify the tasks they want to accomplish there.

focused advertisement • An advertisement that draws attention to a new promotion, special offer, or new product. Compare *alert* and *newsletter*. For more information, see E-MAIL SUBSCRIPTIONS (E2).

fold • An imaginary line on a Web page that delineates what is visible in a browser without making the visitor scroll down. The content below the line is "below the fold." Because a potential customer may not necessarily see content below the fold at first, the most important information should be placed above it. For more information, see ABOVE THE FOLD (I2).

force • A key issue or constraint that comes into play when you're trying to solve a particular design problem.

frequently asked questions • See *FAQ*.

fulfillment • All of the surrounding processes required to deliver and support products that customers have purchased, including logistics, inventory management, parcel management, and customer service. Part of back-end costs.

GIF • (pronounced "jiff") Graphics Interchange Format, a widely supported and popular way to store images. GIF is usually used for small images and images requiring transparency. See also *JPEG, PNG,* and *SVG*. For more information, see FAST-DOWNLOADING IMAGES (L2).

gold-plating • Trying to get a Web site absolutely perfect before launch.

graphic design • Visual communication of information, using elements such as color, images, typography, and layout. Also called *visual design*. Compare *navigation design*.

graphical user interface • See *GUI*.

Graphics Interchange Format • See *GIF*.

greeking • A visual design and usability testing technique in which nonsense text is placed on a Web page. Greeking allows those who view a design or participants testing the interface to focus on the layout and visual design of a page, instead of its content. Typical tasks you would ask participants to do on a greeked page include pointing to what they think is the page title, and pointing to what they believe are the news items. Greeking is often used in low-fidelity prototypes. For more information, see GRID LAYOUT (I1).

grid layout • A technique for organizing Web pages that is borrowed from graphic design (where it is used for organizing page layouts for newspapers, magazines, and other documents). In a grid layout, a page is divided into rows and columns, and every element is made to fit within this grid. Constant design elements, such as titles and logos, always appear in the same place, giving a consistent theme to every page. For more information, see GRID LAYOUT (I1).

GUI • (pronounced "gooey") Graphical user interface. This term often refers to the desktop interface, such as the interface found in Microsoft Windows or the Macintosh operating system. However, GUI can refer to any interface that uses graphics. See also *desktop metaphor*.

guidelines • Suggestions for how to build a Web site, but not as detailed or as rigid as specifications. Guidelines do not have to be as comprehensive, and they can leave more details to your discretion. Compare *specification document*. For more information, see Chapter 5—Processes for Developing Customer-Centered Sites.

Handheld Device Markup Language • See *HDML*.

HCI • Human–computer interaction, a discipline concerned with the design, evaluation, and implementation of interactive computing systems for human use and with the study of major phenomena surrounding them. HCI includes a multitude of other disciplines, such as user interface design, the study of group work, human factors, human physiology, cognitive modeling, and universal accessibility.

HDML • Handheld Device Markup Language. Similar to HTML, HDML is a way to format information for small devices, such as cell phones. WML is considered the successor to HDML. For more information, see SITE ACCESSIBILITY (B9).

B9

headline • A sentence fragment, roughly ten words or less so that it can appear in large type in a small space, that articulates a Web page's hook in the shortest form possible. Compare *blurb*. For more information, see HEADLINES AND BLURBS (D3).

D3

heuristic evaluation • An informal method for evaluating the usability of a Web site, in which three to five expert judges evaluate a site independently, using a list of usability heuristics, or principles.

high-fidelity prototype • A finished and highly detailed prototype, rich with typography, colors, and images. Often presented to clients, high-fidelity prototypes are usually created with computer-based tools. A mock-up is a high-fidelity representation of an individual Web page. Compare *low-fidelity prototype* and *medium-fidelity prototype*. For more information, see Chapter 4—Involving Customers with Iterative Design.

4

hit • A metric that measures the number of requests to a Web server. Hits are generally ineffective as a metric because each image file downloaded also counts as a hit. However, hits can be used as a rough approximation of the popularity of a Web site or pages within a Web site. Compare *impressions*.

horizontal prototype • A prototype that shows a broad swath of what the eventual Web site will support. A horizontal prototype might show the top-level pages, but without much depth behind them. For more information, see Chapter 4—Involving Customers with Iterative Design.

4

hortal • Horizontal portal, a portal that covers a broad range of interests and topics. We hope this terrifying-sounding term never becomes mainstream. This term should not be confused with the art nouveau architect Victor Horta, or the *Star Trek* species known as *horta*. Compare *vortal*.

HTML • HyperText Markup Language, the information that represents the content on a Web page, as well as how the content is displayed.

HTTP • HyperText Transfer Protocol, the means by which HTML Web pages are transferred from the Web server to the Web browser.

human–computer interaction • See *HCI*.

hypertext • Units of information connected and associated with other units. An instance of such an association is called a link or hypertext link. The most pervasive form of hypertext is the Web, though it is by no means the only form.

HyperText Markup Language • See *HTML*.

HyperText Transfer Protocol • See *HTTP*.

I18N • Abbreviation for *internationalization,* the process of adapting a site for international audiences. The *18* comes from the fact that there are 18 letters between the initial *i* and the final *n* in the word *internationalization.* Compare *L10N.* For more information, see INTERNATIONALIZED AND LOCALIZED CONTENT (D10).

identification • Something that states who someone is. One form of identification is a user name. Compare *authentication.* For more information, see PERSISTENT CUSTOMER SESSIONS (H5).

IE • Internet Explorer, Microsoft's standard Web browser. Typically followed by a version number, such as IE4 or IE5.5.

IIS • Internet Information Server, Microsoft's standard Web server. See also *Apache.*

image map • An image on a Web page whose individual parts can be clicked on to take visitors to other Web pages. Image maps can be either client side (where the Web *browser* processes the mouse click) or server side (where the Web *server* processes the mouse click). Client-side image maps are usually faster to process and provide better accessibility.

Implementation phase • The fifth phase of Web development, following Production, in which a software development team creates the HTML, images, database tables, and software necessary for a polished and fully functional Web site that can be rolled out and used by its target customers. For more information, see Chapter 5—Processes for Developing Customer-Centered Sites. See also *Discovery phase, Exploration phase, Refinement phase, Production phase, Launch phase,* and *Maintenance phase.*

impressions • The number of times people see a specific advertisement. Compare *hit.*

index • 1. See *directory.* 2. The data gathered during a search engine Web crawl.

informal evaluation • A quick method for evaluating the effectiveness of a Web site. Typically, five to ten people representative of target customers help you critique your prototype by trying to carry out some tasks from the task analysis.

information architecture • The way information is organized and presented on a Web site. From a usability standpoint, information architecture involves understanding how customers name things, how they categorize and group objects, how they navigate through information, and how they search for information. From an implementation standpoint, information architecture involves creating a structure that scales, or one that can grow as you add more content. Sometimes called *information design.* For more information, see Chapter 4—Involving Customers with Iterative Design and Pattern Group B—Creating a Navigation Framework.

information design • See *information architecture.*

information scent • The perceived proximity to desired information, delivered by cues such as text, link names, images, headings, grouping, page layout, and previous pages seen. For more information, see DESCRIPTIVE, LONGER LINK NAMES (K9).

interactive prototype • A computer-based prototype that is generated to give clients and customers a general understanding of what the completed product should feel like and what it will be capable of doing. See also *wire frame*.

intercept research • A method of recruiting participants to a research study by popping up a short questionnaire on the site to a random sample of visitors or to visitors who performed a targeted action on the site (for example, they reached a particular page or left the site). Intercept research is often used for qualifying research participants for more in-depth research. For more information, see Appendix E—Online Research.

interlaced image • An image that, when loading, appears blurry at first and then is progressively refined. This allows customers to see the image before it fully loads. Compare *progressive-scan image*. For more information, see FAST-DOWNLOADING IMAGES (L2).

internationalization • The process of making software support different languages, dates and times, currencies, weights and measures, and number formats. Sometimes abbreviated *I18N*. Compare *localization*. For more information, see INTERNATIONALIZED AND LOCALIZED CONTENT (D10).

Internet Explorer • See *IE*.

Internet Information Server • See *IIS*.

Internet service provider (ISP) • An ISP sells an Internet connection to customers. Some ISPs provide cable modem, DSL, and modem access. Also called *access provider*.

interstitial • A page inserted in the normal flow of a task, typically for advertising purposes.

intranet • A Web site designed to be used internally within a company. Compare *extranet*. For more information, see ENABLING INTRANETS (A11).

inverse-pyramid writing • A common journalistic style in which the most important idea is stated first and the text continues to the least important idea. For more information, see INVERSE-PYRAMID WRITING STYLE (D7).

IP • Internet protocol.

ISP • See *Internet service provider*.

iterative design • A cyclical design process consisting of three stages: design, prototype, and evaluate. Iterative design is a simple and proven technique for developing useful and usable Web sites. For more information, see Chapter 4—Involving Customers with Iterative Design.

JAR file • A standard way of packaging a collection of Java files into a single file, for faster download. *JAR* stands for *Java archive*.

Java • A general-purpose programming language designed by Sun Microsystems, specifically for network applications. For more information, see www.javasoft.com.

Java archive • See *JAR file*.

JavaScript • A scripting language designed specifically for Web pages. See also *Document Object Model*.

JavaServer Pages • See *JSP*.

Joint Photographic Experts Group • See *JPEG*.

JPEG • (pronounced "jay-peg") Joint Photographic Experts Group, a widely supported file format for saving images with many colors, usually photographs. Sometimes seen as *JPG*. See also *GIF, PNG,* and *SVG*. For more information, see FAST-DOWNLOADING IMAGES (L2).

JSP • JavaServer Pages, a technology created by Sun Microsystems that mixes HTML and Java code together. The code is executed when a site visitor makes a request, enabling the creation of dynamically generated HTML. JSP uses Java servlet technology. Compare *ASP* (definition 1), a competing technology from Microsoft, and *PHP*, a similar Perl-based technology.

kbps • Kilobits per second.

keyword • A significant, illustrative word that describes something about the content or services offered by a site.

L10N • Abbreviation for *localization,* the process of adapting a site to support a local culture. The *10* comes from the fact that there are ten letters between the initial *l* and the final *n* in the word *localization.* Compare *I18N*. For more information, see INTERNATIONALIZED AND LOCALIZED CONTENT (D10).

latency • The amount of time it takes to transfer data from one point to another. Latency should not be confused with *bandwidth*. Here's how it works: The number of lanes in a highway can be considered the bandwidth, and the amount of time it takes to get from one city to another is the latency. In some cases, increasing the number of lanes will decrease the latency, but clearly, this will work only up to a certain point.

Launch phase • The sixth phase of Web development, following Implementation, in which the finished Web site is made available to its intended customers. For more information, see Chapter 5—Processes for Developing Customer-Centered Sites. See also *Discovery phase, Exploration phase, Refinement phase, Production phase, Implementation phase,* and *Maintenance phase.*

lead • The first few paragraphs of a story or longer text. The lead reinforces the headline and entices the visitor to read more. For more information, see INVERSE-PYRAMID WRITING STYLE (D7).

link-based pop-up • A pop-up window that appears when customers click on a link. Compare *automatic pop-up*. For more information, see POP-UP WINDOWS (H6).

link rot • The situation in which a link on your Web site becomes invalid because your site is out of date or the operator of an external site has changed the content of the page or decommissioned the page address without your knowledge.

localization • The process of redesigning a Web interface and translating content to support a local culture. Sometimes abbreviated *L10N*. Compare *internationalization*. For more information, see INTERNATIONALIZED AND LOCALIZED CONTENT (D10).

lossless compression • Reduction in the size of an image file without any loss in image quality. Compare *lossy compression*. For more information, see FAST-DOWN-LOADING IMAGES (L2).

lossy compression • Reduction in the size of an image file that results in some loss of image quality. Compare *lossless compression*. For more information, see FAST-DOWNLOADING IMAGES (L2).

low-fidelity prototype • A quick and informal prototype of a Web site design, often created by sketching on paper, using common art supplies. A low-fidelity prototype contains few details, focusing instead on high-level ideas. It is typically done in the early stages of design. Compare *medium-fidelity prototype* and *high-fidelity prototype*. For more information, see Chapter 4—Involving Customers with Iterative Design.

m-commerce • Mobile e-commerce, such as purchasing items through a cell phone or PDA. As of this writing, m-commerce is still in its early stages, and it is difficult to tell whether it is just hype or has real potential.

Macromedia Flash • See *Flash*.

maintenance document • A document that details how to maintain a completed Web site. For more information, see Chapter 5—Processes for Developing Customer-Centered Sites.

Maintenance phase • The final phase of Web development, following Launch, in which the development team supports the existing site by fixing bugs and making minor improvements, gathers and analyzes metrics of success, and prepares for the next redesign. For more information, see Chapter 5—Processes for Developing Customer-Centered Sites. See also *Discovery phase, Exploration phase, Refinement phase, Production phase, Implementation phase,* and *Launch phase*.

mbps • Megabits per second.

medium-fidelity prototype • A cleaned-up prototype that gives a feel for the final product, without showing too many details, such as typeface, color, and images. Medium-fidelity prototypes are typically done in the early stages of design. Unlike low-fidelity prototypes, they are typically presented to clients. Compare *low-fidelity prototype* and *high-fidelity prototype*. For more information, see Chapter 4—Involving Customers with Iterative Design.

mental model • The way a person believes a system works. People who have used computers extensively, for example, know that most computers consist of a central processing unit (CPU), a monitor, a hard drive, and a keyboard. An engineer will have a more detailed mental model, while a novice may have a much simpler (and possibly incorrect) one. Usability problems often occur when a customer's mental model does not match the actual workings of a system. The mental model helps set expectations, making the system predictable and understandable.

meta-information • Additional information about content, but not part of the content. Examples of meta-information include the author, the creation time, the last modification time, and the type of information, such as document, image, or audio file. Meta-information is sometimes encoded within META tags.

META tag • A marker in a file that indicates to software applications, including search engine crawlers, what a site or page contains. META tags are used on all Web pages to provide additional keywords not included in the text, including synonyms, phrases, and language translations. A META tag is often stored with but is separate from the content it represents. Here's a sample META tag representing the keywords on a Web page:

```
<meta name="keywords" content="chocolate,candy,treats,truffles">
```

For more information, see WRITING FOR SEARCH ENGINES (D6).

metrics • Measurements to determine whether the design team has reached its goals and requirements.

mock-up • A high-fidelity representation of a Web page that shows exactly how the page will appear. Usually produced with a graphics application such as Photoshop, mock-ups are not interactive. Mock-ups contain images, icons, typography, and sophisticated color schemes. Unlike schematics, mock-ups have graphic design that is meant to be taken literally. In some cases, mock-ups are the final deliverable of a design project, perhaps accompanied by written guidelines or specifications.

moderated forum • A forum in which messages are filtered and processed by one or more moderators that must approve all messages to make sure that they follow the established rules and norms. Compare *unmoderated forum*. For more information, see COMMUNITY CONFERENCE (A3).

Mozilla • See *Netscape*.

navigation design • The design of methods to help customers find their way around the information structure of a Web site. Navigation design is one part of information architecture. Compare *graphic design*.

Navigator • See *Netscape*.

NDA • See *nondisclosure agreement*.

Netscape • A Web browser company now owned by America Online. The term *Netscape* is typically used to refer to the Mozilla or Navigator browsers.

network effect • An increase in benefit as more individuals use a particular service. For more information, see NONPROFITS AS NETWORKS OF HELP (A5).

newsletter • A periodic e-mail message sent from a Web site to self-selected customers, informing them of special news, offers, deals, and so on. Compare *alert* and *focused advertisement*. For more information, see E-MAIL SUBSCRIPTIONS (E2).

nondisclosure agreement (NDA) • A legal document specifying that the signer agrees not to discuss any aspect of your product or services with others.

open-source software • Software that is distributed with the source code (the files used to construct the software in the first place), with few limitations on what others can do with the source code.

p2p • 1. Path to profitability, a business term referring to the strategy needed for companies to become profitable and self-sustaining. 2. See *peer-to-peer architecture*.

page template • A sample HTML file that contains the basic structure, layout, and scripts for a set of Web pages of a Web site. Page templates typically contain the navigation elements global to the Web site, as well as sections that can be edited for specific local navigation and specific content. Page templates are used to ensure consistency throughout a site. For more information, see PAGE TEMPLATES

(D1), CONTENT MODULES (D2), and Chapter 5—Processes for Developing Customer-Centered Sites.

participant • A friendly term for someone who helps test an interface design. Meant to replace the not-so-friendly term *subject*.

pattern • A design rule that communicates insight into a design problem, capturing the essence of the problem and its solution in a compact form. Design patterns form a language, or common vocabulary, that allows articulation of an infinite variety of Web designs. Patterns are a powerful conceptual framework for building compelling and effective Web sites that are easy to use.

PDA • Personal digital assistant, a small computing appliance for storing personal information. More and more PDAs include wireless connections, making Web access through these small devices possible.

PDF • Portable Document Format, a common file format for documents. Compare *PostScript*.

peer-to-peer architecture • Sometimes abbreviated *p2p*, peer-to-peer architecture is a communications model in which all customers are at the same level and have the same access to content and capabilities. A common example of peer-to-peer architecture is Napster, a file-sharing application. Many people believe peer-to-peer architecture will become more important in the years to come. Compare *client–server architecture*.

periodic backups • Backups of the entire Web site that are stored far away from the building that contains the Web server.

Perl • A programming language often used as part of the Common Gateway Interface.

persistent cookie • A cookie that is stored on the customer's hard drive, allowing your Web site to track that customer over a relatively long period of time. Compare *session cookie*. For more information, see PERSISTENT CUSTOMER SESSIONS (H5).

persistent customer session • A Web session that lets the Web server remember a customer for a relatively long period of time. Compare *temporary customer session*. For more information, see PERSISTENT CUSTOMER SESSIONS (H5).

persona • A detailed profile of a potential customer, including name, home address, background, and hobbies. The goal in creating personas is to make each customer seem as real as possible. Compare *profile*. For more information, see Chapter 3—Knowing Your Customers: Principles and Techniques.

personal digital assistant • See *PDA*.

personalization • A service-driven process that tailors Web pages to individuals or groups of individuals. Two examples of personalization are having a customer's name on a Web page, and remembering a previously entered mailing address. Personalization makes use of information gathered both explicitly (through customization) and implicitly (such as through server log files and previous purchases). Personalization is typically done on the Web server through dynamically generated HTML. Compare *customization*. For more information, see PERSONALIZED CONTENT (D4).

PHP • PHP: Hypertext Preprocessor (yes, the name is part of the acronym), a technology that mixes HTML and Perl code. The code is executed when a site visitor makes a request, enabling the creation of dynamically generated HTML. Compare *ASP* (definition 1), a competing technology from Microsoft, and *JSP*, a similar Java-based technology.

pilot test data • Data from a quick trial of a proposed evaluation method, such as a survey or a usability test, performed by coworkers and friends, to help solve problems in wording or procedure.

PKI • See *public key infrastructure.*

plug-in • An application that can be embedded into a Web browser. Examples of popular plug-ins include Adobe Acrobat Reader (for PDF files) and Shockwave Flash.

PNG • (pronounced "ping") Portable Network Graphics format, a way of storing images designed specifically for transport across networks. PNG is currently not widely supported by Web browsers, however. See also *GIF, JPEG,* and *SVG.* For more information, see FAST-DOWNLOADING IMAGES (L2).

pop-under • A pop-up window that is positioned under the customer's browser window so that the customer will not see it until the browser is closed. For more information, see POP-UP WINDOWS (H6).

pop-up • A small window that appears in a Web browser, often containing advertising messages or definitions of a term. Pop-ups are created with JavaScript. For more information, see POP-UP WINDOWS (H6).

Portable Document Format • See *PDF.*

Portable Network Graphics • See *PNG.*

portal • A major Web site, designed for a specific audience that uses it to enter the Web, such as America Online (AOL). Portals contain a broad range of content and often make extensive use of customization and personalization. See also *hortal* and *vortal.*

PostScript • A relatively old but common file format for documents that is understood by many printers, typically with file extension *ps,* as in *printout.ps.* Compare *PDF.*

principles • High-level concepts that guide the entire design process and help maintain focus.

process • A well-defined series of steps for accomplishing something. For the purposes of this book, a process is how principles are put into practice.

process data • Qualitative data collected in evaluations, giving an overall gestalt of what works and what does not. Compare *bottom-line data.* For more information, see Chapter 4—Involving Customers with Iterative Design and Appendix A—Running Usability Evaluations.

Production phase • The fourth phase of Web development, following Refinement, in which a fully interactive prototype and/or a design specification are created. Some design firms use the term *production* to mean the actual creation of the Web site—that is, what we have termed *implementation.* For more information, see Chapter 5—Processes for Developing Customer-Centered Sites. See also *Discovery* *phase, Exploration phase, Refinement phase, Implementation phase, Launch phase,* and *Maintenance phase.*

professional respondent • A focus group member who makes money on the side by going from group to group.

profile • 1. On a Web site, details about a customer, including information explicitly provided by that customer (such as an e-mail address) and information implicitly collected (such as which Web pages the person has seen). Profiles are used for personalization. 2. In the Discovery phase of Web development, a profile is a detailed narrative describing an individual. Some profiles are short; others can be long and descriptive. Some profiles are made up in the imagination of the design team; others are based on actual people. Here's an example: "Gail is a 16-year-old teenager interested in reading and talking about insects. She wants to learn more about how to collect insects and how to take care of them. She started using a computer only recently and is new to the Web, but she is a quick learner and eager to learn more." Compare *persona.*

progressive-scan image • An image that loads from top to bottom. Compare *interlaced image.* For more information, see FAST-DOWNLOADING IMAGES (L2).

protocol • A formal and precise definition of what kind of information is transferred and how it is transferred between two or more parties. HTTP is an example of a protocol.

prototype • A first cut at a functional model of a human–computer interface, such as a Web site. Prototypes include site maps, storyboards, schematics, mock-ups, and HTML prototypes. We use the term *interactive prototype* to refer to a prototype that clients can use on a computer. See also *low-fidelity prototype, medium-fidelity prototype,* and *high-fidelity prototype.*

proxy • An intermediate computer between the Web server and the end customer's Web browser. Typical uses of proxies are to cache Web pages for multiple customers and to act as a firewall.

ps • See *PostScript.*

pseudonym • The false name that a person who wants to hide his or her true identity assumes within a given community. For more information, see COMMUNITY CONFERENCE (A3).

psychographics • The beliefs and personality traits of customers.

public key infrastructure (PKI) • An emerging technology for encryption on the Internet.

Python • A programming language sometimes used as part of the Common Gateway Interface.

quality assurance • The group that tests all code, graphics, and HTML code thoroughly, so that the Web site works as intended and downloads quickly.

question bias • Skewing of a research result because the wording of questions leads people to answer in a certain way.

red–green deficiency • A form of color deficiency characterized by the inability to distinguish between red and green. Red–green deficiency affects mostly males.

Refinement phase • The third phase of Web site development, following Exploration, in which the design team polishes the navigation, layout, and flow of the selected design. For more information, see Chapter 5—Processes for Developing Customer-Centered Sites. See also *Discovery phase, Exploration phase, Production phase, Implementation phase, Launch phase,* and *Maintenance phase.*

reliable data • Results that would be found consistently if you ran a survey or a usability test over and over with the same type of audience under the same conditions.

remote usability testing • Online recruitment and usability testing of a Web site, often with many participants. For more information, see Appendix E—Online Research.

response time • The time it takes a customer to initiate an action when given a stimulus. Response times on the order of 100 milliseconds are needed for things like dragging icons and typing text. Response times on the order of 1 second (1,000 milliseconds) are required to maintain an uninterrupted flow of thought when completing a routine action, such as clicking on a button.

rollout • Official deployment of a completed Web site. See also *Launch phase.*

rollover • A graphical icon that changes when the mouse moves over it. Currently, rollovers require visitors to have JavaScript activated in their Web browsers. Compare *tool tip.*

sample bias • Skewing of a research result because the composition of participants does not accurately reflect the demographics or psychographics of the target customers.

Scalable Vector Graphics • See *SVG.*

scale • A measure of how well something works if it increases in size, such as how well an information architecture performs when lots more information is added to a Web site compared to what it was originally designed for, or whether a Web server works as well for 10,000 customers as it does for many fewer customers.

scenario • A story rich in context that focuses more on what people will do than on how they will do it. Also called *use case.* For more information, see Chapters 3—Knowing Your Customers: Principles and Techniques and 4—Involving Customers with Iterative Design.

schematic • A representation of the content that will appear on an individual Web page. Schematics are usually devoid of images, though they may indicate with a label where an image should be placed. Unlike mock-ups, schematics typically do not make heavy use of color, typography, and graphics. Compare *site map* and *storyboard.* For more information, see Chapters 3—Knowing Your Customers: Principles and Techniques and 4—Involving Customers with Iterative Design.

screen reader • A special hardware device or software program, designed to assist people with impaired vision, that takes all the text on a page and uses computer-based speech synthesis to read it out. For more information, see SITE ACCESSIBILITY (B9).

searching • One of two major strategies used to find information on a Web site. Searching makes use of local or Internet-wide search engines. Compare *browsing.* For more information, see Pattern Group J—Making Site Search Fast and Relevant.

Secure Electronic Transaction • See *SET*.

Secure Sockets Layer • See *SSL*.

server • A centralized repository of information or other resources, usually a Web server. Clients send requests to servers, and servers send results back to clients. Compare *client* (definition 1). See also *client–server architecture.*

servlet • A small Java-based application that runs on a server, commonly used in JSP pages. Servlets are similar in concept to the Common Gateway Interface.

session cookie • A cookie that temporarily stores the identity of a person. When a customer closes his or her Web browser, the session cookie is deleted, making it impossible to track people over long periods of time. Compare *persistent cookie* and *session ID.* For more information, see PERSISTENT CUSTOMER SESSIONS (H5).

session ID • A string that temporarily stores the identity of a customer in a Web address. Compare *session cookie.* For more information, see PERSISTENT CUSTOMER SESSIONS (H5).

SET • Secure Electronic Transaction, a relatively new technology supporting secure financial transactions on the Internet.

shopping bag or **shopping cart** • A common mechanism, often symbolized by an icon that pictures a shopping cart, for helping customers on the Web keep track of what they want before they finalize a purchase. For more information, see SHOPPING CART (F3).

shrinking • Reducing the size of an image by resizing the entire image. Compare *cropping.* For more information, see FAST-DOWNLOADING IMAGES (L2).

site map • A high-level diagram showing the overall structure of a site. A site map is used primarily to reflect the information structure of the site, as it is being built, and to a limited extent it shows the navigation structure. Compare *storyboard* and *schematic.* For more information, see Chapter 4—Involving Customers with Iterative Design.

solution diagram • Part of a Web design pattern; a drawing that captures the essence of the pattern in graphical form.

spam • Unwanted and often unsolicited e-mail. The term comes from an old Monty Python skit.

specification document • A detailed document, also called a *spec,* that attempts to describe the intent of a design exhaustively and precisely. The specification document contains a set of exact instructions about how to build a site, usually accompanied by an interactive prototype. Directed toward developers who will implement the site, the specification document gives instructions for how to extrapolate from the prototype to the finished site. Compare *guidelines.* For more information, see Chapter 5—Processes for Developing Customer-Centered Sites.

spider • See *crawler.*

splash screen • An opening screen, often heavy with multimedia, shown before the homepage. Splash screens are often implemented with Flash. Splash screens are often of little value.

SSL • Secure Sockets Layer, a form of encryption designed specifically for Web browsers, with the goal of maintaining the security and integrity of information transferred on the Web. SSL is typically used for e-commerce transactions, such as sending credit card information to a Web site. You can tell you are using SSL if the URL begins with *https://* instead of just *http://*. For more information, see SECURE CONNECTIONS (E6).

statistical validity • A standard for evaluating a study in which it is determined that a study actually measures what it claims to, and that no logical errors have been made in the conclusions drawn from the data. Having enough research participants in a usability study and getting a high enough response rate in a survey are important to achieving validity.

stickiness • The measure of a Web site's ability to retain visitors and drive repeat visits.

storyboard • A sequence of sketches depicting how a customer would accomplish a given task. Typically depicting low-fidelity representations of Web pages, a storyboard is often accompanied by a narrative describing customer tasks. Storyboards are typically not presented to anyone outside the design team, but are used to construct the walk-throughs presented to clients. A walk-through can be thought of as a medium-fidelity or high-fidelity storyboard. Compare *site map* and *schematic*. See also *flow*. For more information, see Chapters 3—Knowing Your Customers: Principles and Techniques and 4—Involving Customers with Iterative Design.

streaming • A method for data transfer, in which small portions of a file are continuously sent to a computer, instead of all at once. The advantage of streaming media is that visitors can view the file as they receive it, instead of having to wait until the entire file is downloaded. Streaming is a common technique used for video and audio files.

style guide • A list of rules for how to spell common words and phrases so that a Web site will have consistent spelling and word usage. It may also specify fonts, colors, and positioning of common design elements (e.g., logos). One of Addison-Wesley's styles, for example, is to spell *Web site* as two words, with a capital *W*. It will appear that way throughout this book.

subsite • A major portion of a Web site in which the individual pages are strongly related in content and navigation.

SVG • Scalable Vector Graphics format, an XML-based graphics format supporting the creation of dynamic images. Site visitors can pan and zoom in on SVG images, for example. SVG holds promise for products beyond the desktop computer, such as handheld devices, interactive television, large wall-sized displays, and even printing, because of the way the graphics data is stored. See also *GIF, JPEG,* and *PNG*. For more information, see FAST-DOWNLOADING IMAGES (L2).

synchronous communication • A communications setup in which all parties have to be online simultaneously and interaction takes place in real time. Compare *asynchronous communication*. For more information, see COMMUNITY CONFERENCE (A3).

T-1 • A piece of hardware needed for a network connection, commonly used to refer to a type of Internet connection provided by telephone companies. T-1 lines transfer data at 1.5 megabits per second and are typically leased by ISPs and businesses.

target customer • See *customer*.

task • A specific goal that a customer wants to accomplish when using a Web site, such as "I want to send my grandmother an online birthday card" or "I want to find the best digital camera for under $500 and buy it."

task and customer analysis • An analysis performed by the design team to articulate who the customers are, what they will do on the Web site, the things they act on, and the things they need to know. For more information, see Chapter 3— Knowing Your Customers: Principles and Techniques.

TCP/IP • Transmission Control Protocol/Internet Protocol, the core set of protocols that control how data is transferred over the Internet. HTTP, used for transferring Web pages, is built on top of TCP/IP.

technology-centered design • Design that is overloaded with animations, audio, and streaming video banners, built with little up-front research about business and customer needs. Compare *company-centered design, customer-centered design,* and *designer-centered design.* For more information, see Chapter 1—Customer-Centered Web Design.

template • See *page template.*

temporary customer session • A Web session that lets the Web server remember a customer for only a short period of time, usually until the customer closes the Web browser. Compare *persistent customer session.* For more information, see PERSISTENT CUSTOMER SESSIONS (H5).

think-aloud protocol • An experimental setup in which participants say out loud what's going on in their minds to give Web site designers an idea of how customers will use the site. Also called *verbal protocol.* For more information, see Chapter 4—Involving Customers with Iterative Design.

thumbnail • A small version of an image that is linked to a larger version. Clicking on a thumbnail brings up the larger image on-screen. For more information, see LOW NUMBER OF FILES (L1) and FAST-DOWNLOADING IMAGES (L2).

tool tip • A piece of text that appears when the mouse cursor hovers over a button or an image. Compare *rollover.*

Transmission Control Protocol/Internet Protocol • See *TCP/IP.*

tutorial • An online, instruction-based class used for training.

UI • User interface, the part of a system with which a customer interacts. See also *GUI.*

undersampling bias • Skewing of a research result because there are not enough participants to have a statistically valid sample.

Uniform Resource Locator • See *URL.*

unmoderated forum • A free-for-all discussion in which anything goes. People can say whatever they want, and it is up to the members of the community to enforce any rules and social norms. Compare *moderated forum.* For more information, see COMMUNITY CONFERENCE (A3).

up-selling • Promoting products that have more features and benefits (and cost more) than the one the customer wants to purchase. Compare *cross-selling*. For more information, see SHOPPING CART (F3) and CROSS-SELLING AND UP-SELLING (G2).

URL • Uniform Resource Locator, the official Web word for *address*. Any address beginning with *http://* is a URL.

use case • See *scenario*.

user-centered design • An effort pioneered in the 1980s for engineering useful and usable computer systems. We have broadened and expanded this concept for Web design into *customer-centered design.*

user experience • See *customer experience.*

user interface • See *UI.*

value proposition • A brief statement of what the Web site offers to target customers. For more information, see UP-FRONT VALUE PROPOSITION (C2).

value ranking • The method a search engine uses to order the different results it returns for a particular search.

verbal protocol • See *think-aloud protocol.*

vertical prototype • A prototype that implements only a few key Web pages along with the path for completing a particular task. Creation of a vertical prototype is appropriate when a complex feature is poorly understood or needs to be explored further. For more information, see Chapter 4—Involving Customers with Iterative Design.

virtual testing • Evaluation of a Web site in which a few select customers see the updated site, and you can watch what they do compared to what they do on the regular Web site.

visual design • See *graphic design.*

vortal • Vertical portal, a portal that specializes in a specific topic, such as law or medicine. Compare *hortal.*

W3C • World Wide Web Consortium, the group that coordinates protocols and standards used on the Web, including HTTP, HTML, and XML. For more information, go to w3c.org.

walk-through • A sequential presentation of Web pages narrated by the designer, who explains what customers will do on each page. Designers can also use a storyboard for a (low-fidelity) walk-through.

WAP • Wireless Application Protocol, used primarily by small devices, such as cell phones, to access e-mail and the Web. See also *WML.* For more information, see SITE ACCESSIBILITY (B9).

Web browser • The software used to navigate Web sites from a computer. The two most popular Web browsers are Internet Explorer and Netscape Navigator, also known as Mozilla. Other browsers include America Online's Web browser, Opera, and the text-based browser Lynx. A Web browser is an example of a client in a client–server architecture.

Web interface guidelines • A checklist to ensure that a final product does not have any obvious problems. Often, these guidelines address only how a Web site is implemented.

Web server • A server, such as Apache or IIS, that delivers Web pages upon request.

white space • The area on a page that is intentionally left blank, to create a feeling of spaciousness and a more readable design. Most bad designs would benefit from more white space.

widget • An interactive object such as a button or slider.

wire frame • A simple but functional interactive prototype of a Web site. Typically a wire frame contains text, layout, links, and overall structure, but few if any graphics.

Wireless Application Protocol • See *WAP*.

Wireless Markup Language • See *WML*.

within-groups experiment • An experiment in which there is one group of test participants, each of whom is assigned to the same condition. For example, when testing two Web sites, each participant uses both sites. Compare *between-groups experiment*. For more information, see Appendix A—Running Usability Evaluations.

WML • Wireless Markup Language. A markup language similar to HTML, WML is designed specifically for small devices, such as cell phones. See also *WAP* and *HDML*. For more information, see SITE ACCESSIBILITY (B9).

World Wide Web Consortium • See *W3C*.

XML • Extensible Markup Language, a standard created by W3C for specifying information formats. Although it is similar to HTML, you can extend XML for use in any domain.

Part I: Foundations of Web Site Design

Chapter 1: Customer-Centered Web Design

Books, Research Papers, and News Articles

Bias, R., and D. Mayhew. (1994) *Cost-Justifying Usability.* San Diego, CA: Academic Press.

> This book is a collection of essays that describe various methods and techniques for quantitatively showing how usability affects the bottom line.

Creative Good. (1999) *Holiday '99 E-Commerce: Bridging the $6 Billion Customer Experience Gap.* (http://www.creativegood.com/research.html)

> This report reviews several of the top e-commerce Web sites, pointing out how simple problems prevented visitors from completing basic tasks, and how these problems could affect the bottom line.

Creative Good. (2000) *Holiday 2000 E-Commerce Report.* (http://www.creativegood.com/research.html)

> This report discusses the results of informal usability evaluations on several top e-commerce Web sites.

Dembeck, C. (2000, January 11) Report: B2B Web sites fail usage test. *E-Commerce Times* [online]. (http://www.ecommercetimes.com/perl/story/2183.html)

> In this news article on a Forrester Report, "Why Web Sites Fail," one of the results described here is that when customers have a bad experience on a Web site, they tell an average of ten other people.

Moore, G. (1999) *Crossing the Chasm: Marketing and Selling High-Tech Products to Mainstream Customers* (rev. ed.). New York: HarperBusiness.

> The author describes how high-tech products sell well initially, mainly to a technically literate customer base, but then hit a lull as marketing professionals try to cross the chasm to mainstream buyers. *Crossing the Chasm* was a milestone in high-tech marketing when it was first released in 1991.

NetRaker Corporation. (2000, April) *EShopping Research Study.* (http://www.netraker.com/nrinfo/company/20000907.asp)

> This study looks at the factors driving repeat visits and purchases at online shopping sites. It found that although a few Web sites offer a great customer

experience, there is still plenty of room for improvement. In a comparison study between Yahoo! Shopping, Amazon.com and AOL Shopping, not one firm scored over an 8.02 on a scale of 0 to 10 when rated by consumers. The lowest score was below 6.5. By comparison, when leaders in offline industries are evaluated on the key components that drive repeat visits and satisfaction, we see scores typically in the high 8s and low 9s.

Tedeschi, B. (1999, August 30) Good Web site design can lead to healthy sales. *New York Times E-Commerce Report.* (**http://www.nytimes.com/library/tech/99/ 08/cyber/commerce/30commerce.html**)

This article reports on IBM's efforts to redesign its Web site and on how sales increased after overall usability was improved.

Web Sites

Creative Good: **http://creativegood.com** *and*

goodexperience.com: **http://www.goodexperience.com**

Creative Good is a strategy firm that helps clients focus on the customer experience. Goodexperience.com is a Web log by Mark Hurst, the founder and president of Creative Good. He provides insights about what is right and wrong with the Web experience today, as well as an occasional tidbit about technology-related issues. The site is updated fairly often, but you may find it more useful to get the weekly e-mail updates instead.

useit.com: Jakob Nielsen's Website: **http://www.useit.com**

Jakob Nielsen is one of the best-known Web personalities today, for his hard-line stance in favor of usability. useit.com is his Web site, where he publishes Alertbox, a biweekly newsletter on Web-related usability issues.

WebWord.com: **http://www.webword.com**

WebWord.com is a great site for those of us who want to keep up with news about Web design and usability but do not have the time to do our own surfing. The WebWord team highlights the best news articles from a bunch of other Web sites.

Chapter 2: Making the Most of Web Design Patterns

Books, Research Papers, and News Articles

Alexander, C., S. Ishikawa, and M. Silverstein. (1977) *A Pattern Language: Towns, Buildings, Construction.* New York: Oxford University Press.

This book originally introduced the idea of patterns in the field of architecture. Alexander has inspired many, including the authors of the book you have in hand, with his idea that patterns could be an effective way of doing design, and a way that customers could express their needs and desires.

Borchers, J. (2001) *A Pattern Approach to Interaction Design.* Chichester, England: Wiley.

This was the first book to bring patterns to user interface design. The Web site for this book, at **http://hcipatterns.org,** includes research and conferences dealing with patterns.

Fry, J. (2001, August 13) Web shoppers' loyalty isn't so crazy after all. *Wall Street Journal.* **(http://ebusiness.mit.edu/news/WSJ_Story8-13-01.html)**

> This article looks at a phenomenon known as *cognitive lock-in,* in which people find things that are familiar more attractive. One result is that people tend not to shop around as much as economists expect, sticking to retailers they already know, because the time to learn a new interface might not be worth the money that might be saved at a competitor's site.

Gamma, E., R. Helm, R. Johnson, and J. Vlissides. (1995) *Design Patterns.* Reading, MA: Addison-Wesley.

> This book brought the concept of patterns to software design and programming.

Web Sites

Erickson, T. (No date) *The Interaction Design Patterns Page.* **(http://www.pliant. org/personal/Tom_Erickson/InteractionPatterns.html)**

> This Web site contains resources on pattern languages for interaction design, including pointers to other pattern Web sites and patterns for user interface design.

Tidwell, J. (1999) *Common Ground: A Pattern Language for Human–Computer Interface Design.* **(http://www.mit.edu/~jtidwell/common_ground.html)**

> This Web site has about 60 patterns targeted at design, running the gamut from content design to navigation to attractiveness.

Welie, M. van. (2001) *Web Design Patterns.* **(http://www.welie.com/patterns)**

> This Web page lists about 20 patterns for Web design, focusing on navigation, searching, page elements, and e-commerce.

Chapter 3: Knowing Your Customers: Principles and Techniques

Books, Research Papers, and News Articles

Beyer, H., and K. Holtzblatt. (1998) *Contextual Design: Defining Customer-Centered Systems.* San Francisco: Morgan Kaufmann.

> Beyer and Holtzblatt have written a fantastic book on their process for customer-centered design. As this philosophical and practical guide explains, their process is centered on gaining a deep understanding of customer needs by interviewing people about the way they work, how their organization works, and other constraints. The ideas they present can be used most effectively in the Discovery phase of the Web site development process, when you're trying to understand who your target audience is and what they want.

Cooper, A. (1999) *The Inmates Are Running the Asylum: Why High-Tech Products Drive Us Crazy and How to Restore the Sanity.* Indianapolis, IN: Sams.

> This book introduces some of the problems with developing user interfaces. Told in narrative form, it also presents techniques to apply for improving the state of the art. In addition, it outlines how to create *personas,* hypothetical and detailed descriptions of typical customers, and why personas are a useful way of thinking about design. (However, we would argue that the personas should be based on interviews and observations of real people instead of being made up.)

Lewis, C., and J. Rieman. (1994) *Task-Centered User Interface Design: A Practical Introduction.* (http://hcibib.org/tcuid)

This shareware book on user interface design has some great material on learning about your customers' tasks. Our Web-based banking example is based on their telephone banking example.

Norman, D. (1988) *The Psychology of Everyday Things.* New York: Basic Books.

This book is an eye-opener, and it should be one of the first books you read to learn about design. Norman points out the importance of design and how it affects our everyday lives. You will never look at doorknobs or oven stoves in the same way again. Also published as *The Design of Everyday Things.*

Palen, L. (1999) Social, individual and technological issues for groupware calendar systems. CHI 1999, ACM Conference on Human Factors in Computing Systems, *CHI Letters,* 2(1): 17–24. (http://doi.acm.org/10.1145/302979.302982)

(This resource requires access to the ACM Digital Library, at http://www.acm.org/dl.) This study examines calendar systems used by groups, finding that current practices have influenced calendaring habits and technology adoption decisions.

Rubinstein, R., and H. Hersh. (1984) *The Human Factor: Designing Computer Systems for People.* Bedford, MA: Digital Press.

This early UI design text includes the list of questions we ask when performing a task analysis.

Saffo, P. (1996) The consumer spectrum. In *Bringing Design to Software,* T. Winograd (Ed.), pp. 87–99. Reading, MA: Addison-Wesley.

This chapter in Winograd's influential book discusses the fact that consumers' willingness to put up with technology products is measured both by how expensive the technology is and by how much complexity they have to deal with to get the benefits of the product.

Shneiderman, B. (1997) *Designing the User Interface: Strategies for Effective Human–Computer Interaction* (3rd ed.). Reading, MA: Addison-Wesley.

This textbook is an overview of academic research in the field of human–computer interaction and it is a great book about the field in general. In addition, the book's Web site, at http://www.awl.com/DTUI, has many lecture notes and overviews, and extensive lists of links.

Software

IBM. *EZSort.* (http://www.ibm.com/ibm/easy/eou_ext.nsf/Publish/410)

EZSort is a free tool that helps designers analyze card-sorting experiments through statistical cluster analysis.

National Institute of Standards and Technology (NIST). *WebCAT: Category Analysis Tool.* (http://zing.ncsl.nist.gov/WebTools/WebCAT/overview.html)

The Web Category Analysis Tool (WebCAT) is a free tool that helps designers set up, run, and analyze card-sorting experiments.

Chapter 4: Involving Customers with Iterative Design

Books, Research Papers, and News Articles

Beyer, H., and K. Holtzblatt. (1998) *Contextual Design: Defining Customer-Centered Systems.* San Francisco: Morgan Kaufmann.

> See description under Chapter 3—Knowing Your Customers: Principles and Techniques.

Kelley, T. (2001) *The Art of Innovation: Lessons in Creativity from IDEO, America's Leading Design Firm.* New York: Currency/Doubleday.

> Skim through the first few chapters, but pay attention when Kelley gets to brainstorming. He describes how the design teams at his company, IDEO, combine their observations of how customers really do things with an extremely creative brainstorming process to create innovative, award-winning products.

McConnell, S. (1996) *Rapid Development: Taming Wild Software Schedules.* Redmond, WA: Microsoft Press.

> McConnell has a chapter about user interface prototyping in his manual for managing the software development process. Although he focuses entirely on software-based prototypes, he lists many of the same advantages of prototyping, including reduced risk, smaller systems, less complex systems, reduction in creeping requirements, and improved schedule visibility.

Mullet, K., and D. Sano. (1994) *Designing Visual Interfaces: Communication Oriented Techniques.* Englewood Cliffs, NJ: Prentice Hall/SunSoft Press.

> Although this book came out before the Web took off, the information on how to create effective visual interfaces is still valuable. This book is handy in the Refinement and Production phases of the Web site development process, as you build polished and high-fidelity mock-ups of your site.

Nielsen, J. (No date) *How to Conduct a Heuristic Evaluation.* (http://www.useit.com/papers/heuristic/heuristic_evaluation.html)

> This tutorial explains a fast and relatively inexpensive method of finding potential usability errors by using a checklist of usability heuristics.

Nielsen, J. (1993) *Usability Engineering.* Boston: Academic Press.

> This book is great for developing products with usability as the key goal. Issues such as prototyping, iterative design, heuristic evaluation, and usability testing are discussed.

Rettig, M. (1994) Prototyping for tiny fingers. *Communications of the ACM,* 37(4): 21–27. (http://www.acm.org/pubs/citations/journals/cacm/1994-37-4/p21-rettig)

> (This resource requires access to the ACM Digital Library, at http://www.acm.org/dl.) This is a great article on the motivation behind low-fidelity prototypes, how to make a low-fidelity prototype, and how to run informal usability tests.

Shneiderman, B. (1997) *Designing the User Interface: Strategies for Effective Human–Computer Interaction* (3rd ed.). Reading, MA: Addison-Wesley.

> See description under Chapter 3—Knowing Your Customers: Principles and Techniques.

Winograd, T. (1996) *Bringing Design to Software.* Reading, MA: Addison-Wesley.
This collection of essays takes a broad look at interaction design as a profession. Issues such as the design process, prototyping, art, and people are discussed.

Software

Group for User Interface Research. *DENIM.* (http://guir.berkeley.edu/denim)
This Web page features DENIM, a sketch-based design tool developed by two of the authors of the book you have in hand for quickly prototyping Web sites.

Chapter 5: Processes for Developing Customer-Centered Sites

Books, Research Papers, and News Articles

Brinck, T., D. Gergle, and S. Wood. (2002) *Usability for the Web: Designing Web Sites That Work.* San Francisco: Morgan Kaufmann.
This book covers a spectrum of topics, including project management, user needs analysis, information architecture, page layout, writing for the Web, visual design, and usability.

McConnell, S. (1996) *Rapid Development: Taming Wild Software Schedules.*
Redmond, WA: Microsoft Press.
This book is really about software development, not Web site development. However, it is an excellent resource on project management, and it is full of best practices, common mistakes, and lessons about planning, scheduling, designing, and creating software. If you are interested in the Discovery and Implementation phases of the Web site development process, this is the book for you.

Newman, M. W., and J. A. Landay. (2000, August) Sitemaps, storyboards, and specifications: A sketch of Web site design practice as manifested through artifacts. In *Proceedings of ACM Conference on Designing Interactive Systems,* pp. 263–274.
New York. (http:guir.berkeley.edu/projects/denim/pubs/iwd-dis-2000.pdf)
This paper reports on our interviews with Web designers, leading to valuable conclusions about the Web design process, the artifacts, and the deliverables.

Part II: Patterns

Pattern Group A: Site Genres

A1 PERSONAL E-COMMERCE

CNET Builder.com. (No date) *E-Business & Strategy.* (http://builder.cnet.com/webbuilding/0-3885.html)
This is a valuable resource on the basics of e-commerce, including managing transactions and purchases, business planning, advertising, and so on.

E-Commerce Times: http://www.ecommercetimes.com
E-Commerce Times offers up-to-date news about e-commerce–related issues from financial, marketing, and management perspectives.

Frenkel, K. (2000, June 7) Portals struggle to convert browsers to shoppers. *New*

York Times E-Commerce Report. (http://www.nytimes.com/library/tech/00/06/ biztech/technology/07fren.html)

> This news article looks at many of the issues confronting e-commerce sites, such as poor usability, lack of support for comparison shopping, privacy, security, and shipping costs. It also discusses the approaches many sites are taking to address these issues.

New York Times, E-Business: http://www.nytimes.com/pages/technology/ ebusiness

> The *New York Times* publishes a daily section on e-business, discussing changes in the financial, legal, and technical landscape that affect online commerce. You can also find a weekly e-commerce report, focusing more on issues like Web site design, e-mail, and online marketing. Many of these e-commerce reports are also archived at http://www.nytimes.com/library/tech/reference/ indexcommerce.html.

Tedeschi, B. (2000, March 29) Now that they've come, what can we sell them? *New York Times E-Commerce Report.* (http://www.nytimes.com/library/tech/00/03/ biztech/technology/29tede.html)

> This piece examines the common lament that it is easy to attract visitors but difficult to make profitable Web sites.

ZDNet Tech Update: http://www.zdnet.com/ecommerce

> ZDNet Tech Update provides news about business strategy and happenings at major technology companies.

A2 NEWS MOSAICS

Pew Internet & American Life Project: http://www.pewinternet.org

> This nonprofit initiative conducts and publishes research on "the impact of the Internet on children, families, communities, the work place, schools, health care and civic/political life."

Pew Research Center for the People and the Press. (2000, December 3) *Youth Vote Influenced by Online Information: Internet Election News Audience Seeks Convenience, Familiar Names.* (http://www.people-press.org/dataarchive)

> This discussion of the impact of the Internet on the 2000 U.S. presidential election shows that 33 percent of online customers took advantage of Internet news sources to help make their election decisions.

Shapiro, A. (1999) *The Control Revolution: How the Internet Is Putting Individuals in Charge and Changing the World We Know.* New York: PublicAffairs.

> Shapiro takes a critical look at the Internet and its impact on society, analyzing a broad range of topics, including copyright, free speech, communities, and personalization. One of his most interesting conclusions is that a high degree of personalization may actually be detrimental to society because people will tend to gravitate toward others with similar interests and beliefs, resulting in pockets of society that talk only to themselves but not to each other.

Coate, J. (1998) *Cyberspace Innkeeping: Building Online Community.* (http://www.
sfgate.com/~tex/innkeeping)
> This article talks about some of the issues in running online communities,
> including anonymity, free speech, and leveling the playing field.

Kim, A. J. (2000) *Community Building on the Web: Secret Strategies for Successful
Online Communities.* Berkeley, CA: Peachpit Press.
> This excellent and practical book provides detailed explanations and case stud-
> ies of why communities form and how they grow. It also provides suggestions
> for how to make your site a nurturing place for communities.

Online Community Report: http://www.onlinecommunityreport.com
> This twice-monthly newsletter offers the latest in online communities, featur-
> ing articles on such topics as distance learning, online auctions, massively mul-
> tiplayer games, and group collaboration.

Pew Internet & American Life Project: http://www.pewinternet.org
> See description under NEWS MOSAICS (A2).

Powazek, D. (2001) *Design for Community: The Art of Connecting Real People in
Virtual Places.* Indianapolis, IN: New Riders.
> This book discusses various aspects of online communities, including design,
> moderation, e-mail, chat, and other issues intrinsic to online communities. It
> also features interviews with many people who run large online communities.

Preece, J. (2000) *Online Communities: Designing Usability and Supporting Sociability.*
New York: Wiley.
> This is one of the best books of academic research on online communities,
> focusing on issues such as sociability, usability, development, and evaluation.

Rheingold, H. (1998) *The Art of Hosting Good Conversations Online.* (http://www.
rheingold.com/texts/artonlinehost.html)
> This Web page outlines the role of the Web site in hosting an online commu-
> nity, describing what the goals should be and ways of achieving those goals.

Rheingold, H. (2000) *The Virtual Community: Homesteading on the Electronic Frontier*
(rev. ed.). Cambridge, MA: MIT Press.
> This book chronicles the start and continued growth of the first thriving online
> community, the WELL. More of a collection of stories than a practical guide,
> the book still contains many insights about the nature of online communities.

A4 SELF-SERVICE GOVERNMENT

Center for Democracy and Technology: http://www.cdt.org
> The Center for Democracy and Technology is devoted to promoting "demo-
> cratic values and constitutional liberties in the digital age." Its interests include
> technology with respect to free speech, privacy, surveillance, cryptography,
> domain names, and international governance.

Federal Computer Week: http://www.fcw.com
> *Federal Computer Week* is a valuable resource for anyone working on informa-
> tion technology for the U.S. government. You will find news articles on a

range of technology-related issues, including accessibility, privacy, telecommunications, and training.

FirstGov: http://www.firstgov.gov
 FirstGov is the official U.S. government portal, a comprehensive directory containing references to all online information created by the U.S. government.

Hart, P., and R. Teeter. (2000) *E-Government: The Next American Revolution.* (http://www.excelgov.org/egovpoll/index.htm)
 This survey on e-government shows that Americans strongly support electronic government, with the ultimate goals of making government "more accountable to citizens," providing "greater public access to information," and making a "more efficient and cost-effective government." However, Americans have many concerns about privacy and security.

Pew Internet & American Life Project: http://www.pewinternet.org
 See description under NEWS MOSAICS (A2).

A5 NONPROFITS AS NETWORKS OF HELP

Internet Nonprofit Center: http://www.nonprofits.org
 The Internet Nonprofit Center provides many links to articles about creating, running, and managing nonprofit organizations. It focuses on logistical, legal, financial, and advertising issues as opposed to Web site design.

Nonprofit Online News: http://news.gilbert.org
 Nonprofit Online News provides news about online nonprofits, and links to such topics as use of e-mail, getting grants, and research about nonprofits.

A7 VALUABLE COMPANY SITES

Nielsen, J., and M. Tahir. (2001) *Homepage Usability: 50 Websites Deconstructed.* Indianapolis, IN: New Riders.
 This text dissects and analyzes 50 different homepages in detail.

Uchitelle, L. (2000, June 7) It's just the beginning. *New York Times E-Commerce Report.* (http://www.nytimes.com/library/tech/00/06/biztech/technology/07uchi.html)
 This article talks about some of the issues that Honeywell, an established company, dealt with in creating its Web site. It focuses on some of the business-to-business aspects involved, including integrating a number of legacy databases, improving access to suppliers and consumers, and managing inventory.

A8 EDUCATIONAL FORUMS

Center for LifeLong Learning and Design: http://www.cs.colorado.edu/~l3d
 The Center for LifeLong Learning and Design is a group at the University of Colorado at Boulder that researches and theorizes about the "scientific foundations for the construction of intelligent systems that amplify human capabilities."

Computer Support for Collaborative Learning: http://www.cscl-home.org
 Computer Support for Collaborative Learning (CSCL) is an international conference devoted to all issues related to computers and learning, including research, education, training, and technology.

Distributed Learning Workshop: http://www.dlworkshop.net
> The Distributed Learning Workshop is a nonprofit group that creates high-quality Web-based instructional materials for college students.

Pew Internet & American Life Project: http://www.pewinternet.org
> See description under NEWS MOSAICS (A2).

Resnick, M., A. Bruckman, and F. Martin. (1996) Pianos not stereos: Creating computational construction kits. *Interactions,* 3(6): 40–50. (http://lcs.www.media.mit.edu/groups/el/Papers/mres/pianos/pianos.html)
> This article argues that computer systems need to be built for more than just ease of use, especially for educational purposes.

A9 STIMULATING ARTS AND ENTERTAINMENT

ACM SIGGRAPH: http://www.acm.org/siggraph
> SIGGRAPH is the Special Interest Group on Graphics. In addition to publishing magazines and maintaining online art galleries, it holds an annual conference that features the latest in tools, research, and computer-based art.

Laurel, B. 1993. *Computers as Theatre.* Reading, MA: Addison-Wesley.
> Although this book was first published before the Web took off, there is still a great deal of relevant material. Laurel's main point is that designing pleasing user interfaces is similar to producing a play in theater, with multiple actors, a story, and a climax.

McCloud, S. (1993) *Understanding Comics: The Invisible Art.* Northampton, MA: Kitchen Sink Press.
> Although this book is a comic about comics, it is really about communicating through text and images in a static medium (just like the many Web pages). It is a fun read that takes a critical look at comics as a medium.

Shedroff, N. (2001) *Experience Design.* Indianapolis, IN: New Riders.
> More of a thought provoker than a how-to guide, this book takes the reader through a diverse set of design ideas, focusing on feeling and emotion and on visual quality.

A10 WEB APPS THAT WORK

Drummond, M. 2001. The end of software as we know it. *Fortune C/Net Tech Review.* (http://fortune.cnet.com/fortune/0-5937473-7-7717969.html)
> This article looks at how software may be delivered as a Web service in the future, looking at issues like standards, intellectual property, maintenance, pricing, and business models.

A11 ENABLING INTRANETS

CIO.com. (No date) *Intranet/Extranet Research Center.* (http://www.cio.com/research/intranet)
> This Web site has a large collection of links, newsletters, interviews, white papers, and reports about building corporate intranets.

Fabris, P. (1999, April 1) You think tomaytoes I think tomahtoes. CIO *Web Business Magazine.* (http://www.cio.com/archive/webbusiness/040199_nort.html)

> This article tells the story of the creation of a large intranet to support over 7,000 employees at Bay Networks. It describes some of the difficulties involved in understanding how information flowed through the company and the different ways in which people organized things.

Nielsen, J. (1999) *Designing Web Usability: The Practice of Simplicity.* Indianapolis, IN: New Riders.

> This book discusses a wide-ranging number of Web usability topics, such as page design, link names, link colors, writing for the Web, search, navigation, intranet design, accessibility, and internationalization. Many screen shots are included to illustrate concepts.

Pattern Group B: Creating a Navigation Framework

B1 MULTIPLE WAYS TO NAVIGATE

Brinck, T., D. Gergle, and S. Wood. (2002) *Usability for the Web: Designing Web Sites That Work.* San Francisco: Morgan Kaufmann.

> See description under Chapter 5—Processes for Developing Customer-Centered Sites.

Garrett, J. (No date) *Information Architecture Resources.* (http://www.jjg.net/ia)

> This is a great resource for learning more about information architecture.

InformationDesign.org: http://www.informationdesign.org

> This Web site is a hub for books, organizations, mailing lists, and other Web sites devoted to information design.

Lakoff, G. (1990) *Women, Fire, and Dangerous Things.* Chicago: University of Chicago Press.

> This book analyzes categories of language and thought from a cognitive science perspective. It also has one of the coolest titles of any book published in the twentieth century, which refers to how an Australian aboriginal language uses the same classifier to describe women, fire, and dangerous things.

Larson, K., and M. Czerwinski. (1998) Web page design: Implications of memory, structure and scent for information retrieval. CHI 1998, ACM Conference on Human Factors in Computing Systems, *CHI Letters,* 1(1): 25–32.

> This study examines the trade-off between breadth and depth for information architectures with respect to preference and performance. Breadth means that the architecture is designed so that many pieces of information are displayed per page (leading to a broad and shallow graph), and depth means that there are fewer pieces of information (leading to a narrow and deep graph). A total of 512 items from Microsoft Encarta were arranged into three Web sites differing in breadth and depth. The overall results were that increased depth led to longer browse times, while a balance between breadth and depth outperformed the broadest and shallowest structure. These findings lend more evidence to the theory that fewer clicks and fewer levels work better for organizing large amounts of information.

Rosenfeld, L., and P. Morville. (1998) *Information Architecture for the World Wide Web.* Cambridge: O'Reilly.

This book describes techniques for organizing, labeling, and indexing the information on a Web site for browsing and searching.

Selingo, J. (2000, August 3) A message to Web designers: If it ain't broke, don't fix it. *New York Times E-Commerce Report.* (http://www.nytimes.com/library/tech/00/08/circuits/articles/03desi.html)

This article looks at the fact that many customers are resistant to change, wanting the power that familiarity and expertise affords. Web sites have had to make changes to accommodate this reality, including homepages that have both directories and search engines, homepages with many organized links instead of just a few, and a consistent structure behind the information.

Special Interest Group on Information Architecture: http://www.asis.org/AboutASIS/SIGEmailLists/ia.html

This e-mail list is devoted to practitioner, researcher, and student issues in information architecture.

Tufte, E. (1984) *The Visual Display of Quantitative Information.* Cheshire, CT: Graphics Press.

Tufte's book is a classic on presenting complex information graphically, stressing simplicity, elegance, and efficiency.

Tufte, E. (1997) *Visual Explanations.* Cheshire, CT: Graphics Press.

Another classic by Tufte, this book presents evidence relevant to cause and effect, for decision making and presentations.

Zaphiris, P., B. Shneiderman, and K. Norman. (1999, June) *Expandable Indexes versus Sequential Menus for Searching Hierarchies on the World Wide Web.* (ftp://ftp.cs.umd.edu/pub/hcil/Reports-Abstracts-Bibliography/99-15html/99-15.html)

This study looks at the effectiveness of expanding menus for Web sites. Expanding menus show top-level hierarchies, revealing the next level of that hierarchy when the mouse is rolled over an item. The results indicate that reducing the depth of hierarchies improves browsing performance, lending more evidence to the theory that fewer clicks and fewer levels work better for organizing large amounts of information.

B2 BROWSABLE CONTENT

See references listed under MULTIPLE WAYS TO NAVIGATE (B1).

B3 HIERARCHICAL ORGANIZATION

See references listed under MULTIPLE WAYS TO NAVIGATE (B1).

B4 TASK-BASED ORGANIZATION

See references listed under MULTIPLE WAYS TO NAVIGATE (B1).

B5 ALPHABETICAL ORGANIZATION

See references listed under MULTIPLE WAYS TO NAVIGATE (B1).

B6 CHRONOLOGICAL ORGANIZATION

See references listed under MULTIPLE WAYS TO NAVIGATE (B1).

B7 POPULARITY-BASED ORGANIZATION

See references listed under MULTIPLE WAYS TO NAVIGATE (B1).

B8 CATEGORY PAGES

See references listed under MULTIPLE WAYS TO NAVIGATE (B1).

B9 SITE ACCESSIBILITY

ASSISTIVETECH.NET: http://www.assistivetech.net
> This Web site provides information about assistive technology devices and services. It features a database of assistive technology products, links to other public and private resources, and a convenient search function.

CAST, Bobby Worldwide: http://www.cast.org/bobby
> Bobby is an online service that checks for the basic accessibility of Web sites. It does not ensure accessibility but does help pinpoint potential problems.

IBM Corporation, Accessibility Center. (No date) *Web Accessibility.*
(http://www.ibm.com/able/accessweb.html)
> IBM offers this checklist for making sure your Web site has basic accessibility built in. The site includes links to further reading.

Section 508: http://www.section508.gov
> This U.S. government Web site provides a wide range of information about Section 508 of the Rehabilitation Act, which requires that electronic and information technology used by federal agencies be made accessible to people with disabilities.

Universal Usability Guide: http://www.universalusability.org
> The ultimate goal of this group is to make technology "affordable, useful, and usable to the vast majority of the global population." Its Web site has some material describing the salient issues, as well as references on long-term social, legal, and technological approaches to addressing the problems.

World Wide Web Consortium (W3C): http://www.w3.org
> The W3C was organized under the mandate of "bringing the Web to its full potential." Thus it has a special interest in making Web sites accessible to everyone. Check out the W3C's Web Accessibility Initiative at http://www.w3.org/wai. You will find tools, checklists, and guidelines at http://www.w3.org/tr/wcag (WCAG stands for Web Content Accessibility Guidelines).

Pattern Group C: Creating a Powerful Homepage

C1 HOMEPAGE PORTAL

Nielsen, J., and M. Tahir. (2001) *Homepage Usability: 50 Websites Deconstructed.* Indianapolis, IN: New Riders.
> See description under VALUABLE COMPANY SITES (A7).

Selingo, J. (2000, August 3) A message to Web designers: If it ain't broke, don't fix it. *New York Times E-Commerce Report.* (http://www.nytimes.com/library/tech/00/08/circuits/articles/03desi.html)

See description under MULTIPLE WAYS TO NAVIGATE (B1).

C2 UP-FRONT VALUE PROPOSITION

Ogilvy, D. (1987) *Ogilvy on Advertising.* New York: Vintage Books.

This is an excellent read on advertising by one of its preeminent creators.

Pattern Group D: Writing and Managing Content

D1 PAGE TEMPLATES

Tedeschi, B. (1999, August 30) Good Web site design can lead to healthy sales. *New York Times E-Commerce Report.* (http://www.nytimes.com/library/tech/99/08/cyber/commerce/30commerce.html)

This article emphasizes how improved Web site designs can improve the bottom line. It looks at issues like having a unified information architecture, page templates to help enforce consistency across large Web sites, and short process funnels to help customers quickly finish tasks.

D2 CONTENT MODULES

Tedeschi, B. (1999, August 30) Good Web site design can lead to healthy sales. *New York Times E-Commerce Report.* (http://www.nytimes.com/library/tech/99/08/cyber/commerce/30commerce.html)

See description under WRITING AND MANAGING CONTENT (D1).

D3 HEADLINES AND BLURBS

Nielsen, J. (1999) *Designing Web Usability: The Practice of Simplicity.* Indianapolis, IN: New Riders.

See description under ENABLING INTRANETS (A11).

D4 PERSONALIZED CONTENT

Eads, S. (2000, August 4) The Web's still-unfulfilled personalization promise. *BusinessWeek Online.* (http://www.businessweek.com/bwdaily/dnflash/aug2000/nf2000084_506.htm)

This article discusses the advantages of personalization but focuses more on the software and financial costs involved in integrating such a system into a Web site, as well as the difficulties involved in measuring effectiveness.

Hansell, S. (2000, December 11) In search for online success, "easy does it" is good theme. *New York Times E-Commerce Report.* (http://www.nytimes.com/2000/12/11/technology/11SIMP.html)

This article talks about simplicity in design as one of the dominant factors of success. It looks at issues such as the fact that underlined text links are more likely to be clicked on than buttons, the fact that basic security systems built into Web browsers work better than sophisticated ones that people have to download and install, and the fact that recommendation systems work only if they are easy and painless to use.

Kramer, J., S. Noronha, and J. Vergo. (2000, August) A user-centered design approach to personalization. *Communications of the ACM*, 43(8): 45–48. (http://doi.acm.org/10.1145/345124.345139)

> (This resource requires access to the ACM Digital Library, at http://www.acm.org/dl.) This article argues that customer-centered design is the key to successful design and implementation of systems that make use of personalization. This is one of several articles about personalization in the August 2000 issue of *Communications of the ACM*.

Manber, U., A. Patel, and J. Robison. (2000, August) Experience with personalization of Yahoo! *Communications of the ACM*, 43(8): 35–39. (http://doi.acm.org/10.1145/345124.345136)

> (This resource requires access to the ACM Digital Library, at http://www.acm.org/dl.) This article discusses the experiences and lessons learned in building and maintaining My Yahoo!, one of the earliest Web sites to use personalization on a large scale. Many interesting points about scalability, privacy and security, and user interface are covered. The article also talks about the fact that people often don't change the defaults. This is one of several articles about personalization in the August 2000 issue of *Communications of the ACM*.

Shapiro, A. (1999) *The Control Revolution: How the Internet Is Putting Individuals in Charge and Changing the World We Know.* New York: PublicAffairs.

> See description under NEWS MOSAICS (A2).

Stellin, S. (2000, August 28) Internet companies learn how to personalize service. *New York Times E-Commerce Report.* (http://nytimes.com/library/tech/00/08/cyber/commerce/28commerce.html)

> This article looks at several ways in which Web sites can apply personalization to improve the customer experience. It also discusses some of the problems involved in personalization, including too much work, bad data, and privacy.

D5 MESSAGE BOARDS

Kim, A. J. (2000) *Community Building on the Web: Secret Strategies for Successful Online Communities.* Berkeley, CA: Peachpit Press.

> See description under COMMUNITY CONFERENCE (A3).

Preece, J. (2000) *Online Communities: Designing Usability and Supporting Sociability.* New York: Wiley.

> See description under COMMUNITY CONFERENCE (A3).

Rheingold, H. (1998) *The Art of Hosting Good Conversations Online.* (http://www.rheingold.com/texts/artonlinehost.html)

> See description under COMMUNITY CONFERENCE (A3).

Rheingold, H. (2000) *The Virtual Community: Homesteading on the Electronic Frontier* (rev. ed.). Cambridge, MA: MIT Press.

> See description under COMMUNITY CONFERENCE (A3).

D6 WRITING FOR SEARCH ENGINES

AltaVista. (No date) *How AltaVista Works.* (http://help.altavista.com/adv_search/ast_haw_index)

This Web site details how the AltaVista search engine works and describes how to write your Web pages to improve search results.

Cunningham, J. P., J. Cantor, S. H. Pearsall, and K. H. Richardson. (2001) Industry briefs: AT&T. *Interactions: New Visions of Human Computer Interaction,* 8(2): 27–31.

This short piece discusses some of the experiences in building AT&T's Web site. Of particular interest is the fact that when people search, they often use the term AT&T, as in "AT&T long distance." Unfortunately, this keyword isn't very useful on the AT&T Web site because every page has AT&T on it! Included in the article is a discussion of the use of META tags to improve searching on this site.

Search Engine Watch: http://searchenginewatch.com

Search Engine Watch provides tips on submitting your Web site to search engines, as well as to newsletters and reviews on search engines.

Tedeschi, B. (2001, December 10) Striving to top the search lists. *New York Times E-Commerce Report.* (http://www.nytimes.com/2001/12/10/technology/ebusiness/10ECOM.html)

This article discusses how shoppers use search engines and describes the difficulties involved in trying to get to the top of the search results.

Webopedia. *Search Engine.* (http://www.webopedia.com/TERM/s/search_engine.html)

Webopedia is an online reference for technical terms. This Web page contains a short explanation of search engines and how they work, as well as references on writing Web pages for search engines.

D7 INVERSE-PYRAMID WRITING STYLE

Brinck, T., D. Gergle, and S. Wood. (2002) *Usability for the Web: Designing Web Sites That Work.* San Francisco: Morgan Kaufmann.

See description under Chapter 5—Processes for Developing Customer-Centered Sites.

Morkes, J., and J. Nielsen. (1997) *Concise, Scannable, and Objective: How to Write for the Web.* (http://www.useit.com/papers/webwriting/writing.html)
and Morkes, J., and J. Nielsen. (1998) *Applying Writing Guidelines to Web Pages.* (http://www.useit.com/papers/webwriting/rewriting.html)

These two Web pages discuss a series of studies on people's attitudes and behaviors toward writing on the Web. Their main recommendations are that text should be concise and easy to scan. They observe that most people skim through text anyway, and that halving the length of the text, using bulleted lists, and highlighting keywords helps the skimming process. In addition, they suggest that text should be objective in tone, avoiding jargon and self-promotion, because it is disliked by readers and negatively affects usability.

Nielsen, J. (1999) *Designing Web Usability: The Practice of Simplicity.* Indianapolis, IN: New Riders.

See description under ENABLING INTRANETS (A11).

D9 *DISTINCTIVE HTML TITLES*

Ivory, M. (2001) *An Empirical Foundation for Automated Web Interface Evaluation.* Doctoral dissertation, University of California, Berkeley, Computer Science Division.

> This Ph.D. dissertation combines quantitative metrics calculated on hundreds of Web sites with the judges' ratings for the 2000 Webby Awards to validate and invalidate many popular Web design guidelines. Distinctive HTML titles were found to be a common trait of highly rated Web sites.

Nielsen, J. (1999) *Designing Web Usability: The Practice of Simplicity.* Indianapolis, IN: New Riders.

> See description under ENABLING INTRANETS (A11).

D10 *INTERNATIONALIZED AND LOCALIZED CONTENT*

IBM Corporation. (2000) *Overview of Software Internationalization.* (http://oss.software.ibm.com/developerworks/opensource/icu/project/userguide/i18n.html)

> This discussion focuses on internationalization and localization issues from a software development perspective, including how to structure the code.

Marcus, A., J. Armitage, and V. Frank. (1999, June 3) Globalization of user-interface design for the Web. In *Proceedings of 5th Human Factors and the Web.* Gaithersburg, MD. (http://www.amanda.com/resources/HFWEB99/HFWEB99.Marcus.html)

> This paper looks at the issues of designing Web sites for a global audience, including metaphors, mental models, navigation, interaction, and appearance.

Marcus, A., and E. Gould. (2000, June 19) Cultural dimensions and global Web user-interface design: What? So What? Now what? In *Proceedings of 6th Conference on Human Factors and the Web.* Austin, TX. (http://www.amanda.com/resources/hfweb2000/hfweb00.marcus.html)

> This paper considers how user interface design might be affected by dimensions of culture, looking at factors like authority, collectivism and individualism, femininity and masculinity, uncertainty, and time.

Nielsen, J. (1999) *Designing Web Usability: The Practice of Simplicity.* Indianapolis, IN: New Riders.

> See description under ENABLING INTRANETS (A11).

World Wide Web Consortium. (No date) *World-Wide Character Sets, Languages, and Writing Systems.* (http://www.w3.org/international)

> This Web page looks at computer-related internationalization and localization issues, including writing HTML in many writing systems, representing dates and times, and fonts.

www.multilingual.com: http://www.multilingual.com

> This Web page contains references to excellent information about Web site internationalization and localization, including featured articles, product reviews, and book reviews.

Pattern Group E: Building Trust and Credibility

E1 SITE BRANDING

Crawford, F. A., and R. Mathews. (2001) *The Myth of Excellence: Why Great Companies Never Try to Be the Best at Everything.* New York: Crown Business.

> Crawford and Matthews surveyed 5,000 consumers to explore their purchasing behavior. The authors found that *values,* such as respect, honesty, trust, and dignity, were more important to consumers than *value.* This finding led to a new model of "consumer relevancy" based on price, service, quality, access, and customer experience. The book suggests that for companies to be successful, they need to dominate on only one of these five factors.

Fry, J. (2001, August 13) Web shoppers' loyalty isn't so crazy after all. *Wall Street Journal.* (http://ebusiness.mit.edu/news/WSJ_Story8-13-01.html)

> See description under Chapter 2—Making the Most of Web Design Patterns.

Johnston, D. (2000, October 23) A glass of wine helps show what buyers want. *New York Times E-Commerce Report.* (http://www.nytimes.com/library/tech/00/10/biztech/technology/25cay.html)

> This article discusses the fact that price is not the only consideration in online shopping. Factors such as convenience, quality, reliability, brand recognition, and good product information also weigh in.

E2 E-MAIL SUBSCRIPTIONS

Stamler, B. (2001, April 18) You want repeat customers? Try e-mail. *New York Times E-Commerce Report.* (http://www.nytimes.com/2001/04/18/technology/18STAM.html)

> This piece looks at the issues that Saturn, Eddie Bauer, and Esperya have had to address when using e-mail for advertising.

Stellin, S. (2000, August 21) Marketers get help from e-mail experts. *New York Times E-Commerce Report.* (http://www.nytimes.com/library/tech/00/08/cyber/commerce/21commerce.html)

> This news article discusses the emergence of an entire industry to help marketers deal with the technical and policy issues involved in e-mail advertising.

Tedeschi, B. (1999, August 9) Personalized e-mail ads: Low cost, high response rate. *New York Times E-Commerce Report.* (http://www.nytimes.com/library/tech/99/08/cyber/commerce/09commerce.html)

> This article reveals that e-mail advertisements are an effective form of advertising for customers who opt in. It also discusses sophisticated marketing techniques, like combining demographics with promotions, or using linked photographs of products to let customers immediately purchase items.

E3 FAIR INFORMATION PRACTICES

European Parliament and the Council of the European Union. (1995) *Directive 95/46/EC of the European Parliament and of the Council of 24 October 1995 on the Protection of Individuals with Regard to the Processing of Personal Data and on the Free*

Movement of Such Data. (http://europa.eu.int/eur-lex/en/lif/dat/1995/
en_395L0046.html)

> This is an online version of the text of a European Parliament directive on fair use of information.

Garfinkel, S. (2001) *Database Nation: The Death of Privacy in the 21st Century.*
Beijing, China: O'Reilly.

> This book describes many of the potential dangers to individuals when companies collect large amounts of information about them.

The Privacy Act of 1974: http://www.usdoj.gov/foia/privstat.htm

> This Web page contains the text of the Privacy Act of 1974.

Privacy.Org: http://www.privacy.org

> Privacy.Org provides news, information, and resources about privacy in general.

U.S. Department of Commerce, Safe Harbor: http://www.export.gov/safeharbor

> The safe harbor Web site contains detailed information on the safe harbor agreement, as well as documents about becoming compliant with safe harbor.

U.S. Federal Trade Commission. (2000, May) *Privacy Online: Fair Information Practices in the Electronic Marketplace: A Report to Congress.* (www.ftc.gov/reports/
privacy2000/privacy2000.pdf)

> This report describes the FTC's conclusion that legislation is necessary to ensure implementation of fair information practices online, and it recommends a framework for such legislation.

U.S. Federal Trade Commission. Privacy Initiatives: http://www.ftc.gov/privacy

> This report details privacy initiatives taken by the U.S. government, including news releases, related laws, reports, and design guidelines for protecting privacy.

E4 PRIVACY POLICY

Pew Internet & American Life. (2000) *Trust and Privacy Online: Why Americans Want to Rewrite the Rules.* (http://www.pewinternet.org/reports/
toc.asp?Report=19)

> This reports details a study looking at Americans' concerns about privacy online.

U.S. Federal Trade Commission, Kidz Privacy: http://www.ftc.gov/bcp/conline/
edcams/kidzprivacy

> The U.S. Federal Trade Commission has created a Web site with additional details and resources on protecting children's privacy online.

See also the references listed under FAIR INFORMATION PRACTICES (E3).

E5 ABOUT US

Fogg, B., J. Marshall, O. Laraki, A. Osipovich, C. Varma, N. Fang, J. Paul,
A. Rangnekar, J. Shon, P. Swani, and M. Treinen. (2001, March 31–April 5) What makes Web sites credible? A report on a large quantitative study. CHI 2000,
ACM Conference on Human Factors in Computing Systems, *CHI Letters,* 3(1):
61–68. (http://www.webcredibility.org/studies/p61-fogg.pdf)

> This paper presents the results of a survey of over 1,400 people from the United States and Europe, reporting how various factors in Web design

affected people's perceptions of credibility. Some interesting results include the facts that providing quick responses to customer service questions, listing the organization's physical address, having a contact phone number and e-mail address, and having photos of the organization's members helped increase credibility.

E6 SECURE CONNECTIONS

UCLA Center for Communication Policy. (2001, November 29) *The UCLA Internet Report 2001: Surveying the Digital Future: Year Two.* (http://www.ccp.ucla.edu)

This survey of over 2,000 people found many interesting results about people's attitudes and behaviors online. One piece of information is that most people waited between 15 and 22 months before purchasing anything online. The single most-cited reason for this was "concerned about giving a credit card number," followed by "no products or services available" and "concerned about deception." Over two-thirds of the people surveyed were also very concerned about privacy when buying online.

Webopedia. SSL. (http://www.webopedia.com/TERM/S/SSL.html)

Webopedia is an online reference for technical terms. This Web page contains a short explanation of how Secure Sockets Layer works, as well as references for further reading.

Pattern Group F: Basic E-Commerce

F1 QUICK-FLOW CHECKOUT

Bidigare, S. (2000, May) *Information Architecture of the Shopping Cart: Best Practices for the Information Architectures of E-Commerce Ordering Systems.* Argus Center for Information Architecture. (http://argus-acia.com/white_papers/shopping_cart_ia.html)

This white paper analyzes four different shopping cart and checkout designs and extracts some design principles for making these processes simple to use.

Tedeschi, B. (1999, August 30) Good Web site design can lead to healthy sales. *New York Times E-Commerce Report.* (http://www.nytimes.com/library/tech/99/08/cyber/commerce/30commerce.html)

See description under PAGE TEMPLATES (D1).

F2 CLEAN PRODUCT DETAILS

Johnston, D. (2000, October 23) A glass of wine helps show what buyers want. *New York Times E-Commerce Report.* (http://www.nytimes.com/library/tech/00/10/biztech/technology/25cay.html)

See description under SITE BRANDING (E1).

Ogilvy, D. (1987) *Ogilvy on Advertising.* New York: Vintage Books.

See description under UP-FRONT VALUE PROPOSITION (C2).

Tedeschi, B. (1999, August 23) Online sales can be messy, especially those pesky returns. *New York Times E-Commerce Report.* (http://www.nytimes.com/library/tech/99/08/cyber/commerce/23commerce.html)

This article looks at the difficulties with handling product returns, as well as at some of the approaches that companies are using to address these problems, including better management, better product details to give customers realistic expectations, and integration of returns with physical stores.

F3 SHOPPING CART

Bidigare, S. (2000, May) *Information Architecture of the Shopping Cart: Best Practices for the Information Architectures of E-Commerce Ordering Systems.* Argus Center for Information Architecture. (http://argus-acia.com/white_papers/shopping_cart_ia.html)
    See description under QUICK-FLOW CHECKOUT (F1).

F9 EASY RETURNS

Tedeschi, B. (1999, August 23) Online sales can be messy, especially those pesky returns. *New York Times E-Commerce Report.* (http://www.nytimes.com/library/tech/99/08/cyber/commerce/23commerce.html)
    See description under CLEAN PRODUCT DETAILS (F2).

Pattern Group G: Advanced E-Commerce

G1 FEATURED PRODUCTS

Ogilvy, D. (1987) *Ogilvy on Advertising.* New York: Vintage Books.
    See description under UP-FRONT VALUE PROPOSITION (C2).

G2 CROSS-SELLING AND UP-SELLING

Ogilvy, D. (1987) *Ogilvy on Advertising.* New York: Vintage Books.
    See description under UP-FRONT VALUE PROPOSITION (C2).

G3 PERSONALIZED RECOMMENDATIONS

    See references listed under PERSONALIZED CONTENT (D4).

G4 RECOMMENDATION COMMUNITY

Kim, A. J. (2000) *Community Building on the Web: Secret Strategies for Successful Online Communities.* Berkeley, CA: Peachpit Press.
    See description under COMMUNITY CONFERENCE (A3).

Preece, J. (2000) *Online Communities: Designing Usability and Supporting Sociability.* New York: Wiley.
    See description under COMMUNITY CONFERENCE (A3).

Sinha, R., and K. Swearingen. (2002) The role of transparency in recommender systems. In *Conference Companion: Proceedings of Human Factors in Computing Systems: CHI 2002.* Minneapolis, MN: ACM Press, pp. 830–31.
    Preliminary results from this research indicate that people felt more confident about recommendations from a recommendation system if they understood why a particular recommendation was made.

See also references listed under PERSONALIZED CONTENT (D4).

Pattern Group H: Helping Customers Complete Tasks

H1 PROCESS FUNNEL

Schwartz, M. (2000, June 12) Sharper Staples. *Computerworld.* (http://www.computerworld.com/cwi/story/0,1199,NAV47_STO45787,00.html)

This short article examines the redesign of the Staples Web site. During the process the designers learned that visitors were suspicious of entering their ZIP code information until being informed about how doing that could help them with shipping information, that the search results had to be culled and organized more efficiently, and that reducing the account creation process from four pages to two reduced the number of customers who balked, among other things. The article also describes how Staples integrated its paper catalogues with its Web site.

Tedeschi, B. (1999, August 30) Good Web site design can lead to healthy sales. *New York Times E-Commerce Report.* (http://www.nytimes.com/library/tech/99/08/cyber/commerce/30commerce.html)

See description under PAGE TEMPLATES (D1).

H2 SIGN-IN/NEW ACCOUNT

Schwartz, M. (2000, June 12) Sharper Staples. *Computerworld.* (http://www.computerworld.com/cwi/story/0,1199,NAV47_STO45787,00.html)

See description under PROCESS FUNNEL (H1).

H5 PERSISTENT CUSTOMER SESSIONS

Persistent Client State: HTTP Cookies. (1999) (http://home.netscape.com/newsref/std/cookie_spec.html)

This Web page describes many of the technical details underlying cookies.

Webopedia. *Cookie.* (http://www.webopedia.com/TERM/c/cookie.html)

Webopedia is an online reference for technical terms. This Web page contains a short explanation of cookies, how they work, and references for further reading.

H7 FREQUENTLY ASKED QUESTIONS

Webopedia. *FAQ.* (http://www.webopedia.com/TERM/F/FAQ.html)

Webopedia is an online reference for technical terms. This Web page contains a short explanation of FAQs, as well as references for further reading.

H8 CONTEXT-SENSITIVE HELP

Greyling, T. (1998, May) Fear and loathing of the help menu: A usability test of online help. *Technical Communication Online,* 45(2): 168–179. (http://www.techcomm-online.org/issues/v45n2/full/0267.html)

This article reports results of a usability test on an online help system. None of the findings are especially surprising: People avoid using online help systems, read any help information hastily, leave quickly if they don't think they're on the right help page, and ignore broad overviews. However, the testers did find that, for their specific application, people liked online help that was context specific and relevant to the current task. They also found that people liked help that was obvious and just one mouse click away.

Pattern Group I: Designing Effective Page Layouts

I1 GRID LAYOUT

Brinck, T., D. Gergle, and S. Wood. (2002) *Usability for the Web: Designing Web Sites That Work.* San Francisco: Morgan Kaufmann.

> See description under Chapter 5—Processes for Developing Customer-Centered Sites.

Krug, S. (2000) *Don't Make Me Think!: A Common Sense Approach to Web Usability.* Indianapolis, IN: Que.

> The title identifies the main point of this fun book, which says that customers usually know what they want to do, but most Web pages force them to think too much about how to do it. Krug describes a host of tips, techniques, and examples for getting this done.

Marcus, A. (1992) *Graphic Design for Electronic Documents and User Interfaces.* Reading, MA: Addison-Wesley.

> This book takes a broad look at visual design. It discusses issues like layout, typography, symbols, icons, color, charts, diagrams, and maps.

Marcus, A., and Aaron Marcus and Associates. (1994) Principles of effective visual communication for graphical user interface design. In *HCI-2000,* R. Baecker, B. Buxton, J. Grudin, and S. Greenberg. (Eds.), pp. 425–441. Palo Alto, CA: Morgan Kaufmann.

> This chapter looks at techniques for achieving effective visual communication, providing an overview of organization, consistency, screen layout, and color use for graphical user interfaces.

Mullet, K., and D. Sano. (1994) *Designing Visual Interfaces: Communication Oriented Techniques.* Englewood Cliffs, NJ: Prentice Hall/SunSoft Press.

> See description under Chapter 4—Involving Customers with Iterative Design.

I2 ABOVE THE FOLD

Krug, S. (2000) *Don't Make Me Think!: A Common Sense Approach to Web Usability.* Indianapolis, IN: Que.

> See description under GRID LAYOUT (I1).

Marcus, A. (1992) *Graphic Design for Electronic Documents and User Interfaces.* Reading, MA: Addison-Wesley.

> See description under GRID LAYOUT (I1).

Marcus, A., and Aaron Marcus and Associates. (1994) Principles of effective visual communication for graphical user interface design. In *HCI-2000,* R. Baecker, B. Buxton, J. Grudin, and S. Greenberg. (Eds.), pp. 425–441. Palo Alto, CA: Morgan Kaufmann.

> See description under GRID LAYOUT (I1).

Mullet, K., and D. Sano. (1994) *Designing Visual Interfaces: Communication Oriented Techniques.* Englewood Cliffs, NJ: Prentice Hall/SunSoft Press.

> See description under GRID LAYOUT (I1).

Spool, J., T. Scanlon, W. Schroeder, C. Snyder, and T. DeAngelo. (1998) *Web Site Usability.* San Francisco: Morgan Kaufmann.

> This book discusses the results of many informal usability tests conducted by the authors. Although the sites that the study evaluated have since evolved, there are still many interesting tidbits here, including link labeling, embedded links, searching, page layout, and keeping important content above the fold.

I3 CLEAR FIRST READS

See references listed under GRID LAYOUT (I1).

I4 EXPANDING-WIDTH SCREEN SIZE

Niederst, J. (1999) *Web Design in a Nutshell: A Desktop Quick Reference.* Beijing, China: O'Reilly.

> This book discusses many of the low-level implementation issues that you will face in the Production and Implementation phases. It covers the different versions of HTML, browser compatibility, forms, and frames.

Weijers, J. (No date) *Jan's Guide to HTML and More.* (http://www.weijers.net/guide)

> This Web site discusses all the basics and some advanced topics of HTML. With a nice clean design, it also provides many useful examples.

I5 FIXED-WIDTH SCREEN SIZE

Niederst, J. (1999) *Web Design in a Nutshell: A Desktop Quick Reference.* Beijing, China: O'Reilly.

> See description under EXPANDING-WIDTH SCREEN SIZE (I4).

Weijers, J. (No date) *Jan's Guide to HTML and More.* http://www.weijers.net/guide)

> See description under EXPANDING-WIDTH SCREEN SIZE (I4).

I6 CONSISTENT SIDEBARS OF RELATED CONTENT

Fogg, B., J. Marshall, O. Laraki, A. Osipovich, C. Varma, N. Fang, J. Paul, A. Rangnekar, J. Shon, P. Swani, and M. Treinen. (2001, March 31–April 5) What makes Web sites credible? A report on a large quantitative study. CHI 2001, ACM Conference on Human Factors in Computing Systems, *CHI Letters,* 3(1): 61–68. (http://www.webcredibility.org/studies/p61-fogg.pdf)

> See description under ABOUT US (E5).

Pattern Group J: Making Site Search Fast and Relevant

J1 SEARCH ACTION MODULE

Bernard, M. (2001) Developing schemas for the location of common Web objects. *Usability News* [online], 3(1). (http://psychology.wichita.edu/surl/usabilitynews/3W/web_object.htm)

> This study asked 304 participants how they expected to see common Web objects on a page, such as the <u>Home</u> link, internal links, external links, the

search engine, and advertisements. The participants expected the <u>Home</u> link to be at the top left and at the center bottom of a Web page, internal links to run along the left side, external links to run on the bottom left and on the right-hand side, search engines to be at the top right or near the top center, and advertisements to be at the top.

English, J., M. Hearst, R. Sinha, K. Swearingen, and K. Yee. (2002) *Flexible Search and Navigation Using Faceted Metadata.* (http://bailando.sims.berkeley.edu/papers/flamenco02.pdf)

This paper describes Flamenco, an advanced search and navigation system that lets nonexperts explore large information spaces. The key idea is to provide a flexible interface that lets people search and navigate through metadata—that is, additional data describing the actual content (for example, the author, date, and publisher of a news article).

Nielsen, J. (1999) *Designing Web Usability: The Practice of Simplicity.* Indianapolis, IN: New Riders.

See description under ENABLING INTRANETS (A11).

Webopedia. *Search Engine.* (http://www.webopedia.com/TERM/s/search_engine.html)

See description under WRITING FOR SEARCH ENGINES (D6).

J2 STRAIGHTFORWARD SEARCH FORMS

Baeza-Yates, R., and B. Ribeiro-Neto. (1999) *Modern Information Retrieval.* Reading, MA: Addison-Wesley.

This book presents extremely technical details about the inner workings of modern information retrieval engines, of which search engines are one type. It includes a great deal of ongoing research in the field. And it looks at many interface techniques related to information retrieval.

Cunningham, J. P., J. Cantor, S. H. Pearsall, and K. H. Richardson. (2001) Industry briefs: AT&T. *Interactions: New Visions of Human Computer Interaction,* 8(2): 27–31.

See description under WRITING FOR SEARCH ENGINES (D6).

English, J., M. Hearst, R. Sinha, K. Swearingen, and K. Yee. (2002) *Flexible Search and Navigation Using Faceted Metadata.* (http://bailando.sims.berkeley.edu/papers/flamenco02.pdf)

See description under SEARCH ACTION MODULE (J1).

J3 ORGANIZED SEARCH RESULTS

Cunningham, J. P., J. Cantor, S. H. Pearsall, and K. H. Richardson. (2001) Industry briefs: AT&T. *Interactions: New Visions of Human Computer Interaction,* 8(2): 27–31.

See description under WRITING FOR SEARCH ENGINES (D6).

English, J., M. Hearst, R. Sinha, K. Swearingen, and K. Yee. (2002) *Flexible Search and Navigation Using Faceted Metadata.* (http://bailando.sims.berkeley.edu/papers/flamenco02.pdf)

See description under SEARCH ACTION MODULE (J1).

Schwartz, M. (2000, June 12) Sharper Staples, *Computerworld.* (http://www. computerworld.com/cwi/story/0,1199,NAV47_STO45787,00.html)

See description under PROCESS FUNNEL (H1).

Tedeschi, B. (2001, December 10) Striving to top the search lists. *New York Times E-Commerce Report.* (http://www.nytimes.com/2001/12/10/technology/ ebusiness/10ECOM.html)

See description under WRITING FOR SEARCH ENGINES (D6).

Pattern Group K: Making Navigation Easy

K2 NAVIGATION BAR

Bernard, M. (2001) Developing schemas for the location of common Web objects. *Usability News* [online], 3(1). (http://psychology.wichita.edu/surl/ usabilitynews/3W/web_object.htm)

See description under SEARCH ACTION MODULE (J1).

Krug, S. (2000) *Don't Make Me Think!: A Common Sense Approach to Web Usability.* Indianapolis, IN: Que.

See description under GRID LAYOUT (I1).

K3 TAB ROWS

Krug, S. (2000) *Don't Make Me Think!: A Common Sense Approach to Web Usability.* Indianapolis, IN: Que.

See description under GRID LAYOUT (I1).

K4 ACTION BUTTONS

Card, S. K., T. P. Moran, and A. Newell. (1983) *The Psychology of Human–Computer Interaction.* Hillsdale, NJ: Lawrence Erlbaum.

This is the classic book on human–computer interaction research, the one that coined the term. It delves deeply into low-level psychological and cognitive research on human performance, including physical motion, memory, and decision making. Of interest here are the sections on evaluating a design using Fitts's Law.

Krug, S. (2000) *Don't Make Me Think!: A Common Sense Approach to Web Usability.* Indianapolis, IN: Que.

See description under GRID LAYOUT (I1).

Raskin, J. (2000) *The Humane Interface.* Boston: Addison-Wesley.

This book looks at user interface development from a fairly low-level, psychological and cognitive science standpoint. It has a short section about Fitts's Law and how it applies to user interfaces.

K5 HIGH-VISIBILITY ACTION BUTTONS

Krug, S. (2000) *Don't Make Me Think!: A Common Sense Approach to Web Usability.* Indianapolis, IN: Que.

See description under GRID LAYOUT (I1).

K7 EMBEDDED LINKS

Bernard, M., S. Hull, and D. Drake. (2001). Where should you put the links? A comparison of four locations. *Usability News* [online], 3(2). (http://psychology. wichita.edu/surl/usabilitynews/3S/links.htm)

> This study compared the placement of links and its effect on performance. Links were embedded in the document, placed at the bottom or top left of the page, or provided in a sidebar right next to their associated content. The study showed no significant differences in the four arrangements in terms of search accuracy, time, or efficiency. However, the 20 participants preferred embedded links because they felt that these links made the test document easier to navigate, and because they made it easier to search for specific information.

Spool, J., T. Scanlon, W. Schroeder, C. Snyder, and T. DeAngelo. (1998) *Web Site Usability*. San Francisco: Morgan Kaufmann.

> See description under ABOVE THE FOLD (I2).

K8 EXTERNAL LINKS

Bernard, M. (2001) Developing schemas for the location of common Web objects. *Usability News* [online], 3(1). (http://psychology.wichita.edu/surl/ usabilitynews/3W/web_object.htm)

> See description under SEARCH ACTION MODULE (J1).

Bernard, M., S. Hull, and D. Drake. (2001). Where should you put the links? A comparison of four locations. *Usability News* [online], 3(2). (http://psychology. wichita.edu/surl/usabilitynews/3S/links.htm)

> See description under EMBEDDED LINKS (K7).

Fogg, B., J. Marshall, O. Laraki, A. Osipovich, C. Varma, N. Fang, J. Paul, A. Rangnekar, J. Shon, P. Swani, and M. Treinen. (2001, March 31–April 5) What makes Web sites credible? A report on a large quantitative study. CHI 2001, ACM Conference on Human Factors in Computing Systems, *CHI Letters*, 3(1): 61–68. (http://www.webcredibility.org/studies/p61-fogg.pdf)

> See description under ABOUT US (E5).

K9 DESCRIPTIVE, LONGER LINK NAMES

Nielsen, J. (1999) *Designing Web Usability: The Practice of Simplicity*. Indianapolis, IN: New Riders.

> See description under ENABLING INTRANETS (A11).

Spool, J., T. Scanlon, W. Schroeder, C. Snyder, and T. DeAngelo. (1998) *Web Site Usability*. San Francisco: Morgan Kaufmann.

> See description under ABOVE THE FOLD (I2).

K10 OBVIOUS LINKS

Hansell, S. (2000, December 11) In search for online success, "easy does it" is good theme. *New York Times E-Commerce Report*. (http://www.nytimes.com/2000/ 12/11/technology/11SIMP.html)

> See description under PERSONALIZED CONTENT (D4).

Nielsen, J. (1999) *Designing Web Usability: The Practice of Simplicity.*
Indianapolis, IN: New Riders.
See description under ENABLING INTRANETS (A11).

K11 FAMILIAR LANGUAGE

See references listed under MULTIPLE WAYS TO NAVIGATE (B1).

K12 PREVENTING ERRORS

37signals. Design Not Found: http://www.37signals.com/dnf
This is a cool site featuring many screen shots of Web error messages, both good and bad. It also has some tips on preventing errors.

K13 MEANINGFUL ERROR MESSAGES

37signals. Design Not Found: http://www.37signals.com/dnf
See description under PREVENTING ERRORS (K12).

K14 PAGE NOT FOUND

404 Research Lab: http://www.plinko.net/404
In addition to containing several humorous examples and jokes about the dreaded "Page not found" error, this Web site has some practical tips for helping customers if they do encounter "Page not found" errors.

Pattern Group L: Speeding Up Your Site

L1 LOW NUMBER OF FILES

Niederst, J. (1999) *Web Design in a Nutshell: A Desktop Quick Reference.* Beijing, China: O'Reilly.
See description under EXPANDING-WIDTH SCREEN SIZE (I4).

Rhodes, J. (2001, July 25) *The Usability of Usability: An Interview with Jared Spool.*
(http://www.webword.com/interviews/spool2.html)
This interview presents an interesting counterpoint to the argument for speedy download times. Jared Spool, a noted usability consultant, claims his research shows that download speed has no correlation with the usability of a site. In fact, his data says that it is the customer's ability to complete tasks that best correlates with the perception of the site's speed.

L2 FAST-DOWNLOADING IMAGES

CNET Builder.com. (No date) *Graphics & Multimedia.* (http://builder.cnet.com/webbuilding/0-3883.html)
This piece gives tips and tricks for creating and publishing images on the Web.

Marcus, A. (1992) *Graphic Design for Electronic Documents and User Interfaces.*
Reading, MA: Addison-Wesley.
See description under GRID LAYOUT (I1).

Marcus, A., and Aaron Marcus and Associates. (1994) Principles of effective visual communication for graphical user interface design. In *HCI-2000*, R. Baecker, B. Buxton, J. Grudin, and S. Greenberg. (Eds.), pp. 425–441. Palo Alto, CA: Morgan Kaufmann.

>This chapter looks at techniques for achieving effective visual communication. Of particular interest here is an overview of creating clear visual languages for icons.

Niederst, J. (1999) *Web Design in a Nutshell: A Desktop Quick Reference.* Beijing, China: O'Reilly.

>See description under EXPANDING-WIDTH SCREEN SIZE (I4).

Spalter, A. (1999) *The Computer in the Visual Arts.* Reading, MA: Addison-Wesley.

>This book looks at many of the technology-related issues involved in creating visual images, including terminology, input devices, displays, projectors, printing, color spaces, three-dimensional worlds, and a little bit about the Web. It is an excellent book for visual designers wanting to learn more about technology, or for technologists wanting to learn more about the visual arts.

Weinman, L. (No date) *The Browser-Safe Color Palette.* (http://www.lynda.com/hex.html)

>You can use the 216-color "browser-safe" color palette in your paint program when you create graphics for the Web. This set of colors was chosen because they look the same both on Macintosh computers and in Microsoft Windows. Some browsers will try to mix pixel colors to obtain colors that are close to the color you want if the color is outside of this palette. There is still some controversy about whether there truly is a browser-safe palette.

L3 SEPARATE TABLES

Niederst, J. (1999) *Web Design in a Nutshell: A Desktop Quick Reference.* Beijing, China: O'Reilly.

>See description under EXPANDING-WIDTH SCREEN SIZE (I4).

Weijers, J. (No date) *Jan's Guide to HTML and More.* http://www.weijers.net/guide)

>See description under EXPANDING-WIDTH SCREEN SIZE (I4).

L4 HTML POWER

Niederst, J. (1999) *Web Design in a Nutshell: A Desktop Quick Reference.* Beijing, China: O'Reilly.

>See description under EXPANDING-WIDTH SCREEN SIZE (I4).

Weijers, J. (No date) *Jan's Guide to HTML and More.* (http://www.weijers.net/guide)

>See description under EXPANDING-WIDTH SCREEN SIZE (I4).

L5 REUSABLE IMAGES

Niederst, J. (1999) *Web Design in a Nutshell: A Desktop Quick Reference.* Beijing, China: O'Reilly.

>See description under EXPANDING-WIDTH SCREEN SIZE (I4).

Part III: Appendixes

Gomoll, K. (1990) Some techniques for observing users. In *The Art of Human–Computer Interface Design,* B. Laurel (Ed.), pp. 85–90. Reading, MA: Addison-Wesley.

> Some of the material in Appendix A (Running Usability Evaluations) of the book you have in hand is based on this chapter's list of ten things to do when running a usability study.

Gonick, L., and W. Smith. (1993) *The Cartoon Guide to Statistics.* New York: HarperPerennial.

> This book is a good introduction to basic statistical terms, as well as procedures, explaining what they're good for and how to do them. It is also presented as a large comic book, with fun illustrations to keep things going.

McQuarrie, E. (1996) *The Market Research Toolbox: A Concise Guide for Beginners.* Thousand Oaks, CA: Sage.

> A great book for people new to market research, discussing the various objectives, techniques for discovering customer needs, and expected payoffs of those techniques. The book looks into secondary research, customer visits, focus groups, surveys, choice modeling, and experimentation, and it details costs, uses, tips, and trade-offs of each.

NetRaker Corporation: http://www.netraker.com

> NetRaker, founded by two of the authors of the book you have in hand (van Duyne and Landay), is a leading provider of end-to-end customer evaluation solutions for Web-based applications.

Rettig, M. (1994) Prototyping for tiny fingers. *Communications of the ACM,* 37(4): 21–27. (http://www.acm.org/pubs/citations/journals/cacm/1994-37-4/p21-rettig)

> See description under Chapter 4—Involving Customers with Iterative Design.

Rubin, J. (1994) *Handbook of Usability Testing: How to Plan, Design, and Conduct Effective Tests.* New York: Wiley.

> This book is a good source that provides step-by-step guidelines on preparing and running usability tests.

Further Reading

CNET Builder.com. (No date) *Web Building.* (http://builder.cnet.com)

> This fairly comprehensive site has a host of resources on building Web sites, including graphics, programming, e-commerce, business strategy, and usability.

Group for User Interface Research (GUIR), University of California at Berkeley: http://guir.berkeley.edu

> GUIR is the research group jointly led by Dr. James Landay, one of the authors of the book you have in hand. GUIR's research thrusts include tools for rapidly prototyping Web and speech user interfaces, novel uses of pen-based interfaces, and mobile computing. Research from GUIR has been published in many premier conferences on human–computer interaction and on design.

HCI Bibliography: Free Access to Human–Computer Interaction Resources: http://www.hcibib.org

> This is a great starting point that links to many, many resources on the Web.

Human–Computer Interaction Resource Network: http://www.hcirn.com
The goal of the Human–Computer Interaction Resource Network is to advance human–computer interaction practices and resources.

IBM: Web Design Guidelines. (http://www.ibm.com/ibm/easy/eou_ext.nsf/publish/572)
Despite its unfortunately long URL, IBM has a good Web design guide that provides tips on the Web design process.

Usable Web: http://www.usableweb.com
Usable Web is another collection of links about Web site design, including information architecture and human factors. The author also provides short descriptions of links and a search engine that finds things quickly.

Usability.gov: http://www.usability.gov
The National Cancer Institute hosts Usability.gov, an online resource for "designing usable, useful and accessible Web sites and user interfaces." Although its primary mission is to improve the communication of cancer research, you will also find guidelines, case studies, and statistics to help guide the development process.

Professional Groups

ACM SIGCHI (Special Interest Group on Computer–Human Interaction): http://www.acm.org/sigchi
The Special Interest Group on Computer–Human Interaction (SIGCHI) holds an annual conference called CHI, the premier forum for research on people and computer systems. SIGCHI also has a Web site that highlights issues such as accessibility, education, and intercultural issues. Finally, SIGCHI maintains a useful mailing list called CHI-WEB that discusses ongoing issues of designing for the Web, at http://sigchi.org/web.

American Center for Design: http://www.ac4d.org
The American Center for Design is a national design organization that looks at both design theory and practice. The emphasis is on "research, ideas, and technologies that are continually shaping, reshaping, and influencing design and design practice." Its site includes links to conferences, membership information, and areas of interest.

American Institute of Graphic Arts: http://www.aiga.org
The American Institute of Graphic Arts is a national organization promoting graphic design. Its site includes links to membership information, events, publications, and local chapters.

Human Factors and Ergonomics Society: http://hfes.org
The Human Factors and Ergonomics Society is an international organization with many special interest groups that are relevant to interface design and evaluation. They also hold an annual conference.

Usability Professionals' Association: http://www.upassoc.org
The Usability Professionals' Association (UPA) promotes usability concepts and techniques. In contrast to ACM SIGCHI, UPA is targeted more at practitioners than at researchers. They hold an annual conference.

Figures 2.5, A1.2, B1.1, B8.2, D1.3, E2.4, E6.4, F1.1, F1.3, F5.2, F6.3, F7.1, F9.2, F9.3, F9.4, F9.5, G1.4, G2.5, G2.6, G3.1, G3.2, G4.1, G4.3, G4.4, G5.3, G5.4, G6.3, G7.3, J1.1, J3.2, K3.4, K4.3
© 2001 Amazon.com, Inc. All rights reserved.

Figures F3.1, F3.2
© 2001 Amazon.com, Inc. All rights reserved. Reprinted with permission from Database Nation © 2000, O'Reilly + Associates, Inc. All rights reserved.

Figure J3.4
© 2001 Amazon.com, Inc. All rights reserved. *Crossing the Quality Chasm,* National Academy Press, 2001.

Figure H6.2
Copyright, Apache Software Foundation

Figures K3.1, L3.2
BabyCenter, LLC © 1997–2002

Figure B7.1
© 2001 BPI Communications Inc. Used with permission.

Figure D6.2
Source: United States' National Cancer Institute

Figure A8.2
© 2001 Carnegie Mellon University. All rights reserved.

Figures A2.2, D7.4
Copyright © 1998–2001 Market-Watch.com, Inc.

Figure H7.3
Lanny Chambers, author/designer

Figure C2.3
The CIENA logo and the CIENA.com Web site have been reprinted with permission from CIENA Corporation. "CIENA" is a trademark or registered trademark of CIENA Corporation in the United States and other countries and is being used with the permission of CIENA Corporation.

Figure A4.3
Courtesy of City of San Jose, California (www.ci.san-jose.ca.us).

Figure A4.1
Courtesy of City of Sydney (www.cityofsydney.new.gov.au).

Figure F2.4
Courtesy of Cooking.com

Figures F2.1, H1.1, H6.3, H8.1, K13.1
Dell Computer Corporation

Figures 2.4, A1.3, E6.1, F1.2, F4.1, F6.1, H2.2, H1.2, H2.3, H2.4, K4.1
These materials have been reproduced with the permission of eBay Inc. Copyright © eBay Inc. All rights reserved.

Figure K11.1
Screen shot courtesy of Edmunds.com, Inc.

Figures C2.1, J2.1, K2.1
Epicurious.com © 2002 CondeNet. All rights reserved. Reprinted by permission.

Figure E4.2
© 2001 Exploratorium (www.exploratorium.edu)

Figure G1.3
Eziba (www.eziba.com)

Figure B3.2
www.FindLaw.com

Figure A10.2
First Internet Bank of Indiana (www.firstib.com) is the first state-chartered, FDIC-insured institution to operate solely via the Internet. Services include checking and savings accounts, CDs, credits cards, and personal loans. First IB also offers online bill payment, real-time transfers between accounts, and the ability to display checking, savings and loan information on a single screen.

Figures K4.3, L2.1
Printed with permission from Geo-caching.com.

Figure D9.4
Google Inc. *Harry Potter,* characters, names, and all related indicia are trademarks of Warner Bros. © 2001.

Figures E5.1, J3.5
Google Inc.

Figure A3.2
Greenpeace

Figure H3.1
healthgiant.com, a division of School Health Corporation

Figure A7.2
Copyright 2001 Hewlett-Packard Company. Reproduced with permission.

Figures A7.1, J3.3
Courtesy IBM Corp.

Figures A9.3, B7.3, I5.2
IFilm International

Figure I4.1
© iWon, Inc. 1999–2001. All rights reserved.

Figure H6.2
Courtesy of *Java Pro Magazine* (www.javapro.com).

Figure A5.3
Reprinted from www.kiwanis.org.

Figures A1.1, E6.6, I3.2
L.L. Bean Inc.

Figures D3.4, D4.6, G3.4, I3.1
© Lands' End, Inc. Used with permission.

Figure E5.3
LEGO is a trademark of the LEGO Group © 2001 The LEGO Group. The LEGO® trademarks and products are used with permission. The LEGO Group does not sponsor or endorse *The Design of Sites.*

Figure E5.4
Reprinted with the permission of LexisNexis, a division of Reed Elsevier Inc.

Figure L4.2
Courtesy of James Lin

Figure L5.2
Lowestfare.com and Globe Design are trademarks of Lowestfare.com, LLC, which also owns all copyright for the Flight Page. Use of this material is pursuant to a license from Lowestfare.com and is strictly

limited under the trademark and copyright laws of the United States.

Figure B7.4
© 2001 Lycos, Inc. Lycos® is a registered trademark of Carnegie Mellon University. All rights reserved.

Figure B8.1
© 2001 Martha Stewart Living Omnimedia, Inc. All rights reserved.

Figures D8.1, G6.1
© 2001 Martha Stewart Living Omnimedia, Inc. All rights reserved. Photographer: Simon Watson

Figure A8.3
Reprinted with permission of The Math Forum @ Drexel, an online community for mathematics education (http://mathforum.org/). Copyright 1996, The Math Forum @ Drexel.

Figures A7.3, A10.3, B9.4, E1.1, H2.1, H8.2, K12.1, K14.1, K2.2
Used by permission from Microsoft Corporation.

Figures D4.5, H8.3
Courtesy of Monster.

Figures D5.2, D5.3, D5.4, D5.6
The Motley Fool, Inc. (www.fool.com)

Figures C1.1, D4.7
Screen shots of MSNBC used by permission from MSNBC. MSNBC is not a sponsor of and does not endorse *The Design of Sites* and/or Addison-Wesley.

Figures D4.7, D9.1, D9.2, D9.3
Screen shots of MSNBC used by permission from MSNBC. MSNBC is not a sponsor of and does not endorse *The Design of Sites* and/or Addison-Wesley. *Harry Potter,* characters, names, and all related indicia are trademarks of Warner Bros. © 2001.

Figure A9.2
Reprinted with the permission of NBA Entertainment.

Figure A1.4
© 2001 Trilegiant Corporation (www.netmarket.com)

Figure K3.2
Reprinted with permission from the publisher, Nolo Copyright 2001, http://www.nolo.com.

Figure A9.1
The screen shot taken from http://www.pbs.org is used herein with permission from The Public Broadcasting Service.

Figure A8.1
Phillips Academy, Andover, Mass. Photographer: Lionel Delevinge

Figure K3.4
Used by permission of Dack Ragus (www.dack.com)

Figure A5.2
Copyright © 2002 Rotary International. All rights reserved. The Rotary International logo is a registered trademark of Rotary International. Used with permission.

Figure A11.1
"SAP" and mySAP.com are trademarks of SAPAktiengesellschaft, Systems, Applications and Products in Data Processing, Neurottstrasse 16, Walldorf, Germany, D-69190. The publisher gratefully acknowledges SAP's kind permission to use its trademark in this publication. SAP AG is not the publisher of this book and is not responsible for it under any aspect of press law.

Figures 5.2, C2.2, G7.2
© Copyright Shutterfly 2001. All rights reserved (www.shutterfly.com).

Figures A7.5, B5.1, D1.4, D2.1, H7.2
Reprinted by permission of Sun Microsystems, Inc. Copyright 2002 Sun Microsystems, Inc. All rights reserved.

Figure H3.3
Steve Brendish: Taxpayers Australia

Figures B2.2, G2.1
The Knot (www.theknot.com. AOL keyword: weddings)

Figure A3.3
Reprinted with the permission of Salon.com.

Figure K10.4
The Chopping Block, Inc. Web designer: Thomas Romer; Illustration: Thomas Romer, Jaylo (www.tmbg.com)

Figure B9.1
Copyright 2000, www.universal usability.org. Permission granted for reprinting.

Figure A5.1
Used with permission of Volunteer-Match.

Figures B2.1, G5.1, G5.2, G62
Images courtesy of Wal-Mart, Inc. Copyright 2000–2002 Wal-Mart.com, Inc. and Wal-Mart Stores, Inc.

Figures B9.2, B9.3
TWC and The Weather Channel and each of their logos are trademarks of The Weather Channel, Inc. All rights reserved.

Figures G1.3, B3.1, B4.1, B7.2, C1.2, D1.1, D2.4, D4.1, D4.4, D5.5, D6.3, D7.1, D8.2, D10.1, E2.3, G4.2, K1.1, L1.1
Reproduced with permission of Yahoo! © 2000 by Yahoo! Inc.

YAHOO! and the YAHOO! logo are trademarks of Yahoo! Inc.

Figure J3.1
© 2001 Zagat Survey, LLC. Zagat, Zagat Survey are registered trademarks of Zagat Survey, LLC and zagat.com is a service mark of Zagat Survey, LLC.

Douglas van Duyne is president, chief executive officer, and cofounder of NetRaker Corporation, a leading provider of customer experience management solutions. He is also founder and principal of Dune Design Group, a strategic digital product design and consulting firm. With 18 years of experience in software design at companies like GO Corporation and KidSoft, he has been an innovator in online shopping, e-commerce, and software and multimedia development. He has also developed Web site designs for companies including Intel Corporation, Safeway, healthshop.com, cooking.com, and ejobs.com. He holds a degree in computer science from the University of California at Berkeley.

van Duyne lives with his wife Arthine, son Max, and two dogs in the Santa Cruz Mountains of California.

James Landay is a professor of computer science at the University of California at Berkeley. He is also the chief technical officer and cofounder of NetRaker. He received his B.S. in electrical engineering and computer science from Berkeley in 1990 and his M.S. and Ph.D. from Carnegie Mellon University in 1993 and 1996, respectively. His Ph.D. dissertation was the first to demonstrate the use of sketching in user interface design tools. He has published extensively in the area of human–computer interaction, including articles on user interface design and evaluation tools, gesture recognition, pen-based user interfaces, mobile computing, and visual languages. He has also consulted for a number of Silicon Valley companies.

Landay lives with his wife Eileen, son Andrew, and their dog in the Oakland Hills of California.

Jason Hong is a researcher at the University of California at Berkeley, specializing in human–computer interaction. Jason received his B.S. in both computer science and discrete mathematics from Georgia Tech. Jason has worked at IBM Research, Fuji Xerox Palo Alto Laboratories, and Xerox Research, where he investigated topics such as collaborative Java applications, paper-based user interfaces, and techniques for viewing and navigating Web pages on cell phones. Jason is also a consultant for eDealFinder.com, a Web site for helping people find electronic coupons.

Jason is a voracious informavore, consuming vast quantities of Web, print, television, film, and musical media, with an emphasis on world history, technology, social impact of technology, and facts that are just plain weird. Jason currently lives with his robotic Aibo dog in Berkeley, California.

External resources, information reference sites,
    149
Extranet, 677
Eziba, rare finds, 413

F

Facilitator role
    usability tests, 634
    Web site evaluation plan, 643
Fair information practices
    applying and adding related features, 333
    choice and, 326
    message boards and, 278
    overview of, 328–329
    personal information, use and protection of,
        331–332
    privacy policies, clarity and conspicuousness,
        331, 332
    privacy policies, overview, 335
    safe harbor principles, 329–331
FAIR INFORMATION PRACTICES (E3), 328–333,
    712–713
False positives, heuristic evaluation, 82, 677
FAMILIAR LANGUAGE (K11), 586–589, 722. *See also*
    Language, familiar
FAQs. *See* Frequently asked questions (FAQs)
FAST-DOWNLOADING IMAGES (L2), 606–613,
    722–723. *See also* Images, downloading
Favorites. *See* Bookmarks
Feature problems, Web site design, 64–65
FEATURED PRODUCTS (G1), 410–416, 715. *See also*
    Products, featured
Federal Trade Commission, privacy policy, 334
Feedback
    design principles and, 68
    giving sense of having "arrived", 216
    Web applications and, 174–175
Field observation, 677
Fields
    optional vs. required, 467, 592
    structured, 591
    validation, 381
Files, 602–605
    applying and adding related features, 604–605
    content organization and, 253
    minimizing number of, 602–603
    removing large, slow files, 603–604

removing unnecessary files, 603
replacing images with HTML, 603
reusing images, 603
FindLaw, categorizing legal information, 196
Firewalls, 677
First impressions, homepages, 229–230
First Internet Bank, graphics of, 173
First reads
    applying and adding related features, 515–516
    defined, 677
    formatting features, 513–514
    homepages and, 233
    overview of, 512–513
    screen resolution and, 514–515
    selecting page elements, 513
    testing, 515
Fitt's Law, 34, 677
FIXED-WIDTH SCREEN SIZE (I5), 521–524, 718. *See
    also* Screen size, fixed width
Flash, Macromedia, 677
Flow, 677
Focus groups, 56–58, 677
Focused advertisements
    defined, 678
    Inverse-pyramid writing style and, 325
    subscribing to, 323
Fold. *See also* Above the fold
    defined, 678
    visibility of action buttons, 563
Fonts
    first reads and, 513
    size and styles, 582–583
Forces
    balancing in design process, 32
    defined, 678
    patterns and, 21–22
Forgotten passwords, 468
Formats
    clarifying expected, 591
    highlighting first reads, 513–514
    images, 607
    multiple, 591–592
Frequently asked questions (FAQs), 493–498
    about us page, 344
    applying and adding related features, 498
    community conferences and, 496–497
    defined, 677
    grouping related, 495

homepage, customer and partner links, 156
navigation bars, 552
page not found message, 598
Misspellings, searches and, 539–540
Mobile Internet devices, accessibility options, 223–224
Mock-ups, 684
Moderated forums
defined, 684
vs. unmoderated forums, 128, 275–276
Monster.com
context-sensitive help and, 501
personalization offered by, 266
The Motley Fool
interface for new posts, 280
saving favorite message boards, 276–277
Mouse, accessibility options, 220
MP3.com, reusable images, 621
MSNBC
homepage, 228
HTML titles, 302, 304
personal information, use of, 268
MULTIPLE DESTINATIONS (G5), 442–446. *See also* Shipping, to multiple destinations
MULTIPLE WAYS TO NAVIGATE (B1), 184–188, 705–706. *See also* Navigation methods
My Yahoo!, personalization and, 265

N
Names
embedded links and, 569–570
weakness of generic names as links, 579–580
Navigation. *See also* Making Navigation Easy (K)
accessibility options, 220
brand space, balancing with navigation space, 154–157, 230–232
consistency of, 216
design, 70
ease of, 233
FAQs and, 495
framework pattern, 183
information, accessibility of, 124
products, multiple ways to locate, 112
Web site structure and, 71
NAVIGATION BAR (K2), 550–553, 720
Navigation bars, 550–553. *See also* Tab rows
applying and adding related features, 552

overview of, 550
types of, 551
Navigation design, 684
Navigation methods, 184–188
adapting methods to different motivations, 185–186
appropriate use of navigation tools, 185
customer intention and impulse and, 185
overview of, 184
providing multiple approaches, 188
tool placement, 186–187
Navigation tools
ease of use, 185
location of, 186
product details and, 362
removing from printer friendly pages, 299
NBA.com, as example of arts and entertainment site, 167
NDAs (nondisclosure agreements), 684
Needs vs. wants, customers, 42–43
Netflix
cross-selling and up-selling, 421
customer ratings, 428
privacy policy, 336
product details, 366
Netmarket, avoiding cost surprises, 115
Netraker.com
cross-tabulation of research data, 662
external links, 572
links for target customers, 156
online research by, 656–657
online research tools, 665–667
reporting research results, 663–664
Netscape, 348, 684
Network effect, 684
Network for Good
civic participation, 144
subscribing to, 322
Network of help, 141
New accounts. *See* Sign-in/new account
Newman, Mark, 74
NEWS MOSAICS (A2), 118–124, 701
News sites
applying and adding related features, 123–124
compared with other news media, 120
getting news updates, 124
importance of time and access, 119–120

Platforms, cross-platform compatibility, 173

Plug-ins, removing unnecessary, 603, 686

PNG (Portable Network Graphics) images, 607, 686

Policies. *See also* Privacy policies
   new content, 181
   return policy, 405
   for writing reviews, 436

Pop-under windows, 686

Pop-up windows, 488–492
   applying and adding related features, 492
   automatic, 489, 670
   context-sensitive help and, 501
   defined, 686
   embedded links and, 570
   link-based, 490
   overview of, 488–489
   process funnel and, 464
   sparing use of, 491

POP-UP WINDOWS (H6), 488–492

POPULARITY-BASED ORGANIZATION (B7), 209–213, 705–706

Portable Document Format (PDF), 685

Portable Network Graphics (PNG) images, 607, 686

Portals, 686

Posts, to message boards, 279–281

PostScript (PS), 686

PREVENTING ERRORS (K12), 590–593, 722. *See also* Error prevention

Price information
   product details and, 362
   removing from gifts, 450

Principles. *See also* Customers, principles
   customer-centered design, 15–16
   defined, 686
   design, 68–70
   safe harbor, 329–331

Print button, printer friendly pages and, 299

Printable pages
   applying and adding related features, 301
   guidelines for use of, 299
   order confirmation and thank-you as, 402
   overview of, 298

PRINTABLE PAGES (D8), 298–301

Privacy
   government services and, 138

message boards and, 275
   personalized recommendations and, 431
   shoppers concern with, 114
   sign-in/new account and, 468
   Web applications and, 175

Privacy policies, 334–339
   applying and adding related features, 338
   availability of, 334–335
   children and, 335–336
   clarity and conspicuousness, 331, 332
   fair information practices and, 335
   legal exceptions, 337
   overview of, 334–335
   personal information and, 337–338
   sign-in/new account and, 468
   U.S. government sites and, 336–337

PRIVACY POLICIES (E4), 334–339, 713

Problems Found reports, 641

Proceed to Checkout button, 371

Process data
   analyzing, 639–640
   defined, 686
   online prototypes and, 635–636
   online testing and, 83
   usability testing and, 628

Process funnel, 462–465
   applying and adding related features, 464–465
   Back button and, 464
   error prevention, 464
   minimizing steps in tasks, 463
   overview of, 462–463
   pop-up windows and, 464
   progress bars and, 463
   removing unnecessary links and content, 463

PROCESS FUNNEL (H1), 462–465, 716

Processes
   customer-centered design, 15–16
   defined, 686

Product availability
   pending orders and, 456
   shopping cart and, 372

Product details, 359–368
   applying and adding related features, 368
   key elements, locating, 361–364
   overview of, 359–360
   product specs, 364–365
   secondary elements, locating, 365

Speeding Up Your Site (L) *(continued)*
   REUSABLE IMAGES (L5), 621–623
   SEPARATE TABLES (L3), 614–616
Spiders, 284, 674
Splash screen, 154–157, 689
SSL (Secure Sockets Layer), 347, 689–690
Standard error of the mean, 640
Standards, mobile Internet, 223–224
Staples.com, shopping carts and, 375
Statistical analysis, 641
Statistical validity
   defined, 690
   measurable goals and, 67
   surveys and, 56
Stickiness, Web sites, 690
STIMULATING ARTS AND ENTERTAINMENT (A9),
     166–170, 704. *See also* Arts and entertain-
     ment sites
Storyboards
   defined, 690
   Exploration phase and, 96
   iterative design and, 74
   scenario building and, 46
STRAIGHTFORWARD SEARCH FORMS (J2), 534–536,
     719. *See also* Search forms
Streaming data, 690
Strings, separating from code, 309
Structured text fields, error prevention and, 591
Student development, educational sites, 160
Style guides, 690
Subcategories, limiting in hierarchies, 195
Subjective metrics, 67–68
Subscription, news mosaics, 124
Subsites, 690
Suggested Improvements reports, 642
Sun Microsystems site
   audience targeted navigation links, 157
   content modules, 251
   variations of page elements, 248
Support community, 39
Surveys
   customer participation in creating value
     propositions, 240
   techniques for knowing customers, 55–56
   usability tests and, 638
Sustainability, community conferences, 132–133
SVG (Scalable Vector Graphics) images, 690

Sydney, Australia, access to government
   information, 135
Synchronous communications, 126–127, 690

T
Tab rows, 554–557
   applying and adding related features, 557
   identifying active tab, 555
   indicator line for, 556
   limitations of, 556
   overview of, 554–555
TAB ROWS (K3), 554–557, 720
Tables. *See also* HTML tables
   absolute and relative widths, 518–519
   removing from printer friendly pages, 299
   simplifying and dividing, 614–616
Target audiences, xxxii
Target customers, 674, xxxi. *See also* Customers
Task analysis
   defined, 691
   Discovery phase and, 93
   techniques for knowing customers, 43–45
   understanding customer tasks, 37
TASK-BASED ORGANIZATION (B4), 198–202,
     705–706. *See also* Organization, task-based
Task-related questions, task analysis, 44
Task training, principles for knowing customers,
   38–39
Tasks. *See also* Helping Customers Complete
     Tasks (H)
   context-sensitive help and, 500
   defined, 691
   linking related, 199, 202
   list for companies, 155
   list for intranets, 180
   process funnel, 463
   selecting for scenario building, 47–49
   selecting for usability tests, 628–630
   simple, medium, and hard difficulty, 629
   tailored for user groups of educational sites
     and, 162
   understanding customer tasks, 36–37
   Web site evaluation plan, 644–645
Taxpayers Australia, guest accounts, 475
TCP/IP (Transmission Control Protocol/Internet
   protocol), 691

Usability *(continued)*
   focus of Web applications on, 175
   intuitive vs. training, 38
   methods for measuring, 84
   unifying with design and marketing, 8–9
Usability research
   online research and, 654–655
   tools for, 665
Usability tests. *See also* Web site evaluation plan
   common mistakes in running, 637
   data analysis, 639–641
   goal setting, 627–628
   key roles, 634
   online prototypes, 635–636
   paper prototypes, 634–635
   participants, recruiting, 630–632
   participants, supporting, 633
   pilot tests, 634
   reporting results, 641–642
   task selection for, 628–630
   test location, 633
   testing process, 636–638
Use case, 692
Use this address button, 378
User-centered design, 9–10, 692
User experience. *See* Customer experience

V

Validate fields, addresses, 381
VALUABLE COMPANY SITES (A7), 152–158, 703. *See also* Company sites
Value propositions
   applying and adding related features, 240–241
   articulation of, 238–239
   defined, 692
   Discovery phase, 91–92
   homepages and, 237
   overview of, 237–238
   requirements of, 238
   selecting, involving customers in, 240
   selecting, picking candidates, 239
   Web applications, 175
Value ranking, 147, 692
van Duyne, Doug, 741, xxvii
Verbal protocol
   defined, 692
   informal evaluations and, 83

Vertical prototypes, 80, 692
Virtual testing, 692
Visitors, Web sites
   bread crumbs and, 566
   educational sites and, 161–162
   inviting personalization by, 265–267
   mapping content to, 269
   tracking visits and history, 271
Visual design. *See* Graphic design

Visual disabilities, accessibility options, 220–222
Vividence, online research tools, 665–667
Volunteer Match, matching volunteers to non-profits, 140
Vortals, 692

W

W3C (World Wide Web Consortium), 607, 692
Walk-through, 692
Wal-Mart site
   ease of navigation, 189
   gift giving and, 448–449
   shipping to multiple addresses, 442, 443
Want vs. needs, customers, 42–43
WAP (Wireless Application Protocol), 692
Weather Channel, use of ALT attribute, 222
Web applications
   applying and adding related features, 176
   converting traditional software to, 173–174
   customer roles supported by, 175
   help functions, 175
   informative feedback, 174–175
   overview of, 171–172
   security and privacy, 175
   trying before buying, 172–173
WEB APPS THAT WORK (A10), 171–177, 704
Web browsers
   cross-browser compatibility, 173
   defined, 692
   downloading from Web servers to, 483
   global access and, 312
   HTML titles and, 303
   inference data and, 426
   reusable images and, 623
   screen size, expanding width, 518
   screen size, fixed width, 522

Thank you for your interest in *The Design of Sites*. Register now at the book's Web site and receive a whitepaper on remote usability testing.

In addition to receiving the whitepaper, you will also receive the NetRaker e-newsletter about Online Usability and Market Research.

 # Plug In To NetRaker!

Now that you're clicking with your customer, see how you can stay connected.

NetRaker provides a suite of automated Web site evaluation tools to help you understand and manage the customer experience effectively and efficiently.

NETRAKER EXPERIENCE EVALUATOR

Create and implement usability tests, task analysis reviews, customer satisfaction studies, and market research studies

NETRAKER EXPERIENCE RECORDER

Enables you to remotely observe and record live customer interactions through screen sharing, chat features, and whiteboard capabilities.

NETRAKER CLICKSTREAM

Tracks Web site visitors as they move through a site and analyzes their navigational paths, identifying page design problems and pinpointing problem areas in a site.

NETRAKER INDEX

Gathers ongoing benchmarks to monitor real-time customer satisfaction and overall site effectiveness, 24/7.

netRaker®

For a demo and more information about NetRaker Solutions:

Visit
www.netraker.com

Email
sales@netraker.com

Call
408.530.8900 option 2
Toll-Free 1.877.483.2114
option 2

Also from Addison-Wesley

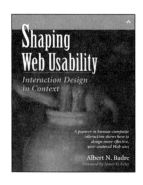

Shaping Web Usability
Interaction Design in Context
By Albert N. Badre

This book provides a concrete methodology for designing a site effectively for the convenience, practicality, and pleasure of its users.

0201729938 • Paperback • 304 pages • © 2002

The Humane Interface
New Directions for Designing Interactive Systems
By Jef Raskin

The creator of the Apple Macintosh goes beyond today's graphic user interfaces to show how the Web, computers, and information appliances can be made easier to learn and use.

0201379376 • Paperback • 256 pages • © 2000

Web Content Management
A Collaborative Approach
By Russell Nakano

With *Web Content Management* as your guide, you will be better prepared to elevate your Web site—whether it is small, growing, or already large—to an information-rich, enterprise-scale solution.

0201657821 • Paperback • 272 pages • © 2002

Collaborative Web Development
Strategies and Best Practices for Web Teams
By Jessica Burdman

Written by a leader in Web development methodologies and processes, *Collaborative Web Development* brings structure and sanity to what is often an overwhelming and chaotic process.

0201433311 • Paperback • 272 pages with CD-ROM • © 1999

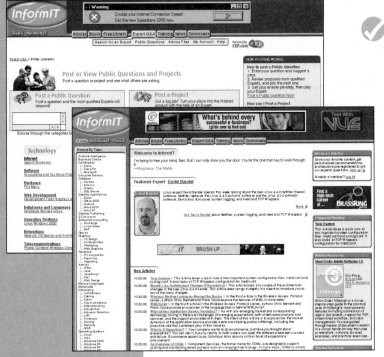